Exploring Writing
Sentences and Paragraphs

John Langan

Atlantic Cape Community College

McGraw
Hill

Boston   Burr Ridge, IL   Dubuque, IA   Madison, WI   New York   San Francisco   St. Louis
Bangkok   Bogotá   Caracas   Kuala Lumpur   Lisbon   London   Madrid   Mexico City
Milan   Montreal   New Delhi   Santiago   Seoul   Singapore   Sydney   Taipei   Toronto

Published by McGraw-Hill, an imprint of The McGraw-Hill Companies, Inc., 1221 Avenue of the Americas, New York, NY, 10020. Copyright © 2008 by The McGraw-Hill Companies, Inc. All rights reserved. No part of this publication may be reproduced or distributed in any form or by any means, or stored in a database or retrieval system, without the prior written consent of The McGraw-Hill Companies, Inc., including, but not limited to, in any network or other electronic storage or transmission, or broadcast for distance learning. Some ancillaries, including electronic and print components, may not be available to customers outside the United States.

This book is printed on acid-free paper.

1 2 3 4 5 6 7 8 9 0 DOW/DOW 0 9 8 7

ISBN 978-0-07-353328-5 (student edition)
ISBN 978-0-07-332741-9 (instructor's edition)
MHID 0-07-353328-9 (student edition)
MHID 0-07-332741-7 (instructor's edition)

Publisher and Editor-in-Chief: *Emily Barrosse*
Sponsoring editor: *John Kindler*
Director of development: *Carla K. Samodulski*
Development editor: *Anne Stameshkin*
Editorial coordinator: *Jesse Hassenger*
Marketing manager: *Tamara Wederbrand*
Manager, publishing services: *Melissa Williams*
Project manager: *Mary Keith Trawick*
Production editor: *Leslie LaDow*
Production supervisor: *Tandra Jorgensen*
Photo researcher: *Emily Tietz*
Design coordinator: *Cassandra Chu*
Interior designer: *Maureen McCutcheon*
Cover designer: *Linda Beaupre*
Media producer: *Alexander Rohrs*
Compositor: *Newgen–Austin*
Typeface: *Palatino*
Printer: *RR Donnelley & Sons*

Library of Congress Cataloging-in-Publication Data

Langan, John
   Exploring writing : sentences and paragraphs / John Langan.
     p. cm.
   Includes bibliographical references and index.
   ISBN-13: 978-0-07-353328-5
   ISBN-10: 0-07-353328-9
     1. English language 2. College readers.   I. Title

2007920742

The Internet addresses listed in the text were accurate at the time of publication. The inclusion of a Web site does not indicate an endorsement by the authors or McGraw-Hill, and McGraw-Hill does not guarantee the accuracy of the information presented at these sites.

www.mhhe.com

John Langan has taught reading and writing at Atlantic Cape Community College near Atlantic City, New Jersey, for more than twenty-five years. The author of a popular series of college textbooks on both writing and reading, John enjoys the challenge of developing materials that teach skills in an especially clear and lively way. Before teaching, he earned advanced degrees in writing at Rutgers University and in reading at Rowan University. He also spent a year writing fiction that, he says, "is now at the back of a drawer waiting to be discovered and acclaimed posthumously." While in school, he supported himself by working as a truck driver, a machinist, a battery assembler, a hospital attendant, and apple packer. John now lives with his wife, Judith Nadell, near Philadelphia. In addition to his wife and Philly sports teams, his passions include reading and turning on nonreaders to the pleasure and power of books. Through Townsend Press, his educational publishing company, he has developed the nonprofit "Townsend Library"—a collection of more than fifty new and classic stories that appeal to readers of any age.

BRIEF CONTENTS

CONTENTS

Appendixes 561

READINGS Listed by Rhetorical Mode

Note: Some selections are listed more than once because they illustrate more than one pattern of development.

Exploring Writing

Emphasizing both process and practice, *Exploring Writing: Sentences and Paragraphs* will help students apply and advance their writing skills. Learning to write effective paragraphs, master essential sentence skills, and read critically are turning points for student writers; these skills will prepare them to write essays in college and tackle many types of writing in the real world. Along the way, there are many small but important skills to develop: using specific and concrete language, selecting good supporting details, writing an effective topic sentence, creating a convincing argument, organizing a paragraph in a way that best fits its purpose, and so on.

Four Bases

Exploring Writing asserts that four principles in particular are keys to effective composition: **unity, support, coherence,** and **sentence skills.** These four principles, or "bases," are highlighted on the inside back cover and are reinforced throughout the book.

- **Unity** means seeing the whole as the sum of its parts; in an effective essay, the student should make one point and stick to it.

- **Support** stresses the importance of using specific evidence to back up that point.

- **Coherence** focuses on the ways writers organize and connect this evidence, as well as how they transition between ideas.

- **Sentence skills** demonstrate an attention to the craft of writing and its elements; clear, error-free sentences maximize the effectiveness of the other three bases.

Countless Possibilities

In this text, I encourage students to see writing as a skill that can be learned *and* a process that must be explored; while the four bases provide a foundation, there are many important factors in writing well. Chapter 1 asks students to examine their attitude toward writing, to write what they know— or can learn about—and to consider keeping a writing journal. Appendix F: A Writer's Journal gives them room to start recording ideas.

Personal Discoveries

A writer's journey is as personal as it is practical; *Exploring Writing* ascribes to the belief that the best way to begin writing is with personal experience. After students have learned to support a point by providing material from their own lives, they are ready to develop an idea by drawing on their own reasoning abilities and on information in reports, articles, and books. In Parts 1 and 2, students are asked to write on topics both from their own experience and from other points of view (for instance, as a real estate agent describing a neighborhood or a store manager giving employees step-by-step instructions).

Realistic Writing

Beginning writers are more likely to learn composition skills through lively, engaging, and realistic models than through materials remote from the common experiences that are part of everyday life. When a writer catalogs various ways to harass an instructor or argues that proms should be banned, students will be more apt to remember and follow the writing principles that are involved.

Student Writing

Students are particularly interested in and challenged by the writing of their peers. After reading effective, engaging papers composed by other students and understanding the power that good writing can have, students will be more encouraged to aim for similar honest realism and detail in their own work.

Organization

Since no two instructors will use a textbook in exactly the same way, the organization of *Exploring Writing* is designed to be flexible. Each of this book's four parts deals with a distinct area of writing, and we have color-coded the outside margins so instructors can turn quickly and easily to the skills they want to present. A sample syllabus is provided in the *Instructor's Manual* (available in print or online at www.mhhe.com/langan).

- **Part 1** introduces key aspects of good writing and the writing process, guiding students through prewriting, drafting, revising, and editing.

- **Part 2** outlines the four bases of effective composition, applies them in nine types of paragraph development, and walks through the transition from paragraph to essay writing.

- **Part 3** serves as an interactive handbook of sentence skills, providing students with ample opportunities to practice and develop as sentence writers. For easy access, topic abbreviations appear on colored bars atop each right-hand page.

- **Part 4** contains fifteen reading selections organized into three themes; a rhetorical Table of Contents **(p. xvi–xvii)** offers an alternative way to group the readings.

Key Features

Over 350 Activities

Exploring Writing features a variety of **Activities,** which appear throughout Parts 1 through 3; these allow students ample opportunities to practice sentence- and paragraph-writing skills. Activities are titled and numbered (starting at 1) within each chapter. Answers to the activities in Part 3 are located in Appendix E so students can check their work; answers to all other activities are located only in the *Instructor's Manual* and the *Annotated Instructor's Edition.*

- **Review Test:** Chapter 2 and all the chapters in Part 3 conclude with tests that cover all content in that chapter; answers to these are available in the *Instructor's Manual* and the *Annotated Instructor's Edition* but not in the student text.

Part 3 features three additional types of activities that focus on sentence skills:

- **Introductory Activity:** These provide hands-on introductions to the topics each chapter will cover. Answers to these exercises are available in Appendix E.

- **Working Together:** These two-part activities give students a chance to collaborate as they develop stronger sentence skills; they can be assigned during or outside of class time.

- **Reflective Activity:** These exercises draw connections between the skills learned in that chapter and the actual process of completing an assignment.

Writing Assignments

Throughout the text, Writing Assignments give students a chance to write about everyday issues such as dating, work, family life, politics, and entertainment. Assignments range from short prompts to step-by-step processes. Through writing paragraphs (and essays), students can try out various processes and patterns of development as they learn about them.

- **A Writer's Checklist:** At the end of Parts 1 through 3, writing checklists encourage students to check their drafts for specific errors or features addressed in that section of the book. Chapter 4 features nine "Four Bases" checklists that students can use when revising paragraphs written in the different patterns of development.

- **Beyond the Classroom:** Throughout Chapter 4, these assignments give students the opportunity to apply the patterns of development to writing situations they will confront outside of the college environment.

Technology Program

Exploring Writing recognizes the need for online support for today's tech-savvy student as well as for students who need to become savvy about technology.

- **Fully integrated Online Learning Center (OLC).** At key points throughout the text, marginal icons direct students to www. mhhe.com/langan, where they can find expanded coverage of a particular topic or hone their skills through completing additional exercises. Access to the site—which is powered by Catalyst 2.0, the premier online resource for writing, research, and editing—is free with every student and instructor copy of *Exploring Writing*.

- **Tech-savvy Writing.** At the end of each chapter in Parts 1 and 2, these prompts give students a chance to apply that chapter's lessons to a specific purpose—while learning to make use of the Internet at all stages of the writing process.

Responding to Images

Because today's students respond so readily to visual images and must learn to evaluate such images critically, this text features over sixty images, each chosen and used for a pedagogical purpose.

- **A Writer's Showcase:** Each showcase in Parts 1 through 3 features images accompanied by writing assignments. (See below for more on this feature.)

- **Chapter- or section-opening images:** Every chapter in Parts 1 and 2 opens and closes with a visual or visuals, all of which are accompanied by writing prompts. Each section in Part 3 also features a visual opener.

- **Images related to concepts and themes:** In Part 2, images are used to help students visualize some concepts (such as comparison-contrast and argument). Part 4 includes Responding to Images writing prompts for featured visuals, which are linked thematically to the professional readings.

Professional Readings

The fifteen selections have been chosen for their content as much as for rhetorical mode. They are organized thematically into three groups: Goals and Values, Education and Self-Improvement, and Human Groups and Society. Some selections reflect important contemporary concerns: for instance, "Let's Really Reform Our Schools," "Rudeness at the Movies," and "What Good Families Are Doing Right." Some provide information students may find helpful: examples are "Anxiety: Challenge by Another Name" and "How They Get You to Do That." Others, such as "All the Good Things," "Rowing the Bus," and "My Daughter Smokes" recount profoundly human experiences.

- **A Writer's Showcase:** Parts 1, 2, and 3 open with a paragraph of professional writing (excerpted from an essay in Part 4), followed by questions and writing assignments that get students thinking about the lessons that section of the text will cover.

- **Apparatus:** In Part 4, each reading is preceded by a **Preview** that introduces the author and reading and a **Words to Watch** vocabulary list. Each reading is followed by **Vocabulary in**

Context, **Questions for Reading Comprehension, Questions for Discussion** (and within the latter, the subsections **About Content, About Structure,** and **About Style and Tone.** There are also three to four **Writing Assignments** per reading, two for paragraphs and one for an essay. Several readings in each thematic section feature a related visual and accompanying **Responding to Images** writing prompt.

Student Work

- **Sample student paragraphs:** In Parts 1 and 2, student work (often accompanied by questions) is used to demonstrate various stages of the writing process, the four bases of effective composition, nine patterns of development, and the progression from paragraph to essay.

- A **Writer's Template:** At the end of each part, a piece of student work is featured; questions prompt commentary on (and suggestions for) revisions appropriate to the topics in that section.

Ease of Use

- **Chapter Preview:** Every chapter opens with an outline of its contents, preparing students for the lessons that follow.

- **Color-coded margins** allow instructors and students to distinguish the four parts at a glance. **Topic abbreviation bars** appear on the outside corner of each right-hand page in Part 3, helping students or instructors who are looking for a specific topic.

- **Tip, Hint,** and **Explanation boxes** in Part 3 offer advice about grammar rules, hints for certain activities, and explanations of why the answers to sample activities are correct, respectively.

- **Teaching Tips** are available throughout the *Annotated Instructor's Edition* in the margins.

- **ESL Teaching Tips,** which offer specific advice for instructing multilingual writers, are featured in the margins of *Exploring Writing.*

Supplements for Instructors

- An **Annotated Instructor's Edition** (ISBN 0-07-332741-7) consists of the student text, complete with answers to all activities and tests. Throughout the text, marginal Teaching Tips offer suggestions for various approaches, classroom activities, discussions, and assignments.

- An **Online Learning Center** (www.mhhe.com/langan) offers a host of instructional aids and additional resources for instructors, including a comprehensive computerized test bank, the downloadable *Instructor's Manual and Test Bank,* online resources for writing instructors, and more.

- **The Virtual Workbook** (ISBN 0-07-299415-0)
  Donna Matsumoto, *Leward Community College*
  This online workbook offers interactive activities and exercises that reinforce the skills students learn in Part 3 of *Exploring Writing.* It is supported by a powerful array of Web-based instructor's tools, including an automated online gradebook.

- **The Classroom Performance System** (CPS by eInstruction) is an easy-to-use, wireless response system that allows instructors to conduct quizzes and polls in class and provide students with immediate feedback. McGraw-Hill provides a database of questions compatible with *Exploring Writing: Sentences and Paragraphs* and *Exploring Writing: Paragraphs and Essays.* To download the database, go to the Online Learning Center at www.mhhe.com/langan. For further details on CPS, go to www.mhhe.com/einstruction.

- **Partners in Teaching** is an online community of composition and basic writing instructors. Two associated listservs, Teaching Composition and Teaching Basic Writing, address issues of pedagogy in theory and in practice. Their goal is to bring together senior members of the college composition community with newer members—junior faculty and teaching assistants—as well as adjuncts. Each month, major figures in the fields of composition and basic writing take turns leading discussions on issues of importance to people in the profession. *We enthusiastically invite you to submit your own ideas for topics and potential contributions to these listservs. Please check out* Teaching Composition *at www.mhhe.com/ tcomp and* Teaching Basic Writing *at www.mhhe.com/tbw and join the discussion.*

Supplements for Students

- An **Online Learning Center** (www.mhhe.com/langan) offers a host of instructional aids and additional resources for students, including self-correcting exercises, writing activities for additional practice, guides to doing research on the Internet and avoiding plagiarism, useful web links, and more. The site is powered by Catalyst 2.0, the premier online resource for writing, research, and editing.

- **The Virtual Workbook** (ISBN 0-07-299415-0)
  Donna Matsumoto, *Leward Community College*
  This online workbook offers interactive activities and exercises that reinforce the skills students learn in Part 3 of *Exploring Writing.*

- **The New McGraw-Hill Exercise Book** (ISBN 0-07-326032-0)
  Santi Buscemi, *Middlesex College*
  This workbook features numerous additional sentence- and paragraph-level editing exercises, as well as research-,

documentation-, and writing-related exercises that can be used for any composition course.

- **The McGraw-Hill Exercise Book for Multilingual Writers** (ISBN 0-07-326030-4)
  Maggie Sokolik, *University of California–Berkeley*
  This workbook features numerous sentence-level and paragraph-level editing exercises tailored specifically for multilingual students.

- **A Writer's Journal** (ISBN 0-07-326031-2)
  Lynee Gaillet, *Georgia State University*
  This elegant journal for students includes quotes on writing from famous authors, as well as advice and tips on writing and the writing process.

- **The McGraw-Hill Student Planner** (ISBN 0-07-322205-4)
  This practical spiral-bound date book and planner for students is organized around the academic year, offering them a handy tool to structure and plan their work. It includes a brief almanac at the back with important facts from a variety of disciplines.

Dictionary and Vocabulary Resources

- **Random House Webster's College Dictionary** (0-07-240011-0): This authoritative dictionary includes over 160,000 entries and 175,000 definitions. The most commonly used definitions are always listed first, so students can find what they need quickly.

- **The Merriam-Webster Dictionary** (0-07-310057-9), based on the best-selling *Merriam-Webster's Collegiate Dictionary*, it contains over 70,000 definitions.

- **The Merriam-Webster's Thesaurus** (0-07-310067-6): This handy paperback thesaurus contains over 157,000 synonyms, antonyms, related and contrasted words, and idioms.

- **Merriam-Webster's Vocabulary Builder** (0-07-310069-2) introduces 3,000 words, and it includes quizzes to test progress.

- **Merriam-Webster's Notebook Dictionary** (0-07-299091-0): This popular dictionary provides an extremely concise reference to the words that form the core of the English vocabulary and is conveniently designed for three-ring binders.

- **Merriam Webster's Notebook Thesaurus** (0-07-310068-4) Designed for three-ring binders, this resource helps students search for words they might need today. It provides concise, clear guidance for over 157,000 word choices.

- **Merriam-Webster's Collegiate Dictionary and Thesaurus, Electronic Edition** (0-07-310070-6): Available on CD-ROM, this online dictionary contains thousands of new words and meanings from all areas of human endeavor, including electronic technology, the sciences, and popular culture.

You can contact your local McGraw-Hill representative or consult McGraw-Hill's Web site at www.mhhe.com/english for more information on the supplements that accompany *Exploring Writing: Sentences and Paragraphs.*

Acknowledgments

I am grateful to my McGraw-Hill editors, John Kindler and Anne Stameshkin, for helping make this book possible. Intern Lauryn Arkin and editorial/marketing team members Jesse Hassenger, Tami Wederbrand, Alyson Watts, and Carla Samodulski also made valuable contributions to this text. Many thanks to the skilled production and design team—Melissa Williams, Mary Keith Trawick at G&S, Leslie LaDow, Cassandra Chu, Maureen McCutcheon, Emily Tietz, and Tandra Jorgensen. Also, I'd like to thank Magdalena Corona and Alex Rohrs for producing the text's media component.

Joyce Stern, Assistant Professor at Nassau Community College, contributed the ESL Tips to this book. Professor Stern is also Assistant to the Chair in the department of Reading and Basic Education. An educator for over thirty years, she holds an advanced degree in TESOL from Hunter College, as well as a New York State Teaching Certificate in TESOL. She is currently coordinating the design, implementation and recruitment of learning communities for both ESL and developmental students at Nassau Community College and has been recognized by the college's Center for Students with Disabilities for her dedication to student learning.

Donna T. Matsumoto, Assistant Professor of English and the Writing Discipline Coordinator at Leeward Community College in Hawaii (Pearl City), wrote the Teaching Tips for the *Instructor's Edition* of *Exploring Writing.* Professor Matsumoto has taught writing, women's studies, and American studies for a number of years throughout the University of Hawaii system, at Hawaii Pacific University, and in community schools for adults. She received a 2005 WebCT Exemplary Course Project award for her online writing course and is the author of McGraw-Hill's *The Virtual Workbook,* an online workbook featuring interactive activities and exercises.

Reviewers who have contributed to this book through their helpful comments include:

Christina Devlin, *Montgomery College–Germantown*

Dane Galloway, *Ozarks Technical Community College*

Richard Gaspar, *Hillsborough Community College*

Charles Gonzalez, *Central Florida Community College*

Joy Hancock, *Mount San Antonio College*

Robert Hellstrom, *Edinboro University of Pennsylvania*

Joshua Mattern, *Waubonsee Community College*

Patty Rogers, *Angelina College*

Cathy Sheeley, *Penn Valley Community College*

Exploring Writing
Sentences and Paragraphs

John Langan *Atlantic Cape Community College*

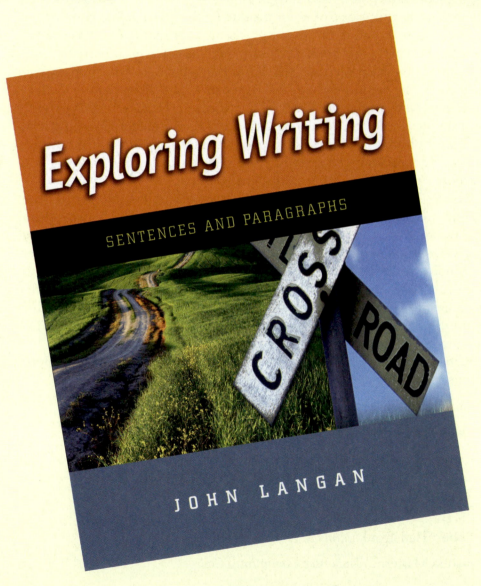

Welcome! The following pages illustrate how *Exploring Writing* will help you learn to write, revise, and edit sentences and paragraphs. To get the most out of this text, spend a few minutes getting to know the book's organization and features.

Organization

Part 1 introduces the elements of good writing and explores the writing process, from prewriting to revising and editing. **Part 2** outlines the four bases of effective composition (**unity, support, coherence,** and **sentence skills**), applies them in nine types of paragraph development, and walks through the transition from paragraph to essay writing.

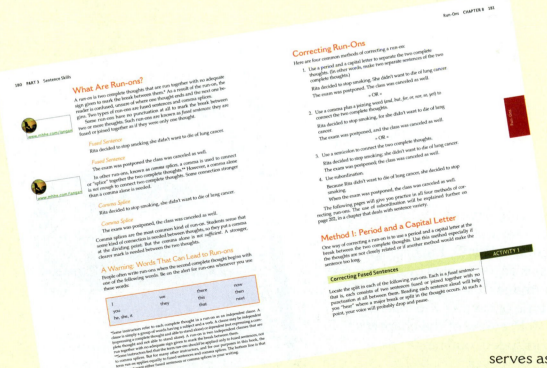

Part 3 serves as an interactive handbook of sentence skills, providing many opportunities to practice and develop as sentence writers. For easy access, topic abbreviations appear on colored bars atop each right-hand page. **Part 4** contains twenty reading selections organized into three themes.

Features

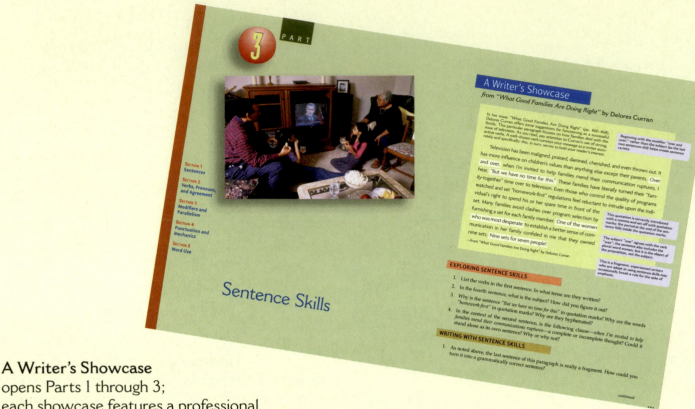

A Writer's Showcase
opens Parts 1 through 3;
each showcase features a professional
paragraph excerpted from a reading in Part 4. Discussion
questions and writing assignments help to introduce lessons
you will learn in the chapters that follow. The reading is accompanied
by a photograph and one or more **Responding to Images** writing prompts.

Chapter and Section Openers—Photographs
or cartoons open every chapter in Parts 1 and
2 and every section in Part 3. Each image (or
group of images) is accompanied by at least one
Responding to Images writing prompt that
introduces the type of writing you will do
in that chapter. A **Preview** of the chapter's
contents is also included, outlining topics
that the chapter will cover.

Abundant sample student paragraphs and two full student essays—These models, often accompanied by questions, demonstrate various stages of the writing process, the four bases of effective writing, the nine patterns of development, and the progression from paragraph to essay.

of specific supporting details, one student writer revised a paper she had done on a restaurant job as the worst job she ever had. In the revised paper, instead of talking about "unsanitary conditions in the kitchen," she referred to such specifics as "green mold on the bacon" and "ants in the potato salad." All your paragraphs should include many vivid details! Using ample support will help you communicate more clearly and effectively in your writing.

> **TIP**   To check a paragraph for support, ask yourself these questions:
> 1. Is there specific evidence to support the opening point?
> 2. Is there enough specific evidence?

www.mhhe.com/langan

Evaluating Paragraphs for Support

ACTIVITY 21   Checking for Specific Details

The paragraph that follows lacks sufficient supporting details. Identify the spot or spots where more specific details are needed.

Culture Conflict

¹I am in a constant tug-of-war with my parents over conflicts between their Vietnamese culture and American culture. ²To begin with, my parents do not like me to have American friends. ³They think that I should spend all my time with other Vietnamese people and speak English only when necessary. ⁴I get into an argument whenever I want to go to a fast-food restaurant or a movie at night with my American friends. ⁵The conflict with my parents is even worse when it comes to plans for a career. ⁶My parents want me to get a degree in science and then go on to medical school. ⁷On the other hand, I think I want to become a teacher. ⁸So far I have been taking both science and education courses, but soon I will have to concentrate on one or the other. ⁹The other night my father made his attitude about what I should do very clear. ¹⁰The most difficult aspect of our cultural differences is the way our family is structured. ¹¹My father is the center of our family, and he expects that I will always listen to him. ¹²Although I am twenty-one years old, I still have a nightly curfew at an hour which I consider insulting. ¹³Also, I am expected to help my mother perform certain household chores that I've really come to hate. ¹⁴My father expects me to live at home until I am married to a Vietnamese man. ¹⁵When that happens, he assumes I will obey my husband just as I obey him. ¹⁶I do not want to be a bad daughter, but I want to live like my American female friends.

Fill in the blanks: The first spot where supporting details are needed occurs after sentence number ____. The second spot occurs after sentence number ____. The third spot occurs after sentence number ____.

Concluding Paragraph

The concluding paragraph often sum____ ing the thesis and, at times, the main ____ sion brings the paper to a natural and ____ reader with a final thought on the sub____

The Concluding Paragraph

1. Which sentence in the concluding ____ Plant" restates the thesis and supp ____

2. Which sentence contains the concl ____

Essays to Consider

Read the following two student essay____ follow.

Giving up ____

¹As I awoke, I overheard a nurse ____ could a mother give him up?" ²"Be q ____ going to wake up soon." ³Then I hea ____ him again. ⁴Three years ago, I gave u____ people who wanted a baby but cou____ my decision, and I can still hear the ____ selfish or crazy. ⁵But the reasons I ga ____ ones, at least to me.

⁶I gave up my baby, first of all, b ____ only seventeen, and I was unmarried ____ not yet feel the desire to have and r ____ be a child raising a child and that, w ____ the baby. I would resent the loss of ____ the baby for that loss. ⁷In addition, I had not had the experiences in life that would make me a responsible, giving parent. ⁸What could I teach my child, when I barely knew what life was all about myself? ⁹Besides my age, another factor in my decision was the problems my parents would have. ¹⁰I had dropped out of high school before graduation, and I did not have a job or even the chance of a job, at least for a while. ¹¹My parents would have to support my child and me, possibly for years. ¹²My mom and dad had already struggled to raise their family and were not well off financially. ¹³Even if I eventually got a job, my parents would have to help raise my child. ¹⁴They would have to be full-time babysitters while I tried to make a life of my own. ¹⁵Because my parents are good people, they would

continued

3. dime   nickel   coin   quarter   half-dollar
4. fax machine   copier   computer   calculator   office machine
5. theft   murder   rape   crime   holdup
6. cracker   snack   carrot stick   cookie   popcorn
7. mascara   cosmetic   foundation   lipstick   eyeshadow
8. yes   no   I don't know   answer   maybe
9. yard work   mowing   planting   trimming hedges   feeding plants
10. job interviews   weddings   car accidents   being fired   stressful times

ACTIVITY 5   Developing Specific Ideas

In each item below, one idea is general and the others are specific. The general idea includes the specific ones. In the spaces provided, write in two more specific ideas that are covered by the general idea.

EXAMPLE
   General: exercises
   Specific: chin-ups, jumping jacks, *sit-____*

1. General: pizza toppings
   Specific: sausa____

2. General: furn____
   Specific: rocki____

3. General: magaz____
   Specific: Reader's ____

4. General: birds
   Specific: eagle, pige____

5. General: music
   Specific: jazz, classical____

6. General: cold symptom
   Specific: aching muscles, ____

7. General: children's games
   Specific: hopscotch, dodge____

8. General: transportation
   Specific: plane, motorcycle, ____

---

www.mhhe.com/langan

Who, Which, and That

When *who*, *which*, and *that* are used as subjects of verbs, they take singular verbs if the word they stand for is singular, and they take plural verbs if the word they stand for is plural. For example, in the sentence

Gary is one of those people who are very private.

the verb is plural because *who* stands for *people*, which is plural. On the other hand, in the sentence

Gary is a person who is very private.

the verb is singular because *who* stands for *person*, which is singular.

Using who, which, or that with Verbs

Write the correct form of the verb in the space provided.

has,
have
goes,
go
becomes,
become
tastes,
taste
is,
are

1. The young man who ____ mowed my grass for years just left for college.

2. The jacket that ____ with those pants is at the cleaners.

3. Women who ____ police officers often have to prove themselves more capable than do their male coworkers.

4. The restaurant serves hamburgers that ____ like dry cereal.

5. The ceiling in Kevin's bedroom is covered with stars, which ____ arranged in the shape of the constellations.

ACTIVITY 5

HINT: Who stands for a singular subject and requires a singular ver____

ACTIVITY 6

Working Together

Part A: Editing and Rewriting

Working with a partner, read the short paragraph below and see if you can underline the five mistakes in subject-verb agreement. Then use the space provided to correct these five errors. Feel free to discuss the rewrite quietly with your partner and refer back to the chapter when necessary.

When most people think about cities, they do not thinks about wild animals. But in my city apartment, there is enough creatures to fill a small forest. In the daytime, I must contend with the pigeons. These unwanted guests at my apartment makes a loud feathery mess on my bedroom windowsill. In the evening, my apartment is visited by roaches. These large insects creep onto my kitchen floor and walls after dark and frighten me with their shiny glistening bodies. Later at

continued

Activities—Over 350 activities appear throughout the text to help you apply and master the **four principles, or bases,** of effective writing. In Part 3, additional types of activities focus on sentence skills: **Working Together** exercises give you the opportunity to collaborate with one or more classmates to complete a sentence-focused writing assignment; **Introductory Activities** provide hands-on introductions to sentence skills covered in that chapter; and **Reflective Activities** draw connections between the skills learned in that chapter and the actual process of completing an assignment.

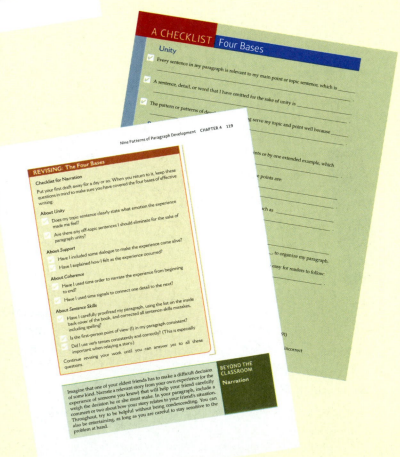

Tech-Savvy Writing prompts in Chapters 1 through 5 draw connections between using the Internet and writing. Additional visuals and **Responding to Images** writing assignments also appear at the end of Chapters 1 through 5; these give you the opportunity to apply the chapter's lessons in a visual context. **Writing Assignments** offer you a chance to write about everyday issues like dating, work, family life, politics, and entertainment. **Beyond the Classroom** assignments throughout Chapter 4 provide the opportunity to apply the patterns of development to real-world writing situations.

A Checklist closes Parts 1 through 3, offering a guide to revising based on lessons covered in that section of the book. The Four Bases: A Checklist accompanies each writing assignment in Chapter 4 to help you make sure you've covered all the bases—unity, support, coherence, and sentence skills—in your writing. Each checklist is tailored to a particular pattern of development.

Tip boxes and Hint boxes throughout the text offer (respectively) advice about grammar rules and clues for completing certain activities. Explanation boxes go beyond *how* to show *why* some examples are correct and others are not. OLC Icons in the margins let you know when you can find more information on a topic or opportunities to practice a skill on the Online Learning Center for *Exploring Writing* (www.mhhe.com/langan).

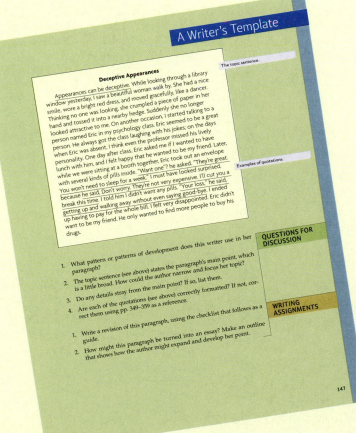

A Writer's Template at the end of Parts 1 and 2 prompts you to apply lessons learned by commenting on a sample student paragraph. Questions guide your review of this paragraph, and writing assignments prompt you to write your own.

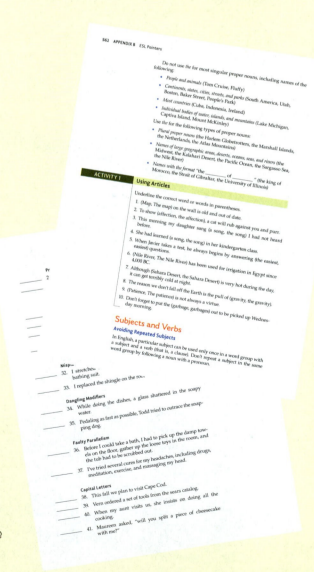

Each of the **twenty professional essays** that appear in Part 4 is preceded by a **Preview** that introduces the author and reading and a list of vocabulary selections called **Words to Watch.** **Questions** that follow each selection— **Vocabulary-in-Context, Reading Comprehension,** and **Discussion (About Content; About Structure; About Style and Tone)**—provide a variety of ways to analyze and respond to the readings, while **Writing Assignments** offer starting points for your own paragraphs and essays. Many readings feature thematically linked images and a corresponding **Responding to Images** writing assignment.

The **Appendixes** include A) an introduction to the parts of speech, B) advice for multilingual writers, C) a diagnostic test, D) an achievement test, E) answers to the sentence skills activities in Part 3 (so you can check your work), and F) A Writer's Journal section where you can record your own thoughts about writing and ideas for specific assignments.

These features will serve as familiar guideposts and handy references as you make your way through the book. The structure will help you in understanding the book's content, even as the activities and writing assignments assist you in learning and remembering the materials.

I hope your experience using *Exploring Writing: Sentences and Paragraphs* will be entirely successful. If you have comments or suggestions for improving the way this textbook works, send an email to english@ mcgraw-hill.com, and my editors will gladly pass it along.

—John Langan

Exploring Writing
Sentences and Paragraphs

PART

1

Writing:
Skills and Process

A Writer's Showcase

from "Rowing the Bus" by Paul Logan

In his essay "Rowing the Bus" (pp. 441–444), Paul Logan looks back at a period of schoolyard cruelty in which he was both a victim and a participant. With unflinching honesty, he describes his behavior then and how it helped to shape the person he has become. In this particular paragraph, Logan offers readers some specific reasons why he was singled out and taunted by bullies.

> Logan's main point is stated here, in the topic sentence.

> The writer defines for us what "the bags" means in this context

I was the perfect target for them*. I was small. I had no father. And my mother, though she worked hard to support me, was unable to afford clothes and sneakers that were "cool." Instead she dressed me in outfits that we got from "the bags"—hand-me-downs given as donations to a local church. Each Wednesday, she'd bring several bags of clothes to the house and pull out musty, wrinkled shirts and worn bell-bottom pants that other families no longer wanted. I knew that people were kind to give things to us, but I hated wearing clothes that might have been donated by my classmates. Each time I wore something from the bags, I feared that the other kids might recognize something that was once theirs. Besides my outdated clothes, I wore thick glasses, had crossed eyes, and spoke with a persistent lisp. For whatever reason, I had never learned to say the "s" sound properly, and I pronounced words that began with "th" as if they began with a "d." In addition, because of my severely crossed eyes, I lacked the hand and eye coordination necessary to hit or catch flying objects.

*bullies (who are mentioned in the previous paragraph. Turn to pp. 441–444 to read the whole essay.)

EXPLORING SUPPORTING DETAILS

1. Paul Logan backs up his main point—"I was the perfect target for them"—with solid support. Identify at least two examples that support this idea.

2. List specific details in this paragraph that help you "see," "smell," and "hear" Logan's point.

WRITING WITH SUPPORTING DETAILS

1. Write a sentence that begins with the phrase: "I was the perfect . . ." This is your topic sentence; now write the rest of the paragraph, supporting your point with specific details. If you need help generating an idea, see pp. 16–24 on prewriting techniques.

2. What are your most vivid memories from childhood? What moments stand out and make you laugh, cringe, or wish you could relive them? Make a list of these moments, and

continued

select a particularly memorable one to write about. Use the drafting strategies starting on page 24 to help you narrow and define your main point.

RESPONDING TO IMAGES

Look carefully at this photograph of a little girl walking next to a school bus. How does the image make you feel, and why? What specific details contribute to establishing this mood? What is the photographer's tone (or attitude toward the subject)?

1

An Introduction to Writing

Responding to Images

Looking carefully at this photograph of a room, what can you determine about who might live here? In a paragraph, describe the space—and the person/ people who might occupy it—to someone who has never seen it. Be as detailed as possible in your description; help your reader "see" what you do (the objects, the decorations, the layout).

Exploring Writing grows out of experiences I had when learning how to write. My early memories of writing in school are not pleasant. In the middle grades I remember getting back paper after paper on which the only comment was "Handwriting very poor." In high school, the night before a book report was due, I would work anxiously at a card table in my bedroom. I was nervous and sweaty because I felt out of my element, like a person who knows only how to open a can of soup being asked to cook a five-course meal. The act of writing was hard enough, and my feeling that I wasn't any good at it made me hate the process all the more.

Luckily, in college I had an instructor who changed my negative attitude about writing. During my first semester in composition, I realized that my instructor repeatedly asked two questions about any paper I wrote: "What is your point?" and "What is your support for that point?" I learned that sound writing consists basically of making a point and then providing evidence to support or develop that point. As I understood, practiced,

Now look at this other cartoon about Snoopy as a writer.

PEANUTS: © United Feature Syndicate, Inc

See if you can answer the following questions:

• What is Snoopy's point about the hero in his writing?

Your answer: His point is that _____

• What is his support for his point?

Your answer: _____

Snoopy's point is that the hero's life has been a disaster. This time, Snoopy has an abundance of support for his point: the hapless hero never had any luck, money, friends, love, laughter, applause, fame, or answers. The remaining flaw in Snoopy's composition is that he does not use enough supporting *details* to really prove his point. Instead, he plays the opposites game with his support ("He wanted to be loved. He died unloved."). As readers, we wonder who the hero wanted to be loved by: his mother? a heroine? a beagle? To sympathize with the hero and understand the nature of his disastrous life, we need more specifics. In the final panel of the cartoon, Snoopy has that guilty expression again. Why might he have a hard time ending this paragraph?

Point and Support in a Paragraph

Suppose you and a friend are talking about jobs you have had. You might say about a particular job, "That was the worst one I ever had. A lot of hard work and not much money." For your friend, that might be enough to make

your point, and you would not really have to explain your statement. But in writing, your point would have to be backed up with specific reasons and details.

Below is a paragraph, written by a student named Gene Hert, about his worst job. A *paragraph* is a short paper of 150 to 200 words. It usually consists of an opening point called a *topic sentence* followed by a series of sentences supporting that point.

My Job in an Apple Plant

Working in an apple plant was the worst job I ever had. First of all, the work was physically hard. For ten hours a night, I took cartons that rolled down a metal track and stacked them onto wooden skids in a tractor trailer. Each carton contained twenty-five pounds of bottled apple juice, and they came down the track almost nonstop. The second bad feature of the job was the pay. I was getting the minimum wage at that time, $3.65 an hour, plus a quarter extra for working the night shift. I had to work over sixty hours a week to get decent take-home pay. Finally, I hated the working conditions. We were limited to two ten-minute breaks and an unpaid half hour for lunch. Most of my time was spent outside on the loading dock in near-zero-degree temperatures. I was very lonely on the job because I had no interests in common with the other truck loaders. I felt this isolation especially when the production line shut down for the night, and I spent two hours by myself cleaning the apple vats. The vats were an ugly place to be on a cold morning, and the job was a bitter one to have.

Notice what the specific details in this paragraph do. They provide you, the reader, with a basis for understanding *why* the writer makes the point that is made. Through this specific evidence, the writer has explained and successfully communicated the idea that this job was his worst one.

The evidence that supports the point in a paragraph often consists of a series of reasons followed by examples and details that support the reasons. That is true of the paragraph above: three reasons are provided, with examples and details that back up those reasons. Supporting evidence in a paper can also consist of anecdotes, personal experiences, facts, studies, statistics, and the opinions of experts.

Point and Support   ACTIVITY 1

The paragraph on the apple plant, like almost any piece of effective writing, has two essential parts: (1) a point is advanced, and (2) that point is then supported. Taking a minute to outline the paragraph will help you understand these basic parts clearly. Add the words needed to complete the outline that follows.

Point: Working in an apple plant is the worst job I ever had.

Reason 1: _____

    a. Loaded cartons onto skids for ten hours a night

    b. _____

Reason 2: _____

    a. _____

    b. Had to work sixty hours for decent take-home pay

Reason 3: _____

    a. Two ten-minute breaks and an unpaid lunch

    b. _____

    c. Loneliness on job

        (1) No interests in common with other workers

        (2) By myself for two hours cleaning the apple vats

ACTIVITY 2 — Fill in the Blanks

See if you can complete the following statements.

1. An important difference between writing and talking is that in writing we absolutely must _____ any statement we make.

2. A _____ is made up of a point and a collection of specifics that support the point.

WRITING ASSIGNMENT

An excellent way to get a feel for the paragraph is to write one. Your instructor may ask you to do that now. The only guidelines you need to follow are the ones described here. There is an advantage to writing a paragraph right away, at a point where you have had almost no instruction. This first paragraph will give a quick sense of your needs as a writer and will provide a baseline—a standard of comparison that you and your instructor can use to measure your writing progress during the semester.

Here, then, is your topic: Write a paragraph on the best or worst job you have ever had. Provide three reasons why your job was the best or the worst, and give plenty of details to develop each of your three reasons.

Notice that the sample paragraph, "My Job in an Apple Plant," has the same format your paragraph should have. You should do what this author has done:

- State a point in the first sentence.

- Give three reasons to support the point.

- Introduce each reason clearly with signal words (such as *First of all, Second,* and *Finally*).

- Provide details that develop each of the three reasons.

Write or type your paragraph on a separate sheet of paper. After completing the paragraph, hand it in to your instructor.

Writing as a Skill

A realistic attitude about writing must build on the idea that *writing is a skill*. It is a skill like driving, typing, or cooking, and like any skill, it can be learned. If you have the determination to learn, this book will give you the extensive practice needed to develop your writing skills.

People who believe that writing is a "natural gift" rather than a learned skill may think that they are the only ones for whom writing is unbearably difficult. They might feel that everyone else finds writing easy or at least tolerable. Such people typically say, "I'm not any good at writing" or "English was not one of my good subjects." The result of this attitude is that people try to avoid writing, and when they do write, they don't try their best. Their attitude becomes a self-fulfilling prophecy: Their writing fails chiefly because they have convinced themselves that they don't have the "natural talent" needed to write. Unless their attitude changes, they probably will not learn how to write effectively.

Many people find it difficult to do the intense, active thinking that clear writing demands. It is frightening to sit down before a blank sheet of paper or a computer screen and know that an hour later, little on it may be worth keeping. It is frustrating to discover how much of a challenge it is to transfer thoughts and feelings from one's head into words. It is upsetting to find that an apparently simple writing subject often turns out to be complicated. But writing is not an automatic process; for almost everyone, competent writing comes from plain hard work—from determination, sweat, and head-on battle. The good news is that the skill of writing can be mastered, and if you are ready to work, you will learn what you need to know.

Why Does Your Attitude toward Writing Matter?

How Do You Feel about Writing?	**ACTIVITY 3**

Your attitude toward writing is an important part of learning to write well. To get a sense of just how you feel about writing, read the following statements. Put a check beside those statements with which you agree. (This activity is not a test, so try to be as honest as possible.)

_____ 1. A good writer should be able to sit down and write a paper straight through without stopping.

_____ 2. Writing is a skill that anyone can learn with practice.

_____ 3. I'll never be good at writing because I make too many mistakes in spelling, grammar, and punctuation.

_____   4. Because I dislike writing, I always start a paper at the last possible minute.

_____   5. I've always done poorly in English, and I don't expect that to change.

Now read the following comments about the five statements. The comments will help you see if your attitude is hurting or helping your efforts to become a better writer.

1. **A good writer should be able to sit down and write a paper straight through without stopping.**

   The statement is *false*. Writing is, in fact, a process. It is done not in one easy step but in a series of steps, and seldom at one sitting. If you cannot do a paper all at once, that simply means you are like most of the other people on the planet. It is harmful to carry around the false idea that writing should be an easy matter.

2. **Writing is a skill that anyone can learn with practice.**

   This statement is absolutely true. Writing is a skill, like driving or typing, that you can master with hard work. If you want to learn to write, you can. It is as simple as that. If you believe this, you are ready to learn how to become a competent writer.

   Some people hold the false belief that writing is a natural gift that some have and others do not. Because of this belief, they never make a truly honest effort to learn to write—and so they never learn.

3. **I'll never be good at writing because I make too many mistakes in spelling, grammar, and punctuation.**

   The first concern in good writing should be *content*—what you have to say. Your ideas and feelings are what matter most. You should not worry about spelling, grammar, or punctuation while working on content.

   Unfortunately, some people are so self-conscious about making mistakes that they do not focus on what they want to say. They need to realize that a paper is best done in stages, and that applying the rules can and should wait until a later stage in the writing process. Through review and practice, you will eventually learn how to follow the rules with confidence.

4. **Because I dislike writing, I always start a paper at the last possible minute.**

   This is all too common. You feel you are *going to* do poorly, and then your behavior ensures that you *will* do poorly! Your attitude is so negative that you defeat yourself—not even allowing enough time to really try.

   Again, what you need to realize is that writing is a process. Because it is done in steps, you don't have to get it right all at once. Just get started well in advance. If you allow yourself enough time, you'll find a way to make a paper come together.

5. **I've always done poorly in English, and I don't expect that to change.**

   How you may have performed in the *past* does not control how you can perform in the *present*. Even if you did poorly in English in high school, it is in your power to make this one of your best subjects in college. If you believe writing can be learned, and if you work hard at it, you will become a better writer.

In brief, your attitude is crucial. If you believe you are a poor writer and always will be, chances are you will not improve. If you realize you can become a better writer, chances are you *will* improve. Depending on how you allow yourself to think, you can be your own best friend or your own worst enemy.

Writing as a Process of Discovery

In addition to believing that writing is a natural gift, many people believe, mistakenly, that writing should flow in a simple, straight line from the writer's head onto the page. But writing is seldom an easy, one-step journey in which a finished paper comes out in a first draft. The truth is that *writing is a process of discovery* that involves a series of steps, and those steps are very often a zigzag journey. Look at the following illustrations of the writing process:

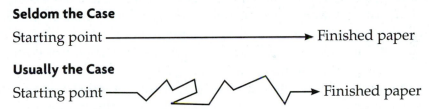

Seldom the Case

Starting point ⟶ Finished paper

Usually the Case

Starting point ⟶ Finished paper

Very often, writers do not discover just what they want to write about until they explore their thoughts in writing. For example, Gene Hert had been asked to write about a best or worst job. Only after he did some free-writing on jobs he liked and disliked did he realize that the most interesting details centered on his job at an apple plant. He discovered his subject in the course of writing.

Another student, Rhonda, talking afterward about a paper she wrote, explained that at first her topic was how she relaxed with her children. But as she accumulated details, she realized after a page of writing that the words *relax* and *children* simply did not go together. Her details were really examples of how she *enjoyed* her children, not how she *relaxed* with them. She sensed that the real focus of her writing should be what she did by herself to relax, and then she thought suddenly that the best time of her week was Thursday after school. "A light clicked on in my head," she explained. "I knew I had my paper." Then it was a matter of detailing exactly what she did to relax on Thursday evenings.

The point is that writing is often a process of exploration and continuing discovery. As you write, you may suddenly switch direction or double back. You may be working on a topic sentence and realize that it could be your concluding thought. Or you may be developing a supporting idea and then decide that it should be the main point of your paper. Chapter 2 will treat the writing process directly. It is important to remember that writers frequently do not know their exact destination as they begin to write. Very often they discover the direction and shape of a paper *during* the process of writing.

Keeping a Journal

Because writing is a skill, it makes sense that the more you practice writing, the better you will write. One excellent way to get practice in writing, even before you begin composing formal paragraphs, is to keep a daily or almost daily journal. Keeping a journal will help you develop the habit of thinking on paper and will show you how ideas can be discovered in the process of writing. A journal can make writing a familiar part of your life and can serve as a continuing source of ideas for papers.

At some point during the day—perhaps during a study period after your last class of the day, or right before dinner, or right before going to bed—spend fifteen minutes or so writing in your journal. Keep in mind that you do not have to plan what to write about, or be in the mood to write, or worry about making mistakes as you write; just write down whatever words come out. You should write at least one page in each session.

You may want to use a notebook that you can easily carry with you for on-the-spot writing. Or you may decide to write on loose-leaf paper that can be transferred later to a journal folder. No matter how you proceed, be sure to date all entries.

Your instructor may ask you to make journal entries a specific number of times a week for a specific number of weeks. He or she may have you turn in your journal every so often for review and feedback. If you are keeping the journal on your own, try to make entries three to five times a week every week of the semester. Your journal can serve as a sourcebook of ideas for possible papers. More important, keeping a journal will help you develop the habit of thinking on paper, and it can help you make writing a familiar part of your life.

| ACTIVITY 4 | Using a Journal to Generate Ideas |

Following is an excerpt from one student's journal. (Sentence-skills mistakes have been corrected to improve readability.) As you read, look for a general point and supporting material that could be the basis for an interesting paper.

October 6

Today a woman came into our department at the store and wanted to know if we had any scrap lumber ten feet long. Ten feet! "Lady," I said, "anything we have that's ten feet long sure as heck isn't scrap." When the boss heard me say that, he almost canned me. My boss is a company man, down to his toe tips. He wants to make a big impression on his bosses, and he'll run us around like mad all night to make himself look good. He's the most ambitious man I've ever met. If I don't transfer out of Hardware soon, I'm going to go crazy on this job. I'm not ready to quit, though. The time is not right. I want to be here for a year and have another job lined up and have other things right before I quit. It's good the boss wasn't around tonight when another customer wanted me to carry a bookcase he had bought out to his car. He didn't ask me to help him—he <u>expected</u> me to help him. I hate that kind of "You're my servant" attitude, and I told him that carrying stuff out to cars wasn't my job. Ordinarily I go out of my way to give people a hand, but not guys like him. . . .

- If the writer of this journal is looking for an idea for a paper, he can probably find several in this single entry. For example, he might write a narrative supporting the point that "In my sales job I have to deal with some irritating customers." See if you can find another idea in this entry that might be the basis for an interesting paragraph. Write your point in the space below.

  _____

- Take fifteen minutes to prepare a journal entry right now on this day in your life. On a separate sheet of paper, just start writing about anything that you have said, heard, thought, or felt, and let your thoughts take you where they may.

TECH-SAVVY WRITING

Go to each of the following pages:

www.yahoo.com

www.nationalgeographic.com

www.rottentomatoes.com

www.youtube.com

www.myspace.com

www.firstgov.gov

What is the main point of each site? How would you state it in a sentence? Next, describe **one** Web site's purpose in a paragraph. Use plenty of specific evidence to support your point.

RESPONDING TO IMAGES

A lot is happening in this photograph, but we are immediately drawn to one particular interaction. What is the focus (or central point), and how does the photographer guide our eyes and attention to it?

The Writing Process

Final Version
from "O Captain! My Captain!" by Walt Whitman (second stanza)

O Captain! My Captain! rise up and hear the bells;
Rise up—for you the flag is flung—for you the bugle trills;
For you bouquets and ribbon'd wreaths —for you the shores a-crowding;
For you they call, the swaying mass, their eager faces turning;
    Here Captain! dear father!
        This arm beneath your head;
            It is some dream that on the deck,
                You've fallen cold and dead.

Chapter Preview

How Do You Reach the Goals of Effective Writing?

Prewriting

- Technique 1: Freewriting
- Technique 2: Questioning
- Technique 3: Making a List
- Technique 4: Clustering
- Technique 5: Preparing a Scratch Outline

Writing the First Draft

Revising

Editing and Proofreading

Tips on Using a Computer

Using Peer Review

Responding to Images

Even the famous poem "O Captain, My Captain" by Walt Whitman was once a rough draft. Compare this excerpted draft with its final version; what has changed? Choose one revision and explain why and how it makes the poem a stronger work.

How Do You Reach the Goals of Effective Writing?

Even professional writers do not sit down and write a paper automatically, in one draft. Instead, they have to work on it a step at a time. Writing a paper is a process that can be divided into the following steps:

- Prewriting
- Writing the First Draft
- Revising
- Editing and Proofreading

These steps are described on the following pages.

Prewriting

If you are like many people, you may have trouble getting started writing. A mental block may develop when you sit down before a blank sheet of paper or a blank screen. You may not be able to think of an interesting topic or a point to make about your topic. Or you may have trouble coming up with specific details to support your point. And even after starting a composition, you may hit snags—moments when you wonder "What else can I say?" or "Where do I go next?"

The following pages describe five techniques that will help you think about and develop a topic and get words on paper: (1) freewriting, (2) questioning, (3) making a list, (4) clustering, and (5) preparing a scratch outline. These prewriting techniques help you think about and create material, and they are a central part of the writing process.

Technique 1: Freewriting

www.mhhe.com/langan

When you do not know what to write about a subject or when you are blocked in writing, freewriting sometimes helps. In *freewriting*, you write on your topic for ten minutes. You do not worry about spelling or punctuating correctly, about erasing mistakes, about organizing material, or about finding exact words. You just write without stopping. If you get stuck for words, you write "I am looking for something to say" or repeat words until something comes. There is no need to feel inhibited, since mistakes *do not count* and you do not have to hand in your paper.

Freewriting will limber up your writing muscles and make you familiar with the act of writing. It is a way to break through mental blocks about writing. Since you do not have to worry about mistakes, you can focus on discovering what you want to say about a subject. Your initial ideas and impressions will often become clearer after you have gotten them down on paper, and they may lead to other impressions and ideas. Through continued practice in freewriting, you will develop the habit of thinking as you write. And you will learn a technique that is a helpful way to get started on almost any piece of writing.

Freewriting: A Student Model

Gene Hert's paragraph "My Job in an Apple Plant" on page 7 in Chapter 1 was written in response to an assignment to write a composition on the best or worst job he ever had. Gene began by doing some general freewriting and thinking about his jobs. Here is his freewriting:

> I have had good and bad jobs, that's for sure. It was great earning money for the first time. I shoveled snow for my neighbor, a friend of mine and I did the work and had snowball fights along the way. I remember my neighbor reaching into his pocket and pulling out several dollars and handing us the money, it was like magic. Then there was the lawnmowing, which was also a good job. I mowed my aunts lawn while she was away at work. Then I'd go sit by myself in her cool living room and have a coke she left in the refrigarator for me. And look through all her magazines. Then there was the apple plant job I had after high school. That was a worst job that left me totaly wiped out at the end of my shift. Lifting cartons and cartons of apple juice for bosses that treated us like slaves. The cartons coming and coming all night long. I started early in the evening and finished the next morning. I still remember how tired I was. Driving back home the first time. That was a lonely job and a hard job and I don't eat apples anymore.

At this point, Gene read over his notes, and as he later commented, "I realized that I had several potential topics. I said to myself, 'What point can I make that I can cover in a paragraph? What do I have the most information about?' I decided to narrow my topic down to my awful job at the apple plant. I figured I would have lots of interesting details for that topic." Gene then did a more focused freewriting to accumulate details for a paragraph on this job:

> The job I remember most is the worst job I ever had. I worked in an apple plant, I put in very long hours and would be totaly beat after ten hours of work. All the time lifting cartons of apple juice which would come racing down a metal track. The guy with me was a bit lazy at times, and I would be one man doing a two-man job. The cartons would go into a tracter trailer, we would have to throw down wooden skids to put the cartons on, then wed have to move the metal track as we filled up the truck. There is no other job I have had that even compares to this job, it was a lot worse than it seems. The bosses treated us like slaves and the company paid us like slaves. I would work all night from 7 p.m. and drive home in the morning at 5 a.m. and be bone tired. I remember my arms and sholders were so tired after the first night. I had trouble turning the steering wheel of my father's car.

TIP   Notice that there are problems with spelling, grammar, and punctuation in Gene's freewriting. Gene was not worried about such matters, nor should he have been. At this stage, he just wanted to do some thinking on paper and get some material down on the page. He knew that this was a good first step, a good way of getting started, and that he would then be able to go on and shape that material.

You should take the same approach when freewriting: Explore your topic without worrying at all about being "correct." Figuring out what you want to say and getting raw material down on the page should have all of your attention at this early stage of the writing process.

ACTIVITY 1   Freewriting

To get a sense of the freewriting process, take a sheet of paper and freewrite about different jobs you have had and what you liked or did not like about them. See how much material you can accumulate in ten minutes. And remember not to worry about "mistakes"; you're just thinking on paper.

Technique 2: Questioning

In *questioning*, you generate ideas and details by asking as many questions as you can think of about your subject. Such questions include *Why? When? Where? Who? How? In what ways?*

www.mhhe.com/langan

Here are questions that Gene Hert asked while further developing his paragraph:

Questioning: A Student Model

Questions	Answers
What did I hate about the job?	Very hard work.
	Poor pay.
	Mean bosses.
How was the work hard?	Nonstop cartons of apple juice.
	Cartons became very heavy.
Why was pay poor?	$3.65 an hour (minimum wage at the time).
	Only a quarter more for working the second shift.
	Only good money was in overtime—where you got time and a half.
	No double time.
How were the bosses mean?	Yelled at some workers.
	Showed no appreciation.
	Created bad working conditions.
In what ways were working conditions bad?	Unheated truck in zero-degree weather.
	Floor of tractor trailer was cold steel.
	Breaks were limited—only two of them.
	Lonely job.

> **TIP**   Asking questions can be an effective way of getting yourself to think about a topic from different angles. The questions can help you generate details about a topic and get ideas on how to organize those details. Notice how asking questions gives Gene a better sense of the different reasons why he hated the job.

ACTIVITY 2   Questioning

To get a feel for the questioning process, use a sheet of paper to ask yourself a series of questions about your best and worst jobs. See how many details you can accumulate in ten minutes. And remember again not to be concerned about "mistakes," because you are just thinking on paper.

www.mhhe.com/langan

Technique 3: Making a List

In *making a list*, also known as *brainstorming*, you create a list of ideas and details that relate to your subject. Pile these items up, one after another, without trying to sort out major details from minor ones, or trying to put the details in any special order, or even trying to spell words correctly. Your goal is to accumulate raw material by making up a list of everything about your subject that occurs to you.

After freewriting and questioning, Gene made up the following list of details.

Making a List: A Student Model

Apple factory job—worst one I ever had

Bosses were mean

Working conditions were poor

Went to work at 5 P.M., got back at 7 A.M.

Lifted cartons of apple juice for ten hours

Cartons were heavy

Only two ten-minute breaks a night

Pay was only $3.65 an hour

Just quarter extra for night shift

Cost of gas money to and from work

No pay for lunch break

continued

Had to work 60 hours for good take-home pay

Loaded onto wooden skids in a truck

Bosses yelled at some workers

Temperature zero outside

Floors of trucks ice-cold metal

Nonstop pace

Had to clean apple vats after work

Slept, ate, and worked—no social life

No real friends at work

TIP   One detail led to another as Gene expanded his list. Slowly but surely, more details emerged, some of which he could use in developing his paragraph. By the time you finish making a list, you should be ready to plan an outline of your paragraph and then to write your first draft.

Listing

ACTIVITY 3

To get a sense of making a list, use a sheet of paper to list a series of details about one of the best or worst jobs you ever had. Don't worry about deciding whether the details are major or minor; instead, just get down as many details as you can think of in five or ten minutes.

Technique 4: Clustering

Clustering, also known as *diagramming* or *mapping,* is another strategy that can be used to generate material for a paper of any length. This method is helpful for people who like to think in a visual way. In clustering, you use lines, boxes, arrows, and circles to show relationships among the ideas and details that occur to you.

Begin by stating your subject in a few words in the center of a blank sheet of paper. Then, as ideas and details occur to you, put them in boxes or circles around the subject and draw lines to connect them to each other and to the subject. Put minor ideas or details in smaller boxes or circles, and use connecting lines to show how they relate as well.

Keep in mind that there is no right or wrong way of clustering. It is a way to think on paper about how various ideas and details relate to one another. What follows is an example of what Gene might have done to develop his ideas:

Clustering: A Student Model

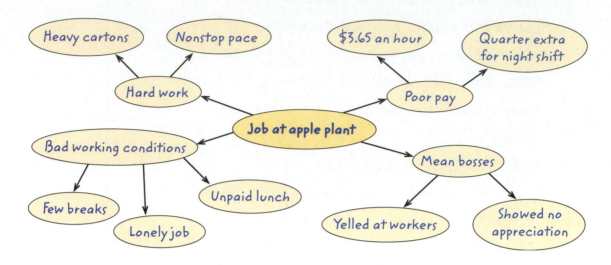

> ┌─────┐
> │ TIP │   In addition to helping generate material, clustering often suggests
> └─────┘ ways to organize ideas and details.

ACTIVITY 4   **Clustering/Diagramming**

Use clustering or diagramming to organize the details that you created for the previous activity about a best or worst job (page 21).

www.mhhe.com/langan

Technique 5: Preparing a Scratch Outline

A scratch outline can be the *single most helpful technique* for writing a good paper. A scratch outline often follows freewriting, questioning, making a list, or clustering, but it may also gradually emerge in the midst of these strategies. In fact, trying to make a scratch outline is a good way to see if you need to do more prewriting. If you cannot come up with a solid outline, then you know you need to do more prewriting to clarify your main point and its several kinds of support.

In a scratch outline, you think carefully about the point you are making, the supporting items for that point, and the order in which you will arrange those items. The scratch outline is a plan or blueprint to help you achieve a unified, supported, and well-organized composition.

Scratch Outline: A Student Model

In Gene's case, as he was working on his list of details, he suddenly realized what the plan of his paragraph could be. He could organize many of his details into one of three supporting groups: (1) the job itself, (2) the pay, and (3) the working conditions. He then went back to the list, crossed out items that he now saw did not fit, and numbered the items according to the group where they fit. Here is what Gene did with his list:

Apple factory job—worst one I ever had

~~Bosses were mean~~

3   Working conditions were poor

~~Went to work at 5 P.M., got back at 7 A.M.~~

1   Lifted cartons of apple juice for ten hours

1   Cartons were heavy

3   Only two ten-minute breaks a night

2   Pay was only $3.65 an hour

2   Just quarter extra for night shift

~~Cost of gas money to and from work~~

2   Had to work 60 hours for good take-home pay

1   Loaded onto wooden skids in a truck

~~Bosses yelled at some workers~~

3   Temperature zero outside

~~Floors of trucks ice-cold metal~~

1   Nonstop pace

3   No pay for lunch break

3   Had to clean apple vats after work

~~Slept, ate, and worked—no social life~~

3   No real friends at work

Under the list, Gene was now able to prepare his scratch outline:

The apple plant was my worst job.

1. Hard work

2. Poor pay

3. Poor working conditions

> **TIP**   After all his prewriting, Gene was pleased. He knew that he had a promising composition—one with a clear point and solid support. He saw that he could organize the material into a paragraph with a topic sentence, supporting points, and vivid details. He was now ready to write the first draft of his paragraph, using his outline as a guide. Chances are that if you do enough prewriting and thinking on paper, you will eventually discover the point and support of your paragraph.

ACTIVITY 5   Making a Scratch Outline

Create a scratch outline that could serve as a guide if you were to write a paragraph on your best or worst job experience.

Writing the First Draft

When you write a first draft, be prepared to put in additional thoughts and details that did not emerge during prewriting. And don't worry if you hit a snag. Just leave a blank space or add a comment such as "Do later" and press on to finish the paper. Also, don't worry yet about grammar, punctuation, or spelling. You don't want to take time correcting words or sentences that you may decide to remove later. Instead, make it your goal to state your main idea clearly and develop the content of your paragraph with plenty of specific details.

Writing a First Draft: A Student Model

Here is Gene's first draft, done in longhand:

> ~~The apple plant job was my worst.~~ Working in an apple plant was the worst job I ever had. The work was physicaly hard. For ~~a long time~~ ten hours a night, I stacked cartons that rolled down a metal track in a tracter trailer. Each carton had cans or bottles of apple juice, and they were heavy. At the same time, I had to keep a mental count of all the cartons I had loaded. The pay for the job was a bad feature. I was getting the minamum wage at that time plus a quarter extra for night shift. I had to work a lot to get a decent take-home pay. Working conditions were poor at the apple plant, we were limited to ~~short breaks~~ two ten-minute breaks. The truck-loading dock where I was most of the time was a cold and lonely place. Then by myself cleaning up. DETAILS!

> **TIP**   After Gene finished the first draft, he was able to put it aside until the next day. You will benefit as well if you can allow some time between finishing a draft and starting to revise.

Drafting   ACTIVITY 6

See if you can fill in the missing words in the following explanation of Gene's first draft.

1. Gene presents his _____ in the first sentence and then crosses it out and revises it right away to make it read smoothly and clearly.

2. Notice that he continues to accumulate specific supporting details as he writes the draft. For example, he crosses out and replaces "a long time"

    with the more specific _____; he crosses out and re-

    places "short breaks" with the more specific _____.

3. There are various misspellings—for example, _____.
    Gene doesn't worry about spelling at this point. He just wants to get down as much of the substance of his paper as possible.

4. There are various punctuation errors, especially the run-on and the

    fragment near the *(beginning, middle, end)* _____ of the paragraph.

5. Near the close of his paragraph, Gene can't think of added details to

    insert, so he simply prints _____ as a reminder to himself for the next draft.

Revising

Revising is as much a stage in the writing process as prewriting, outlining, and doing the first draft. *Revising* means that you rewrite a paragraph or paper, building upon what has already been done in order to make it stronger. One writer has said about revision, "It's like cleaning house—getting rid of all the junk and putting things in the right order." It is not just "straightening up"; instead, you must be ready to roll up your sleeves and do whatever is needed to create an effective paper. Too many students think that a first draft *is* the final one. They start to become writers when they realize that revising a rough draft three or four times is often at the heart of the writing process.

Here are some quick hints that can help make revision easier. First, set your first draft aside for a while. You can then come back to it with a fresher, more objective point of view. Second, work from typed or printed text, preferably double-spaced so you'll have room to handwrite changes later. You'll be able to see the paragraph or paper more impartially if it

3. To add more (*unity, support, organization*) _____, he changes "a lot of hours" to "_____"; he changes "on the dock" to "_____"; he changes "cold temperatures" to "_____."

4. In the interest of eliminating wordiness, he removes the words "_____" from the sixth sentence.

5. To achieve parallelism, Gene changes "the half hour for lunch was not paid" to "_____."

6. For greater sentence variety, Gene combines two short sentences, beginning the second part of the sentence with the subordinating word "_____."

7. To create a consistent point of view, Gene changes "You felt this isolation" to "_____."

8. Finally, Gene replaces the somewhat vague "bad" in "The vats were a bad place to be on a cold morning, and the job was a bad one to have" with two more precise words: "_____" and "_____."

www.mhhe.com/langan

Editing and Proofreading

The next-to-last major stage in the writing process is editing—checking a paper for mistakes in grammar, punctuation, usage, and spelling. Students often find it hard to edit a paper carefully. They have put so much work into their writing, or so little, that it's almost painful for them to look at the paper one more time. You may simply have to *will* yourself to carry out this important closing step in the writing process. Remember that eliminating sentence-skills mistakes will improve an average paper and help ensure a strong grade on a good paper. Further, as you get into the habit of checking your papers, you will also get into the habit of using sentence skills consistently. They are an integral part of clear, effective writing.

The checklist of sentence skills on the inside back cover of the book will serve as a guide while you are editing your paper.

Here are tips that can help you edit the next-to-final draft of a paper for sentence-skills mistakes:

Editing Tips

1. Have at hand two essential tools: a good dictionary (see pages 381–389) and a grammar handbook (you can use Part 3 of this book).

2. Use a sheet of paper to cover your essay so that you can expose only one sentence at a time. Look for errors in grammar,

spelling, and typing. It may help to read each sentence out loud. If the sentence does not read clearly and smoothly, chances are something is wrong.

3. Pay special attention to the kinds of errors you tend to make. For example, if you tend to write run-ons or fragments, be especially on the lookout for these errors.

4. Try to work on a typed or word-processed draft, where you'll be able to see your writing more objectively than you could on a handwritten page; use a pen with colored ink so that your corrections will stand out.

Proofreading, the final stage in the writing process, means checking a paper carefully for spelling, grammar, punctuation, and other errors. You are ready for this stage when you are satisfied with your choice of supporting details, the order in which they are presented, and the way they and your topic sentence are worded.

www.mhhe.com/langan

At this point in your work, use your dictionary to do final checks on your spelling. Use a grammar handbook (such as the one in Part 3 of this text) to be sure about grammar, punctuation, and usage. Also read through your paper carefully, looking for typing errors, omitted words, and any other errors you may have missed before. Proofreading is often hard to do—again, students have spent so much time with their work, or so little, that they want to avoid it. But if it is done carefully, this important final step will ensure that your paper looks as good as possible.

Proofreading Tips

1. One helpful trick at this stage is to read your paper out loud. You will probably hear awkward wordings and become aware of spots where the punctuation needs to be changed. Make the improvements needed for your sentences to read smoothly and clearly.

2. Another helpful technique is to take a sheet of paper and cover your paragraph so that you can expose just one line at a time and check it carefully.

3. A third strategy is to read your paper backward, from the last sentence to the first. This helps keep you from getting caught up in the flow of the paper and missing small mistakes—which is easy to do, since you're so familiar with what you meant to say.

Editing and Proofreading: A Student Model

After typing into his word-processing file all the revisions in his paragraph, Gene printed out another clean draft of the paper. He then turned his attention to editing changes, as shown below:

My Job in an Apple Plant

Working in an apple plant was the worst job I ever had. First of all, the work was ~~phsicaly~~ *physically* hard. For ten hours a night, I took cartons that rolled down a metal track and stacked them onto wooden skids in a ~~tracter~~ *tractor* trailer. Each carton contained ~~25~~ *twenty-five* pounds of bottled apple juice, and they came down the track almost nonstop. The second bad feature of the job was the pay. I was getting the ~~minamum~~ *minimum* wage at that time, $3.65 an hour. *P*lus a quarter extra for working the night shift. I had to work over sixty hours a week to get a decent take-home pay. Finally, I hated the working conditions. We were limited to two ten-minute breaks and an unpaid half hour for lunch. Most of my time was spent outside on the loading dock in near-zero-degree temperatures. And I was very lonely on the job because I had no interests in common with the other workers. I felt this isolation especially when the production line shut down for the night, and I ~~had to clean~~ *spent two hours by myself cleaning* the apple vats. The vats were an ugly place to be on a cold morning, and the job was a bitter one to have.

TIP   You can make your changes (as Gene did) in longhand right on the printout of your paper. To note Gene's changes, complete the activity that follows.

ACTIVITY 8   **Editing and Proofreading a Draft**

Fill in the missing words.

1. As part of his editing, Gene checked and corrected the _____ of three words, *physically*, *tractor*, and *minimum*.

2. He added _____ to set off an introductory phrase ("First of all") and an introductory word ("Finally") and also to connect the two complete thoughts in the final sentence.

3. He corrected a fragment ("_____") by using a comma to attach it to the preceding sentence.

4. He realized that a number like "25" should be _____ as "twenty-five."

5. Since revision can occur at any stage of the writing process, including editing, Gene makes one of his details more vivid by adding the descriptive words "_____."

At this point, all Gene had to do was to enter his corrections, print out the final draft of the paper, and proofread it for any typos or other careless errors. He was then ready to hand it in to his instructor.

Tips on Using a Computer

- If you are using your school's computer center, allow enough time. You may have to wait for a computer or printer to be free. In addition, you may need several sessions at the computer and printer to complete your paper.

- Every word-processing program allows you to save your writing by hitting one or more keys. Save your work file frequently as you write your draft. A saved file is stored safely on the computer or network. A file that is not saved will be lost if the computer crashes or if the power is turned off.

- Keep your work in two places—the hard drive or network you are working on and, if you have one, a backup USB drive. At the end of each session with the computer, copy your work onto the USB drive or e-mail a copy to yourself. Then if the hard drive or network becomes damaged, you'll have the backup copy.

- Print out your work at least at the end of every session. Then not only will you have your most recent draft to work on away from the computer, you'll also have a copy in case something should happen to your electronic copy.

- Work in single spacing so that you can see as much of your writing on the screen at one time as possible. Just before you print out your work, change to double spacing.

Drafting

☑ My main point is expressed in the topic sentence, which is _____

_____

_____.

☑ My main point is supported by several specific examples or by one extended example, which

are/is _____.

☑ I appeal to my readers' five senses with vivid details, such as _____

and _____.

☑ The tone of my paragraph could be described as _____.

Revising

☑ I waited _____ hours/days between finishing my first draft and revising it.

☑ My paragraph is unified; all the supporting points serve to back up the topic sentence. I

eliminated this point/sentence/word because it did not contribute to the main idea:

_____

_____.

☑ My paragraph is well supported; there is plenty of specific evidence for each supporting point.

For one of my supporting points, _____ , I use the following evidence:

_____.

☑ My paragraph is well organized. First, I have a clear method of organizing my thoughts, which

is list order/time order (circle one.) Also, I used the following transition words or signals to

make the organization of my paragraph easy for readers to follow: _____.

Editing / Proofreading

Grammar

☑ I use verb tenses correctly throughout the paragraph (pp. 239–242).

☑ My subjects agree with their verbs (pp. 230–238).

☑ I used a spell-checker and looked up words that I was unsure how to spell in an online or print

dictionary (pp. 381–389).

✔ One grammar or spelling mistake I corrected (or one word I looked up) was _____

_____

_____ .

Style

✔ I used words effectively by avoiding slang, clichés, pretentious language, and wordiness (pp. 418–426).

✔ I varied my sentences in length and structure (pp. 195–208).

Notes

_____

_____

_____

_____

_____

_____

_____

_____

_____

_____

_____

_____

_____

_____

_____

_____

_____

_____

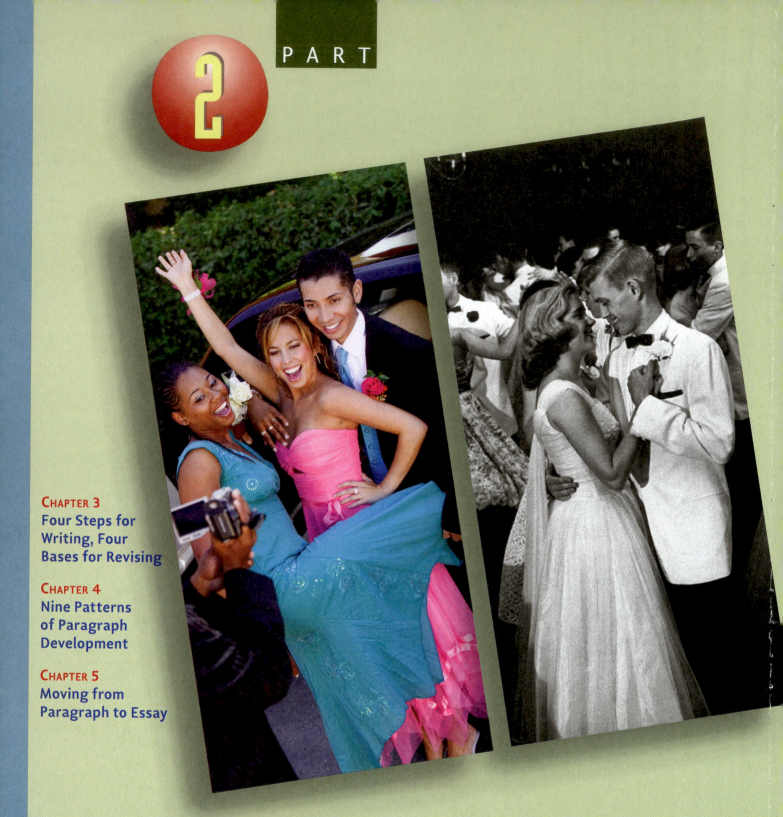

2

PART

Writing Effective Paragraphs

A Writer's Showcase

from "Let's Really Reform Our Schools" by Anita Garland

In her essay "Let's Really Reform Our Schools" (pp. 488–491), Anita Garland criticizes the practices and priorities of American high schools, offering some radical suggestions for improvement. This particular paragraph focuses on getting rid of proms; the author argues that prom distracts from—rather than contributes to—the goals of a high school education.

The transition word *Another* indicates that this paragraph, as part of a larger essay, refers back to the previous paragraph.

Garland's topic sentence. Every sentence in this paragraph contributes to the argument stated here, establishing a sense of UNITY.

Another school-related activity that should get the ax is the fluff-headed, money-eating, misery-inducing event known as the prom. How in the world did the schools of America get involved in this showcase of excess? Proms have to be the epitome of everything that is wrong, tasteless, misdirected, inappropriate, and just plain sad about the way we bring up our young people. Instead of simply letting the kids put on a dance, we've turned the prom into a bloated nightmare that ruins young people's budgets, their self-image, and even their lives. The pressure to show up at the prom with the best-looking date, in the most expensive clothes, wearing the most exotic flowers, riding in the most extravagant form of transportation, dominates the thinking of many students for months before the prom itself. Students cling to doomed, even abusive romantic relationships rather than risk being dateless for this night of nights. They lose any concept of meaningful values as they implore their parents for more, more, more money to throw into the jaws of the prom god. The adult trappings of the prom—the slinky dresses, emphasis on romance, slow dancing, nightclub atmosphere—all encourage kids to engage in behavior that can have tragic consequences. Who knows how many unplanned pregnancies and alcohol-related accidents can be directly attributed to the pressures of prom night? And yet, not going to the prom seems a fate worse than death to many young people.

Garland uses SENTENCE SKILLS correctly and effectvely. In particular, note her use of sentence variety (see pp. 195–208 for more on this topic).

Specific details like these back up the author's point, offering SUPPORT.

Garland saves her strongest point for last, using emphatic order. This organizational choice contributes to a sense of paragraph COHERENCE.

READING FOR PATTERNS

1. Are any words or phrases *defined* in this paragraph? If so, what are they? (For more on definition, see pp. 104–107.)

2. What are some vivid *descriptions* the writer uses? Which senses do they appeal to? (For more on description, see pp. 111–115.)

3. Is there a *cause-effect* relationship in this paragraph? (For more on cause and effect, see pp. 95–98.)

continued

47

Identifying Topics, Topic Sentences, and Support

The following activity will sharpen your sense of the differences between topics, topic sentences, and supporting sentences.

ACTIVITY 3	Breaking Down the Parts of a Paragraph

Each group of items below includes one topic, one main idea (expressed in a topic sentence), and two supporting details for that idea. In the space provided, label each item with one of the following:

T	topic
MI	main idea
SD	supporting details

1. _____ a. The weather in the summer is often hot and sticky.

   _____ b. Summer can be an unpleasant time of year.

   _____ c. Summer.

   _____ d. Bug bites, poison ivy, and allergies are a big part of summertime.

2. _____ a. The new Ultimate sports car is bound to be very popular.

   _____ b. The company has promised to provide any repairs needed during the first three years at no charge.

   _____ c. Because it gets thirty miles per gallon of gas, it offers real savings on fuel costs.

   _____ d. The new Ultimate sports car.

3. _____ a. Decorating an apartment doesn't need to be expensive.

   _____ b. A few plants add a touch of color without costing a lot of money.

   _____ c. Inexpensive braided rugs can be bought to match nearly any furniture.

   _____ d. Decorating an apartment.

4. _____ a. Long practice sessions and busy game schedules take too much time away from schoolwork.

   _____ b. High school sports.

   _____ c. The competition between schools may become so intense that, depending on the outcome of one game, athletes are either adored or scorned.

   _____ d. High school sports put too much pressure on young athletes.

5. _____ a. After mapping out the best route to your destination, phone ahead for motel reservations.

_____ b. A long car trip.

_____ c. Following a few guidelines before a long car trip can help you avoid potential problems.

_____ d. Have your car's engine tuned as well, and have the tires, brakes, and exhaust system inspected.

Step 2: Back Up Your Point

To support your point, you need to provide specific reasons, examples, and other details that explain and develop it. The more precise and particular your supporting details are, the better your readers can "see," "hear," and "feel" them.

Understanding General versus Specific Ideas

A paragraph is made up of a main idea, which is general, and the specific ideas that support it. So to write well, you must understand the difference between general and specific ideas.

It is helpful to realize that you use general and specific ideas all the time in your everyday life. For example, in choosing a film to rent, you may think, "Which should I rent, an action movie, a comedy, or a romance?" In such a case, *film* is the general idea, and *action movie, comedy,* and *romance* are the specific ideas.

Or you may decide to begin an exercise program. In that case, you might consider walking, jumping rope, or lifting weights. In this case, *exercise* is the general idea, and *walking, jumping rope,* and *lifting weights* are the specific ideas.

Or if you are talking to a friend about a date that didn't work out well, you may say, "The dinner was terrible, the car broke down, and we had little to say to each other." In this case, the general idea is *the date didn't work out well,* and the specific ideas are the three reasons you named.

The following activities will give you experience in recognizing the relationship between general and specific. They will also provide a helpful background for the information and additional activities that follow.

Identifying General Ideas   ACTIVITY 4

Each group of words consists of one general idea and four specific ideas. The general idea includes all the specific ideas. Underline the general idea in each group.

EXAMPLE

jeep   van   truck   <u>vehicle</u>   sedan

1. salty   bitter   flavor   sweet   sour

2. jewelry   necklace   ring   earrings   bracelet

3. dime nickel coin quarter half-dollar

4. fax machine copier computer calculator office machine

5. theft murder rape crime holdup

6. cracker snack carrot stick cookie popcorn

7. mascara cosmetic foundation lipstick eyeshadow

8. yes no I don't know answer maybe

9. yard work mowing planting trimming hedges feeding plants

10. job interviews weddings car accidents being fired stressful times

ACTIVITY 5 — Developing Specific Ideas

In each item below, one idea is general and the others are specific. The general idea includes the specific ones. In the spaces provided, write in two more specific ideas that are covered by the general idea.

EXAMPLE

General: exercises

Specific: chin-ups, jumping jacks, ___sit-ups___ , ___push-ups___

1. *General:* pizza toppings

   Specific: sausage, mushrooms, _____ , _____

2. *General:* furniture

   Specific: rocking chair, coffee table, _____ , _____

3. *General:* magazines

   Specific: Reader's Digest, Newsweek, _____ , _____

4. *General:* birds

   Specific: eagle, pigeon, _____ , _____

5. *General:* music

   Specific: jazz, classical, _____ , _____

6. *General:* cold symptoms

   Specific: aching muscles, watery eyes, _____ , _____

7. *General:* children's games

   Specific: hopscotch, dodgeball, _____ , _____

8. *General:* transportation

   Specific: plane, motorcycle, _____ , _____

9. *General:* city problems

   Specific: overcrowding, pollution, _____ , _____

10. *General:* types of TV shows

    Specific: cartoons, situation comedies, _____ , _____

What Ideas Have in Common

ACTIVITY 6

Read each group of specific ideas below. Then circle the letter of the general idea that tells what the specific ideas have in common. Note that the general idea should not be too broad or too narrow. Begin by trying the example item, and then read the explanation that follows.

EXAMPLE

Specific ideas: peeling potatoes, washing dishes, cracking eggs, cleaning out refrigerator

The general idea is

   a. household jobs.

   (b.) kitchen tasks.

   c. steps in making dinner.

> **EXPLANATION:** It is true that the specific ideas are all household jobs, but they have in common something even more specific—they are all tasks done in the kitchen. Therefore answer *a* is too broad, and the correct answer is *b*. Answer *c* is too narrow because it doesn't cover all the specific ideas. While two of them could be steps in making a dinner ("peeling potatoes" and "cracking eggs"), two have nothing to do with making dinner.

1. *Specific ideas:* crowded office, rude coworkers, demanding boss, unreasonable deadlines

   The general idea is

   a. problems.

   b. work problems.

   c. problems with work schedules.

2. *Specific ideas:* cactus, rosebush, fern, daisy

   The general idea is

   a. plants.

   b. plants that have thorns.

   c. plants that grow in the desert.

3. *Specific ideas:* Band-Aids, gauze, smelling salts, aspirin

   The general idea is

   a. supplies.

   b. first-aid supplies.

   c. supplies for treating a headache.

4. *Specific ideas:* trout, whales, salmon, frogs

   The general idea is

   a. animals.

   b. fish.

   c. animals living in water.

5. *Specific ideas:* Hershey bar, lollipop, mints, fudge

   The general idea is

   a. food.

   b. candy.

   c. chocolate.

6. *Specific ideas:* "Go to bed," "Pick up that trash," "Run twenty laps," "Type this letter."

   The general idea is

   a. remarks.

   b. orders.

   c. the boss's orders.

7. *Specific ideas:* "I had no time to study," "The questions were unfair," "I had a headache," "The instructor didn't give us enough time."

   The general idea is

   a. statements.

   b. excuses for being late.

   c. excuses for not doing well on a test.

8. *Specific ideas:* candle, sun, headlight, flashlight

   The general idea is

   a. things that are very hot.

   b. light sources for a home.

   c. sources of light.

9. *Specific ideas:* driving with expired license plates, driving over the speed limit, parking without putting money in the meter, driving without a license

   The general idea is:

   a. ways to cause a traffic accident.

   b. traffic problems.

   c. ways to get a ticket.

10. *Specific ideas:* "Are we there yet?" "Where do people come from?" "Can I have that toy?" "Do I have to go to bed now?"

    The general idea is

    a. Things adults say to one another.

    b. Things children ask adults.

    c. Things children ask at school.

What Is the General Idea? ACTIVITY 7

In the following items, the specific ideas are given but the general ideas are unstated. Fill in the blanks with the general ideas.

EXAMPLE

General idea: _____ car problems _____

Specific ideas: flat tire   dented bumper
                cracked windshield   dirty oil filter

1. General idea: _____
   Specific ideas: nephew   grandmother
                   aunt   cousin

2. General idea: _____
   Specific ideas: boots   sneakers
                   moccasins   slippers

3. General idea: _____
   Specific ideas: camping   hiking
                   fishing   hunting

4. General idea: _____
   Specific ideas: broom   sponge
                   mop   glass cleaner

5. General idea: _____
   Specific ideas: cloudy   sunny
                   snowy   rainy

6. General idea: _____
   Specific ideas: Spread mustard on slice of bread
                   Add turkey and cheese
                   Put lettuce on top of cheese
                   Cover with another slice of bread

7. General idea: _____
   Specific ideas: thermos of lemonade   insect repellent
                   basket of food   blanket

8. General idea: _____
   Specific ideas: fleas in carpeting   loud barking
                   tangled fur   veterinary bills

9. *General idea:* _____

   Specific ideas: diabetes   cancer
                       appendicitis   broken leg

10. *General idea:* _____

   Specific ideas: flooded basements   wet streets
                       rainbow   overflowing rivers

Recognizing Specific Details

Specific details are examples, reasons, particulars, and facts. Such details are needed to support and explain a topic sentence effectively. They provide the evidence needed for us to understand, as well as to feel and experience, a writer's point.

Below is a topic sentence followed by two sets of supporting sentences. Write a check mark next to the set that provides sharp, specific details.

Topic sentence: Ticket sales for a recent Rolling Stones concert proved that the classic rock band is still very popular.

_____ a. Fans came from everywhere to buy tickets to the concert. People wanted good seats and were willing to endure a great deal of various kinds of discomfort as they waited in line for many hours. Some people actually waited for days, sleeping at night in uncomfortable circumstances. Good tickets were sold out extremely quickly.

_____ b. The first person in the long ticket line spent three days standing in the hot sun and three nights sleeping on the concrete without even a pillow. The man behind her waited equally long in his wheelchair. The ticket window opened at 10:00 A.M., and the tickets for the good seats—those in front of the stage—were sold out an hour later.

> **EXPLANATION:** The second set (b) provides specific details. Instead of a vague statement about fans who were "willing to endure a great deal of various kinds of discomfort," we get vivid details we can see and picture clearly: "three days standing in the hot sun," "three nights sleeping on the concrete without even a pillow," "The man behind her waited equally long in his wheelchair."
>
> Instead of a vague statement that tickets were "sold out extremely quickly," we get exact and vivid details: "The ticket window opened at 10:00 A.M., and the tickets for the good seats—those in front of the stage—were sold out an hour later."

Specific details are often like a movie script. They provide us with such clear pictures that we could make a film of them if we wanted to. You would know just how to film the information given in the second set of sentences. You would show the fans in line under a hot sun and, later, sleeping on the concrete. The first person in line would be shown sleeping without a pillow under her head. You would show tickets finally going on sale, and after an hour you could show the ticket seller explaining that all of the seats in front of the stage were sold out.

In contrast, the writer of the first set of sentences (*a*) fails to provide the specific information needed. If you were asked to make a film based on set *a*, you would have to figure out on your own just what particulars to show.

When you are working to provide specific supporting information in a paper, it might help to ask yourself, "Could someone easily film this information?" If the answer is yes, your supporting details are specific enough for your readers to visualize.

Specific vs. General Support   ACTIVITY 8

Each topic sentence below is followed by two sets of supporting details. Write *S* (for *specific*) in the space next to the set that provides specific support for the point. Write *G* (for *general*) next to the set that offers only vague, general support.

1. *Topic sentence:* The West Side Shopping Mall is an unpleasant place.

   _____ a. The floors are covered with cigarette butts, dirty paper plates, and spilled food. The stores are so crowded I had to wait twenty minutes just to get a dressing room to try on a shirt.

   _____ b. It's very dirty, and not enough places are provided for trash. The stores are not equipped to handle the large number of shoppers that often show up.

> **HINT** Which set of supporting details could you more readily use in a film?

2. *Topic sentence:* Our golden retriever is a wonderful pet for children.

   _____ a. He is gentle, patient, eager to please, and affectionate. Capable of following orders, he is also ready to think for himself and find solutions to a problem. He senses children's moods and goes along with their wishes.

   _____ b. He doesn't bite, even when children pull his tail. After learning to catch a ball, he will bring it back again and again, seemingly always ready to play. If the children don't want to play anymore, he will just sit by their side, gazing at them with his faithful eyes.

3. *Topic sentence:* My two-year-old daughter's fearlessness is a constant source of danger to her.

   _____ a. She doesn't realize that certain activities are dangerous. Even when I warn her, she will go ahead and do something that could hurt her. I have to constantly be on the lookout for dangerous situations and try to protect her from them.

_____ b. For instance, she loves going to the swimming pool. That's great. But she will jump into water that is way over her head. She likes animals and will run to pet any dog that wanders by, no matter how unfriendly it seems.

4. *Topic sentence:* People's views of scientists are often more fiction than fact.

_____ a. Scientists are portrayed in movies as crazy guys with long hair, thick glasses, and shabby clothes. Incapable of remembering the time of day, these imaginary scientists skip meals and prefer the company of laboratory animals to that of their own children. In reality, scientists get hungry at mealtime, love their children, and go to work in suits.

_____ b. People don't know exactly what scientists do and fantasize a lot about their work. Instead of thinking of scientists as real people who do a particular type of work, people think of them as weird, antisocial geniuses whom one could spot a mile away. In reality, most scientists look and act much like their neighbors.

5. *Topic sentence:* Early theories of child raising were very different from today's theories.

_____ a. The first books on child raising came out hundreds of years ago. The advice they contained was based almost entirely on superstitions and other untrue beliefs. Some of the advice was harmless, but some could lead to long-term effects. They told parents to do things to their children that seem to us to make no sense at all.

_____ b. One early book, for example, advised mothers not to breast-feed their babies right after feeling anger because the anger would go into the milk and injure the child. Another told parents to begin toilet-training their children at the age of three weeks and to tie their babies' arms down for several months to prevent thumb sucking.

ACTIVITY 9   **Specific vs. General Support in a Paragraph**

At several points in each of the following paragraphs, you are given a choice of two sets of supporting details. Write *S* (for *specific*) in the space next to the set that provides specific support for the point. Write *G* (for *general*) next to the set that offers only vague, general support.

Paragraph 1

My daughter is as shy as I am, and it breaks my heart to see her dealing with the same problems I had to deal with in my childhood because of my shyness. I feel very sad for her when I see the problems she has making friends.

_____ a. It takes her a long time to begin to do the things other children do to make friends, and her feelings get hurt very easily over one thing or another. She is not at all comfortable about making connections with her classmates at school.

_____ b. She usually spends Christmas vacation alone because by that time of year she doesn't have friends yet. Only when her birthday comes in the summer is she confident enough to invite school friends to her party. Once she sends out the invitations, she almost sleeps by the telephone, waiting for the children to respond. If they say they can't come, her eyes fill with tears.

I recognize very well her signs of shyness, which make her look smaller and more fragile than she really is.

_____ c. When she has to talk to someone she doesn't know well, she speaks in a whisper and stares sideways. Pressing her hands together, she lifts her shoulders as though she wished she could hide her head between them.

_____ d. When she is forced to talk to anyone other than her family and her closest friends, the sound of her voice and the position of her head change. Even her posture changes in a way that makes it look as if she's trying to make her body disappear.

It is hard for me to watch her passing unnoticed at school.

_____ e. She never gets chosen for a special job or privilege, even though she tries her best, practicing in privacy at home. She just doesn't measure up. Worst of all, even her teacher seems to forget her existence much of the time.

_____ f. Although she rehearses in our basement, she never gets chosen for a good part in a play. Her voice is never loud or clear enough. Worst of all, her teacher doesn't call on her in class for days at a time.

Paragraph 2

It is said that the dog is man's best friend, but I strongly believe that the honor belongs to my computer. A computer won't fetch a stick for me, but it can help me entertain myself in many ways.

_____ a. If I am bored, tired, or out of ideas, the computer allows me to explore things that interest me, such as anything relating to the world of professional sports.

_____ b. The other day, I used my computer to visit the National Football League's Web site. I was then able to get injury updates for players on my favorite team, the Philadelphia Eagles.

While the dog is a faithful friend, it does not allow me to be a more responsible person the way my computer does.

_____ c. I use my computer to pay all my bills automatically over the Internet. I also use it to balance my checkbook and keep track of my expenses. Now I always know how much money is in my account at the end of the month.

_____ d. The computer helps me be responsible with financial matters because it records my transactions. With the computer, I have access to more information, which allows me to make good decisions with my money.

A dog might help me meet strangers I see in the park, but the computer helps me meet people who share my interests.

_____ e. With my computer, I can go online and find people with every type of hobby or interest. Thousands of online chat rooms and discussion groups are available featuring people from all over the country—and the world. The computer can even allow me to develop meaningful personal relationships with others.

_____ f. Two months ago, I discovered a Web site for people in my community who enjoy hiking. I'm planning to meet a group next Saturday for a day hike. And earlier this year, I met my wonderful fiancée, Shelly, through an online dating service.

Providing Specific Details

ACTIVITY 10   Getting Specific

Each of the following sentences contains a general word or words, set off in *italic* type. Substitute sharp, specific words in each case.

EXAMPLE

After the parade, the city street was littered with *garbage*.

After the parade, the city street was littered with multicolored

confetti, dirty popcorn, and lifeless balloons.

1. If I had enough money, I'd visit *several places.*

   _____

   _____

2. It took her *a long time* to get home.

   _____

   _____

3. Ron is often stared at because of his *unusual hair color and hairstyle.*

   _____

   _____

4. After you pass *two buildings,* you'll see my house on the left.

   _____

   _____

5. Nia's purse is crammed with *lots of stuff.*

   _____

   _____

6. I bought *some junk food* for the long car trip.

   _____

   _____

7. The floor in the front of my car is covered with *things.*

   _____

   _____

8. When his mother said no to his request for a toy, the child *reacted strongly.*

   _____

   _____

9. Devan gave his girlfriend a *surprise present* for Valentine's Day.

   _____

   _____

10. My cat can *do a wonderful trick.*

    _____

    _____

Selecting Details That Fit

The details in your paper must all clearly relate to and support your opening point. If a detail does not support your point, leave it out. Otherwise,

www.mhhe.com/langan

your paper will lack unity. For example, see if you can circle the letter of the two sentences that do *not* support the topic sentence below.

Topic sentence: **Mario is a very talented person.**

   a. Mario is always courteous to his professors.
   b. He has created beautiful paintings in his art course.
   c. Mario is the lead singer in a local band.
   d. He won an award in a photography contest.
   e. He is hoping to become a professional photographer.

EXPLANATION: Being courteous may be a virtue, but it is not a talent, so sentence *a* does not support the topic sentence. Also, Mario's desire to become a professional photographer tells us nothing about his talent; thus sentence *e* does not support the topic sentence either. The other three statements all clearly back up the topic sentence. Each in some way supports the idea that Mario is talented—in art, as a singer, or as a photographer.

| ACTIVITY 11 | **Details That Don't Fit** |

In each group below, circle the two items that do *not* support the topic sentence.

1. *Topic sentence:* Carla seems attracted only to men who are unavailable.
   a. She once fell in love with a man serving a life sentence in prison.
   b. Her parents worry about her inability to connect with a nice single man.
   c. She wants to get married and have kids before she is thirty.
   d. Her current boyfriend is married.
   e. Recently she had a huge crush on a Catholic priest.

2. *Topic sentence:* Some dog owners have little consideration for other people.
   a. Obedience lessons can be a good experience for both the dog and the owner.
   b. Some dog owners let their dogs leave droppings on the sidewalk or in other people's yards.
   c. They leave the dog home alone for hours, and it barks and howls and wakes the neighbors.
   d. Some people keep very large dogs in small apartments.
   e. Even when small children are playing nearby, owners let their bad-tempered dogs run loose.

3. *Topic sentence:* Dr. Eliot is a very poor teacher.
   a. He cancels class frequently with no explanation.
   b. When a student asks a question that he can't answer, he becomes irritated with the student.
   c. He got his PhD at a university in another country.
   d. He's taught at the college for many years and is on a number of faculty committees.
   e. He puts off grading papers until the end of the semester, and then returns them all at once.

4. *Topic sentence:* Some doctors seem to think it is all right to keep patients waiting.
   a. Pharmaceutical sales representatives sometimes must wait hours to see a doctor.
   b. The doctors stand in the hallway chatting with nurses and secretaries even when they have a waiting room full of patients.
   c. Patients sometimes travel long distances to consult with a particular doctor.
   d. When a patient calls before an appointment to see if the doctor is on time, the answer is often yes even when the doctor is two hours behind schedule.
   e. Some doctors schedule appointments in a way that ensures long lines, to make it appear that they are especially skillful.

5. *Topic sentence:* Several factors were responsible for the staggering loss of lives when the *Titanic* sank.
   a. Over 1,500 people died in the *Titanic* disaster; only 711 survived.
   b. Despite warnings about the presence of icebergs, the captain allowed the *Titanic* to continue at high speed.
   c. If the ship had hit the iceberg head-on, its watertight compartments might have kept it from sinking; however, it hit on the side, resulting in a long, jagged gash through which water poured in.
   d. The *Titanic*, equipped with the very best communication systems available in 1912, sent out SOS messages.
   e. When the captain gave orders to abandon the *Titanic*, many passengers refused because they believed the ship was unsinkable, so many lifeboats were only partly filled.

Providing Details That Fit

Writing Specific Details   ACTIVITY 12

Each topic sentence in this activity is followed by one supporting detail. See if you can add a second detail in each case. Make sure your detail supports the topic sentence.

1. *Topic sentence:* There are good reasons why the video store is losing so many customers.

    a. The store stocks only one copy of every movie, even the most popular titles.

    b. _____

2. *Topic sentence:* The little boy did some dangerous stunts on his bicycle.

    a. He rode down a flight of steps at top speed.

    b. _____

3. *Topic sentence:* Craig has awful table manners.

    a. He stuffs his mouth with food and then begins a conversation.

    b. _____

4. *Topic sentence:* There are many advantages to living in the city.

    a. One can meet many new people with interesting backgrounds.

    b. _____

5. *Topic sentence:* All high school students should have summer jobs.

    a. Summer jobs help teens learn to handle a budget.

    b. _____

ACTIVITY 13   **Providing Support**

See if you can add *two* supporting details for each of the topic sentences below.

1. *Topic sentence:* The managers of this apartment building don't care about their renters.

    a. Mrs. Harris has been asking them to fix her leaky faucet for two months.

    b. _____

    c. _____

2. *Topic sentence:* None of the shirts for sale were satisfactory.

    a. Some were attractive but too expensive.

    b. _____

    c. _____

3. *Topic sentence:* After being married for forty years, Mr. and Mrs. Lambert have grown similar in odd ways.

    a. They both love to have a cup of warm apple juice just before bed.

    b. _____

    c. _____

4. *Topic sentence:* It is a special time for me when my brother is in town.

   a. We always go bowling together and then stop for pizza.

   b. _____

   c. _____

5. *Topic sentence:* Our neighbor's daughter is very spoiled.

   a. When anyone else in the family has a birthday, she gets several presents too.

   b. _____

   c. _____

Providing Details in a Paragraph

Adding Details to a Paragraph   ACTIVITY 14

The following paragraph needs specific details to back up its three supporting points. In the spaces provided, write two or three sentences of convincing details for each supporting point.

A Disappointing Concert

   Although I had looked forward to seeing my favorite musical group in concert, the experience was disappointing. For one thing, our seats were terrible, in two ways. _____

_____

_____

_____

   In addition, the crowd made it hard to enjoy the music. _____

_____

_____

_____

_____

   And finally, the band members acted as if they didn't want to be there. _____

_____

_____

_____

Omitting and Grouping Details in Planning a Paragraph

One common way to develop material for a paper involves three steps: (1) First, make up a list of details about your point, (2) Then omit details that don't truly support your point, (3) Finally, group remaining details together in logical ways. Omitting details that don't fit and grouping related details together are part of learning how to write effectively.

ACTIVITY 15	Grouping Details

See if you can figure out a way to put the following details into three groups. Write *A* in front of the details that go with one group, *B* in front of the details that go with a second group, and *C* in front of the details that make up a third group. Cross out the four details that do not relate to the topic sentence.

Topic sentence: My brother Sean caused our parents lots of headaches when he was a teenager.

_____ In constant trouble at school

_____ While playing a joke on his lab partner, nearly blew up the chemistry lab

_____ Girlfriend was eight years older than he and had been married twice

_____ Girlfriend had a very sweet four-year-old son

_____ Parents worried about people Sean spent his time with

_____ Several signs that he was using drugs

_____ Failed so many courses that he had to go to summer school in order to graduate

_____ Was suspended twice for getting into fights between classes

_____ Our father taught math at the high school we attended

_____ His money just disappeared, and he never had anything to show for it

_____ His best pal had been arrested for armed robbery

_____ Often looked glassy-eyed

_____ Hung around with older kids who had dropped out of school

_____ Until he was in eighth grade, he had always been on the honor roll

_____ No one was allowed in his room, which he kept locked whenever he was away from home

_____ Has managed to turn his life around now that he's in college

EXPLANATION: After thinking about the list for a while, you probably realized that the details about Sean's trouble at school form one group. He got in trouble at school for nearly blowing up the chemistry lab, failing courses, and fighting between classes. Another group of details has to do with his parents' worrying about the people he spent time with. His parents were worried because he had an older girlfriend, a best friend who was arrested for armed robbery, and older friends who were school dropouts. Finally, there are the details about signs that he was using drugs: his money disappearing, his glassy-eyed appearance, and not allowing others in his room.

The main idea—that as a teenager, the writer's brother caused their parents lots of headaches—can be supported with three kinds of evidence: the trouble he got into at school, his friends, and the signs indicating he was on drugs. The other four items in the list do not logically go with any of these three types of evidence and so should be omitted.

Omitting and Grouping Details   ACTIVITY 16

This activity will give you practice in omitting and grouping details. See if you can figure out a way to put the following details into three groups. Write *A* in front of the details that go with one group, *B* in front of the details that go with a second group, and *C* in front of the details that make up a third group. Cross out the four details that do not relate to the topic sentence.

Topic sentence: There are interesting and enjoyable ways for children to keep their classroom skills strong over summer vacation.

_____ Kids can help figure out how big a tip to leave in a restaurant.

_____ They can keep their reading skills sharp in various ways.

_____ Summer is a good time for learning to swim.

_____ Reading the newspaper with Mom or Dad will keep kids in touch with challenging reading.

_____ Adults can ask a child to do such tasks as count their change.

_____ Kids can have fun improving their writing skills.

_____ A child might enjoy writing a diary of his or her summer activities.

_____ Weekly visits to the library will keep them in touch with good books.

_____ After returning to school, children can write about their summer vacation.

_____ Kids should also have plenty of physical exercise over the summer.

_____ Arithmetic skills can be polished over the summer.

_____   Parents can encourage kids to write letters to relatives.

_____   Parents should take children to the library during the school year, too.

_____   In the grocery store, a child can compare prices and choose the best bargains.

_____   Even the comic strips provide reading practice for a young child.

_____   Getting a pen pal in another state can give a child an enjoyable reason to write over the summer.

www.mhhe.com/langan

Step 3: Organize the Support

You will find it helpful to learn two common ways of organizing support in a paragraph—*listing order* and *time order*. You should also learn the signal words, known as *transitions*, that increase the effectiveness of each method.

Transitions are words and phrases that indicate relationships between ideas. They are like signposts that guide travelers, showing them how to move smoothly from one spot to the next. Be sure to take advantage of transitions. They will help organize and connect your ideas, and they will help your readers follow the direction of your thoughts.

Listing Order

A writer can organize supporting evidence in a paper by providing a list of two or more reasons, examples, or details. Often the most important or interesting item is saved for last because the reader is most likely to remember the last thing read.

Transition words that indicate listing order include the following:

one	second	also	next	last of all
for one thing	third	another	moreover	finally
first of all	next	in addition	furthermore	

Gene's paragraph about working at the apple plant (Chapter 1, p. 7) uses a listing order: it lists three reasons why it was the worst job he ever had, and each of those three reasons is introduced by one of the above transitions. In the spaces below, write in the three transitions:

_____   _____   _____

The first reason in the paragraph about working at the plant is introduced with *first of all*, the second reason by *second*, and the third reason by *finally*.

Using Listing Order

ACTIVITY 17

Use *listing order* to arrange the scrambled list of sentences below. Number each supporting sentence 1, 2, 3, . . . so that you go from the least important item to what is presented as the most important item.

Note that transitions will help by making clear the relationships between some of the sentences.

Topic sentence: I am no longer a big fan of professional sports, for a number of reasons.

_____ Basketball and hockey continue well into the baseball season, and football doesn't have its Super Bowl until the middle of winter, when basketball should be at center stage.

_____ In addition, I detest the high fives, taunting, and trash talk that so many professional athletes now indulge in during games.

_____ Second, I am bothered by the length of professional sports seasons.

_____ Also, professional athletes have no loyalty to a team or city, as they greedily sell their abilities to the highest bidder.

_____ For one thing, greed is the engine running professional sports.

_____ There are numerous news stories of professional athletes in trouble with the law because of drugs, guns, fights, traffic accidents, or domestic violence.

_____ After a good year, athletes making millions become unhappy if they aren't rewarded with a new contract calling for even more millions.

_____ But the main reason I've become disenchanted with professional sports is the disgusting behavior of so many of its performers.

Time Order

When a writer uses time order, supporting details are presented in the order in which they occurred. *First* this happened; *next* this; *after* that, this; and so on. Many paragraphs, especially paragraphs that tell a story or give a series of directions, are organized in a time order.

Transition words that show time relationships include the following:

first	before	after	when	then
next	during	now	while	until
as	soon	later	often	finally

Read the following paragraph, which is organized in time order. See if you can underline the six transition words that show the time relationships.

> Della had a sad experience while driving home last night. She traveled along the dark, winding road that led toward her home. She was only two miles from her house when she noticed a glimmer of light in the road. The next thing she knew, she heard a sickening thud and realized she had struck an animal. The light, she realized, had been its eyes reflected in her car's headlights. Della stopped the car and ran back to see what she had hit. It was a handsome cocker spaniel, with blond fur and long ears. As she bent over the still form, she realized there was nothing to be done. The dog was dead. Della searched the dog for a collar and tags. There was nothing. Before leaving, she walked to several nearby houses, asking if anyone knew who owned the dog. No one did. Finally Della gave up and drove on. She was sad to leave someone's pet lying there alone.

The main point of the paragraph is stated in its first sentence: "Della had a sad experience while driving home last night." The support for this point is all the details of Della's experience. Those details are presented in the order in which they occurred. The time relationships are highlighted by these transitions: *while, when, next, as, before,* and *finally.*

ACTIVITY 18	Using Time Order

Use *time order* to arrange the scrambled sentences below. Number the supporting sentences in the order in which they occur in time (1, 2, 3, . . .).

Note that transitions will help by making clear the relationships between sentences.

Topic sentence: If you are a smoker, the following steps should help you quit.

_____ Before your "quit day" arrives, have a medical checkup to make sure it will be all right for you to begin an exercise program.

_____ You should then write down on a card your decision to quit and the date of your "quit day."

_____ When your "quit day" arrives, stop smoking and start your exercise program.

_____ Finally, remind yourself repeatedly how good you will feel when you can confidently tell yourself and others that you are a nonsmoker.

_____ Place the card in a location where you will be sure to see it every day.

_____ When you begin this exercise program, be sure to drink plenty of water every day and to follow a sensible diet.

_____ After making a definite decision to stop smoking, select a specific "quit day."

_____ Eventually, your exercise program should include activities strenuous enough to strengthen your lung capacity and your overall stamina.

More about Using Transitions

As already stated, transitions are signal words that help readers follow the direction of the writer's thoughts. To see the value of transitions, look at the two versions of the short paragraph below. Check the version that is easier to read and understand.

www.mhhe.com/langan

_____ a. Where will you get the material for your writing assignments? There are several good sources. Your own experience is a major resource. For an assignment about childhood, for instance, you can draw on your own numerous memories of childhood. Other people's experiences are extremely useful. You may have heard people you know or even people on TV or radio talking about their childhoods. Or you can interview people with a specific writing assignment in mind. Books and magazines are a good source of material for assignments. Many experts, for example, have written about various aspects of childhood.

_____ b. Where will you get the material for your writing assignments? There are several good sources. First of all, your own experience is a major resource. For an assignment about childhood, for instance, you can draw on your own numerous memories of childhood. In addition, other people's experiences are extremely useful. You may have heard people you know or even people on TV or radio talking about their childhoods. Or you can interview people with a specific writing assignment in mind. Finally, books and magazines are a good source of material for assignments. Many experts, for example, have written about various aspects of childhood.

EXPLANATION: You no doubt chose the second version, _b._ The listing transitions—_first of all, in addition,_ and _finally_—make it clear when the author is introducing a new supporting point. The reader of paragraph _b_ is better able to follow the author's line of thinking and to note that three main sources of material for assignments are being listed: your own experience, other people's experiences, and books and magazines.

| **ACTIVITY 19** | **Using Transitions** |

The following paragraphs use listing order or time order. In each case, fill in the blanks with appropriate transitions from the box above the paragraph. Use each transition once.

1.

| after | now | first | soon | while |

My husband has developed an involving hobby, in which I, unfortunately, am unable to share. He _____ enrolled in ground flight instruction classes at the local community college. The lessons were all about air safety regulations and procedures. _____ passing a difficult exam, he decided to take flying lessons at the city airport. Every Monday he would wake at six o'clock in the morning and drive happily to the airport, eager to see his instructor. _____ he was taking lessons, he started to buy airplane magazines and talk about them constantly. "Look at that Cessna 150," he would say. "Isn't she a beauty?" _____, after many lessons, he is flying by himself. _____ he will be able to carry passengers. That is my biggest nightmare. I know he will want me to fly with him, but I am not a lover of heights. I can't understand why someone would leave the safety of the ground to be in the sky, defenseless as a kite.

2.

| finally | for one thing | second |

The karate class I took last week convinced me that martial arts may never be my strong point. _____, there is the issue of balance. The instructor asked everyone in class to stand on one foot to practice kicking. Each time I tried, I wobbled and had to spread my arms out wide to avoid falling. I even stumbled into Mr. Kim, my instructor, who glared at me. _____, there was the issue of flexibility. Mr. Kim asked us to stretch and touch our toes. Everyone did this without a problem—except me. I could barely reach my knees before pain raced up and down my back. _____, there was my lack of coordination. When everyone started practicing blocks, I got confused. I couldn't figure out where to move my arms and legs. By the time I got the first move right, the whole group had finished three more. By the end of my first lesson, I was completely lost.

3.

| later | soon | when | then |

At the age of thirty-one I finally had the opportunity to see snow for the first time in my life. It was in New York City on a cloudy afternoon in November. My daughter and I had gone to the American Museum of Natural History. _____ we left the museum, snow was falling gently. I thought that it was so beautiful! It made me remember movies I had seen countless times in my native Brazil. We decided to find a taxi. _____ we were crossing Central Park, snuggled in the cozy cab, watching the snow cover trees, bushes, branches, and grass. We were amazed to see the landscape quickly change from fall to winter. _____ we arrived in front of our hotel, and I still remember stepping on the crisp snow and laughing like a child who is touched by magic. _____ that day, I heard on the radio that another snowstorm was coming. I was naive enough to wait for thunder and the other sounds of a rainstorm. I did not know yet that snow, even a snowstorm, is silent and soft.

4.

| last of all | another | first of all | in addition |

Public school students who expect to attend school from September to June, and then have a long summer vacation, may be in for a big surprise before long. For a number of reasons, many schools are switching to a year-round calendar. _____, many educators point out that the traditional school calendar was established years ago when young people had to be available during the summer months to work on farms, but this necessity has long since passed. _____ reason is that a longer school year accommodates individual learning rates more effectively—that is, fast learners can go into more depth about a subject that interests them, while those who learn at a slower pace have more time to master the essential material. _____, many communities have gone to year-round school to relieve overcrowding, since students can be put on different schedules throughout the year. _____, and perhaps most important, educators feel that year-round schools eliminate the loss of learning that many students experience over a long summer break.

Step 4: Write Clear, Error-Free Sentences

If you use correct spelling and follow the rules of grammar, punctuation, and usage, your sentences will be clear and well written. But by no means must you have all that information in your head. Even the best writers need to use reference materials to be sure their writing is correct. So when you write your papers, keep a good dictionary and grammar handbook nearby.

In general, however, save them for after you've gotten your ideas firmly down in writing. You'll find as you write paragraphs that you will make a number of sentence errors. Simply ignore them until you get to a later draft of your paper, when there will be time enough to make the needed corrections. Part 3 of this text will focus on sentence skills.

Four Bases for Revising Writing

In this chapter, you've learned four essential steps in writing an effective paragraph. The following box shows how these steps lead to four standards, or bases, you can use in evaluating and revising paragraphs.

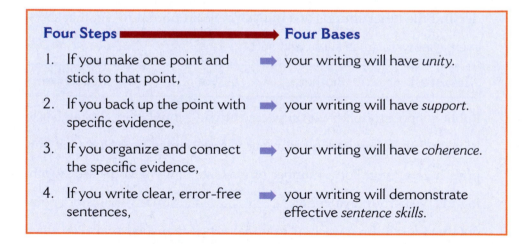

Four Steps ➡️ **Four Bases**

1. If you make one point and stick to that point, ➡️ your writing will have *unity*.

2. If you back up the point with specific evidence, ➡️ your writing will have *support*.

3. If you organize and connect the specific evidence, ➡️ your writing will have *coherence*.

4. If you write clear, error-free sentences, ➡️ your writing will demonstrate effective *sentence skills*.

Base 1: Unity

Understanding Unity

To achieve unity is to have all the details in your paper related to the single point expressed in the topic sentence, the first sentence. Each time you think of something to put in, ask yourself whether it relates to your main point. If if does not, leave it out. For example, if you were writing about a certain job as the worst job you ever had and then spent a couple of sentences talking about the interesting people you met there, you would be missing the first and most essential base of good writing.

> **TIP** To check a paragraph for unity, ask yourself these questions:
> 1. Is there a clear opening statement of the point of the paper?
> 2. Is all the material on target in support of the opening point?

Evaluating a Paragraph for Unity

Omitting Off-Target Sentences

ACTIVITY 20

The following paragraph contains two sentences that are off target—sentences that do not support the opening point—and so the paragraph is not unified. In the interest of paragraph unity, such sentences must be omitted.

Cross out the irrelevant sentences and write the numbers of those sentences in the spaces provided.

A Kindergarten Failure

[1]In kindergarten I experienced the fear of failure that haunts many schoolchildren. [2]My moment of panic occurred on my last day in kindergarten at Charles Foos Public School in Riverside, California. [3]My family lived in California for three years before we moved to Omaha, Nebraska, where my father was a personnel manager for Mutual of Omaha. [4]Our teacher began reading a list of names of all those students who were to line up at the door in order to visit the first-grade classroom. [5]Our teacher was a pleasant-faced woman who had resumed her career after raising her own children. [6]She called off every name but mine, and I was left sitting alone in the class while everyone else left, the teacher included. [7]I sat there in absolute horror. [8]I imagined that I was the first kid in human history who had flunked things like crayons, sandbox, and sliding board. [9]Without getting the teacher's permission, I got up and walked to the bathroom and threw up into a sink. [10]Only when I ran home in tears to my mother did I get an explanation of what had happened. [11]Since I was to go to a parochial school in the fall, I had not been taken with the other children to meet the first-grade teacher at the public school. [12]My moment of terror and shame had been only a misunderstanding.

The numbers of the irrelevant sentences: _____   _____

Base 2: Support

Understanding Support

The second base of effective writing, *support*, provides specific examples that illustrate the main point of a paragraph. Readers want to see and judge for ourselves whether a writer is making a valid point about a subject, but without specific details we cannot do so. After realizing the importance of specific supporting details, one student writer revised a paper she had done on a restaurant job as the worst job she ever had. In the revised paper, instead of talking about "unsanitary conditions in the kitchen," she referred to such specifics as "green mold on the bacon" and "ants in the potato salad." All your paragraphs should include many vivid details! Using ample support will help you communicate more clearly and effectively in your writing.

www.mhhe.com/langan

> **TIP**   To check a paragraph for support, ask yourself these questions:
> 1. Is there *specific* evidence to support the opening point?
> 2. Is there *enough* specific evidence?

Evaluating Paragraphs for Support

ACTIVITY 21   **Checking for Specific Details**

The paragraph that follows lacks sufficient supporting details. Identify the spot or spots where more specific details are needed.

Culture Conflict

[1]I am in a constant tug-of-war with my parents over conflicts between their Vietnamese culture and American culture. [2]To begin with, my parents do not like me to have American friends. [3]They think that I should spend all my time with other Vietnamese people and speak English only when necessary. [4]I get into an argument whenever I want to go to a fast-food restaurant or a movie at night with my American friends. [5]The conflict with my parents is even worse when it comes to plans for a career. [6]My parents want me to get a degree in science and then go on to medical school. [7]On the other hand, I think I want to become a teacher. [8]So far I have been taking both science and education courses, but soon I will have to concentrate on one or the other. [9]The other night my father made his attitude about what I should do very clear. [10]The most difficult aspect of our cultural differences is the way our family is structured. [11]My father is the center of our family, and he expects that I will always listen to him. [12]Although I am twenty-one years old, I still have a nightly curfew at an hour which I consider insulting. [13]Also, I am expected to help my mother perform certain household chores that I've really come to hate. [14]My father expects me to live at home until I am married to a Vietnamese man. [15]When that happens, he assumes I will obey my husband just as I obey him. [16]I do not want to be a bad daughter, but I want to live like my American female friends.

Fill in the blanks: The first spot where supporting details are needed occurs after sentence number _____. The second spot occurs after sentence number _____. The third spot occurs after sentence number _____.

Base 3: Coherence

Understanding Coherence

Once you have determined that a paragraph is unified and supported, check to see if the writer has a clear and consistent way of organizing the material.

The third base of effective writing is *coherence.* The supporting ideas and sentences in a composition must be organized in a consistent way so that they cohere, or "stick together." Key techniques for tying material together are choosing a clear method of organization (such as time order or emphatic order) and using transitions and other connecting words as signposts.

> **TIP** To check a paragraph for coherence, ask yourself these questions:
> 1. Does the paragraph have a clear method of organization?
> 2. Are transitions and other connecting words used to tie the material together?

www.mhhe.com/langan

Evaluating Paragraphs for Coherence

Looking for Organization and Coherence	ACTIVITY 22

Answer the questions about coherence that follow the paragraph below.

> **Why I Bought a Handgun**
>
> [1]I bought a handgun to keep in my house for several reasons. [2]Most important, I have had a frightening experience with an obscene phone caller. [3]For several weeks, a man has called me once or twice a day, sometimes as late as three in the morning. [4]As soon as I pick up the phone, he whispers something obscene or threatens me by saying, "I'll get you." [5]I decided to buy a gun because crime is increasing in my neighborhood. [6]One neighbor's house was burglarized while she was at work; the thieves not only stole her appliances but also threw paint around her living room and slashed her furniture. [7]Not long after this incident, an elderly woman from the apartment house on the corner was mugged on her way to the supermarket. [8]The man grabbed her purse and threw her to the ground, breaking her hip. [9]Buying a gun was my response to listening to the nightly news. [10]It seemed that every news story involved violence of some kind—rapes, murders, muggings, and robberies. [11]I wondered if some of the victims in the stories would still be alive if they had been able to frighten the criminal off with a gun. [12]As time passed, I became more convinced that I should keep a gun in the house.

a. The paragraph should use emphatic order. Write *1* before the reason that seems slightly less important than the other two, *2* before the second-most-important reason, and *3* before the most important reason.

_____   Obscene phone caller

_____   Crime increase in neighborhood

_____   News stories about crime

b. Before which of the three reasons should the transitional words *first of all* be added? _____

c. Before which of the three reasons could the transition *in addition* be added? _____

d. Which words show emphasis in sentence 2? _____

e. In sentence 8, to whom does the pronoun *her* refer? _____

_____

f. How often does the key word *gun* appear in the paragraph?

_____

g. What is a synonym for *burglarized* in sentence 6? _____

Base 4: Sentence Skills

Understanding Sentence Skills

Errors in grammar, punctuation, sentence structure, mechanics, and even formatting can detract greatly from your writing; the fourth base, **sentence skills,** requires that you identify, fix, and avoid these types of mistakes. Error-free sentence allow readers to focus on the content of a paragraph as a whole. Poor grammar and sentence skills can be merely distracting, or they can change the meaning of a sentence entirely; they also lessen a writer's credibility. For instance, a potential employer might think, "If he can't spell the word *political,* does he really have an interest in working on my campaign?"

Part 3 of this book focuses on a wide range of sentence skills. You should review all the skills carefully. Doing so will ensure that you know the most important rules of grammar, punctuation, and usage—rules needed to write clear, error-free sentences.

Checking for Sentence Skills

Sentence skills and the other bases of effective writing are summarized in the following chart and on the inside front cover of the book.

A Summary of the Four Bases of Effective Writing

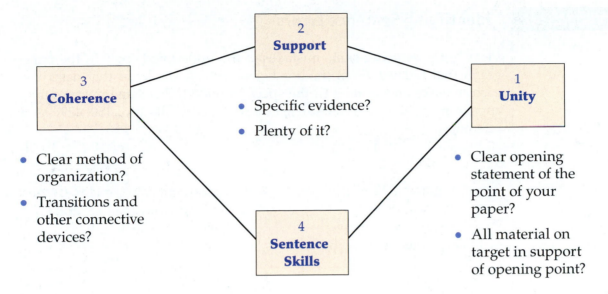

- Fragments eliminated? (162–178)

- Run-ons eliminated? (179–194)

- Correct verb forms? (210–229, 239–249)

- Subject and verb agreement? (230–238)

- Faulty modifiers and faulty parallelism eliminated? (281–285, 292–299)

- Faulty pronouns eliminated? (250–260, 261–272)

- Capital letters used correctly? (320–328)

- Punctuation marks where needed?

  (a) Apostrophe (337–348)   (d) Semicolon; colon (374–376)

  (b) Quotation marks (349–359)   (e) Hyphen; dash (376–377)

  (c) Comma (360–373)   (f) Parentheses (378)

- Correct paper format? (315–319)

- Needless words eliminated? (423–424)

www.mhhe.com/langan

Evaluating Paragraphs for Sentence Skills

| ACTIVITY 23 | Identifying Sentence Errors |

Identify the sentence-skills mistakes at the underlined spots in the paragraph that follows. From the box below, choose the letter that describes each mistake and write it in the space provided. The same mistake may appear more than once. Use Part 3: Sentence Skills (pp. 150–429) as a reference.

a. fragment (162–178)
b. run-on (179–194)
c. mistake in subject-verb agreement (230–238)

d. apostrophe mistake (337–348)
e. faulty parallelism (292–299)

Looking Out for Yourself

It's sad but true: "If you don't look out for yourself, no one else will." For example, some people have a false idea about the power of a college degree, they think that once they possesses the degree, the
<u>1</u>   <u>2</u>
world will be waiting on their doorstep. In fact, nobody is likely to be on their doorstep unless, through advance planning, they has prepared
                                                <u>3</u>
themselves for a career. The kind in which good job opportunities ex-
                                  <u>4</u>
ist. Even after a person has landed a job, however, a healthy amount of self-interest is needed. People who hide in corners or with hesitation
                                              <u>5</u>
to let others know about their skills doesn't get promotions or raises.
                                          <u>6</u>
Its important to take credit for a job well done, whether the job in-
<u>7</u>
volves writing a report, organized the office filing system, or calming
                          <u>8</u>
down an angry customer. Also, people should feel free to ask the boss for a raise. If they work hard and really deserve it. Those who look out
                                              <u>9</u>
for themselves get the rewards, people who depend on others to help
                                    <u>10</u>
them along get left behind.

1. _____   2. _____   3. _____   4. _____   5. _____

6. _____   7. _____   8. _____   9. _____   10. _____

TECH-SAVVY WRITING

Visit any Web site and evaluate it using the following criteria: unity, support, coherence, and sentence skills. Write a critique, recommending what could improve the site. Questions to consider: Can you easily identify what the site's goals are? Is it well organized and easy to navigate? Does it seem credible? Does it contain valuable information, and is this information presented in an appealing way? Do you see any typos, spelling errors, or awkward sentences?

RESPONDING TO IMAGES

Focusing on the third base, *coherence*, describe the organizing principles of this site, as introduced on its home page.

4

Nine Patterns of Paragraph Development

Responding to Images

(1) How do these photographs describe the devastating effects of Hurricane Katrina and its aftermath? What story or stories do the images narrate? (2) Compare and contrast the photographs from before and after the hurricane struck. Why do you think the photographer chose to juxtapose these particular images?

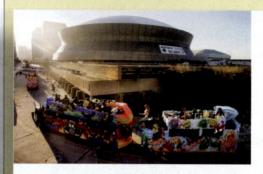

Important Considerations in Paragraph Development

Before you begin work on particular types of paragraphs, there are several general considerations about writing to keep in mind.

Knowing Your Subject

Whenever possible, write on a subject that interests you. You will then find it easier to put more time into your work. Even more important, try to write on a subject that you already know something about. If you do not have direct experience with the subject, you should at least have indirect experience—knowledge gained through thinking, prewriting, reading, or talking about the subject.

If you are asked to write on a topic about which you have no experience or knowledge, you should do whatever research is required to gain the information you need. Without direct or indirect experience, or the information you gain through research, you may not be able to provide the specific evidence needed to develop whatever point you are trying to make. Your writing will be starved for specifics.

Knowing Your Purpose and Audience

The three most common purposes of writing are to inform, to persuade, and to entertain. Each is described briefly below.

- To **inform**—to give information about a subject. Authors who are writing to inform want to provide facts that will explain or teach something to readers. For example, an informative paragraph about sandwiches might begin, "Eating food between two slices of bread—a sandwich—is a practice that has its origins in eighteenth-century England."

- To **persuade**—to convince the reader to agree with the author's point of view on a subject. Authors who are writing to persuade may give facts, but their main goal is to argue or prove a point to readers. A persuasive paragraph about sandwiches might begin, "There are good reasons why every sandwich should be made with whole-grain bread."

- To **entertain**—to amuse and delight; to appeal to the reader's senses and imagination. Authors write to entertain in various ways, through fiction and nonfiction. An entertaining paragraph about sandwiches might begin, "What I wanted was a midnight snack, but what I got was better—the biggest, most magical sandwich in the entire world."

Your audience will be primarily your instructor and sometimes other students. Your instructor is really a symbol of the larger audience you should see yourself writing for—an audience of educated adults who expect you to present your ideas in a clear, direct, organized way. If you can learn to write to persuade or inform such a general audience, you will have accomplished a great deal.

A Note on Tone

It will also be helpful for you to write some paragraphs for a more specific audience. By so doing, you will develop an ability to choose words and adopt a tone of voice that is just right for a given purpose and a given group of people. *Tone* reveals the attitude that a writer has toward a subject. It is expressed through the words and details the writer selects. Just as a speaker's voice can project a range of feelings, a writer's voice can project one or more tones, or feelings: anger, sympathy, hopefulness, sadness, respect, dislike, and so on.

Patterns of Development

Traditionally, writing has been divided into the following patterns of development:

- Exposition
  Examples
  Process
  Cause and effect
  Comparison and contrast
  Definition
  Division and classification

- Description

- Narration

- Argumentation

www.mhhe.com/langan

In *exposition*, the writer provides information about and explains a particular subject. Patterns of development within exposition include giving *examples*, detailing a *process* of doing or making something, analyzing *causes and effects*, *comparing* and *contrasting*, *defining* a term or concept, and *dividing* something into parts or *classifying* it into categories.

In addition to exposition, three other patterns of development are common: description, narration, and argumentation. A *description* is a verbal picture of a person, place, or thing. In *narration*, a writer tells the story of something that happened. Finally, in *argumentation*, a writer attempts to support a controversial point or defend a position on which there is a difference of opinion.

Each pattern has its own internal logic and provides its own special strategies for imposing order on your ideas.

> **TIP**   As you practice each pattern, you should remember the following:
>
> - While each paragraph that you write will involve one predominant pattern, very often one or more additional patterns may be involved as well. For instance, the paragraph "My Job in an Apple Plant" that you have already read (page 7) presents a series of examples showing why Gene disliked his job. There is also an element of narration, as the writer recounts his experience as a story.
>
> - Additionally, the paragraph shows how conditions caused this negative effect. No matter which pattern or patterns you use, each paragraph will probably involve some form of argumentation. You will advance a point and then go on to support your point. To convince the reader that your point is valid, you may use a series of examples, or narration, or description, or some other pattern of organization. For instance, a writer could advance the opinion that good horror movies can be easily distinguished from bad horror movies and then supply comparative information about both to support her claim. Much of your writing, in short, will have the purpose of persuading your reader that the idea you have advanced is valid.

1. Exemplification

In our daily conversations, we often provide *examples*—that is, details, particulars, specific instances—to explain statements that we make. Consider the several statements and supporting examples in the following box:

Statement	Examples
Wal-Mart was crowded today.	There were at least four carts waiting at each of the checkout counters, and it took me forty-five minutes to get through a line.
The corduroy shirt I bought is poorly made.	When I washed it, the colors began to fade, one button cracked and another fell off, a shoulder seam opened, and the sleeves shrank almost two inches.
My son Peter is unreliable.	If I depend on him to turn off a pot of beans in ten minutes, the family is likely to eat burned beans. If I ask him to turn down the thermostat before he goes to bed, the heat is likely to stay on all night.

In each case, the examples help us *see for ourselves* the truth of the statement that has been made. In paragraphs, too, explanatory examples help the audience fully understand a point. Lively, specific examples also add interest to a piece of writing.

A Paragraph to Consider

An Egotistical Neighbor

¹I have an egotistical neighbor named Alice. ²If I tell Alice how beautiful her dress is, she will take the time to tell me the name of the store where she bought it, the type of material that was used in making it, and the price. ³Alice is also egotistical when it comes to her children. ⁴Because they are hers, she thinks they just have to be the best children on the block. ⁵I am wasting my time by trying to tell her I have seen her kids expose themselves on the street or take things from parked cars. ⁶I do not think parents should praise their children too much. ⁷Kids have learned how to be good at home and simply awful when they are not at home. ⁸Finally, Alice is quick to describe the furnishings of her home for someone who is meeting her for the first time. ⁹She tells how much she paid for the paneling in her dining

continued

room. [10]She mentions that she has three flat-screen television sets and that they were bought at an expensive electronics store. [11]She lets the person know that the entertainment system in her living room cost more than two thousand dollars and that she has such a large collection of DVDs that she would not be able to watch them all in one week. [12]Poor Alice is so self-centered that she never realizes how boring she can be.

QUESTIONS

About Unity

1. Which two sentences in "An Egotistical Neighbor" are irrelevant to the point that Alice is egotistical? (*Write the sentence numbers here.*)

   _____   _____

About Support

2. How many specific examples are given that show Alice is egotistical?

   _____ two   _____ four   _____ six   _____ seven

About Coherence

3. What two transition words are used to introduce examples in "An Egotistical Neighbor"?

   _____   _____

Writing an Examples Paragraph

WRITING ASSIGNMENT

The assignment here is to complete an unfinished paragraph (in the box), which has as its topic sentence, "My husband Roger is a selfish person." Provide the supporting details needed to develop the examples of Roger's selfishness. The first example has been done for you.

A Selfish Person

My husband Roger is a selfish person. For one thing, he refuses to move out of the city, even though it is a bad place to raise the children. *We inherited some money when my parents died, and it might be enough for a down payment on a small house in a nearby town. But Roger says he would miss his buddies in the neighborhood.*

_____

---

continued

Also, when we go on vacation, we always go where Roger wants

to go.   _____

_____

_____

_____

Another example of Roger's selfishness is that he always spends

any budget money that is left over.   _____

_____

_____

_____

Finally, Roger leaves all the work of caring for the children to me.

_____

_____

_____

_____

PREWRITING

a. On a separate piece of paper, jot down a couple of answers for each of the following questions:

- What specific vacations did the family go on because Roger wanted to go? Write down particular places, length of stay, time of year. What vacations has the family never gone on (for example, to visit the wife's relatives), even though the wife wanted to?

- What specific items has Roger bought for himself (rather than for the whole family's use) with leftover budget money?

- What chores and duties involved in the everyday caring for the children has Roger never done?

Your instructor may ask you to work with one or two other students in generating the details needed to develop the three examples in the paragraph. The groups may then be asked to read their details aloud, with the class deciding which details are the most effective for each example.

Here, and in general in your writing, try to generate *more* supporting material than you need. You are then in a position to choose the most convincing details for your paper.

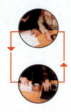

b. Read over the details you have generated and decide which sound most effective. Jot down additional details as they occur to you.

c. Take your best details, reshape them as needed, and use them to complete the paragraph about Roger.

REVISING: The Four Bases

Checklist for Exemplification

Read the paragraph with these questions in mind to make sure you have covered the four bases of effective writing:

About *Unity*

☑ Do all of the examples I provide support the central idea that Roger is selfish?

About *Support*

☑ Are there enough examples to make my point about Roger and convince others to agree with me?

☑ Do I appeal to my readers' senses with vivid, specific examples?

About *Coherence*

☑ Have I presented the examples in my paragraph in the most effective order?

About *Sentence Skills*

☑ Have I used specific rather than general words?

☑ Are my sentences varied in length and structure?

☑ Have I checked for spelling and other sentence skills, as listed on the inside back cover of the book?

Continue revising your work until you and your reader can answer *yes* to all these questions.

BEYOND THE CLASSROOM

Exemplification

Imagine that you are a television critic who has been asked to write a paragraph-long article about the "best show on television." Tell us what the show is and why it is entertaining, groundbreaking, well-acted, and so on. Make sure to give plenty of examples that support your point.

2. Process

Every day we perform many activities that are *processes*—that is, series of steps carried out in a definite order. Many of these processes are familiar and automatic: for example, tying shoelaces, changing bed linen, using a vending machine, and starting a car. We are thus seldom aware of the sequence of steps making up each activity. In other cases, such as when we are asked for directions to a particular place, or when we try to read and follow the directions for a new table game, we may be painfully conscious of the whole series of steps involved in the process.

> **TIP**   In process writing, you are often giving instruction to the reader, so the pronoun *you* can appropriately be used. As a general rule, though, do not use *you* in your writing.

A Paragraph to Consider

How to Harass an Instructor

¹There are several steps you can take to harass an instructor during a class. ²First of all, show up late so that you can interrupt the beginning of the instructor's presentation. ³Saunter in nonchalantly and try to find a seat next to a friend. ⁴In a normal tone of voice, speak some words of greeting to your friends as you sit down, and scrape your chair as loudly as possible while you make yourself comfortable in it. ⁵Then just sit there and do anything but pay attention. ⁶When the instructor sees that you are not involved in the class, he or she may pop a quick question, probably hoping to embarrass you. ⁷You should then say, in a loud voice, "I DON'T KNOW THE ANSWER." ⁸This declaration of ignorance will throw the instructor off guard. ⁹If the instructor then asks you why you don't know the answer, say, "I don't even know what page we're on" or "I thought the assignment was boring, so I didn't do it." ¹⁰After the instructor calls on someone else, get up loudly from your seat, walk to the front of the classroom, and demand to be excused for an emergency visit to the washroom. ¹¹Stay there at least fifteen minutes and take your time coming back. ¹²On your way back, find a vending machine and buy yourself a snack; this class is boring, so you deserve a pick-me-up. ¹³If the instructor asks you where you've been when you reenter the room, simply ignore the question and go to your seat. ¹⁴Flop into your chair, slouching back and extending your legs as far out as possible. ¹⁵When the instructor informs you of the assignment that the class is working on, heave an exaggerated sigh and very slowly open up your book and start turning the pages. ¹⁶About a half hour before class is over, begin to look at the clock every few minutes. ¹⁷Ten minutes before dismissal time, start noisily packing up your books and papers. ¹⁸Then get up and begin walking to the door a couple of minutes before the class is supposed to end. ¹⁹The instructor will look at you and wonder whether it wouldn't have been better to go into business instead of education.

QUESTIONS

About Unity

1. Which sentence should be eliminated in the interest of paragraph unity? (*Write the sentence number here.*)

   _____

About Support

2. After which sentence in "How to Harass an Instructor" are supporting details (examples) needed?

   _____

About Coherence

3. Does this paragraph use time order or emphatic order?

   _____

Writing a Process Paragraph

WRITING ASSIGNMENT

Choose one of the following topics to write about in a process paragraph.

   How to feed a family on a budget

   How to break up with a boyfriend or girlfriend

   How to balance a checkbook

   How to change a car or bike tire

   How to get rid of house or garden pests, such as mice, roaches, or wasps

   How to play a simple game such as checkers, tic-tac-toe, or an easy card game

   How to shorten a skirt or pants

   How to meet new people, for either dating or friendship

   How to plant a garden

   How to deal with a nosy person

   How to fix a leaky faucet, a clogged drain, or the like

   How to build a campfire or start a fire in a fireplace

   How to study for an important exam

   How to conduct a yard or garage sale

   How to wash dishes efficiently, clean a bathroom, or do laundry

PREWRITING

a. Begin by freewriting on your topic for ten minutes. Do not worry about spelling, grammar, organization, or other matters of form. Just write whatever comes into your head regarding the topic. Keep writing for more than ten minutes if ideas keep coming to you. This freewriting will give you a base of raw material to draw from during the next phase of your work on the paragraph. After freewriting, you should have a sense of whether there is enough material available for you to write a process paragraph about the topic. If so, continue as explained below. If there is not enough material, choose another topic and freewrite about *it* for ten minutes.

b.   Write a clear, direct topic sentence stating the process you are going to describe. For instance, if you are going to describe a way to study for major exams, your topic sentence might be "My study-skills instructor has suggested a good way to study for major exams." Or you can state in your topic sentence the process and the number of steps involved: "My technique for building a campfire involves four main steps."

c.   List all the steps you can think of that may be included in the process. At this point, don't worry about how each step fits or whether two steps overlap. Here, for example, is the list prepared by a student who is writing about how to sneak into the house at night.

Quiet on stairs

Come in after Dad's asleep

House is freezing at night

Bring key

Know which steps to avoid

Lift up front door

Late dances on Saturday night

Don't turn on bathroom light

Avoid squeaky spots on floor

Get into bed quietly

Undress quietly

d.   Number your items in the order in which they occur; strike out items that do not fit in the list; add others that come to mind. The student writer did this step as follows:

Quiet on stairs

Come in after Dad's asleep

House is freezing at night

Bring key

Know which steps to avoid

Lift up front door

Late dances on Saturday night

Don't turn on bathroom light

Avoid squeaky spots on floor

Get into bed quietly

Undress quietly

e. Use your list as a guide to write the first draft of your paragraph. As you write, try to think of additional details that will support your opening sentence. Do not expect to finish your paragraph in one draft. After you complete your first rough draft, in fact, you should be ready to write a series of drafts as you work toward the goals of unity, support, and coherence.

REVISING: The Four Bases

Checklist for Process

After you have written the first draft of your paragraph, set it aside for a while if you can. Then read it out loud, either to yourself or (better yet) to a friend or classmate who will be honest with you about how it sounds. Reexamine your paragraph with these questions in mind to make sure you have covered the four bases of effective writing:

About *Unity*

 An effective process composition describes a series of events in a way that is clear and easy to follow. Are the steps in your paragraph described in a clear, logical way?

About *Support*

 Does your paragraph explain every necessary step so that a reader could perform the task described?

About *Coherence*

 Have you used transitions such as *first, next, also, then, after, now, during,* and *finally* to make the paper move smoothly from one step to another?

About *Sentence Skills*

 Is the point of view consistent? For example, if you begin by writing "This is how I got rid of mice" (first person), do not switch to "You must buy the right traps" (second person). Write this paragraph either from the first-person point of view (using *I* and *we*) or from the second-person point of view (*you*)—do not jump back and forth between the two.

 Have you corrected any sentence-skills mistakes that you noticed while reading the paragraph out loud? Have you checked the composition for sentence skills, including spelling, as listed on the inside back cover of this book?

Continue revising your work until you and your reader can answer *yes* to all these questions.

BEYOND THE CLASSROOM

Process

Imagine that you have to train someone to take your place in any job you've held (or currently hold); if you have never held a job, you can train this person to take your place as a student. Write a process paragraph that describes what a day on the job entails. Break the day's activities down into steps, making sure to include what advance preparation your replacement might need.

3. Cause and Effect

What caused Pat to drop out of school? Why are soap operas so popular? Why does our football team do so poorly each year? How has retirement affected Dad? What effects does divorce have on children? Every day we ask such questions and look for answers. We realize that situations have causes and effects—good or bad. By examining causes and effects, we seek to understand and explain things.

A Paragraph to Consider

New Puppy in the House

[1]Buying a new puppy can have significant effects on a household. [2]For one thing, the puppy keeps the entire family awake for at least two solid weeks. [3]Every night when the puppy is placed in its box, it begins to howl, yip, and whine. [4]Even after the lights go out and the house quiets down, the puppy continues to moan. [5]A second effect is that the puppy tortures the family by destroying material possessions. [6]Every day something different is damaged. [7]Family members find chewed belts and shoes, gnawed table legs, and ripped sofa cushions leaking stuffing. [8]In addition, the puppy often misses the paper during the paper-training stage of life, thus making the house smell like the public restroom at a city bus station. [9]Maybe the most serious problem, though, is that the puppy causes family arguments. [10]Parents argue with children about who is supposed to feed and walk the dog. [11]Children argue about who gets to play with the puppy first. [12]Puppies are adorable, and no child can resist their charm. [13]Everyone argues about who left socks and shoes around for the puppy to find. [14]These continual arguments, along with the effects of sleeplessness and the loss of valued possessions, can really disrupt a household. [15]Only when the puppy gets a bit older does the household settle back to normal.

www.mhhe.com/langan

QUESTIONS

About Unity

1. Which sentence does not support the opening idea and should be omitted? (*Write the sentence number here.*)

   _____

About Support

2. How many effects of bringing a new puppy into the house are given in this paragraph?

   _____ one   _____ two   _____ three   _____ four

About Coherence

3. What words signal the effect that the author feels may be the most important?

   _____

Writing a Cause-and-Effect Paragraph

WRITING ASSIGNMENT

Choose one of the following three topic sentences and brief outlines. Each is made up of three supporting points (causes or effects). Your task is to turn the topic sentence and outline into a cause-or-effect paragraph.

Option 1
Topic sentence: There are several reasons why some high school graduates are unable to read.

(1) Failure of parents (*cause*)
(2) Failure of schools (*cause*)
(3) Failure of students themselves (*cause*)

Option 2
Topic sentence: Attending college has changed my personality in positive ways.

(1) More confident (*effect*)
(2) More knowledgeable (*effect*)
(3) More adventurous (*effect*)

Option 3
Topic sentence: Living with roommates (or family) makes attending college difficult.

(1) Late-night hours (*cause*)
(2) More temptations to cut class (*cause*)
(3) More distractions from studying (*cause*)

PREWRITING

a. After you've chosen the option that appeals to you most, jot down all the details you can think of that might go under each of the supporting points. Use separate paper for your lists. Don't worry yet about whether you can use all the items—your goal is to generate more material than you need. Here, for example, are some of the details generated by the author of "New Puppy in the House" to back up her supporting points.

Topic sentence: Having a new puppy disrupts a household.

1. Keeps family awake
   a. Whines at night
   b. Howls
   c. Loss of sleep
2. Destroys possessions
   a. Chews belts and shoes
   b. Chews furniture
   c. Tears up toys it's supposed to fetch
3. Has accidents in house
   a. Misses paper
   b. Disgusting cleanup
   c. Makes house smell bad
4. Causes arguments
   a. Arguments about walking dog
   b. Arguments about feeding dog
   c. Arguments about who gets to play with dog
   d. Arguments about vet bills

b. Now go through the details you have generated and decide which are most effective. Strike out the ones you decide are not worth using. Do other details occur to you? If so, jot them down as well.

c. Now you are ready to write your paragraph. Begin the paragraph with the topic sentence you chose. Make sure to develop each of the supporting points from the outline into a complete sentence, and then back it up with the best of the details you have generated.

REVISING: The Four Bases

Checklist for Cause and Effect

Review your paragraph with these questions in mind to make sure you have covered the four bases of effective writing:

About *Unity*

- ✔ Have I begun the paragraph with the topic sentence provided?
- ✔ Are any sentences in my paragraph not directly relevant to this topic sentence?

About *Support*

- ✔ Is each supporting point stated in a complete sentence?
- ✔ Have I provided effective details to back up each supporting point?

About *Coherence*

- ✔ Have I used transitions such as *in addition*, *another thing*, and *also* to make the relationships between the sentences clear?

About *Sentence Skills*

- ✔ Have I avoided wordiness?
- ✔ Have I proofread the paragraph for sentence-skills errors, including spelling, as listed on the inside back cover of the book?

Continue revising your work until you can answer *yes* to all these questions.

BEYOND THE CLASSROOM

Cause and Effect

Your roommate has been complaining that it's impossible to succeed in Mr. X's class because the class is too stressful. You volunteer to attend the class and see for yourself. Afterward, you decide to write a letter to the instructor calling attention to the stressful conditions and suggesting concrete ways to deal with them. Write this letter, explaining in detail the causes and effects of stress in the class.

4. Comparison and Contrast

Comparison and contrast are two everyday thought processes. When we *compare* two things, we show how they are similar; when we *contrast* two things, we show how they are different. We might compare or contrast two brand-name products (for example, Nike versus Adidas running shoes), two television shows, two instructors, two jobs, two friends, or two courses of action we could take in a given situation. The purpose of comparing and contrasting is to understand each of the two things more clearly and, at times, to make judgments about them.

There are two common methods, or formats, of development in a comparison or contrast paper. One format presents the details *one side at a time.* The other presents the details *point by point.*

Two Paragraphs to Consider

Read these sample paragraphs of comparison or contrast and then answer the questions that follow.

Two Views on Toys

¹Children and adults have very different preferences. ²First, there is the matter of taste. ³Adults pride themselves on taste, while children ignore the matter of taste in favor of things that are fun. ⁴Adults, especially grandparents, pick out tasteful toys that go unused, while children love the cheap playthings advertised on television. ⁵Second, of course, there is the matter of money. ⁶The new games on the market today are a case in point. ⁷Have you ever tried to lure a child away from some expensive game in order to get him or her to play with an old-fashioned game or toy? ⁸Finally, there is a difference between an adult's and a child's idea of what is educational. ⁹Adults, filled with memories of their own childhood, tend to be fond of the written word. ¹⁰Today's children, on the other hand, concentrate on anything electronic. ¹¹These things mean much more to them than to adults. ¹²Next holiday season, examine the toys that adults choose for children. ¹³Then look at the toys the children prefer. ¹⁴You will see the difference.

Mike and Helen

¹Mike and Helen, a married couple we know, look very much alike. ²They are both short, dark-haired, and slightly pudgy. ³Like his wife, Mike has a good sense of humor. ⁴Both Mike and Helen can be charming when they want to be, and they seem to handle small crises in a calm, cool way. ⁵A problem such as an overflowing washer, a stalled car, or a sick child is not a cause for panic; they seem to take such events in stride. ⁶In contrast to Helen, though, Mike tends to be disorganized. ⁷He is late for appointments and unable to keep important documents—bank records, receipts, and insurance papers— where he can find them. ⁸Also unlike Helen, Mike tends to hold a grudge. ⁹He is slow to forget a cruel remark, a careless joke, or an unfriendly slight. ¹⁰Another difference between these two is how they like to spend their free time; while Mike enjoys swimming, camping, and fishing, Helen prefers to stay inside and read or play chess.

QUESTIONS

About Unity

1. Which paragraph lacks a topic sentence?

   _____

2. Which paragraph has a topic sentence that is too broad?

   _____

About Support

3. Which paragraph contains almost no specific details?

   _____

4. Which paragraph provides more complete support?

   _____

About Coherence

5. What method of development (one side at a time or point by point) is used in "Mike and Helen"?

   _____

6. What method of development is used in "Two Views in Toys"?

   _____

RESPONDING TO IMAGES

Compare or contrast these two photographs of men cooking:

Writing a Comparison or Contrast Paragraph

Write a comparison or contrast paragraph on one of the following topics:

Two holidays	Two characters in the same movie or TV show
Two instructors	Two homes
Two children	Two neighborhoods
Two kinds of eaters	Two cartoon strips
Two drivers	Two cars
Two coworkers	Two friends
Two members of a team (or two teams)	Two crises
Two singers or groups	Two bosses or supervisors
Two pets	Two magazines
Two parties	
Two jobs	

PREWRITING

a. Choose your topic, the two subjects you will write about.

b. Decide whether your paragraph will *compare* the two subjects (discuss their similarities), *contrast* them (discuss their differences), or do both. If you choose to write about differences, you might write about how a musical group you enjoy differs from a musical group you dislike. You might discuss important differences between two employers you have had or between two neighborhoods you've lived in. You might contrast a job you've had in a car factory with a job you've had as a receptionist.

c. Write a direct topic sentence for your paragraph. Here's an example: "My job in a car-parts factory was very different from my job as a receptionist."

d. Come up with at least three strong points to support your topic sentence. If you are contrasting two jobs, for example, your points might be that they differed greatly (1) in their physical setting, (2) in the skills they required, and (3) in the people they brought you into contact with.

e. Use your topic sentence and supporting points to create a scratch outline for your paragraph. For the paragraph about jobs, the outline would look like this:

Topic sentence: My job in a car-parts factory was very different from my job as a receptionist.

1. The jobs differed in physical setting.
2. The jobs differed in the skills they required.
3. The jobs differed in the people they brought me into contact with.

f. Under each of your supporting points, jot down as many details as occur to you. Don't worry yet about whether the details all fit perfectly or whether you will be able to use them all. Your goal is to generate a wealth of material to draw on. An example:

Topic sentence: My job in a car-parts factory was very different from my job as a receptionist.

1. The jobs differed in physical setting.
   Factory loud and dirty
   Office clean and quiet
   Factory full of machines, hunks of metal, tools
   Office full of desks, files, computers
   Factory smelled of motor oil
   Office smelled of new carpet
   Windows in factory too high and grimy to look out of
   Office had clean windows onto street

2. The jobs differed in the skills and behavior they required.
   Factory required physical strength
   Office required mental activity
   Didn't need to be polite in factory
   Had to be polite in office
   Didn't need to think much for self in factory
   Constantly had to make decisions in office

3. The jobs differed in the people they brought me into contact with.
   In factory, worked with same crew every day
   In office, saw constant stream of new customers
   Most coworkers in factory had high school education or less
   Many coworkers and clients in office well educated
   Coworkers in factory spoke variety of languages
   Rarely heard anything but English in office

g. Decide which format you will use to develop your paragraph: one side at a time or point by point. Either is acceptable; it is up to you to decide which you prefer. The important thing is to be consistent: whichever format you choose, be sure to use it throughout the entire paragraph.

h. Write the first draft of your paragraph.

REVISING: The Four Bases

Checklist for Comparison and Contrast

Put your composition away for a day or so. You will return to it with a fresh perspective and a better ability to critique what you have written. Reread your paragraph with these questions in mind to make sure you have covered the four bases of effective writing:

About *Unity*

☑ Does my topic sentence make it clear what two things I am comparing or contrasting?

☑ Do all sentences in the paragraph stay on topic?

About *Support*

☑ Have I compared or contrasted the subjects in at least three important ways?

☑ Have I provided specific details that effectively back up my supporting points?

About *Coherence*

☑ If I have chosen the point-by-point format, have I consistently discussed a point about one subject, then immediately discussed the same point about the other subject before moving on to the next point?

☑ If I have chosen the one-side-at-a-time format, have I discussed every point about one of my subjects, then discussed the same points *in the same order* about the second subjects?

☑ Have I used appropriate transitions, such as *first, in addition, also,* and *another way,* to help readers follow my train of thought?

About *Sentence Skills*

☑ Have I carefully proofread my paragraph, using the guidelines on the inside back cover of the book, and corrected all sentence-skills mistakes, including spelling?

Continue revising your work until you can answer *yes* to all these questions.

BEYOND THE CLASSROOM

Comparison and Contrast

Imagine that a new club has opened in the building next to your house/apartment/dorm. At first, you were thrilled—but then loud music and screaming patrons started making it nearly impossible for you to study or sleep. Seven days a week, the club stays open until 2:00 A.M.

1. Write a paragraph-long letter of complaint to the club owners, contrasting life before and after the club opened.
2. Write an e-mail on the same topic to one of your friends.
3. How do the two pieces of writing (for two different purposes/audiences) differ from each other? How are they similar?

5. Definition

In talking with other people, we sometimes offer informal definitions to explain just what we mean by a particular term. Suppose, for example, we say to a friend, "Karen can be so clingy." We might then expand on our idea of "clingy" by saying, "You know, a clingy person needs to be with someone every single minute. If Karen's best friend makes plans that don't include her, she becomes hurt. And when she dates someone, she calls him several times a day and gets upset if he even goes to the grocery store without her. She hangs on to people too tightly." In a written definition, we make clear in a more complete and formal way our own personal understanding of a term. Such a definition typically starts with one meaning of a term. The meaning is then illustrated with a series of examples or a story.

A Paragraph to Consider

Luck

[1]Luck is putting $1.75 into a vending machine and getting the money back with your snake. [2]It is an instructor's decision to give a retest on a test on which you first scored thirty. [3]Luck refers to moments of good fortune that happen in everyday life. [4] It is not going to the dentist for two years and then going and finding out that you do not have any cavities. [5]It is calling up a plumber to fix a leak on a day when the plumber has no other work to do. [6] Luck is finding a used car for sale at good price at exactly the time when your car rolls its last mile. [7] Luck is driving into a traffic bottleneck and choosing the lane that winds up moving most rapidly. [8]Luck is being late for work on a day when your boss arrives later than you do. [9]It is having a new checkout aisle at the supermarket open up just as your cart arrives. [10]The best kind of luck is winning a new flat-screen TV on a chance for which you paid only a quarter.

About Unity

1. Where is the topic sentence in this paragraph? Where would it be more appropriately placed?

   _____

   _____

About Support

2. How does this paragraph develop its definition of *luck?* Is it through a series of short examples or through a single extended example?

   _____

About Coherence

3. What does it mean that "Luck" uses emphatic order?

   _____

Writing a Definition Paragraph

Write a paragraph that defines the term *TV addict*. Base your paragraph on the topic sentence and three supporting points provided below.

Topic sentence: Television addicts are people who will watch all the programs they can, for as long as they can, without doing anything else.

(1)   TV addicts, first of all, will watch anything on the tube, no matter how bad it is. . . .

(2)   In addition, addicts watch more hours of TV than normal people do. . . .

(3)   Finally, addicts feel that TV is more important than other people or any other activities that might be going on. . . .

PREWRITING

a. Generate as many examples as you can for each of the three qualities of a TV addict. You can do this by asking yourself the following questions:

   • What are some truly awful shows that I (or TV addicts I know) watch just because the television is turned on?

   • What are some examples of the large amounts of time that I (or TV addicts I know) watch television?

   • What are some examples of ways that I (or TV addicts I know) neglect people or give up activities in order to watch TV?

   Write down every answer you can think of for each question. At this point, don't worry about writing full sentences or even about grammar or spelling. Just get your thoughts down on paper.

Shoebox greeting card © Hallmark Cards, Kansas City

DEFINE "GOOD."

Responding to Images

Explain to someone who doesn't know what "good" means why this cartoon is funny.

b. Look over the list of examples you have generated. Select the strongest examples you have thought of. You should have at least two or three for each quality. If not, ask yourself the questions in step *a* again.

c. Write out the examples you will use, this time expressing them in full, grammatically correct sentences.

d. Start with the topic sentence and three points provided in the assignment. Fill in the examples you've generated to support each point and write a first draft of your paragraph.

REVISING: The Four Bases

Checklist for Definition

Put your first draft away for a day or so. When you come back to it, reread it critically, asking yourself these questions to make sure you have covered the four bases of effective writing:

About *Unity*

☑ Have I used the topic sentence and the three supporting points that were provided?

☑ Does every sentence in my paragraph help define the term *TV addict?*

About *Support*

☑ Have I backed up each supporting point with at least two examples?

☑ Does each of my examples effectively illustrate the point that it backs up?

About *Coherence*

☑ Have I used appropriate transitional language (*another, in addition, for example*) to tie my thoughts together?

☑ Are all transitional words correctly used?

About *Sentence Skills*

☑ Have I carefully proofread my paragraph, using the guidelines on the inside back cover of the book, and corrected all sentence-skills mistakes, including spelling?

☑ Have I used a consistent point of view throughout my paragraph?

Continue revising your work until you can answer *yes* to all these questions.

Imagine that you are applying for a grant from your town or city government to build a community garden in an urban area, or a community theater in a rural/suburban one. To make such an appeal effective, you will need to define *community*; such a definition will help you to show that the garden or theater will enhance the lives of everyone in this particular community. Use examples or one extended example to illustrate each of your general points.

BEYOND THE CLASSROOM

Definition

6. Classification and Division

If you were doing the laundry, you might begin by separating the clothing into piles. You would then put all the whites in one pile and all the colors in another. Or you might classify the laundry, not according to color, but according to fabric—putting all cottons in one pile, polyesters in another, and so on. *Classifying* is the process of taking many things and separating them into categories. We generally classify to better manage or understand many things. Librarians classify books into groups (novels, travel, health, etc.) to make them easier to find. A scientist sheds light on the world by classifying all living things into two main groups: animals and plants.

Dividing, in contrast, is taking one thing and breaking it down into parts. We often divide, or analyze, to better understand, teach, or evaluate something. For instance, a tinkerer might take apart a clock to see how it works; a science text might divide a tree into its parts to explain their functions. A music reviewer may analyze the elements of a band's performance—for example, the skill of the various players, rapport with the audience, selections, and so on.

In short, if you are classifying, you are sorting *numbers of things* into categories. If you are dividing, you are breaking *one thing* into parts. It all depends on your purpose—you might classify flowers into various types or divide a single flower into its parts.

Two Paragraphs to Consider

Types of E-Mail

[1]As more and more people take advantage of e-mailing, three categories of e-mail have emerged. [2]One category of e-mail is junk mail. [3]When most people sign on to their computers, they are greeted with a flood of get-rich-quick schemes, invitations to pornographic Web sites, and ads for a variety of unwanted products. [4]E-mail users quickly become good at hitting the "delete" button to get rid of this garbage. [5]The second category that clogs most people's electronic mailbox is forwarded mail, most of which also gets deleted without being read. [6]The third and best category of e-mail is genuine personal e-mail from genuine personal friends. [7]Getting such real, thoughtful e-mail can almost make up for the irritation of the other two categories.

Planning a Trip

[1]Designating a destination where the political and societal conditions are healthy and secure is the first and most important step in planning a trip. [2]Unstable governments very often lead to social unrest and violence. [3]Once settling on a general location, devising a budget is the next step. [4]The cost of living in some countries can be drastically higher than others. [5]When the destination is settled on, becoming familiar with the religious and cultural customs of the country is highly recommended. [6]What is accepted in the United States may be considered illegal or insulting in a foreign country. [7]For example, in Islamic countries, women are expected to cover their entire body and head. [8]In many instances, women wear veils across the face with a small slit positioned in front of the eyes. [9]Showing up in a tank top and shorts will very likely jeopardize one's sense of security and safety. [10]Now it is time to purchase an airline ticket and again, research is strongly advised in order to obtain the best possible deal. [11]Depending on one's idea of fun, planning an itinerary can be exceedingly complicated or relatively simple. [12]If lying on a lounge chair and sipping a cocktail by the water's edge is the desired activity, then planning the itinerary will be quite effortless. [13]But if a traveler is interested in involving himself or herself in some rigorous activities such as mountain climbing, scuba diving, or kayaking, planning the itinerary will probably require a lot more time. [14]Many people do not realize that there is in fact a lot of research involved in planning a trip. [15]These people should not be so careless, as they could expose themselves to extremely dangerous situations. [16]It is frustrating that so few people take research seriously.

QUESTIONS

About Unity

1. Which paragraph lacks a topic sentence?

   _____

2. Which sentence(s) in "Planning a Trip" should be eliminated in the interest of paragraph unity? (*Write the sentence number here.*) _____

About Support

3. Which aspect of "Planning a Trip" lacks specific details?

   _____

4. After which sentence in "Types of E-Mail" are supporting details needed? (*Write the sentence number here.*) _____

About Coherence

5. Which paragraph uses emphatic order to organize its details?

_____

6. Which words in "Types of E-mail" signal the most important detail?

_____

Writing a Division-Classification Paragraph

WRITING ASSIGNMENT

Below are four options to develop into a classification paragraph. Each one presents a topic to classify into three categories. Choose one option to develop into a paragraph.

Option 1
Supermarket shoppers

(1) Slow, careful shoppers

(2) Average shoppers

(3) Hurried shoppers

Option 2
Eaters

(1) Very conservative eaters

(2) Typical eaters

(3) Adventurous eaters

Option 3
Types of housekeepers

(1) Never clean

(2) Clean on a regular basis

(3) Clean constantly

Option 4
Attitudes toward money

(1) Tightfisted

(2) Reasonable

(3) Extravagant

PREWRITING

a. Begin by doing some freewriting on the topic you have chosen. For five or ten minutes, simply write down everything that comes into your head when you think about "types of housekeepers, "attitudes toward money," or whichever option you choose. Don't worry about grammar, spelling, or organization—just write.

b. Now that you've "loosened up your brain" a little, try asking yourself questions about the topic and writing down your answers. If you are writing about supermarket shoppers, for instance, you might ask questions like these:

How do the three kinds of shoppers prepare for their shopping trip?

How many aisles will each kind of shopper visit?

What do the different kinds of shoppers bring along with them—lists, calculators, coupons, and so on?

How long does each type of shopper spend in the store?

Write down whatever answers occur to you for these and other questions. Again, do not worry at this stage about writing correctly. Instead, concentrate on getting down all the information you can think of that supports your three points.

c. Reread the material you have accumulated. If some of the details you have written make you think of even better ones, add them. Select the details that best support your three points. Number them in the order you will present them.

d. Restate your topic as a grammatically complete topic sentence. For example, if you're writing about eaters, your topic sentence might be "Eaters can be divided into three categories." Turn each of your three supporting points into a full sentence as well.

e. Using your topic sentence and three supporting sentences and adding the details you have generated, write the first draft of your paragraph.

REVISING: The Four Bases

Checklist for Classification-Division

Put your work away for a couple of days. Then reread it with a critical eye; keep these questions in mind to make sure you have covered the four bases of effective writing:

About *Unity*

 • Does my paragraph include a complete topic sentence and three supporting points?

About *Support*

 • Have I backed up each supporting point with strong, specific details?

About *Coherence*

 • Does the paragraph successfully classify types of shoppers, housekeepers, eaters, or attitudes toward money?

About *Sentence Skills*

 • Have I carefully proofread my paragraph, using the list on the inside back cover of the book, and corrected all sentence-skills mistakes, including spelling?

 • Have I used specific rather than general words?

Continue revising your work until you can answer *yes* to all these questions.

BEYOND THE CLASSROOM

Classification and Division

Imagine that you are a real estate agent and someone new to the area has asked you for suggestions about where to look for a home. Write a paragraph classifying local neighborhoods into three or more types. For each type, include an explanation with one or more examples.

7. Description

When you describe something or someone, you give your readers a picture in words. To make this "word picture" as vivid and real as possible, you must observe and record specific details that appeal to your readers' senses (sight, hearing, taste, smell, and touch). More than any other type of writing, a descriptive paragraph needs sharp, colorful details.

Here is a description in which only the sense of sight is used:

A rug covers the living-room floor.

In contrast, here is a description rich in sense impressions:

A thick, reddish-brown shag rug is laid wall to wall across the living-room floor. The long, curled fibers of the shag seem to whisper as you walk through them in your bare feet, and when you squeeze your toes into the deep covering, the soft fibers push back at you with a spongy resilience.

Sense impressions include sight (*thick, reddish-brown shag rug; laid wall to wall; walk through them in your bare feet; squeeze your toes into the deep covering; push back*), hearing (*whisper*), and touch (*bare feet, soft fibers, spongy resilience*). The sharp, vivid images provided by the sensory details give us a clear picture of the rug and enable us to share the writer's experience.

A Paragraph to Consider

My Teenage Son's Room

[1]I push open the door with difficulty. [2]The doorknob is loose and has to be jiggled just right before the catch releases from the doorjamb. [3]Furthermore, as I push at the door, it runs into a basketball shoe lying on the floor. [4]I manage to squeeze in through the narrow opening. [5]I am immediately aware of a pungent odor in the room, most of which is coming from the closet, to my right. [6]That's the location of a white wicker clothes hamper, heaped with grass-stained jeans, sweat-stained T-shirts, and smelly socks. [7]But the half-eaten burrito, lying dried and unappetizing on the bedside table across the room, contributes a bit of aroma, as does the glass of curdled, sour milk sitting on the sunny windowsill. [8]To my left, the small wire cage on Greg's desk is also fragrant, but pleasantly. [9]From its nest of sweet-smelling cedar chips, the gerbil peers out at me with its bright eyes, its tiny claws scratching against the cage wall. [10]The floor around the wastebasket that is next to the desk is surrounded by what appears to be a sprinkling of snowballs. [11]They're actually old wadded-up school papers, and I can picture Greg sitting on his bed, crushing them into balls and aiming them at the "basket"—the trash can. [12]I glance at the bed across from the desk and chuckle because pillows stuffed under the tangled nest of blankets make it look as if someone is still sleeping there, though I know Greg is in history class right now. [13]I

continued

step carefully through the room, trying to walk through the obstacle course of science-fiction paperbacks, a wristwatch, sports magazines, and a dust-covered computer on which my son stacks empty soda cans. [14]I leave everything as I find it, but tape a note to Greg's door saying, "Isn't it about time to clean up?"

QUESTIONS

About Unity

1. Does this paragraph have a topic sentence?

_____

About Support

2. Label as *sight, touch, hearing,* or *smell* all the sensory details in the following sentences.

    That's the location of a white wicker clothes hamper, heaped with

    grass-stained jeans, sweat-stained T-shirts, and smelly socks.

About Coherence

3. Spatial signals (*above, next to, to the right,* and so on) are often used to help organize details in a descriptive paragraph. List four space signals that appear in "My Teenage Son's Room":

_____

Writing a Descriptive Paragraph

WRITING ASSIGNMENT

Write a paragraph describing a certain person's room. Use as your topic sentence "I could tell by looking at the room that a _____ lived there." There are many kinds of people who could be the focus for such a paragraph. You can select any one of the following, or think of another type of person.

Photographer	Music lover	Carpenter
Cook	TV addict	Baby
Student	Camper	Cat or dog lover
Musician	Computer expert	World traveler
Hunter	Cheerleader	Drug addict
Slob	Football player	Little boy or girl
Outdoors person	Actor	Alcoholic
Doctor	Dancer	In-line skater

PREWRITING

a. After choosing a topic, spend a few minutes making sure it will work. Prepare a list of all the details you can think of that support the topic. For example, a student who planned to describe a soccer player's room made this list:

soccer balls

shin guards

posters of professional soccer teams

soccer trophies

shirt printed with team name and number

autographed soccer ball

medals and ribbons

photos of player's own team

sports clippings

radio that looks like soccer ball

soccer socks

soccer shorts

If you don't have enough details, choose another type of person. Check your new choice by listing details before committing yourself to the topic.

b. You may want to use other prewriting techniques, such as freewriting or questioning, to develop more details for your topic. As you continue prewriting, keep the following in mind:

- Everything in the paragraph should support your point. For example, if you are writing about a soccer player's room, every detail should serve to show that the person who lives in that room plays and loves soccer. Other details—for example, the person's computer, tropical fish tank, or daily "to-do" list—should be omitted.

- Description depends on the use of specific rather than general descriptive words. For example:

General	Specific
Mess on the floor	The obstacle course of science-fiction paperbacks, a wristwatch, sports magazines, and a dust-covered computer on which my son stacks empty soda cans.
Ugly turtle tub	Large plastic tub of dirty, stagnant-looking water containing a few motionless turtles
Bad smell	Unpleasant mixture of strong chemical deodorizers, urine-soaked newspapers, and musty sawdust
Nice skin	Soft, velvety brown skin

Remember that you want your readers to experience the room vividly. Your words should be as detailed as a clear photograph, giving readers a real feel for the room. Appeal to as many senses as possible. Most of your description will involve the sense of sight, but you may be able to include details about touch, hearing, and smell as well.

- Spatial order is a good way to organize a descriptive paragraph. Move as a visitor's eye might move around the room, from right to left or from larger items to smaller ones. Here are a few transition words of the sort that show spatial relationships.

to the left	across from	on the opposite side
to the right	above	nearby
next to	below	

Such transitions will help prevent you—and your reader—from getting lost as the description proceeds.

c. Before you write, see if you can make a scratch outline based on your list. Here is one possible outline of the paragraph about the soccer player's room. Note that the details are organized according to spatial order—from the edges of the room in toward the center.

Topic sentence: I could tell by looking at the room that a soccer player lived there.

1. Walls
2. Bookcase
3. Desk
4. Chair
5. Floor

d. Then proceed to write a first draft of your paragraph.

REVISING: The Four Bases

Checklist for Description

Read your descriptive paragraph slowly out loud to a friend or classmate. Ask the friend to close his or her eyes and try to picture the room as you read. Read it out loud a second time. To ensure you have covered the four bases of effective writing, ask your friend to answer these questions:

About *Unity*

 Does every detail in the paragraph support the topic sentence? Here's one way to find out: Ask your friend to imagine omitting the key word or words (in the case of our example, *soccer player*) in your topic sentence. Would readers know what word should fit in that empty space?

About *Support*

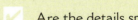 Are the details specific and vivid rather than general?

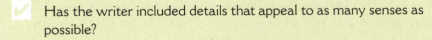 Has the writer included details that appeal to as many senses as possible?

About *Coherence*

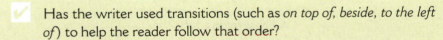 Does the paragraph follow a logical spatial order?

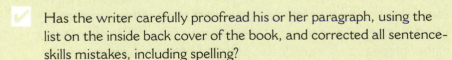 Has the writer used transitions (such as *on top of, beside, to the left of*) to help the reader follow that order?

About *Sentence Skills*

Has the writer carefully proofread his or her paragraph, using the list on the inside back cover of the book, and corrected all sentence-skills mistakes, including spelling?

Continue revising your work until you can answer *yes* to all these questions.

Imagine that you are an interior designer. Write a paragraph describing a design for one of the following: a child's bedroom, a kitchen, a small restaurant, a porch, or a bakery. In your prewriting, you might list all the relevant needs of the people who live or work in the space you are designing. Consider issues such as storage space, appropriate lighting and colors, and the first thing people should or would notice when they walk in. Then put all the parts together so that they work well as a whole. Use a spatial order in your paragraph to help readers "see" your room.

BEYOND THE CLASSROOM

Description

8. Narration

At times we make a statement clear by relating in detail something that has happened. In the story we tell, we present the details in the order in which they happened. A person might say, for example, "I was embarrassed yesterday," and then go on to illustrate the statement with the following narrative:

> I was hurrying across campus to get to a class. It had rained heavily all morning, so I was hopscotching my way around puddles in the pathway. I called to two friends ahead to wait for me, and right before I caught up to them, I came to a large puddle that covered the entire path. I had to make a quick choice of either stepping into the puddle or trying to jump over it. I jumped, wanting to seem cool, since my friends were watching, but didn't clear the puddle. Water splashed everywhere, drenching my shoe, sock, and pants cuff, and spraying the pants of my friends as well. "Well done, Dave!" they said. My embarrassment was all the greater because I had tried to look so casual.

The speaker's details have made his moment of embarrassment vivid and real for us, and we can see and understand just why he felt as he did.

A Paragraph to Consider

A Frustrating Job

¹Working as a babysitter was the most frustrating job I ever had. ²I discovered this fact when my sister asked me to stay with her two sons for the evening. ³I figured I would get them dinner, let them watch a little TV, and then put them to bed early. ⁴The rest of the night I planned to watch TV and collect an easy twenty dollars. ⁵It turned out to be anything but easy. ⁶First, right before we were about to sit down for a pizza dinner, Rickie let the parakeet out of its cage. ⁷This bird is really intelligent and can repeat almost any phrase. ⁸The dog started chasing it around the house, so I decided to catch it before the dog did. ⁹Rickie and Jeff volunteered to help, following at my heels. ¹⁰We had the bird cornered by the fireplace when Rickie jumped for it and knocked over the hamster cage. ¹¹Then the bird escaped again, and the hamsters began scurrying around their cage like crazy creatures. ¹²The dog had disappeared by this point, so I decided to clean up the hamsters' cage and try to calm them down. ¹³While I was doing this, Rickie and Jeff caught the parakeet and put it back in its cage. ¹⁴It was time to return to the kitchen and eat cold pizza. ¹⁵But upon entering the kitchen, I discovered why the dog had lost interest in the bird chase. ¹⁶What was left of the pizza was lying on the floor, and tomato sauce was dripping from the dog's chin. ¹⁷I cleaned up the mess and then served chicken noodle soup and ice cream to the boys. ¹⁸Only at nine o'clock did I get the kids to bed. ¹⁹I then returned downstairs to find that the dog had thrown up pizza

continued

on the living-room rug. [20]When I finished cleaning the rug, my sister returned. [21]I took the twenty dollars and told her that she should get someone else next time.

About Unity

1. Which sentence in this paragraph should be omitted in the interest of unity? (*Write the sentence number here.*) _____

About Support

2. What do you think is the best (most real and vivid) detail or image in the paragraph "A Frustrating Job"?

_____

About Coherence

3. Does this paragraph use time order or emphatic order to organize details?

_____

4. What are four transition words used in this paragraph?

_____

Writing a Narrative Paragraph

Write a paragraph about an experience in which a certain emotion was predominant. The emotion might be fear, pride, satisfaction, embarrassment, or any of these:

Frustration	Sympathy	Shyness
Love	Bitterness	Disappointment
Sadness	Violence	Happiness
Terror	Surprise	Jealousy
Shock	Nostalgia	Anger
Relief	Loss	Hate
Envy	Silliness	Nervousness

The experience you write about should be limited in time. Note that the paragraph presented in this chapter details an experience that occurred within a relatively short period of time: one frustrating night of babysitting.

A good way to bring an event to life for your readers is to include some dialogue, as the writers of two of the three paragraphs in this chapter have done. Words that you said, or that someone else said, help make a situation come alive. First, though, be sure to check the section on quotation marks on pages 349–359.

PREWRITING

a. Begin by freewriting. Think of an experience or event that caused you to feel a certain emotion strongly. Then spend ten minutes writing freely about the experience. Do not worry at this point about spelling or grammar or putting things in the right order. Instead, just try to get down all the details you can think of that seem related to the experience.

b. This preliminary writing will help you decide whether your topic is promising enough to develop further. If it is not, choose another emotion and repeat step *a*. If it does seem promising, do two things:

   • First, write your topic sentence, underlining the emotion you will focus on. For example, "My first day in kindergarten was one of the *scariest* days of my life."

   • Second, make up a list of all the details involved in the experience. Then number these details according to the order in which they occurred.

c. Referring to your list of details, write a rough draft of your paragraph. Use time signals such as *first, then, after, next, while, during,* and *finally* to help connect details as you move from the beginning to the middle to the end of your narrative. Be sure to include not only what happened but also how you felt about what was going on.

REVISING: The Four Bases

Checklist for Narration

Put your first draft away for a day or so. When you return to it, keep these questions in mind to make sure you have covered the four bases of effective writing:

About *Unity*

☑ Does my topic sentence clearly state what emotion the experience made me feel?

☑ Are there any off-topic sentences I should eliminate for the sake of paragraph unity?

About *Support*

☑ Have I included some dialogue to make the experience come alive?

☑ Have I explained how I felt as the experience occurred?

About *Coherence*

☑ Have I used time order to narrate the experience from beginning to end?

☑ Have I used time signals to connect one detail to the next?

About *Sentence Skills*

☑ Have I carefully proofread my paragraph, using the list on the inside back cover of the book, and corrected all sentence-skills mistakes, including spelling?

☑ Is the first-person point of view (I) in my paragraph consistent?

☑ Did I use verb tenses consistently and correctly? (This is especially important when relaying a story.)

Continue revising your work until you can answer *yes* to all these questions.

Imagine that one of your oldest friends has to make a difficult decision of some kind. Narrate a relevant story from your own experience (or the experience of someone you know) that will help your friend carefully weigh the decision he or she must make. In your paragraph, include a comment or two about how your story relates to your friend's situation. Throughout, try to be helpful without being condescending. You can also be entertaining, as long as you are careful to stay sensitive to the problem at hand.

BEYOND THE CLASSROOM

Narration

9. Argument

Most of us know someone who enjoys a good argument. Such a person usually challenges any sweeping statement we might make. "Why do you say that?" he or she will ask. "Give your reasons." Our questioner then listens carefully as we cite our reasons, waiting to see if we really do have solid evidence to support our point of view. In an argument, the two parties each present their supporting evidence. The goal is to determine who has the more solid evidence to support his or her point of view. A questioner may make us feel a bit nervous, but we may also appreciate the way he or she makes us think through our opinions.

The ability to advance sound, compelling arguments is an important skill in everyday life. We can use argument to get an extension on a term paper, obtain a favor from a friend, or convince an employer that we are the right person for a job. Understanding persuasion based on clear, logical reasoning can also help us see through the sometimes-faulty arguments advanced by advertisers, editors, politicians, and others who try to bring us over to their side.

A Paragraph to Consider

Living Alone

[1]Living alone is quite an experience. [2]People who live alone, for one thing, have to learn to do all kinds of tasks by themselves. [3]They must learn—even if they have had no experience—to change fuses, put up curtains and shades, temporarily dam an overflowing toilet, cook a meal, and defrost a refrigerator. [4]When there is no father, husband, mother, or wife to depend on, a person can't fall back on the excuse, "I don't know how to do that." [5]Those who live alone also need the strength to deal with people. [6]Alone, singles must face noisy neighbors, unresponsive landlords, dishonest repair people, and aggressive bill collectors. [7]Because there are no buffers between themselves and the outside world, people living alone have to handle every visitor—friendly or unfriendly—alone. [8]Finally, singles need a large dose of courage to cope with occasional panic and unavoidable loneliness. [9]That weird thump in the night is even more terrifying when there is no one in the next bed or the next room. [10]Frightening weather or unexpected bad news is doubly bad when the worry can't be shared. [11]Even when life is going well, little moments of sudden loneliness can send shivers through the heart. [12]Struggling through such bad times taps into reserves of courage that people may not have known they possessed. [13]Facing everyday tasks, confronting all types of people, and handling panic and loneliness can shape singles into brave, resourceful, and more independent people.

About Unity

1. The topic sentence in "Living Alone" is too broad. Circle the topic sentence below that states accurately what the paragraph is about.

    a. Living alone can make one a better person.

    b. Living alone can create feelings of loneliness.

    c. Living alone should be avoided.

2. How many reasons are given to support the topic sentence in this paragraph?

    _____ one _____ two _____ three _____ four

About Coherence

3. What are the three main transition words in this paragraph?

    _____

Writing an Argument Paragraph

Develop an argument paragraph based on one of the following statements:

Condoms should (*or* should not) be made available in schools.

_____ (*name a specific athlete*) is the athlete most worthy of admiration in his *or* her sport.

Television is one of the best (*or* worst) inventions of this century.

_____ make the best (*or* worst) pets.

Cigarette and alcohol advertising should (*or* should not) be banned.

Teenagers make poor parents.

_____ is one public figure today who can be considered a hero.

This college needs a better _____ (cafeteria *or* library *or* student center *or* grading policy *or* attendance policy).

"Gentlemen, it's time we gave some serious thought to the effects of global warming."

Responding to Images

What argument does this cartoon make? Is it persuasive? Why or why not?

PREWRITING

a. Make up brief outlines for any three of the preceding statements. Make sure you have three separate and distinct reasons for each statement. Below is an example of a brief outline for a paragraph making another point.

Large cities should outlaw passenger cars.

1. Cut down on smog and pollution
2. Cut down on noise
3. Make more room for pedestrians

b. Decide, perhaps through discussion with your instructor or class-mates, which of your outlines is the most promising for development into a paragraph. Make sure your supporting points are logical by asking yourself in each case, "Does this item truly support my topic sentence?"

c. Do some prewriting. Prepare a list of all the details you can think of that might actually support your point. Don't limit yourself; include more details than you can actually use. Here, for example, are details generated by the writer of "Living Alone":

Deal with power failures	Noisy neighbors
Nasty landlords	Develop courage
Scary noises at night	Do all the cooking
Spiders	Home repairs
Bill collectors	Obscene phone calls
Frightening storms	Loneliness

d. Decide which details you will use to develop your paragraph. Number the details in the order in which you will present them. Because pre-senting the strongest reason last (emphatic order) is the most effective way to organize an argument paragraph, be sure to save your most powerful reason for last. Here is how the author of "Living Alone" made decisions about details:

Deal with power failures

Nasty landlords

Scary noises at night

Spiders

Bill collectors

Frightening storms

Noisy neighbors

Develop courage

Do all the cooking

Home repairs

Obscene phone calls

Loneliness

e. Write the first draft of your paragraph. As you write, develop each reason with specific details. For example, in "Living Alone," notice how the writer makes the experience of living alone come alive with phrases like "That weird thump in the night" or "little moments of sudden loneliness can send shivers through the heart."

REVISING: The Four Bases

Checklist for Argument

Put your paragraph away for a day or so. When you reread it, ask yourself these questions to make sure you have covered the four bases of effective writing:

About *Unity*

☑ Imagine that your audience is a jury who will ultimately render a verdict on your argument. Have you presented a convincing case? If you were on the jury, would you both understand and be favorably impressed by this argument?

☑ Does every one of your supporting points help prove the argument stated in your topic sentence?

About *Support*

☑ Have you backed up your points of support with specific details?

☑ Have you appealed to your readers' senses with these details?

About *Coherence*

☑ Have you used emphatic order in your paragraph, saving the most important, strongest detail for last?

About *Sentence Skills*

☑ Have you used strong verbs (rather than *is* and *to be*) throughout?

☑ Have you written your argument in the active, rather than passive, voice?

☑ Have you checked your paper for sentence-skills mistakes, including spelling?

Continue revising your work until you can answer *yes* to all these questions.

BEYOND THE CLASSROOM

Argument

Imagine that you have adopted a wonderful pet (dog, cat, snake, etc.) but your landlord, roommate, or boyfriend/girlfriend has asked that you get rid of it. Write a letter to this naysayer, explaining in detail why you chose to adopt this pet and why you should be allowed to keep it. Do your best to convince your landlord, roommate, or significant other that it is a good choice.

TECH-SAVVY WRITING

Examine your college's home page and consider what patterns of development it uses—and for what purposes. In your response, consider some of the following questions: How does the home page describe and/or define your school, and does it serve to narrate your college's story? As a prospective student, what kind of first impression does this page (not the site as a whole) offer? How is it an *argument* or advertisement for you school? How does it use *classification* and/or *division* as organizing principles? Does the site seem easy to navigate? What might you, as a current student, use the site for?

RESPONDING TO IMAGES

The images that follow address the topic of same-sex marriage. Why do you think the photographs were taken? Consider issues of purpose and audience. What patterns of development are at work in each image? How might the reason a photograph is taken differ from how it is used in a textbook?

5

Moving from Paragraph to Essay

Responding to Images

What can an artist learn about drawing the human form by focusing on one particular aspect of it, such as a hand?

What Is an Essay?

Differences between an Essay and a Paragraph

An essay is simply a paper composed of several paragraphs, rather than one paragraph. In an essay, subjects can and should be treated more fully than they would be in a single-paragraph paper.

The main idea or point developed in an essay is called the *thesis statement* or *thesis sentence* (rather than, as in a paragraph, the *topic sentence*). The thesis statement appears in the introductory paragraph, and it is then developed in the supporting paragraphs that follow. A short concluding paragraph closes the essay.

The Form of an Essay

The diagram that follows shows the form of an essay.

Introductory paragraph

> Introduction
> Thesis statement
> Plan of development:
> Points 1, 2, 3

The *introduction* attracts the reader's interest.

The *thesis statement* (or *thesis sentence*) states the main idea advanced in the paper.

The *plan of development* is a list of points that support the thesis. The points are presented in the order in which they will be developed in the paper.

First supporting paragraph

> Topic sentence (point 1)
> Specific evidence

The *topic sentence* advances the first supporting point for the thesis, and the *specific evidence* in the rest of the paragraph develops that first point.

Second supporting paragraph

> Topic sentence (point 2)
> Specific evidence

The *topic sentence* advances the second supporting point for the thesis, and the *specific evidence* in the rest of the paragraph develops that second point.

Third supporting paragraph

> Topic sentence (point 3)
> Specific evidence

The *topic sentence* advances the third supporting point for the thesis, and the *specific evidence* in the rest of the paragraph develops that third point.

Concluding paragraph

> Summary,
> Conclusion,
> or both

A *summary* is a brief restatement of the thesis and its main points. A *conclusion* is a final thought or two stemming from the subject of the paper.

A Model Essay

Gene, the writer of the paragraph on working in an apple plant (page 7), later decided to develop his subject more fully. Here is the essay that resulted.

My Job in an Apple Plant

[1]In the course of working my way through school, I have taken many jobs I would rather forget. [2]I have spent nine hours a day lifting heavy automobile and truck batteries off the end of an assembly belt. [3]I have risked the loss of eyes and fingers working a punch press in a textile factory. [4]I have served as a ward aide in a mental hospital, helping care for brain-damaged men who would break into violent fits at unexpected moments. [5]But none of these jobs was as dreadful as my job in an apple plant. [6]The work was physically hard; the pay was poor; and, most of all, the working conditions were dismal.

[7]First, the job made enormous demands on my strength and energy. [8]For ten hours a night, I took cartons that rolled down a metal track and stacked them onto wooden skids in a tractor trailer. [9]Each carton contained twelve heavy bottles of apple juice. [10]A carton shot down the track about every fifteen seconds. [11]I once figured out that I was lifting an average of twelve tons of apple juice every night. [12]When a truck was almost filled, I or my partner had to drag fourteen bulky wooden skids into the empty trailer nearby and then set up added sections of the heavy metal track so that we could start routing cartons to the back of the empty van. [13]While one of us did that, the other performed the stacking work of two men.

[14]I would not have minded the difficulty of the work so much if the pay had not been so poor. [15]I was paid the minimum wage at that time, $3.65 an hour, plus just a quarter extra for working the night shift. [16]Because of the low salary, I felt compelled to get as much overtime pay as possible. [17]Everything over eight hours a night was time-and-a-half, so I typically worked twelve hours a night. [18]On Friday I would sometimes work straight through until Saturday at noon—eighteen hours. [19]I averaged over sixty hours a week but did not take home much more than $230.

[20]But even more than the low pay, what upset me about my apple plant job was the working conditions. [21]Our humorless supervisor cared only about his production record for each night and tried to keep the assembly line moving at breakneck pace. [22]During work I was limited to two ten-minute breaks and an unpaid half hour for lunch. [23]Most of my time was spent outside on the truck loading dock in near-zero-degree temperatures. [24]The steel floors of the trucks were like ice; the quickly penetrating cold made my feet feel like stone. [25]I had no shared interests with the man I loaded cartons with, and so I had to work without companionship on the job. [26]And after the production line shut down and most people left, I had to spend two hours alone scrubbing clean the apple vats, which were coated with a sticky residue.

[27]I stayed on the job for five months, all the while hating the difficulty of the work, the poor money, and the conditions under which I worked. [28]By the time I quit, I was determined never to do such degrading work again.

Introductory paragraph

First supporting paragraph

Second supporting paragraph

Third supporting paragraph

Concluding paragraph

Important Points about the Essay

Introductory Paragraph

An introductory paragraph has certain purposes or functions and can be constructed using various methods.

Purposes of the Introduction

An introductory paragraph should do three things:

1. Attract the reader's *interest.* Using one of the suggested methods of introduction described under "Common Methods of Introduction" can help draw the reader into your paper.

2. Present a *thesis sentence*—a clear, direct statement of the central idea that you will develop in your paper. The thesis statement, like a topic sentence, should have a keyword or keywords reflecting your attitude about the subject. For example, in the essay on the apple plant job, the keyword is *dreadful.*

3. Indicate a *plan of development*—a preview of the major points that will support your thesis statement, listed in the order in which they will be presented. In some cases, the thesis statement and plan of development may appear in the same sentence. In other cases, the plan of development may be omitted.

ACTIVITY 1	Introductory Paragraphs

1. In "My Job in an Apple Plant," which sentences are used to attract the reader's interest?

    _____ sentences 1 to 3   _____ 1 to 4   _____ 1 to 5

2. The thesis in "My Job in an Apple Plant" is presented in

    _____ sentence 4   _____ sentence 5   _____ sentence 6

3. Is the thesis followed by a plan of development?

    _____ Yes   _____ No

4. Which words in the plan of development announce the three major supporting points in the essay? Write them below.

    a. _____

    b. _____

    c. _____

Common Methods of Introduction

Four common methods of introducing an essay are as follows:

a. Begin with a broad statement and narrow it down to your thesis statement.

b. Present an idea or situation that is the opposite of the one you will develop.

c. Tell a brief story.

d. Ask one or more questions.

| **Identifying Methods of Introduction** | **ACTIVITY 2** |

Following are four introductions. In the space provided, write the letter of the method of introduction used in each case.

_____ 1. One morning twenty-nine years ago, my father backed out of his parking space, smashed into the Cadillac parked across the street, put the car into drive, and kept going. "Take it easy, Floyd," yelled Mom. "Better to be late than to die!" But that didn't keep him from accelerating, weaving in and out of traffic, and running into a telephone booth. As a result, I was born in my parents' old green-and-white Chevy instead of at Bradley Hospital. Perhaps it's no surprise, then, that my own car was the location of other key events in my life—an accident that almost killed me, the place where I made a crucial job decision, and my proposal to my wife.

_____ 2. I have had a lot of interesting teachers through the years. Some have taught me useful and interesting facts. Even better, some have shown me how to learn. Some have even inspired me. But of all the wonderful teachers I've had, my favorite is Mrs. Rogers, who taught me how to write, showed me the pleasures of reading, and most important, helped me realize I could do just about anything I put my mind to.

_____ 3. Most mornings at my office pass in a rather typical—and peaceful—fashion. First, I go over the calendar and write reminders to myself about my day's schedule. I also go through the list of orders that were taken the day before, checking to be sure everything is clear. Other tasks follow until it's time for lunch. However, life at my office was not so typical this morning because of a black cloud, a loud alarm, and a visitor wearing a mask.

_____ 4. Does your will to study collapse when someone suggests getting a pizza? Does your social life compete with your class attendance? Is there a huge gap between your intentions and your actions? If the answers to these questions are yes, yes, and yes, read on. You can benefit from three powerful ways to motivate yourself: setting goals and working consciously to reach them, using rational thinking, and developing a positive personality.

Supporting Paragraphs

Most essays have three supporting points, developed in three separate paragraphs. (Some essays will have two supporting points; others, four or more.) Each of the supporting paragraphs should begin with a topic sentence that states the point to be detailed in that paragraph. Just as the thesis provides a focus for the entire essay, topic sentences provide a focus for each supporting paragraph.

ACTIVITY 3	Supporting Paragraphs

1. What is the topic sentence for the first supporting paragraph of "My Job in an Apple Plant"? (*Write the sentence number here.*) _____

2. What is the topic sentence for the second supporting paragraph? _____

3. What is the topic sentence for the third supporting paragraph? _____

Transitional Sentences

In paragraphs, transitions and other connective devices (pages 70–76) are used to help link sentences. Similarly, in an essay, *transitional sentences* are used to help tie the supporting paragraphs together. Such transitional sentences usually occur near the end of one paragraph or the beginning of the next.

In "My Job in an Apple Plant," the first transitional sentence is

> I would not have minded the difficulty of the work so much if the pay had not been so poor.

In this sentence, the keyword *difficulty* reminds us of the point of the first supporting paragraph, while *pay* tells us the point to be developed in the second supporting paragraph.

ACTIVITY 4	Transitional Sentences

Here is the other transitional sentence in "My Job in an Apple Plant":

> But even more than the low pay, what upset me about my apple plant job was the working conditions.

Complete the following statement: In the preceding sentence, the keywords

_____ echo the point of the second supporting para-

graph, and the keywords _____ announce the topic

of the third supporting paragraph.

Concluding Paragraph

The concluding paragraph often summarizes the essay by briefly restating the thesis and, at times, the main supporting points. Also, the conclusion brings the paper to a natural and graceful end, sometimes leaving the reader with a final thought on the subject.

The Concluding Paragraph	ACTIVITY 5

1. Which sentence in the concluding paragraph of "My Job in an Apple Plant" restates the thesis and supporting points of the essay? _____

2. Which sentence contains the concluding thought of the essay? _____

Essays to Consider

Read the following two student essays and then answer the questions that follow.

Giving up a Baby

[1]As I awoke, I overheard a nurse say, "It's a lovely baby boy. [2]How could a mother give him up?" [3]"Be quiet," another voice said. [4]"She's going to wake up soon." [5]Then I heard the baby cry, but I never heard him again. [6]Three years ago, I gave up my child to two strangers, people who wanted a baby but could not have one. [7]I was in pain over my decision, and I can still hear the voices of people who said I was selfish or crazy. [8]But the reasons I gave up my child were important ones, at least to me.

[9]I gave up my baby, first of all, because I was very young. [10]I was only seventeen, and I was unmarried. [11]Because I was so young, I did not yet feel the desire to have and raise a baby. [12]I knew that I would be a child raising a child and that, when I had to stay home to care for the baby, I would resent the loss of my freedom. [13]I might also blame the baby for that loss. [14]In addition, I had not had the experiences in life that would make me a responsible, giving parent. [15]What could I teach my child, when I barely knew what life was all about myself?

[16]Besides my age, another factor in my decision was the problems my parents would have. [17]I had dropped out of high school before graduation, and I did not have a job or even the chance of a job, at least for a while. [18]My parents would have to support my child and me, possibly for years. [19]My mom and dad had already struggled to raise their family and were not well off financially. [20]I knew I could not burden them with an unemployed teenager and her baby. [21]Even if I eventually got a job, my parents would have to help raise my child. [22]They would have to be full-time babysitters while I tried to make a life of my own. [23]Because my parents are good people, they would

continued

have done all this for me. ²⁴But I felt I could not ask for such a big sacrifice from them.

²⁵The most important factor in my decision was, I suppose, a selfish one. ²⁶I was worried about my own future. ²⁷I didn't want to marry the baby's father. ²⁸I realized during the time I was pregnant that we didn't love each other. ²⁹My future as an unmarried mother with no education or skills would certainly have been limited. ³⁰I would be struggling to survive, and I would have to give up for years my dreams of getting a job and my own car and apartment. ³¹It is hard to admit, but I also considered the fact that, with a baby, I would not have the social life most young people have. ³²I would not be able to stay out late, go to parties, or feel carefree and irresponsible, for I would always have an enormous responsibility waiting for me at home. ³³With a baby, the future looked limited and insecure.

³⁴In summary, thinking about my age, my responsibility to my parents, and my own future made me decide to give up my baby. ³⁵As I look back today at my decision, I know that it was the right one for me at the time.

An Interpretation of Lord of the Flies

¹Modern history has shown us the evil that exists in human beings. ²Assassinations are common, governments use torture to discourage dissent, and six million Jews were exterminated during World War II. ³In Lord of the Flies, William Golding describes a group of schoolboys shipwrecked on an island with no authority figures to control their behavior. ⁴One of the boys soon yields to dark forces within himself, and his corruption symbolizes the evil in all of us. ⁵First, Jack Merridew kills a living creature; then, he rebels against the group leader; and finally, he seizes power and sets up his own murderous society.

⁶The first stage in Jack's downfall is his killing of a living creature. ⁷In Chapter 1, Jack aims at a pig but is unable to kill. ⁸His upraised arm pauses "because of the enormity of the knife descending and cutting into living flesh, because of the unbearable blood," and the pig escapes. ⁹Three chapters later, however, Jack leads some boys on a successful hunt. ¹⁰He returns triumphantly with a freshly killed pig and reports excitedly to the others, "I cut the pig's throat." ¹¹Yet Jack twitches as he says this, and he wipes his bloody hands on his shorts as if eager to remove the stains. ¹²There is still some civilization left in him.

¹³After the initial act of killing the pig, Jack's refusal to cooperate with Ralph shows us that this civilized part is rapidly disappearing. ¹⁴With no adults around, Ralph has made some rules. ¹⁵One is that a signal fire must be kept burning. ¹⁶But Jack tempts the boys watching the fire to go hunting, and the fire goes out. ¹⁷Another rule is that at

continued

a meeting, only the person holding a special seashell has the right to speak. [18]In Chapter 5, another boy is speaking when Jack rudely tells him to shut up. [19]Ralph accuses Jack of breaking the rules. [20]Jack shouts: "Bollocks to the rules! We're strong—we hunt! If there's a beast, we'll hunt it down! We'll close in and beat and beat and beat—!" [21]He gives a "wild whoop" and leaps off the platform, throwing the meeting into chaos. [22]Jack is now much more savage than civilized.

[23]The most obvious proof of Jack's corruption comes in Chapter 8, when he establishes his own murderous society. [24]Insisting that Ralph is not a "proper chief" because he does not hunt, Jack asks for a new election. [25]After he again loses, Jack announces, "I'm going off by myself. . . . Anyone who wants to hunt when I do can come too." [26]Eventually, nearly all the boys join Jack's "tribe." [27]Following his example, they paint their faces like savages, sacrifice to "the beast," brutally murder two of their schoolmates, and nearly succeed in killing Ralph as well. [28]Jack has now become completely savage—and so have the others.

[29]Through Jack Merridew, then, Golding shows how easily moral laws can be forgotten. [30]Freed from grown-ups and their rules, Jack learns to kill living things, defy authority, and lead a tribe of murdering savages. [31]Jack's example is a frightening reminder of humanity's potential for evil. [32]The "beast" the boys try to hunt and kill is actually within every human being.

QUESTIONS

1. In which essay does the thesis statement appear in the last sentence of the introductory paragraph?

   _____

2. In the essay on *Lord of the Flies,* which sentence of the introductory paragraph contains the plan of development? _____

3. Which method of introduction is used in "Giving up a Baby"?

   a. General to narrow   c. Incident or story

   b. Stating importance of topic   d. Questions

4. Complete the following brief outline of "Giving up a Baby":
   I gave up my baby for three reasons:

   a. _____

   b. _____

   c. _____

5. How do both essays connect their first supporting paragraphs with the second ones?

   _____

6. *Complete the following statement:* Emphatic order is shown in the last supporting paragraph of "Giving up a Baby" with the words *most important factor;* and in the last supporting paragraph of "An Interpretation of *Lord of the Flies*" with the words _____.

7. Which essay uses time order as well as emphatic order to organize its three supporting paragraphs? _____

8. List four major transitions used in the supporting paragraphs of "An Interpretation of *Lord of the Flies*."

a. _____   c. _____

b. _____   d. _____

Planning the Essay

Outlining the Essay

When you write an essay, planning is crucial for success. You should plan your essay by outlining in two ways:

1. Prepare a scratch outline. This should consist of a short statement of the thesis followed by the main supporting points for the thesis. Here is Gene's scratch outline for his essay on the apple plant:

> Working at an apple plant was my worst job.
>
> 1. Hard work
>
> 2. Poor pay
>
> 3. Bad working conditions

Do not underestimate the value of this initial outline—or the work involved in achieving it. Be prepared to do a good deal of plain hard thinking at this first and most important stage of your paper.

2. Prepare a more detailed outline. The outline form that follows will serve as a guide. Your instructor may ask you to submit a copy of this form either before you actually write an essay or along with your finished essay.

Form for Planning an Essay

To write an effective essay, use a form like the one that follows.

Opening remarks

Thesis statement _____

_____

Plan of development

Introduction

Topic sentence 1 _____

_____

Specific supporting evidence

Topic sentence 2 _____

_____

Specific supporting evidence

Body

Topic sentence 3 _____

_____

Specific supporting evidence

Summary, closing remarks, or both

Conclusion

Practice in Writing the Essay

In this section, you will expand and strengthen your understanding of the essay form as you work through the following activities.

Understanding the Two Parts of a Thesis Statement

In this chapter, you have learned that effective essays center on a thesis, or main point, that a writer wishes to express. This central idea is usually presented as a *thesis statement* in an essay's introductory paragraph.

A good thesis statement does two things. First, it tells readers an essay's *topic*. Second, it presents the *writer's attitude, opinion, idea,* or *point* about that topic. For example, look at the following thesis statement:

Celebrities are often poor role models.

In this thesis statement, the topic is *celebrities;* the writer's main point is *that celebrities are often poor role models.*

ACTIVITY 6	Topics and Main Points

For each thesis statement, single-underline the topic and double-underline the main point that the writer wishes to express about it.

1. Several teachers have played important roles in my life.

2. A period of loneliness in life can actually have certain benefits.

3. Owning an old car has its own special rewards.

4. Learning to write takes work, patience, and a sense of humor.

5. Advertisers use several clever sales techniques to promote their message.

6. Anger in everyday life often results from a lack of time, a frustration with technology, and a buildup of stress.

7. The sale of handguns in this country should be sharply limited for several reasons.

8. My study habits in college benefited greatly from a course on note-taking, textbook study, and test-taking skills.

9. Retired people must cope with the mental, emotional, and physical stresses of being "old."

10. Parents should take certain steps to encourage their children to enjoy reading.

Supporting the Thesis with Specific Evidence

The first essential step in writing a successful essay is to form a clearly stated thesis. The second basic step is to support the thesis with specific reasons or details.

To ensure that your essay will have adequate support, you may find an informal outline very helpful. Write down a brief version of your thesis idea, and then work out and jot down the three points that will support your thesis.

Here is the scratch outline that was prepared for one essay:

> The college cafeteria is poorly managed.
>
> The checkout lines are always long.
>
> The floor and tables are often dirty.
>
> Food choices are often limited.

A scratch outline like the one above looks simple, but developing it often requires a good deal of careful thinking. The time spent on developing a logical outline is invaluable, though. Once you have planned the steps that logically support your thesis, you will be in an excellent position to go on to write an effective essay.

Using Specific Evidence   ACTIVITY 7

Following are five informal outlines in which two points (*a* and *b*) are already provided. Complete each outline by adding a third logical supporting point (*c*).

1. Poor grades in school can have various causes.

    a. Family problems

    b. Study problems

    c. _____

2. My landlord adds to the stress in my life.

    a. Keeps raising the rent

    b. Expects me to help maintain the apartment

    c. _____

3. My mother (*or some other adult*) has three qualities I admire.

    a. Sense of humor

    b. Patience

    c. _____

4. The first day in college was nerve-racking.

    a. Meeting new people

    b. Dealing with the bookstore

    c. _____

5. Getting married at nineteen was a mistake.

    a. Not finished with my education

    b. Not ready to have children

    c. _____

Identifying Introductions

The following box lists the six common methods for introducing an essay that are discussed in this chapter.

1. Broad statement	4. Incident or story
2. Contrast	5. Question
3. Relevance	6. Quotation

ACTIVITY 8	Methods of Introduction

After reviewing the methods of introduction on pages 128–129, refer to the box preceding and read the following six introductory paragraphs. Then, in the space provided, write the number of the kind of introduction used in each paragraph. Each kind of introduction is used once.

Paragraph A _____

Is bullying a natural, unavoidable part of growing up? Is it something that everyone has to either endure as a victim, practice as a bully, or tolerate as a bystander? Does bullying leave deep scars on its victims, or is it fairly harmless? Does being a bully indicate some deep-rooted problems, or is it not a big deal? These and other questions need to be looked at as we consider the three forms of bullying: physical, verbal, and social.

Paragraph B _____

In a perfect school, students would treat each other with affection and respect. Differences would be tolerated, and even welcomed. Kids would become more popular by being kind and supportive. Students would go out of their way to make sure one another felt happy and comfortable. But most schools are not perfect. Instead of being places of respect and tolerance, they are places where the hateful act of bullying is widespread.

Paragraph C _____

Students have to deal with all kinds of problems in schools. There are the problems created by difficult classes, by too much homework, or by personality conflicts with teachers. There are problems with scheduling the classes you need and still getting some of the ones you want. There are problems with bad cafeteria food, grouchy principals, or overcrowded classrooms. But one of the most difficult problems of all has to do with a terrible situation that exists in most schools: bullying.

Paragraph D _____

Eric, a new boy at school, was shy and physically small. He quickly became a victim of bullies. Kids would wait after school, pull out his shirt, and punch and shove him around. He was called such names as "Mouse Boy" and "Jerk Boy." When he sat down during lunch hour, others would leave his table. In gym games he was never thrown the ball, as if he didn't exist. Then one day he came to school with a gun. When the police were called, he told them he just couldn't take it anymore. Bullying had hurt him badly, just as it hurts many other students. Every member of a school community should be aware of bullying and the three hateful forms that it takes: physical, verbal, and social bullying.

Paragraph E _____

A British prime minister once said, "Courage is fire, and bullying is smoke." If that is true, there is a lot of "smoke" present in most schools today. Bullying in schools is a huge problem that hurts both its victims and the people who practice it. Physical, verbal, and social bullying are all harmful in their own ways.

Paragraph F _____

A pair of students bring guns and homemade bombs to school, killing a number of their fellow students and teachers before taking their own lives. A young man hangs himself on Sunday evening rather than attend school the following morning. A junior high school girl is admitted to the emergency room after cutting her wrists. What do all these horrible reports have to do with each other? All were reportedly caused by a terrible practice that is common in schools: bullying.

Revising an Essay for All Four Bases: Unity, Support, Coherence, and Sentence Skills

You know from your work on paragraphs that there are four bases a paper must cover to be effective. In the following activity, you will evaluate and revise an essay in terms of all four bases: *unity, support, coherence,* and *sentence skills.*

Revising an Essay   ACTIVITY 9

Comments follow each supporting paragraph and the concluding paragraph. Circle the letter of the *one* statement that applies in each case.

Paragraph 1: Introduction

> **A Hateful Activity: Bullying**
>
> Eric, a new boy at school, was shy and physically small. He quickly became a victim of bullies. Kids would wait after school, pull out his shirt, and punch and shove him around. He was called such names as "Mouse Boy" and "Jerk Boy." When he sat down during lunch hour, others would leave his table. In gym games he was never thrown the ball, as if he didn't exist. Then one day he came to school with a gun. When the police were called, he told them he just couldn't take it anymore. Bullying had hurt him badly, just as it hurts many other students. Every member of a school community should be aware of bullying and the three hateful forms that it takes: physical, verbal, and social bullying.

Paragraph 2: First Supporting Paragraph

Bigger or meaner kids try to hurt kids who are smaller or unsure of themselves. They'll push kids into their lockers, knock books out of their hands, or shoulder them out of the cafeteria line. In gym class, a bully often likes to kick kids' legs out from under them while they are running. In the classroom, bullies might kick the back of the chair or step on the foot of the kids they want to intimidate. Bullies will corner a kid in a bathroom. There the victim will be slapped around, will have his or her clothes half pulled off, and might even be shoved into a trash can. Bullies will wait for kids after school and bump or wrestle them around, often while others are looking on. The goal is to frighten kids as much as possible and try to make them cry. Physical bullying is more common among boys, but it is not unknown for girls to be physical bullies as well. The victims are left bruised and hurting, but often in even more pain emotionally than bodily.

a. Paragraph 2 contains an irrelevant sentence.
b. Paragraph 2 lacks transition words.
c. Paragraph 2 lacks supporting details at one key spot.
d. Paragraph 2 contains a fragment and a run-on.

Paragraph 3: Second Supporting Paragraph

Perhaps even worse than physical attack is verbal bullying, which uses words, rather than hands or fists, as weapons. We may be told that "sticks and stones may break my bones, but words can never harm me," but few of us are immune to the pain of a verbal attack. Like physical bullies, verbal bullies tend to single out certain targets. From that moment on, the victim is subject to a hail of insults and put-downs. These are usually delivered in public, so the victim's humiliation will be greatest: "Oh, no, here comes the nerd!" "Why don't you lose some weight, blubber boy?" "You smell as bad as you look!" "Weirdo." "Fairy." "Creep." " Dork." "Slut." "Loser." Verbal bullying is an equal-opportunity activity, with girls as likely to be verbal bullies as boys. If parents don't want their children to be bullies like this, they shouldn't be abusive themselves. Meanwhile, the victim retreats farther and farther into his or her shell, hoping to escape further notice.

a. Paragraph 3 contains an irrelevant sentence.
b. Paragraph 3 lacks transition words.
c. Paragraph 3 lacks supporting details at one key spot.
d. Paragraph 3 contains a fragment and a run-on.

Paragraph 4: Third Supporting Paragraph

As bad as verbal bullying is, many would agree that the most painful type of bullying of all is social bullying. Many students have a strong need for the comfort of being part of a group. For social bullies, the pleasure of belonging to a group is increased by the sight of someone who is refused entry into that group. So, like wolves targeting the weakest sheep in a herd, the bullies lead the pack in isolating people who they decide are different. Bullies do everything they can to make those people feel sad and lonely. In class and out of it, the bullies make it clear that the victims are ignored and unwanted. As the victims sink further into isolation and depression, the social bullies—who seem to be female more often than male—feel all the more puffed up by their own popularity.

a. Paragraph 4 contains an irrelevant sentence.
b. Paragraph 4 lacks transition words.
c. Paragraph 4 lacks supporting details at one key spot.
d. Paragraph 4 contains a fragment and a run-on.

Paragraph 5: Concluding Paragraph

Whether bullying is physical, verbal, or social, it can leave deep and lasting scars. If parents, teachers, and other adults were more aware of the types of bullying, they might help by stepping in. Before the situation becomes too extreme. If students were more aware of the terrible pain that bullying causes, they might think twice about being bullies themselves, their awareness could make the world a kinder place.

a. Paragraph 5 contains an irrelevant sentence.
b. Paragraph 5 lacks transition words.
c. Paragraph 5 lacks supporting details at one key spot.
d. Paragraph 5 contains a fragment and a run-on.

Essay Assignments

Write an essay about the best or worst features of your apartment or house. In your introduction, you might begin with a general description of where you live. Then end the paragraph with your thesis statement and plan of development.

Here are some thesis statements that may help you think about and develop your own paper.

Thesis statement: I love my apartment because of its wonderful location, its great kitchen, and my terrific neighbors.

(*A supporting* paragraph on the apartment's location, for example, might focus on the fact that it's in the middle of a lively, interesting neighborhood with a good supermarket, a drugstore, a variety of restaurants, and so on.)

Thesis statement: My house has three key advantages: a wonderful landlord, a beautiful yard, and housemates that are like family.

(*A supporting* paragraph about the landlord might explain how he or she fixes things promptly and once, in a special circumstance, allowed you to pay your rent late.)

Thesis statement: A tiny kitchen, dismal decor, and noisy neighbors are the three main disadvantages of my apartment.

(*A supporting* paragraph on the apartment's dismal decor could begin with this topic sentence: "The dark and poorly kept walls and floorings are ugly and, even worse, gloomy." Such a sentence might then be followed by some very carefully worded, concrete specifics and perhaps a revealing anecdote.)

> **HINT**   Listing transitions such as *first of all, second, another, also, in addition, finally,* and so on may help you introduce your supporting paragraphs as well as set off different supporting details within those paragraphs.

There are many theories about what children need from the adults in their lives. Give some thought to your own childhood, your own children, or your observations of children you know. Decide on three things that *you* believe are essential to a child's growth and development. Then write a five-paragraph essay on those three qualities.

Your introductory paragraph should arouse your readers' interest. For instance, you might explain how important a person's childhood is to the rest of his or her life. The introductory paragraph should also include a thesis statement made up of your central idea and the three necessities you think are so important. For instance, one student's thesis was this: "I feel that three things all children need are love, approval, and a sense of belonging."

Devote each of the following three supporting paragraphs to one of these important things. Begin each paragraph with a clearly stated topic sentence, and use concrete examples to show how adults can provide each quality to children. Be equally specific in showing what you believe happens when children are not provided with these things. To help your reader make the transition from paragraph to paragraph, use such words as *another thing, in addition,* and *a final quality.* You may wish to consider writing about some of the following things many people feel children need for healthy growth and development:

Unconditional love

Approval

Sense of belonging

Opportunities to experiment

Feeling of safety

Clearly defined limits to behavior

Sense of responsibility

In a concluding paragraph, provide a summary of the points in your paper as well as a final thought to round off your discussion.

WRITING ASSIGNMENT 3

Something Special

Imagine that your apartment or house is burning down. Of course, the best strategy would be to get yourself and others out of the building as quickly as possible. But suppose you knew for sure that you had time to rescue three of your possessions. Which three would you choose? Write an essay in which you discuss the three things in your home that you would most want to save from a fire.

Begin by doing some prewriting to find the items you want to write about. You could, for instance, try making a list and then choosing several of the most likely candidates. Then you could freewrite about each of those candidates. In this way, you are likely to find three possessions that will make strong subjects for this essay. Each will be the basis of a supporting paragraph. Each supporting paragraph will focus on why the object being discussed is so important to you. Make your support as specific and colorful as possible, perhaps using detailed descriptions, anecdotes, or quotations to reveal the importance of each object.

In planning your introduction, consider beginning with a broad, general idea and then narrowing it down to your thesis statement. Here, for example, is one such introduction for this paper:

> I have many possessions that I would be sad to lose. Because I love to cook, I would miss various kitchen appliances that provide me with so many happy cooking adventures. I would also miss the wonderful electronic equipment that entertains me every day, including my large-screen television set and my XBox 360. I would miss the various telephones on which I have spent many interesting hours chatting in every part of my apartment, including the bathtub. But if my apartment were burning down, I would most want to rescue three things that are irreplaceable and hold great meaning for me—the silverware set that belonged to my grandmother, my mother's wedding gown, and my giant photo album.

WRITING ASSIGNMENT 4

Teaching the Basics

What are you experienced in? Fixing cars? Growing flowers? Baking? Waiting on customers? Solving math problems? Write an essay teaching readers the basics of an activity in which you have some experience. If you're not sure about which activity to choose, use prewriting to help you find a topic you can support strongly. Once you've chosen your topic, continue to prewrite as a way to find your key points and organize them into three supporting paragraphs. The key details of waiting on customers in a diner, for instance, might be divided according to time order, as seen in the following topic sentences:

Topic sentence for supporting paragraph 1: Greeting customers and taking their orders should not be done carelessly.

Topic sentence for supporting paragraph 2: There are right and wrong ways to bring customers their food and to keep track of them during their meal.

Topic sentence for supporting paragraph 3: The final interaction with customers may be brief, but it is important.

HINT   To make your points clear, be sure to use detailed descriptions and concrete examples throughout your essay. Also, you may want to use transitional words such as *first, then, also, another, when, after, while,* and *finally* to help organize your details.

WRITING ASSIGNMENT 5

Advantages or Disadvantages of Single Life

More and more people are remaining single longer, and almost half of the people who marry eventually divorce and become single again. Write an essay on the advantages or disadvantages of single life. Each of your three supporting paragraphs will focus on one advantage or one disadvantage. To decide which approach to take, begin by making two lists. A list of advantages might include:

More freedom of choice

Lower expenses

Fewer responsibilities

Dating opportunities

A list of disadvantages could include:

Loneliness

Depression on holidays

Lack of support in everyday decisions

Disapproval of parents and family

Go on to list as many specific details as you can think of to support your advantages and disadvantages. Those details will help you decide whether you want your thesis to focus on benefits or drawbacks. Then create a scratch outline made up of your thesis statement and each of your main supporting points. Put the most important or most dramatic supporting point last.

In your introduction, you might gain your reader's interest by asking several questions or by telling a brief, revealing story about single life. As you develop your supporting paragraphs, make sure that each paragraph begins with a topic sentence and focuses on one advantage or disadvantage of single life. While writing the essay, continue developing details that vividly support each of your points.

In a concluding paragraph, provide a summary of the points in your paper as well as a final thought to round off your discussion. Your final thought might be in the form of a prediction or a recommendation.

Additional Writing Assignments

Detailed writing assignments follow each of the fifteen readings in Part 4. As you work on those assignments, you will find it helpful to turn back to the writing activities in this chapter.

TECH-SAVVY WRITING

How is a home page like an introductory paragraph for a Web site? Choose any Web site and, in a paragraph, describe what introductory techniques (as described on pp. 128–129) its home page employs. Next, make an outline for an essay that compares and contrasts the goals of an introductory paragraph with those of a home page. What is the purpose of each? How does each gain an audience? Why do (or don't) certain words or phrases make you want to turn the page or click on a link?

HINT   Go to Part 4 to see fifteen examples of introductory paragraphs within the essays they introduce.

RESPONDING TO IMAGES

These three photographs of the Sistine Chapel's ceiling zoom in closer and closer to focus on Michelangelo's famous depiction of God's finger touching Adam's. Write a paragraph describing any one of these images. Then make an outline for a larger essay that compares and contrasts the three photographs.

Deceptive Appearances

The topic sentence.

Appearances can be deceptive. While looking through a library window yesterday, I saw a beautiful woman walk by. She had a nice smile, wore a bright red dress, and moved gracefully, like a dancer. Thinking no one was looking, she crumpled a piece of paper in her hand and tossed it into a nearby hedge. Suddenly she no longer looked attractive to me. On another occasion, I started talking to a person named Eric in my psychology class. Eric seemed to be a great person. He always got the class laughing with his jokes; on the days when Eric was absent, I think even the professor missed his lively personality. One day after class, Eric asked me if I wanted to have lunch with him, and I felt happy that he wanted to be my friend. Later, while we were sitting at a booth together, Eric took out an envelope with several kinds of pills inside. "Want one"? he asked. "They're great. You won't need to sleep for a week." I must have looked surprised, because he said, Don't worry. They're not very expensive. I'll cut you a break this time. I told him I didn't want any pills. "Your loss," he said, getting up and walking away without even saying good-bye. I ended up having to pay for the whole bill. I felt very disappointed. Eric didn't want to be my friend. He only wanted to find more people to buy his drugs.

Examples of quotations.

QUESTIONS FOR DISCUSSION

1. What pattern or patterns of development does this writer use in her paragraph?

2. The topic sentence (see above) states the paragraph's main point, which is a little broad. How could the author narrow and focus her topic?

3. Do any details stray from the main point? If so, list them.

4. Are each of the quotations (see above) correctly formatted? If not, correct them using pp. 349–359 as a reference.

WRITING ASSIGNMENTS

1. Write a revision of this paragraph, using the checklist that follows as a guide.

2. How might this paragraph be turned into an essay? Make an outline that shows how the author might expand and develop her point.

Unity

✔ Every sentence in my paragraph is relevant to my main point or topic sentence, which is _____ _____ .

✔ A sentence, detail, or word that I have omitted for the sake of unity is _____ _____ .

✔ The pattern or patterns of development I'm using serve my topic and point well because _____ _____ .

Support

✔ My main idea is supported by several supporting points or by one extended example, which are/is _____ .

✔ Several examples of specific evidence for this point/these points are:

_____

_____ .

✔ I appeal to my readers' five senses with vivid descriptions, such as _____

and _____ .

Coherence

✔ I use one or more patterns of development, which is/are _____

_____ , to organize my paragraph.

✔ I use the following transition words or signals to make my paragraph easy for readers to follow:

_____ .

Sentence Skills

Grammar

✔ I use parallelism to balance my words and ideas. (pp. 292–299)

✔ I use pronouns and their antecedents correctly. (pp. 250–260, 261–272)

✔ My paragraph includes no misplaced or dangling modifiers. (pp. 281–285, 286–291)

✔ I read my paragraph out loud to help catch typos and awkward or grammatically incorrect sentences.

Style

✔ I use active verbs, rather than "is" and "to be." Some examples of active verbs I use are

_____ and _____ . (pp. 247–248)

✔ I use a consistent point of view throughout the paragraph. It is written in the _____

person. (pp. 256–260)

✔ I use specific, concrete language throughout, avoiding vague or abstract words.

Notes

_____

_____

_____

_____

_____

_____

_____

_____

_____

_____

_____

_____

_____

_____

_____

_____

_____

_____

_____

_____

_____

_____

_____

_____

PART

3

Sentence Skills

A Writer's Showcase

from "What Good Families Are Doing Right" by Delores Curran

In her essay "What Good Families Are Doing Right" (pp. 460–468), Delores Curran offers some suggestions for functioning as a successful family. This particular paragraph focuses on how families deal with the issue of television. As you read, pay attention to Curran's use of strong, active verbs. A well-chosen verb conveys your message as a writer accurately and specifically; this, in turn, serves to hold your reader's interest.

Television has been maligned, praised, damned, cherished, and even thrown out. It has more influence on children's values than anything else except their parents. Over and over, when I'm invited to help families mend their communication ruptures, I hear, "But we have no time for this." These families have literally turned their "family-together" time over to television. Even those who control the quality of programs watched and set "homework-first" regulations feel reluctant to intrude upon the individual's right to spend his or her spare time in front of the set. Many families avoid clashes over program selection by furnishing a set for each family member. One of the women who was most desperate to establish a better sense of communication in her family confided in me that they owned nine sets. Nine sets for seven people!

—from "What Good Families Are Doing Right" by Delores Curran

> Beginning with the modifier "over and over," rather than the subject (as the last two sentences did) helps create sentence variety.

> This quotation is correctly introduced with a comma and set off with quotation marks; the period at the end of the sentence falls inside the quotation marks.

> The subject "one" agrees with the verb "was"; the sentence also includes the plural word *women*, but it is the object of the preposition, not the subject.

> This is a fragment; experienced writers who are adept at using sentence skills may occasionally break a rule for the sake of emphasis.

EXPLORING SENTENCE SKILLS

1. List the verbs in the first sentence. In what tense are they written?

2. In the fourth sentence, what is the subject? How did you figure it out?

3. Why is the sentence *"But we have no time for this"* in quotation marks? Why are the words *"homework-first"* in quotation marks? Why are they hyphenated?

4. In the context of the second sentence, is the following clause—*when I'm invited to help families mend their communications ruptures*—a complete or incomplete thought? Could it stand alone as its own sentence? Why or why not?

WRITING WITH SENTENCE SKILLS

1. As noted above, the last sentence of this paragraph is really a fragment. How could you turn it into a grammatically correct sentence?

continued

WRITING WITH SENTENCE SKILLS

2. Read the essay "What Good Families Are Doing Right" in its entirety on pp. 460–468. Then write a paragraph discussing the author's use of any one of the following: point of view, effective word choice, sentence variety, modifiers, adjectives, and active verbs. Use specific examples from the reading to show how the author's mastery of this particular sentence skill contributes to the essay's unity, coherence, and support. Make sure you check your own paragraph carefully for sentence errors.

RESPONDING TO IMAGES

Write a paragraph describing the photographer's attitude toward the people in this scene. Use specific details from the image to support your claims. Proof your work carefully for sentence-level errors, and make sure you use language clearly and effectively.

Sentences

Responding to Images

1. *Why is the writing in the child's drawing a fragment? How might you make it a complete sentence? For more on fragments, see pp. 162–178.*
2. *This sign features a comma splice, which is a type of run-on sentence. What are two ways in which you could fix this error? For more on comma splices, see p. 180.*
3. *Would you pay less attention to a sign that was confusing or grammatically incorrect? Why or why not?*

6

Subjects and Verbs

INTRODUCTORY ACTIVITY

Understanding subjects and verbs is a big step toward mastering many sentence skills. As a speaker of English, you already have an instinctive feel for these basic building blocks of English sentences. See if you can insert an appropriate word in each space that follows. The answer will be a subject.

1. The _____ will soon be over.

2. _____ cannot be trusted.

3. A strange _____ appeared in my backyard.

4. _____ is one of my favorite activities.

Now insert an appropriate word in the following spaces. Each answer will be a verb.

5. The prisoner _____ at the judge.

6. My sister _____ much harder than I do.

7. The players _____ in the locker room.

8. Rob and Marilyn _____ with the teacher.

Finally, insert appropriate words in the following spaces. Each answer will be a subject in the first space and a verb in the second.

9. The _____ almost _____ out of the tree.

10. Many_____today_____sex and violence.

11. The _____ carefully _____ the patient.

12. A _____ quickly _____ the ball.

The basic building blocks of English sentences are subjects and verbs. Understanding them is an important first step toward mastering a number of sentence skills.

Every sentence has a subject and a verb. Who or what the sentence speaks about is called the *subject;* what the sentence says about the subject is called the *verb*. In the following sentences, the subject is underlined once and the verb twice:

People gossip.

The truck belched fumes.

He waved at me.

Alaska contains the largest wilderness area in the United States.

That woman is a millionaire.

The pants feel itchy.

A Simple Way to Find a Subject

To find a subject, ask *who* or *what* the sentence is about. As shown below, your answer is the subject.

Who is the first sentence about? People

What is the second sentence about? The truck

Who is the third sentence about? He

What is the fourth sentence about? Alaska

Who is the fifth sentence about? That woman

What is the sixth sentence about? The pants

It helps to remember that the subject of a sentence is always a *noun* (any person, place, or thing) or a pronoun. A *pronoun* is simply a word like *he, she, it, you,* or *they* used in place of a noun. In the preceding sentences, the subjects are persons (*People, He, woman*), a place (*Alaska*), and things (*truck, pants*). And note that one pronoun (*He*) is used as a subject.

A Simple Way to Find a Verb

To find a verb, ask what the sentence *says about* the subject. As shown below, your answer is the verb.

www.mhhe.com/langan

What does the first sentence *say about* people? They gossip.

What does the second sentence *say about* the truck? It belched (fumes).

What does the third sentence *say about* him? He waved (at me).

What does the fourth sentence *say about* Alaska? It contains (the largest wilderness area in the United States).

What does the fifth sentence *say about* that woman? She is (a millionaire).

What does the sixth sentence *say about* the pants? They feel (itchy).

A second way to find the verb is to put *I, you, he, she, it,* or *they* in front of the word you think is a verb. If the result makes sense, you have a verb.

For example, you could put *they* in front of *gossip* in the first sentence above, with the result, *they gossip,* making sense. Therefore, you know that *gossip* is a verb. You could use the same test with the other verbs as well.

Finally, it helps to remember that most verbs show action. In "People gossip," the action is *gossiping.* In "The truck belched fumes," the action is *belching.* In "He waved at me," the action is *waving.* In "Alaska contains the largest wilderness area in the United States," the action is *containing.*

Certain other verbs, known as *linking verbs,* do not show action. They do, however, give information about the subject of the sentence. In "That woman is a millionaire," the linking verb *is* tells us that the woman is a millionaire. In "The pants feel itchy," the linking verb *feel* gives us the information that the pants are itchy.

ACTIVITY 1 — Finding Subjects and Verbs

www.mhhe.com/langan

HINT: Who is item 1 about? What does the sentence say about him, her, or them?

In each of the following sentences, draw one line under the subject and two lines under the verb.

To find the subject, ask *who* or *what* the sentence is about. Then to find the verb, ask what the sentence *says about* the subject.

1. Carl spilled cocoa on the pale carpet.

2. A ladybug landed on my shoulder.

3. Nick eats cold pizza for breakfast.

4. The waitress brought someone else's meal by mistake.

5. I found a blue egg under the tree in my backyard.

6. Diane stapled her papers together.

7. The audience applauded before the song was finished.

8. My boss has a lot of patience.

9. I tasted poached eggs today for the first time.

10. The new paperboy threw our newspaper under the car.

ACTIVITY 2 — Subjects and Linking Verbs

HINT: Who is item 1 about? What linking verb gives us information about them?

Follow the directions given for Activity 1. Note that all the verbs here are linking verbs.

1. My parents are not very sociable.

2. I am always nervous on the first day of classes.

3. Tri Lee was the first person to finish the exam.

4. Our dog becomes friendly after a few minutes of growling.

5. Estelle seems ready for a nervous breakdown.

6. That plastic hot dog looks good enough to eat.

7. Most people appear slimmer in clothes with vertical stripes.

8. Many students felt exhausted after finishing the placement exam.

9. A cheeseburger has more than seven times as much sodium as French fries.

10. Yesterday, my telephone seemed to be ringing constantly.

Subjects and Verbs

ACTIVITY 3

Follow the directions given for Activity 1.

1. The rabbits ate more than their share of my garden.

2. My father prefers his well-worn jeans to new ones.

3. A local restaurant donated food for the homeless.

4. Stanley always looks ready for a fight.

5. An elderly couple relaxed on a bench in the shopping mall.

6. Lightning brightened the dark sky for a few seconds.

7. Our town council voted for a curfew on Halloween.

8. Lola's sore throat kept her home from work today.

9. Surprisingly, Vonda's little sister decided not to go to the circus.

10. As usual, I chose the slowest checkout line in the supermarket.

HINT: What is item 1 about? What did they do?

www.mhhe.com/langan

More about Subjects and Verbs

Distinguishing Subjects from Prepositional Phrases

The subject of a sentence never appears within a prepositional phrase. A *prepositional phrase* is simply a group of words beginning with a preposition and ending with the answer to the question *what, when,* or *where.* Here is a list of common prepositions.

		Common Prepositions		
about	before	by	inside	over
above	behind	during	into	through
across	below	except	of	to
among	beneath	for	off	toward
around	beside	from	on	under
at	between	in	onto	with

When you are looking for the subject of a sentence, it is helpful to cross out prepositional phrases.

~~In the middle of the night~~, we heard footsteps ~~on the roof~~.

The magazines ~~on the table~~ belong ~~in the garage~~.

~~Before the opening kickoff~~, a brass band marched ~~onto the field~~.

The hardware store ~~across the street~~ went ~~out of business~~.

~~In spite of our advice~~, Sally quit her job ~~at Burger King~~.

ACTIVITY 4	Subjects and Prepositional Phrases

Cross out prepositional phrases. Then draw a single line under subjects and a double line under verbs.

HINT: What are the two prepositional phrases in item 1? What is the subject? What does the sentence say about her?

1. By accident, Anita dropped her folder into the mailbox.

2. Before the test, I glanced through my notes.

3. My car stalled on the bridge at rush hour.

4. I hung a photo of Whitney Houston above my bed.

5. On weekends, we visit my grandmother at a nursing home.

6. During the movie, some teenagers giggled at the love scenes.

7. A pedestrian tunnel runs beneath the street to the train station.

8. The parents hid their daughter's Christmas gifts in the garage.

9. All the teachers, except Mr. Blake, wear ties to school.

10. The strawberry jam in my brother's sandwich dripped onto his lap.

Verbs of More than One Word

Many verbs consist of more than one word. Here, for example, are some of the many forms of the verb *help*:

Some Forms of the Verb *Help*

helps	should have been helping	will have helped
helping	can help	would have been helped
is helping	would have been helping	has been helped
was helping	will be helping	had been helped
may help	had been helping	must have helped
should help	helped	having helped
will help	have helped	should have been helped
does help	has helped	had helped

Below are sentences that contain verbs of more than one word:

Yolanda is working overtime this week.

Another book has been written about the Kennedy family.

We should have stopped for gas at the last station.

The game has just been canceled.

Words such as *not, just, never, only,* and *always* are not part of the verb, although they may appear within the verb.

Yolanda is not working overtime next week.

The boys should just not have stayed out so late.

The game has always been played regardless of the weather.

No verb preceded by *to* is ever the verb of a sentence.

Sue wants to go with us.

The newly married couple decided to rent a house for a year.

The store needs extra people to help out at Christmas.

No *-ing* word by itself is ever the verb of a sentence. (It may be part of the verb, but it must have a helping verb in front of it.)

We planning the trip for months. (This is not a sentence, because the verb is not complete.)

We were planning the trip for months. (This is a complete sentence.)

Verbs of More than One Word   ACTIVITY 5

Draw a single line under subjects and a double line under verbs. Be sure to include all parts of the verb.

1. Ellen has chosen blue dresses for her bridesmaids.

2. You should plan your weekly budget more carefully.

3. Felix has been waiting in line for tickets all morning.

4. We should have invited Terri to the party.

5. I would have preferred a movie with a happy ending.

6. Classes were interrupted three times today by a faulty fire alarm.

7. Sam can touch his nose with his tongue.

8. I have been encouraging my mother to quit smoking.

9. Tony has just agreed to feed his neighbor's fish over the holiday.

10. Many students have not been giving much thought to selecting a major.

HINT: Who or what is item 1 about? What does it say about him, her, or them? What two words make up the verb?

Compound Subjects and Verbs

A sentence may have more than one verb:

The dancer stumbled and fell.

Lola washed her hair, blew it dry, and parted it in the middle.

A sentence may have more than one subject:

Cats and dogs are sometimes the best of friends.

The striking workers and their bosses could not come to an agreement.

A sentence may have several subjects and several verbs:

Holly and I read the book and reported on it to the class.

Pete, Nick, and Fran caught the fish in the morning, cleaned them in the afternoon, and ate them that night.

ACTIVITY 6	Compound Subjects and Verbs

Draw a single line under subjects and a double line under verbs. Be sure to mark *all* the subjects and verbs.

HINT: What two things is item 1 about? What does it say about them?

1. Boards and bricks make a nice bookcase.

2. We bought a big bag of peanuts and finished it by the movie's end.

3. A fly and a bee hung lifelessly in the spider's web.

4. The twins look alike but think, act, and dress quite differently.

5. Canned salmon and tuna contain significant amounts of calcium.

6. I waited for the bubble bath to foam and then slipped into the warm tub.

7. The little girl in the next car waved and smiled at me.

8. The bird actually dived under the water and reappeared with a fish.

9. Singers, dancers, and actors performed at the heart-association benefit.

10. The magician and his assistant bowed and disappeared in a cloud of smoke.

REVIEW TEST 1

Draw one line under the subjects and two lines under the verbs. To help find subjects, cross out prepositional phrases as necessary. Underline all the parts of a verb. You may find more than one subject and verb in a sentence.

1. Most breakfast cereals contain sugar.

2. The drawer of the bureau sticks on rainy days.

3. Our local bus company offers special rates for senior citizens.

4. Drunk drivers in Norway must spend three weeks in jail at hard labor.

5. On weekends, the campus bookstore closes at five o'clock.

6. We wrapped and labeled all the Christmas gifts over the weekend.

7. Motorcycles have been banned from the expressway.

8. Episodes of this old television series are in black and white.

9. The computer sorted, counted, and recorded the ballots within minutes after the closing of the polls.

10. Eddie stepped to the foul line and calmly sank both free throws to win the basketball game.

REVIEW TEST 2

Follow the directions given for Review Test 1.

1. Gasoline from the broken fuel line dripped onto the floor of the garage.

2. All the carrot tops in the garden had been eaten by rabbits.

3. An old man with a plastic trash bag collected aluminum cans along the road.

4. The majority of people wait until April 15 to file their income tax.

5. My mother became a college freshman at the age of forty-two.

6. At the delicatessen, Linda and Paul ate corned beef sandwiches and drank root beer.

7. The window fan made a clanking sound during the night and kept us from sleeping.

8. An umbrella tumbled across the street in the gusty wind and landed between two cars.

9. Telephones in the mayor's office rang continuously with calls from angry citizens about the city tax increase.

10. A teenager pushed a woman, grabbed her purse, and ran off through the crowd.

Fragments

INTRODUCTORY ACTIVITY

Every sentence must have a subject and a verb and must express a complete thought. A word group that lacks a subject or a verb and does not express a complete thought is a *fragment.*

What follows are a number of fragments and sentences. See if you can complete the statement that explains each fragment.

1. Telephones.   *Fragment*

    Telephones ring.   *Sentence*

"Telephones" is a fragment because, while it has a subject (*Telephones*),

it lacks a _____ (*ring*) and so does not express a complete thought.

2. Explains.   *Fragment*

    Darrell explains.   *Sentence*

"Explains" is a fragment because, while it has a verb (*Explains*), it lacks

a _____ (*Darrell*) and does not express a complete thought.

3. Scribbling notes in class.   *Fragment*

    Jayne was scribbling notes in class.   *Sentence*

"Scribbling notes in class" is a fragment because it lacks a _____

(*Jayne*) and also part of the _____ (*was*). As a result, it does not express a complete thought.

4. When the dentist began drilling.   *Fragment*

    When the dentist began drilling, I closed my eyes.   *Sentence*

"When the dentist began drilling" is a fragment because we want to know *what happened when* the dentist began drilling. The word group

does not follow through and _____.

Answers are on page 596.

What Fragments Are

Every sentence must have a subject and a verb and must express a complete thought. A word group that lacks a subject or a verb and does not express a complete thought is a *fragment*. Following are the most common types of fragments that people write:

- Dependent-word fragments
- *-ing* and *to* fragments
- Added-detail fragments
- Missing-subject fragments

Once you understand the specific kind or kinds of fragments that you might write, you should be able to eliminate them from your writing. The following pages explain all four types of fragments.

Dependent-Word Fragments

Some word groups that begin with a dependent word are fragments. Here is a list of common dependent words:

Common Dependent Words	
after	unless
although, though	until
as	what, whatever
because	when, whenever
before	where, wherever
even though	whether
how	which, whichever
if, even if	while
in order that	who
since	whose
that, so that	

Whenever you start a sentence with one of these dependent words, you must be careful that a dependent-word fragment does not result. The word group beginning with the dependent word *After* in the selection below is a fragment.

  After I stopped drinking coffee. I began sleeping better at night.

A *dependent statement*—one starting with a dependent word such as *After*—cannot stand alone. It depends on another statement to complete the thought. "After I stopped drinking coffee" is a dependent statement. It leaves us hanging. We expect in the same sentence to find out *what happened after* the writer stopped drinking coffee. When a writer does not follow through and complete a thought, a fragment results.

To correct the fragment, simply follow through and complete the thought:

> After I stopped drinking coffee, I began sleeping better at night.

Remember, then, that *dependent statements by themselves* are fragments. They must be attached to a statement that makes sense standing alone.*

Here are two other examples of dependent-word fragments that need to be corrected.

> Brian sat nervously in the dental clinic. While waiting to have his wisdom tooth pulled.

> Maria decided to throw away the boxes. That had accumulated for years in the basement.

> **EXPLANATION:** "While waiting to have his wisdom tooth pulled" is a fragment; it does not make sense standing by itself. We want to know in the same statement *what Brian did* while waiting to have his tooth pulled. The writer must complete the thought. Likewise, "That had accumulated for years in the basement" is not in itself a complete thought. We want to know in the same statement what *that* refers to.

How to Correct Dependent-Word Fragments

In most cases, you can correct a dependent-word fragment by attaching it to the sentence that comes after it or to the sentence that comes before it:

> After I stopped drinking coffee, I began sleeping better at night.
>
> (The fragment has been attached to the sentence that comes after it.)

> Brian sat nervously in the dental clinic while waiting to have his wisdom tooth pulled.
>
> (The fragment has been attached to the sentence that comes before it.)

> Maria decided to throw away the boxes that had accumulated for years in the basement.
>
> (The fragment has been attached to the sentence that comes before it.)

Another way of correcting a dependent-word fragment is to eliminate the dependent word and make a new sentence:

> I stopped drinking coffee.

> He was waiting to have his wisdom tooth pulled.

> They had accumulated for years in the basement.

*Some instructors refer to a dependent-word fragment as a dependent clause. A clause is simply a group of words having a subject and a verb. A clause may be independent (expressing a complete thought and able to stand alone) or dependent (not expressing a complete thought and not able to stand alone). A dependent clause by itself is a fragment. It can be corrected simply by adding an independent clause.

Do not use this second method of correction too frequently, however, for it may cut down on interest and variety in your writing style.

Use a comma if a dependent-word group comes at the *beginning* of a sentence:

> After I stopped drinking coffee, I began sleeping better at night.

However, do not generally use a comma if the dependent-word group comes at the end of a sentence:

> Brian sat nervously in the dental clinic while waiting to have his wisdom tooth pulled.

> Maria decided to throw away the boxes that had accumulated for years in the basement.

Sometimes the dependent words *who, that, which,* or *where* appear not at the very start but *near* the start of a word group. A fragment often results.

> Today I visited Hilda Cooper. A friend who is in the hospital.

"A friend who is in the hospital" is not in itself a complete thought. We want to know in the same statement *who* the friend is. The fragment can be corrected by attaching it to the sentence that comes before it:

> Today I visited Hilda Cooper, a friend who is in the hospital.

> **EXPLANATION:** Here a comma is used to set off "a friend who is in the hospital," which is extra material placed at the end of the sentence.

Correcting Dependent-Word Fragments   ACTIVITY 1

Turn each of the dependent-word groups into a sentence by adding a complete thought. Put a comma after the dependent-word group if a dependent word starts the sentence.

EXAMPLES

After I got out of high school

After I got out of high school, I spent a year traveling.

The watch that I got fixed

The watch that I got fixed has just stopped working again.

1. Before I go to work

_____

_____

HINT: For item 1, describe something you do before you go to work.

2. Because I have a test tomorrow

_____

_____

3. Since it was such a hot day

_____

_____

4. The sandwich that I bought

_____

_____

5. When the department store closed

_____

_____

| ACTIVITY 2 | **Combining Sentences to Correct Dependent-Word Fragments** |

Underline the dependent-word fragment (or fragments) in each selection. Then correct each fragment by attaching it to the sentence that comes before or the sentence that comes after—whichever sounds more natural. Put a comma after the dependent-word group if it starts the sentence.

HINT: In item 1, which word group begins with a dependent word?

1. When the waitress coughed in his food. Frank lost his appetite. He didn't even take home a doggy bag.

_____

_____

2. Our power went out. During a thunderstorm. I lost the paper I was writing on the computer.

_____

_____

3. Tony doesn't like going to the ballpark. If he misses an exciting play. There's no instant replay.

_____

_____

4. After the mail carrier comes. I run to our mailbox. I love to get mail. Even if it is only junk mail.

_____

_____

5. Even though she can't read. My little daughter likes to go to the library. She chooses books with pretty covers. While I look at the latest magazines.

_____

_____

-ing and *to* Fragments

When a word ending in *-ing* or the word *to* appears at or near the start of a word group, a fragment may result. Such fragments often lack a subject and part of the verb.

Underline the word groups in the following examples that contain *-ing* words. Each of these is an *-ing* fragment.

EXAMPLE 1

I spent all day in the employment office. <u>Trying to find a job that suited me.</u> The prospects looked bleak.

EXAMPLE 2

Lola surprised Tony on the nature hike. <u>Picking blobs of resin off pine trees.</u> Then she chewed them like bubble gum.

EXAMPLE 3

Mel took an aisle seat on the bus. <u>His reason being that he had more legroom.</u>

> **TIP**   People sometimes write *-ing* fragments because they think the subject in one sentence will work for the next word group as well. In Example 1, they might think the subject *I* in the opening sentence will also serve as the subject for "Trying to find a job that suited me." But the subject must actually be *in* the sentence.

How to Correct *-ing* Fragments

1. Attach the fragment to the sentence that comes before it or the sentence that comes after it, whichever makes sense. Example 1 could read, "I spent all day in the employment office, trying to find a job that suited me." (Note that here a comma is used to set off "trying to find a job that suited me," which is extra material placed at the end of the sentence.)

» OR «

2. Add a subject and change the *-ing* verb part to the correct form of the verb. Example 2 could read, "She picked blobs of resin off pine trees."

» OR «

3. Change *being* to the correct form of the verb *be* (*am, are, is, was, were*). Example 3 could read, "His reason was that he had more legroom."

How to Correct *to* Fragments

As previously noted, when *to* appears at or near the start of a word group, a fragment sometimes results.

> Fragment: <u>To remind people of their selfishness.</u> Otis leaves handwritten notes on cars that take up two parking spaces.

The first word group in the preceding example is a *to* fragment. It can be corrected by adding it to the sentence that comes after it.

> Correct: To remind people of their selfishness, Otis leaves handwritten notes on cars that take up two parking spaces.

EXPLANATION: Here a comma is used to set off "To remind people of their selfishness," which is introductory material in the sentence.

ACTIVITY 3	**Correcting *-ing* Fragments**

Underline the *-ing* fragment in each of the three items that follow. Then make the fragment a sentence by rewriting it, using the method described in parentheses.

EXAMPLE

> The dog eyed me with suspicion. <u>Not knowing whether its master was at home.</u> I hesitated to open the gate.

(Add the fragment to the sentence that comes after it.)

Not knowing whether its master was at home, I hesitated to open the gate.

_____

HINT: In item 1, add the *-ing* fragment to the preceding sentence.

1. Vince sat nervously in the dentist's chair. Waiting for his X-rays to be developed. He prayed there would be no cavities.

_____

_____

HINT: In item 2, add fragment to the sentence that comes after it.

2. Looking through the movie ads for twenty minutes. Lew and Marian tried to find a film they both wanted to see.

_____

_____

HINT: In item 3, add the subject *it* and change the verb *tipping* to the correct form, *tipped*.

3. The jeep went too fast around the sharp curve. As a result, tipping over.

_____

_____

Correcting *-ing* or *to* Fragments

Underline the *-ing* or *to* fragment in each selection. Then rewrite each selection correctly, using one of the methods of correction described on pages 167–168.

1. Some workers dug up the street near our house. Causing frequent vibrations inside. By evening, all the pictures on our walls were crooked.

   _____

   _____

   HINT: In item 1, add the *-ing* fragment to the preceding sentence.

2. I had heard about the surprise party for me. I therefore walked slowly into the darkened living room. Preparing to look shocked.

   _____

   _____

3. Dribbling skillfully up the court. Luis looked for a teammate who was open. Then he passed the ball.

   _____

   _____

4. As I was dreaming of a sunny day at the beach, the alarm clock rang. Wanting to finish the dream. I pushed the Snooze button.

   _____

   _____

5. To get back my term paper. I went to see my English instructor from last semester. I also wanted some career advice.

   _____

   _____

Added-Detail Fragments

Added-detail fragments lack a subject and a verb. They often begin with one of the following words or phrases.

also	except	including
especially	for example	such as

See if you can underline the one added-detail fragment in each of these examples:

EXAMPLE 1

Tony has trouble accepting criticism. Except from Lola. She has a knack for tact.

EXAMPLE 1

One example of my father's generosity is that he visits sick friends in the hospital. And takes along get-well cards with a few dollars folded in them.

EXAMPLE 2

The weight lifter grunted as he heaved the barbells into the air. Then, with a loud groan, dropped them.

> **TIP** People write missing-subject fragments because they think the subject in one sentence will apply to the next word group as well. But the subject, as well as the verb, must be in *each* word group to make a sentence.

How to Correct Missing-Subject Fragments

1. Attach the fragment to the preceding sentence. Example 1 could read: "One example of my father's generosity is that he visits sick friends in the hospital and takes along get-well cards with a few dollars folded in them."

» OR «

2. Add a subject (which can often be a pronoun standing for the subject in the preceding sentence). Example 2 could read: "Then, with a loud groan, he dropped them."

| ACTIVITY 7 | **Correcting Missing-Subject Fragments** |

Underline the missing-subject fragment in each selection. Then rewrite that part of the selection needed to correct the fragment. Use one of the two methods of correction previously described.

1. Artie tripped on his shoelace. Then looked around to see if anyone had noticed.

   _____

   _____

HINT: In item 1, the missing subject is *he.*

2. I started the car. And quickly turned down the blaring radio.

   _____

   _____

3. The fire in the fireplace crackled merrily. Its orange-red flames shot high in the air. And made strange shadows all around the dark room.

   _____

   _____

4. The receptionist at that office is not very well trained. She was chewing gum and talking with a coworker at the same time she took my call. And forgot to take my name.

_____

_____

5. My elderly aunt never stands for long on a bus ride. She places herself in front of a seated young man. And stands on his feet until he gets up.

_____

_____

TIP   **How to Check for Fragments**

1. Read your paper aloud from the *last* sentence to the *first*. You will be better able to see and hear whether each word group you read is a complete thought.
2. If you think any word group is a fragment, ask yourself: Does this contain a subject and a verb and express a complete thought?
3. More specifically, be on the lookout for the most common fragments.
    - Dependent-word fragments (starting with words such as *after, because, since, when,* and *before*)
    - *-ing* and *to* fragments (*-ing* or *to* at or near the start of a word group)
    - Added-detail fragments (starting with words such as *for example, such as, also,* and *especially*)
    - Missing-subject fragments (a verb is present but not the subject)

www.mhhe.com/langan

Working Together

ACTIVITY 8

Part A: Editing and Rewriting

Working with a partner, read the short paragraph below and underline the five fragments. Then use the space provided to correct the fragments. Feel free to discuss the rewrite quietly with your partner and refer back to the chapter when necessary.

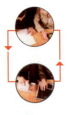

> [1]I can't remember a time when my sister didn't love to write. [2]In school, when teachers assigned a composition or essay. [3]Her classmates often groaned. [4]She would join them in their protests. [5]Because she didn't want to seem different. [6]Secretly, though, her spirit would dance. [7]Words were special to her. [8]I remember an incident when she was in third grade. [9]She wrote a funny story. [10]About the time my dog made a mess of our kitchen. [11]The teacher made my sister stand in front

continued

> of the class and read it aloud. ¹²By the time she finished. ¹³The class-room was bedlam. ¹⁴Even the teacher wiped away tears of laughter. ¹⁵It was a magic moment. ¹⁶Which made my sister more in love with writing than ever.

_____

_____

_____

_____

_____

_____

_____

Part B: Creating Sentences

Working with a partner, make up your own short fragments test as directed.

1. Write a dependent-word fragment in the space below. Then correct the fragment by making it into a complete sentence. You may want to begin your fragment with the word *before, after, when, because,* or *if.*

    Fragment _____

    Sentence _____

2. In the space below, write a fragment that begins with a word that has an *-ing* ending. Then correct the fragment by making it into a complete sentence. You may want to begin your fragment with the word *laughing, walking, shopping,* or *talking.*

    Fragment _____

    Sentence _____

3. Write an added-detail fragment in the space below. Then correct the fragment by making it into a complete sentence. You may want to begin your fragment with the word *also, especially, except,* or *including.*

    Fragment _____

    Sentence _____

REFLECTIVE ACTIVITY

1. Look at the paragraph that you revised in Activity 8. How has removing fragments affected the paragraph? Explain.

2. Explain what it is about fragments that you find most difficult to remember and apply. Use an example to make your point clear. Feel free to refer to anything in this chapter.

Turn each of the following word groups into a complete sentence. Use the space provided.

EXAMPLES

Feeling very confident

Feeling very confident, I began my speech.

Until the rain started

We played softball until the rain started.

1. After we ate dinner

2. Whenever the instructor is late

3. Under the bed

4. If the weather is bad

5. Dave, who is not very organized

6. To get to know each other better

7. Which was annoying

8. Will meet me later

9. Staring at the computer screen

10. Waiting in the long line

REVIEW TEST 2

Underline the fragment in each item that follows. Then correct the fragment in the space provided.

EXAMPLE

Sam received all kinds of junk mail. <u>Then complained to the post office.</u> Eventually, some of the mail stopped coming.

Then he complained to the post office.

1. Fascinated, Nina stared at the stranger. Who was standing in the doorway. She wondered if she could convince him they had met before.

_____

_____

2. Trees can survive on a steep mountain slope if they obey two rules. They must grow low to the ground. And bend with the wind.

_____

_____

3. While waiting in line at the supermarket. I look in people's baskets. Their food choices give hints about their personalities.

_____

_____

4. I saw spectacular twin rainbows through the kitchen window. So I rushed to get my camera. To take a picture before they vanished.

_____

_____

5. Whenever you buy cotton clothes, get them one size too large. By allowing for shrinkage. You will get a longer life out of them.

_____

_____

6. My nutty cousin cuts the address labels off his magazines. Then pastes them on envelopes. This way, he doesn't have to write his return address.

_____

_____

7. Marian never has to buy ketchup or mustard. Because she saves the extra packets that come with fast-food orders.

_____

_____

8. The soccer players were amazing. Using their feet as well as most people use their hands.

_____

_____

9. My husband climbed his first mountain yesterday. Now he's calling all our friends. To tell them about his peak experience.

_____

_____

10. The trivia book listed some interesting facts about Babe Ruth. For instance, he spoke German fluently. Also, kept cool on hot days by putting wet cabbage leaves under his cap.

_____

_____

REVIEW TEST 3

In the space provided, write C if a word group is a complete sentence; write *frag* if it is a fragment. The first two are done for you.

frag   1. When the bus drivers went on strike.

C   2. I saw many people giving rides to strangers.

_____ 3. Some even drove out of their way for others.

_____ 4. Especially when the weather was bad.

_____ 5. One rainy day, I saw an elderly woman pull her cab over to the curb.

_____ 6. Yelling and waving for five shivering students to get into her car.

_____ 7. Until the strike finally ended.

_____ 8. Scenes like that were not uncommon.

_____ 9. It seems that community problems bring people together.

_____ 10. By weakening the feeling that we live very separate lives.

Now correct the *fragments* you have found. Attach each fragment to the sentence that comes before or after it, or make whatever other change is needed to turn the fragment into a sentence. Use the space provided. The first one is corrected for you.

1. <u>When the bus drivers went on strike, I saw many people giving rides</u>
<u>to strangers.</u>

2. _____

_____

3. _____

_____

4. _____

_____

5. _____

_____

REVIEW TEST 4

Write quickly for five minutes about the town or city where you live. Don't worry about spelling, punctuation, finding exact words, or organizing your thoughts. Just focus on writing as many words as you can without stopping.

After you have finished, go back and make whatever changes are needed to correct any fragments in your writing.

Run-Ons

INTRODUCTORY ACTIVITY

A run-on occurs when two sentences are run together with no adequate sign given to mark the break between them. Shown below are four run-on sentences, each followed by a correct sentence. See if you can complete the statement that explains how each run-on is corrected.

1. A man coughed in the movie theater the result was a chain reaction of copycat coughing.

    A man coughed in the movie theater. The result was a chain reaction of copycat coughing.

The run-on has been corrected by using a _____ and a capital letter to separate the two complete thoughts.

2. I heard laughter inside the house, no one answered the bell.

    I heard laughter inside the house, but no one answered the bell.

The run-on has been corrected by using a joining word, _____, to connect the two complete thoughts.

3. A car sped around the corner, it sprayed slush all over the pedestrians.

    A car sped around the corner; it sprayed slush all over the pedestrians.

The run-on has been corrected by using a _____ to connect the two closely related thoughts.

4. I had a campus map, I still could not find my classroom building.

    Although I had a campus map, I still could not find my classroom building.

The run-on has been corrected by using the subordinating word

_____ to connect the two closely related thoughts.

Answers are on page 597.

What Are Run-Ons?

A *run-on* is two complete thoughts that are run together with no adequate sign given to mark the break between them.* As a result of the run-on, the reader is confused, unsure of where one thought ends and the next one begins. Two types of run-ons are fused sentences and comma splices.

www.mhhe.com/langan

Some run-ons have no punctuation at all to mark the break between two or more thoughts. Such run-ons are known as *fused sentences:* they are fused or joined together as if they were only one thought.

Fused Sentence

Rita decided to stop smoking she didn't want to die of lung cancer.

Fused Sentence

The exam was postponed the class was canceled as well.

www.mhhe.com/langan

In other run-ons, known as *comma splices,* a comma is used to connect or "splice" together the two complete thoughts.** However, a comma alone is *not enough* to connect two complete thoughts. Some connection stronger than a comma alone is needed.

Comma Splice

Rita decided to stop smoking, she didn't want to die of lung cancer.

Comma Splice

The exam was postponed, the class was canceled as well.

Comma splices are the most common kind of run-on. Students sense that some kind of connection is needed between thoughts, so they put a comma at the dividing point. But the comma alone is *not sufficient.* A stronger, clearer mark is needed between the two thoughts.

A Warning: Words That Can Lead to Run-Ons

People often write run-ons when the second complete thought begins with one of the following words. Be on the alert for run-ons whenever you use these words:

I	we	there	now
you	they	this	then
he, she, it		that	next

*Some instructors refer to each complete thought in a run-on as an *independent clause.* A *clause* is simply a group of words having a subject and a verb. A clause may be *independent* (expressing a complete thought and able to stand alone) or *dependent* (not expressing a complete thought and not able to stand alone). A run-on is two independent clauses that are run together with no adequate sign given to mark the break between them.

**Some instructors feel that the term *run-ons* should be applied only to fused sentences, not to comma splices. But for many other instructors, and for our purposes in this book, the term *run-on* applies equally to fused sentences and comma splices. The bottom line is that you do not want either fused sentences or comma splices in your writing.

Correcting Run-Ons

Here are four common methods of correcting a run-on:

1. Use a period and a capital letter to separate the two complete thoughts. (In other words, make two separate sentences of the two complete thoughts.)

   Rita decided to stop smoking. She didn't want to die of lung cancer.

   The exam was postponed. The class was canceled as well.

   » OR «

2. Use a comma plus a joining word (*and, but, for, or, nor, so, yet*) to connect the two complete thoughts.

   Rita decided to stop smoking, for she didn't want to die of lung cancer.

   The exam was postponed, and the class was canceled as well.

   » OR «

3. Use a semicolon to connect the two complete thoughts.

   Rita decided to stop smoking; she didn't want to die of lung cancer.

   The exam was postponed; the class was canceled as well.

4. Use subordination.

   Because Rita didn't want to die of lung cancer, she decided to stop smoking.

   When the exam was postponed, the class was canceled as well.

The following pages will give you practice in all four methods of correcting run-ons. The use of subordination will be explained further on page 202, in a chapter that deals with sentence variety.

Method 1: Period and a Capital Letter

One way of correcting a run-on is to use a period and a capital letter at the break between the two complete thoughts. Use this method especially if the thoughts are not closely related or if another method would make the sentence too long.

Correcting Fused Sentences   ACTIVITY 1

Locate the split in each of the following run-ons. Each is a *fused sentence*—that is, each consists of two sentences fused or joined together with no punctuation at all between them. Reading each sentence aloud will help you "hear" where a major break or split in the thought occurs. At such a point, your voice will probably drop and pause.

> **HINT** Correct the run-on by putting a period at the end of the first thought and a capital letter at the start of the second thought.

EXAMPLE

Gary was not a success at his job ⋅H his mouth moved faster than his hands.

HINT: In item 1, *The fern hadn't been watered in a month* is a complete thought. *Its leaves looked like frayed brown shoelaces* is also a complete thought.

1. The fern hadn't been watered in a month its leaves looked like frayed brown shoelaces.

2. Newspapers are piled up on the neighbors' porch they must be out of town.

3. Joyce's recipe for chocolate fudge is very easy to make it is also very expensive.

4. Watching television gave the old man something to do he didn't have many visitors anymore.

5. Jon accidentally ruined his favorite black shirt a few drops of bleach spilled onto it in the laundry room.

6. The first Olympic Games were held in 776 BC. the only event was a footrace.

7. Gloria decorated her apartment creatively and cheaply she papered her bedroom walls with magazine covers.

8. There were papers scattered all over Lena's desk she spent twenty minutes looking for a missing receipt.

9. Spring rain dripped into the fireplace the room smelled like last winter's fires.

10. The car swerved dangerously through traffic its rear bumper sticker read, "School's Out—Drive Carefully."

ACTIVITY 2 — Correcting Run-Ons—Fused Sentences and Comma Splices

Locate the split in each of the following run-ons. Some of the run-ons are fused sentences, and some of them are *comma splices*—run-ons spliced or joined together only with a comma. Correct each run-on by putting a period at the end of the first thought and a capital letter at the start of the next thought.

HINT: In item 1, *My father* is the subject of the first complete thought. *He* is the subject of the second one.

1. My father is a very sentimental man he still has my kindergarten drawings.

2. Sue dropped the letter into the mailbox then she regretted mailing it.

3. Certain street names are very common the most common is "Park."

4. Bacteria are incredibly tiny a drop of liquid may contain fifty million of them.

5. The fastest dog in the world is the greyhound it can run over forty-one miles an hour.

6. Mandy's parents speak only Chinese she speaks Chinese, English, and French.

7. My iPod stopped working its battery was worn out.

8. A shadow on the kitchen wall was lovely it had the shape of a plant on the windowsill.

9. The little girl hated seeing her father drink one day, she poured all his liquor down the kitchen drain.

10. Children have been born at odd times for instance, James was born on February 29 during leap year.

Writing the Next Sentence

ACTIVITY 3

Write a second sentence to go with each sentence that follows. Start the second sentence with the word given at the left.

EXAMPLE

He   My dog's ears snapped up.   He had heard a wolf howling on television.

_____

He   1. Carlos likes going to the mall.

_____

_____

They 2. Ants marched across our kitchen floor.

_____

_____

Now   3. Our car just broke down.

_____

_____

There 4. Raccoons knocked over our garbage cans.

_____

_____

Then 5. First I stopped at the bakery.

_____

_____

Run-Ons

Method 2: Comma and a Joining Word

Another way of correcting a run-on is to use a comma plus a joining word to connect the two complete thoughts. Joining words (also called *coordinating conjunctions*) include *and, but, for, or, nor, so,* and *yet.* Here is what the four most common joining words mean:

and   in addition, along with

Lola was watching Monday night football, and she was doing her homework.

> **TIP**   *And* means *in addition:* Lola was watching Monday night football; *in addition,* she was doing her homework.

but   however, except, on the other hand, just the opposite

I voted for the president two years ago, but I would not vote for him today.

> **TIP**   *But* means *however:* I voted for the president two years ago; *however,* I would not vote for him today.

for   because, the reason why, the cause for something

Saturday is the worst day to shop, for people jam the stores.

> **TIP**   *For* means *because:* Saturday is the worst day to shop *because* people jam the stores. If you are not comfortable using *for,* you may want to use *because* instead of *for* in the activities that follow. If you do use *because,* omit the comma before it.

so   as a result, therefore

Our son misbehaved again, so he was sent upstairs without dessert.

> **TIP**   *So* means *as a result:* Our son misbehaved again; *as a result,* he was sent upstairs without dessert.

Connecting Two Thoughts

Insert the comma and the joining word (*and, but, for, so*) that logically connects the two thoughts in each sentence.

EXAMPLE

A trip to the zoo always depresses me **, for** I hate to see animals in cages.

1. I want to stop smoking I don't want to gain weight.

2. Packages are flown to distant cities during the night vans deliver them the next morning.

3. The grass turned brown in the summer's heat the grapes shriveled and died on the vine.

4. Woody wanted to buy his girlfriend a ring he began saving ten dollars a week.

5. I enjoy watching television I feel guilty about spending so much time in front of the tube.

6. It was too hot indoors to study I decided to go down to the shopping center for ice cream.

7. I don't like to go to the doctor's office I'm afraid one of the other patients will make me really sick.

8. This world map was published only three years ago the names of some countries are already out of date.

9. Nate is color-blind his wife lays out his clothes every morning.

10. We knew there had been a power failure all our digital clocks were blinking "12:00."

Using Commas and Joining Words

Add a complete, closely related thought to each of the following statements. When you write the second thought, use a comma plus the joining word shown at the left.

EXAMPLE

but   I was sick with the flu, _____but I still had to study for the test._____

but   1. We have the same taste in clothes

_____

_____

so   2. Keisha needed a little break from studying

_____

_____

HINT: In item 1, "car" and "payments" are the subjects of the two complete thoughts.

1. A new car is always fun to drive ＿＿＿＿＿ the payments are never fun to make.

2. The fork that fell into our garbage disposal looks like a piece of modern art ＿＿＿＿＿ it is useless.

3. Auto races no longer use gasoline ＿＿＿＿＿ spectators have nothing to fear from exhaust fumes.

4. We got to the stadium two hours before the game started ＿＿＿＿＿ all the parking spaces were already taken.

5. Mice use their sensitive whiskers as feelers ＿＿＿＿＿ they scurry along close to walls.

ACTIVITY 8   Using Semicolons and Commas

Punctuate each sentence by using a semicolon and a comma.

EXAMPLE

Our tap water has a funny taste; consequently, we buy bottled water to drink.

HINT: To correctly punctuate item 1, first locate the transitional word that joins the two complete thoughts.

1. Nora lives two blocks from the grocery store nevertheless she always drives there.

2. The little boy ate too much Halloween candy as a result he got a stomachache.

3. Our dog protects us by barking at strangers however he also barks at our friends.

4. Jeff cut back a few hours on his work schedule otherwise he would have had very little time for studying.

5. My sister invited her ex-husband over to celebrate the holiday with the children furthermore she bought a gift for him from the children.

Method 4: Subordination

A fourth method of joining related thoughts is to use subordination. *Subordination* is a way of showing that one thought in a sentence is not as important as another thought. Here are three sentences where one idea is subordinated to (made less emphatic than) the other idea:

Because Rita didn't want to die of lung cancer, she decided to stop smoking.

The wedding reception began to get out of hand when the guests started to throw food at each other.

Although my brothers wanted to watch a *Law and Order* rerun, the rest of the family insisted on turning to the network news.

Dependent Words

Notice that when we subordinate, we use dependent words such as *because*, *when*, and *although*. Following is a brief list of common dependent words (see also the list on page 197). Subordination is explained in full on page 202.

Common Dependent Words

after	before	unless
although	even though	until
as	if	when
because	since	while

Using Dependent Words

ACTIVITY 9

Choose a logical dependent word from the preceding box and write it in the space provided.

EXAMPLE

_____Until_____ I was six, I thought chocolate milk came from brown cows.

1. Will hasn't had a cigarette _____ July 4, 2000.

2. _____ you're willing to work hard, don't sign up for Professor Dunn's class.

3. The lines at that supermarket are so long _____ there are too few cashiers.

4. _____ reading the scary novel, my sister had nightmares for days.

5. My boss gave me smoked salmon for my birthday _____ he knows I'm a vegetarian.

HINT: In item 1, which dependent word best signals that something extends from the past (July 4, 2000) to the present?

Using Subordination

ACTIVITY 10

Rewrite the five sentences that follow (all taken from this chapter) so that one idea is subordinate to the other. Use one of the dependent words from the box "Common Dependent Words".

EXAMPLE

Auto races no longer use gasoline; spectators have nothing to fear from exhaust fumes.

Since auto races no longer use gasoline, spectators have nothing to fear from

exhaust fumes.

HINT: For item 1, select a dependent word that logically connects the two ideas (a wish to stop smoking and a wish not to gain weight).

1. I want to stop smoking; I don't want to gain weight.

   _____

   _____

2. It was too hot indoors to study; I decided to go down to the shopping center for ice cream.

   _____

   _____

3. The puppy quickly ate; the baby watched with interest.

   _____

   _____

4. The elderly woman smiled at me; her face broke into a thousand wrinkles.

   _____

   _____

5. This world map was published only three years ago; the names of some countries are already out of date.

   _____

   _____

ACTIVITY 11   Working Together

Part A: Editing and Rewriting

Working with a partner, read carefully the short paragraph that follows and underline the five run-ons. Then use the space provided to correct the five run-ons. Feel free to discuss the rewrite quietly with your partner and refer back to the chapter when necessary.

> [1]When Mark began his first full-time job, he immediately got a credit card, a used sports car was his first purchase. [2]Then he began to buy expensive clothes that he could not afford he also bought impressive gifts for his parents and his girlfriend. [3]Several months passed before Mark realized that he owed an enormous amount of money. [4]To make matters worse, his car broke down, a stack of bills suddenly seemed to be due at once. [5]Mark tried to cut back on his purchases, he soon realized he had to cut up his credit card to prevent himself from using it. [6]He also began keeping a careful record of his spending he had no idea where his money had gone till then. [7]He hated to admit to his family and friends that he had to get his budget under control. [8]However, his girlfriend said she did not mind inexpensive dates, and his parents were proud of his growing maturity.

_____

_____

_____

_____

_____

_____

_____

_____

_____

Part B: Creating Sentences

Working with a partner, make up your own short run-ons test as directed.

1. Write a run-on sentence. Then rewrite it, using a period and a capital letter to separate the thoughts into two sentences.

   Run-on

   _____

   Rewrite

   _____

2. Write a sentence that has two complete thoughts. Then rewrite it, using a comma and a joining word to correctly join the complete thoughts.

   Two complete thoughts

   _____

   Rewrite

   _____

3. Write a sentence that has two complete thoughts. Then rewrite it, using a semicolon to correctly join the complete thoughts.

   Two complete thoughts

   _____

   Rewrite

   _____

Run-Ons

REFLECTIVE ACTIVITY

1. Look at the paragraph that you revised in Activity 11. Explain how run-ons affect the paragraph.

2. In your own written work, which type of run-on are you most likely to write: comma splices or fused sentences? Why do you tend to make this kind of mistake?

3. Which method for correcting run-ons are you most likely to use in your own writing? Which are you least likely to use? Why?

REVIEW TEST 1

Correct the following run-ons by using either (1) a period and a capital letter or (2) a comma and the joining word *and, but, for,* or *so.* Do not use the same method of correction for each sentence.

EXAMPLE

Fred pulled the cellophane off the cake the icing came along with it. *(and)*

1. I put a dollar in the soda machine all I got was an empty can.

2. I tore open a ketchup packet a bright red streak flew across the front of my new white shirt.

3. Yolanda wanted to sleep late her dog woke her up at dawn.

4. The theater's parking lot was full we missed the first ten minutes of the movie.

5. Helen bites her nails she tries to keep her hands hidden.

6. The waiter cheerfully filled our coffee cups three times we left him a generous tip.

7. I love to wander through old cemeteries I enjoy reading the gravestones and taking pictures of them.

8. Travel to distant planets has long been a dream of humanity the technology to achieve that dream will soon be available.

9. Gordon no longer has to worry about missing the bus he rides to work in a car pool.

10. The baby wouldn't stop crying all the passengers on the bus gave the mother dirty looks.

Correct each run-on by using subordination. Choose from among the following dependent words.

after	before	unless
although	even though	until
as	if	when
because	since	while

EXAMPLE

Tony hated going to a new barber, he was afraid of butchered hair.

Because Tony was afraid of butchered hair, he hated going to a new barber.

1. Mom was frying potatoes, the heat set off the smoke alarm.

   _____

   _____

2. I love animals I'm not ready to take on the responsibility of a pet.

   _____

   _____

3. Lani leaves a lecture class, she reviews and clarifies her notes.

   _____

   _____

4. Matthew jogs, he thinks over his day's activities.

   _____

   _____

5. My mother puts apples in the fruit bowl she first washes the wax off them.

   _____

   _____

6. I began to shake on the examining table the nurse reached out and held my hand.

   _____

   _____

7. Some pets are easy to care for, others require patience and lots of hard work.

_____

_____

8. Molly forgot to turn the oven off her homemade bread looked like burned toast.

_____

_____

9. A wheel hit a crack in the sidewalk the skateboard shot out from under Danny.

_____

_____

10. John Grisham and Stephen King make huge fortunes with their novels most writers barely make a living.

_____

_____

REVIEW TEST 3

On a separate piece of paper, write six sentences, each of which has two complete thoughts. In two of the sentences, use a period and a capital letter between the thoughts. In another two sentences, use a comma and a joining word (*and, but, or, nor, for, so, yet*) to join the thoughts. In the final two sentences, use a semicolon to join the thoughts.

REVIEW TEST 4

Write for five minutes about something that makes you angry. Don't worry about spelling, punctuation, finding exact words, or organizing your thoughts. Just focus on writing as many words as you can without stopping.

After you have finished, go back and make whatever changes are needed to correct any run-on sentences in your writing.

Sentence Variety I

Four Traditional Sentence Patterns

Sentences in English are traditionally described as *simple, compound, complex,* or *compound-complex.*

The Simple Sentence

A simple sentence has a single subject-verb combination.

> Children play.
>
> The game ended early.
>
> My car stalled three times last week.
>
> The lake has been polluted by several neighboring streams.
>
> A simple sentence may have more than one subject:
>
> Lola and Tony drove home.
>
> The wind and water dried my hair.

or more than one verb:

> The children smiled and waved at us.
>
> The lawn mower smoked and sputtered.

or several subjects and verbs:

> Manny, Moe, and Jack lubricated my car, replaced the oil filter, and cleaned the spark plugs.

The Simple Sentence	ACTIVITY 1

On separate paper, write:

> Three sentences, each with a single subject and verb
>
> Three sentences, each with a single subject and a double verb
>
> Three sentences, each with a double subject and a single verb

In each case, underline the subject once and the verb twice. (See pages 154–161 if necessary for more information on subjects and verbs.)

The Compound Sentence

A compound, or "double," sentence is made up of two (or more) simple sentences. The two complete statements in a compound sentence are usually connected by a comma plus a joining word (*and, but, for, or, nor, so, yet*).

A compound sentence is used when you want to give equal weight to two closely related ideas. The technique of showing that ideas have equal importance is called *coordination*.

Following are some compound sentences. Each sentence contains two ideas that the writer considers equal in importance.

The rain increased, so the officials canceled the game.

Martha wanted to go shopping, but Fred refused to drive her.

Hollis was watching television in the family room, and April was upstairs on the phone.

I had to give up wood carving, for my arthritis had become very painful.

ACTIVITY 2	**The Compound Sentence**

Combine the following pairs of simple sentences into compound sentences. Use a comma and a logical joining word (*and, but, for, so*) to connect each pair.

> **HINT**   If you are not sure what *and, but, for,* and *so* mean, review page 184.

EXAMPLE
- We hung up the print.
- The wall still looked bare.

  We hung up the print, but the wall still looked bare.

1. • Cass tied the turkey carcass to a tree.

   • She watched the birds pick at bits of meat and skin.

   _____

   _____

HINT: In item 1, use *and* to connect the two thoughts of equal importance.

2. • I ran the hot water faucet for two minutes.

   • Only cold water came out.

   _____

   _____

3. • Nathan orders all his Christmas gifts through the Internet.

   • He dislikes shopping in crowded stores.

   _____

   _____

4. • I need to buy a new set of tires.

   • I will read *Consumer Reports* to learn about various brands.

   _____

   _____

5. • I asked Cecilia to go out with me on Saturday night.

   • She told me she'd rather stay home and watch TV.

   _____

   _____

Writing Compound Sentences

ACTIVITY 3

On a separate piece of paper, write five compound sentences of your own. Use a different joining word (*and, but, for, or, nor, so, yet*) to connect the two complete ideas in each sentence.

The Complex Sentence

A complex sentence is made up of a simple sentence (a complete statement) and a statement that begins with a dependent word.* Here is a list of common dependent words:

Dependent Words		
after	if, even if	when, whenever
although, though	in order that	where, wherever
as	since	whether
because	that, so that	which, whichever
before	unless	while
even though	until	who
how	what, whatever	whose

*The two parts of a complex sentence are sometimes called an *independent clause* and a *dependent clause*. A *clause* is simply a word group that contains a subject and a verb. An *independent clause* expresses a complete thought and can stand alone. A *dependent clause* does not express a complete thought in itself and "depends on" the independent clause to complete its meaning. Dependent clauses always begin with a dependent or subordinating word.

Sentence Variety I

A complex sentence is used when you want to emphasize one idea over another in a sentence. Look at the following complex sentence:

Because I forgot the time, I missed the final exam.

The idea that the writer wants to emphasize here—*I missed the final exam*—is expressed as a complete thought. The less important idea—*Because I forgot the time*—is subordinated to the complete thought. The technique of giving one idea less emphasis than another is called *subordination*.

Following are other examples of complex sentences. In each case, the part starting with the dependent word is the less emphasized part of the sentence.

While Aisha was eating breakfast, she began to feel sick.

I checked my money *before* I invited Pedro for lunch.

When Jerry lost his temper, he also lost his job.

Although I practiced for three months, I failed my driving test.

| ACTIVITY 4 | Creating Complex Sentences |

Use logical dependent words to combine the following pairs of simple sentences into complex sentences. Place a comma after a dependent statement when it starts the sentence.

EXAMPLE

- I obtained a credit card.
- I began spending money recklessly.

When I obtained a credit card, I began spending money recklessly   .

- Alan dressed the turkey.
- His brother greased the roasting pan.

Alan dressed the turkey while his brother greased the roasting pan.

HINT: In item 1, use the dependent word *when*.

1. • Cindy opened the cutlery drawer.
   • A bee flew out.

2. • I washed the windows thoroughly.
   • They still looked dirty.

3. • I never opened a book all semester.

   • I guess I deserved to flunk.

   _____

   _____

4. • Manny gets up in the morning.

   • He does stretching exercises for five minutes.

   _____

   _____

5. • My son spilled the pickle jar at dinner.

   • I had to wash the kitchen floor.

   _____

   _____

Using Subordination

ACTIVITY 5

Rewrite the following sentences, using subordination rather than coordination. Include a comma when a dependent statement starts a sentence.

EXAMPLE

   The hair dryer was not working right, so I returned it to the store.
   Because the hair dryer was not working right, I returned it to the store.

   _____

1. Carlo set the table, and his wife finished cooking dinner.

   _____

   _____

HINT: In item 1, use the dependent word *as*.

2. Maggie could have gotten good grades, but she did not study enough.

   _____

   _____

3. I watered my drooping African violets, and they perked right up.

   _____

   _____

4. The little boy kept pushing the "down" button, but the elevator didn't come any more quickly.

   _____

   _____

5. I never really knew what pain was, and then I had four impacted wisdom teeth pulled at once.

_____

_____

| ACTIVITY 6 | Using *Who, Which,* or *That* |

Combine the following simple sentences into complex sentences. Omit repeated words. Use the dependent words *who, which,* or *that.*

> **HINT**
> - The word *who* refers to persons.
> - The word *which* refers to things.
> - The word *that* refers to persons or things.

Use commas around the dependent statement only if it seems to interrupt the flow of thought in the sentence. (See pages 360–373 for more about commas.)

EXAMPLES

- Clyde picked up a hitchhiker.
- The hitchhiker was traveling around the world.

  Clyde picked up a hitchhiker who was traveling around the world.

  _____

- Larry is a sleepwalker.
- Larry is my brother.

  Larry, who is my brother, is a sleepwalker.

  _____

HINT: In item 1, use commas and *who.*

1. - Karen just gave birth to twins.
   - Karen is an old friend of mine.

   _____

   _____

2. - The tea burned the roof of my mouth.
   - The tea was hotter than I expected.

   _____

   _____

3. - I dropped the camera.
   - My sister had just bought the camera.

   _____

   _____

4. • Ernie brought us some enormous oranges.

   • Ernie is visiting from California.

   _____

   _____

5. • Liz used a steam cleaner to shampoo her rugs.

   • The rugs were dirtier than she realized.

   _____

   _____

Writing Complex Sentences   ACTIVITY 7

On a separate piece of paper, write eight complex sentences, using, in turn, the dependent words *unless, if, after, because, when, who, which,* and *that.*

The Compound-Complex Sentence

A compound-complex sentence is made up of two (or more) simple sentences and one or more dependent statements. In the following examples, there is a solid line under the simple sentences and a dotted line under the dependent statements.

> When the power line snapped, Jack was listening to the stereo, and Linda was reading in bed.

> After I returned to school following a long illness, the math teacher gave me makeup work, but the history teacher made me drop her course.

Using Joining Words and Dependent Words   ACTIVITY 8

Read through each sentence to get a sense of its overall meaning. Then insert a logical joining word (*and, or, but, for,* or *so*) and a logical dependent word (*because, since, when,* or *although*).

1. _____ you paint the closet, remember to open a window,

   _____ you might get a headache from the smell.

   HINT: In item 1, use *after* and *for.*

2. _____ I get into bed at night, I try to read a book, _____ I always fall asleep within minutes.

3. Russell ate less butter _____ he learned that his cholesterol

   level was a little too high, _____ he also included some bran in his diet.

4. _____ she made the honor roll, Molly received a library pass

   from the principal, _____ she didn't have to sit in study hall the whole semester.

5. We planned to go to a concert tonight, _____ it was canceled _____ the lead singer was arrested.

Writing Compound-Complex Sentences

On a separate piece of paper, write five compound-complex sentences.

www.mhhe.com/langan

Review of Subordination and Coordination

Subordination and coordination are ways of showing the exact relationship of ideas within a sentence. Through **subordination,** we show that one idea is less important than another. When we subordinate, we use dependent words such as *when, although, while, because,* and *after.* (A list of common dependent words has been given on page 197.) Through **coordination,** we show that ideas are of equal importance. When we coordinate, we use the words *and, but, for, or, nor, so, yet.*

Using Subordination or Coordination

Use subordination or coordination to combine the following groups of simple sentences into one or more longer sentences. Be sure to omit repeated words. Since various combinations are possible, you might want to jot down several combinations on a separate piece of paper. Then read them aloud to find the combination that sounds best.

Keep in mind that, very often, the relationship among ideas in a sentence will be clearer when subordination rather than coordination is used.

EXAMPLE

- My car does not start on cold mornings.
- I think the battery needs to be replaced.
- I already had it recharged once.
- I don't think charging it again would help.

  Because my car does not start on cold mornings, I think the battery needs to be replaced. I already had it recharged once, so I don't think charging it again would help.

> **HINT**   Use a comma at the end of a word group that starts with a dependent word (as in "Because my car does not start on cold mornings, . . .").

> **HINT**   Use a comma between independent word groups connected by *and, but, for, or, nor, so, yet* (as in "I already had it recharged once, so . . .").

1. • Sidney likes loud music.
   • His parents can't stand it.
   • He wears earphones.

   _____

   _____

   _____

   HINT: In item 1, use *although*, two commas, and the joining word *so*.

2. • The volcano erupted.
   • The sky turned black with smoke.
   • Nearby villagers were frightened.
   • They clogged the roads leading to safety.

   _____

   _____

   _____

   _____

3. • Glenda had a haircut today.
   • She came home and looked in the mirror.
   • She decided to wear a hat for a few days.
   • She thought she looked like a bald eagle.

   _____

   _____

   _____

   _____

4. • I ran out of gas on the way to work.
   • I discovered how helpful strangers can be.
   • A passing driver saw I was stuck.
   • He drove me to the gas station and back to my car.

   _____

   _____

   _____

   _____

Sentence Variety I

5. • Our dog often rests on the floor in the sunshine.
    • He waits for the children to get home from school.
    • The sunlight moves along the floor.
    • He moves with it.

    _____

    _____

    _____

    _____

6. • My father was going to be late from work.
    • We planned to have a late dinner.
    • I was hungry before dinner.
    • I ate a salami and cheese sandwich.
    • I did this secretly.

    _____

    _____

    _____

    _____

7. • A baseball game was scheduled for early afternoon.
    • It looked like rain.
    • A crew rolled huge tarps to cover the field.
    • Then the sun reappeared.

    _____

    _____

    _____

    _____

8. • Cassy worries about the pesticides used on fruit.
    • She washes apples, pears, and plums in soap and water.
    • She doesn't rinse them well.
    • They have a soapy flavor.

    _____

    _____

    _____

    _____

9. • Charlene needed to buy stamps.

   • She went to the post office during her lunch hour.

   • The line was long.

   • She waited there for half an hour.

   • She had to go back to work without stamps.

   _____

   _____

   _____

   _____

10. • The weather suddenly became frigid.

   • Almost everyone at work caught a cold.

   • Someone brought a big batch of chicken soup.

   • She poured it into one of the office coffeepots.

   • The pot was empty by noon.

   _____

   _____

   _____

   _____

REVIEW TEST 1

Combine each group of short sentences into one sentence. Various combinations are possible. Choose the combination that reads most smoothly and clearly and that sounds most appropriate in the context of surrounding sentences. Use a separate piece of paper.

Here is an example of a group of sentences and some possible combinations:

EXAMPLE

   • Martha moved in the desk chair.

   • Her moving was uneasy.

   • The chair was hard.

   • She worked at the assignment.

   • The assignment was for her English class.

   Martha moved uneasily in the hard desk chair, working at the assignment for her English class.

   Moving uneasily in the hard desk chair, Martha worked at the assignment for her English class.

Martha moved uneasily in the hard desk chair as she worked at the assignment for her English class.

While she worked at the assignment for her English class, Martha moved uneasily in the hard desk chair.

> **HINT**   In combining short sentences into one sentence, omit repeated words where necessary.

Doctor's Waiting Room

- People visit the doctor.
- Their ordeal begins.

- A patient has an appointment for 2:00.
- He is told he will have to wait.
- The wait will be at least one hour.

- Other people arrive.
- Everyone takes a seat.
- Soon the room becomes crowded.

- Some people read old magazines.
- Others count the stripes.
- The stripes are in the wallpaper.

- Some people look at each other.
- Some people may smile.
- No one talks to anyone else.

- Some people are very sick.
- They cough a lot.
- They hold tissues to their noses.

- The people around them turn away.
- They hold their breath.
- They are afraid of becoming infected.

- Time passes.
- It passes slowly.
- All the people count.
- They count the number of people ahead of them.

- The long-awaited moment finally arrives.
- The receptionist comes into the waiting area.

- She looks at the patient.
- She says the magic words.
- "The doctor will see you now."

Combine each group of short sentences into one sentence. Various combinations are possible. Choose the combination that reads most smoothly and clearly and that sounds most appropriate in the context of surrounding sentences. Use a separate piece of paper.

> **HINT** In combining short sentences into one sentence, omit repeated words where necessary.

A Remedy for Shyness

- Linda Nelson was shy.
- She seldom met new people.
- She spent a lot of time alone.

- Too often Linda avoided speaking.
- She did not want to take a risk.
- The risk was embarrassing herself.

- Luckily, Linda got some advice.
- The advice was good.
- She got the advice from her cousin Rose.
- Linda decided to try to change.
- She would change her behavior.

- Rose told Linda not to blame herself for being shy.
- She told her the shyness made her seem attractive.
- She told her the shyness made her seem modest.

- Rose encouraged her to talk to others.
- Linda began to join conversations at school.
- Linda began to join conversations at work.

- Gradually, Linda learned something.
- She could start conversations.
- She could start them herself.
- She could do this even though her heart pounded.
- She could do this even though her stomach churned.

- Linda still feels uncomfortable sometimes.
- She is doing things that once seemed impossible.

- Linda joined a bowling league.
- She did this recently.
- Some of her new friends invited her to join.
- The friends were from work.

- She is not the best bowler on the team.
- She is winning a victory over shyness.
- She is winning, thanks to her cousin's help.
- She is winning, thanks to her own determination.

- Linda is a happier person today.
- She has taken charge of her life.
- She has made herself a more interesting person.

Verbs, Pronouns, and Agreement

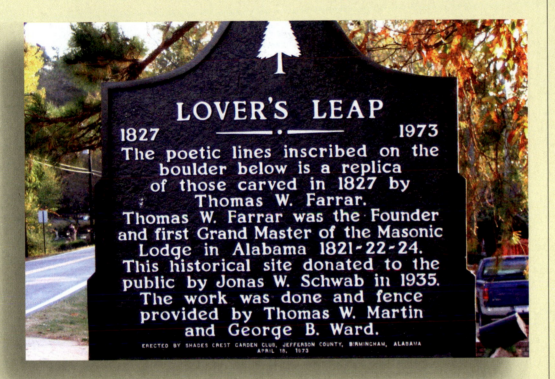

Responding to Images

How could you change this sign's wording to make it grammatically correct? What specific errors have been made?

Standard English Verbs

INTRODUCTORY ACTIVITY

Underline what you think is the correct form of the verb in each pair of sentences that follows.

That radio station once (play, played) top-forty hits.

It now (play, plays) classical music.

When Jean was a little girl, she (hope, hoped) to become a movie star.

Now she (hope, hopes) to be accepted at law school.

At first, my father (juggle, juggled) with balls of yarn.

Now that he is an expert, he (juggle, juggles) raw eggs.

On the basis of the previous examples, see if you can complete the following statements.

1. The first sentence in each pair refers to an action in the (past time, present time), and the regular verb has an _____ ending.

2. The second sentence in each pair refers to an action in the (past time, present time), and the regular verb has an _____ ending.

Answers are on page 585.

Many people have grown up in communities where nonstandard verb forms are used in everyday life. Such nonstandard forms include *they be, it done, we has, you was, she don't,* and *it ain't.* Community dialects have richness and power, but in college and the world at large, Standard English verb forms must be used. Standard English helps ensure clear communication among English-speaking people everywhere, and it is especially important in the world of work.

This chapter compares the community dialect and the standard English forms of a regular verb and three common irregular verbs.

Regular Verbs: Dialect and Standard Forms

The following chart compares community dialect (nonstandard) and standard English forms of the regular verb *talk*.

TALK			
Community Dialect		**Standard English**	
(Do not use in your writing)		(Use for clear communication)	
PRESENT TENSE			
I talks	we talks	I talk	we talk
you talks	you talks	you talk	you talk
he, she, it talk	they talks	he, she, it talks	they talk
PAST TENSE			
I talk	we talk	I talked	we talked
you talk	you talk	you talked	you talked
he, she, it talk	they talk	he, she, it talked	they talked

One of the most common nonstandard forms results from dropping the endings of regular verbs. For example, people might say "Rose work until ten o'clock tonight" instead of "Rose work*s* until ten o'clock tonight." Or they'll say "I work overtime yesterday" instead of "I work*ed* overtime yesterday." To avoid such nonstandard usage, memorize the forms shown above for the regular verb *talk*. Then do the activities that follow. These activities will help you make it a habit to include correct verb endings in your writing.

Present Tense Endings

The verb ending *-s* or *-es* is needed with a regular verb in the present tense when the subject is *he, she, it,* or any one person or thing.

www.mhhe.com/langan

He	He lift<u>s</u> weights.
She	She run<u>s</u>.
It	It amaze<u>s</u> me.
One person	Their son Ted swim<u>s</u>.
One person	Their daughter Terri dance<u>s</u>.
One thing	Their house jump<u>s</u> at night with all the exercise.

| ACTIVITY 1 | **Using Standard Verb Forms** |

www.mhhe.com/langan

HINT: Add *s* to *drive* in item 1.

All but one of the ten sentences that follow need *-s* or *-es* endings. Cross out the nonstandard verb forms and write the standard forms in the spaces provided. Mark with a *C* the one sentence that needs no change.

EXAMPLE

_____ends_____   The sale ~~end~~ tomorrow.

_____   1. Tim drive too fast for me.

_____   2. Our washing machine always get stuck at the rinse cycle.

_____   3. Roberto practice his saxophone two hours each day.

_____   4. Whenever I serve meat loaf, my daughter make a peanut butter sandwich.

_____   5. My grandfather brush his teeth with baking soda.

_____   6. While watching television in the evening, Kitty usually fall asleep.

_____   7. Mom always wakes me by saying, "Get up, the day is growing older."

_____   8. On my old car radio, a static sound come from every station but one.

_____   9. My little sister watch fireworks with her hands over her ears.

_____   10. The broken computer buzz like an angry wasp.

| ACTIVITY 2 | **Using Present Tense -s Verb Endings** |

Rewrite the short selection that follows, adding present tense *-s* verb endings in the ten places where they are needed.

> My little sister want to be a singer when she grow up. She constantly hum and sing around the house. Sometimes she make quite a racket. When she listen to music on the radio, for example, she sing very loudly in order to hear herself over the radio. And when she take a shower, her voice ring through the whole house because she think nobody can hear her from there.

_____

_____

_____

_____

_____

Past Tense Endings

The verb ending -*d* or -*ed* is needed with a regular verb in the past tense.

> Yesterday we finish<u>ed</u> painting the house.
>
> I complet<u>ed</u> the paper an hour before class.
>
> Fred's car stall<u>ed</u> on his way to work this morning.

www.mhhe.com/langan

| **Using Standard Verb Forms: -*d* and -*ed* Endings** | **ACTIVITY 3** |

All but one of the ten sentences that follow need -*d* or -*ed* endings. Cross out the nonstandard verb forms and write the standard forms in the spaces provided. Mark with a *C* the one sentence that needs no change.

EXAMPLE

<u>jumped</u>   The cat ~~jump~~ onto my lap when I sat down.

_____   1. A waiter at the new restaurant accidentally spill ice water into Phil's lap.

_____   2. In a prim Indiana town, a couple was actually jail for kissing in public.

_____   3. While ironing my new shirt this morning, I burn a hole right through it.

_____   4. Fran wrapped the gag gift in waxed paper and tie it with dental floss.

_____   5. Pencil marks dotted Matt's bedroom wall where he measure his height each month.

_____   6. My brother was eating too fast and almost choked on a piece of bread.

_____   7. Last summer, a burglar smash my car window and stole my jacket.

_____   8. The kids construct an obstacle course in the basement out of boxes and toys.

_____   9. The rain came down so hard it level the young cornstalks in our garden.

_____   10. As Alfonso pulled up to the red light, he suddenly realize his brakes were not working.

HINT: In item 1, add *ed* to *spill.*

| **Using Past Tense Verb Endings** | **ACTIVITY 4** |

Rewrite the following selection, adding past tense -*d* or -*ed* verb endings in the fifteen places where they are needed.

My cousin Joel complete a course in home repairs and offer one day to fix several things in my house. He repair a screen door that squeak, a dining room chair that wobble a bit, and a faulty electrical outlet. That night when I open the screen door, it loosen from its hinges. When I seat myself in the chair Joel had fix, one of its legs crack off. Remembering that Joel had also fool around with the electrical outlet, I quickly call an electrician and ask him to stop by the next day. Then I pray the house would not burn down before he arrive.

_____

_____

_____

_____

_____

_____

Three Common Irregular Verbs: Dialect and Standard Forms

The following charts compare the community dialect (nonstandard) and Standard English forms of the common irregular verbs *be, have,* and *do.*

> **TIP** For more on irregular verbs, see Chapter 11, beginning on page 219.

BE			
Community Dialect		**Standard English**	
(Do not use in your writing)		(Use for clear communication)	
PRESENT TENSE			
I be (or is)	we be	I am	we are
you be	you be	you are	you are
he, she, it be	they be	he, she, it is	they are
PAST TENSE			
I were	we was	I was	we were
you was	you was	you were	you were
he, she, it were	they was	he, she, it was	they were

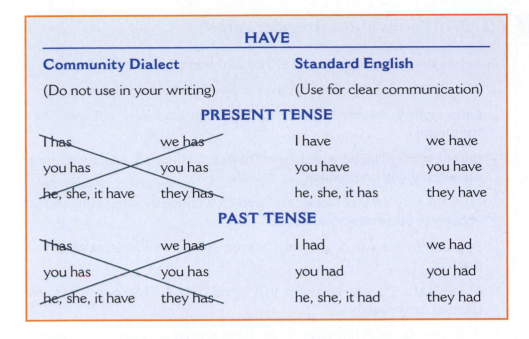

HAVE

Community Dialect		Standard English	
(Do not use in your writing)		(Use for clear communication)	

PRESENT TENSE

~~I has~~	~~we has~~	I have	we have
you has	you has	you have	you have
~~he, she, it have~~	~~they has~~	he, she, it has	they have

PAST TENSE

~~I has~~	~~we has~~	I had	we had
you has	you has	you had	you had
~~he, she, it have~~	~~they has~~	he, she, it had	they had

DO

Community Dialect		Standard English	
(Do not use in your writing)		(Use for clear communication)	

PRESENT TENSE

~~I does~~	~~we does~~	I do	we do
you does	you does	you do	you do
~~he, she, it do~~	~~they does~~	he, she, it does	they do

PAST TENSE

~~I done~~	~~we done~~	I did	we did
you done	you done	you did	you did
~~he, she, it done~~	~~they done~~	he, she, it did	they did

TIP   Many people have trouble with one negative form of *do*. They will say, for example, "She don't listen" instead of "She doesn't listen," or they will say "This pen don't work" instead of "This pen doesn't work." Be careful to avoid the common mistake of using *don't* instead of *doesn't*.

ACTIVITY 5 — Standard Forms of the Irregular Verbs

HINT: *Be* is never a verb by itself.

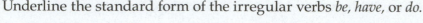
www.mhhe.com/langan

Underline the standard form of the irregular verbs *be*, *have*, or *do*.

1. The piranha (be, is) a fish that lives in South American rivers.

2. Only eight to twelve inches long, piranhas (do, does) not look very frightening.

3. But the smell of blood in the water (have, has) the effect of driving piranhas crazy with excitement.

4. Even the tiny drop of blood produced by a single mosquito bite (be, is) enough to attract the vicious fish.

5. Piranhas (has, have) double rows of teeth, which make them dangerous hunters.

6. Those teeth (be, are) so sharp that some Native American tribes use them as arrowheads.

7. A single piranha's bite (has, have) the potential to cause severe injury, such as the loss of a finger or toe.

8. However, piranhas (does, do) their greatest damage when they attack in large numbers.

9. Some travelers (was, were) boating on the Amazon when they saw a school of piranhas strip a four-hundred-pound hog to a skeleton in minutes.

10. "What the piranha (does, do) is believable only if you see it," reported one witness.

ACTIVITY 6 — Identifying and Correcting Nonstandard Verbs

HINT: *You does* is never a correct form.

Cross out the nonstandard verb form in each sentence. Then write the standard form of *be*, *have*, or *do* in the space provided.

_____ 1. If you does your assignments on time, you may not understand my friend Albert.

_____ 2. Albert be the world's worst procrastinator.

_____ 3. Procrastinators be people who always put things off.

_____ 4. They has problems with deadlines of all kinds.

_____ 5. Albert were a procrastinator at the age of six.

_____ 6. The boy next door have a few friends over for lunch one day.

_____ 7. Albert's parents was upset when they learned Albert got there three hours late.

_____ 8. They done the neighbors a favor by taking Albert home at once.

_____ 9. Today, Albert still do everything at the last minute or even later.

_____ 10. He have plans to join Procrastinators Anonymous—when he gets around to it.

Using Standard Forms of *be, have,* and *do*

Fill in each blank with the standard form of *be, have,* or *do.*

My cousin Rita _____ decided to lose thirty pounds, so she _____ put herself on a rigid diet that _____ not allow her to eat anything that she enjoys. Last weekend, while the family _____ at Aunt Jenny's house for dinner, all Rita _____ to eat _____ a can of Diet Delight peaches. We _____ convinced that Rita meant business when she joined an exercise club whose members _____ to work out on enormous machines and _____ twenty sit-ups just to get started. If Rita _____ reach her goal, we _____ all going to be very proud of her. But I would not be surprised if she _____ not succeed, because this _____ her fourth diet this year.

Underline the standard verb form.

1. A cake in the oven (make, makes) the whole house smell good.

2. My brother deliberately (wear, wears) socks that clash with his clothes.

3. Our boss (don't, doesn't) want us to take any extra coffee breaks.

4. After I got home from the movie theater, I (realize, realized) I had lost my wallet.

5. The cheap ballpoint pen (leak, leaked) ink on my favorite shirt.

6. If they (was, were) my children, I wouldn't let them play near that creek.

7. We have to be quiet, because my sister (is, be) studying for her sociology test.

8. A neighbor (watch, watched) our house while we were away on vacation.

A Brief Review of Regular Verbs

Every verb has four principal forms: present, past, past participle, and present participle. These forms can be used to build all the verb tenses (the times shown by a verb).

Most verbs in English are regular. The past and past participle of a regular verb are formed by adding *-d* or *-ed* to the present. The *past participle* is the form of the verb used with the helping verbs *have, has,* or *had* (or some form of *be* with passive verbs, which are explained on page 247). The *present participle* is formed by adding *-ing* to the present.

Here are the principal forms of some regular verbs:

Present	Past	Past Participle	Present Participle
laugh	laughed	laughed	laughing
ask	asked	asked	asking
touch	touched	touched	touching
decide	decided	decided	deciding
explode	exploded	exploded	exploding

List of Irregular Verbs

Irregular verbs have irregular forms in the past tense and past participle. For example, the past tense of the irregular verb *grow* is *grew;* the past participle is *grown.*

Almost everyone has some degree of trouble with irregular verbs. When you are unsure about the form of a verb, you can check the following list of irregular verbs. (The present participle is not shown on this list, because it is formed simply by adding *-ing* to the base form of the verb.) Or you can check a dictionary, which gives the principal forms of irregular verbs.

Present	Past	Past Participle
arise	arose	arisen
awake	awoke *or* awaked	awoke *or* awaked
be (am, are, is)	was (were)	been
become	became	become
begin	began	begun
bend	bent	bent
bite	bit	bitten
blow	blew	blown
break	broke	broken
bring	brought	brought
build	built	built
burst	burst	burst

Present	Past	Past Participle
buy	bought	bought
catch	caught	caught
choose	chose	chosen
come	came	come
cost	cost	cost
cut	cut	cut
do (does)	did	done
draw	drew	drawn
drink	drank	drunk
drive	drove	driven
eat	ate	eaten
fall	fell	fallen
feed	fed	fed
feel	felt	felt
fight	fought	fought
find	found	found
fly	flew	flown
freeze	froze	frozen
get	got	got *or* gotten
give	gave	given
go (goes)	went	gone
grow	grew	grown
have (has)	had	had
hear	heard	heard
hide	hid	hidden
hold	held	held
hurt	hurt	hurt
keep	kept	kept
know	knew	known
lay	laid	laid
lead	led	led
leave	left	left
lend	lent	lent
let	let	let
lie	lay	lain
light	lit	lit
lose	lost	lost
make	made	made
meet	met	met
pay	paid	paid
ride	rode	ridden
ring	rang	rung
rise	rose	risen
run	ran	run
say	said	said
see	saw	seen
sell	sold	sold

Present	Past	Past Participle
send	sent	sent
shake	shook	shaken
shrink	shrank	shrunk
shut	shut	shut
sing	sang	sung
sit	sat	sat
sleep	slept	slept
speak	spoke	spoken
spend	spent	spent
stand	stood	stood
steal	stole	stolen
stick	stuck	stuck
sting	stung	stung
swear	swore	sworn
swim	swam	swum
take	took	taken
teach	taught	taught
tear	tore	torn
tell	told	told
think	thought	thought
wake	woke *or* waked	woken *or* waked
wear	wore	worn
win	won	won
write	wrote	written

ACTIVITY 1   Identifying Incorrect Verb Forms

Cross out the incorrect verb form in the following sentences. Then write the correct form of the verb in the space provided.

EXAMPLE

_____began_____   When the mud slide started, the whole neighborhood ~~begun~~ going downhill.

HINT: In item 1, use the past tense of *come.*

_____   1. The coach caught Otto when he come in two hours after curfew.

_____   2. We standed out in the rain all night to buy tickets to the concert.

_____   3. The Romans had builded a network of roads so the army could travel more quickly from place to place.

_____   4. Our championship team has swam in every important meet this year.

_____   5. The nervous mother holded her child's hand tightly as they crossed the busy street.

_____ 6. Hakeem drived in circles for an hour before he admitted that he was lost.

_____ 7. He had wrote the answers to all the questions before anyone else had finished the first page.

_____ 8. The tornado blowed the sign from the top of the bank, and it landed five blocks away in the motel swimming pool.

_____ 9. Kathy buyed school clothes with the money she earned from her summer job.

_____ 10. The poker players knowed they were in trouble when the stranger shuffled the cards with one hand.

Using Present Tense, Past Tense, and Past Participle Verbs   ACTIVITY 2

For each of the italicized verbs in the following sentences, fill in the three missing forms in the order shown in the box:

> a. Present tense, which takes an -s ending when the subject is *he, she, it,* or any *one person or thing* (see page 211)
>
> b. Past tense
>
> c. Past participle—the form that goes with the helping verb *have, has,* or *had*

EXAMPLE

My little nephew loves to *break* things. Every Christmas he (a) ____breaks____ his new toys the minute they're unwrapped. Last year he (b) ____broke____ five toys in seven minutes and then went on to smash his family's new china platter. His mother says he won't be happy until he has (c) ____broken____ their hearts.

1. Did you ever go to *sleep* on a water bed? My cousin Nancy (a) _____ on one. Last year I spent the weekend at Nancy's apartment, and I (b) _____ on it. Since then I have (c) _____ on it several more times, without once getting seasick.

2. A dreadful little boy in my neighborhood loves to *ring* my doorbell and run away. Sometimes he (a) _____ it several times a day. The last time it (b) _____ over and over, I finally refused to answer the door. Then I found out that the mail carrier had (c) _____ the doorbell to deliver a gift from my boyfriend.

HINT: In item 1, add an *s* to *sleep* in choice a. Use the past tense of *sleep* for b and c.

3. Why does every teacher ask us to *write* about our summer vacations? Most students (a) _____ about what really happened, but that is usually too dull. I (b) _____ an essay about being taken aboard an alien spacecraft. I bet it was the most interesting essay anybody has ever (c) _____ for my teacher's English class.

4. My sister never has to *stand* in line for a movie very long. She always (a) _____ for a few minutes and then walks straight to the entrance. "I (b) _____ in line as long as I could," she tells the ticket taker. "In fact," she continues in a weak voice, "I have (c) _____ in line too long already. I feel faint." She is always ushered inside immediately.

5. As usual, Ron planned to *swim* at least a hundred laps before breakfast. He knew that an Olympic hopeful (a) _____ while others sleep. That morning he (b) _____ with a deliberate stroke, counting the rhythm silently. He had (c) _____ this way daily for the last two years. It was a price he was willing to pay to be one of the best.

6. I know a woman who likes to *buy* things and return them after she uses them. For example, she always (a) _____ new shoes to wear for special occasions. Then she wears them for the event and returns them the next day. Once she (b) _____ a complete outfit, wore it twice, and returned it a week later. Whenever I shop, I worry that I have (c) _____ something that she has used and returned.

7. Craig sat in his car at the rural crossroads and wondered which direction to *choose*. Should he (a) _____ left or right? He sighed and turned right, knowing that if he (b) _____ the wrong way, he would run out of gas before finding his way back to the highway. After several anxious minutes, he spotted an Exxon sign. He pulled into the service station, grateful that he had (c) _____ the right direction after all.

8. My friend Alice loves to *eat*. But no matter how much she (a) _____, she stays thin. Her husband, on the other hand, is fat. "Why?" he jokingly complains. "I (b) _____ very little today. In fact," he adds with a grin, "all my life I have (c) _____ just one meal a day. Of course, it usually lasts from morning till night."

9. All the kids in the neighborhood waited each winter for Mahoney's pond to *freeze*. They knew that a sudden cold snap (a) _____ only the surface. It took at least a week of low temperatures before the pond (b) _____ more than a few inches deep. Mr. Mahoney checked the ice each day. When it had finally (c) _____ to a depth of six inches, he gave his permission for the children to skate on it.

10. It is important for people to *give* blood. A healthy person can (a)

_____ a pint of blood in less than fifteen minutes with little or

no discomfort. The first time I (b) _____ blood, I was afraid
the needle would hurt, but all I felt was a slight pinch. I have (c)

_____ blood many times since then. Each time I do, I feel good,
knowing that my gift will help other people.

Troublesome Irregular Verbs

Three common irregular verbs that often give people trouble are *be, have,*
and *do.* See pages 214–215 for a discussion of these verbs. Three sets of other
irregular verbs that can lead to difficulties are *lie-lay, sit-set,* and *rise-raise.*

Lie-Lay

The principal forms of *lie* and *lay* are as follows:

Present	Past	Past Participle
lie	lay	lain
lay	laid	laid

TIP   *To lie* means *to rest* or *recline. To lay* means *to put something down.*

To Lie	**To Lay**
Tony *lies* on the couch.	I *lay* the mail on the table.
This morning he *lay* in the tub.	Yesterday I *laid* the mail on the counter.
He has *lain* in bed all week with the flu.	I have *laid* the mail where everyone will see it.

Using *lie* and *lay*

ACTIVITY 3

Underline the correct verb.

HINT   Use a form of *lie* if you can substitute *recline.* Use a form of *lay* if
you can substitute *place.*

HINT: Since the kitten is resting, what is the correct answer?

1. On warm sunny days, Serena's kitten often (lies, lays) on the bedroom windowsill.

2. (Lying, Laying) too long in bed in the morning can give me a headache.

3. The Magna Carta (lay, laid) the foundation for the establishment of the English Parliament.

4. He was certain he had (lain, laid) the tiles in a straight line until he stepped back to look.

5. I (lay, laid) down on the couch and pressed my face into the pillow.

Sit-Set

The principal forms of *sit* and *set* are as follows:

Present	Past	Past Participle
sit	sat	sat
set	set	set

TIP   *To sit* means *to take a seat* or *to rest. To set* means *to put* or *to place.*

To Sit	**To Set**
I *sit* down during work breaks.	Tony *sets* out the knives, forks, and spoons.
I *sat* in the doctor's office for three hours.	His sister already *set* out the dishes.
I have always *sat* in the last desk.	They have just *set* out the dinner ware.

ACTIVITY 4   **Using *set* and *sit***

Underline the correct form of the verb.

HINT   Use a form of *sit* if you can substitute *rest*. Use a form of *set* if you can substitute *place*.

HINT: Since the movers placed the boxes, what is the correct verb?

1. The movers have (sat, set) all the smaller boxes on the kitchen table.

2. When I'm on a bus, I like (sitting, setting) in front.

3. The aircraft carrier (sat, set) five miles offshore as helicopters shuttled to and from the island.

4. (Sit, Set) the plant on the windowsill so it will get the morning sun.

5. Lupe helped decorate for the party by (sitting, setting) vases of fresh flowers on each of the tables.

Rise-Raise

The principal forms of *rise* and *raise* are as follows:

Present	Past	Past Participle
rise	rose	risen
raise	raised	raised

> **TIP**   To *rise* means *to get up* or *to move up*. To *raise* (which is a regular verb with simple *-ed* endings) means *to lift up* or *to increase in amount*.

To Rise	To Raise
The soldiers *rise* at dawn.	I'm going to *raise* the stakes in the card game.
The crowd *rose* to applaud the batter.	I *raised* the shades to let in the sun.
Dracula has *risen* from the grave.	I would have quit if the company had not *raised* my salary.

Using *rise* and *raise*

ACTIVITY 5

Underline the correct verb.

> **HINT**   Use a form of *rise* if you can substitute *get up* or *move up*. Use a form of *raise* if you can substitute *lift up* or *increase*.

1. It is usually warmer upstairs because heat (rises, raises).

2. The new owner (rose, raised) the rent, so now I will have to look for another apartment.

3. We (rose, raised) at three o'clock in the morning to watch the meteor shower.

HINT: Since heat moves upward, what is the correct verb?

4. After four days of rain, the river had (risen, raised) over its banks and threatened to flood the highway.

5. A single sailboat made them (rise, raise) the drawbridge, stopping traffic in both directions for fifteen minutes.

REVIEW TEST 1

Cross out the incorrect verb form in each sentence. Then write the correct form of the verb in the space provided.

_____ 1. The spare key under the mat falled through a crack in the porch floor.

_____ 2. When he blowed out the dozens of candles on his cake, the old man used a hair dryer.

_____ 3. Many residents fighted the city's plan to build a new stadium in their neighborhood.

_____ 4. Oscar said he could have swam ten more laps if he hadn't gotten leg cramps.

_____ 5. After he had broke the vase, the little boy hid the pieces under the sofa.

_____ 6. People looked away from the homeless man who was laying on the sidewalk.

_____ 7. You should have saw Ann's face when she passed her driving test.

_____ 8. After I lended Dave money, I remembered that he seldom pays people back.

_____ 9. My grandmother has growed tomatoes and peppers in her backyard for many years.

_____ 10. The health inspector come into the kitchen as the cook picked up a hamburger from the floor.

REVIEW TEST 2

Write short sentences using the form noted for the following irregular verbs.

EXAMPLE

Past of _ride_ _The Lone Ranger rode into the sunset._

1. Present of _shake_ _____

2. Past participle of _write_ _____

3. Past participle of _begin_ _____

4. Past of _go_ _____

5. Past participle of *grow* _____

6. Present of *speak* _____

7. Past of *bring* _____

8. Present of *do* _____

9. Past participle of *give* _____

10. Past of *drink* _____

12

Subject-Verb Agreement

INTRODUCTORY ACTIVITY

As you read each pair of sentences, write a check mark beside the sentence that you think uses the underlined word correctly.

The pictures in that magazine is very controversial. _____

The pictures in that magazine are very controversial. _____

There was many applicants for the job. _____

There were many applicants for the job. _____

Everybody usually watch the lighted numbers in an elevator. _____

Everybody usually watches the lighted numbers in an elevator. _____

On the basis of the above examples, see if you can complete the following statements.

1. In the first two pairs of sentences, the subjects are _____

    and _____. Since both these subjects are plural, the verb
    must be plural.

2. In the last pair of sentences, the subject, *Everybody,* is a word that
    is always (singular, plural), so its accompanying verb must be
    (singular, plural).

Answers are on page 586.

A verb must agree with its subject in number. A *singular subject* (one person or thing) takes a singular verb. A *plural subject* (more than one person or thing) takes a plural verb. Mistakes in subject-verb agreement are sometimes made in the following situations:

*   When words come between the subject and the verb

*   When a verb comes before the subject

*   With indefinite pronouns

- With compound subjects
- With *who, which,* and *that*

Each situation is explained in depth on the following pages.

Words between the Subject and the Verb

Words that come between the subject and the verb do not change subject-verb agreement. In the following sentence

> The breakfast cereals in the pantry are made mostly of sugar.

the subject (*cereals*) is plural, so the verb (*are*) is plural. The words *in the pantry* that come between the subject and the verb do not affect subject-verb agreement. To help find the subject of certain sentences, cross out prepositional phrases (explained on page 157):

> One of the crooked politicians was jailed for a month.

> The boxes in my grandmother's attic contained old family photos and long-forgotten toys.

Following is a list of common prepositions.

www.mhhe.com/langan

Subject-Verb Agreement

COMMON PREPOSITIONS

about	before	by	inside	over
above	behind	during	into	through
across	below	except	of	to
among	beneath	for	off	toward
around	beside	from	on	under
at	between	in	onto	with

Words between Subjects and Verbs

ACTIVITY 1

Draw one line under the subject. Then lightly cross out any words that come between the subject and the verb. Finally, draw two lines under the correct verb in parentheses.

EXAMPLE

The price of the stereo speakers (is, are) too high for my wallet.

1. A trail of bloodstains (leads, lead) to the spot where the murder was committed.

2. The winter clothes in the hall closet (takes, take) up too much room.

3. A basket of fancy fruit and nuts (was, were) delivered to my house.

4. The garbled instructions for assembling the bicycle (was, were) almost impossible to follow.

HINT: In item 1, cross out the preposition between the subject and verb.

5. Smoke from the distant forest fires (is, are) visible from many miles away.

6. Workers at that automobile plant (begins, begin) each day with a period of exercise.

7. The earliest date on any of the cemetery gravestones (appears, appear) to be 1804.

8. The line of cars in the traffic jam (seems, seem) to extend for miles.

9. Several boxes in the corner of the attic (contains, contain) old family pictures.

10. Sleeping bags with the new insulation material (protects, protect) campers even in subzero temperatures.

Verb before the Subject

www.mhhe.com/langan

A verb agrees with its subject even when the verb comes *before* the subject. Words that may precede the subject include *there, here,* and, in questions, *who, which, what,* and *where.*

Inside the storage shed are the garden tools.

At the street corner were two panhandlers.

There are times when I'm ready to quit my job.

Where are the instructions for the DVD player?

> TIP   If you are unsure about the subject, ask *who* or *what* of the verb. With the first sentence above, you might ask, "What is inside the storage shed?" The answer, garden *tools,* is the subject.

ACTIVITY 2   Verbs That Precede Subjects

Draw one line under the subject. Then draw two lines under the correct verb in parentheses.

HINT: To find the subject in item 1, ask "What is coming from behind the wall?"

1. There (is, are) a scratching noise coming from behind this wall.

2. On the bottom of the jar of preserves (is, are) the berries.

3. Floating near the base of the dock (was, were) several discarded aluminum cans.

4. In the middle of the woods behind our home (sits, sit) an abandoned cabin.

5. There (was, were) so many students talking at once that the instructor shouted for quiet.

6. Outside the novelty shop at the mall (stands, stand) a life-size cutout of W. C. Fields.

7. Coming out of the fog toward the frightened boys (was, were) the menacing shape of a large dog.

8. In the rear of the closet (was, were) the basketball sneakers that I thought I had lost.

9. On the table in the doctor's office (is, are) some magazines that are five years old.

10. Lining one wall of the gym (was, were) a row of lockers for the team members.

www.mhhe.com/langan

Indefinite Pronouns

The following words, known as *indefinite pronouns,* always take singular verbs.

INDEFINITE PRONOUNS

(-*one* words)	(-*body* words)	(-*thing* words)	
one	nobody	nothing	each
anyone	anybody	anything	either
everyone	everybody	everything	neither
someone	somebody	something	

> **TIP** *Both* always takes a plural verb.

Using Verbs with Indefinite Pronouns

ACTIVITY 3

Write the correct form of the verb in the space provided.

keeps, keep
1. Something always _____ me from getting to bed on time.

works, work
2. Nobody that I know _____ as hard as Manuel.

pays, pay
3. Neither of the jobs offered to me _____ more than six dollars an hour.

has, have
4. Both of the speakers _____ told us more than we care to know about the dangers of water pollution.

slips, slip
5. Someone in Inez's apartment house _____ an unsigned valentine under her door every year.

HINT: The indefinite pronoun *something* requires a singular verb.

leans, lean	6. Anything sitting on the old wooden floor _____ to one side.
expects, expect	7. Each of my friends _____ to be invited to my new backyard pool.
was, were	8. Not one of the three smoke detectors in the house _____ working properly.
stops, stop	9. Only one of all the brands of waxes _____ the rust on my car from spreading.
has, have	10. Just about everybody who hates getting up early for work _____ jumped out of bed at 6:00 a.m. to go on vacation.

Compound Subjects

Subjects joined by *and* generally take a plural verb.

> Yoga and biking are Lola's ways of staying in shape.

> Ambition and good luck are the keys to his success.

When subjects are joined by *either . . . or, neither . . . nor, not only . . . but also,* the verb agrees with the subject closer to the verb.

> Either the restaurant manager or his assistants deserve to be fired for the spoiled meat used in the stew.

www.mhhe.com/langan

> **EXPLANATION:** The nearer subject, *assistants*, is plural, and so the verb is plural.

ACTIVITY 4	**Using Verbs with Compound Subjects**

Write the correct form of the verb in the space provided.

HINT: The compound subject *shivering and crying* requires a plural verb.

| saddens, sadden |
| needs, need |
| has, have |
| continues, continue |
| tears, tear |

1. The shivering and crying of animals in pet stores _____ me very much.

2. The floor and cabinets in the kitchen _____ to be cleaned.

3. Her best friend and her coach _____ more influence on Sally than her parents do.

4. Crabgrass and dandelions _____ to spread across the lawn despite my efforts to wipe them out.

5. Either the neighborhood kids or an automatic car-wash machine always _____ the antenna off my car.

Who, Which, and *That*

www.mhhe.com/langan

When *who, which,* and *that* are used as subjects of verbs, they take singular verbs if the word they stand for is singular, and they take plural verbs if the word they stand for is plural. For example, in the sentence

Gary is one of those people <u>who</u> <u>are</u> very private.

the verb is plural because *who* stands for *people,* which is plural. On the other hand, in the sentence

Gary is a person <u>who</u> <u>is</u> very private.

the verb is singular because *who* stands for *person,* which is singular.

Using *who, which,* or *that* with Verbs

ACTIVITY 5

Write the correct form of the verb in the space provided.

has,
have

1. The young man who _____ mowed my grass for years just left for college.

goes,
go

2. The jacket that _____ with those pants is at the cleaners.

HINT: *Who* stands for a singular subject and requires a singular verb.

becomes,
become

3. Women who _____ police officers often have to prove themselves more capable than do their male coworkers.

tastes,
taste

4. The restaurant serves hamburgers that _____ like dry cereal.

is,
are

5. The ceiling in Kevin's bedroom is covered with stars, which _____ arranged in the shape of the constellations.

Working Together

ACTIVITY 6

Part A: Editing and Rewriting

Working with a partner, read the short paragraph below and see if you can underline the five mistakes in subject-verb agreement. Then use the space provided to correct these five errors. Feel free to discuss the rewrite quietly with your partner and refer back to the chapter when necessary.

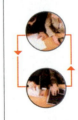

> When most people think about cities, they do not thinks about wild animals. But in my city apartment, there is enough creatures to fill a small forest. In the daytime, I must contend with the pigeons. These unwanted guests at my apartment makes a loud feathery mess on my bedroom windowsill. In the evening, my apartment is visited by roaches. These large insects creep onto my kitchen floor and walls after dark and frighten me with their shiny glistening bodies. Later at

continued

night, my apartment is invaded by mice. Waking from sleep, I can hear their little feet tapping as they scurry behind walls and above my ceiling. Everybody I know think I should move into a new apartment. What I really need is to go somewhere that have less wild creatures—maybe a forest!

_____

_____

_____

_____

_____

Part B: Creating Sentences

Working with a partner, write sentences as directed. Use a separate piece of paper. For each item, pay special attention to subject-verb agreement.

1. Write a sentence in which the words *in the cafeteria* or *on the table* come between the subject and verb. Underline the subject of your sentence and circle the verb.

2. Write a sentence that begins with the words *There is* or *There are.* Underline the subject of your sentence and circle the verb.

3. Write a sentence in which the indefinite pronoun *nobody* or *anything* is the subject.

4. Write a sentence with the compound subject *manager and employees.* Underline the subject of your sentence and circle the verb.

REFLECTIVE ACTIVITY

1. Look at the paragraph about the apartment that you revised in Activity 6. Which rule involving subject-verb agreement gave you the most trouble? How did you figure out the correct answer?

2. Five situations involving subject-verb agreement have been discussed in this chapter. Explain which one is most likely to cause you problems.

REVIEW TEST 1

Complete each of the following sentences, using *is, are, was, were, have,* or *has.* Underline the subject of each of these verbs. In some cases you will need to provide that subject.

EXAMPLE

The hot dogs in that luncheonette ____*are hazardous to your health.*____

1. In my glove compartment _____

2. The cat and her three kittens _____

3. I frequently see people who _____

4. Neither of the wrestlers _____

5. Scattered across the parking lot _____

6. The dust balls under my bed _____

7. There are _____

8. My friend and his brother _____

9. The newspapers that accumulate in my garage _____

_____

10. It was one of those movies that _____

_____

Draw one line under the subject. Then draw two lines under the correct verb in parentheses.

1. The plants in the window (grows, grow) quickly because they have plenty of sunlight.

2. Nobody (walks, walk) on the streets of this neighborhood at night.

3. Here (is, are) the keys you need to get into the apartment.

4. A dropped pass and two fumbles (was, were) the reasons the team lost the football game.

5. There (is, are) billboards all along the road warning drivers to stay sober.

6. A paper plate fitted over the dog's head (prevents, prevent) the animal from biting its stitches.

7. Since I gained weight, neither my old suits nor my new shirt (fits, fit) me.

8. What (does, do) my marital status have to do with my qualifications for the job?

9. Sitting silently off in the distance in the bright moonlight (was, were) the wolf and his mate.

10. Neither the security guard nor the police officer (was, were) able to figure out how the thief got into the building.

REVIEW TEST 3

There are ten mistakes in subject-verb agreement in the following passage. Cross out each incorrect verb and write the correct form above it. In addition, underline the subject of each of the verbs that must be changed.

After more than thirty years on television, there is few honors that *Sesame Street* has not won. The awards are deserved, for *Sesame Street* is a show that treat children with respect. Most children's programs consists of cheaply made cartoons that is based on the adventures of a superhero or a video-game character. Unfortunately, children's TV programs are generally so poor because quality kids' shows does not make the profits that the networks demand. Both the superhero story and the video-game story is easy to slap together. By contrast, the producers of *Sesame Street* spends enormous amounts of time and money researching how children learn. Another reason for the low profits are the nature of the audience. Because children have little money to spend on sponsors' products, each of the networks charge bottom rates for advertising during children's programs. *Sesame Street*, a nonprofit show, does not even accept ads. And income from the sale of *Sesame Street* products are used to do an even better job of producing the show.

Consistent Verb Tense

INTRODUCTORY ACTIVITY

See if you can find and underline the two mistakes in verb tense in the following selection.

> When Computer Warehouse had a sale, Alex decided to buy a new computer. He planned to set up the machine himself and hoped to connect to the Internet right away. When he arrived home, however, Alex discovers that setting up a wireless hub could be complicated and confusing. The directions sounded as if they had been written for engineers. After two hours of frustration, Alex gave up and calls a technician for help.

Now try to complete the following statement:

> Verb tenses should be consistent. In the selection above, two verbs have to be changed because they are mistakenly in the (*present, past*)

_____ tense while all the other verbs in the selection are in the

(*present, past*) _____ tense.

Answers are on page 586.

Keeping Tenses Consistent

Do not shift tenses unnecessarily. If you begin writing a paper in the present tense, don't shift suddenly to the past. If you begin in the past, don't shift without reason to the present. Notice the inconsistent verb tenses in the following example:

www.mhhe.com/langan

incorrect   Smoke spilled from the front of the overheated car. The driver opens up the hood, then jumped back as steam billows out.

The verbs must be consistently in the present tense:

correct   Smoke spills from the front of the overheated car. The driver opens up the hood, then jumps back as steam billows out.

Or the verbs must be consistently in the past tense:

correct   Smoke spilled from the front of the overheated car. The driver opened up the hood, then jumped back as steam billowed out.

| ACTIVITY 1 | Avoiding Unnecessary Tense Shifts |

In each item, one verb must be changed so that it agrees in tense with the other verbs. Cross out the incorrect verb and write the correct form in the space at the left.

EXAMPLE

looked   I gave away my striped sweater after three people told me I ~~look~~ like a giant bee.

HINT: Change *rolls* to past tense to agree with the rest of the sentence.

_____   1. The wet dog, delighted that its bath was over, raced madly around the living room and rolls all over the carpet.

_____   2. On vacation, I couldn't face another restaurant meal, so I purchase cheese and crackers and ate in my room.

_____   3. The excited crowd clapped and cheered when the performers step onto the stage.

_____   4. Before the rain stopped, mud slid down the hill and crashes into the houses in the valley.

_____   5. When my little brother found my new box of markers, he snatches one and made green circles all over our front steps.

_____   6. The old house looked as if it hadn't been cleaned in years. Dust cover everything, and the smell of mildew hung in the air.

_____   7. The outfielder tumbled, made a spectacular catch, and lifts the ball up for the umpire to witness.

_____   8. Annie talks aloud to her favorite soap opera character; she argued and fights with the woman over her decisions.

_____   9. At the pie-eating contest, Leo stuffed in the last piece of blueberry pie, swallows it all, and then flashed a purple grin for the photographer.

_____ 10. The supermarket seemed empty on Sunday morning; shopping carts stood in long lines, bakery shelves were bare, and the lights over the meat counter glow dimly.

Change the verbs where needed in the following selection so that they are consistently in the past tense. Cross out each incorrect verb and write the correct form above it, as shown in the example. You will need to make ten corrections.

Years ago, I live in an old apartment house where I got little peace and quiet. For one thing, I often heard the constant fights that went on in the adjoining apartment. The husband yells about killing his wife, and she screamed right back about leaving him or having him arrested. In addition, the people in the apartment above me have four noisy kids. Sometimes it seem as if football games were going on upstairs. The noise reach a high point when I got home from work, which also happened to be the time the kids return from school. If the kids and neighbors were not disturbing me, I always had one other person to depend on—the superintendent, who visits my apartment whenever he felt like it. He always had an excuse, such as checking the water pipes or caulking the windows. But each time he came, I suspect he just wants to get away from his noisy family, which occupied the basement apartment. I move out of that apartment as soon as I was able to.

REVIEW TEST 2

Change verbs as necessary in the following selection so that they are consistently in the past tense. Cross out each incorrect verb and write the correct form above it. You will need to make ten corrections in all.

As a kid, I never really enjoyed the public swimming pool. First, there were all sorts of rules that prevent me from having much fun in the water. One was that children under the age of fourteen had to be accompanied by an adult. I didn't like having to beg a parent or a neighbor to take me swimming every time I want to go. Another rule was that girls are not allowed in the water without bathing caps. The required bathing cap was so tight that it cause a heavy pressure mark on my forehead. Also, it often gives me a headache. Second, I wasn't a very good swimmer then. Most of the time I find myself hanging on to the side of the pool. And whenever I attempted a graceful dive, I end up doing a belly flop. Finally, many of the kids tease me. Some of them liked splashing water into my face, which force me to swallow chlorine and a dead bug or two. Even worse was the boy who sneaks up behind me all summer long to dump ice cubes down the back of my swimsuit.

CHAPTER 14

Additional Information about Verbs

Verb Tense

Verbs tell us the time of an action. The time that a verb shows is usually called *tense*. The most common tenses are the simple present, past, and future. In addition, there are nine other tenses that enable us to express more specific ideas about time than we could with the simple tenses alone. Following are the twelve verb tenses, with examples. Read them to increase your sense of the many different ways of expressing time in English.

www.mhhe.com/langan

Tenses	Examples
Present	I *work*.
	Jill *works*.
Past	Howard *worked* on the lawn.
Future	You *will work* overtime this week.
Present perfect	Gail *has worked* hard on the puzzle.
	They *have worked* well together.
Past perfect	They *had worked* eight hours before their shift ended.
Future perfect	The volunteers *will have worked* many unpaid hours.
Present progressive	I *am* not *working* today.
	You *are working* the second shift.
	The dryer *is* not *working* properly.
Past progressive	She *was working* outside.
	The plumbers *were working* here this morning.
Future progressive	The sound system *will be working* by tonight.
Present perfect progressive	Married life *has* not *been working* out for that couple.
Past perfect progressive	I *had been working* overtime until recently.
Future perfect progressive	My sister *will have been working* at that store for eleven straight months by the time she takes a vacation next week.

The perfect tenses are formed by adding *have, has,* or *had* to the past participle (the form of the verb that ends, usually, in *-ed*). The progressive tenses are formed by adding *am, is, are, was,* or *were* to the present participle (the form of the verb that ends in *-ing*). The perfect progressive tenses are formed by adding *have been, has been,* or *had been* to the present participle.

Certain tenses are explained in more detail on the following pages.

Present Perfect
(*have* or *has* + past participle)

The present perfect tense expresses an action that began in the past and has recently been completed or is continuing in the present.

The city *has* just *agreed* on a contract with the sanitation workers.

Tony's parents *have lived* in that house for twenty years.

Lola *has enjoyed* mystery novels since she was a little girl.

Past Perfect
(*had* + past participle)

The past perfect tense expresses a past action that was completed before another past action.

Lola *had learned* to dance by the time she was five.

The class *had* just *started* when the fire bell rang.

Bad weather *had* never *been* a problem on our vacations until last year.

Present Progressive
(*am, is,* or *are* + the *-ing* form)

The present progressive tense expresses an action still in progress.

I *am taking* an early train into the city every day this week.

Karl *is playing* softball over at the field.

The vegetables *are growing* rapidly.

Past Progressive
(*was* or *were* + the *-ing* form)

The past progressive expresses an action that was in progress in the past.

I *was spending* forty dollars a week on cigarettes before I quit.

Last week, the store *was selling* many items at half price.

My friends *were driving* over to pick me up when the accident occurred.

Using the Correct Verb Tense

For the sentences that follow, fill in the present or past perfect or the present or past progressive of the verb shown. Use the tense that seems to express the meaning of each sentence best.

EXAMPLE

park   This summer, Mickey ___is parking___ cars at a French restaurant.

dry   1. The afternoon sun was so hot it _____ our jeans in less than an hour.

plan   2. My parents _____ a trip to the seashore until they heard about the sharks.

grow   3. This year, Aunt Anita _____ tomatoes; she must have two hundred already.

throw   4. The pitcher _____ the ball to second; unfortunately, the runner was on third.

carve   5. Everyone at the dinner table continued to complain about the way Henry _____ the Thanksgiving turkey.

open   6. The excited child _____ all her birthday presents before her father could load his camera.

care   7. Erica answered an ad for a babysitter and now _____ for three children, two dogs, and twenty houseplants.

watch   8. Helen is a television athlete; she _____ almost every football and baseball game televised this year.

walk   9. The hiker _____ for over twenty miles before she stopped for a short rest.

try   10. Last winter my brothers _____ to get a job bagging groceries at the supermarket.

Verbals

Verbals are words formed from verbs. Verbals, like verbs, often express action. They can add variety to your sentences and vigor to your writing style. The three kinds of verbals are *infinitives, participles,* and *gerunds*.

www.mhhe.com/langan

Infinitive

An infinitive is *to* plus the base form of the verb.

I started *to practice*.

Don't try *to lift* that table.

I asked Russ *to drive* me home.

Participle

A participle is a verb form used as an adjective (a descriptive word). The present participle ends in -ing. The past participle ends in -ed or has an irregular ending.

Favoring his *cramped* leg, the *screaming* boy waded out of the pool.

The *laughing* child held up her *locked* piggy bank.

Using a shovel and a bucket, I scooped water out of the *flooded* basement.

Gerund

A gerund is the -ing form of a verb used as a noun.

Studying wears me out.

Playing basketball is my main pleasure during the week.

Through *jogging,* you can get yourself in shape.

ACTIVITY 2   **Using Infinitives, Participles, and Gerunds**

In the space beside each sentence, identify the italicized word as a participle (*P*), an infinitive (*I*), or a gerund (*G*).

> **HINT**   In item 1, *reclining* is used as a descriptive word.

_____   1.   Carmine preferred the *reclining* chair for his bad back.

_____   2.   Doctors believe that *walking* is one of the most beneficial forms of exercise.

_____   3.   Once the pan was hot enough, Granddad was ready *to cook* his famous blueberry pancakes.

_____   4.   It isn't *flying* that makes Elsa anxious but the airline food.

_____   5.   *Scratching* its back against a tree, the bear looked deceptively harmless.

_____   6.   *To make* the room more cheerful, Alice painted the dark cabinets yellow.

_____   7.   *Observing* gorillas' mating behavior is part of that zookeeper's job.

_____   8.   During the entire movie, the man continued *to talk* loudly on his cell phone.

_____   9.   My brother's *receding* hairline makes him look older than he really is.

_____ 10. At the front door of the hospital, workers found a blanket *containing* a healthy newborn baby.

Active and Passive Verbs

www.mhhe.com/langan

When the subject of a sentence performs the action of a verb, the verb is in the *active voice*. When the subject of a sentence receives the action of a verb, the verb is in the *passive voice*.

The passive form of a verb consists of a form of the verb *be* plus the past participle of the main verb. Look at the active and passive forms of the verbs below.

Active	Passive
Lola *ate* the vanilla pudding. (The subject, *Lola,* is the doer of the action.)	The vanilla pudding *was eaten* by Lola. (The subject, *pudding,* does not act. Instead, something happens to it.)
The plumber *replaced* the hot water heater. (The subject, *plumber,* is the doer of the action.)	The hot water heater *was replaced* by the plumber. (The subject, *heater,* does not act. Instead, something happens to it.)

In general, active verbs are more effective than passive verbs. Active verbs give your writing a simpler and more vigorous style. The passive form of verbs is appropriate, however, when the performer of an action is unknown or is less important than the receiver of the action. For example:

My house was vandalized last night.
(The performer of the action is unknown.)

Mark was seriously injured as a result of your negligence.
(The receiver of the action, *Mark,* is being emphasized.)

Making Sentences Active

ACTIVITY 3

Change the following sentences from passive voice to active voice. Note that in some cases you may have to add a subject.

EXAMPLES

The motorcycle was ridden by Tony.

Tony rode the motorcycle.

The basketball team was given a standing ovation.

The crowd gave the basketball team a standing ovation.

> **EXPLANATION** In the second example, a subject had to be added.

Verbals/Active and Passive Verbs

> **HINT** Who boarded the bus? Make him the subject of item 1.

1. The bus was boarded by a man with a live parrot on his shoulder.

   _____

   _____

2. The stained-glass window was broken by a large falling branch.

   _____

   _____

3. Baseballs for hospitalized children were autographed by the entire team.

   _____

   _____

4. The hotel was destroyed by a fire that started with a cigarette.

   _____

   _____

5. The pressures of dealing with life and death must be faced by doctors.

   _____

   _____

6. The missile was directed to its target by a sophisticated laser system.

   _____

   _____

7. The kitchen shelves were covered by a thick layer of yellowish grease.

   _____

   _____

8. Trash in the neighborhood park was removed by a group of volunteers.

   _____

   _____

9. Most of the escaped convicts were captured within a mile of the jail by the state police.

   _____

   _____

10. Prizes were awarded by the judges for hog-calling and stone-skipping.

   _____

   _____

REVIEW TEST

On a separate piece of paper, write three sentences for each of the following forms:

1. Present perfect tense

2. Past perfect tense

3. Present progressive tense

4. Past progressive tense

5. Infinitive

6. Participle

7. Gerund

8. Passive voice (when the performer of the action is unknown or is less important than the receiver of an action—see page 247)

Verbals/Active and Passive Verbs

Unclear	**Clear**
Our instructor did not explain the assignment, which made me angry. (Does *which* mean that the instructor's failure to explain the assignment made you angry, or that the assignment itself made you angry? Be clear.)	I was angry that our instructor did not explain the assignment.

ACTIVITY 1   Pronoun Reference

Rewrite each of the following sentences to make clear the vague pronoun reference. Add, change, or omit words as necessary.

EXAMPLE

Lana thanked Amy for the gift, which was very thoughtful of her.

Lana thanked Amy for the thoughtful gift.

 HINT   In item 1, what does *it* stand for?

1. Fran removed the blanket from the sofa bed and folded it up.

   _____

   _____

2. The defendant told the judge he was mentally ill.

   _____

   _____

3. Before the demonstration, they passed out signs for us to carry.

   _____

   _____

4. Cindy complained to Rachel that her boyfriend was being dishonest.

   _____

   _____

5. Because I didn't rinse last night's dishes, it smells like a garbage can.

   _____

   _____

6. The students watched a film on endangered species, which really depressed them.

   _____

   _____

7. The veterinarian said that if I find a tick on my dog, I should get rid of it immediately.

_____

_____

8. My sister removed the curtains from the windows so that she could wash them.

_____

_____

9. Richard said his acupuncture therapist could help my sprained shoulder, but I don't believe in it.

_____

_____

10. I discovered when I went to sell my old textbooks that they've put out new editions, and nobody wants to buy them.

_____

_____

Pronoun Agreement

www.mhhe.com/langan

A pronoun must agree in number with the word or words it replaces. If the word a pronoun refers to is singular, the pronoun must be singular; if the word is plural, the pronoun must be plural. (The word a pronoun refers to is known as the *antecedent*.)

Lola agreed to lend me her Coldplay albums.

The gravediggers sipped coffee during their break.

In the first example, the pronoun *her* refers to the singular word *Lola*; in the second example, the pronoun *their* refers to the plural word *gravediggers*.

Pronoun Agreement   ACTIVITY 2

Write the appropriate pronoun (*they, their, them, it*) in the blank space in each of the following sentences.

EXAMPLE

My credit cards got me into debt, so I burned _____them_____.

HINT   In item I, which word best takes the place of *the two girls?*

1. The two girls in identical dresses were surprised when _____ saw each other at the prom.

2. Flies often lay _____ eggs on the bodies of dead animals.

3. I put my family pictures in a photo album, but then I lost _____.

4. I used to collect baseball cards and comic books, but then I gave _____ to my little brother.

5. When the children are watching television, it's impossible to get _____ attention.

Indefinite Pronouns

www.mhhe.com/langan

The following words, known as *indefinite pronouns,* are always singular.

INDEFINITE PRONOUNS

(*-one* words)	(*-body* words)	
one	nobody	each
anyone	anybody	either
everyone	everybody	neither
someone	somebody	

Either of the apartments has *its* drawbacks

One of the girls lost *her* skateboard

Everyone in the class must hand in *his* paper tomorrow.

In each example, the pronoun is singular because it refers to one of the indefinite pronouns. There are two important points to remember about indefinite pronouns.

1: Using Gender-Appropriate Pronouns

The previous example suggests that everyone in the class is male. If the students were all female, the pronoun would be *her.* If the students were a mixed group of males and females, the pronoun form would be *his or her.*

Everyone in the class must hand in *his or her* paper tomorrow.

Some writers still follow the traditional practice of using *his* to refer to both men and women. Many now use *his or her* to avoid an implied sexual bias. Perhaps the best practice, though, is to avoid using either *his* or the somewhat awkward *his or her.* This can often be done by rewriting a sentence in the plural:

All students in the class must hand in *their* papers tomorrow.

Here are some examples of sentences that can be rewritten in the plural.

Singular: A young child is seldom willing to share her toys with others.

Plural: Young children are seldom willing to share their toys with others.

Singular: Anyone who does not wear his seat belt will be fined.

Plural: People who do not wear their seat belts will be fined.

Singular: A newly elected politician should not forget his or her campaign promises.

Plural: Newly elected politicians should not forget their campaign promises.

2: Using Plural Pronouns with Indefinite Pronouns

In informal spoken English, *plural* pronouns are often used with indefinite pronouns. Instead of saying

Everybody has *his or her* own idea of an ideal vacation.

we are likely to say

Everybody has *their* own idea of an ideal vacation.

Here are other examples:

Everyone in the class must pass in *their* papers.

Everybody in our club has *their* own idea about how to raise money.

No one in our family skips *their* chores.

In such cases, the indefinite pronouns are clearly plural in meaning. Also, the use of such plurals helps people avoid the awkward *his or her*. In time, the plural pronoun may be accepted in formal speech or writing. Until that happens, however, you should use the grammatically correct singular form in your writing. Note: some instructors *do* accept plural pronouns with indefinite pronouns; check with yours.

Using Pronouns Correctly	**ACTIVITY 3**

Underline the correct pronoun.

EXAMPLE

Neither of those houses has (its, their) own garage.

> **EXPLANATION:** *Neither* is a singular subject and requires a singular pronoun.

 HINT   In item I, *neither* requires a singular pronoun.

1. Neither of the men was aware that (his, their) voice was being taped.

2. One of the waiters was fired for failing to report all (his, their) tips.

3. We have three dogs, and each of them has (its, their) own bowl.

4. During the intermission, everyone had to wait a while for (her, their) turn to get into the ladies' room.

5. All of the presents on the table had tiny gold bows on (it, them).

6. Mr. Alvarez refuses to let anyone ride in his car without using (his or her, their) seat belt.

7. It seems that neither of the mothers is comfortable answering (her, their) teenager's questions about sex.

8. If anybody in the men's club objects to the new rules, (he, they) should speak up now.

9. Nobody on the women's basketball team had enough nerve to voice (her, their) complaints to the coach.

10. Before being allowed to go on the class trip, each student had to have (his or her, their) parents sign a permission form.

Pronoun Point of View

Pronouns should not shift their point of view unnecessarily. When writing a paper, be consistent in your use of first-, second-, or third-person pronouns.

Type of Pronoun	Singular	Plural
First-person pronouns	I (my, mine, me)	we (our, us)
Second-person pronouns	you (your)	you (your)
Third-person pronouns	he (his, him)	they (their, them)
	she (her)	
	it (its)	

TIP   Any person, place, or thing, as well as any indefinite pronoun such as *one*, *anyone*, *someone*, and so on (see page 254), is a third-person word.

For instance, if you start writing in the first-person *I*, don't jump suddenly to the second-person *you*. Or if you are writing in the third-person *they*, don't shift unexpectedly to *you*. Look at the following examples.

Inconsistent	**Consistent**
One reason that *I* like living in the city is that *you* always have a wide choice of sports events to attend. (The most common mistake people make is to let a *you* slip into their writing after they start with another pronoun.)	One reason that *I* like living in the city is that *I* always have a wide choice of sports events to attend.
Someone who is dieting should have the support of friends; *you* should also have plenty of willpower.	*Someone* who is dieting should have the support of friends; *he* or *she* should also have plenty of willpower.
Students who work while *they* are going to school face special challenges. For one thing, *you* seldom have enough study time.	Students who work while *they* are going to school face special challenges. For one thing, *they* seldom have enough study time.

Correcting Inconsistent Pronouns

ACTIVITY 4

Cross out inconsistent pronouns in the following sentences and write the correction above the error.

EXAMPLE

I work much better when the boss doesn't hover over ~~you~~ me with instructions on what to do.

> **HINT**   Since the sentence in item 1 begins in first person, change *your* to a first-person pronoun.

1. A good horror movie makes my bones feel like ice and gets your blood running cold.

2. People buy groceries from that supermarket because you know it has the best prices in the area.

3. One experience that almost everyone fears is when you have to speak in front of a crowd of people.

4. If students attend class regularly and study hard, you should receive good grades.

5. I drive on back roads instead of major highways because you can avoid traffic.

Pronoun Ref/ Agreement/ Point of View

6. The spread of many illnesses, such as the flu and common cold, could be reduced if people just washed your hands.

7. Andy enjoys watching soap operas because then you can worry about someone else's problems instead of your own.

8. Our street was so slippery after the ice storm that you could barely take a step without falling down.

9. Mrs. Almac prefers working the three-to-eleven shift because that way you can still have a large part of your day free.

10. All of us at work voted to join the union because we felt it would protect your rights.

REVIEW TEST 1

Underline the correct word in the parentheses.

1. Devan slammed the phone down on the table so hard that (it, the phone) broke.

2. During the boring movie, people started to squirm in (his or her, their) seats.

3. I love living alone because (you, I) never have to answer to anyone else.

4. Almost all the magazines I subscribe to arrive with (its, their) covers torn.

5. My father disagrees with my husband about almost everything because (he, my father) is so stubborn.

6. I like driving on that turnpike because (they, state officials) don't allow billboards there.

7. Neither one of the umpires wanted to admit that (he, they) had made a mistake.

8. When Ed went to the bank for a home improvement loan, (they, the loan officers) asked him for three credit references.

9. Even if you graduate from that business school, (they, the placement officers) don't guarantee they will find you a job.

10. Not one of the women in the audience was willing to raise (her, their) hand when the magician asked for a female volunteer.

Cross out the pronoun error in each sentence and write the correction in the space provided. Then circle the letter that correctly describes the type of error that was made.

EXAMPLES

~~Anyone~~ turning in their papers late will be penalized.

_____*Students*_____

Mistake in: a. pronoun reference   ⓑ pronoun agreement

When Clyde takes his son Paul to the park, ~~he~~ enjoys himself.

_____*Paul (or Clyde)*_____

Mistake in: ⓐ pronoun reference   b. pronoun point of view

From where we stood, ~~you~~ could see three states.

_____*we*_____

Mistake in: a. pronoun agreement   ⓑ pronoun point of view

1. A good salesperson knows that you should be courteous to customers.

    _____

    Mistake in: a. pronoun agreement   b. pronoun point of view

2. Neither of the girls who flunked bothered to bring their grades home.

    _____

    Mistake in: a. pronoun reference   b. pronoun agreement

3. When the shabbily dressed woman walked into the fancy hotel, they weren't very polite to her.

    _____

    Mistake in: a. pronoun agreement   b. pronoun reference

4. Nobody seems to add or subtract without their calculator anymore.

    _____

    Mistake in: a. pronoun agreement   b. pronoun point of view

5. Denise went everywhere with Nita until she moved to Texas last year.

    _____

    Mistake in: a. pronoun agreement   b. pronoun reference

6. Everyone on my street believes they saw a strange glow in the sky last night.

    _____

    Mistake in: a. pronoun agreement   b. pronoun point view

7. In baking desserts, people should follow the directions carefully or you are likely to end up with something unexpected.

_____

Mistake in: a. pronoun reference   b. pronoun point of view

8. When Jerry added another card to the delicate structure, it fell down.

_____

Mistake in: a. pronoun reference   b. pronoun point of view

9. Anyone who wants to join the car pool should leave their name with me.

_____

Mistake in: a. pronoun agreement   b. pronoun reference

10. Any working mother knows that you need at least a twenty-five-hour day.

_____

Mistake in: a. pronoun agreement   b. pronoun point of view

HINT   In item 10, you will also need to correct a verb form.

Pronoun Types

INTRODUCTORY ACTIVITY

In each pair, write a check beside the sentence that you think uses pronouns correctly.

Andy and *I* enrolled in a Web design course. _____

Andy and *me* enrolled in a Web design course. _____

The police officer pointed to my sister and *me*. _____

The police officer pointed to my sister and *I*. _____

Lola prefers men *whom* take pride in their bodies. _____

Lola prefers men *who* take pride in their bodies. _____

The players are confident that the league championship is *theirs'*.

_____

The players are confident that the league championship is *theirs*.

_____

Them concert tickets are too expensive. _____

Those concert tickets are too expensive. _____

Our parents should spend some money on *themself* for a change. _____

Our parents should spend some money on *themselves* for a

change. _____

Answers are on page 587.

Subject and Object Pronouns

Pronouns change their form depending on the place they occupy in a sentence. What follows is a list of subject and object pronouns:

Subject Pronouns	Object Pronouns
I	me
you	you (no change)
he	him
she	her
it	it (no change)
we	us
they	them

www.mhhe.com/langan

Subject Pronouns

Subject pronouns are subjects of verbs.

> *They* are getting tired. (*They* is the subject of the verb *are getting*.)

> *She* will decide tomorrow. (*She* is the subject of the verb *will decide*.)

> *We* organized the game. (*We* is the subject of the verb *organized*.)

Several rules for using subject pronouns and some common mistakes people make in using them are explained below.

Rule 1

Use a subject pronoun in a sentence with a compound (more than one) subject.

Incorrect	**Correct**
Nate and *me* went shopping yesterday.	Nate and *I* went shopping yesterday.
Him and *me* spent lots of money.	*He* and *I* spent lots of money.

If you are not sure which pronoun to use, try each pronoun by itself in the sentence. The correct pronoun will be the one that sounds right. For example, "*Me* went shopping yesterday" does not sound right; "*I* went shopping yesterday" does.

Rule 2

Use a subject pronoun after forms of the verb *be*. Forms of *be* include *am, are, is, was, were, has been, have been*, and others.

> It was *I* who telephoned.

> It may be *they* at the door.

> It is *she*.

The sentences above may sound strange and stilted to you, since this rule is seldom actually followed in conversation. When we speak with one another, forms such as "It was me," "It may be them," and "It is her" are widely accepted. In formal writing, however, the grammatically correct forms are still preferred. You can avoid having to use a subject pronoun after *be* simply by rewording a sentence. Here is how the preceding examples could be reworded:

I was the one who telephoned.

They may be at the door.

She is here.

Rule 3

Use subject pronouns after *than* or *as* when a verb is understood after the pronoun.

You read faster than I (read). (The verb *read* is understood after *I*.)

Tom is as stubborn as I (am). (The verb *am* is understood after *I*.)

We don't go out as much as they (do). (The verb *do* is understood after *they*.)

> **TIP**   Avoid mistakes by mentally adding the "missing" verb to the end of the sentence.

> **TIP**   Use object pronouns after *as* or *than* when a verb is not understood after the pronoun.
>
> The law applies to you as well as me.
>
> Our boss paid Monica more than me.

Object Pronouns

Object pronouns (*me, him, her, us, them*) are objects of verbs or prepositions. (Prepositions are connecting words such as *for, at, about, to, before, by, with,* and *of.* See also page 157.)

www.mhhe.com/langan

Raisa chose *me.* (*Me* is the object of the verb *chose.*)

We met *them* at the ballpark. (*Them* is the object of the verb *met.*)

Don't mention UFOs to *us.* (*Us* is the object of the preposition *to.*)

I live near *her.* (*Her* is the object of the preposition *near.*)

People are sometimes uncertain about what pronoun to use when two objects follow the verb.

Incorrect	**Correct**
I spoke to George and *he.*	I spoke to George and *him.*
She pointed at Linda and *I.*	She pointed at Linda and *me.*

Pronoun Types

If you are not sure which pronoun to use, try each pronoun by itself in the sentence. The correct pronoun will be the one that sounds right. For example, "I spoke to he" doesn't sound right; "I spoke to him" does.

ACTIVITY 1 — Identifying Subject and Object Pronouns

Underline the correct subject or object pronoun in each of the following sentences. Then show whether your answer is a subject or an object pronoun by circling the *S* or *O* in the margin.

 In item 1, the correct pronoun is the object of the preposition *to*.

S   O   1.   I left the decision to (her, she).

S   O   2.   (She, Her) and Louise look enough alike to be sisters.

S   O   3.   Just between you and (I, me), these rolls taste like sawdust.

S   O   4.   The certified letter was addressed to both (she, her) and (I, me).

S   O   5.   If (he, him) and Vic are serious about school, why are they absent so much?

S   O   6.   Practically everyone is better at crossword puzzles than (I, me).

S   O   7.   It was (they, them) who left the patio furniture outside during the rainstorm.

S   O   8.   The creature who climbed out of the coffin scared Boris and (I, me) half to death.

S   O   9.   (We, Us) tenants are organizing a protest against the dishonest landlord.

S   O   10. When we were little, my sister and (I, me) invented a secret language.

ACTIVITY 2 — Using Subject or Object Pronouns

For each sentence, write an appropriate subject or object pronoun in the space provided. Try to use as many different pronouns as possible.

 Along with *Gerald*, this pronoun is part of the sentence's subject in item 1.

1. Gerald and _____ forgot to lock the door the night our restaurant was robbed.

2. The referee disqualified Tyray and _____ for fighting.

3. I have seldom met two people as boring as _____ .

4. If you and _____ don't lose patience, we'll finish sanding this floor by tonight.

5. Our professor told _____ students that our final exam would be a take-home test.

6. Ernie and _____ drove on the interstate highway for ten hours with only one stop.

7. I don't follow sports as much as _____ .

8. You know better than _____ how to remove lipstick stains.

9. Maggie and _____ spent several hours yesterday looking for the lost puppy.

10. The store manager praised _____ for being the best cashiers in the department.

Relative Pronouns

Relative pronouns do two things at once. First, they refer to someone or something already mentioned in the sentence. Second, they start a short word group that gives additional information about this someone or something. Here is a list of relative pronouns:

RELATIVE PRONOUNS

who	which
whose	that
whom	

Here are some sample sentences:

The only friend *who* really understands me is moving away.

The child *whom* Ben and Arlene adopted is from Korea.

Chocolate, *which* is my favorite food, upsets my stomach.

I guessed at half the questions *that* were on the test.

In the example sentences, *who* refers to *friend*, *whom* refers to *child*, *which* refers to *chocolate*, and *that* refers to *questions*. In addition, each of the relative pronouns begins a group of words that describes the person or thing being referred to. For example, the words *whom Ben and Arlene adopted* tell which child the sentence is about, and the words *which is my favorite food* give added information about chocolate.

> **TIP**   Phrases using the relative pronoun *which* are set off by commas, while phrases using *that* are not.

Points to Remember about Relative Pronouns

- *Whose* means *belonging to whom.* Be careful not to confuse *whose* with *who's,* which means *who is.*

- *Who, whose,* and *whom* all refer to people. *Which* refers to things. *That* can refer to either people or things.

      I don't know *whose* book this is.

      Don't sit on the chair, *which* is broken.

      Let's elect a captain *who* cares about winning.

- *Who, whose, whom,* and *which* can also be used to ask questions. When they are used in this way, they are called *interrogative pronouns:*

      Who murdered the secret agent?

      Whose fingerprints were on the bloodstained knife?

      To *whom* have the detectives been talking?

      Which suspect is going to confess?

> **TIP**   In informal usage, *who* is generally used instead of *whom* as an interrogative pronoun. Informally, we can say or write, "*Who* are you rooting for in the game?" or "*Who* did the instructor fail?" More formal usage would call for *whom:* "*Whom* are you rooting for in the game?" "*Whom* did the instructor fail?"

- *Who* and *whom* are used differently. *Who* is a subject pronoun. Use *who* as the subject of a verb:

      Let's see *who* will be teaching the course.

Whom is an object pronoun. Use *whom* as the object of a verb or a preposition:

      Dr. Kelsey is the instructor *whom* I like best.

      I haven't decided for *whom* I will vote.

You may want to review the material on subject and object pronouns on pages 261–265.

Here is an easy way to decide whether to use *who* or *whom*. Find the first verb after the place where the *who* or *whom* will go. See if it already has a subject. If it does have a subject, use the object pronoun *whom*. If there is no subject, give it one by using the subject pronoun *who*. Notice how *who* and *whom* are used in the sentences that follow:

> I don't know *who* sideswiped my car.

> The suspect *whom* the police arrested finally confessed.

In the first sentence, *who* is used to give the verb *sideswiped* a subject. In the second sentence, the verb *arrested* already has a subject, *police*. Therefore, *whom* is the correct pronoun.

Identifying Correct Relative Pronouns   ACTIVITY 3

Underline the correct pronoun in each of the following sentences.

> **HINT**   *Who* refers only to people; it cannot refer to the word *activity* in item 1.

1. One activity (that, who) my father and I both enjoy is cooking.

2. On a bright, sunny day, some office buildings (who, that) have glass walls look like giant icicles.

3. My sister, (who, whom) loves ballet, walks around the house on her toes.

4. The new highway, (who, which) was supposed to lessen traffic jams, only made them worse.

5. The supervisor (who, whom) everybody dislikes was just given thirty days' notice.

Using Relative Pronouns   ACTIVITY 4

On a separate piece of paper, write five sentences using *who, whose, whom, which,* and *that.*

Possessive Pronouns

Possessive pronouns show ownership or possession.

> Clyde shut off the engine of *his* motorcycle.

> The keys are *mine.*

Following is a list of possessive pronouns:

www.mhhe.com/langan

POSSESSIVE PRONOUNS

my, mine	our, ours
your, yours	your, yours
his	their, theirs
her, hers	
its	

> **TIP**   A possessive pronoun *never* uses an apostrophe. (See also page 339.)
>
> **Incorrect**   **Correct**
>
> That coat is *hers'*.   That coat is *hers*.
>
> The card table is *theirs'*.   The card table is *theirs*.

ACTIVITY 5   Correcting Possessive Pronouns

Cross out the incorrect pronoun form in each of the sentences that follow. Write the correct form in the space at the left.

EXAMPLE

___My___   ~~Me~~ car has broken down again.

> **HINT**   The possessive pronoun *yours* never uses an apostrophe.

_____   1. Is this pen yours' or mine?

_____   2. Only relatives of him are allowed to visit while he is in the hospital.

_____   3. My sisters think that every new dress I buy is theirs' too.

_____   4. Are you going to eat all of you hamburger, or can I have half?

_____   5. The thermos that is mines is held together with duct tape.

Demonstrative Pronouns

Demonstrative pronouns point to or single out a person or thing. There are four demonstrative pronouns:

DEMONSTRATIVE PRONOUNS

this	these
that	those

Generally speaking, *this* and *these* refer to things close at hand; *that* and *those* refer to things farther away.

Is anyone using *this* spoon?

I am going to throw away *these* magazines.

I just bought *that* old white pickup at the curb.

Pick up *those* toys in the corner.

Do not use *them, this here, that there, these here,* or *those there* to point something out. Use only *this, that, these,* or *those.*

Incorrect	**Correct**
Them tires are badly worn.	*Those* tires are badly worn.
This here book looks hard to read.	*This* book looks hard to read.
That there candy is delicious.	*That* candy is delicious.
Those there squirrels are pests.	*Those* squirrels are pests.

Correcting Demonstrative Pronouns   ACTIVITY 6

Cross out the incorrect form of the demonstrative pronoun and write the correct form in the space provided.

EXAMPLE

Those   ~~Them~~ clothes need washing.

_____   1. This here town isn't big enough for both of us, Tex.

_____   2. Let's hurry and get them seats before someone else does.

_____   3. That there dress looked better on the hanger than it does on you.

_____   4. Let me try one of those there chocolates before they're all gone.

_____   5. Watch out for them potholes the next time you drive my car.

Pronoun Types

| ACTIVITY 7 | Using Demonstrative Pronouns |

Write four sentences using *this*, *that*, *these*, and *those*.

_____

_____

_____

_____

Reflexive Pronouns

Reflexive pronouns are pronouns that refer to the subject of a sentence. Here is a list of reflexive pronouns:

REFLEXIVE PRONOUNS

myself	ourselves
yourself	yourselves
himself	themselves
herself	
itself	

Sometimes a reflexive pronoun is used for emphasis:

You will have to wash the dishes *yourself*.

We *ourselves* are willing to forget the matter.

The manager *himself* stole merchandise from the store.

Points to Remember about Reflexive Pronouns

• In the plural, *-self* becomes *-selves*.

Lola covered *herself* with insect repellent.

They treated *themselves* to a Bermuda vacation.

• Be careful that you do not use any of the following incorrect forms as reflexive pronouns.

Incorrect	**Correct**
He believes in *hisself*.	He believes in *himself*.
We drove the children *ourself*.	We drove the children *ourselves*.
They saw *themself* in the fun house mirror.	They saw *themselves* in the fun house mirror.
I'll do it *meself*.	I'll do it *myself*.

Using Reflexive Prounouns

ACTIVITY 8

Cross out the incorrect form of the reflexive pronoun and write the correct form in the space at the left.

EXAMPLE

themselves   She believes that God helps those who help ~~themself.~~

> **HINT**   *Themself* is a not a standard word.

_____ 1. Shoppers stop and stare when they see themself on the closed-circuit TV overhead.

_____ 2. The restaurant owner herselve came out to apologize to us.

_____ 3. When my baby brother tries to dress hisself, the results are often funny.

_____ 4. The waiter was busy, so we poured ourself coffee from a nearby pot.

_____ 5. These housepainters seem to be making more work for theirselves than is necessary.

REVIEW TEST 1

Underline the correct pronoun in the parentheses.

1. The waitress finally brought Dolores and (I, me) our order.

2. I hope my son behaves (hisself, himself) at preschool.

3. Hand me (that, that there) fiddle and I'll play you a tune.

4. If it were up to (she, her), men wouldn't have the right to vote.

5. Roger, (who, whom) has worked here for almost thirty years, is ready to retire.

6. Vera dressed much more casually than (I, me) for the party.

7. You won't get very far on the bike unless you add more air to (its, it's) tires.

8. We'll be reading (this, this here) stack of books during the semester.

9. The apartment of (his, him) is next to a chemical processing plant.

10. The ducks circled the lake until they were sure that no one was around but (theirselves, themselves).

REVIEW TEST 2

Cross out the pronoun error in each sentence and write the correct form in the space at the left.

EXAMPLE

_____I_____   Terry and ~~me~~ have already seen the movie.

_____ 1. The chili that Manny prepared was too spicy for we to eat.

_____ 2. I checked them wires, but I couldn't find any faulty connections.

_____ 3. The old Chevy, who has 110,000 miles on it, is still running well.

_____ 4. When him and his partner asked me to step out of my car, I knew I was in trouble.

_____ 5. Omar realized that he would have to change the tire hisself.

_____ 6. My husband is much more sentimental than me.

_____ 7. I hope you'll come visit us in July while the garden is looking its' best.

_____ 8. The CDs are mines, but you can listen to them whenever you wish.

_____ 9. This here dog is friendly as long as you move slowly.

_____ 10. Vicky and me are going to the concert at the fairgrounds.

REVIEW TEST 3

On a separate piece of paper, write sentences that use each of the following words or phrases.

EXAMPLE

Peter and him _The coach suspended Peter and him._

1. yourselves
2. Jasmine and me
3. these
4. the neighbors and us
5. Victor and he
6. slower than I
7. its
8. which
9. you and I
10. Maria and them

SECTION

Modifiers and Parallelism

© Luc Cromheecke, used by permission .

Responding to Images

If you had to diagnose this real-life error in grammatical language, what might you call it? (Hint: It's one of the chapter titles in this section.)

273

4. more impulsive _____

_____

5. better _____

_____

6. cleverly _____

_____

7. worst _____

_____

8. rough _____

_____

9. most annoying _____

_____

10. sweeter _____

_____

Misplaced Modifiers

Chapter Preview

What Misplaced Modifiers Are and How to Correct Them

INTRODUCTORY ACTIVITY

Because of misplaced words, each of the sentences below has more than one possible meaning. In each case, see if you can explain both the intended meaning and the unintended meaning.

1. The farmers sprayed the apple trees wearing masks.

    Intended meaning: _____

    Unintended meaning: _____

2. The woman reached out for the faith healer who had a terminal disease.

    Intended meaning: _____

    Unintended meaning: _____

Answers are on page 588.

What Misplaced Modifiers Are and How to Correct Them

www.mhhe.com/langan

Misplaced modifiers are words that, because of awkward placement, do not describe the words the writer intended them to describe. Misplaced modifiers often confuse the meaning of a sentence. To avoid them, place words as close as possible to what they describe.

Misplaced Words	**Correctly Placed Words**
They could see the Goodyear blimp *sitting on the front lawn.* (The *Goodyear blimp* was sitting on the front lawn?)	Sitting on the front lawn, they could see the Goodyear blimp. (The intended meaning—that the Goodyear blimp was visible from the front lawn—is now clear.)
We had a hamburger after the movie, *which was too greasy for my taste.* (The *movie* was too greasy for my taste?)	After the movie, we had a hamburger, which was too greasy for my taste. (The intended meaning—that the hamburger was greasy—is now clear.)

Our phone *almost rang* fifteen times last night.

Our phone rang almost fifteen times last night.

(The phone *almost rang* fifteen times, but in fact did not ring at all?)

(The intended meaning—that the phone rang a little under fifteen times—is now clear.)

Other single-word modifiers to watch out for include *only, even, hardly, nearly,* and *often.* Such words should be placed immediately before the word they modify.

| ACTIVITY 1 | Fixing Misplaced Modifiers |

Underline the misplaced word or words in each sentence. Then rewrite the sentence, placing related words together to make the meaning clear.

EXAMPLE

Anita returned the hamburger to the supermarket <u>that was spoiled</u>.

Anita returned the hamburger that was spoiled to the supermarket.

 HINT   Who is *at the back of the cage* in item 1?

1. The tiger growled at a passerby at the back of his cage.

   _____

   _____

2. Lee hung colorful scarves over her windows made of green and blue silk.

   _____

   _____

3. We watched the fireworks standing on our front porch.

   _____

   _____

4. Jason almost has two hundred baseball cards.

   _____

   _____

5. The salesclerk exchanged the blue sweater for a yellow one with a smile.

   _____

   _____

6. We all stared at the man in the front row of the theater with curly purple hair.

   _____

   _____

7. I love the cookies from the bakery with the chocolate frosting.

_____

_____

8. The faculty decided to strike during their last meeting.

_____

_____

9. Larry looked on as his car burned with disbelief.

_____

_____

10. My cousin sent me instructions on how to get to her house in a letter.

_____

_____

Misplaced Modifiers

Placing Modifiers Correctly   ACTIVITY 2

Rewrite each sentence, adding the *italicized* words. Make sure that the intended meaning is clear and that two different interpretations are not possible.

EXAMPLE

I borrowed a pen for the essay test. (Insert *that ran out of ink.*)

For the essay test, I borrowed a pen that ran out of ink.

> **HINT**   Who has the *glass of lemonade* in item 1?

1. My mother sat lazily in the hot sun watching her grandchildren play. (Insert *with a glass of lemonade.*)

_____

_____

2. My father agreed to pay for the car repairs. (Insert *over the phone.*)

_____

_____

3. I found a note on the kitchen bulletin board. (Insert *from Jeff.*)

_____

_____

4. The fires destroyed the entire forest. (Insert *almost.*)

_____

_____

5. Jon read about how the American Revolution began. (Insert *during class*.)

_____

_____

REVIEW TEST 1

Write *M* for *misplaced* or *C* for *correct* in front of each sentence.

_____ 1. I keep a ten-dollar bill under the car seat for emergencies.

_____ 2. I keep a ten-dollar bill for emergencies under the car seat.

_____ 3. This morning, I planned my day in the shower.

_____ 4. In the shower this morning, I planned my day.

_____ 5. While skating, Bert ran over a dog's tail.

_____ 6. Bert ran over a dog's tail skating.

_____ 7. I could hear my neighbors screaming at each other through the apartment wall.

_____ 8. Through the apartment wall, I could hear my neighbors screaming at each other.

_____ 9. For the family reunion, we cooked hamburgers and hot dogs on an outdoor grill.

_____ 10. For the family reunion on an outdoor grill we cooked hamburgers and hot dogs.

_____ 11. Virgil visited the old house, still weak with the flu.

_____ 12. Virgil, still weak with the flu, visited the old house.

_____ 13. While still weak with the flu, Virgil visited the old house.

_____ 14. My teenage son nearly grew three inches last year.

_____ 15. My teenage son grew nearly three inches last year.

_____ 16. The instructor explained how to study for the final exam at the end of her lecture.

_____ 17. The instructor explained how to study at the end of her lecture for the final exam.

_____ 18. At the end of her lecture, the instructor explained how to study for the final exam.

_____ 19. In the library, I read that a deadly virus was spread through an air-conditioning system.

_____ 20. I read that a deadly virus was spread through an air-conditioning system in the library.

Underline the five misplaced modifiers in the following passage. Then, in the spaces that follow, show how you would correct them.

¹The young teenagers who almost hang out in our town library every night are becoming a major nuisance. ²They show up every weeknight and infuriate the otherwise mild librarians throwing spitballs and paper airplanes. ³Some of the kids hide out behind stacks of bookcases; others indulge in continual adolescent flirting games. ⁴The noise many of these teenagers make is especially offensive to some of the older library patrons, who often give looks to the clusters of young people that are disapproving. ⁵One time there was so much noise that a librarian lost her temper and yelled at some boys to be quiet or leave the library at the top of her lungs. ⁶The worst recent offense took place when a soaking-wet dog was led into the middle of the library by a junior high school boy with a stubby tail and the meanest-looking face one could ever imagine.

Sentence number: _____

Correction:

_____

Sentence number: _____

Correction:

_____

Sentence number: _____

Correction:

_____

Sentence number: _____

Correction:

_____

Sentence number: _____

Correction:

_____

_____

Dangling Modifiers

INTRODUCTORY ACTIVITY

Because of dangling modifiers, each of the sentences below has more than one possible meaning. In each case, see if you can explain both the intended meaning and the unintended meaning.

1. Munching leaves from a tall tree, the children were fascinated by the eighteen-foot-tall giraffe.

    Intended meaning: _____

    _____

    Unintended meaning: _____

    _____

2. Arriving home after ten months in the army, Michael's neighbors threw a block party for him.

    Intended meaning: _____

    _____

    Unintended meaning: _____

    _____

Answers are on page 589.

www.mhhe.com/langan

What Dangling Modifiers Are and How to Correct Them

A modifier that opens a sentence must be followed immediately by the word it is meant to describe. Otherwise, the modifier is said to be *dangling,* and the sentence takes on an unintended meaning. For example, look at this sentence:

> While sleeping in his backyard, a Frisbee hit Bill on the head.

The unintended meaning is that the *Frisbee* was sleeping in his backyard. What the writer meant, of course, was that *Bill* was sleeping in his backyard. The writer should have placed *Bill* right after the modifier, revising the rest of the sentence as necessary:

While sleeping in his backyard, *Bill* was hit on the head by a Frisbee.

The sentence could also be corrected by adding the missing subject and verb to the opening word group:

While *Bill* was sleeping in his backyard, a Frisbee hit him on the head.

Other sentences with dangling modifiers follow. Read the explanations of why they are dangling and look carefully at how they are corrected.

Dangling Modifiers

Dangling	**Correct**
Having almost no money, my survival depended on my parents.	Having almost no money, *I* depended on my parents for survival.
(*Who* has almost no money? The answer is not *survival* but *I*. The subject *I* must be added.)	*Or:* Since *I* had almost no money, I depended on my parents for survival.
Riding his bike, a German shepherd bit Tony on the ankle.	Riding his bike, *Tony* was bitten on the ankle by a German shepherd.
(*Who* is riding the bike? The answer is not *German shepherd*, as it unintentionally seems to be, but *Tony*. The subject *Tony* must be added.)	*Or:* While *Tony* was riding his bike, a German shepherd bit him on the ankle.
When trying to lose weight, all snacks are best avoided.	When trying to lose weight, *you* should avoid all snacks.
(*Who* is trying to lose weight? The answer is not *snacks* but *you* The subject *you* must be added.)	*Or:* When *you* are trying to lose weight, avoid all snacks.

These examples make clear two ways of correcting a dangling modifier. Decide on a logical subject and do one of the following:

1. Place the subject *within* the opening word group:

   Since *I* had almost no money, I depended on my parents for survival.

> **TIP**   In some cases an appropriate subordinating word such as *since* must be added, and the verb may have to be changed slightly as well.

2. Place the subject right *after* the opening word group:

   Having almost no money, *I* depended on my parents for survival.

Sometimes even more rewriting is necessary to correct a dangling modifier. What is important to remember is that a modifier must be placed as close as possible to the word that it modifies.

| ACTIVITY 1 | Correcting Dangling Modifiers |

Rewrite each sentence to correct the dangling modifier. Mark the one sentence that is correct with a *C*.

>   **HINT**   What is *hanging safely on a wall* in item 1?

1. Hanging safely on a wall, a security guard pointed to the priceless painting.

   _____

   _____

2. At the age of five, my mother bought me a chemistry set.

   _____

   _____

3. While it was raining, shoppers ran into the stores.

   _____

   _____

4. Having turned sour, I would not drink the milk.

   _____

   _____

5. Talking on the phone, my hot tea turned cold.

   _____

   _____

6. Piled high with dirty dishes, Pete hated to look at the kitchen sink.

   _____

   _____

7. Having locked my keys in the car, the police had to open it for me.

   _____

   _____

8. Drooping and looking all dried out, the children watered the plants.

   _____

   _____

9. After sitting through a long lecture, my foot was asleep.

   _____

   _____

10. Being late, stopping for coffee was out of the question.

   _____

   _____

Placing Modifiers Correctly   ACTIVITY 2

Complete the following sentences. In each case, a logical subject should follow the opening words.

EXAMPLE
   Checking the oil stick, _I saw that my car was a quart low._

1. While taking a bath, _____

2. Before starting the car, _____

3. Frightened by the noise in the basement, _____

4. Realizing it was late, _____

5. Though very expensive, _____

REVIEW TEST 1

Write *D* for *dangling* or *C* for *correct* in front of each sentence. Remember that the opening words are a dangling modifier if they are not followed immediately by a logical subject.

_____ 1. Burning quickly, the firefighters turned several hoses on the house.

_____ 2. Because the house was burning quickly, firefighters turned several hoses on it.

_____ 3. While focusing the camera, several people wandered out of view.

_____ 4. While I focused the camera, several people wandered out of view.

_____ 5. When I peered down from the thirtieth floor, the cars looked like toys.

_____ 6. Peering down from the thirtieth floor, the cars looked like toys.

_____ 7. The cars looked like toys peering down from the thirtieth floor.

_____ 8. Riding in the rear of the bus, the sudden starts and stops were sickening.

_____ 9. For passengers riding in the rear of the bus, the sudden starts and stops were sickening.

————— 10. Speaking excitedly, the phone seemed glued to Sara's ear.

————— 11. The phone seemed glued to Sara's ear as she spoke excitedly.

————— 12. In a sentimental frame of mind, the music brought tears to Beth's eyes.

————— 13. As Beth was in a sentimental frame of mind, the music brought tears to her eyes.

————— 14. When Helen suddenly became sick, I drove her to the doctor's office.

————— 15. Suddenly sick, I drove Helen to the doctor's office.

————— 16. The pancake was browned on one side, so Mark flipped it over.

————— 17. Browned on one side, Mark flipped the pancake over.

————— 18. Hanging by her teeth, the acrobat's body swung back and forth.

————— 19. Hanging by her teeth, the acrobat swung back and forth.

————— 20. While hanging by her teeth, the acrobat's body swung back and forth.

REVIEW TEST 2

Underline the five dangling modifiers in this passage. Then correct them in the spaces provided.

¹Have you ever thought about what life was like for the first generation of your family to come to America? ²Or have you wondered what your grandparents did for fun when they were your age? ³Family stories tend to be told for two or three generations and then disappear because no one ever records them. ⁴Using a tape recorder, these stories can be saved for the future. ⁵Here are some hints for conducting interviews with older members of your family. ⁶Thinking hard about what you really want to know, good questions can be prepared in advance. ⁷Try to put the people you interview at ease by reassuring them that you value what they have to say. ⁸Nervous about the tape recorder, stories might not come so easily to them otherwise. ⁹Remember that most people have never been interviewed before. ¹⁰Listening carefully to everything the person says, your interview will be more successful. ¹¹By respecting their feelings, your older relatives will be delighted to share their stories. ¹²The tapes you make will be valued by your family for many years to come.

Sentence number: _____

Correction:

_____

_____

Sentence number: _____

Correction:

_____

_____

Sentence number: _____

Correction:

_____

_____

Sentence number: _____

Correction:

_____

_____

Sentence number: _____

Correction:

_____

_____

Faulty Parallelism

INTRODUCTORY ACTIVITY

Read aloud each pair of sentences below. Write a check mark beside the sentence that reads more smoothly and clearly and sounds more natural.

Pair 1

_____ I use my TV remote control to change channels, to adjust the volume, and for turning the set on and off.

_____ I use my TV remote control to change channels, to adjust the volume, and to turn the set on and off.

Pair 2

_____ One option the employees had was to take a cut in pay; the other was longer hours of work.

_____ One option the employees had was to take a cut in pay; the other was to work longer hours.

Pair 3

_____ The refrigerator has a cracked vegetable drawer, one of the shelves is missing, and a strange freezer smell.

_____ The refrigerator has a cracked vegetable drawer, a missing shelf, and a strange freezer smell.

Answers are on page 589.

www.mhhe.com/langan

Parallelism Explained

Words in a pair or series should have parallel structure. By balancing the items in a pair or series so that they have the same kind of structure, you will make the sentence clearer and easier to read. Notice how the parallel sentences that follow read more smoothly than the nonparallel ones.

Nonparallel (Not Balanced)	Parallel (Balanced)
Brit spends her free time reading, listening to music, and she works in the garden.	Brit spends her free time reading, listening to music, and working in the garden. (A balanced series of -ing words: *reading, listening, working.*)
After the camping trip I was exhausted, irritable, and wanted to eat.	After the camping trip I was exhausted, irritable, and hungry. (A balanced series of descriptive words: *exhausted, irritable, hungry.*)
My hope for retirement is to be healthy, to live in a comfortable house, and having plenty of money.	My hope for retirement is to be healthy, to live in a comfortable house, and to have plenty of money. (A balanced series of *to* verbs: *to be, to live, to have.*)
Nightly, Fred puts out the trash, checks the locks on the doors, and the burglar alarm is turned on.	Nightly, Fred puts out the trash, checks the locks on the doors, and turns on the burglar alarm. (Balanced verbs and word order: *puts out the trash, checks the locks, turns on the burglar alarm.*)

Balanced sentences are not a skill you need to worry about when you are writing first drafts. But when you rewrite, you should try to put matching words and ideas into matching structures. Such parallelism will improve your writing style.

Using Parallelism   ACTIVITY 1

The one item in each list that is not parallel in form to the other items is crossed out. In the space provided, rewrite that item in parallel form. The first one has been done for you as an example.

1. fresh food

   attractive setting

   ~~service that is fast~~

   fast service
   _____

2. screaming children

   dogs that howl

   blaring music

   _____

3. slow

   speaks rudely

   careless

   _____

4. to hike

   swimming

   boating

   _____

5. noisy neighbors

   high rent

   security that is poor

   _____

8. healthy soups

   tasty sandwiches

   desserts that are inexpensive

   _____

6. cleaning of the apartment

   paid the bills

   did the laundry

   _____

9. under the desk drawers

   the floor of the closet

   behind the bedroom curtains

   _____

7. looking good

   to have fun

   feeling fine

   _____

10. works at the supermarket

    member of the church choir

    coaches the Little League team

    _____

ACTIVITY 2 | **Correcting Nonparallel Sentences**

The unbalanced part of each sentence is *italicized.* Rewrite this part so that it matches the rest of the sentence.

EXAMPLE

In the afternoon, I changed two diapers, ironed several shirts, and *was watching* soap operas. watched _____

1. Taiyaba dropped a coin into the slot machine, pulled the lever, and *was waiting* to strike it rich.

   _____

2. Studying a little each day is more effective than *to cram.*

   _____

3. Many old people fear loneliness, *becoming ill,* and poverty.

   _____

4. My pet peeves are screeching chalk, *buses that are late,* and dripping sinks.

   _____

5. The magazine cover promised stories on losing weight quickly, *how to attract* a rich spouse, and finding the perfect haircut.

   _____

6. As smoke billowed around her, Paula knew her only choices were to jump or *suffocation.*

   _____

7. The principal often pestered students, yelled at teachers, and *was interrupting* classes.

   _____

8. People immigrate to America with hopes of finding freedom, happiness, and *in order to become financially secure.*

   _____

9. Once inside the zoo gates. Julio could hear lions roaring, *the chirping of birds,* and elephants trumpeting.

   _____

10. As a child, I had nightmares about a huge monster that came out of a cave, *was breathing fire,* and wanted to barbecue me.

    _____

Writing Parallel Sentences   ACTIVITY 3

Complete the following statements. The first two parts of each statement are parallel in form; the part that you add should be parallel in form as well.

EXAMPLE

Three things I like about myself are my sense of humor, my thoughtfulness, and <u>my self-discipline.</u>

1. I always celebrate my birthday by sleeping late, eating a good dinner, and _____

   _____

2. When Anita gets home from work, she likes to kick off her shoes, turn on some soft music, and _____

   _____

3. Despite the salesman's pitch, I could see that his "wonderful" used car had worn tires, rusting fenders, and _____

   _____

4. Trying to realize that it was only a machine, Tina sat down in front of the computer, took a deep breath, and _____

   _____

5. Three qualities I look for in a friend are loyalty, a sense of humor, and

   _____

   _____

ACTIVITY 4   Working Together

Part A: Editing and Rewriting

Working with a partner, read carefully the short paragraph below and cross out the five instances of faulty parallelism. Then use the space provided to correct the instances of faulty parallelism. Feel free to discuss the rewrite quietly with your partner and refer back to the chapter when necessary.

> Running is an exercise that can be good for you mentally, physically, and also be helpful for your emotions. A beginning runner should keep three things in mind: the warm-up session, the actual time that you are running, and the cool-down period. Never start a run without first having warmed up through stretching exercises. Stretching reduces muscle stiffness, decreases the possibility of injury, and it's a good method to gradually increase the heart rate. During the run itself, move at a comfortable pace. Your breathing should be steady and with depth. Finally, remember to cool down after a run. An adequate cool-down period allows time for the body to relax and the normalizing of the heart rate.

_____

_____

_____

_____

_____

_____

_____

_____

_____

_____

Part B: Creating Sentences

Working with a partner, make up your own short test on faulty parallelism, as directed.

1. Write a sentence that includes three things you want to do tomorrow. One of those things should not be in parallel form. Then correct the faulty parallelism.

    Nonparallel _____

    _____

    Parallel _____

    _____

2. Write a sentence that names three positive qualities of a person you like or three negative qualities that you don't like.

    Nonparallel _____

    _____

    Parallel _____

    _____

3. Write a sentence that includes three everyday things that annoy you.

    Nonparallel _____

    _____

    Parallel _____

    _____

REFLECTIVE ACTIVITY

1. Look at the paragraph that you just revised. How does parallel form improve the paragraph?

2. How would you evaluate your own use of parallel form? When you write, do you use it almost never, at times, or often? How would you benefit from using it more?

REVIEW TEST 1

Faulty Parallelism

Cross out the unbalanced part of each sentence. Then rewrite the unbalanced part so that it matches the other item or items in the sentence.

EXAMPLE

I enjoy watering the grass and ~~to work~~ in the garden.

working _____

1. When someone gives you advice, do you listen, laugh, or are you just ignoring it?

    _____

2. After finding an apartment, we signed a lease, made a deposit, and preparing to move in.

    _____

3. The little girl came home from school with a tear-streaked face, a black eye, and her shirt was torn.

    _____

4. Ruby watched television, was talking on the phone, and studied all at the same time.

    _____

5. My Halloween shopping list included one bottle of blue nail polish, fake blood, and a wig that was colored purple.

    _____

6. Carmen went to class prepared to take notes, to volunteer answers, and with questions to ask.

    _____

7. The severe thunderstorm brought winds that were strong, dangerous lightning, and heavy rain to the entire county.

    _____

8. When I got back from vacation, my refrigerator contained rotting vegetables, milk that was soured, and moldy cheese.

    _____

9. The guide demonstrated how colonial Americans made iron tools, crushed grain for flour, and were making their own cloth.

    _____

10. When my roommate blasts her stereo, I shut her door, put cotton in my ears, and am running the vacuum cleaner.

    _____

REVIEW TEST 2

Each group of sentences contains two errors in parallelism. Underline these errors. Then, on the lines below, rewrite each item that doesn't match to make it parallel with the other item or items in the sentence.

1. When Phil left for work, he felt bright and cheerful. But by midafternoon he was coughing, wheezing, and shivers ran throughout his body. He left work, drove home, and was crawling into bed, where he stayed for the next four days.

    a. _____

    b. _____

2. I never spend money on fancy wrapping paper. When people get a present, they generally want to rip off the paper and be looking at what's inside. So I wrap my gifts in either plain brown grocery bags or Sunday comics that are colorful.

    a. _____

    b. _____

3. Failing students can be kinder than to pass them. There is little benefit to passing a student to a level of work he or she can't do. In addition, it is cruel to graduate a student from high school who has neither the communication skills nor the skills at math needed to get along in the world.

a. _____

b. _____

4. The little boy drew back from his new babysitter. Her long red nails, black eye makeup, and jewelry that jangled all frightened him. He was sure she was either a bad witch or a queen who was evil.

    a. _____

    b. _____

5. An actress stopped in the middle of a Broadway show and scolded flash photographers in the audience. She said they can either have a photo session or they can be enjoying the show, but they can't do both. The photographers sank down in their seats, their cameras were put away, and quietly watched the show.

    a. _____

    b. _____

REVIEW TEST 3

Cross out the five nonparallel parts in the following passage. Correct them in the spaces between the lines.

When a few people in one community decided to form a homeowners' association, many of their neighbors were skeptical. Some objected to stirring things up, and others were feeling the dues were too high. But many neighbors joined, and their first big success was a garage sale. They scheduled a day for everybody in the neighborhood to bring unwanted items to a community center. Big appliances and other items that are heavy were picked up by volunteers with trucks. The association promoted the sale by placing ads in newspapers and with the distribution of fliers at local shopping centers. Dozens of families took part. After that, the association helped plant trees, start a Crime Watch Program, and in repairing cracked sidewalks. Members now receive discounts from local merchants and theater owners. This association's success has inspired many more neighbors to join and people in other neighborhoods, who are starting their own organizations.

Sentence Variety II

Like Chapter 9, this chapter will show you a variety of ways to write effective and varied sentences. You will learn more about the many ways you can express your ideas. The practices here will also reinforce much of what you have learned in this section about modifiers and the use of parallelism.

-ing Word Groups

Use an *-ing* word group at some point in a sentence. Here are examples:

> The doctor, *hoping* for the best, examined the X-rays.

> *Jogging* every day, I soon raised my energy level.

> **TIP** More information about *-ing* words, also known as *present participles*, appears on page 246.

ACTIVITY 1 | **Combining Sentences with -ing Words**

Combine each pair of sentences below into one sentence by using an *-ing* word and omitting repeated words. Use a comma or commas to set off the *-ing* word group from the rest of the sentence.

EXAMPLE

• The diesel truck chugged up the hill.

• It spewed out smoke.

  Spewing out smoke, the diesel truck chugged up the hill.

or The diesel truck, spewing out smoke, chugged up the hill.

1. • The tourists began to leave the bus.

   • They picked up their cameras.

   _____

   _____

2. • I was almost hit by a car.

   • I was jogging on the street.

   _____

   _____

3. • Barbara untangled her snarled hair from the brush.

   • She winced with pain.

   _____

   _____

4. • The singer ran to the front of the stage.

   • She waved her arms at the excited crowd.

   _____

   _____

5. • The team braced itself for a last-ditch effort.

   • It was losing by one point with thirty seconds left to play.

   _____

   _____

Using -ing Word Groups

ACTIVITY 2

On a separate piece of paper, write five sentences of your own that contain *-ing* word groups.

-ed Word Groups

Use an *-ed* word group at some point in a sentence. Here are examples:

Tired of studying, I took a short break.

Mary, *amused* by the joke, told it to a friend.

I opened my eyes wide, *shocked* by the red "F" on my paper.

> **TIP**   More information about *-ed* words, also known as *past participles*, appears on page 246.

Combining Sentences with -ed Words

ACTIVITY 3

Combine each of the following pairs of sentences into one sentence by using an *-ed* word and omitting repeated words. Use a comma or commas to set off the *-ed* word group from the rest of the sentence.

EXAMPLE

- Tim woke up with a start.

- He was troubled by a dream.

  Troubled by a dream, Tim woke up with a start.

  or Tim, troubled by a dream, woke up with a start.

1. • Mary sat up suddenly in bed.

   • She was startled by a thunderclap.

   _____

   _____

2. • My parents decided to have a second wedding.

   • They have been married for fifty years.

   _____

   _____

3. • Erica wouldn't leave her car.

   • She was frightened by the large dog near the curb.

   _____

   _____

4. • The old orange felt like a marshmallow.

   • It was dotted with mold.

   _____

   _____

5. • Ernie made a huge sandwich and popped popcorn.

   • He was determined to have plenty to eat during the movie.

   _____

   _____

ACTIVITY 4   Using -*ed* Word Groups

On a separate piece of paper, write five sentences of your own that contain -*ed* word groups.

-*ly* Openers

Use an -*ly* word to open a sentence. Here are examples:

Gently, he mixed the chemicals together.

Anxiously, the contestant looked at the game clock.

Skillfully, the quarterback rifled a pass to his receiver.

TIP   More information about *-ly* words, which are also known as *adverbs*, appears on page 277.

Combining Sentences with *-ly* Words

Combine each of the following pairs of sentences into one sentence by starting with an *-ly* word and omitting repeated words. Place a comma after the opening *-ly* word.

EXAMPLE

- I gave several yanks to the starting cord of the lawn mower.
- I was angry.

  Angrily, I gave several yanks to the starting cord of the lawn mower.

HINT   Begin your revised sentence in item 1 with *Noisily.*

1. • We ate raw carrots and celery sticks.
   • We were noisy.

   _____

   _____

2. • Cliff spoke to his sobbing little brother.
   • He was gentle.

   _____

   _____

3. • The father picked up his baby daughter.
   • He was tender.

   _____

   _____

4. • I paced up and down the hospital corridor.
   • I was anxious.

   _____

   _____

5. • Anita repeatedly dived into the pool to find her engagement ring.
   • She was frantic.

   _____

   _____

Sentence Variety

| ACTIVITY 6 | Using -*ly* Words |

On a separate piece of paper, write five sentences of your own that begin with -*ly* words.

To Openers

Use a *to* word group to open a sentence. Here are examples:

> *To* succeed in that course, you must attend every class.
>
> *To* help me sleep better, I learned to quiet my mind through meditation.
>
> *To* get good seats, we went to the game early.

> **TIP** The combination of *to* and a verb, also known as an *infinitive*, is explained on page 245.

| ACTIVITY 7 | Combining Sentences with *to* Word Groups |

Combine each of the following pairs of sentences into one sentence by starting with a *to* word group and omitting repeated words. Use a comma after the opening *to* word group.

EXAMPLE

- I fertilize the grass every spring.
- I want to make it greener.

  To make the grass greener, I fertilize it every spring.

> In item 1, your combined sentence should omit these words: *she did this.*

1. • Sally put a thick towel on the bottom of the tub.

   • She did this to make the tub less slippery.

   _____

   _____

2. • We now keep our garbage in the garage.

   • We do this to keep raccoons away.

   _____

   _____

3. • Bill pressed two fingers against the large vein in his neck.

   • He did this to count his pulse.

   _____

   _____

4. • My aunt opens her dishwasher when it begins drying.

   • She does this to steam her face.

   _____

   _____

5. • We looked through our closets for unused clothing.

   • We did this to help out the homeless.

   _____

   _____

Using *to*   ACTIVITY 8

On a separate piece of paper, write five sentences of your own that begin with *to* word groups.

Prepositional Phrase Openers

Use prepositional phrase openers. Here are examples:

> *From the beginning,* I disliked my boss.
>
> *In spite of her work,* she failed the course.
>
> *After the game,* we went to a movie.

> **TIP**   Prepositional phrases include words such as *in, from, of, at, by,* and *with.* A list of common prepositions appears on page 157.

Combining Sentences by Opening with Prepositional Phrases   ACTIVITY 9

Combine each of the following groups of sentences into one sentence by omitting repeated words. Start each sentence with a suitable prepositional phrase and put the other prepositional phrases in places that sound right. Generally, you should use a comma after the opening prepositional phrase.

EXAMPLE

   • A fire started.

   • It did this at 5:00 a.m.

   • It did this inside the garage.

   At 5:00 a.m., a fire started inside the garage.

> **HINT**   Begin item 1's sentence with *About once a week.*

1. • We have dinner with my parents.
    • We do this about once a week.
    • We do this at a restaurant.

    _____

    _____

2. • I put the dirty cups away.
    • I did this before company came.
    • I put them in the cupboard.

    _____

    _____

3. • My eyes roamed.
    • They did this during my English exam.
    • They did this around the room.
    • They did this until they met the instructor's eye.

    _____

    _____

4. • The little boy drew intently.
    • He did this in a comic book.
    • He did this for twenty minutes.
    • He did this without stopping once.

    _____

    _____

5. • A playful young orangutan wriggled.
    • He did this at the zoo.
    • He did this in a corner.
    • He did this under a paper sack.

    _____

    _____

ACTIVITY 10   Using Prepositional Phrases

On a separate piece of paper, write five sentences of your own, each beginning with a prepositional phrase and containing at least one other prepositional phrase.

Series of Items

Use a series of items. Following are two of the many items that can be used in a series: adjectives and verbs.

Adjectives in Series

Adjectives are descriptive words. Here are examples:

The *husky young* man sanded the *chipped, weather-worn* paint off the fence.

Husky and *young* are adjectives that describe *man; chipped* and *weather-worn* are adjectives that describe *paint*. More information about adjectives appears in Appendix B.

Using Adjectives in a Series	ACTIVITY 11

Combine each of the following groups of sentences into one sentence by using adjectives in a series and omitting repeated words. Use a comma between adjectives only when *and* inserted between them sounds natural.

EXAMPLE

- I sewed a set of buttons onto my coat.
- The buttons were shiny.
- The buttons were black.
- The coat was old.
- The coat was green.

   I sewed a set of shiny black buttons onto my old green coat.

 HINT   Begin the sentence in item 1 with *The old, peeling shingles.*

1. • The shingles blew off the roof during the storm.
   • The shingles were old.
   • The shingles were peeling.
   • The storm was blustery.

   _____

   _____

2. • The dancer whirled across the stage with his partner.
   • The dancer was lean.
   • The dancer was powerful.
   • The partner was graceful.
   • The partner was elegant.

   _____

   _____

3. • A rat scurried into the kitchen of the restaurant.
   • The rat was large.
   • The rat was furry.
   • The kitchen was crowded.

   _____

   _____

4. • The moon lit up the sky like a streetlamp.
   • The moon was full.
   • The moon was golden.
   • The sky was cloudy.
   • The streetlamp was huge.
   • The streetlamp was floating.

   _____

   _____

5. • The doorbell of the house played a tune.
   • The doorbell was oval.
   • The doorbell was plastic.
   • The house was large.
   • The house was ornate.
   • The tune was loud.
   • The tune was rock.

   _____

   _____

ACTIVITY 12   **Writing with Adjectives in Series**

On a separate piece of paper, write five sentences of your own that contain a series of adjectives.

Verbs in Series

Verbs are words that express action. Here are examples:

In my job as a cook's helper, I *prepared* salads, *sliced* meat and cheese, and *made* all kinds of sandwiches.

Basic information about verbs appears in Appendix A.

Combining Sentences with Verbs in a Series

ACTIVITY 13

Combine each group of sentences below into one sentence by using verbs in a series and omitting repeated words. Use a comma between verbs in a series.

EXAMPLES

- In the dingy bar, Sam shelled peanuts.
- He sipped a beer.
- He talked up a storm with friends.

  In the dingy bar, Sam shelled peanuts, sipped a beer, and talked up a

  storm with friends.

 HINT   What three things did the dog do in item 1?

1. • The flea-ridden dog rubbed itself against the fence.
   • It bit its tail.
   • It scratched its neck with its hind leg.

   _____

   _____

2. • I put my homework on the table.
   • I made a cup of coffee.
   • I turned the radio up full blast.

   _____

   _____

3. • The driver stopped the school bus.
   • He walked to the back.
   • He separated two children.

   _____

   _____

4. • I rolled up my sleeve.
   • I glanced at the nurse nervously.
   • I shut my eyes.
   • I waited for the worst to be over.

   _____

   _____

Sentence Variety

5.
  • The parents applauded politely at the program's end.
  • They looked at their watches.
  • They exchanged looks of relief.
  • They reached for their coats.

  _____

  _____

ACTIVITY 14 — Using Verbs in Series

On a separate piece of paper, write five sentences of your own that use verbs in a series.

> **TIP** The chapter on parallelism (pages 292–299) gives you practice in some of the other kinds of items that can be used in a series.

REVIEW TEST 1

Combine each group of short sentences into one sentence. Various combinations are possible. Choose the combination that reads most smoothly and clearly and that sounds most appropriate in the context of the surrounding sentences.

> **HINT** In combining short sentences into one sentence, omit repeated words where necessary. Use separate paper. The story continues in the next review test.

Dracula's Revenge
  • Mickey Raines had a dislike.
  • The dislike was of horror movies.
  • His friends were different.
  • They loved to see such movies.
  • They would always invite Mickey to go with them.
  • He would always refuse.
  • He thought horror films were stupid.
  • The actors were covered with fake blood.
  • They were pretending to writhe in agony.

- Mickey thought their behavior was disgusting.

- He did not think their behavior was frightening.

- Once his friends persuaded him to come with them.

- They went to see a movie.

- The movie was called *Halloween 14—The Horror Continues*.

- Mickey found it ridiculous.

- He laughed aloud through parts of the movie.

- They were the scariest parts.

- His friends were embarrassed.

- They were so embarrassed they moved.

- They moved away from him.

- They moved to another part of the theater.

- Then one night Mickey was alone.

- He was alone in his house.

- His mother was out for the evening.

- He turned on the television.

- A movie was playing.

- It was called *Nosferatu*.

- It was the original film version of the Dracula story.

- The film version was silent.

- It was made in Germany.

- It was made in 1922.

REVIEW TEST 2

Combine each group of short sentences into one sentence. Various combinations are possible. Choose the combination that reads most smoothly and clearly and that sounds most appropriate in the context of the surrounding sentences.

> **HINT**   In combining short sentences into one sentence, omit repeated words where necessary. Use a separate piece of paper. The story continues from the previous review test.

- The movie was not gory at all.
- There were no teenage girls in it getting chased.
- There were no teenage girls in it getting murdered.

- The villain was a vampire.
- He was hideous.
- He was shriveled.
- He was terrifying.

- His victims did not die.
- His victims grew weaker.
- They grew weaker after every attack.

- The vampire reminded Mickey of a parasite.
- The parasite was terrible.
- It was a dead thing.
- It was feeding off the living.

- Mickey trembled.
- He was trembling at the thought of such a creature.
- It could be lurking just out of sight.
- It could be lurking in the darkness.

- Then he heard a scraping noise.
- The noise was at the front door.
- He almost cried out in terror.

- The door opened quickly.
- Cold air rushed in.
- His mother appeared.
- She was back from her date.

- His mother smiled at him.
- She called out, "Hello."
- She paused in the foyer to take off her coat.

- Mickey was relieved to see her.
- His relief was enormous.
- He rushed up to greet her.

- The spell of the movie was broken.
- Mickey locked the door on the night.

Sentence Variety

SECTION

Punctuation and Mechanics

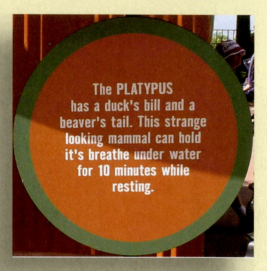

Responding to Images

How does each of the signs above misuse punctuation, capitalization, and/or mechanics—and how is the direction or information in each sign changed or confused because of this error or errors? Have you seen similar mistakes in signs posted on campus? On the road? In a restaurant? In a newspaper or book?

Paper Format

INTRODUCTORY ACTIVITY

Check the paper opening below that seems clearer and easier to read.

_____ A

	Dangers of Prescription Drugs
	Careless consumers can harm themselves with
	prescription drugs. To begin with, consumers should always
	be aware of the possible side effects of a prescription drug.

_____ B

	"dangers of prescription drugs"
	Careless consumers can harm themselves with prescription drugs.
	To begin with, consumers should always be aware of the possible
	side effects of a prescription drug. They should take the time.

What are four reasons for your choice?

_____

_____

_____

_____

Answers are on page 590.

Guidelines for Preparing a Paper

Here are guidelines to follow in preparing a paper for an instructor.

1. Use standard letter-sized 8½ by 11 paper.

2. Leave wide margins (1 to 1½ inches) all around the paper. In particular, do not crowd the right-hand or bottom margin. This white space makes your paper more readable and leaves the instructor room for comments.

3. Always use black as your font color, and choose a font style that is easy to read, such as Times New Roman. Avoid fancy or distracting colors and fonts. Make sure the type is large enough to be readable but not overwhelming. Most instructors prefer fonts in the 10–12 point range.

4. If you write by hand (your instructor permits it):
   - Use a pen with blue or black ink (*not* a pencil).
   - Be careful not to overlap letters and not to make decorative loops on letters.
   - On narrow-ruled paper, write on every other line.
   - Make all your letters distinct. Pay special attention to *a, e, i, o,* and *u*—five letters that people sometimes write illegibly.

5. Center the title of your paper on the first line of the first page. Do not put quotation marks around the title. Do not underline the title. Capitalize all the major words in a title, including the first word. Short connecting words within a title, such as *of, for, the, in, to,* and all prepositions, are not capitalized.

6. Skip a line between the title and the first line of your text. Indent the first line of each paragraph about five spaces (half an inch) from the left-hand margin.

7. Make commas, periods, and other punctuation marks firm and clear. Leave a slight space after each period.

8. If you break a word at the end of a line, break only between syllables. Do not break words of one syllable.

9. Put your name, date, and course number where your instructor asks for them.

Remember these points about the title and the first sentence of your paper.

10. The title should be one or several words that tell what the paper is about. It should usually *not* be a complete sentence. For example, if you are writing a paper about your jealous sister, the title could simply be "My Jealous Sister."

11. Do not rely on the title to help explain the first sentence of your paper. The first sentence must be independent of the title. For instance, if the title of your paper is "My Jealous Sister," the first sentence should *not* be, "She has been this way as long as I can remember." Rather, the first sentence might be, "My sister has always been a jealous person."

Paper Format

Correcting Formatting Errors   ACTIVITY 1

Identify the mistakes in format in the following lines from a student composition. Explain the mistakes in the spaces provided. One mistake is described for you as an example.

	"Being a younger sister"
	When I was young, I would gladly have donated my older sister to ano-
	ther family. First of all, most of my clothes were hand-me-downs. I ra-
	rely got to buy anything new to wear. My sister took very good care
	of her clothes,which only made the problem worse. Also, she was always
	very critical of everything.

1. Break words at correct syllable divisions (an-other). _____

2. _____

3. _____

4. _____

5. _____

6. _____

Writing Titles   ACTIVITY 2

As already stated, a title should tell in several words what a paper is about.
Often a title can be based on the sentence that expresses the main idea of
a paper.

   Following are five main-idea sentences from student papers. Write a
suitable specific title for each paper, basing the title on the main idea.

EXAMPLE

   Title: Aging Americans as Outcasts _____

Our society treats aging Americans as outcasts in many ways.

 HINT   What is a three-word subject for the paper in item 1?

1. Title: _____

   Pets offer a number of benefits to their owners.

2. Title: _____

   Since I have learned to budget carefully, I no longer run out of money at
   the end of the week.

3. Title: _____

    Studying regularly with a study group has helped me raise my grades.

4. Title: _____

    Grandparents have a special relationship with their grandchildren.

5. Title: _____

    My decision to eliminate junk food from my diet has been good for my health and my budget.

| ACTIVITY 3 | Rewriting Dependent Sentences |

In four of the five following sentences, the writer has mistakenly used the title to help explain the first sentence. But as previously noted, you must *not* rely on the title to explain your first sentence. Rewrite the sentences so that they are independent of the title. Write *Correct* under the one sentence that is independent.

EXAMPLE

Title: Flunking an Exam

First sentence: I managed to do this because of several bad habits.

Rewritten: I managed to flunk an exam because of several bad habits.

HINT   Indicate the words that *they* stands for in item 1.

---

1. Title: The Best Children's Television Shows

    First sentence: They educate while they entertain, and they are not violent.

    Rewritten: _____

    _____

2. Title: Women in the Workplace

    First sentence: They have made many gains there in the last twenty-five years.

    Rewritten: _____

    _____

3. Title: The Generation Gap

    First sentence: It results from differing experiences of various age groups.

    Rewritten: _____

    _____

4. Title: My Ideal Job

    First sentence: My ideal job would be to manage a pop singer and make a lot of money.

    Rewritten: _____

    _____

5. Title: Important Accomplishments

    First sentence: One of them was to finish high school despite my parents' divorce.

    Rewritten: _____

    _____

REVIEW TEST

Use the space below to rewrite the following sentences from a student paper, correcting the mistakes in format.

"my nursing-home friends"
I now count some of them among my good friends. I first went
there just to keep a relative of mine company. That is when I
learned some of them rarely got any visitors. Many were star-
ved for conversation and friendship. At the time, I did not
want to get involved. But what I discovered was that they had
very interesting stories to tell, and one woman, Mildred, taught
me to play chess. She was a good listener, and she gave me exc-
ellent advice about how to ask my parents for money.

Capital Letters

INTRODUCTORY ACTIVITY

You probably know a good deal about the uses of capital letters. Answering the questions below will help you check your knowledge.

1. Write the full name of a person you know: _____

2. In what city and state were you born? _____

3. What is your present street address? _____

4. Name a country where you would like to travel: _____

5. Name a school that you attended: _____

6. Give the name of a store where you buy food: _____

7. Name a company where you or anyone you know works: _____

8. Which day of the week is the busiest for you? _____

9. What holiday is your favorite? _____

10. Which brand of toothpaste do you use? _____

11. Give the brand name of a candy you like: _____

12. Name a song or a television show you enjoy: _____

13. Write the title of a magazine or newspaper you read: _____

Items 14–16

Three capital letters are needed in the example below. Underline the words you think should be capitalized. Then write them, capitalized, in the spaces provided.

on Super Bowl Sunday, my roommate said, "let's buy some snacks and invite a few friends over to watch the game." i knew my plans to write a term paper would have to be changed.

14. _____ 15. _____ 16. _____

Answers are on page 590.

Main Uses of Capital Letters

Capital letters are used with:

1. First word in a sentence or direct quotation
2. Names of persons and the word *I*
3. Names of particular places
4. Names of days of the week, months, and holidays
5. Names of commercial products
6. Titles of books, magazines, articles, films, television shows, songs, poems, stories, papers that you write, and the like
7. Names of companies, associations, unions, clubs, religious and political groups, and other organizations

Each use is illustrated on the pages that follow.

First Word in a Sentence or Direct Quotation

Our company has begun laying people off.

The doctor said, "This may hurt a bit."

"My husband," said Martha, "is a light eater. When it's light, he starts to eat."

> **EXPLANATION:** In the third example above, *My* and *When* are capitalized because they start new sentences. But *is* is not capitalized, because it is part of the first sentence.

Names of Persons and the Word *I*

At the picnic, I met Tony Curry and Lola Morrison.

Names of Particular Places

After graduating from Gibbs High School in Houston, I worked for a summer at a nearby Holiday Inn on Clairmont Boulevard.

But   Use small letters if the specific name of a place is not given.

After graduating from high school in my hometown, I worked for a summer at a nearby hotel on one of the main shopping streets.

Names of Days of the Week, Months, and Holidays

This year, Memorial Day falls on the last Thursday in May.

But   Use small letters for the seasons—summer, fall, winter, spring.

In the early summer and fall, my hay fever bothers me.

Names of Commercial Products

The consumer magazine gave high ratings to Cheerios breakfast cereal, Breyer's ice cream, and Progresso chicken noodle soup.

But   Use small letters for the *type* of product (breakfast cereal, ice cream, chicken noodle soup, and the like).

Titles of Books, Magazines, Articles, Films, Television Shows, Songs, Poems, Stories, Papers That You Write, and the Like

My oral report was on *The Diary of a Young Girl,* by Anne Frank.

While watching *The Young and the Restless* on television, I thumbed through *Cosmopolitan* magazine and the *New York Times.*

Names of Companies, Associations, Unions, Clubs, Religious and Political Groups, and Other Organizations

A new bill before Congress is opposed by the National Rifle Association.

My wife is Jewish; I am Roman Catholic. We are both members of the Democratic Party.

My parents have life insurance with Prudential, auto insurance with Allstate, and medical insurance with Blue Cross and Blue Shield.

ACTIVITY 1	Capitalizing Names and Titles

In the sentences that follow, cross out the words that need capitals. Then write the capitalized forms of the words in the space provided. The number of spaces tells you how many corrections to make in each case.

EXAMPLE

Rhoda said, "~~why~~ should I bother to *eat* this ~~hershey~~ bar? I should just

apply it directly to my hips."   _____Why_____   _____Hershey_____

HINT: The word *I* and names of organizations are capitalized.

1. Sometimes i still regret not joining the boy scouts when I was in grade school.

   _____   _____   _____

2. On the friday after thanksgiving, Carole went to target to buy gifts for her family.

   _____   _____   _____

3. In the box office of the regal cinema is a sign saying, "if you plan to see an R-rated movie, be ready to show your ID."

   _____   _____   _____

4. In many new england towns, republicans outnumber democrats five to one.

_____ _____ _____ _____

5. Nelson was surprised to learn that both state farm and nationwide have insurance offices in the prudential building.

_____ _____ _____ _____ _____

6. Magazines such as *time* and *newsweek* featured articles about the fires that devastated part of southern california.

_____ _____ _____

7. The rose grower whom Manny works for said that the biggest rose-selling holidays are valentine's day and mother's day.

_____ _____ _____ _____

8. With some pepsis and fritos nearby, the kids settled down to play a game on the macintosh computer.

_____ _____ _____

9. Bob's ford taurus was badly damaged when he struck a deer last saturday.

_____ _____ _____

10. Though Julie Andrews excelled in the broadway version of *my fair lady,* Audrey Hepburn was cast as the female lead in the movie version.

_____ _____ _____ _____

Other Uses of Capital Letters

Capital letters are also used with:

- Names that show family relationships
- Titles of persons when used with their names
- Specific school courses
- Languages
- Geographic locations
- Historic periods and events
- Races, nations, and nationalities
- Opening and closing of a letter

Each use is illustrated on the pages that follow.

Names That Show Family Relationships

Aunt Fern and Uncle Jack are selling their house.

I asked Grandfather to start the fire.

Is Mother feeling better?

But   Do not capitalize words such as *mother, father, grandmother, grandfather, uncle, aunt,* and so on when they are preceded by *my* or another possessive word.

My aunt and uncle are selling their house.

I asked my grandfather to start the fire.

Is my mother feeling better?

Titles of Persons When Used with Their Names

I wrote an angry letter to Senator Blutt.

Can you drive to Dr. Stein's office?

We asked Professor Bushkin about his attendance policy.

But   Use small letters when titles appear by themselves, without specific names.

I wrote an angry letter to my senator.

Can you drive to the doctor's office?

We asked our professor about his attendance policy.

Specific School Courses

My courses this semester include Accounting I, Introduction to Data Processing, Business Law, General Psychology, and Basic Math.

But   Use small letters for general subject areas.

This semester I'm taking mostly business courses, but I have a psychology course and a math course as well.

Languages

Lydia speaks English and Spanish equally well.

Geographic Locations

I lived in the South for many years and then moved to the West Coast.

But   Use small letters in giving directions.

Go south for about five miles and then bear west.

Historic Periods and Events

One essay question dealt with the Battle of the Bulge in World War II.

Races, Nations, and Nationalities

The census form asked whether I was African American, Native American, Hispanic, or Asian.

Last summer I hitchhiked through Italy, France, and Germany.

The city is a melting pot for Koreans, Vietnamese, and Mexican Americans.

But   Use small letters when referring to *whites* or *blacks.*

Both whites and blacks supported our mayor in the election.

Opening and Closing of a Letter

Dear Sir:	Sincerely yours,
Dear Madam:	Truly yours,

Capitalize only the first word in a closing.

| **Where Is Capitalization Needed?** | ACTIVITY 2 |

Cross out the words that need capitals in the following sentences. Then write the capitalized forms of the words in the spaces provided. The number of spaces tells you how many corrections to make in each case.

1. The nervous game show contestant couldn't remember how long the hundred years' war lasted.

   _____   _____   _____

   HINT: Capitalize the name of the historic event in item 1.

2. My sister and I always plead with aunt sophie to sing polish songs whenever she visits us.

   _____   _____   _____

3. While in Philadelphia, we visited independence hall and saw the liberty bell.

   _____   _____   _____   _____

4. The readings for the first semester of world history end with the middle ages.

   _____   _____   _____   _____

5. The Miami area has many fine cuban restaurants, several spanish-language newspapers, and annual hispanic cultural festivals.

   _____   _____   _____

Unnecessary Use of Capitals

| **Where Is Capitalization Unnecessary?** | ACTIVITY 3 |

Many errors in capitalization are caused by adding capitals where they are not needed. Cross out the incorrectly capitalized letters in the following sentences and write the correct forms in the spaces provided. The number of spaces tells you how many corrections to make in each sentence.

1. Antonio's Grandmother makes the best Spaghetti with Meatballs I've ever tasted.

   _____   _____   _____

   HINT: No words need capitals in item 1.

2. In our High School, the American history teacher was also the Basketball Coach.

    _____ _____ _____ _____

3. A Shop at Westville Mall sells copies of all the trendy clothes shown in various Fashion Magazines.

    _____ _____ _____

4. Several Parents' Groups protested the Ads for the new horror movie, which showed Santa Claus as a Maniac with a knife.

    _____ _____ _____ _____

5. When I complained to the Manager of the Restaurant about the poor service, she gave me a free Dessert.

    _____ _____ _____

ACTIVITY 4   Working Together

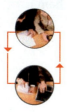

Part A: Editing and Rewriting

Working with a partner, read the short paragraph below and mark off the fifteen spots where capital letters are missing. Then use the space provided to rewrite the passage, adding capital letters where needed. Feel free to discuss the passage quietly with your partner and refer back to the chapter when necessary.

> The morning that I visited the lincoln memorial, it was raining. It was a quiet thursday in late october, and the air was cold. I was with uncle walt, and we had spent the morning visiting the smithsonian institution together. After lunch, my uncle said to me, "now we're going to go someplace that you'll never forget." When we arrived, I was overwhelmed by lincoln's massive statue, which dwarfed everything around it—just as the man had done in life. To my left I was aware of the silently flowing potomac river. Engraved on one of the marble walls was the gettysburg address. I read those familiar words and remained there for a time in silence, touched by the simple eloquence of that speech. I then snapped just one picture with my kodak camera and walked down the stone steps quietly. The photograph still sits on my desk today as a reminder of that special visit.

    _____

    _____

    _____

    _____

    _____

_____

_____

_____

_____

_____

_____

Part B: Creating Sentences

Working with a partner, write a sentence (or two) as directed. Pay special attention to capital letters.

1. Write about a place you like (or want) to visit. Be sure to give the name of the place, including the city, state, or country, where it is located.

2. Write a sentence (or two) in which you state the name of your elementary school, your favorite teacher or subject, and your least favorite teacher or subject.

3. Write a sentence (or two) that includes the names of three brand-name products that you often use. You may begin the sentence with the words, "Three brand-name products I use every day are . . ."

4. Think of the name of your favorite musical artist or performer. Then write a sentence in which you include the musician's name and the title of one of his or her songs.

5. Write a sentence in which you describe something you plan to do two days from now. Be sure to include the date and day of the week.

REFLECTIVE ACTIVITY

1. What would writing be like without capital letters? Use an example or two to help show how capital letters are important to writing.

2. What three uses of capital letters are most difficult for you to remember? Explain, giving examples.

REVIEW TEST 1

Cross out the words that need capitals in the following sentences. Then write the capitalized forms of the words in the spaces provided. The number of spaces tells you how many corrections to make in each sentence.

EXAMPLE

During halftime of the ~~saturday~~ afternoon football game, my sister said, "~~let's~~ get some hamburgers from ~~wendy's~~ or put a pizza in the oven."

Saturday   _Let's_   _Wendy's_

1. When he saw the commercial that said "just do it," Lance put on his nike running shoes and went to the store to get some ice cream.

   _____   _____

2. Millions of years ago, america's midwest was covered by a great inland sea.

   _____   _____

3. One of our thanksgiving traditions is sending a check to an organization such as greenpeace, which helps protect the environment.

   _____   _____

4. If you drive onto route 10 in tallahassee, florida, and stay on that road, you'll eventually end up in california.

   _____   _____   _____   _____

5. Just before english class this morning, Arlene titled her final paper "my argument for an A."

   _____   _____   _____

6. I read in the book *royal lives* that when an ancient egyptian king died, his servants were often killed and buried with him.

   _____   _____   _____

7. dear mr. Bradford:
   This is the third and final time I will write to complain about the leak in my bathroom.
   sincerely,
   Anne Morrison

   _____   _____   _____

8. "After age eighty," grandma ida would say, "time passes very quickly. it seems as though it's time for breakfast every fifteen minutes."

   _____   _____   _____

9. Dr. Green, who teaches a course called cultural anthropology, spent last summer on an archaeological dig in israel.

   _____   _____   _____

10. During the singing of "the star-spangled banner," many fans at yankee stadium drank sodas, read their programs, or chatted with each other.

    _____   _____   _____

    _____   _____   _____

REVIEW TEST 2

On a separate piece of paper, write:

- seven sentences demonstrating the seven main uses of capital letters.
- eight sentences demonstrating the eight other uses of capital letters.

Numbers and Abbreviations

INTRODUCTORY ACTIVITY

Write a check mark beside the item in each pair that you think uses numbers correctly.

I finished the exam by 8:55, but my grade was only 65

percent. _____

I finished the exam by eight-fifty-five, but my grade was only

sixty-five percent. _____

9 people are in my biology lab, but there are 45 in my lecture

group. _____

Nine people are in my biology lab, but there are forty-five in my

lecture group. _____

Write a check mark beside the item in each pair that you think uses abbreviations correctly.

Both of my bros. were treated by Dr. Lewis after the mt. climbing

accident. _____

Both of my brothers were treated by Dr. Lewis after the mountain

climbing accident. _____

I spent two hrs. finishing my Eng. paper and handed it to my

teacher, Ms. Peters, right at the deadline. _____

I spent two hours finishing my English paper and handed it to

my teacher, Ms. Peters, right at the deadline. _____

Answers are on page 591.

www.mhhe.com/langan

Numbers

Keep the following three rules in mind when using numbers.

Rule 1

Spell out numbers that take no more than two words. Otherwise, use numerals—the numbers themselves.

> Last year Tina bought nine new records.

> Ray struck out fifteen batters in Sunday's softball game.

But

> Tina now has 114 records in her collection.

> Already this season Ray has recorded 168 strikeouts.

You should also spell out a number that begins a sentence.

> One hundred fifty first-graders throughout the city showed flu symptoms today.

Rule 2

Be consistent when you use a series of numbers. If some numbers in a sentence or paragraph require more than two words, then use numbers themselves throughout the selection.

> That executive who tried to cut 250 employees' salaries owns 8 cars, 4 homes, 3 boats, and 1 jet.

Rule 3

Use numbers to show dates, times, addresses, percentages, exact sums of money, and parts of a book.

> John F. Kennedy was killed on November 22, 1963.

> My job interview was set for 10:15. (*But:* Spell out numbers before *o'clock*. For example: The time was then changed to eleven o'clock.)

> Janet's new address is 118 North 35 Street.

> Almost 40 percent of my meals are eaten at fast-food restaurants.

> The cashier rang up a total of $18.35. (*But:* Round amounts may be expressed as words. For example: The movie has an eight-dollar admission charge.)

> Read Chapter 6 in your math textbook and answer questions 1 to 5 on page 250.

ACTIVITY 1 | **Using Numbers**

Use the three rules to make the corrections needed in these sentences.

HINT In item 1, use numerals to show time.

1. Almost every morning I get up at exactly six-fifteen.

2. But on Sunday mornings, I sleep until 9 o'clock.

3. Sue and George got married on July twenty-eighth, 2004.

4. Joanne got really nervous when she saw there were only 6 other people in her English class.

5. Please send your complaints to sixteen hundred Pennsylvania Avenue.

6. 43 stores in the New England area were closed by a retail workers' strike.

7. Martin's computer system, including a printer, cost nine hundred thirty dollars and twenty cents.

8. Pages sixty through sixty-four of my biology book are stuck together.

9. Hollywood starlet Fifi LaFlamme's closet stores twenty-seven evening gowns, fifty-two designer suits, and 132 pairs of shoes.

10. Since over fifty percent of the class failed the midterm exam, the instructor decided not to count the grades.

Abbreviations

While abbreviations are a helpful time-saver in note-taking, you should avoid most abbreviations in formal writing. Listed below are some of the few abbreviations that are acceptable in compositions. Note that a period is used after most abbreviations.

- Mr., Mrs., Ms., Jr., Sr., Dr., when used with proper names:

  Mr. Rollin   Ms. Peters   Dr. Coleman

- Time references:

  A.M. or AM or a.m.   P.M. or PM or p.m.   BC/AD or B.C./A.D.

- First or middle initial in a name:

  T. Alan Parker   Linda M. Evans

- Organizations, technical words, and trade names known primarily by initials:

  ABC   CIA   UNESCO   GM   AIDS   DNA

Using Abbreviations

ACTIVITY 2

Cross out the words that should not be abbreviated and correct them in the spaces provided.

> **HINT**   No words should be abbreviated in item 1.

1. After I placed the "bike for sale" ad in the newsp., the tele. rang nonstop for a week.

   _____   _____

2. Sharon bought two bush. of ripe tomatoes at the farm mkt. on Rt. 73.

   _____   _____   _____

3. On Mon., NASA will announce its plans for a Sept. flight to Mars.

   _____   _____

4. The psych class was taught by Dr. Aronson, a noted psychiatrist from Eng.

   _____   _____

5. The best things on the menu are the chick. pot pie and the mac. and cheese.

   _____   _____

6. Several baby opossums (each of which weighs less than an oz.) can fit into a tbsp.

   _____   _____

7. I didn't have time to study for my chem. test on Sun., but I studied for four hrs. yesterday.

   _____   _____   _____

8. Every Jan., our co. gives awards for the best employee suggestions of the previous yr.

   _____   _____   _____

9. Lawrence T. Johnson lost his lic. to practice medicine when the state board discovered he never went to med. school.

   _____   _____

10. Mick, a vet. who served in Iraq, started his own photography bus. after graduating from a community coll.

    _____   _____   _____

REVIEW TEST

Cross out the mistake or mistakes in numbers and abbreviations and correct them in the spaces provided.

1. Sears' 4-day sale starts this coming Thurs.

   _____   _____

2. One suspect had blue eyes and brn. hair and was over 6 ft. tall.

_____ _____ _____

3. Answers to the chpt. questions start on p. two hundred and ninety-three.

_____ _____ _____

4. With Dec. twenty-fifth only hrs. away, little Rhonda couldn't eat or sleep.

_____ _____ _____

5. Over 200 children helped in the collection of seven hundred and thirty-two dollars for UNICEF.

_____ _____

6. My growing 15-year-old son wears sz. 11 shoes that look like boats.

_____ _____

7. My 3 years of Spanish in h.s. helped me to get a job in the city health clinic.

_____ _____ _____

8. The robber was sentenced to 10 yrs. in prison for holding up a bank on Pacific Blvd.

_____ _____ _____

9. I canceled my appt. when I got an emerg. call that my mother had been taken to the hosp.

_____ _____ _____

10. When city employees staged a strike on Mon., more than 70 pct. of them didn't show up for work.

_____ _____

25

End Marks

INTRODUCTORY ACTIVITY

Add the end mark needed in each of the following sentences.

1. All week I have been feeling depressed_

2. What is the deadline for handing in the paper_

3. The man at the door wants to know whose car is double-parked_

4. That truck ahead of us is out of control_

Answers are on page 591.

A sentence always begins with a capital letter. It always ends with a period, a question mark, or an exclamation point.

www.mhhe.com/langan

Period (.)

Use a period after a sentence that makes a statement.

> More single parents are adopting children.
>
> It has rained for most of the week.

Use a period after most abbreviations.

Mr. Brady	B.A.	Dr. Ballard
Ms. Peters	a.m.	Tom Ricci, Jr.

www.mhhe.com/langan

Question Mark (?)

Use a question mark after a *direct* question.

> When is your paper due?
>
> How is your cold?
>
> Tom asked, "When are you leaving?"
>
> "Why can't we all stop arguing?" Rosa asked.

Do *not* use a question mark after an *indirect* question (a question not in the speaker's exact words).

> She asked when the paper was due.
>
> He asked how my cold was.
>
> Tom asked when I was leaving.
>
> Rosa asked why we couldn't all stop arguing.

Exclamation Point (!)

Use an exclamation point after a word or sentence that expresses strong feeling.

> Come here!
>
> Ouch! This pizza is hot!
>
> That truck just missed us!

www.mhhe.com/langan

 TIP   Be careful not to overuse exclamation points.

Using End Punctuation   **ACTIVITY 1**

Add a period, question mark, or exclamation point as needed to each of the following sentences.

 HINT   Item 1 is a *direct* question.

---

1. Is it possible for a fish to drown _____

2. Thomas Jefferson was a redhead _____

3. I asked Jill for the time of day, but she wouldn't give it to me _____

4. When Eva learned she had won the lottery, she jumped up and down, yelling, "I don't believe it _____"

5. Because Americans watch so much television, one writer has called us a nation of "vidiots _____"

6. I questioned whether the police officer's report was accurate _____

7. If you had one year left to live, what would you do with the rest of your life _____

8. The last thing I heard before waking up in the hospital was someone screaming, "Look out for that truck _____"

End Marks (.!?)

9. On the plane from New York to Chicago, Dominic said, "Must I turn my watch back one hour—or forward ____"

10. Carlos asked himself on the way to his wedding whether he was sure he wanted to get married ____

REVIEW TEST

Add a period, question mark, or exclamation point as needed to each of the following sentences.

1. My birthday present was wrapped in old newspapers and yellowed Scotch tape ____

2. Did you know that washing in very hot water can dry out your skin ____

3. The bride stunned everyone when she appeared in a purple lace gown ____

4. Don't eat that poisonous mushroom ____

5. How did you get a wad of gum in your hair ____

6. That boy is waving a loaded gun ____

7. All through the interview, my stomach grumbled and my hands shook ____

8. If you won the lottery, what would you do with the prize money ____

9. I wonder if we should have a New Year's Eve party this year ____

10. Look out for that swerving car ____

Apostrophes

INTRODUCTORY ACTIVITY

Look carefully at the three items below. Then see if you can answer the questions that follow each item.

1. the desk of the manager   = the manager's desk

    the car of Hakim   = Hakim's car

    the teeth of my dog   = my dog's teeth

    the smile of the woman   = the woman's smile

    the briefcase of my mother = my mother's briefcase

    What is the purpose of the apostrophe in each example above?

    _____

2. He is my best friend.   = He's my best friend.

    I am afraid of spiders.   = I'm afraid of spiders.

    Do not watch too much TV.   = Don't watch too much TV.

    They are an odd couple.   = They're an odd couple.

    It is a wonderful movie.   = It's a wonderful movie.

    What is the purpose of the apostrophe in each example above?

    _____

3. Several buildings were damaged by the severe storm. One building's roof was blown off and dropped in a nearby field.

    Why does the apostrophe belong in the second sentence but not the first?

    _____

    _____

Answers are on page 591.

The two main uses of the apostrophe are:

- To show the omission of one or more letters in a contraction
- To show ownership or possession

Each use is explained on the pages that follow.

www.mhhe.com/langan

Apostrophes in Contractions

A contraction is formed when two words are combined to make one word. An apostrophe is used to show where letters are omitted in forming the contraction. Here are two contractions:

have + not   = haven't (the *o* in *not* has been omitted)

I   + will   = I'll (the *wi* in *will* has been omitted)

The following are some other common contractions:

I	+ am	= I'm	it	+ is	= it's
I	+ have	= I've	it	+ has	= it's
I	+ had	= I'd	is	+ not	= isn't
who	+ is	= who's	could	+ not	= couldn't
do	+ not	= don't	I	+ would	= I'd
did	+ not	= didn't	they	+ are	= they're
let	+ us	= let's	there	+ is	= there's

> **TIP**   The combination *will* + *not* has an unusual contraction: *won't*.

ACTIVITY 1	**Combining Words**

Combine the following words into contractions. One is done for you.

she	+ is	= __she's__	you	+ will	= _____
you	+ have	= _____	we	+ would	= _____
have	+ not	= _____	could	+ not	= _____
he	+ has	= _____	they	+ will	= _____
we	+ are	= _____	does	+ not	= _____

ACTIVITY 2	**Forming Contractions**

Write the contraction for the words in parentheses.

EXAMPLE

He (could not) ___couldn't___ come.

> **HINT**   An apostrophe replaces the letter *o* in both answers in item 1.

1. I (did not) _____ like the movie, but the popcorn (was not) _____ bad.

2. Tara (does not) _____ hide her feelings well, so if (she is) _____ angry, you will know it.

3. (You are) _____ taking the wrong approach with Len, as he (cannot) _____ stand being lectured.

4. This (is not) _____ the first time (you have) _____ embarrassed me in public.

5. (We would) _____ love to have you stay for dinner if you (do not) _____ mind eating leftovers.

> **TIP**   Even though contractions are common in everyday speech and in written dialogue, usually it is best to avoid them in formal writing.

Using the Apostrophe   ACTIVITY 3

Write five sentences using the apostrophe in different contractions.

1. _____

2. _____

3. _____

4. _____

5. _____

Four Contractions to Note Carefully

Four contractions that deserve special attention are *they're, it's, you're,* and *who's.* Sometimes these contractions are confused with the possessive words *their, its, your,* and *whose.* The following list shows the difference in meaning between the contractions and the possessive words.

Contractions	Possessive Words
they're (means *they are*)	their (means *belonging to them*
it's (means *it is* or *it has*)	its (means *belonging to it*)
you're (means *you are*)	your (means *belonging to you*)
who's (means *who is*)	whose (means *belonging to whom*)

Apostrophes (')

> **TIP**   Possessive words are explained further below.

ACTIVITY 4 — Using Apostrophes Correctly

Underline the correct form (the contraction or the possessive word) in each of the following sentences. Use the contraction whenever the two words of the contraction (*they are, it is, you are, who is*) would also fit.

> **HINT**   The sentence in item 1 contains one contraction and one possessive word.

1. (It's, Its) wonderful that (you're, your) grandmother is still so strong and active at eighty.

2. I don't know (who's, whose) fault it is that the car battery is dead, but I know (who's, whose) the primary suspect.

3. (You're, Your) feeling nauseated because you did not open any windows while staining (you're, your) living-room floor.

4. (They're, There) are some people who insist on acting gloomy no matter how well (they're, their) lives are going.

5. (It's, Its) hard to be pleasant to neighbors who always keep (they're, their) stereo on too loud.

Apostrophes to Show Ownership or Possession

To show ownership or possession, we can use such words as *belongs to, owned by,* or (most commonly) *of.*

> the knapsack *that belongs to* Uwem
>
> the grades *possessed by* Travis
>
> the house *owned by* my mother
>
> the sore arm *of* the pitcher

But the apostrophe plus *s* (if the word does not end in *-s*) is often the quickest and easiest way to show possession. Thus we can say:

> Uwem's knapsack
>
> Travis's grades
>
> my mother's house
>
> the pitcher's sore arm

Points to Remember

1. The 's goes with the owner or possessor (in the examples given, *Uwem*, *Travis*, *mother*, and *pitcher*). What follows is the person or thing possessed (in the examples given, *knapsack*, *grades*, *house*, and *sore arm*). An easy way to determine the owner or possessor is to ask the question "Who owns it?" In the first example, the answer to the question "Who owns the knapsack?" is *Uwem*. Therefore, the 's goes with *Uwem*.

2. In handwriting, there should always be a break between the word and the 's.

Yes   No

3. A singular word ending in -s (such as *Travis* in the earlier example) also shows possession by adding an apostrophe plus s (Travis's).

Using 's to Show Possession	ACTIVITY 5

Rewrite the italicized part of each sentence below, using 's to show possession. Remember that the 's goes with the **owner** or **possessor**.

EXAMPLES

The motorcycle owned by Clyde is a frightening machine.

Clyde's motorcycle

The roommate of my brother is a sweet and friendly person.

My brother's roommate

 HINT   In item 1, who owns the *voice*?

1. The *voice of the singer* had a relaxing effect on the crowd.

   _____

2. *The garage of Dawn* has so much furniture stored in it that there's no room for her car.

   _____

3. *The law of Murphy* states, "Anything that can go wrong will go wrong."

   _____

4. All the financial-planning information has been stored in the *memory of the computer*.

   _____

5. Because *the mother of my wife* is in jail for forgery, I call her my motheroutlaw.

   _____

6. Where is the rest of *the meat loaf of yesterday,* which I was planning to eat for lunch?

   _____

7. *The promotion of my sister* to vice president of the company was well earned.

   _____

8. *The bratty little brother of Alexis* has grown up to become a charming young man.

   _____

9. The judges reversed *the call of the referee* after they viewed the replay.

   _____

10. Thousands of gallons of crude oil spilled into the ocean when *the hull of the tanker* ruptured in the storm.

   _____

ACTIVITY 6   Indentifying Possessive Nouns

Underline the word in each sentence that needs 's. Then write the word correctly in the space at the left.

> **HINT**   In item 1, the hoof belongs to the horse.

_____   1. The trainer removed a nail from the horse hoof.

_____   2. My brother appetite is like a bottomless pit.

_____   3. Arnie pulled his young son hand away from the kerosene heater.

_____   4. The comedian trademarks were long cigars and red socks.

_____   5. No matter when you dial the landlord number, nobody answers the phone.

_____   6. The assistant manager always takes credit for Ted ideas.

_____   7. We all froze when the bank teller wig fell off.

_____   8. Some people never feel other people problems are their concern.

_____   9. Nita hires an accountant to prepare her dance studio tax returns each year.

_____   10. The screen door slammed on the little girl fingers.

Making Words Possessive

Add 's to each of the following words to make it the possessor or owner of something. Then write sentences using the words. Your sentences can be serious or playful. One is done for you as an example.

1. Cary _____Cary's_____

   Cary's hair is bright red.

2. teacher _____

   _____

3. insect _____

   _____

4. husband _____

   _____

5. salesperson _____

   _____

Apostrophes versus Possessive Pronouns

Do not use an apostrophe with possessive pronouns. They already show ownership. Possessive pronouns include *his, hers, its, yours, ours,* and *theirs.*

Incorrect	Correct
The bookstore lost its' lease.	The bookstore lost its lease.
The racing bikes were theirs'.	The racing bikes were theirs.
The change is yours'.	The change is yours.
His' problems are ours', too.	His problems are ours, too.
Her' cold is worse than his'.	Her cold is worse than his.

Apostrophe versus Simple Plurals

When you want to make a word plural, just add *s* at the end of the word. Do *not* add an apostrophe. For example, the plural of the word *movie* is *movies,* not *movie's* or *movies'.*

Look at this sentence:

When Sally's cat began catching birds, the neighbors called the police.

The words *birds* and *neighbors* are simple plurals, meaning more than one bird, more than one neighbor. The plural is shown by adding -*s* only. (More information about plurals starts on page 392.) On the other hand, the 's after *Sally* shows possession—that Sally owns the cat.

| ACTIVITY 8 | **Apostrophes vs. Simple Plurals** |

In the spaces provided under each sentence, add the one apostrophe needed and explain why the other words ending in *s* are simple plurals.

EXAMPLE

Originally, the cuffs of mens pants were meant for cigar ashes.

cuffs: simple plural meaning more than one cuff

mens: men's, meaning "belonging to men"

ashes: simple plural meaning more than one ash

> **HINT** In item 1, what possesses the *aromas*?

1. The pizza parlors aromas seeped through the vents to our second-floor apartment.

   parlors: _____

   aromas: _____

   vents: _____

2. A police cars siren echoed through the streets and buildings of the city.

   cars: _____

   streets: _____

   buildings: _____

3. Karens tomato plants are taller than the six-foot stakes she used to support them.

   Karens: _____

   plants: _____

   stakes: _____

4. Because of the lakes high bacteria level, officials prohibited boating, swimming, and fishing there.

   lakes: _____

   officials: _____

5. I have considered applying for many positions, but an exterminators job is not one of them.

   positions: _____

   exterminators: _____

6. The candlelights glow fell gently on the pale white plates and ruby-red goblets.

   candlelights: _____

   plates: _____

   goblets: _____

7. Crackers layered with cheese and apple slices are my fathers favorite snack.

   Crackers: _____

   slices: _____

   fathers: _____

8. Within a day, that insects eggs will turn into glistening white worms.

   insects: _____

   eggs: _____

   worms: _____

9. Seabirds skidding along the oceans edge at midnight looked like miniature moonlight surfers.

   Seabirds: _____

   oceans: _____

   surfers: _____

10. My daughters prayers were answered when the heavy snow caused all the schools in the area to close for the rest of the week.

   daughters: _____

   prayers: _____

   schools: _____

Apostrophes with Plural Words Ending in -s

Plurals that end in -s show possession simply by adding the apostrophe, rather than an apostrophe plus *s*.

Both of my *neighbors'* homes have been burglarized recently.

The many *workers'* complaints were ignored by the company.

All the *campers'* tents were damaged by the hailstorm.

Missing Apostrophes	ACTIVITY 9

Add an apostrophe where needed in each sentence that follows.

HINT   In item 1, whose *union* is it?

1. The nurses union protested my layoff.

2. My two sisters feet are the same size, so they share their shoes.

3. The lions keeper has worked with those lions since birth.

4. The Tylers new television set was mistakenly delivered to our house.

5. The photo album that was lost contained my parents wedding pictures.

ACTIVITY 10	**Working Together**

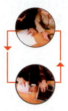

Part A: Editing and Rewriting

Working with a partner, read the short paragraph below. Underline ten places where you could rewrite, using apostrophes to indicate contractions and possessives. Then rewrite those parts in the spaces that follow. Feel free to discuss the rewrite quietly with your partner and refer back to the chapter when necessary.

> The dog of my neighbor is evil. For one thing, it barks constantly, even when there is nothing to bark at. Because of the constant barking of the dog, I cannot sleep at night. The dog also growls menacingly whenever it sees me. One time, it tried to charge at me through the fence of my landlord. Luckily for me, the fence was strong enough to restrain the dog. I have tried to talk to my neighbor about the problem, but he refuses to listen. He thinks there is nothing wrong with the behavior of the dog. But that is because the dog does not show its fangs to him.

_____

_____

_____

_____

_____

Part B: Creating Sentences

Working with a partner, write sentences that use apostrophes as directed.

1. Write a sentence describing something a friend owns. For instance, you might mention a pet or a material possession.

_____

2. Using an apostrophe to show a contraction, write a sentence about something at school or work that you feel is wrong and needs to be changed.

_____

3. Write a sentence that correctly uses the word *teachers*. Then write a second sentence that correctly uses the word *teacher's*.

_____

_____

REFLECTIVE ACTIVITY

1. Look at the paragraph about the dog that you just revised. How has adding apostrophes affected the paragraph?

2. Explain what it is about apostrophes that you find most difficult to remember and apply. Use an example to make your point clear.

In each sentence, cross out the two words that need apostrophes. Then write the words correctly in the spaces provided.

1. That authors latest horror novel isnt so horrifying.

_____   _____

2. "I dont get it," I confessed after hearing Pams long, complicated joke.

_____   _____

3. Luckily the motorcycles gas tank handnt been scratched in the collision.

_____   _____

4. Whos been stealing the Sunday papers from my doorsteps before Im awake?

_____   _____

5. Nadias aunts never start the day without asking an astrologers advice.

_____   _____

6. I, too, would like to take a shower, if theres any water left by the time youre finished.

_____   _____

7. Olivia watched sadly as the highway departments bulldozer demolished the house shed grown up in.

_____   _____

8. Sylvia wasnt on time for her first day of work because her mothers car broke down on the highway.

_____   _____

9. The coach said theres no room on the team for players who dont want to win.

    _____   _____

10. The authorities guess is that a radical protest group put the toxic chemical in the towns water supply.

    _____   _____

Rewrite the following sentences, changing each underlined phrase into either a contraction or a possessive.

1. Joe was not happy to hear the high-pitched sound of the drill of the dentist.

    _____

    _____

2. The weather forecast of today assured us that it is definitely going to be sunny, cloudy, or rainy.

    _____

    _____

3. The enthusiasm of my brother Manny for baseball is so great that he will even wear his glove and cap when he watches a game on TV.

    _____

    _____

4. Many parents think the influence of television is to blame for the poor performance of their children in school.

    _____

    _____

5. I was shocked by the announcement of my friend that he was going to marry a girl he had dated for only two months.

    _____

    _____

Quotation Marks

INTRODUCTORY ACTIVITY

Read the following scene and underline all the words enclosed within quotation marks. Your instructor may also have you dramatize the scene with one person reading the narration and three persons acting the speaking parts—Clyde, Charlotte, and Sam. The two speakers should imagine the scene as part of a stage play and try to make their words seem as real and true-to-life as possible.

At a party that Clyde and his wife, Charlotte, recently hosted, Clyde got angry at a guy named Sam who kept bothering Charlotte. "Listen, man," Clyde said, "what's this thing you have for my wife? There are lots of other women at this party."

"Relax," Sam replied. "Charlotte is very attractive, and I enjoy talking with her."

"Listen, Sam," Charlotte said, "I've already told you three times that I don't want to talk to you anymore. Please leave me alone."

"Look, there's no law that says I can't talk to you if I want to," Sam challenged.

"Sam, I'm only going to say this once," Clyde warned. "Lay off my wife, or leave this party *now*."

Sam grinned at Clyde smugly. "You've got good liquor here. Why should I leave? Besides, I'm not done talking with Charlotte."

Clyde went to his basement and was back a minute later holding a two-by-four. "I'm giving you a choice," Clyde said. "Leave by the door or I'll slam you out the window."

Sam left by the door.

1. On the basis of the above selection, what is the purpose of quotation marks?

   _____

2. Do commas and periods that come after a quotation go inside or outside the quotation marks?

   _____

Answers are on page 592.

The two main uses of quotation marks are as follows. Each use is explained here.

1. To set off the exact words of a speaker or writer
2. To set off the titles of short works

www.mhhe.com/langan

Quotation Marks to Set Off the Words of a Speaker or Writer

Use quotation marks when you want to show the exact words of a speaker or writer.

"Who left the cap off the toothpaste?" Lola demanded.

(Quotation marks set off the exact words that Lola spoke.)

Ben Franklin wrote, "Keep your eyes wide open before marriage, half shut afterward."

(Quotation marks set off the exact words that Ben Franklin wrote.)

"You're never too young," Aunt Fern told me, "to have a heart attack."

(Two pairs of quotation marks are used to enclose the aunt's exact words.)

Maria complained, "I look so old some days. Even makeup doesn't help. I feel as though I'm painting a corpse!"

(Note that the end quotes do not come until the end of Maria's speech. Place quotation marks before the first quoted word of a speech and after the last quoted word. As long as no interruption occurs in the speech, do not use quotation marks for each new sentence.)

> **EXPLANATION:** In the four preceding examples, notice that a comma sets off the quoted part from the rest of the sentence. Also observe that commas and periods at the end of a quotation always go inside the quotation marks.

Complete the following statements, which explain how capital letters, commas, and periods are used in quotations. Refer to the four examples as guides.

- Every quotation begins with a _____ letter.

- When a quotation is split (as in the sentence about Aunt Fern), the second part does not begin with a capital letter unless it is a

  _____ sentence.

- _____ are typically used to separate the quoted part of a sentence from the rest of the sentence.

- Commas and periods that come at the end of a quotation

  go _____ quotation marks.

The answers are *capital, new, Commas,* and *inside.*

Using Quotation Marks

Insert quotation marks where needed in the sentences that follow.

 HINT In item 1, put quotes around the words on the sticker.

1. The chilling bumper sticker read, You can't hug children with nuclear arms.

2. One day we'll look back on this argument, and it will seem funny, Bruce assured Rosa.

3. Hey, lady, this is an express line! shouted the cashier to the woman with a full basket.

4. My grandfather was fond of saying, Happiness is found along the way, not at the end of the road.

5. When will I be old enough to pay the adult fare? the child asked.

6. On his deathbed, Oscar Wilde is supposed to have said, Either this wallpaper goes or I do.

7. The sign on my neighbor's front door reads, Never mind the dog. Beware of owner.

8. I'm not afraid to die, said Woody Allen. I just don't want to be there when it happens.

9. My son once told me, Sometimes I wish I were little again. Then I wouldn't have to make so many decisions.

10. I don't feel like cooking tonight, Eve said to Adam. Let's just have fruit.

Formatting Quotations

Rewrite the following sentences, adding quotation marks where needed. Use a capital letter to begin a quotation and use a comma to set off a quoted part from the rest of the sentence.

EXAMPLE

I'm getting tired Sally said.

"I'm getting tired," Sally said.

 HINT In item 1, add a comma and put quotes around Simon's words.

1. Simon said take three giant steps forward.

_____

_____

2. Please don't hang up before leaving a message stated the telephone recording.

_____

_____

3. Clark Kent asked a man on the street where is the nearest phone booth?

_____

_____

4. You dirtied every pan in the kitchen just to scramble some eggs Rico said in disgust.

_____

_____

5. Nothing can be done for your broken little toe, the doctor said. You have to wait for it to heal.

_____

_____

| ACTIVITY 3 | **Writing with Quotation Marks** |

1. Write three quotations that appear in the first part of a sentence.

   EXAMPLE "Let's go shopping," I suggested. _____

   a. _____

   b. _____

   c. _____

2. Write three quotations that appear at the end of a sentence.

   EXAMPLE Bob asked, "Have you had lunch yet?" _____

   a. _____

   b. _____

   c. _____

3. Write three quotations that appear at the beginning and end of a sentence.

   EXAMPLE "If the bus doesn't come soon," Mary said, "we'll freeze." _____

   a. _____

   b. _____

   c. _____

Indirect Quotations

An indirect quotation is a rewording of someone else's comments rather than a word-for-word direct quotation. The word *that* often signals an indirect quotation.

Direct Quotation	Indirect Quotation
George said, "My son is a daredevil."	George said that his son is a daredevil.
(George's exact spoken words are given, so quotation marks are used.)	(We learn George's words indirectly, so no quotation marks are used.)
Carol's note to Arnie read, "I'm at the neighbors'. Give me a call."	Carol left a note for Arnie saying that she would be at the neighbors' and he should give her a call.
(The exact words that Carol wrote in the note are given, so quotation marks are used.)	(We learn Carol's words indirectly, so no quotation marks are used.)

Using Dialogue   ACTIVITY 4

Rewrite the following sentences, changing words as necessary to convert the sentences into direct quotations. The first one is done for you as an example.

1. Agnes told me as we left work that Herb got a raise.

   Agnes said to me as we left work, "Herb got a raise."

2. I said that it was hard to believe, since Herb is a do-nothing.

   _____

   _____

3. Agnes replied that even so, he's gone up in the world.

   _____

   _____

4. I told her that she must be kidding.

   _____

   _____

5. Agnes laughed and said that Herb was moved from the first to the fourth floor today.

   _____

   _____

Converting Quotations into Indirect Statements   ACTIVITY 5

Rewrite the following sentences, converting each direct quotation into an indirect statement. In each case, you will have to add the word *that* or *if* and change other words as well.

EXAMPLE

The barber asked Fred, "Have you noticed how your hair is thinning?"

The barber asked Fred if he had noticed how his hair was thinning.

 HINT   Begin the sentence in item 1 with *My doctor said that.*

1. My doctor said, "You need to lose weight."

2. Latoya asked Tony, "Don't you ever wash your car?"

3. The police officer asked me, "Do you know how fast you were going?"

4. Jane whispered, "Harold's so boring he lights up a room when he leaves it."

5. The instructor said, "Movies are actually a series of still pictures."

Quotation Marks to Set Off the Titles of Short Works

Titles of short works are usually set off by quotation marks, while titles of long works are underlined or italicized. Use quotation marks to set off the titles of short works such as articles in books, newspapers, or magazines; chapters in a book; and short stories, poems, and songs. On the other hand, you should underline or italicize the titles of books, newspapers, magazines, plays, movies, music albums, and television shows. See the following examples.

Quotation Marks	**Underlines**
the article "The Toxic Tragedy"	in the book Who's Poisoning America

the article "New Cures for Headaches"	in the newspaper the New York Times
the article "When the Patient Plays Doctor"	in the magazine Family Health
the chapter "Connecting with Kids"	in the book Straight Talk
the story "The Dead"	in the book Dubliners
the poem "Birches"	in the book The Complete Poems of Robert Frost
the song "Some Enchanted Evening"	in the album South Pacific
	the television show Arrested Development the movie Rear Window

---

TIP   In printed form, the titles of long works are usually set off by italics—slanted type that looks *like this*.

Using Quotations in Titles

ACTIVIY 6

Use quotation marks or underlines as needed.

HINT   Underline the name of the TV show in item 1.

---

1. My sister programmed her TiVo so she won't have to miss any more episodes of General Hospital.

2. Rita grabbed the National Enquirer and eagerly began to read the article I Had a Space Alien's Baby.

3. Our exam will cover two chapters, The Study of Heredity and The Origin of Diversity, in our biology textbook, Life.

4. The last song on the bluegrass program was called I Ain't Broke but I'm Badly Bent.

5. The classic 1980s movie Stand by Me was actually based on The Body, a short story written by Stephen King.

6. At last night's performance of Annie Get Your Gun, the audience joined the cast in singing There's No Business Like Show Business.

7. A typical article in Cosmopolitan has a title like How to Hook a Man without Letting Him Know You're Fishing.

8. One way Joanne deals with depression is to get out her Man of La Mancha album and play the song The Impossible Dream.

Quotation Marks
(" ")

9. I read the article How Good Is Your Breakfast? in Consumer Reports while munching a doughnut this morning.

10. According to a Psychology Today article titled Home on the Street, there are 36,000 people living on New York City's sidewalks.

Other Uses of Quotation Marks

Here are two more uses of quotation marks.

1. To set off special words or phrases from the rest of a sentence (italics can also be used for this purpose):

   Many people spell the words "all right" as one word, "alright," instead of correctly spelling them as two words.

   I have trouble telling the difference between "principal" and "principle."

2. To mark off a quotation within a quotation. For this purpose, single quotation marks (' ') are used:

   Ben Franklin said, "The noblest question in the world is, 'What good may I do in it?'"

   "If you want to have a scary experience," Nick told Fran, "read Stephen King's story 'The Mangler' in his book *Night Shift*."

| ACTIVITY 7 | Working Together |

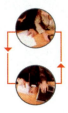

Part A: Editing and Rewriting

Working with a partner, read the short paragraph below and circle the places where quotation marks are needed. Then use the space provided to rewrite the paragraph, adding quotation marks where necessary. Feel free to discuss the rewrite quietly with your partner and refer back to the chapter if you have questions.

Harry and his friend Susan got stuck in an elevator. Another man was stuck with them. Harry turned to Susan and asked, Has this ever happened to you before?

Once, she said, About ten years ago in a department store. We weren't stuck long.

Harry took a deep breath. We're lucky only three of us are here. I don't like being closed up in small places, especially crowded ones.

Then the other man asked, Is there a phone or something here so we can talk to somebody?

Susan looked around and noticed a small panel in the corner of the elevator. A sign just over the panel read Open in Case of Emergency.

I think it might be in there, she said, pointing to the sign.

The man opened the panel, found a telephone, and dialed the security number written nearby.   Can anyone hear me? he asked.

A voice on the phone said, Yes, and we know you're stuck.   Just wait a few minutes.

When Harry heard that people knew about their problem, he let out a sigh.   I sure hope they can fix this quickly, he said softly, wringing his hands.

Susan put her arm around him and smiled.   Don't worry.   We'll be out of here in no time.

_____

_____

_____

_____

_____

_____

_____

_____

_____

_____

_____

Part B: Creating Sentences

Working with a partner, write sentences that use quotation marks as directed.

1. Write a sentence in which you quote a favorite expression of someone you know. Identify the person's relationship to you.

EXAMPLE

My brother Sam often says after a meal, "That wasn't bad at all."

_____

_____

2. Write a quotation that contains the words *Tony asked Lola*. Write a second quotation that includes the words *Lola replied*.

_____

_____

3. Write a sentence that interests or amuses you from a book, magazine, or newspaper. Identify the title and author of the book, magazine article, or newspaper article.

EXAMPLE

In her book <u>At Wit's End,</u> Erma Bombeck advises, "Never go to a doctor whose office plants have died."

_____

_____

REFLECTIVE ACTIVITY

1. Look at the paragraph about the elevator that you previously revised. Explain how adding quotation marks has affected the paragraph.

2. What would writing be like without quotation marks? Explain, using an example, how quotation marks are important to understanding writing.

3. Explain what it is about quotation marks that is most difficult for you to remember and apply. Use an example to make your point clear. Feel free to refer back to anything in this chapter.

REVIEW TEST 1

Place quotation marks around the exact words of a speaker or writer in the sentences that follow.

1. Give me a break! Charlie shouted to no one in particular.

2. My mother always says, Some are wise, and some are otherwise.

3. Why do men continue to wear ties when they serve no purpose? asked Paul.

4. Take all you want, but eat all you take, read the sign in the cafeteria.

5. One of Mark Twain's famous lines is, Man is the only animal that blushes—or needs to.

6. My friend the radio announcer loses his voice every time we drive under a bridge, said the comedian.

7. The first time my daughter had a headache, she told me, Mommy, I have a pain in my brain.

8. If your parachute doesn't open, the skydiving instructor joked, bring it back, and we'll give you a new one.

9. The novelist ended a letter to his brother by saying, I'm sorry for writing such a long letter. I didn't have time for a shorter one.

10. Work fascinates me, said the comedian. I could sit and watch it for hours.

Place quotation marks around the exact words of a speaker in the sentences that follow. Three of the sentences contain indirect quotations and do not require quotation marks.

EXAMPLE

Soon after moving into their new house, Mike said to Marian, "Why don't we have a party? It'd be a good way to meet all our neighbors."

1. Nice idea, said Marian, but way too much work.

2. It won't be that bad. We'll grill hamburgers and ask everybody to bring a side dish, Mike answered.

3. Marian said that she would agree to the idea if Mike called all the guests.

4. Hi, this is Mike Josephs, your new neighbor in 44B, Mike said each time he called someone.

5. Afterward, he told Marian that everything was under control.

6. I told them we'd provide burgers and plenty of drinks, Mike explained, and they'll bring everything else.

7. When the party started, the first guests arrived saying, We brought potato salad—we hope that's all right!

8. Then guests number two, three, and four arrived, also announcing that they had brought potato salad.

9. As the sixth bowl of potato salad arrived, Mike mumbled to Marian Maybe I should have made some more suggestions about what people should bring.

10. Oh, well, I really love potato salad, Marian said.

Go through the comics section of a newspaper to find a comic strip that amuses you. Be sure to choose a strip where two or more characters are speaking to each other. Write a full description that will enable people who have not read the comic strip to visualize it clearly and appreciate its humor. Describe the setting and action in each panel and enclose the words of the speakers in quotation marks.

28

Commas

INTRODUCTORY ACTIVITY

Commas often (though not always) signal a minor break or pause in a sentence. Each of the six pairs of sentences below illustrates one of six main uses of the comma. Read each pair of sentences aloud and place a comma wherever you feel a slight pause occurs. Then choose the rule that applies from the box at the bottom of the page, and write its letter on the line provided.

_____ 1. You can use a credit card write out a check or provide cash.

The old house was infested with red ants roaches and mice.

_____ 2. To start the car depress the accelerator and turn the ignition key.

Before you go hiking buy a comfortable pair of shoes.

_____ 3. Leeches creatures that suck human blood are valuable to medical science.

George Derek who was just arrested was a classmate of mine.

_____ 4. Our professor said the exam would be easy but I thought it was difficult.

Wind howled through the trees and rain pounded against the window.

_____ 5. Emily asked "Why is it so hard to remember your dreams the next day?"

"I am so tired after work" Lily said "that I fall asleep right away."

_____ 6. Bert has driven 1500000 accident-free miles in his job as a trucker.

The Gates Trucking Company of Newark New Jersey gave Bert an award on August 26 2006 for his superior safety record.

---

a. separate items in a list
b. separate introductory material from the sentence
c. separate words that interrupt the sentence
d. separate complete thoughts in a sentence
e. separate direct quotations from the rest of the sentence
f. separate numbers, addresses, and dates in everyday writing

---

Answers are on page 593.

Six Main Uses of the Comma

www.mhhe.com/langan

Commas are used mainly as follows:

- To separate items in a series

- To set off introductory material

- On both sides of words that interrupt the flow of thought in a sentence

- Between two complete thoughts connected by *and, but, for, or, nor, so, yet*

- To set off a direct quotation from the rest of a sentence

- To set off certain everyday material

You may find it helpful to remember that the comma often marks a slight pause, or break, in a sentence. These pauses or breaks occur at the points where the six main comma rules apply. Sentence examples for each of the comma rules are given on the following pages; read these sentences aloud and listen for the minor pauses or breaks that are signaled by commas.

However, you should keep in mind that commas are far more often overused than underused. As a general rule, you should *not* use a comma unless a given comma rule applies or unless a comma is otherwise needed to help a sentence read clearly. A good rule of thumb is that "when in doubt" about whether to use a comma, it is often best to "leave it out."

After reviewing each of the comma rules that follow, you will practice adding commas that are needed and omitting commas that are not needed.

Commas between Items in a Series

Use a comma to separate items in a series.

Magazines, paperback novels, and textbooks crowded the shelves.

Hard-luck Sam needs a loan, a good-paying job, and a close friend.

Pat sat in the doctor's office, checked her watch, and flipped nervously through a magazine.

Mira bit into the ripe, juicy apple.

More and more people entered the crowded, noisy stadium.

> **TIP**   A comma is used between two descriptive words in a series only if the word *and* inserted between the words sounds natural. You could say:
>
> Mira bit into the ripe *and* juicy apple.
>
> More and more people entered the crowded *and* noisy stadium.
>
> But notice in the following sentences that the descriptive words do not sound natural when *and* is inserted between them. In such cases, no comma is used.
>
> The model wore a classy black dress. ("A classy *and* black dress" doesn't sound right, so no comma is used.)
>
> Dr. Van Helsing noticed two tiny puncture marks on the patient's neck. ("Two *and* tiny puncture marks" doesn't sound right, so no comma is used.)

ACTIVITY 1   Commas between Items in a Series

Place commas between items in each series.

1. Many of the refugees wandered around without work food or a place to live.

2. Ice cream crushed candy Pepsi and popcorn formed a gluelike compound on the movie theater's floor.

3. We finally drove across the Arizona–New Mexico border after eight hours four hundred miles and three rest stops.

ACTIVITY 2   Necessary and Unnecessary Commas

For each item, cross out the one comma that is not needed. Add the one comma that is needed between items in a series.

1. I discovered gum wrappers, pennies and a sock hidden, under the seats when I vacuumed my car.

2. Squirrels Canadian geese, two white swans, and clouds of mosquitoes, populate Farwell Park.

3. Lewis dribbled twice, spun to his left and lofted his patented hook shot over the outstretched arms, of the Panthers' center.

Commas after Introductory Material

Use a comma to set off introductory material.

Fearlessly, Lola picked up the slimy slug.

Just to annoy Tony, she let it crawl along her arm.

Although I have a black belt in karate, I decided to go easy on the demented bully who had kicked sand in my face.

Mumbling under her breath, the woman picked over the tomatoes.

> **TIP**   If the introductory material is brief, the comma is sometimes omitted. In the activities here, you should include the comma.

Commas after Introductory Clauses

Place commas after introductory material.

>   In item 1, the last introductory word is *done*.

1. When all is said and done a lot more is said than done.

2. If you mark your suitcase with colored tape it will be easier to find at the baggage counter.

3. Feeling brave and silly at the same time Anita volunteered to go onstage and help the magician.

More Necessary and Unnecessary Commas

For each item, cross out the one comma that is not needed. Add the one comma that is needed after introductory material.

> **HINT**   In item 1, add a comma to the first sentence and omit the comma in the second.

1. Using metallic cords from her Christmas presents young Ali made several bracelets for herself. After that, she took a long ribbon, and tied a bow around her dog's head.

2. As the bride smiled and strolled past me down the aisle I saw a bead of sweat roll, from her forehead down her cheek. Remembering my own wedding, I knew she wasn't sweating from the heat.

3. When my children were young, I wrote interesting anecdotes about them in a notebook. For example I wrote a note to remind me, that my son once wanted to be a yo-yo maker.

Commas around Words Interrupting the Flow of Thought

Use a comma before and after words that interrupt the flow of thought in a sentence.

The car, cleaned and repaired, is ready to be sold.

Martha, our new neighbor, used to work as a bouncer at Rexy's Tavern.

Taking long walks, especially after dark, helps me sort out my thoughts.

Usually you can "hear" words that interrupt the flow of thought in a sentence. However, when you are not sure if certain words are interrupters, remove them from the sentence. If it still makes sense without the words, you know that the words are interrupters and that the information they give is nonessential. Such nonessential information is set off with commas. In the following sentence

Susie Hall, who is my best friend, won a new car in the *Reader's Digest* sweepstakes.

the words *who is my best friend* are extra information, not needed to identify the subject of the sentence, *Susie Hall.* Put commas around such nonessential information. On the other hand, in the sentence

The woman who is my best friend won a new car in the *Reader's Digest* sweepstakes.

The words *who is my best friend* supply essential information that we need to identify the woman. If the words were removed from the sentence, we would no longer know which woman won the sweepstakes. Commas are not used around such essential information.

Here is another example:

The Shining, a novel by Stephen King, is the scariest book I've ever read.

Here the words *a novel by Stephen King* are extra information, not needed to identify the subject of the sentence, *The Shining.* Commas go around such nonessential information. On the other hand, in the sentence

Stephen King's novel *The Shining* is the scariest book I've ever read.

the words *The Shining* are needed to identify the novel because he has written more than one. Commas are not used around such essential information.

Most of the time you will be able to "hear" words that interrupt the flow of thought in a sentence and will not have to think about whether the words are essential or nonessential.*

ACTIVITY 5   Commas That Set Off Interrupters

Add commas to set off interrupting words.

 In item 1, the interrupting words are *aided by members of the chorus.*

*Some instructors refer to nonessential or extra information that is set off by commas as a *nonrestrictive clause.* Essential information that interrupts the flow of thought is called a *restrictive clause.* No commas are used to set off a restrictive clause.

1. The dancer aided by members of the chorus hobbled across the stage toward the wings.

2. Mr. and Mrs. Anderson who were married on the Fourth of July named their first child "Freedom."

3. The repairman unaware of the grease on his shoes left a black trail from our front door to the washing machine.

More Necessary and Unnecessary Commas

ACTIVITY 6

For each item, cross out the one comma that is not needed. Add the comma that is needed to completely set off the interrupting words.

 HINT   In item 1, the interrupting words are *even the most gigantic.*

1. All trees, even the most gigantic are only 1 percent living tissue; the rest, is deadwood.

2. The city council in a rare fit, of wisdom, established a series of bicycle paths around town.

3. John Adams and Thomas Jefferson, the second and third presidents, of the United States died on the same day in 1826.

4. My aunt, a talkative, woman married a patient man who is a wonderful listener.

Commas between Complete Thoughts Connected by Joining Words

Use a comma between two complete thoughts connected by *and, but, for, or, nor, so,* or *yet* (joining words).

> My parents threatened to throw me out of the house, so I had to stop playing the drums.

> The polyester bedsheets had a gorgeous design, but they didn't feel as comfortable as plain cotton sheets.

> The teenage girls walked along the hot summer streets, and the teenage boys drove by in their shiny cars.

 TIP   The comma is optional when the complete thoughts are short:

Hal relaxed but Bob kept working.

The soda was flat so I poured it away.

We left school early for the furnace had broken down.

Commas (,)

Be careful not to use a comma in sentences having *one* subject and a *double* verb. The comma is used only in sentences made up of two complete thoughts (two subjects and two verbs). In the sentence

> Mary lay awake that stormy night and listened to the thunder crashing.

there is only one subject (*Mary*) and a double verb (*lay* and *listened*). No comma is needed. Likewise, the sentence

> The quarterback kept the ball and plunged across the goal line for a touchdown.

has only one subject (*quarterback*) and a double verb (*kept* and *plunged*); therefore, no comma is needed.

| ACTIVITY 7 | Commas That Connect Complete Thoughts |

Place a comma before a joining word that connects two complete thoughts (two subjects and two verbs). Remember, do *not* place a comma within sentences that have only one subject and a double verb. Mark sentences that are correct with a *C*.

> **HINT**   In item 1, *but* connects two complete thoughts.

1. The apartment Kate looked at was clean and spacious but the rent was too expensive for her budget.

2. Our power went out during the thunderstorm so we decided to eat dinner by candlelight.

3. Eddie is building a kayak in his garage and plans to take it down the Columbia River next year.

4. I desperately need more storage space for I can't seem to throw anything away.

5. The helicopter hovered overhead and lowered a rescue line to the downed pilot.

6. Travis was going to quit his job at the supermarket but he changed his mind after getting a raise.

7. One of the men got ready to leave work at four but put his coat away upon seeing his boss.

8. The family expected Valerie to go to college but she went to work after eloping with her boyfriend.

9. Bobby pleaded with his parents to buy him a computer for his schoolwork but he spends most of his time playing games on it.

10. The doctor examined me for less than ten minutes and then presented me with a bill for ninety dollars.

Commas with Direct Quotations

Use a comma or commas to set off a direct quotation from the rest of a sentence.

"Please take a number," said the deli clerk.

Fred told Martha, "I've just signed up for a course on Web-page design."

"Those who sling mud," a famous politician once said, "usually lose ground."

"Reading this book," complained Stan, "is about as interesting as watching paint dry."

> **TIP** Commas and periods at the end of a quotation go inside quotation marks. See also page 350.

Setting Off Quotations with Commas   ACTIVITY 8

In each sentence, add the one or more commas needed to set off the quoted material.

> **HINT** In item 1, add a comma before the quoted material.

1. The five-year-old boy said "Mommy, I have a bad headache in my tummy."

2. "The best way to get rid of a temptation" Oscar Wilde advised "is to yield to it."

3. "The movie will scare the whole family" wrote the reviewer.

More Necessary and Unnecessary Commas   ACTIVITY 9

In each item, cross out the one comma that is not needed to set off a quotation. Add the comma(s) needed to set off a quotation from the rest of the sentence.

> **HINT** In item 1, add a comma before the quoted material.

1. "If you're looking for a career change," read the poster, in the subway station "consider the US Armed Forces."

2. "Your arms look fine" said the swimming instructor, "but you keep forgetting, to kick."

Commas (,)

3. "Did you really think" the judge asked, the defendant, "you could kill both your parents and then ask for mercy because you're an orphan?"

Commas with Everyday Material

Use commas to set off certain everyday material, as shown in the following sections.

Persons Spoken to

I think, Sally, that you should go to bed.

Please turn down the stereo, Mark.

Please, sir, can you spare a dollar?

Dates

Our house was burglarized on June 28, 2004, and two weeks later on July 11, 2004.

Addresses

Lola's sister lives at 342 Red Oak Drive, Los Angeles, California 90057. She is moving to Manchester, Vermont, after her divorce.

 TIP   No comma is used before a zip code.

Openings and Closings of Letters

Dear Marilyn,   Sincerely,

Dear John,   Truly yours,

In formal letters, a colon is used after the opening:

Dear Sir:

Dear Madam:

Numbers

Government officials estimate that Americans spend about 785,000,000 hours a year filling out federal forms.

ACTIVITY 10   **Adding Commas**

Place commas where needed.

 HINT   Two commas are needed in item 1.

1. Excuse me madam but your scarf is in my soup.

2. Before age eighteen, the average child spends 6000 hours in school and 15000 hours watching television.

3. The famous ocean liner *Titanic* sank in the Atlantic Ocean on April 15 1912.

4. Dear Teresa
   What do you think of this psychology lecture? Will you meet me for lunch after class? I'll treat. Pass me your answer right away.
   > Love
   > Jeff

5. The zoo in Washington D.C. purchases 50000 pounds of meat; 6500 loaves of bread; 114000 live crickets; and other foods for its animals each year.

Unnecessary Use of Commas

Remember that if no clear rule applies for using a comma, it is usually better not to use one. As stated earlier, "When in doubt, leave it out." Following are some typical examples of unnecessary commas.

Incorrect

Sharon told me, that my socks were different colors.

(A comma is not used before *that* unless the flow of thought is interrupted.)

The union negotiations, dragged on for three days.

(Do not use a comma between a simple subject and verb.)

I waxed all the furniture, and cleaned the windows.

(Use a comma before *and* only with more than two items in a series or when *and* joins two complete thoughts.)

Sharon carried, the baby into the house.

(Do not use a comma between a verb and its object.)

I had a clear view, of the entire robbery.

(Do not use a comma before a prepositional phrase.)

Eliminating Unnecessary Commas   ACTIVITY 11

Cross out commas that do not belong. Some commas are correct. Do not add any commas.

1. We grew a pumpkin last year, that weighed over one hundred pounds.

2. Anyone with a failing grade, must report to the principal.

3. Last weekend a grizzly bear attacked a hiker, who got too close to its cubs.

4. After watching my form, on the high-diving board, Mr. Riley, my instructor, asked me if I had insurance.

5. Rosa flew first to Los Angeles, and then she went to visit her parents, in Mexico City.

6. The tall muscular man wearing the dark sunglasses, is a professional wrestler.

7. Onions, radishes, and potatoes, seem to grow better in cooler climates.

8. Whenever Vincent is in Las Vegas, you can find him at the blackjack table, or the roulette wheel.

9. While I watched in disbelief, my car rolled down the hill, and through the front window of a Chinese restaurant.

10. The question, sir, is not, whether you committed the crime, but, when you committed the crime.

ACTIVITY 12   **Working Together**

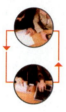

Part A: Editing and Rewriting

Working with a partner, read carefully the short paragraph below and cross out the five misplaced commas. Then insert the ten additional commas needed. Feel free to discuss the rewrite quietly with your partner and refer back to the chapter when necessary.

Dear Teresa,

On Tuesday, May 4 2004 my husband, and I were unable to sleep because of the loud music coming from your apartment. When I first heard the music I didn't say anything to you because it was still early. But the music, along with loud, laughter and talking, continued until around four o'clock in the morning. At midnight, my husband went into the hallway to see what was happening and he ran into one of your guests. The man who seemed very drunk stared at him, and said "Go back to bed, old man." The next morning, we found beer cans pizza boxes, and cigarette butts, piled outside our door. This is unacceptable. We have written this letter to you as a warning. The next time something like this happens we will call the police, and the building manager. We don't want to cause trouble with you but we will not tolerate another incident like what happened that night.

Sincerely,

Rose Connelly

Part B: Creating Sentences

Working with a partner, write sentences that use commas as directed.

1. Write a sentence mentioning three items you want to get the next time you go to the store.

   _____

   _____

2. Write two sentences describing how you relax after getting home from school or work. Start the first sentence with *After* or *When*. Start the second sentence with *Next*.

   _____

   _____

3. Write a sentence that tells something about your favorite movie, book, television show, or song. Use the words *which is my favorite movie* (or *book, television show,* or *song*) after the name of the movie, book, television show, or song.

   _____

   _____

4. Write two complete thoughts about a person you know. The first thought should mention something that you like about the person. The second thought should mention something you don't like. Join the two thoughts with *but.* Do not use the name of a classmate.

   _____

   _____

5. Invent a line that Lola might say to Tony. Use the words *Lola said* in the sentence. Then include Tony's reply, using the words *Tony responded.*

   _____

   _____

6. Write a sentence about an important event in your life. Include the day, month, and year of the event.

   _____

   _____

REFLECTIVE ACTIVITY

1. Look at the letter that you revised on the previous page. Explain how adding commas has affected the paragraph.

2. What would writing be like without the comma? How do commas help writing?

3. What is the most difficult comma rule for you to remember and apply? Explain, giving an example.

Commas (,)

REVIEW TEST 1

Insert commas where needed. In the space provided under each sentence, summarize briefly the rule that explains the use of the comma or commas.

1. As the usher turned his head two youngsters darted into the movie theater.

   _____

2. My boss it is rumored is about to be fired.

   _____

3. I found my father's dusty water-stained yearbook behind some pipes in the basement.

   _____

4. "Be careful what you wish for" an old saying goes "or you may get it."

   _____

5. My final mortgage payment on December 3 2011 seems light-years away.

   _____

6. We sat together on the riverbank watched the sun disappear and made plans for our divorce.

   _____

7. I panicked when I saw the flashing red lights behind me but the policeman just wanted to pass.

   _____

8. The burly umpire his shoes and trousers now covered with dirt pulled off his mask and angrily ejected the St. Louis manager from the game.

   _____

9. "Knock off the noise" Sam yelled to the children. "I'm talking long distance to your grandmother."

   _____

10. Rubbing her eyes and clearing her throat Stella tried to sound human as she answered the early morning call.

    _____

Insert commas where needed. One sentence does not need commas. Mark it with a C.

1. Some people believe that television can be addictive but I think they're wrong.

2. While there are people who turn on their sets upon waking up in the morning I don't do that.

3. I turn on my set only upon sitting down for breakfast and then I watch the *Today Show*.

4. I don't need to watch game shows soap operas and situation comedies to get through the day.

5. Instead I watch all these programs simply because I enjoy them.

6. I also keep the television turned on all evening because thanks to cable there is always something decent to watch.

7. If I did not have good viewing choices I would flick off the set without hesitation.

8. Lots of people switch channels rapidly to preview what is on.

9. I on the other hand turn immediately to the channel I know I want.

10. In other words I am not addicted; I am a selective viewer who just happens to select a lot of shows.

On a separate piece of paper, write six sentences, with each sentence demonstrating one of the six main comma rules.

CHAPTER

29

Other Punctuation Marks

INTRODUCTORY ACTIVITY

Each sentence below needs one of the following punctuation marks.

See if you can insert the correct mark(s) in each case.

1. The following items were on my mother's grocery list eggs, tomatoes, milk, and cereal.

2. A life size statue of her cat adorns the living room of Diana's penthouse.

3. Sigmund Freud, the pioneer of psychoanalysis 1856–1939, was a habitual cocaine user.

4. As children, we would put pennies on the railroad track we wanted to see what they would look like after being run over by a train.

5. The stuntwoman was battered, broken, barely breathing but alive.

Answers are on page 607.

www.mhhe.com/langan

Colons (:)

The colon is a mark of introduction. Use the colon at the end of a complete statement to do the following:

- Introduce a list.

    My little brother has three hobbies: playing video games, racing his Hot Wheels cars all over the floor, and driving me crazy.

- Introduce a long quotation.

    Janet's paper was based on a passage from George Eliot's novel *Middlemarch:* "If we had a keen vision and feeling of all ordinary human life, it would be like hearing the grass grow and the squirrel's heart beat, and we should die of that roar which lies on the other side of silence. As it is, the quickest of us walk about well wadded with stupidity."*

*In formal writing, indent long quotations, and do not set them off with quotation marks; a "long quotation" is generally four lines or longer.

374

- Introduce an explanation.

  There are two ways to do this job: the easy way and the right way.

Two minor uses of the colon are after the opening in a formal letter (*Dear Sir or Madam:*) and between the hour and the minute in writing the time (*The bus will leave for the game at 11:45*).

Using Colons

Place colons where needed.

 HINT   Add a colon before the explanation in item 1.

1. Roger is on a "see-food" diet if he sees food, he eats it.

2. Brenda had some terrible problems last summer her mother suffered a heart attack, her husband lost his job, and one of her children was arrested for shoplifting.

3. Andy Rooney wrote in one of his columns "Doctors should never talk to ordinary people about anything but medicine. When doctors talk politics, economics, or sports, they reveal themselves to be ordinary mortals, idiots just like the rest of us. That isn't what any of us wants our doctors to be."

Semicolons (;)

The semicolon signals more of a pause than the comma alone but not quite the full pause of a period. Use a semicolon to do the following:

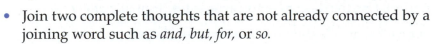
www.mhhe.com/langan

- Join two complete thoughts that are not already connected by a joining word such as *and, but, for,* or *so.*

  The chemistry lab blew up; Professor Thomas was fired.

  I once stabbed myself with a pencil; a black mark has been under my skin ever since.

- Join two complete thoughts that include a transitional word such as *however, otherwise, moreover, furthermore, therefore,* or *consequently.*

  I changed and made the bed; moreover, I cleaned the entire bedroom.

  Sally finished typing the paper; however, she forgot to bring it to class.

TIP   The first two uses of the semicolon are treated in more detail on pages 186–188.

3. Separate items in a series when the items themselves contain commas.

This fall I won't have to work on Labor Day, September 7; Veterans Day, November 11; or Thanksgiving Day, November 26.

At the final Weight Watchers' meeting, prizes were awarded to Sally Johnson, for losing 20 pounds; Irving Ross, for losing 26 pounds; and Betty Mills, the champion loser, who lost 102 pounds.

ACTIVITY 2   **Using Semicolons**

Place semicolons where needed.

> **HINT**   Add a semicolon before the transitional word in item 1.

1. Manny worked four extra hours at his job last night consequently, he has been like a zombie in class today.

2. We could tell it was still raining all the puddles looked as if they were being shot at.

3. My grocery shopping has to take into account my daughter, who's a vegetarian my mother, who is diabetic, and my husband, who wants meat at every meal.

www.mhhe.com/langan

Dashes (—)

A dash signals a degree of pause longer than a comma but not as complete as a period. Use the dash to set off words for dramatic effect.

I suggest—no, I insist—that you stay for dinner.

The prisoner walked toward the electric chair—grinning.

A meaningful job, a loving wife, and a car that wouldn't break down all the time—these are the things he wanted in life.

ACTIVITY 3   **Using the Dash**

Place dashes where needed.

> **HINT**   One dash is needed in item 1.

1. The members of the Polar Bear Club marched into the icy sea shivering.

2. The actress's wedding her third in three years included a dozen brides-maids and a flock of white doves.

3. My sociology class meets at the worst possible time eight o'clock on Monday morning.

Hyphens (-)

Use a hyphen in the following ways:

www.mhhe.com/langan

- With two or more words that act as a single unit describing a noun:

  The society ladies nibbled at the deep-fried grasshoppers.

  A white-gloved waiter then put some snails on their table.

  Your dictionary will often help when you are unsure about whether to use a hyphen between words.

- To divide a word at the end of a line of writing or typing:

  Although it had begun to drizzle, the teams decided to play the championship game that day.

 TIP   Divide a word only between syllables. Use your dictionary (see page 382) to be sure of correct syllable divisions.

 TIP   Do not divide words of one syllable.

TIP   Do not divide a word if you can avoid dividing it.

Using Hyphens

ACTIVITY 4

Place hyphens where needed.

 HINT   Two hyphens are needed in item 1.

1. Why do I always find myself behind a slow moving car when I'm in a no passing zone?

2. To convince herself that she was still on a diet, Paula ordered a sugar free cola with her double cheese pizza.

3. Twirling his mustache, the hard hearted villain chuckled as he tied the teary eyed heroine to the railroad tracks.

www.mhhe.com/langan

Parentheses ( )

Use parentheses to do the following:

- Set off extra or incidental information from the rest of a sentence:

  The chapter on drugs in our textbook (pages 234–271) contains some frightening statistics.

  The normal body temperature of a cat (101° to 102°) is 3° higher than the temperature of its owner.

- Enclose letters or numbers that signal items in a series:

  Three steps to follow in previewing a textbook are to (1) study the title, (2) read the first and last paragraphs, and (3) study the headings and subheadings.

> **TIP**   Do not use parentheses too often in your writing.

ACTIVITY 5   **Using Parentheses**

Add parentheses where needed.

> **HINT**   Put the extra information in item 1 in parentheses.

1. According to the 2000 Census, a majority of Americans 80 percent had earned a high school diploma.

2. That instructor's office hours 3:00 to 4:00 p.m. are impossible for any student with an afternoon job.

3. Since I am forgetful, I often 1 make a list and then 2 check off items I have done. Now, where did I put my list?

REVIEW TEST 1

At the appropriate spot or spots, insert the punctuation mark shown in the margin.

EXAMPLE

;   The singles dance was a success; I met several people I wanted to see again.

:   1. That catalog lists some unusual items a sausage stuffer, an electric foot warmer, and a remote-control car starter.

—   2. My brother's jokes none of which I can repeat are unfunny and tasteless.

-    3. These days, many two career couples have decided not to have children.

( )   4. The section on space travel in my daughter's science book Chapters 10–11 is sadly out of date.

:   5. Anne Frank wrote in her diary "It's a wonder I haven't abandoned all my ideals; they seem so absurd and impractical. Yet I cling to them because I still believe, in spite of everything, that people are truly good at heart."

;   6. The frightened hamster darted from room to room finally, it crawled under a dresser.

—   7. Credit card bills, the mortgage payment, and car repairs no wonder my paycheck doesn't last till the end of the month.

-    8. Someone once defined a self confident person as one who does crossword puzzles in pen instead of pencil.

( )   9. Three ways to save money on home repairs are 1 get several estimates, 2 avoid costly designer products, and 3 do it yourself.

;   10. I ordered several items from Sears: two suitcases, one maroon and one blue; an extra-large, machine-washable sweater and a canvas gym bag.

REVIEW TEST 2

On a separate piece of paper, write two sentences using each of the following punctuation marks: colon, semicolon, dash, hyphen, parentheses.

SECTION

V

Word Use

Responding to Images

1. Which of these signs misuses a homonym? How should the word be spelled?
2. Why is the mistake in each sign particularly funny?

380

Dictionary Use

INTRODUCTORY ACTIVITY

The dictionary is an indispensable tool, as will be apparent if you try to answer the following questions *without* using one.

1. Which one of the following words is spelled incorrectly?

   fortutious   macrobiotics   stratagem

2. If you wanted to hyphenate the following word correctly, at which points would you place the syllable divisions?

   h i e r o g l y p h i c s

3. What common word has the sound of the first *e* in the word

   chameleon? _____

4. Where is the primary accent in the following word?

   o c t o g e n a r i a n

5. What are the two separate meanings of the word *earmark?*

   _____

   _____

Your dictionary is a quick and sure authority on all these matters: spelling, syllabication, pronunciation, and word meanings. And as this chapter will show, it is also a source for many other kinds of information.

Answers are on page 608.

The dictionary is a valuable tool. To take advantage of it, you need to understand the main kinds of information that a dictionary gives about a word. Look at the information provided for the word *dictate* in the following entry from the *American Heritage Dictionary,* fourth paperback edition.*

*©2001 Houghton Mifflin Company. Reprinted by permission from *American Heritage Dictionary of the English Language,* Fourth Paperback Edition.

Spelling and syllabication   *Pronunciation*   *Part of speech*

dic•tate (dĭk′tāt′, dĭk-tāt′) *v.* **-tat•ed, -tat•ing.** — *Meanings*
1. To say or read aloud for transcription.
2. To prescribe or command with author-
ity. —*n.* (dĭk′tāt′). **1.** A directive; command. — *Example*
2. A guiding principle: *the dictates of con-*
science. [< Lat. *dictāre.* < *dīcere, say*]
—**dic•ta′tion** *n.* — *Etymology*

Other form of the word

Spelling

The first bit of information, in the **boldface** (heavy type) entry itself, is the
spelling of *dictate.* You probably already know the spelling of *dictate,* but if
you didn't, you could find it by pronouncing the syllables in the word carefully and then looking it up in the dictionary.

| ACTIVITY 1 | **Using a Dictionary** |

Use your dictionary to correct the spelling of the following words:

wellcome _____   persistant _____

quiting _____   proformance _____

consentration _____   oppurtinity _____

perfessional _____   desision _____

recieving _____   roomate _____

aranged _____   envolvment _____

extremly _____   diferance _____

nesasary _____   catagory _____

exciteing _____   priveledge _____

Syllabication

The second bit of information that the dictionary gives, also within the
boldface entry, is the syllabication of *dic•tate.* Note that a dot separates each
syllable (or part) of the word.

| ACTIVITY 2 | **Marking Syllable Divisions** |

Use your dictionary to mark the syllable divisions in the following
words. Also indicate how many syllables are in each word.

venture	(_____ syllables)
obsession	(_____ syllables)
energetic	(_____ syllables)
inspirational	(_____ syllables)

Noting syllable divisions will enable you to *hyphenate* a word: divide it at the end of one line of writing and complete it at the beginning of the next line. You can correctly hyphenate a word only at a syllable division, and you may have to check your dictionary to make sure of the syllable divisions for a particular word.

Pronunciation

The third bit of information in the sample dictionary entry is the pronunciation of *dictate: (dik′tat′)* or (*dik-tat′*). You already know how to pronounce *dictate,* but if you did not, the information within the parentheses would serve as your guide.

Vowel Sounds

You will probably use the pronunciation key in your dictionary mainly as a guide to pronouncing different vowel sounds (*vowels* are the letters *a, e, i, o,* and *u*). Here is the pronunciation key that appears on every other page of the paperback *American Heritage Dictionary:*

ă pat   ā pay   â care   ä father   ĕ pet   ē be   ĭ pit   ī tie   î pier
ŏ pot   ō toe   ô paw, for   oi noise   ŏŏ took   ōō boot   ou out
th thin   *th* this   ŭ cut   û urge   yōō abuse   zh vision
ə about, item, edible, gallop, circus

This key tells you, for example, that the short *a* is pronounced like the *a* in *pat,* the long *a* is like the *a* in *pay,* and the short *i* is like the *i* in *pit.*

Understanding Vowel Sounds   ACTIVITY 3

Look at the pronunciation key in your own dictionary. The key is probably located in the front of the dictionary or at the bottom of every page. What common word in the key tells you how to pronounce each of the following sounds?

ĕ _____   ō _____

ī _____   ŭ _____

ŏ _____   ōō _____

TIP: A long vowel always has the sound of its own name.

The Schwa (ə)

The symbol ə looks like an upside-down *e*. It is called a *schwa*, and it stands for the unaccented sound in such words as *about, item, edible, gallop,* and *circus.* More approximately, it stands for the sound *uh*—like the *uh* that speakers sometimes make when they hesitate. Perhaps it would help to remember that *uh*, as well as ə, could be used to represent the schwa sound.

Here are three of the many words in which the schwa sound appears: *socialize* (sō´shə līz or sō´shuh līz); *legitimate* (lə jǐt´ ə mǐt or luh jǐt´ uh mǐt); *oblivious* (ə blǐv´ē əs or uh blǐv´ē uhs).

ACTIVITY 4   **Using the Schwa**

Open your dictionary to any page, and you will almost surely be able to find three words that make use of the schwa in the pronunciation in parentheses after the main entry. Write three such words and their pronunciations in the following spaces:

1. _____

2. _____

3. _____

Accent Marks

Some words contain both a primary accent, shown by a heavy stroke (´), and a secondary accent, shown by a lighter stroke (´). For example, in the word *vicissitude* (vǐ sǐs´ ǐ to͞od´), the stress, or accent, goes chiefly on the second syllable (sǐs´), and, to a lesser extent, on the last syllable (to͞od´).

Use your dictionary to add stress marks to the following words:

notorious (nō tôr´ ē əs)   enterprise (ĕn´ tər prīz)

instigate (ǐn´ stǐ gāt)   irresistible (ǐr´ ǐ zǐs´ tə bəl)

equivocate (ǐ kwǐv´ ə kāt)   probability (prŏb´ ə bǐl´ ǐ tē)

millennium (mə lĕn´ ē əm)   representative (rĕp´ rǐ zen´ tə tǐv)

Full Pronunciation

Use your dictionary to write out the full pronunciation (the information given in parentheses) for each of the following words:

1. magnate _____

2. semblance _____

3. satiate _____

4. bastion _____

5. celestial _____

6. extraneous _____

7. edifice _____

8. incipient _____

9. fallacious _____

10. ostracize _____

11. phlegmatic _____

12. proximity _____

13. anachronism _____

14. felicitous _____

15. extemporaneous _____

Now practice pronouncing each word. Use the pronunciation key in your dictionary as an aid to sounding out each syllable. Do *not* try to pronounce a word all at once; instead, work on mastering *one syllable at a time*. When you can pronounce each of the syllables in a word successfully, then say them in sequence, add the accent, and pronounce the entire word.

Other Information about Words

Parts of Speech

The dictionary entry for *dictate* includes the abbreviation *v*. This indicates that the meanings of *dictate* as a verb will follow. The abbreviation *n*. is then followed by the meanings of *dictate* as a noun.

Using a Dictionary's Abbreviations Key	ACTIVITY 5

At the front of your dictionary, you will probably find a key that will explain the meanings of abbreviations used in the dictionary. Use the key to fill in the meanings of the following abbreviations:

pl.   = _____

sing. = _____

adj.   = _____

adv.   = _____

Principal Parts of Irregular Verbs

Dictate is a regular verb and forms its principal parts by adding -*d*, -*d*, and -*ing* to the stem of the verb. When a verb is irregular, the dictionary lists its principal parts. For example, with *begin* the present tense comes first (the entry itself, *begin*). Next comes the past tense (*began*), and then the past participle (*begun*)— the form of the verb used with such helping words as *have, had,* and *was*. Then comes the present participle (*beginning*)—the -*ing* form of the word.

ACTIVITY 6 — Principal Parts

Look up the principal parts of the following irregular verbs and write them in the spaces provided. The first one has been done for you.

Present	Past	Past Participle	Present Participle
see	saw	seen	seeing
choose	_____	_____	_____
know	_____	_____	_____
speak	_____	_____	_____

Plural Forms of Irregular Nouns

The dictionary supplies the plural forms of all irregular nouns. (Regular nouns form the plural by adding -s or -es.)

ACTIVITY 7 — Writing Plural Forms

Write the plurals of the following nouns:

thief   _____

cavity   _____

hero   _____

thesis   _____

 TIP: See pages 392–394 for more information about plurals.

Meanings

When a word has more than one meaning, its meanings are numbered in the dictionary, as with the sample verb *dictate*. In many dictionaries, the most common meanings are presented first. The introductory pages of your dictionary will explain the order in which meanings are presented.

ACTIVITY 8 — Using Sentence Context

Use the sentence context to try to explain the meaning of the underlined word in each of the following sentences. Write your definition in the space provided. Then look up and record the dictionary meaning of the word. Be sure to select the meaning that best fits the word as it is used in the sentence.

1. Honesty is a cardinal rule in my family.

    Your definition:

    _____

Dictionary definition: _____

_____

2. The union strike put management in a ticklish situation.

Your definition: _____

Dictionary definition: _____

3. Ben lacks confidence, probably because his parents constantly railed at him.

Your definition: _____

_____

Dictionary definition: _____

_____

Etymology

Etymology refers to the history of a word. Many words have origins in foreign languages, such as Greek (abbreviated Gk in the dictionary) or Latin (L). Such information is usually enclosed in brackets and is more likely to be present in an online or hardbound desk dictionary than in a paperback one. A good desk dictionary will tell you, for example, that the word *cannibal* derives from the name of the man-eating tribe, the Caribs, that Christopher Columbus discovered on Cuba and Haiti.

The following are some good desk dictionaries:

The American Heritage Dictionary

Random House College Dictionary

Webster's New Collegiate Dictionary

Webster's New World Dictionary

Etymology	**ACTIVITY 9**

See if your dictionary says anything about the origins of the following words.

magazine _____

anatomy _____

frankfurter _____

Usage Labels

As a general rule, use only Standard English words in your writing. If a word is not Standard English, your dictionary will probably give it a usage label such as *informal, nonstandard, slang, vulgar, obsolete, archaic,* or *rare.*

| ACTIVITY 10 | **Usage** |

Look up the following words and record how your dictionary labels them. Remember that a recent hardbound desk dictionary or the online *Oxford English Dictionary* will always be the best source of information about usage.

sharp (meaning *attractive*)

_____

hard-nosed

_____

sass (meaning *to talk impudently*)

_____

ain't

_____

put-down

_____

Synonyms

A *synonym* is a word that is close in meaning to another word. Using synonyms helps you avoid unnecessary repetition of the same word in a paper. A paperback dictionary is not likely to give you synonyms for words, but a good desk dictionary will. (You might also want to own a *thesaurus,* a book that lists synonyms and antonyms. An *antonym* is a word approximately opposite in meaning to another word.)

| ACTIVITY 11 | **Synonyms** |

Consult a desk dictionary that gives synonyms for the following words, and write some of the synonyms in the spaces provided.

desire _____

ask _____

cry _____

| **REVIEW TEST** |

Items 1–5
Use your dictionary to answer the following questions.

1. How many syllables are in the word *neurosurgery?* _____

2. Where is the primary accent in the word *elevation?* _____

3. In the word *evasion,* the *a* is pronounced like

   a. short *o*

   b. short *a*

   c. schwa

   d. long *a*

4. In the word *nobility,* the *y* is pronounced like

   a. schwa

   b. short *a*

   c. long *e*

   d. short *e*

5. In the word *data,* the second *a* is pronounced like

   a. short *a*

   b. schwa

   c. short *i*

   d. long *e*

Items 6–10

There are five misspelled words in the following sentence. Cross out each misspelled word and write the correct spelling in the spaces provided.

Some freinds and I are planning to go to the libary on Wensday to do some research for an importent paper for our litrature class.

6. _____

7. _____

8. _____

9. _____

10. _____

Spelling Improvement

INTRODUCTORY ACTIVITY

See if you can circle the word that is misspelled in each of the following pairs:

akward	*or*	awkward
exercise	*or*	exercize
business	*or*	buisness
worried	*or*	worryed
shamful	*or*	shameful
begining	*or*	beginning
partys	*or*	parties
sandwichs	*or*	sandwiches
heroes	*or*	heros

Answers are on page 608.

Poor spelling often results from bad habits developed in early grade-school years. With work, such habits can be corrected. If you can write your name without misspelling it, there is no reason why you can't do the same with almost any word in the English language. Following are seven steps you can take to improve your spelling.

Step 1: Using the Dictionary

Get into the habit of using the dictionary. When you write a paper, allow yourself time to look up the spelling of all the words you are unsure about. Do not underestimate the value of this step just because it is such a simple one. By using the dictionary, you can probably make yourself a 95 percent better speller.

Step 2: Keeping a Personal Spelling List

Keep a list of words you misspell, and study those words regularly. You might use the space in Appendix F: A Writer's Journal to keep track of these words (see pp. 611–620).

> **TIP**   When you have trouble spelling long words, try to break each word into syllables and see whether you can spell the syllables. For example, *mis-demeanor* can be spelled easily if you can hear and spell in turn its four syllables: *mis-de-mean-or.* The word *formidable* can be spelled more easily if you hear and spell in turn its four syllables: *for-mi-da-ble.* Remember: try to see, hear, and spell long words in terms of their syllables.

Step 3: Mastering Commonly Confused Words

Master the meanings and spellings of the commonly confused words on pages 402–417. Your instructor may assign twenty words for you to study at a time and give you a series of quizzes until you have mastered all the words.

Step 4: Using a Computer's Spell-Checker

Most word-processing programs feature a *spell-checker* that will identify incorrect words and suggest correct spellings. If you are unsure how to use yours, consult the program's "help" function. Spell-checkers are not foolproof; they will fail to catch misused homonyms like the words *your* and *you're.*

Step 5: Understanding Basic Spelling Rules

Explained briefly here are three rules that may improve your spelling. While exceptions sometimes occur, these rules hold true most of the time.

1. *Change y to i.*   When a word ends in a consonant plus *y*, change *y* to *i* when you add an ending.

try + ed = tried	marry + es = marries
worry + es = worries	lazy + ness = laziness
lucky + ly = luckily	silly + est = silliest

2. *Final silent e.*   Drop a final *e* before an ending that starts with a vowel (the vowels are *a, e, i, o,* and *u*).

hope + ing = hoping	sense + ible = sensible
fine + est = finest	hide + ing = hiding

Keep the final *e* before an ending that starts with a consonant.

use + ful = useful   care + less = careless

life + like = lifelike   settle + ment = settlement

3. ***Doubling a final consonant.***   Double the final consonant of a word when all the following are true:

a. The word is one syllable or is accented on the last syllable.
b. The word ends in a single consonant preceded by a single vowel.
c. The ending you are adding starts with a vowel.

sob   + ing = sobbing   big   + est = biggest

drop   + ed = dropped   omit   + ed   = omitted

admit + ing = admitting   begin + ing = beginning

| ACTIVITY 1 | Using Correct Endings |

Combine the following words and endings by applying the previous three rules.

HINT: Change *y* to *i* in item 1.

1. hurry   + ed   = _____   6. commit + ed   = _____

2. admire   + ing = _____   7. dive   + ing = _____

3. deny   + es   = _____   8. hasty   + ly = _____

4. jab   + ing = _____   9. propel   + ing = _____

5. magnify + ed   = _____   10. nudge   + es = _____

Step 6: Understanding Plurals

Most words form their plurals by adding *-s* to the singular.

Singular	Plural
blanket	blankets
pencil	pencils
street	streets

Some words, however, form their plurals in special ways, as shown in the rules that follow.

- Words ending in *-s, -ss, -z, -x, -sh,* or *-ch* usually form the plural by adding *-es.*

kiss	kisses	inch	inches
box	boxes	dish	dishes

- Words ending in a consonant plus *y* form the plural by changing *y* to *i* and adding *-es.*

| party | parties | county | counties |
| baby | babies | city | cities |

- Some words ending in *f* change the *f* to *v* and add *-es* in the plural.

| leaf | leaves | life | lives |
| wife | wives | yourself | yourselves |

- Some words ending in *o* form their plurals by adding *-es*.

| potato | potatoes | mosquito | mosquitoes |
| hero | heroes | tomato | tomatoes |

- Some words of foreign origin have irregular plurals. When in doubt, check your dictionary.

| antenna | antennae | crisis | crises |
| criterion | criteria | medium | media |

- Some words form their plurals by changing letters within the word.

| man | men | foot | feet |
| tooth | teeth | goose | geese |

- Combined words (words made up of two or more words) form their plurals by adding *-s* to the main word.

| brother-in-law | brothers-in-law |
| passerby | passersby |

Using Plural Endings or Forms   ACTIVITY 2

Complete these sentences by filling in the plural of the word at the left.

> **HINT**   A word ending in *s* forms the plural by adding *-es*.

bus   1. No _____ are permitted on the Channel Bridge.

grocery   2. Many of the _____ spilled out of the bags in my trunk when I braked suddenly.

potato   3. Baked _____ complement almost any main dish.

taxi   4. Just after I decided to take the crowded bus, four _____ passed us on Market Street.

themself   5. The owners of the failed curried-pizza restaurant have no one but _____ to blame.

theory   6. The essay question asked us to describe two _____ of evolution.

passerby

7. When I had a flat tire after work, several _____ stopped to ask if they could help.

alumnus

8. More presidents of the United States were _____ of Harvard than of any other university.

sandwich

9. The best short-order cook I ever met could make thirty bacon, lettuce, and tomato _____ in ten minutes.

mouse

10. During the sanitation workers' strike, _____ scurried along the street between bags of uncollected trash.

Step 7: Mastering a Basic Word List

Make sure you can spell all the words in the following list. They are some of the words used most often in English. Again, your instructor may assign twenty words for you to study at a time and give you a series of quizzes until you have mastered the words.

ability	beautiful	daughter
absent	because	death
accident	become	decide
across	before	deposit
address	begin	describe
advertise	being	different
advice	believe	direction
after	between	distance
again	bottom 40	doubt
against	breathe	dozen
all right	building	during
almost	business	each
a lot	careful	early
although	careless	earth
always	cereal	education
among	certain	either
angry	change	English
animal	cheap	enough 80
another	chief	entrance
answer 20	children	everything
anxious	church	examine
apply	cigarette	exercise
approve	clothing	expect
argue	collect	family
around	color	flower
attempt	comfortable	foreign
attention	company	friend
awful	condition	garden
awkward	conversation 60	general
balance	daily	grocery
bargain	danger	guess

Spelling

happy	ocean	sleep
heard	offer	smoke
heavy	often	something
height	omit	soul
himself	only	started
holiday	operate	state
house 100	opportunity	straight
however	original	street
hundred	ought	strong 200
hungry	pain	student
important	paper	studying
instead	pencil	success
intelligence	people	suffer
interest	perfect	surprise
interfere	period	teach
kitchen	personal	telephone
knowledge	picture	theory
labor	place 160	thought
language	pocket	thousand
laugh	possible	through
leave	potato	ticket
length	president	tired
lesson	pretty	today
letter	problem	together
listen	promise	tomorrow
loneliness	property	tongue
making 120	psychology	tonight
marry	public	touch
match	question	travel 220
matter	quick	truly
measure	raise	understand
medicine	ready	unity
middle	really	until
might	reason	upon
million	receive	usual
minute	recognize	value
mistake	remember	vegetable
money	repeat 180	view
month	restaurant	visitor
morning	ridiculous	voice
mountain	said	warning
much	same	watch
needle	sandwich	welcome
neglect	send	window
newspaper	sentence	would
noise	several	writing
none 140	shoes	written
nothing	should	year
number	since	yesterday 240

REVIEW TEST

Items 1–10
Use the three basic spelling rules to spell the following words.

1. admire   + able   = _____
2. drop   + ing   = _____
3. big   + est   = _____
4. gamble   + ing   = _____
5. luxury   + es   = _____
6. immediate   + ly   = _____
7. imply   + es   = _____
8. plan   + ed   = _____
9. involve   + ment   = _____
10. refer   + ed   = _____

Items 11–14
Circle the correctly spelled plural in each pair.

11. daisies   daisys
12. bookshelfs   bookshelves
13. mosquitos   mosquitoes
14. crisis   crises

Items 15–20
Circle the correctly spelled word (from the basic word list) in each pair.

15. tommorrow   tomorrow
16. height   hieght
17. needel   needle
18. visiter   visitor
19. hungry   hungery
20. writting   writing

Omitted Words and Letters

INTRODUCTORY ACTIVITY

Some people drop small connecting words such as *of, and,* or *in* when they write. They may also drop the *-s* endings of plural nouns. See if you can find the six places in the passage below where letters or words have been dropped. Supply whatever is missing.

Two glass bottle of apple juice lie broken the supermarket aisle.

Suddenly, a toddler who has gotten away from his parents appears at

the head of the aisle. He spots the broken bottles and begins to run

toward them. His chubby body lurches along like wind-up toy, and

his arm move excitedly up and down. Luckily, alert shopper quickly

reacts to the impending disaster and blocks the toddler's path. Then

the shopper waits with crying, frustrated little boy until his parents

show up.

Answers are on page 608.

Be careful not to leave out words or letters when you write. The omission of words such as *a, an, of, to,* or *the* or the *-s* ending needed on nouns or verbs may confuse and irritate your readers. They may not want to read what they regard as careless work.

Finding Omitted Words and Letters

Finding omitted words and letters, like finding many other sentence-skills mistakes, is a matter of careful proofreading. You must develop your ability to look carefully at a page to find places where mistakes may exist.

The exercises here will give you practice in finding omitted words and omitted *-s* endings on nouns. Another section of this book (pages 211–212) gives you practice in finding omitted *-s* endings on verbs.

Omitted Words

ACTIVITY 1	Adding Missing Words

Add the omitted word (*a*, *an*, *the*, *of*, or *to*) as needed.

EXAMPLE

Some people regard television as ^a tranquilizer that provides temporary relief from ^the pain and anxiety ^of modern life.

> **HINT** Four changes are needed in item 1.

1. I grabbed metal bar on roof of subway car as the train lurched into
   station.
2. For most our country's history, gold was basis the monetary system.
3. Maggie made about a quart French-toast batter—enough soak few
   dozen slices.
4. Several pairs sneakers tumbled around in dryer and banged against
   glass door.
5. To err is human and to forgive is divine, but never make a mistake in
   the first place takes lot of luck.
6. Raccoons like wash their food in stream with their nimble, glovelike
   hands before eating.
7. When I got the grocery store, I realized I had left my shopping list in
   glove compartment my car.
8. Game shows are inexpensive way for networks make high profit.
9. Soap operas, on other hand, are very expensive to produce because the
   high salaries of many cast members.
10. One memorable Friday the thirteenth, a friend mine bought black cat
    and broken mirror and walked under ladder. He had a wonderful day!

Omitted -s Endings

The plural form of regular nouns usually ends in *-s*. One common mistake
that some people make with plurals is to omit this *-s* ending. People who
drop the ending from plurals when speaking also tend to do it when writing. This tendency is especially noticeable when the meaning of the sentence shows that a word is plural.

Ed and Mary pay two hundred dollar a month for an apartment that has only two room.

The *-s* ending has been omitted from *dollars* and *rooms*.

The activities that follow will help you correct the habit of omitting the *-s* endings from plurals.

Using *-s* Endings	ACTIVITY 2

Add *-s* endings where needed.

EXAMPLE

Bill beat me at several game^s of darts.

> **HINT**   Two *-s* endings are needed in item 1.

1. Many sightseer flocked around the disaster area like ghoul.

2. Martha has two set of twins, and all of their name rhyme.

3. Dozen of beetle are eating away at the rosebush in our yard.

4. Since a convention of dentist was in town, all the restaurant had waiting line.

5. Until the first of the year, worker in all department will not be permitted any overtime.

6. Blinking light, such as those on video game or police car, can trigger seizures in person with epilepsy.

7. Ray and his friends invented several game using an old rubber radiator hose and two plastic ball.

8. My thirteen-year-old has grown so much lately that she doesn't fit into the shoe and jean I bought for her a couple of month ago.

9. While cleaning out her desk drawers, Ann found a page of postage stamp stuck together and a couple of dried-up pen.

10. Worker fed large log and chunk of wood into the huge machine, which spit out chip and sawdust from its other end.

ACTIVITY 3	Writing with Plural Forms

Write sentences that use plural forms of the following pairs of words.

EXAMPLE

girl, bike ___The little girls raced their bikes down the street.___

1. college, student

    _____

    _____

2. shopper, bargain

    _____

    _____

3. car, driver

    _____

    _____

4. instructor, grade

    _____

    _____

5. vampire, victim

    _____

    _____

> **TIP** People who drop the *-s* ending on nouns also tend to omit endings on verbs. Pages 211–212 will help you correct the habit of dropping verb endings.

REVIEW TEST 1

Insert the two small connecting words needed in each sentence.

1. When I opened freezer door, box of ice cream fell out.

2. Hiking along trail next to the lake, we came to very muddy stretch.

3. The newlyweds rented apartment with two rooms and bath.

4. I had walk all the way up to our fifth-floor office because elevator was broken.

5. Unfortunately, the road leading wealth is a lot longer than one leading to poverty.

Insert the two -*s* endings needed in each sentence.

1. The tallest building in the city has 67 floor and 75,010 doorknob.

2. Student who receive the highest grades are usually the one who study the most.

3. The trash cans by the picnic benches attracted dozen of bee.

4. Tiny crack were visible in all the wall of the building after the earthquake.

5. The fruit basket we received included instruction for ripening fresh fruit and a booklet of recipe.

Commonly Confused Words

INTRODUCTORY ACTIVITY

Circle the five words that are misspelled in the following passage. Then write their correct spellings in the spaces provided.

If your a resident of a temperate climate, you may suffer from feelings of depression in the winter and early spring. Scientists are now studying people who's moods seem to worsen in winter, and there findings show that the amount of daylight a person receives is an important factor in "seasonal depression." When a person gets to little sunlight, his or her mood darkens. Its fairly easy to treat severe cases of seasonal depression; the cure involves spending a few hours a day in front of full-spectrum fluorescent lights that contain all the components of natural light.

1. _____
2. _____
3. _____
4. _____
5. _____

Answers are on page 609.

Homonyms

The commonly confused words shown below are known as *homonyms;* they have the same sounds but different meanings and spellings. Complete the activities for each set of words, and check off and study any words that give you trouble.

COMMON HOMONYMS

all ready	knew	principal	to
already	new	principle	too
			two
brake	know	right	
break	no	write	wear
			where
coarse	pair	than	
course	pear	then	weather
			whether
hear	passed	their	
here	past	there	whose
		they're	who's
hole	peace		
whole	piece	threw	your
		through	you're
its	plain		
it's	plane		

Homonyms

Commonly Confused Words

all ready   completely prepared

already   previously, before

We were *all ready* to go, for we had eaten and packed *already* that morning.

Fill in the blanks: Phil was _____ for his driver's test, since he had _____ memorized the questions and regulations.

Write sentences using *all ready* and *already.*

_____

_____

brake   stop

break   come apart

Dot slams the *brake* pedal so hard that I'm afraid I'll *break* my neck in her car.

Fill in the blanks: While attempting to _____ a speed record, the race-car driver had to _____ for a spectator who had wandered onto the track.

Write sentences using *brake* and *break.*

_____

_____

coarse	rough
course	part of a meal; a school subject; direction; certainly (with *of*)

During the *course* of my career as a waitress, I've dealt with some very *coarse* customers.

Fill in the blanks: The instructor in my electronics _____ is known to use _____ language.

Write sentences using *coarse* and *course.*

_____

_____

hear	perceive with the ear
here	in this place

If I *hear* another insulting ethnic joke *here,* I'll leave.

Fill in the blanks: Unless you sit right _____ in one of the front rows, you won't be able to _____ a single thing the soft-spoken lecturer says.

Write sentences using *hear* and *here.*

_____

_____

hole	empty spot
whole	entire

If there is a *hole* in the tailpipe, I'm afraid we will have to replace the *whole* exhaust assembly.

Fill in the blanks: If you eat the _____ portion of chili, it will probably burn a _____ in your stomach.

Write sentences using *hole* and *whole.*

_____

_____

its	belonging to it
it's	contraction of *it is* or *it has*

The kitchen floor has lost *its* shine because *it's* been used as a rollerskating rink by the children.

Fill in the blanks: Our living-room carpet has lost _____ vivid color since_____ been exposed to so much sunlight.

Write sentences using *its* and *it's.*

_____

_____

knew   past tense of *know*

new   not old

We *knew* that the *new* television comedy would be canceled quickly.

Fill in the blanks: As soon as we brought our _____ microwave home,

we _____ it wouldn't fit where we planned to put it.

Write sentences using *knew* and *new.*

_____

_____

know   to understand

no   a negative

I never *know* who might drop in even though *no* one is expected.

Fill in the blanks: I _____ there are _____ openings in your

company at present, but please keep my résumé in case anything turns up.

Write sentences using *know* and *no.*

_____

_____

pair   set of two

pear   fruit

The dessert consisted of a *pair* of thin biscuits topped with vanilla ice cream and poached *pear* halves.

Fill in the blanks: We spotted a _____ of bluejays on our dwarf

_____ tree.

Write sentences using *pair* and *pear.*

_____

_____

passed   went by; succeeded in; handed to

past   time before the present; by, as in "I drove past the house."

After Edna *passed* the driver's test, she drove *past* all her friends' houses and honked the horn.

Fill in the blanks: Norman couldn't understand why he'd been

_____ over for the promotion, because his _____ work had

been very good.

Write sentences using *passed* and *past.*

_____

_____

peace   calm

piece   part

The *peace* of the little town was shattered when a *piece* of a human body was found in the town dump.

Fill in the blanks: We ate in _____ until my two brothers started fighting over who would get the last _____ of blueberry pie.

Write sentences using *peace* and *piece*.

_____

_____

plain   simple

plane   aircraft

The *plain* box contained a very expensive model *plane* kit.

Fill in the blanks: The _____ truth is that unless you can land this _____ within the next twenty minutes, it will run out of fuel and crash.

Write sentences using *plain* and *plane*.

_____

_____

principal   main; a person in charge of a school; amount of money
            borrowed

principle   law or standard

My *principal* goal in child rearing is to give my daughter strong *principles* to live by.

Fill in the blanks: My _____ reason for turning down the part-time job is that it's against my _____s to work on weekends.

Write sentences using *principal* and *principle*.

_____

_____

HINT   It might help to remember that the *e* in *principle* is also in *rule*—the meaning of *principle*.

right   correct; opposite of *left;* something to which one is entitled

write   to put words on paper

It is my *right* to refuse to *write* my name on your petition.

Fill in the blanks: The instructor said if the students' outlines were

not _____, they would have to _____ them again.

Write sentences using *right* and *write.*

_____

_____

than   used in comparisons

then   at that time

I glared angrily at my boss, and *then* I told him our problems were more
serious *than* he suspected.

Fill in the blanks: Felix hiked seven miles and _____ chopped fire-

wood; he was soon more tired _____ he'd been in years.

Write sentences using *than* and *then.*

_____

_____

> **HINT**   It might help to remember that *then* (the word spelled with an *e*) is
> a time signal (*time* also has an *e*).

their   belonging to them

there   at that place; a neutral word used with verbs such as *is, are, was,*
            were, have, and *had*

they're   contraction of *they are*

The tenants *there* are complaining because *they're* being cheated by *their*
landlords.

Fill in the blanks: The music next door is so loud that I'm going over

_____ to tell my neighbors to turn _____ stereo down

before _____ arrested for disturbing the peace.

Write sentences using *their, there,* and *they're.*

_____

_____

threw   past tense of *throw*

through from one side to the other; finished

When a character in a movie *threw* a cat *through* the window, I had to close my eyes.

Fill in the blanks: When Lee was finally _____ studying for her psychology final, she _____ her textbook and notes into her closet.

Write sentences using *threw* and *through*.

_____

_____

to   verb part, as in *to smile*; toward, as in "I'm going to school."

too   overly, as in "The pizza was too hot"; also, as in "The coffee was hot, too."

two   the number 2

Lola drove *to* the store *to* get some ginger ale. (The first *to* means *toward*; the second *to* is a verb part that goes with *get*.)

The jacket is *too* tight; the pants are tight, *too*. (The first *too* means *overly*; the second *too* means *also*.)

The *two* basketball players leaped for the jump ball. (the number 2)

Fill in the blanks: My _____ daughters are _____ young _____ wear much makeup.

Write sentences using *to, too,* and *two*.

_____

_____

wear   to have on

where   in what place

I work at a nuclear reactor, *where* one must *wear* a radiation-detection badge at all times.

Fill in the blanks: At the college _____ Ann goes, almost all the students _____ very casual clothes to class.

Write sentences using *wear* and *where*.

_____

_____

weather   atmospheric conditions

whether   if it happens that; in case; if

Because of the threatening *weather*, it's not certain *whether* the game will be played.

Fill in the blanks: After I hear the _____ report, I'll decide _____ I'll drive or take the train to my sister's house.

Write sentences using *weather* and *whether.*

_____

_____

whose   belonging to whom

who's   contraction of *who is* and *who has*

    The man *who's* the author of the latest diet book is a man *whose* ability to cash in on the latest craze is well known.

Fill in the blanks: The cousin _____ visiting us is the one _____ car was just demolished by a tractor trailer.

Write sentences using *whose* and *who's.*

_____

_____

your   belonging to you

you're   contraction of *you are*

    Since *your* family has a history of heart disease, *you're* the kind of person who should take extra health precautions.

Fill in the blanks: If _____ not going to eat any more, could I have what's left on _____ plate?

Write sentences using *your* and *you're.*

_____

_____

Other Words Frequently Confused

Following is a list of other words that people frequently confuse. Complete the activities for each set of words, and check off and study the ones that give you trouble.

COMMONLY CONFUSED WORDS			
a	among	desert	learn
an	between	dessert	teach
accept	beside	does	loose
except	besides	dose	lose
advice	can	fewer	quiet
advise	may	less	quite
affect	clothes	former	though
effect	cloths	latter	thought

ACTIVITY 2   Commonly Confused Words

a, an   Both *a* and *an* are used before other words to mean, approximately, *one.*

Generally you should use *an* before words starting with a vowel (*a, e, i, o, u*):

an absence   an exhibit   an idol   an offer   an upgrade

Generally you should use *a* before words starting with a consonant (all other letters):

a pen   a ride   a digital clock   a movie   a neighbor

Fill in the blanks: When it comes to eating, I am lucky; I can eat like _____ elephant and stay as thin as _____ snake.

Write sentences using *a* and *an.*

_____

_____

accept   receive; agree to

except   exclude; but

If I *accept* your advice, I'll lose all my friends *except* you.

Fill in the blanks: Everyone _____ my parents was delighted when I decided to _____ the out-of-town job offer.

Write sentences using *accept* and *except.*

_____

_____

advice   noun meaning *an opinion*

advise   verb meaning *to counsel, to give advice*

Jake never listened to his parents' *advice,* and he ended up listening to a cop *advise* him of his rights.

Fill in the blanks: My father once gave me some good _____: never _____ people on anything unless they ask you to.

Write sentences using *advice* and *advise.*

_____

_____

affect   verb meaning *to influence*

effect   verb meaning *to bring about something;* noun meaning *result*

My sister Sally cries for *effect,* but her act no longer *affects* my parents.

Fill in the blanks: Some school officials think suspension will

_____ students positively, but many students think its main

_____ is time off from school.

Write sentences using *affect* and *effect.*

_____

_____

among   implies three or more

between   implies only two

We selfishly divided the box of candy *between* the two of us rather than *among* all the members of the family.

Fill in the blanks: _____ my souvenirs from high school is a scrapbook with a large pink rose pressed _____ two of its pages.

Write sentences using *among* and *between.*

_____

_____

beside   along the side of

besides   in addition to

Fred sat *beside* Martha. *Besides* them, there were ten other people at the Tupperware party.

Fill in the blanks: Elena refused to sit _____ Carlos in class because

he always fidgeted, and, _____, he couldn't keep his mouth shut.

Write sentences using *beside* and *besides.*

_____

_____

can   refers to the ability to do something

may   refers to permission or possibility

If you *can* work overtime on Saturday, you *may* take Monday off.

Fill in the blanks: Joanne certainly _____ handle the project, but

she _____ not have time to complete it by the deadline.

Write sentences using *can* and *may.*

_____

_____

clothes   articles of dress

cloths   pieces of fabric

   I tore up some old *clothes* to use as polishing *cloths.*

Fill in the blanks: I keep a bag of dust _____ in the corner of my _____ closet.

Write sentences using *clothes* and *cloths.*

_____

_____

desert   a stretch of dry land; to abandon one's post or duty

dessert   last part of a meal

   Don't *desert* us now; order a sinful *dessert* along with us.

Fill in the blanks: I know my willpower will _____ me whenever there are brownies for _____.

Write sentences using *desert* and *dessert.*

_____

_____

does   form of the verb *do*

dose   amount of medicine

   Martha *does* not realize that a *dose* of brandy is not the best medicine for the flu.

Fill in the blanks: A _____ of aspirin _____ wonders for Sally's arthritis.

Write sentences using *does* and *dose.*

_____

_____

fewer   used with things that can be counted

less   refers to amount, value, or degree

   I missed *fewer* writing classes than Rafael, but I wrote *less* effectively than he did.

Fill in the blanks: Florence is taking _____ courses this semester because she has _____ free time than she did last year.

Write sentences using *fewer* and *less.*

_____

_____

former   refers to the first of two items named

latter   refers to the second of two items named

I turned down both the job in the service station and the job as a shipping clerk; the *former* involved irregular hours and the *latter* offered very low pay.

Fill in the blanks: My mother does both calisthenics and yoga; the

_____ keeps her weight down while the _____ helps her relax.

Write sentences using *former* and *latter.*

_____

_____

> **HINT**   Be sure to distinguish *latter* from *later* (meaning *after some time*).

learn   to gain knowledge

teach   to give knowledge

   After Roz *learns* the new dance, she is going to *teach* it to me.

Fill in the blanks: My dog is very smart; she can _____ any new trick

I _____ her in just minutes.

Write sentences using *learn* and *teach.*

_____

_____

loose   not fastened; not tight-fitting

lose   misplace; fail to win

   I am afraid I'll *lose* my ring; it's too *loose* on my finger.

Fill in the blanks: Those slippers are so _____ that every time I take a

step, I _____ one.

Write sentences using *loose* and *lose.*

_____

_____

quiet   peaceful

quite   entirely; really; rather

   After a busy day, the children were not *quiet,* and their parents were *quite* tired.

Fill in the blanks: After moving furniture all day, Vince was _____

exhausted, so he found a _____ place and lay down for a nap.

Write sentences using *quiet* and *quite.*

_____

_____

though despite the fact that

thought past tense of *think*

  Though I enjoyed the dance, I *thought* the cover charge of forty dollars was too high.

Fill in the blanks: Even _____ my paper was two weeks late, I _____ the instructor would accept it.

Write sentences using *though* and *thought*.

_____

_____

Incorrect Word Forms

Following is a list of incorrect word forms that people sometimes use in their writing. Complete the activities for each word, and check off and study any words that give you trouble.

INCORRECT WORD FORMS

being that	could of	should of
can't hardly	irregardless	would of
couldn't hardly	must of	

ACTIVITY 3 Incorrect Word Forms

being that Incorrect! Use *because* or *since*.

                                                because

  I'm going to bed now ~~being that~~ I must get up early tomorrow.

Correct the following sentences.

1. Being that our stove doesn't work, we'll have tuna salad for dinner.

2. I never invite both of my aunts over together, being that they don't speak to each other.

3. I'm taking a day off tomorrow being that it's my birthday.

can't hardly Incorrect! Use *can hardly* or *could hardly*.

couldn't hardly

                              can

  Small store owners ~~can't~~ hardly afford to offer large discounts.

Correct the following sentences.

1. I can't hardly concentrate when the teacher looks over my shoulder.

2. James couldn't hardly believe the bill for fixing his car's brakes.

3. You couldn't hardly hear the music because the audience was so loud.

could of   Incorrect! Use *could have.*

           have

I could ~~of~~ done better on that test.

Correct the following sentences.

1. The sidewalk was so hot you could of toasted bread on it.

2. The moon was so bright you could of read by it.

3. The peach pie was so good that I could of eaten it all.

irregardless   Incorrect! Use *regardless.*

    Regardless

~~Irregardless~~ of what anyone says, he will not change his mind.

Correct the following sentences.

1. Irregardless of your feelings about customers, you must treat them with courtesy.

2. Jay jogs every day irregardless of the weather.

3. Anyone can learn to read irregardless of age.

must of   Incorrect! Use *must have, should have, would have.*

should of

would of

         have

I should ~~of~~ applied for a loan when my credit was good.

Correct the following sentences.

1. I must of dozed off during the movie.

2. If Marty hadn't missed class yesterday, he would of known about today's test.

3. You should of told me to stop at the supermarket.

REVIEW TEST 1

These sentences check your understanding of *its, it's; there, their, they're; to, too, two;* and *your, you're.* Underline the correct word in the parentheses. Rather than guess, look back at the explanations of the words when necessary.

1. It seems whenever (your, you're) at the doctor's office, (your, you're) symptoms disappear.

2. The boss asked his assistant (to, too, two) rearrange the insurance files, placing each in (its, it's) proper sequence.

3. You'll get (your, you're) share of the pizza when (its, it's) cool enough (to, too, two) eat.

4. (Its, It's) a terrible feeling when (your, you're) (to, too, two) late (to, too, two) help someone.

5. (To, Too, Two) eat insects, most spiders use their (to, too, two) fangs to inject a special poison that turns (there, their, they're) victim's flesh into a soupy liquid they can drink.

6. (Its, It's) a fact that (there, their, they're) are (to, too, two) many violent shows on TV.

7. (There, Their, They're) is no valid reason for the (to, too, two) of you (to, too, two) have forgotten about turning in (your, you're) assignments.

8. If you (to, too, two) continue (to, too, two) drive so fast, (its, it's) likely you'll get ticketed by the police.

9. "My philosophy on guys is that (there, their, they're) just like buses," said Lola. "If you miss one, (there, their, they're) is always another one coming by in a little while."

10. "(Its, It's) about time you (to, too, two) showed up," the manager huffed. "(There, Their, They're) is already a line of customers waiting outside."

REVIEW TEST 2

The following sentences check your understanding of a variety of commonly confused words. Underline the correct word in the parentheses. Rather than guess, look back at the explanations of the words when necessary.

1. When (your, you're) (plain, plane) arrives, call us (weather, whether) (its, it's) late or not.

2. You (should have, should of) first found out (whose, who's) really (to, too, two) blame before coming in (hear, here) and making false accusations.

3. When Jack drove (threw, through) his old neighborhood, he (could hardly, couldn't hardly) recognize some of the places he (knew, new) as a child.

4. The (affect, effect) of having drunk (to, too, two) much alcohol last night was something like having (a, an) jackhammer drilling (among, between) my ears.

5. I was (quiet, quite) surprised to learn that in the (passed, past), (our, are) town was the site of (a, an) Revolutionary War battle.

6. Of (coarse, course) (its, it's) important to get good grades while (your, you're) in school, but it (does, dose) not hurt to (know, now, no) the (right, write) people when (your, you're) looking for a job.

7. If (your, you're) interested in listening to a great album, take my (advice, advise) and pick up a copy of *Sgt. Pepper's Lonely Hearts Club Band;* (its, it's) been voted the most popular rock album in history.

8. (Being that, Since) Barry has failed all five quizzes and one major exam and didn't hand in the midterm paper, he (though, thought) it would be a good idea (to, too, two) drop the (coarse, course).

9. (Their, There, They're) is (know, no) greater feeling (than, then) that of walking (threw, through) a forest in the spring.

10. I spent the (hole, whole) day looking (threw, through) my history notes, but when it came time to take the exam, I still (could hardly, couldn't hardly) understand the similarities (among, between) the Korean War, World War I, and World War II.

On a separate piece of paper, write short sentences using the ten words shown below.

their	effect
your	passed
it's	here
then	brake
too (meaning *also*)	whose

Commonly
Confused Words

CHAPTER

34

Effective Word Choice

Chapter Preview

Slang

Clichés

Pretentious Words

Wordiness

INTRODUCTORY ACTIVITY

Put a check beside the sentence in each pair that makes more effective and appropriate use of words.

1. After a bummer of a movie, we pigged out on a pizza. _____

   After a disappointing movie, we devoured a pizza. _____

2. Feeling blue about the death of his best friend, Tennyson wrote the tearjerker "In Memoriam." _____

   Mourning the death of his best friend, Tennyson wrote the moving poem "In Memoriam." _____

3. The personality adjustment inventories will be administered on Wednesday in the Student Center. _____

   Psychological tests will be given on Wednesday in the Student Center. _____

4. The referee in the game, in my personal opinion, made the right decision in the situation. _____

   I think the referee made the right decision. _____

Now see if you can circle the correct number in each case:

Pair (1, 2, 3, 4) contains a sentence with slang; pair (1, 2, 3, 4) contains a sentence with a cliché; pair (1, 2, 3, 4) contains a sentence with pretentious words; and pair (1, 2, 3, 4) contains a wordy sentence.

Answers are on page 610.

Choose your words carefully when you write. Always take the time to think about your word choices, rather than simply using the first word that comes to mind. You want to develop the habit of selecting words that are appropriate and exact for your purposes. One way you can show sensitivity to language is by avoiding slang, clichés, pretentious words, and wordiness.

418

Slang

We often use slang expressions when we talk because they are so vivid and colorful. However, slang is usually out of place in formal writing. Here are some examples of slang expressions:

www.mhhe.com/langan

> Last night's party was a *real train wreck.*
>
> I don't want to *lay a guilt trip* on you.
>
> My boss *dissed* me last night when he said I was a bad employee.
>
> Dad *flipped out* when he learned that Jan had *totaled* the car.
>
> Someone *ripped off* Ken's new running shoes from his locker.
>
> After the game, we *stuffed our faces* at the diner.
>
> I finally told my parents to *get off my case.*
>
> The movie really *grossed me out.*

Slang expressions have a number of drawbacks. They go out of date quickly, they become tiresome if used excessively in writing, and they may communicate clearly to some readers but not to others. Also, the use of slang can be an evasion of the specific details that are often needed to make one's meaning clear in writing. For example, in "the party was a real train wreck," the writer has not provided the specific details about the party necessary for us to understand the statement clearly. Was it the setting, the food and drink (or lack of them), the guests, the music, or the hosts that made the party such a dreadful experience? In general, then, you should avoid slang in your writing. If you are in doubt about whether an expression is slang, it may help to check a recently published hardbound dictionary.

Avoiding Slang   ACTIVITY 1

Rewrite the following sentences, replacing the italicized slang words with more formal ones.

EXAMPLE

> I was *so beat* Friday night that I decided *to ditch* the birthday party.
> I was so exhausted Friday night that I decided not to go to the birthday party.

 HINT   In item 1, consider: what do "putting it away" and "blimp" mean?

1. If you keep *putting it away,* you're going to be *a blimp.*

   _____

   _____

Effective Word Choice

2. My parents always *shoot me down* when I ask them for some *bucks* to buy new clothes.

   _____

   _____

3. The entire city was *psyched up* when the basketball team *creamed* its opponent in the play-offs.

   _____

   _____

4. If Ellen would *lighten up* and stop talking about her troubles, a date with her wouldn't be such a *downer*.

   _____

   _____

5. I'm going to have to *sweat it out* for the next couple of days, hoping the boss doesn't discover the *goof* I made.

   _____

   _____

Clichés

Clichés are expressions that have been worn out through constant use. Some typical clichés are listed below.

COMMON CLICHÉS

all work and no play	sad but true
at a loss for words	saw the light
better late than never	short and sweet
drop in the bucket	sigh of relief
easier said than done	singing the blues
had a hard time of it	taking a big chance
in the nick of time	time and time again
in this day and age	too close for comfort
it dawned on me	too little, too late
it goes without saying	took a turn for the worse
last but not least	under the weather
make ends meet	where he (*or* she) is coming from
needless to say	word to the wise
on top of the world	work like a dog

Clichés are common in speech but make your writing seem tired and stale. Also, they are often an evasion of the specific details that you must work to provide in your writing. You should, then, avoid clichés and try to express your meaning in fresh, original ways.

| **Avoiding Clichés** | **ACTIVITY 2** |

Underline the cliché in each of the following sentences. Then substitute specific, fresh words for the trite expression.

EXAMPLE

My parents supported me through some <u>trying times</u>.
rough years
_____

1. To make a long story short, my sister decided to file for divorce.

    _____

2. As quick as a wink, the baby tipped over the open box of oatmeal.

    _____

3. Any advice my friends give me goes in one ear and out the other.

    _____

4. I felt like a million dollars when I got my first A on a college test.

    _____

5. These days, well-paying jobs for high school graduates are few and far between.

    _____

HINT: In item 1, *to make a long story short* is a cliché.

| **WRITING ASSIGNMENT** |

Write a short paragraph describing the kind of day you had yesterday. Try to put as many clichés as possible into your writing. For example, "I had a long hard day. I had a lot to get done, and I kept my nose to the grindstone." By making yourself aware of clichés in this way, you should lessen the chance that they will appear in your writing.

Pretentious Words

Some people feel that they can improve their writing by using fancy, elevated words rather than simpler, more natural words. But artificial and stilted language more often obscures their meaning than communicates it clearly.

Here are some unnatural-sounding sentences:

The football combatants left the gridiron.

His instructional technique is a very positive one.

At the counter, we inquired about the arrival time of the aircraft.

I observed the perpetrator of the robbery depart from the retail establishment.

The same thoughts can be expressed more clearly and effectively by using plain, natural language:

The football players left the field.

His teaching style energizes students.

At the counter, we asked when the plane would arrive.

I saw the robber leave the store.

Following is a list of some other inflated words and the simple words that could replace them.

Inflated Words	Simpler Words
component	part
delineate	describe
facilitate	help
finalize	finish
initiate	begin
manifested	shown
subsequent to	after
to endeavor	to try
transmit	send

ACTIVITY 3   Avoiding Pretentious Words

Cross out the two pretentious words in each sentence. Then substitute clear, simple language for the pretentious words.

EXAMPLE

Sally was ~~terminated~~ from her ~~employment~~.

Sally was fired from her job.

> **HINT**   In item 1, replace *query* and *associates* with simpler words.

1. Please query one of our sales associates.

   _____

   _____

2. The meteorological conditions are terrible today.

   _____

   _____

3. My parents desire me to obtain a college degree.

   _____

   _____

4. Do not protrude your arm out of the car, or an accident might ensue.

   _____

   _____

5. Many conflagrations are caused by the careless utilization of portable heaters.

   _____

   _____

Wordiness

www.mhhe.com/langan

Wordiness—using more words than necessary to express a meaning—is often a sign of lazy or careless writing. Your readers may resent the extra time and energy they must spend when you have not done the work needed to make your writing direct and concise.

Here is a list of some wordy expressions that could be reduced to single words.

Wordy Form	Short Form
a large number of	many
a period of a week	a week
arrive at an agreement	agree
at an earlier point in time	before
at the present time	now
big in size	big
due to the fact that	because
during the time that	while
five in number	five
for the reason that	because
good benefit	benefit
in every instance	always
in my opinion	I think
in the event that	if
in the near future	soon
in this day and age	today
is able to	can
large in size	large
plan ahead for the future	plan
postponed until later	postponed
red in color	red
return back	return

Here are examples of wordy sentences:

At this point in time in our country, the amount of violence seems to be increasing every day.

I called to the children repeatedly to get their attention, but my shouts did not get any response from them.

Omitting needless words improves these sentences:

Violence is increasing in our country.

I called to the children repeatedly, but they didn't respond.

| ACTIVITY 4 | Omitting Unnecessary Words |

Rewrite the following sentences, cutting unnecessary words.

EXAMPLE

Starting as of the month of June, I will be working at the store on a fulltime basis.

As of June, I will be working at the store full time.

>   In item 1, the first part of the sentence and *as of yet* are wordy.

1. It is a well-known and proven fact that there is no cure as of yet for the common cold.

   _____

2. The main point that I will try to make in this paper is that our state should legalize and permit gambling.

   _____

3. Due to the fact that Chen's car refused to start up, he had to take public transportation by bus to his place of work.

   _____

4. When I was just a little boy, I already knew in my mind that my goal was to be a stockbroker in the future of my life.

   _____

5. The exercises that Susan does every day of the week give her more energy with which to deal with the happenings of everyday life.

   _____

Certain words are italicized in the following sentences. In the space provided, identify whether the words are slang (*S*), clichés (*C*), or pretentious words (*PW*). Then replace them with more effective words.

_____   1.   Donna *came out of her shell* after she joined a singing group at school.

_____

_____   2.   I *totally lost it* when my little brother *got busted* for underage drinking.

_____

_____   3.   I'm *suffering from a temporary depletion of all cash reserves.*

_____

_____   4.   Our manager *flipped out* when a cashier gave the wrong change to a customer.

_____

_____   5.   I got angry at the park visitors who did not put their *waste materials* in the *trash receptacle.*

_____

_____   6.   Hearing I had passed the accounting final really *took a load off my mind.*

_____

_____   7.   We all thought it was *too good to be true* when the instructor said that most of us would get As in the course.

_____

_____   8.   Fred *asserted to* the collection agency that he had sent the *remuneration.*

_____

_____   9.   My old Toyota just *bit the dust,* so I'm *checking out* new cars.

_____

_____   10.   This book was written by a millionaire who *didn't have a dime to his name* as a boy.

_____

REVIEW TEST 2

Rewrite the following sentences, omitting unnecessary words.

1. At 6:00 early this morning, I suddenly heard a loud and noisy banging by someone at the front door of my apartment.

   _____

   _____

2. The fact of the matter is that I did not remember until, of course, just now that I had an appointment to meet you.

   _____

   _____

3. We are very pleased to have the opportunity to inform you that your line of credit on your credit card with us has just been increased.

   _____

   _____

4. At this point in time, the company has no plan of adding to anyone's salary by giving a raise in pay in the near or distant future.

   _____

   _____

5. If you are out on the job market seeking a job, you just might benefit from professional help to assist you in your search for employment.

   _____

   _____

Correction Symbols

Here is a list of symbols your instructor may use when marking papers. The numbers in parentheses refer to the pages that explain the skill involved.

agr	Correct the mistake in agreement of subject and verb (230–238) or pronoun and the word the pronoun refers to (250–260).
apos	Correct the apostrophe mistake (337–348).
bal	Balance the parts of the sentence so they have the same (parallel) form (292–299).
cap	Correct the mistake in capital letters (320–328).
coh	Revise to improve coherence (70–75; 79–80).
comma	Add a comma (360–373).
CS	Correct the comma splice (179–193).
DM	Correct the dangling modifier (286–291).
det	Support or develop the topic more fully by adding details (53–70; 77–78).
frag	Attach the fragment to a sentence or make it a sentence (162–178).
lc	Use a lowercase (small) letter rather than a capital (320–328).
MM	Correct the misplaced modifier (281–285).
¶	Indent for a new paragraph.
no ¶	Do not indent for a new paragraph.
pro	Correct the pronoun mistake (250–272).
quot	Correct the mistake in quotation marks (349–359).
R-O	Correct the run-on (179–193).
sp	Correct the spelling error (381–417).
trans	Supply or improve a transition (70–75).
und	Underline (354–355).
verb	Correct the verb or verb form (210–229; 239–249).
wordy	Omit needless words (423–426).
WC	Replace the word marked with a more accurate one (word choice).
?	Write the illegible word clearly.
/	Eliminate the word, letter, or punctuation mark so slashed.
^	Add the omitted word or words.
; / : / - / —	Add semicolon (375), colon (374); hyphen (377), or dash (376).
✓	You have something fine or good here: an expression, a detail, an idea.

Walking Billboards

[1]Many Americans have turned into driving, walking billboards. [2]As much as we all claim to hate commercials on television we dont seem to have any qualms about turning ourselves into commercials. [3]Our car bumpers for example advertise lake resorts underground caverns, and amusement parks. [4]Also, we wear clothes marked with other peoples initials and slogans. [5]Our fascination with the names of designers show up on the backs of our sneakers, the breast pockets of our shirts, and the right rear pockets of our blue jeans. [6]And we wear T-shirts filled with all kinds of advertising messages. [7]For instance, people are willing to wear shirts that read, "Dillon Construction," "Nike," or even I Got Crabs at Ed's Seafood Palace. [8]In conclusion, we say we hate commercials, we actually pay people for the right to advertise their products.

See if you can locate and correct the ten sentence-skills mistakes in the preceding passage by a student writer. The mistakes are listed in the box below. As you locate each mistake, write the number of the word group containing that mistake. Use the spaces provided. Then (on a separate piece of paper) correct the mistakes.

1 run-on ____	2 missing commas around an interrupter ____ ____
1 mistake in subject-verb agreement ____	1 missing comma between items in a series ____
1 missing comma after introductory words ____	2 apostrophe mistakes ____ ____
	2 missing quotation marks ____ ____

Clear and Correct Sentences

✔ My paragraph/essay is free of fragments.

✔ My paragraph/essay contains no comma splices or fused sentences.

✔ Throughout, my sentence structure is varied.

Verbs, Pronouns, and Agreement

✔ In every sentence, my subjects agree with my verbs.

✔ I use verb tenses consistently.

✔ When I use pronouns, it is clear what (or which) noun they refer to.

Modifiers and Parallelism

✔ I use adjectives and adverbs correctly.

✔ My sentences contain no misplaced or dangling modifiers; it is clear what each modifier refers to.

✔ I have avoided faulty parallelism in my paragraph/essay.

Punctuation and Mechanics

✔ I use capitalization in appropriate places.

✔ I use end punctuation, apostrophes, quotation marks, commas, and other forms of punctuation correctly.

✔ I formatted my paper according to my instructor's guidelines or the instructions in Chapter 22.

Word Use

✔ I looked up any words whose meanings or spellings I was unsure of in a dictionary. I also used a spell-checker.

✔ I did not misuse any of the commonly confused words listed in Chapter 33.

✔ Throughout, I was careful to choose my words effectively, according to the guidelines in Chapter 34. I have avoided slang, clichés, and wordiness.

Readings for Writers

Introduction to the Readings

The reading selections in Part Four will help you find topics for writing. Some of the selections provide helpful practical information. For example, you'll learn how to discuss problems openly with others and how to avoid being manipulated by clever ads. Other selections deal with thought-provoking aspects of contemporary life, exploring why people play the lottery or behave in certain ways at the movies. Still other selections are devoted to a celebration of human goals and values; one essay, for example, examines what a "good family" really is. The varied subjects should inspire lively class discussions as well as serious individual thought. The selections should provide a continuing source of high-interest material for a wide range of writing assignments.

They will also help develop reading skills, which offer direct benefits to you as a writer. First, through close reading, you will learn how to recognize the main idea or point of a selection and how to identify and evaluate the supporting material that develops that main idea. In your writing, you will aim to achieve the same essential structure: an overall point followed by detailed, valid support for that point. Second, close reading will help you explore a selection and its possibilities thoroughly. The more you understand about what is said in a piece, the more ideas and feelings you may have about writing on an assigned topic or a related topic of your own. A third benefit of close reading is becoming more aware of authors' stylistic devices—for example, their introductions and conclusions, their ways of presenting and developing a point, their use of transitions, and their choice of language to achieve a particular tone. Recognizing these devices in other people's writing will help you expand your own range of writing techniques.

The Format of Each Selection

Each selection begins with a short **Preview** that gives helpful background information about the author and the work. This is followed by **Words to Watch,** a list of difficult words in the selection, with their paragraph numbers. You may find it helpful to look up the definitions of these words in a dictionary to remind yourself of meanings or to learn new ones. Within the reading itself, each listed word is marked with a small colored bullet (•). When you're reading, if you are not sure of the definition of a word marked with this bullet, don't hesitate to look it up. The selection is then followed by several sets of questions.

- First, there are **Vocabulary in Context** questions to help you expand your knowledge of selected words. **Reading Comprehension Questions** foster several important reading skills: recognizing a subject or topic, determining the thesis or main idea, identifying key supporting points, and making inferences. Answering the questions will enable you and your instructor to check quickly your basic understanding of a selection. More significantly, as you move from one selection to the next, you will sharpen your reading skills as well as strengthen your thinking skills—two key factors in becoming a better writer.

- Following the comprehension questions are several **Discussion Questions.** In addition to dealing with content, these questions focus on **Structure, Style,** and **Tone.**

Finally, several **Writing Assignments** accompany each selection. Many of the assignments provide suggestions for prewriting and appropriate methods of development. Some readings also feature related images and **Responding to Images** writing prompts. When writing your responses to the readings, you will have opportunities to apply all the methods of development presented in Chapter 4 of this book.

How to Read Well: Four General Steps

Skillful reading is an important part of becoming a skillful writer. Following are four steps that will help make you a better reader—both of the selections here and in your reading at large.

1 Concentrate as You Read

To improve your concentration, follow these tips. First, read in a place where you can be quiet and alone. Don't choose a spot where a TV or stereo is on or where friends or family are talking nearby. Next, sit in an upright position when you read. If your body is in a completely relaxed position, sprawled across a bed or nestled in an easy chair, your mind is also going to be completely relaxed. The light muscular tension that comes from sitting upright in a chair promotes concentration and keeps your mind ready to work. Finally, consider using your index finger (or a pen) as a pacer while you read. Lightly underline each line of print with your index finger as you read down a page. Hold your hand slightly above the page and move your finger at a speed that is a little too fast for comfort. This pacing with your index finger, like sitting upright on a chair, creates a slight physical tension that will keep your body and mind focused and alert.

2 Skim Material before You Read It

In skimming, you spend about two minutes rapidly surveying a selection, looking for important points and skipping secondary material. Follow this sequence when skimming:

- Begin by reading the overview that precedes the selection.

- Then study the title of the selection for a few moments. A good title is the shortest possible summary of a selection; it often tells you in several words what a selection is about.

- Next, form a basic question (or questions) based on the title. Forming questions out of the title is often a key to locating a writer's main idea—your next concern in skimming.

- Read the first two or three paragraphs and the last two or three paragraphs in the selection. Very often a writer's main idea, if it is directly stated, will appear in one of these paragraphs and will relate to the title.

- Finally, look quickly at the rest of the selection for other clues to important points. Are there any subheads you can relate in some way to the title? Are there any words the author has decided to emphasize by setting them off in *italic* or **boldface** type? Are there any major lists of items signaled by words such as *first, second, also, another,* and so on?

3 Read the Selection Straight through with a Pen Nearby

Don't slow down or turn back; just aim to understand as much as you can the first time through. Place a check or star beside answers to basic questions you formed from the title, and beside other ideas that seem important; you can also mark the passage or page with a tab or bookmark. Number lists of important points *1, 2, 3. . . .* Circle words you don't understand. Put question marks in the margin next to passages that are unclear and that you will want to reread.

4 Work with the Material

Go back and reread passages that were not clear the first time through. Look up words that block your understanding of ideas and write their meanings in the margin. Also, carefully reread the areas you identified as most important; doing so will deepen your understanding of the material. Now that you have a sense of the whole, prepare a short outline of the selection by answering the following questions on a sheet of paper:

- What is the main idea?

- What key points support the main idea?

- What seem to be other important points in the selection?

By working with the material in this way, you will significantly increase your understanding of a selection. Effective reading, just like effective writing, does not happen all at once. Rather, it is a process. Often you begin with a general impression of what something means, and then, by working at it, you move to a deeper level of understanding of the material.

How to Answer the **Vocabulary in Context** Questions

To decide on the meaning of an unfamiliar word, consider its context. Ask yourself, "Are there any clues in the sentence that suggest what this word means?"

How to Answer the **Reading Comprehension Questions**

Several important reading skills are involved in the reading comprehension questions that follow each selection. The skills are:

- Summarizing the selection by providing a title for it
- Determining the main idea
- Recognizing key supporting details
- Making inferences

The following hints will help you apply each of these reading skills:

- *Subject or title.* Remember that the title should accurately describe the *entire* selection. It should be neither too broad nor too narrow for the material in the selection. It should answer the question "What is this about?" as specifically as possible. Note that you may at times find it easier to do the "title" question *after* the "main idea" question.

- *Main idea.* Choose the statement that you think best expresses the main idea or thesis of the entire selection. Remember that the title will often help you focus on the main idea. Then ask yourself, "Does most of the material in the selection support this statement?" If you can answer *yes* to this question, you have found the thesis.

- *Key details.* If you were asked to give a two-minute summary of a selection, the major details are the ones you would include in that summary. To determine the key details, ask yourself, "What are the major supporting points for the thesis?"

- *Inferences.* Answer these questions by drawing on the evidence presented in the selection and on your own common sense. Ask yourself, "What reasonable judgments can I make on the basis of the information in the selection?"

* * *

The readings begin on the next page. Enjoy!

All the Good Things

Sister Helen Mrosla

<table>
<tr><td>

PREVIEW

Sometimes the smallest things we do have the biggest impact. A teacher's impulsive idea, designed to brighten a dull Friday-afternoon class, affected her students more than she ever dreamed. Sister Helen Mrosla's moment of classroom inspiration took on a life of its own, returning to visit her at a most unexpected time. Her account of the experience reminds us of the human heart's endless hunger for recognition and appreciation.

</td><td>

WORDS TO WATCH

mischievousness (1)
incessantly (2)
accustomed (2)
novice (3)
edgy (8)
pallbearer (17)

</td></tr>
</table>

1   He was in the first third-grade class I taught at Saint Mary's School in Morris, Minnesota. All thirty-four of my students were dear to me, but Mark Eklund was one in a million. He was very neat in appearance but had that happy-to-be-alive attitude that made even his occasional mischievousness• delightful.

2   Mark talked incessantly.• I had to remind him again and again that talking without permission was not acceptable. What impressed me so much, though, was his sincere response every time I had to correct him for misbehaving—"Thank you for correcting me, Sister!" I didn't know what to make of it at first, but before long I became accustomed• to hearing it many times a day.

3   One morning my patience was growing thin when Mark talked once too often, and then I made a novice• teacher's mistake. I looked at him and said, "If you say one more word, I am going to tape your mouth shut!"

4   It wasn't ten seconds later when Chuck blurted out, "Mark is talking again." I hadn't asked any of the students to help me watch Mark, but since I had stated the punishment in front of the class, I had to act on it.

5   I remember the scene as if it had occurred this morning. I walked to my desk, very deliberately opened my drawer, and took out a roll of masking tape. Without saying a word, I proceeded to Mark's desk, tore off two pieces of tape and made a big X with them over his mouth. I then returned to the front of the room. As I glanced at Mark to see how he was doing, he winked at me.

6   That did it! I started laughing. The class cheered as I walked back to Mark's desk, removed the tape, and shrugged my shoulders. His first words were, "Thank you for correcting me, Sister."

7   At the end of the year I was asked to teach junior-high math. The years flew by, and before I knew it Mark was in my classroom again. He was more handsome than ever and just as polite. Since he had to listen carefully to my instruction in the "new math," he did not talk as much in ninth grade as he had talked in the third.

8   One Friday, things just didn't feel right. We had worked hard on a new concept all week, and I sensed that the students were frowning, frustrated with themselves—and edgy• with one another. I had to stop this crankiness before it got out of hand. So I asked them to list the names of the other students in the room on two sheets of paper, leaving a space after each name. Then I told them to think of the nicest thing they could say about each of their classmates and write it down.

435

It took the remainder of the class period to finish the assignment, and as the 9 students left the room, each one handed me the papers. Charlie smiled. Mark said, "Thank you for teaching me, Sister. Have a good weekend."

That Saturday, I wrote down the name of each student on a separate sheet of 10 paper, and I listed what everyone else had said about that individual.

On Monday I gave each student his or her list. Before long, the entire class 11 was smiling. "Really?" I heard whispered. "I never knew that meant anything to anyone!" "I didn't know others liked me so much!"

No one ever mentioned those papers in class again. I never knew if the stu- 12 dents discussed them after class or with their parents, but it didn't matter. The exercise had accomplished its purpose. The students were happy with themselves and one another again.

That group of students moved on. Several years later, after I returned from 13 a vacation, my parents met me at the airport. As we were driving home, Mother asked me the usual questions about the trip—the weather, my experiences in general. There was a slight lull in the conversation. Mother gave Dad a sideways glance and simply said, "Dad?" My father cleared his throat as he usually did before something important. "The Eklunds called last night," he began. "Really?" I said. "I haven't heard from them in years. I wonder how Mark is."

Dad responded quietly. "Mark was killed in Vietnam," he said. "The funeral is 14 tomorrow, and his parents would like it if you could attend." To this day I can still point to the exact spot on I-494 where Dad told me about Mark.

I had never seen a serviceman in a military coffin before. Mark looked so 15 handsome, so mature. All I could think at that moment was, Mark, I would give all the masking tape in the world if only you would talk to me.

The church was packed with Mark's friends. Chuck's sister sang "The Battle 16 Hymn of the Republic." Why did it have to rain on the day of the funeral? It was difficult enough at the graveside. The pastor said the usual prayers, and the bugler played "Taps." One by one, those who loved Mark took a last walk by the coffin and sprinkled it with holy water.

I was the last one to bless the coffin. As I stood there, one of the soldiers who 17 had acted as pallbearer• came up to me. "Were you Mark's math teacher?" he asked. I nodded as I continued to stare at the coffin. "Mark talked about you a lot," he said.

After the funeral, most of Mark's former classmates headed to Chuck's farm- 18 house for lunch. Mark's mother and father were there, obviously waiting for me. "We want to show you something," his father said, taking a wallet out of his pocket. "They found this on Mark when he was killed. We thought you might recognize it."

Opening the billfold, he carefully removed two worn pieces of notebook pa- 19 per that had obviously been taped, folded and refolded many times. I knew without looking that the papers were the ones on which I had listed all the good things each of Mark's classmates had said about him. "Thank you so much for doing that," Mark's mother said. "As you can see, Mark treasured it."

Mark's classmates started to gather around us. Charlie smiled rather sheep- 20 ishly and said, "I still have my list. It's in the top drawer of my desk at home." Chuck's wife said, "Chuck asked me to put his list in our wedding album." "I have mine too," Marilyn said. "It's in my diary." Then Vicki, another classmate, reached into her pocketbook, took out her wallet, and showed her worn and frazzled list to the group. "I carry this with me at all times," Vicki said without batting an eyelash. "I think we all saved our lists."

That's when I finally sat down and cried. I cried for Mark and for all his friends 21 who would never see him again.

VOCABULARY IN CONTEXT

1. The word *incessantly* in "Mark talked incessantly. I had to remind him again and again that talking without permission was not acceptable" (paragraph 2) means

    a. slowly.

    b. quietly.

    c. constantly.

    d. pleasantly.

2. The word *edgy* in "We had worked hard on a new concept all week, and I sensed that the students were frowning, frustrated with themselves—and edgy with one another. I had to stop this crankiness before it got out of hand" (paragraph 8) means

    a. funny.

    b. calm.

    c. easily annoyed.

    d. dangerous.

READING COMPREHENSION QUESTIONS

1. Which of the following would be the best alternative title for this selection?

    a. Talkative Mark

    b. My Life as a Teacher

    c. More Important Than I Knew

    d. A Tragic Death

2. Which sentence best expresses the main idea of the selection?

    a. Although Sister Helen sometimes scolded Mark Eklund, he appreciated her devotion to teaching.

    b. When a former student of hers died, Sister Helen discovered how important one of her assignments had been to him and his classmates.

    c. When her students were cranky one day, Sister Helen had them write down something nice about each of their classmates.

    d. A pupil whom Sister Helen was especially fond of was tragically killed while serving in Vietnam.

3. Upon reading their lists for the first time, Sister Helen's students

    a. were silent and embarrassed.

    b. were disappointed.

    c. pretended to think the lists were stupid, although they really liked them.

    d. smiled and seemed pleased.

4. In the days after the assignment to write down something nice about one another,

    a. students didn't mention the assignment again.

    b. students often brought their lists to school.

    c. Sister Helen received calls from several parents complaining about the assignment.

    d. Sister Helen decided to repeat the assignment in every one of her classes.

5. According to Vicki,

   a. Mark was the only student to have saved his list.

   b. Vicki and Mark were the only students to have saved their lists.

   c. Vicki, Mark, Charlie, Chuck, and Marilyn were the only students to have saved their lists.

   d. all the students had saved their lists.

6. The author implies that

   a. she was surprised to learn how much the lists had meant to her students.

   b. Mark's parents were jealous of his affection for Sister Helen.

   c. Mark's death shattered her faith in God.

   d. Mark's classmates had not stayed in touch with one another over the years.

7. *True or false?* _____ The author implies that Mark had gotten married.

8. We can conclude that when Sister Helen was a third-grade teacher, she

   a. was usually short-tempered and irritable.

   b. wasn't always sure how to discipline her students.

   c. didn't expect Mark to do well in school.

   d. had no sense of humor.

DISCUSSION QUESTIONS

About Content

1. What did Sister Helen hope to accomplish by asking her students to list nice things about one another?

2. At least some students were surprised by the good things others wrote about them. What does this tell us about how we see ourselves and how we communicate our views of others?

3. "All the Good Things" has literally traveled around the world. Not only has it been reprinted in numerous publications, but many readers have sent it out over the Internet for others to read. Why do you think so many people love this story? Why do they want to share it with others?

About Structure

4. This selection is organized according to time. What three separate time periods does it cover? What paragraphs are included in the first time period? The second? The third?

5. Paragraph 8 includes a cause-and-effect structure. What part of the paragraph is devoted to the cause? What part is devoted to the effect? What transition word signals the break between the cause and the effect?

6. What does the title "All the Good Things" mean? Is this a good title for the essay? Why or why not?

About Style and Tone

7. Sister Helen is willing to let her readers see her weaknesses as well as her strengths. Find a place in the selection in which the author shows herself as less than perfect.

8. What does Sister Helen accomplish by beginning her essay with the word "he"? What does that unusual beginning tell the reader?

9. How does Sister Helen feel about her students? Find evidence that backs up your opinion.

10. Sister Helen comments on Mark's "happy-to-be-alive" attitude. What support does she provide that makes us understand what Mark was like?

RESPONDING TO IMAGES

From looking at the photograph below, what can you tell about the relationship between the students and their instructor? What specific visual clues help you draw these conclusions?

WRITING ASSIGNMENTS

Assignment 1: Writing a Paragraph

Early in her story, Sister Helen refers to a "teacher's mistake" that forced her to punish a student in front of the class. Write a paragraph about a time you gave in to pressure to do something because others around you expected it. Explain what the situation was, just what happened, and how you felt afterward. Here are two sample topic sentences:

> Even though I knew it was wrong, I went along with some friends who shoplifted at the mall.

Just because my friends did, I made fun of a kid in my study hall who was a slow learner.

Assignment 2: Writing a Paragraph

Sister Helen's students kept their lists for many years. What souvenir of the past have you kept for a long time? Why? Write a paragraph describing the souvenir, how you got it, and what it means to you. Begin with a topic sentence such as this:

> I've kept a green ribbon in one of my dresser drawers for over ten years because it reminds me of an experience I treasure.

Assignment 3: Writing an Essay

It's easy to forget to let others know how much they have helped us. Only after one of the students died did Sister Helen learn how important the list of positive comments had been to her class. Write an essay about someone to whom you are grateful and explain what that person has done for you. In your thesis statement, introduce the person and describe his or her relationship to you. Also include a general statement of what that person has done for you. Your thesis statement can be similar to any of these:

> My brother Roy has been an important part of my life.

> My best friend Ginger helped me through a major crisis.

> Mrs. Morrison, my seventh-grade English teacher, taught me a lesson for which I will always be grateful.

Use freewriting to help you find interesting details to support your thesis statement. You may find two or three separate incidents to write about, each in a paragraph of its own. Or you may find it best to use several paragraphs to give a detailed narrative of one incident or two or three related events. (Note how Sister Helen uses several separate "scenes" to tell her story.) Whatever your approach, use some dialogue to enliven key parts of your essay. (Review the reading to see how Sister Helen uses dialogue throughout her essay.)

Alternatively, write an essay about three people to whom you are grateful. In that case, each paragraph of the body of your essay would deal with one of those people. The thesis statement in such an essay might be similar to this:

> There are three people who have made a big difference in my life.

Rowing the Bus

Paul Logan

PREVIEW	WORDS TO WATCH
There is a well-known saying that goes something like this: All that is necessary in order for evil to triumph is for good people to do nothing. Even young people are forced to face cruel behavior and to decide how they will respond to it. In this essay, Paul Logan looks back at a period of schoolyard cruelty in which he was both a victim and a participant. With unflinching honesty, he describes his behavior then and how it helped to shape the person he has become.	simulate (1) feigning (5) taunted (6) belittled (6) gait (7) rift (9) stoic (13)

When I was in elementary school, some older kids made me row the bus. 1 Rowing meant that on the way to school I had to sit in the dirty bus aisle littered with paper, gum wads, and spitballs. Then I had to simulate• the motion of rowing while the kids around me laughed and chanted, "Row, row, row the bus." I was forced to do this by a group of bullies who spent most of their time picking on me.

I was the perfect target for them. I was small. I had no father. And my mother, 2 though she worked hard to support me, was unable to afford clothes and sneakers that were "cool." Instead she dressed me in outfits that we got from "the bags"— hand-me-downs given as donations to a local church.

Each Wednesday, she'd bring several bags of clothes to the house and pull out 3 musty, wrinkled shirts and worn bell-bottom pants that other families no longer wanted. I knew that people were kind to give things to us, but I hated wearing clothes that might have been donated by my classmates. Each time I wore something from the bags, I feared that the other kids might recognize something that was once theirs.

Besides my outdated clothes, I wore thick glasses, had crossed eyes, and spoke 4 with a persistent lisp. For whatever reason, I had never learned to say the "s" sound properly, and I pronounced words that began with "th" as if they began with a "d." In addition, because of my severely crossed eyes, I lacked the hand and eye coordination necessary to hit or catch flying objects.

As a result, footballs, baseballs, soccer balls and basketballs became my en- 5 emies. I knew, before I stepped onto the field or court, that I would do something clumsy or foolish and that everyone would laugh at me. I feared humiliation so much that I became skillful at feigning• illnesses to get out of gym class. Eventually I learned how to give myself low-grade fevers so the nurse would write me an excuse. It worked for a while, until the gym teachers caught on. When I did have to play, I was always the last one chosen to be on any team. In fact, team captains did everything in their power to make their opponents get stuck with me. When the unlucky team captain was forced to call my name, I would trudge over to the team, knowing that no one there liked or wanted me. For four years, from second through fifth grade, I prayed nightly for God to give me school days in which I would not be insulted, embarrassed, or made to feel ashamed.

I thought my prayers were answered when my mother decided to move dur- 6 ing the summer before sixth grade. The move meant that I got to start sixth grade in a different school, a place where I had no reputation. Although the older kids laughed and snorted at me as soon as I got on my new bus—they couldn't miss my thick glasses and strange clothes—I soon discovered that there was another kid who received the brunt of their insults. His name was George, and everyone made fun of him. The kids taunted• him because he was skinny; they belittled• him because he had acne that pocked and blotched his face; and they teased him because his voice was squeaky. During my first gym class at my new school, I wasn't the last one chosen for kickball; George was.

George tried hard to be friends with me, coming up to me in the cafeteria on 7 the first day of school. "Hi. My name's George. Can I sit with you?" he asked with a peculiar squeakiness that made each word high-pitched and raspy. As I nodded for him to sit down, I noticed an uncomfortable silence in the cafeteria as many of the students who had mocked George's clumsy gait• during gym class began watching the two of us and whispering among themselves. By letting him sit with me, I had violated an unspoken law of school, a sinister code of childhood that demands there must always be someone to pick on. I began to realize two things. If I befriended George, I would soon receive the same treatment that I had gotten at my old school. If I stayed away from him, I might actually have a chance to escape being at the bottom.

Within days, the kids started taunting us whenever we were together. "Who's your new little buddy, Georgie?" In the hallways, groups of students began mumbling about me just loud enough for me to hear, "Look, it's George's ugly boyfriend." On the bus rides to and from school, wads of paper and wet chewing gum were tossed at me by the bigger, older kids in the back of the bus. 8

It became clear that my friendship with George was going to cause me several more years of misery at my new school. I decided to stop being friends with George. In class and at lunch, I spent less and less time with him. Sometimes I told him I was too busy to talk; other times I acted distracted and gave one-word responses to whatever he said. Our classmates, sensing that they had created a rift• between George and me, intensified their attacks on him. Each day, George grew more desperate as he realized that the one person who could prevent him from being completely isolated was closing him off. I knew that I shouldn't avoid him, that he was feeling the same way I felt for so long, but I was so afraid that my life would become the hell it had been in my old school that I continued to ignore him. 9

Then, at recess one day, the meanest kid in the school, Chris, decided he had had enough of George. He vowed that he was going to beat up George and anyone else who claimed to be his friend. A mob of kids formed and came after me. Chris led the way and cornered me near our school's swing sets. He grabbed me by my shirt and raised his fist over my head. A huge gathering of kids surrounded us, urging him to beat me up, chanting "Go, Chris, go!" 10

"You're Georgie's new little boyfriend, aren't you?" he yelled. The hot blast of his breath carried droplets of his spit into my face. In a complete betrayal of the only kid who was nice to me, I denied George's friendship. 11

"No, I'm not George's friend. I don't like him. He's stupid," I blurted out. Several kids snickered and mumbled under their breath. Chris stared at me for a few seconds and then threw me to the ground. 12

"Wimp. Where's George?" he demanded, standing over me. Someone pointed to George sitting alone on top of the monkey bars about thirty yards from where we were. He was watching me. Chris and his followers sprinted over to George and yanked him off the bars to the ground. Although the mob quickly encircled them, I could still see the two of them at the center of the crowd, looking at each other. George seemed stoic,• staring straight through Chris. I heard the familiar chant of "Go, Chris, go!" and watched as his fists began slamming into George's head and body. His face bloodied and his nose broken, George crumpled to the ground and sobbed without even throwing a punch. The mob cheered with pleasure and darted off into the playground to avoid an approaching teacher. 13

Chris was suspended, and after a few days, George came back to school. I wanted to talk to him, to ask him how he was, to apologize for leaving him alone and for not trying to stop him from getting hurt. But I couldn't go near him. Filled with shame for denying George and angered by my own cowardice, I never spoke to him again. 14

Several months later, without telling any students, George transferred to another school. Once in a while, in those last weeks before he left, I caught him watching me as I sat with the rest of the kids in the cafeteria. He never yelled at me or expressed anger, disappointment, or even sadness. Instead he just looked at me. 15

In the years that followed, George's silent stare remained with me. It was there in eighth grade when I saw a gang of popular kids beat up a sixth-grader because, they said, he was "ugly and stupid." It was there my first year in high school, when I saw a group of older kids steal another freshman's clothes and throw them into the showers. It was there a year later, when I watched several seniors press a wad of chewing gum into the hair of a new girl on the bus. Each time that I witnessed another awkward, uncomfortable, scared kid being tormented, I thought of 16

George, and gradually his haunting stare began to speak to me. No longer silent, it told me that every child who is picked on and taunted deserves better, that no one—no matter how big, strong, attractive, or popular—has the right to abuse another person.

Finally, in my junior year when a loudmouthed, pink-skinned bully named Donald began picking on two freshmen on the bus, I could no longer deny George. Donald was crumpling a large wad of paper and preparing to bounce it off the back of the head of one of the young students when I interrupted him. **17**

"Leave them alone, Don," I said. By then I was six inches taller and, after two years of high-school wrestling, thirty pounds heavier than I had been in my freshman year. Though Donald was still two years older than me, he wasn't much bigger. He stopped what he was doing, squinted, and stared at me. **18**

"What's your problem, Paul?" **19**

I felt the way I had many years earlier on the playground when I watched the mob of kids begin to surround George. **20**

"Just leave them alone. They aren't bothering you," I responded quietly. **21**

"What's it to you?" he challenged. A glimpse of my own past, of rowing the bus, of being mocked for my clothes, my lisp, my glasses, and my absent father flashed in my mind. **22**

"Just don't mess with them. That's all I am saying, Don." My fingertips were tingling. The bus was silent. He got up from his seat and leaned over me, and I rose from my seat to face him. For a minute, both of us just stood there, without a word, staring. **23**

"I'm just playing with them, Paul," he said, chuckling. "You don't have to go psycho on me or anything." Then he shook his head, slapped me firmly on the chest with the back of his hand, and sat down. But he never threw that wad of paper. For the rest of the year, whenever I was on the bus, Don and the other trouble-makers were noticeably quiet. **24**

Although it has been years since my days on the playground and the school bus, George's look still haunts me. Today, I see it on the faces of a few scared kids at my sister's school—she is in fifth grade. Or once in a while I'll catch a glimpse of someone like George on the evening news, in a story about a child who brought a gun to school to stop the kids from picking on him, or in a feature about a teenager who killed herself because everyone teased her. In each school, in almost every classroom, there is a George with a stricken face, hoping that someone nearby will be strong enough to be kind—despite what the crowd says—and brave enough to stand up against people who attack, tease, or hurt those who are vulnerable. **25**

If asked about their behavior, I'm sure the bullies would say, "What's it to you? It's just a joke. It's nothing." But to George and me, and everyone else who has been humiliated or laughed at or spat on, it is everything. No one should have to row the bus. **26**

VOCABULARY IN CONTEXT

1. The word *simulate* in "Then I had to simulate the motion of rowing while the kids around me laughed and chanted, 'Row, row, row the bus'" (paragraph 1) means

   a. sing.

   b. ignore.

   c. imitate.

   d. release.

2. The word *rift* in "I decided to stop being friends with George. . . . Our class-mates, sensing that they had created a rift between George and me, intensified their attacks on him" (paragraph 9) means

   a. friendship.

   b. agreement.

   c. break.

   d. joke.

READING COMPREHENSION QUESTIONS

1. Which of the following would be the best alternative title for this selection?

   a. A Sixth-Grade Adventure

   b. Children's Fears

   c. Dealing with Cruelty

   d. The Trouble with Busing

2. Which sentence best expresses the main idea of the selection?

   a. Although Paul Logan was the target of other students' abuse when he was a young boy, their attacks stopped as he grew taller and stronger.

   b. When Logan moved to a different school, he discovered that another student, George, was the target of more bullying than he was.

   c. Logan's experience of being bullied and his shame at how he treated George eventually made him speak up for someone else who was teased.

   d. Logan is ashamed that he did not stand up for George when George was being attacked by a bully on the playground.

3. When Chris attacked George, George reacted by

   a. fighting back hard.

   b. shouting for Logan to help him.

   c. running away.

   d. accepting the beating.

4. Logan finally found the courage to stand up for abused students when he saw

   a. Donald about to throw paper at a younger student.

   b. older kids throwing a freshman's clothes into the shower.

   c. seniors putting bubble gum in a new student's hair.

   d. a gang beating up a sixth-grader whom they disliked.

5. *True or false?* _____ After Logan confronted Donald on the bus, Donald began picking on Logan as well.

6. *True or false?* _____ The author suggests that his mother did not care very much about him.

7. The author implies that, when he started sixth grade at a new school,

   a. he became fairly popular.

   b. he decided to try out for athletic teams.

   c. he was relieved to find a kid who was more unpopular than he.

   d. he was frequently beaten up.

8. We can conclude that

   a. the kids who picked on George later regretted what they had done.

   b. George and the author eventually talked together about their experience in sixth grade.

   c. the author thinks kids today are kinder than they were when he was in sixth grade.

   d. the author is a more compassionate person now because of his experience with George.

DISCUSSION QUESTIONS

About Content

1. Logan describes a number of incidents involving students' cruelty to other students. Find at least three such incidents. What do they seem to have in common? Judging from such incidents, what purpose does cruel teasing seem to serve?

2. Throughout the essay, Paul Logan talks about cruel but ordinary school behavior. But in paragraph 25, he briefly mentions two extreme and tragic consequences of such cruelty. What are those consequences, and why do you think he introduces them? What is he implying?

About Structure

3. Overall, the author uses narration to develop his points. Below, write three time transitions he uses to advance his narration.

_____   _____   _____

4. Logan describes the gradual change within him that finally results in his standing up for two students who are being abused. Where in the narrative does Logan show how internal changes may be taking place within him? Where in the narrative does he show that his reaction to witnessing bullying has changed?

5. Paul Logan titled his selection "Rowing the Bus." Yet very little of the essay actually deals with the incident the title describes. Why do you think Logan chose that title?

About Style and Tone

6. Good descriptive writing involves the reader's senses. Give examples of how Logan appeals to our senses in paragraphs 1–4 of "Rowing the Bus."

Sight _____

Smell _____

Hearing _____

7. What is Logan's attitude toward himself regarding his treatment of George? Find three phrases that reveal his attitude and write them here.

WRITING ASSIGNMENTS

Assignment 1: Writing a Paragraph

Logan writes, "In each school, in almost every classroom, there is a George with a stricken face." Think of a person who filled the role of George in one of your classes. Then write a descriptive paragraph about that person, explaining why he or she was a target and what form the teasing took. Be sure to include a description of your own thoughts and actions regarding the student who was teased. Your topic sentence might be something like one of these:

> A girl in my fifth-grade class was a lot like George in "Rowing the Bus."

> Like Paul Logan, I suffered greatly in elementary school from being bullied.

Try to include details that appeal to two or three of the senses.

Assignment 2: Writing a Paragraph

Paul Logan feared that his life at his new school would be made miserable if he continued being friends with George. So he ended the friendship, even though he felt ashamed of doing so. Think of a time when you have wanted to do the right thing but felt that the price would be too high. Maybe you knew a friend was doing something dishonest and wanted him to stop but were afraid of losing his friendship. Or perhaps you pretended to forget a promise you had made because you decided it was too difficult to keep. Write a paragraph describing the choice you made and how you felt about yourself afterward.

Assignment 3: Writing an Essay

Logan provides many vivid descriptions of incidents in which bullies attack her students. Reread these descriptions, and consider what they teach you about the nature of bullies and bullying. Then write an essay that supports the following main idea:

> Bullies seem to share certain qualities.

Identify two or three qualities; then discuss each in a separate paragraph. You may use two or three of the following as the topic sentences for your supporting paragraphs, or come up with your own supporting points:

> Bullies are cowardly.

> Bullies make themselves feel big by making other people feel small.

> Bullies cannot feel very good about themselves.

> Bullies are feared but not respected.

> Bullies act cruelly in order to get attention.

Develop each supporting point with one or more anecdotes or ideas from any of the following: your own experience, your understanding of human nature, and "Rowing the Bus."

The Scholarship Jacket
Marta Salinas

PREVIEW	WORDS TO WATCH
All of us have suffered disappointments and moments when we have felt we've been treated unfairly. In "The Scholarship Jacket," originally published in *Growing Up Chicana: An Anthology*, Marta Salinas writes about one such moment in her childhood in southern Texas. By focusing on an award that school authorities decided she should not receive, Salinas shows us the pain of discrimination as well as the need for inner strength.	valedictorian (1) agile (2) falsify (5) coincidence (7) dismay (10) muster (12) mesquite (15) withdrawn (21) gaunt (25) adrenaline (31)

1   The small Texas school that I attended carried out a tradition every year during the eighth-grade graduation: a beautiful jacket in gold and green, the school colors, was awarded to the class valedictorian,• the student who had maintained the highest grades for eight years. The scholarship jacket had a big gold *S* on the left front side, and the winner's name was written in gold letters on the pocket.

2   My oldest sister, Rosie, had won the jacket a few years back, and I fully expected to win also. I was fourteen and in the eighth grade. I had been a straight-A student since the first grade, and the last year I had looked forward to owning that jacket. My father was a farm laborer who couldn't earn enough money to feed eight children, so when I was six I was given to my grandparents to raise. We couldn't participate in sports at school because there were registration fees, uniform costs, and trips out of town; so even though we were quite agile• and athletic, there would never be a sports school jacket for us. This one, the scholarship jacket, was our only chance.

3   In May, close to graduation, spring fever struck, and no one paid any attention to class; instead we stared out the windows and at each other, wanting to speed up the last few weeks of school. I despaired every time I looked in the mirror. Pencil-thin, with not a curve anywhere, I was called "Beanpole" and "String Bean," and I knew that's what I looked like. A flat chest, no hips, and a brain, that's what I had. That really isn't much for a fourteen-year-old to work with, I thought, as I absentmindedly wandered from my history class to the gym. Another hour of sweating during basketball and displaying my toothpick legs was coming up. Then I remembered my P.E. shorts were still in a bag under my desk where I'd forgotten them. I had to walk all the way back and get them. Coach Thompson was a real bear if anyone wasn't dressed for P.E. She had said I was a good forward and once she even tried to talk Grandma into letting me join the team. Grandma, of course, said no.

4   I was almost back at my classroom door when I heard angry voices and arguing. I stopped. I didn't mean to eavesdrop; I just hesitated, not knowing what to do. I needed those shorts and I was going to be late, but I didn't want to interrupt an argument between my teachers. I recognized the voices: Mr. Schmidt, my history teacher; and Mr. Boone, my math teacher. They seemed to be arguing about me. I couldn't believe it. I still remember the shock that rooted me flat against the wall as if I were trying to blend in with the graffiti written there.

5   "I refuse to do it! I don't care who her father is; her grades don't even begin to compare to Martha's. I won't lie or falsify• records. Martha has a straight-A-plus

average and you know it." That was Mr. Schmidt, and he sounded very angry. Mr. Boone's voice sounded calm and quiet.

"Look, Joann's father is not only on the Board, he owns the only store in town; we could say it was a close tie and—" 6

The pounding in my ears drowned out the rest of the words, only a word here and there filtered through. ". . . Martha is Mexican . . . resign . . . won't do it. . . ." Mr. Schmidt came rushing out, and luckily for me went down the opposite way toward the auditorium, so he didn't see me. Shaking, I waited a few minutes and then went in and grabbed my bag and fled from the room. Mr. Boone looked up when I came in but didn't say anything. To this day I don't remember if I got in trouble in P.E. for being late or how I made it through the rest of the afternoon. I went home very sad and cried into my pillow that night so Grandmother wouldn't hear me. It seemed a cruel coincidence• that I had overheard that conversation. 7

The next day when the principal called me into his office, I knew what it would be about. He looked uncomfortable and unhappy. I decided I wasn't going to make it any easier for him, so I looked him straight in the eye. He looked away and fidgeted with the papers on his desk. 8

"Martha," he said, "there's been a change in policy this year regarding the scholarship jacket. As you know, it has always been free." He cleared his throat and continued. "This year the Board decided to charge fifteen dollars—which still won't cover the complete cost of the jacket." 9

I stared at him in shock and a small sound of dismay• escaped my throat. I hadn't expected this. He still avoided looking in my eyes. 10

"So if you are unable to pay the fifteen dollars for the jacket, it will be given to the next one in line." 11

Standing with all the dignity I could muster,• I said, "I'll speak to my grandfather about it, sir, and let you know tomorrow." I cried on the walk home from the bus stop. The dirt road was a quarter of a mile from the highway, so by the time I got home, my eyes were red and puffy. 12

"Where's Grandpa?" I asked Grandma, looking down at the floor so she wouldn't ask me why I'd been crying. She was sewing on a quilt and didn't look up. 13

"I think he's out back working in the bean field." 14

I went outside and looked out at the fields. There he was. I could see him walking between the rows, his body bent over the little plants, hoe in hand. I walked slowly out to him, trying to think how I could best ask him for the money. There was a cool breeze blowing and a sweet smell of mesquite• in the air, but I didn't appreciate it. I kicked at a dirt clod. I wanted that jacket so much. It was more than just being a valedictorian and giving a little thank-you speech for the jacket on graduation night. It represented eight years of hard work and expectation. I knew I had to be honest with Grandpa; it was my only chance. He saw me and looked up. 15

He waited for me to speak. I cleared my throat nervously and clasped my hands behind my back so he wouldn't see them shaking. "Grandpa, I have a big favor to ask you," I said in Spanish, the only language he knew. He still waited silently. I tried again. "Grandpa, this year the principal said the scholarship jacket is not going to be free. It's going to cost fifteen dollars and I have to take the money in tomorrow, otherwise it'll be given to someone else." The last words came out in an eager rush. Grandpa straightened up tiredly and leaned his chin on the hoe handle. He looked out over the field that was filled with the tiny green bean plants. I waited, desperately hoping he'd say I could have the money. 16

He turned to me and asked quietly, "What does a scholarship jacket mean?" 17

I answered quickly; maybe there was a chance. "It means you've earned it by having the highest grades for eight years and that's why they're giving it to you." Too late I realized the significance of my words. Grandpa knew that I understood 18 it was not a matter of money. It wasn't that. He went back to hoeing the weeds that sprang up between the delicate little bean plants. It was a time-consuming job; sometimes the small shoots were right next to each other. Finally he spoke again.

"Then if you pay for it, Marta, it's not a scholarship jacket, is it? Tell your prin- **19** cipal I will not pay the fifteen dollars."

I walked back to the house and locked myself in the bathroom for a long time. **20** I was angry with Grandfather even though I knew he was right, and I was angry with the Board, whoever they were. Why did they have to change the rules just when it was my turn to win the jacket?

It was a very sad and withdrawn• girl who dragged into the principal's office **21** the next day. This time he did look me in the eyes.

"What did your grandfather say?"   **22**

I sat very straight in my chair.   **23**

"He said to tell you he won't pay the fifteen dollars."   **24**

The principal muttered something I couldn't understand under his breath, **25** and walked over to the window. He stood looking out at something outside. He looked bigger than usual when he stood up; he was a tall, gaunt• man with gray hair, and I watched the back of his head while I waited for him to speak.

"Why?" he finally asked. "Your grandfather has the money. Doesn't he own a **26** small bean farm?"

I looked at him, forcing my eyes to stay dry. "He said if I had to pay for it, then **27** it wouldn't be a scholarship jacket," I said, and stood up to leave. "I guess you'll just have to give it to Joann." I hadn't meant to say that; it had just slipped out. I was almost to the door when he stopped me.

"Martha—wait."   **28**

I turned and looked at him, waiting. What did he want now? I could feel my **29** heart pounding. Something bitter and vile-tasting was coming up in my mouth; I was afraid I was going to be sick. I didn't need any sympathy speeches. He sighed loudly and went back to his big desk. He looked at me, biting his lip, as if thinking.

"OK, damn it. We'll make an exception in your case. I'll tell the Board, you'll **30** get your jacket."

I could hardly believe it. I spoke in a trembling rush. "Oh, thank you, sir!" **31** Suddenly I felt great. I didn't know about adrenaline• in those days, but I knew something was pumping through me, making me feel as tall as the sky. I wanted to yell, jump, run the mile, do something. I ran out so I could cry in the hall where there was no one to see me. At the end of the day, Mr. Schmidt winked at me and said, "I hear you're getting a scholarship jacket this year."

His face looked as happy and innocent as a baby's, but I knew better. Without **32** answering I gave him a quick hug and ran to the bus. I cried on the walk home again, but this time because I was so happy. I couldn't wait to tell Grandpa and ran straight to the field. I joined him in the row where he was working and with-out saying anything I crouched down and started pulling up the weeds with my hands. Grandpa worked alongside me for a few minutes, but he didn't ask what had happened. After I had a little pile of weeds between the rows, I stood up and faced him.

"The principal said he's making an exception for me, Grandpa, and I'm getting **33** the jacket after all. That's after I told him what you said."

Grandpa didn't say anything; he just gave me a pat on the shoulder and a **34** smile. He pulled out the crumpled red handkerchief that he always carried in his back pocket and wiped the sweat off his forehead.

"Better go see if your grandmother needs any help with supper."   **35**

I gave him a big grin. He didn't fool me. I skipped and ran back to the house **36** whistling some silly tune.

VOCABULARY IN CONTEXT

1. The word *falsify* in "I won't lie or falsify records. Martha has a straight-A-plus average and you know it" (paragraph 5) means

   a. make untrue.

   b. write down.

   c. keep track of.

   d. sort alphabetically.

2. The word *dismay* in "I stared at him in shock and a small sound of dismay escaped my throat. I hadn't expected this" (paragraph 10) means

   a. joy.

   b. comfort.

   c. relief.

   d. disappointment.

READING COMPREHENSION QUESTIONS

1. Which sentence best expresses the central point of the selection?

   a. It is more important to be smart than good-looking or athletic.

   b. People who are willing to pay for an award deserve it more than people who are not.

   c. By refusing to give in to discrimination, the author finally received the award she had earned.

   d. Always do what the adults in your family say, even if you don't agree.

2. Which sentence best expresses the main idea of paragraph 2?

   a. Marta wanted to win the scholarship jacket to be like her sister Rosie.

   b. The scholarship jacket was especially important to Marta because she was unable to earn a jacket in any other way.

   c. The scholarship jacket was better than a sports school jacket.

   d. Marta resented her parents for sending her to live with her grandparents.

3. Which sentence best expresses the main idea of paragraph 7?

   a. Marta was shocked and saddened by the conversation she overheard.

   b. Marta didn't want her grandmother to know she was crying.

   c. Mr. Schmidt didn't see Marta when he rushed out of the room.

   d. Marta didn't hear every word of Mr. Schmidt's and Mr. Boone's conversation.

4. Marta was raised by her grandparents because

   a. she wanted to learn to speak Spanish.

   b. her father did not earn enough money to feed all his children.

   c. she wanted to learn about farming.

   d. her parents died when she was six.

5. *True or false?* _____ Marta was called by a different name at school.

6. We can infer from paragraph 8 that the principal was "uncomfortable and unhappy" because
   a. the students had not been paying attention in class during the last few weeks before graduation.
   b. his office was very hot.
   c. he was ashamed to tell Marta that she had to pay fifteen dollars for a jacket that she had earned.
   d. Mr. Boone and Mr. Schmidt were fighting in the hallway

7. The author implies that the Board members were not going to give Marta the scholarship jacket because
   a. she was late for P.E. class.
   b. they wanted to award the jacket to the daughter of an important local citizen.
   c. another student had better grades.
   d. they didn't think it was fair to have two members of the same family win the jacket.

8. *True or false?* _____ The author implies that the Board's new policy to require a fee for the scholarship jacket was an act of discrimination.

DISCUSSION QUESTIONS

About Content

1. Why was winning the scholarship jacket so important to Marta?

2. What seemed to be the meaning of the argument between Mr. Schmidt and Mr. Boone?

3. After Marta's grandfather asks her what the scholarship jacket is, the author writes, "'It means you've earned it by having the highest grades for eight years and that's why they're giving it to you.' Too late I realized the significance of my words." What is the significance of her words?

About Structure

4. Why do you think Salinas begins her essay with a detailed description of the scholarship jacket? How does her description contribute to our interest in her story?

5. At what point does Salinas stop providing background information and start giving a time-ordered narration of a particular event in her life?

6. In the course of the essay, Salinas rides an emotional roller coaster. Find and write here three words or phrases she uses to describe her different emotional states:

   _____   _____   _____

About Style and Tone

7. As you read the essay, what impression do you form of Salinas's grandfather? What kind of man does he seem to be? What details does Salinas provide in order to create that impression?

8. In paragraph 12, Salinas writes, "Standing with all the dignity I could muster, I said, 'I'll speak to my grandfather about it, sir, and let you know tomorrow.'" What other evidence does Salinas give us that her dignity is important to her?

WRITING ASSIGNMENTS

Assignment 1: Writing a Paragraph

Write a paragraph about a time when you experienced or witnessed an injustice. Describe the circumstances surrounding the incident and why you think the people involved acted as they did. In your paragraph, describe how you felt at the time and any effect the incident has had on you. Your topic sentence could be something like one of the following:

> I was angry when my supervisor promoted his nephew even though I was more qualified.

> A friend of mine recently got into trouble with authorities even though he was innocent of any wrongdoing.

Assignment 2: Writing a Paragraph

Marta stresses again and again how important the scholarship jacket was to her and how hard she worked to win it. Write a paragraph about something you worked hard to achieve when you were younger. How long did you work toward that goal? How did you feel when you finally succeeded? Or as an alternative, write about not achieving the goal. How did you cope with the disappointment? What lessons, if any, did you learn from the experience?

Assignment 3: Writing an Essay

This story contains several examples of authority figures—specifically, the two teachers, the principal, and Marta's grandfather. Write an essay describing three qualities that you think an authority figure should possess. Such qualities might include honesty, fairness, compassion, and knowledge.

In the body of your essay, devote each supporting paragraph to one of those qualities. Within each paragraph, give an example or examples of how an authority figure in your life has demonstrated that quality.

You may write about three different authority figures who have demonstrated those three qualities to you. Alternatively, one authority figure may have demonstrated all three.

Your thesis statement might be similar to one of these:

> My older brother, my grandmother, and my football coach have been models of admirable behavior for me.

> My older brother's honesty, courage, and kindness to others have set a valuable example for me.

Tickets to Nowhere

Andy Rooney

<table>
<tr><td>PREVIEW</td><td>WORDS TO WATCH</td></tr>
<tr><td>

Who doesn't love a "get rich quick" story? We eagerly read the accounts of lucky people who've become wealthy overnight just by buying the right lottery ticket. The hope that we might do the same keeps many of us "investing" in the lottery week after week. But syndicated columnist Andy Rooney thinks there's another lottery story that also deserves our attention.

</td><td>

gushed (6)
digits (9)
stowed (10)
fidgeted (12)
clutched (13)

</td></tr>
</table>

1   Things never went very well for Jim Oakland. He dropped out of high school because he was impatient to get rich, but after dropping out he lived at home with his parents for two years and didn't earn a dime.

2   He finally got a summer job working for the highway department holding up a sign telling oncoming drivers to be careful of the workers ahead. Later that same year, he picked up some extra money putting fliers under the windshield wipers of parked cars.

3   Things just never went very well for Jim, and he was twenty-three before he left home and went to Florida hoping his ship would come in down there. He never lost his desire to get rich; but first he needed money for the rent, so he took a job near Fort Lauderdale for $4.50 an hour servicing the goldfish aquariums kept near the cashier's counter in a lot of restaurants.

4   Jim was paid in cash once a week by the owner of the goldfish business, and the first thing he did was go to the little convenience store near where he lived and buy $20 worth of lottery tickets. He was really determined to get rich.

5   A week ago, the lottery jackpot in Florida reached $54 million. Jim woke up nights thinking what he could do with $54 million. During the days, he daydreamed about it. One morning he was driving along the main street in the boss's old pickup truck with six tanks of goldfish in back. As he drove past a BMW dealer, he looked at the new models in the window.

6   He saw the car he wanted in the showroom window, but unfortunately he didn't see the light change. The car in front of him stopped short and Jim slammed on his brakes. The fish tanks slid forward. The tanks broke, the water gushed° out, and the goldfish slithered and flopped all over the back of the truck. Some fell off into the road.

7   It wasn't a good day for the goldfish or for Jim, of course. He knew he'd have to pay for the tanks and 75 cents each for the fish, and if it weren't for the $54 million lottery, he wouldn't have known which way to turn. He had that lucky feeling.

8   For the tanks and the dead goldfish, the boss deducted $114 of Jim's $180 weekly pay. Even though he didn't have enough left for the rent and food, Jim doubled the amount he was going to spend on lottery tickets. He never needed $54 million more.

9   Jim had this system. He took his age and added the last four digits° of the telephone number of the last girl he dated. He called it his lucky number . . . even though the last four digits changed quite often and he'd never won with his system. Everyone laughed at Jim and said he'd never win the lottery.

Jim put down $40 on the counter that week and the man punched out his tick- 10
ets. Jim stowed• them safely away in his wallet with last week's tickets. He never
threw away his lottery tickets until at least a month after the drawing just in case
there was some mistake. He'd heard of mistakes.

Jim listened to the radio all afternoon the day of the drawing. The people at 11
the radio station he was listening to waited for news of the winning numbers to
come over the wires and, even then, the announcers didn't rush to get them on.
The station manager thought the people running the lottery ought to pay to have
the winning numbers broadcast, just like any other commercial announcement.

Jim fidgeted• while they gave the weather and the traffic and the news. Then 12
they played more music. All he wanted to hear were those numbers.

"Well," the radio announcer said finally, "we have the lottery numbers some 13
of you have been waiting for. You ready?" Jim was ready. He clutched• his ticket
with the number 274802.

"The winning number," the announcer said, "is 860539. I'll repeat that. 860539." 14
Jim was still a loser.

I thought that, with all the human interest stories about lottery winners, we 15
ought to have a story about one of the several million losers.

VOCABULARY IN CONTEXT

1. The word *gushed* in "The tanks broke, the water gushed out, and the goldfish
   slithered and flopped all over the back of the truck" (paragraph 6) means
   a. dripped slowly.
   b. steamed.
   c. poured.
   d. held.

2. The word *digits* in "He took his age and added the last four digits of the telephone number of the last girl he dated" (paragraph 9) means
   a. letters.
   b. single numbers.
   c. rings.
   d. area codes.

READING COMPREHENSION QUESTIONS

1. Which of the following would be the best alternative title for this selection?
   a. A $54 Million Jackpot
   b. An Unnecessary Accident
   c. Foolish Dreams
   d. Moving to Florida

2. Which sentence best expresses the main idea of the selection?
   a. Everyone dreams of winning the lottery.
   b. The more money you invest in lottery tickets, the better your chances of
      winning.
   c. Jim Oakland's dreams of getting rich by winning the lottery were
      unrealistic.
   d. Jim Oakland is a very unlucky man.

3. *True or false?* _____ Jim dropped out of school because he was offered a good-paying job in Florida.

4. When Jim lost money as a result of his accident with the goldfish, he
    a. put himself on a strict budget.
    b. spent even more on lottery tickets.
    c. got a second job.
    d. moved back in with his parents to save money.

5. Jim never threw away his lottery tickets
    a. at all.
    b. until his next paycheck.
    c. until at least a month after the drawing.
    d. so that he could write off his losses on his tax return.

6. We can infer from paragraphs 6–7 that
    a. Jim's daydreams about getting rich made him careless.
    b. the driver in front of Jim should have gotten a ticket.
    c. the brakes on Jim's pickup truck were faulty.
    d. Jim slammed on his brakes because he'd suddenly realized that he'd never win the lottery.

7. In paragraph 9, the author suggests that Jim
    a. was good in math.
    b. did not date very often.
    c. never told anyone about his dreams of winning the lottery.
    d. never dated the same girl for very long.

8. Andy Rooney suggests that
    a. although few people win the lottery, it's still worth trying.
    b. most of what the public hears about lotteries shows how harmful they are.
    c. Jim Oakland gave up playing the lottery after losing the $54 million jackpot.
    d. playing the lottery harms far more people than it helps.

DISCUSSION QUESTIONS

About Content

1. Jim Oakland seemed to feel that lotteries were entirely good. Andy Rooney takes a more negative view. What is your opinion? On balance, are lotteries good or bad? On what are you basing your opinion?

2. Do you know anyone like Jim, someone who depends on luck more than on hard work or ability? If so, why do you think this person relies so much on luck? How lucky has he or she been?

3. What would be the good points of suddenly winning a large amount of money? What might be the downside? All in all, would you prefer to win or to earn the money you have? Why?

About Structure

4. As Rooney's piece went on, did you think that it was going to be about Jim Oakland winning the lottery—or losing it? What details contributed to your expectations?

About Style and Tone

5. At only one point in the essay does Rooney use a direct quotation. What is that point? Why do you think he chooses to dramatize that moment with the speaker's exact words?

6. One meaning of *irony* is a contradiction between what might be expected and what really happens. Rooney uses this type of irony in an understated way to contrast Oakland's goal with his actions. For instance, in paragraph 1, he states that Oakland was "impatient to get rich." In the same sentence he states, "he lived at home with his parents for two years and didn't earn a dime." Find one other spot in the selection where Rooney uses irony and write its paragraph number here:

_____

7. Rooney refers to himself only one time in the essay, in the final paragraph. Why do you think he chooses to use "I" at that point? What is the effect?

8. How do you think Rooney feels about Jim? Does he admire his continued optimism about striking it rich? Does he think Jim is a bad person? Find passages in the essay that support your opinion about how Rooney regards Jim.

WRITING ASSIGNMENTS

Assignment 1: Writing a Paragraph

Write a paragraph about a time when you had good luck. Perhaps you found a twenty-dollar bill, or you happened to meet the person you are currently dating or are married to, or you were fortunate enough to find a job you like. Provide plenty of detail to let readers know why you consider your experience so fortunate. Your topic sentence may begin like this:

A time I had incredibly good luck was the day that _____.

Assignment 2: Writing a Paragraph

As Andy Rooney describes him, Jim is a man who has relied on luck to make good things happen in his life, rather than on hard work or realistic planning. Do you know someone who drifts along in life, hoping for a lucky break but doing little to make it happen? Write a paragraph describing how this person goes about his or her life. Introduce that person in your topic sentence, as in these examples:

My sister's former husband relies on luck, not work or planning, to get ahead in life.

Instead of studying, my roommate hopes that luck will be enough to help her pass her courses.

Then give several specific examples of the person's behavior. Conclude by providing a suggestion about what this person might do in order to take the responsibility of creating his or her own "good luck."

Alternatively, write a paragraph about a person who plans logically and works hard to achieve his or her goals.

Assignment 3: Writing an Essay

Rooney uses just one example—Jim Oakland's story—to suggest the general point that people should not count on the lottery to make them rich. Write an essay in which you, like Rooney, defend an idea that many oppose or have given little thought to. Perhaps you will argue that high schools should distribute forms of birth-control to students or that alcohol should be banned on your college campus.

Develop your essay by describing in detail the experiences of one person. Your three supporting paragraphs may be organized by time order, describing the person's experience from an early to a later point; or they may be organized as a list—for example, showing how the person's experience affected him or her in three different ways. In your conclusion, make it clear, as Rooney does, that the one person you're writing about is intended to illustrate a general point.

Here is a sample outline for one such essay:

Thesis statement: Alcoholic beverages should be banned on this campus.

Topic sentence 1: Drinking affected Beverly's academic life.

Topic sentence 2: Drinking also affected Beverly's social life.

Topic sentence 3: Finally, drinking jeopardized Beverly's work life.

Conclusion: Many students, like Beverly, have their lives damaged and even ruined by alcohol.

What Good Families Are Doing Right

Delores Curran

PREVIEW	WORDS TO WATCH
It isn't easy to be a successful parent these days. Pressured by the conflicting demands of home and workplace, confused by changing moral standards, and drowned out by the constant barrage of new media, today's parents seem to be facing impossible odds in their struggle to raise healthy families. Yet some parents manage to "do it all"—and even remain on speaking terms with their children. How do they do it? Delores Curran's survey offers some significant suggestions; her article could serve as a recipe for a successful family.	dominate (9) submissive (9) maligned (12) aghast (14) fidelity (15) engrossing (17) denigrating (22) nuances (25) fettered (33) rebuke (36) jest (37)

I have worked with families for fifteen years, conducting hundreds of semi- 1
nars, workshops, and classes on parenting, and I meet good families all the time.
They're fairly easy to recognize. Good families have a kind of visible strength.
They expect problems and work together to find solutions, applying common
sense and trying new methods to meet new needs. And they share a common
shortcoming—they can tell me in a minute what's wrong with them, but they
aren't sure what's right with them. Many healthy families with whom I work, in
fact, protest at being called *healthy*. They don't think they are. The professionals
who work with them do.

To prepare the book on which this article is based, I asked respected work- 2
ers in the fields of education, religion, health, family counseling, and voluntary
organizations to identify a list of possible traits of a healthy family. Together we
isolated fifty-six such traits, and I sent this list to five hundred professionals who
regularly work with families—teachers, doctors, principals, members of the clergy,
scout directors, YMCA leaders, family counselors, social workers—asking them to
pick the fifteen qualities they most commonly found in healthy families.

While all of these traits are important, the one most often cited as central to 3
close family life is communication: The healthy family knows how to talk—and
how to listen.

"Without communication you don't know one another," wrote one family 4
counselor. "If you don't know one another, you don't care about one another, and
that's what the family is all about."

"The most familiar complaint I hear from wives I counsel is 'He won't talk to 5
me' and 'He doesn't listen to me,'" said a pastoral marriage counselor. "And when
I share this complaint with their husbands, they don't hear *me,* either."

"We have kids in classes whose families are so robotized by television that 6
they don't know one another," said a fifth-grade teacher.

Professional counselors are not the only ones to recognize the need. The phe- 7
nomenal growth of communication groups such as Parent Effectiveness Training, Parent Awareness, Marriage Encounter, Couple Communication, and literally
hundreds of others tells us that the need for effective communication—the sharing of deepest feelings—is felt by many.

Healthy families have also recognized this need, and they have, either instinc- 8
tively or consciously, developed methods of meeting it. They know that conflicts
are to be expected, that we all become angry and frustrated and discouraged. And
they know how to reveal those feelings—good and bad—to each other. Honest
communication isn't always easy. But when it's working well, there are certain rec-
ognizable signs or symptoms, what I call the hallmarks of the successfully communicating family.

The Family Exhibits a Strong Relationship between the Parents

According to Dr. Jerry M. Lewis—author of a significant work on families, *No* 9
Single Thread—healthy spouses complement, rather than dominate,• each other.
Either husband or wife could be the leader, depending on the circumstances. In
the unhealthy families he studied, the dominant spouse had to hide feelings of
weakness while the submissive• spouse feared being put down if he or she exposed a weakness.

Children in the healthy family have no question about which parent is boss. 10
Both parents are. If children are asked who is boss, they're likely to respond,
"Sometimes Mom, sometimes Dad." And, in a wonderful statement, Dr. Lewis
adds, "If you ask if they're comfortable with this, they look at you as if you're
crazy—as if there's no other way it ought to be."

My survey respondents echo Dr. Lewis. One wrote, "The healthiest families I [11] know are ones in which the mother and father have a strong, loving relationship. This seems to flow over to the children and even beyond the home. It seems to breed security in the children and, in turn, fosters the ability to take risks, to reach out to others, to search for their own answers, become independent and develop a good self-image."

The Family Has Control over Television

Television has been maligned,• praised, damned, cherished, and even thrown [12] out. It has more influence on children's values than anything else except their parents. Over and over, when I'm invited to help families mend their communication ruptures, I hear "But we have no time for this." These families have literally turned their "family-together" time over to television. Even those who control the quality of programs watched and set "homework-first" regulations feel reluctant to intrude upon the individual's right to spend his or her spare time in front of the set. Many families avoid clashes over program selection by furnishing a set for each family member. One of the women who was most desperate to establish a better sense of communication in her family confided to me that they owned nine sets. Nine sets for seven people!

Whether the breakdown in family communication leads to excessive viewing [13] or whether too much television breaks into family lives, we don't know. But we do know that we can become out of one another's reach when we're in front of a TV set. The term *television widow* is not humorous to thousands whose spouses are absent even when they're there. One woman remarked, "I can't get worried about whether there's life after death. I'd be satisfied with life after dinner."

In family-communication workshops, I ask families to make a list of phrases [14] they most commonly hear in their home. One parent was aghast• to discover that his family's most familiar comments were "What's on?" and "Move." In families like this one, communication isn't hostile—it's just missing.

But television doesn't have to be a villain. A 1980 Gallup Poll found that the [15] public sees great potential for television as a positive force. It can be a tremendous device for initiating discussion on subjects that may not come up elsewhere, subjects such as sexuality, corporate ethics, sportsmanship, and marital fidelity.•

Even very bad programs offer material for values clarification if family mem- [16] bers view them together. My sixteen-year-old son and his father recently watched a program in which hazardous driving was part of the hero's characterization. At one point, my son turned to his dad and asked, "Is that possible to do with that kind of truck?"

"I don't know," replied my husband, "but it sure is dumb. If that load shifted [17] . . ." With that, they launched into a discussion on the responsibility of drivers that didn't have to originate as a parental lecture. Furthermore, as the discussion became more engrossing• to them, they turned the sound down so that they could continue their conversation.

Parents frequently report similar experiences; in fact, this use of television [18] was recommended in the widely publicized 1972 Surgeon General's report as the most effective form of television gatekeeping by parents. Instead of turning off the set, parents should view programs with their children and make moral judgments and initiate discussion. Talking about the problems and attitudes of a TV family can be a lively, nonthreatening way to risk sharing real fears, hopes, and dreams.

The Family Listens and Responds

"My parents say they want me to come to them with problems, but when I do, [19] either they're busy or they only half-listen and keep on doing what they were doing—like shaving or making a grocery list. If a friend of theirs came over to talk, they'd stop, be polite, and listen," said one of the children quoted in a *Christian Science Monitor* interview by Ann McCarroll. This child put his finger on the most difficult problem of communicating in families: the inability to listen.

It is usually easier to react than to respond. When we react, we reflect our own 20 experiences and feelings; when we respond, we get into the other person's feelings. For example:

> *Tom, age seventeen:* "I don't know if I want to go to college. I don't think I'd do very well there."

> *Father:* "Nonsense. Of course you'll do well."

That's reacting. This father is cutting off communication. He's refusing either 21 to hear the boy's fears or to consider his feelings, possibly because he can't accept the idea that his son might not attend college. Here's another way of handling the same situation:

> *Tom:* "I don't know if I want to go to college. I don't think I'd do very well there."

> *Father:* "Why not?"

> *Tom:* "Because I'm not that smart."

> *Father:* "Yeah, that's scary. I worried about that, too."

> *Tom:* "Did you ever come close to flunking out?"

> *Father:* "No, but I worried a lot before I went because I thought college would be full of brains. Once I got there, I found out that most of the kids were just like me."

This father has responded rather than reacted to his son's fears. First, he 22 searched for the reason behind his son's lack of confidence and found it was fear of academic ability (it could have been fear of leaving home, of a new environment, of peer pressure, or of any of a number of things); second, he accepted the fear as legitimate; third, he empathized by admitting to having the same fear when he was Tom's age; and, finally, he explained why his, not Tom's, fears turned out to be groundless. He did all this without denigrating• or lecturing.

And that's tough for parents to do. Often we don't want to hear our children's 23 fears, because those fears frighten us; or we don't want to pay attention to their dreams because their dreams aren't what we have in mind for them. Parents who deny such feelings will allow only surface conversation. It's fine as long as a child says, "School was OK today," but when she says, "I'm scared of boys," the parents are uncomfortable. They don't want her to be afraid of boys, but since they don't quite know what to say, they react with a pleasant "Oh, you'll outgrow it." She probably will, but what she needs at the moment is someone to hear and understand her pain.

In Ann McCarroll's interviews, she talked to one fifteen-year-old boy 24 who said he had *"some* mother. Each morning she sits with me while I eat breakfast. We talk about anything and everything. She isn't refined or elegant or educated. She's a terrible housekeeper. But she's interested in everything I do, and she always listens to me—even if she's busy or tired."

That's the kind of listening found in families that experience real commu- 25 nication. Answers to the routine question, "How was your day?" are heard with the eyes and heart as well as the ears. Nuances• are picked up and questions are asked, although problems are not necessarily solved. Members of a family who really listen to one another instinctively know that if people listen to you, they are interested in you. And that's enough for most of us.

The Family Recognizes Unspoken Messages

Much of our communication—especially our communication of feelings—is non- 26
verbal. Dr. Lewis defines *empathy* as "someone responding to you in such a way
that you feel deeply understood." He says, "There is probably no more important dimension in all of human relationships than the capacity for empathy. And
healthy families teach empathy." Their members are allowed to be mad, glad, and
sad. There's no crime in being in a bad mood, nor is there betrayal in being happy
while someone else is feeling moody. The family recognizes that bad days and
good days attack everyone at different times.

Nonverbal expressions of love, too, are the best way to show children that par- 27
ents love each other. A spouse reaching for the other's hand, a wink, a squeeze on
the shoulder, a "How's-your-back-this-morning?" a meaningful glance across the
room—all these tell children how their parents feel about each other.

The most destructive nonverbal communication in marriage is silence. Silence 28
can mean lack of interest, hostility, denigration, boredom, or outright war. On the
part of a teen or preteen, silence usually indicates pain, sometimes very deep pain.
The sad irony discovered by so many family therapists is that parents who seek
professional help when a teenager becomes silent have often denied the child any
other way of communicating. And although they won't permit their children to
become angry or to reveal doubts or to share depression, they do worry about the
withdrawal that results. Rarely do they see any connection between the two.

Healthy families use signs, symbols, body language, smiles, and other ges- 29
tures to express caring and love. They deal with silence and withdrawal in a positive, open way. Communication doesn't mean just talking or listening; it includes
all the clues to a person's feelings—his bearing, her expression, their resignation.
Family members don't have to say, "I'm hurting," or, "I'm in need." A quick glance
tells that. And they have developed ways of responding that indicate caring and
love, whether or not there's an immediate solution to the pain.

The Family Encourages Individual Feelings and Independent Thinking

Close families encourage the emergence of individual personalities through open 30
sharing of thoughts and feelings. Unhealthy families tend to be less open, less accepting of differences among members. The family must be Republican, or Bronco
supporters, or gun-control advocates, and woe to the individual who says, "Yes,
but . . . ."

Instead of finding differing opinions threatening, the healthy family finds 31
them exhilarating. It is exciting to witness such a family discussing politics, sports,
or the world. Members freely say, "I don't agree with you," without risking ridi-
cule or rebuke. They say, "I think it's wrong . . ." immediately after Dad says, "I
think it's right. . ."; and Dad listens and responds.

Give-and-take gives children practice in articulating their thoughts at home 32
so that eventually they'll feel confident outside the home. What may seem to be
verbal rambling by preteens during a family conversation is a prelude to sorting
out their thinking and putting words to their thoughts.

Rigid families don't understand the dynamics of give-and-take. Some label 33
it disrespectful and argumentative; others find it confusing. Dr. John Meeks,
medical director of the Psychiatric Institute of Montgomery County, Maryland,
claims that argument is a way of life with normally developing adolescents. "In
early adolescence they'll argue with parents about anything at all; as they grow
older, the quantity of argument decreases but the quality increases." According to
Dr. Meeks, arguing is something adolescents need to do. If the argument doesn't
become too bitter, they have a good chance to test their own beliefs and feelings.

"Incidentally," says Meeks, "parents can expect to 'lose' most of these arguments, because adolescents are not fettered• by logic or even reality." Nor are they likely to be polite. Learning how to disagree respectfully is a difficult task, but good families work at it.

Encouraging individual feelings and thoughts, of course, in no way presumes 34 that parents permit their children to do whatever they want. There's a great difference between permitting a son to express an opinion on marijuana and allowing him to use it. That his opinion conflicts with his parents' opinion is OK as long as his parents make sure he knows their thinking on the subject. Whether he admits it or not, he's likely at least to consider their ideas if he respects them.

Permitting teenagers to sort out their feelings and thoughts in open discus- 35 sions at home gives them valuable experience in dealing with a bewildering array of situations they may encounter when they leave home. Cutting off discussion of behavior unacceptable to us, on the other hand, makes our young people feel guilty for even thinking about values contrary to ours and ends up making those values more attractive to them.

The Family Recognizes Turn-Off Words and Put-Down Phrases

Some families deliberately use hurtful language in their daily communication. 36 "What did you do all day around here?" can be a red flag to a woman who has spent her day on household tasks that don't show unless they're not done. "If only we had enough money" can be a rebuke• to a husband who is working as hard as he can to provide for the family. "Flunk any tests today, John?" only discourages a child who may be having trouble in school.

Close families seem to recognize that a comment made in jest• can be in- 37 sulting. A father in one of my groups confided that he could tease his wife about everything but her skiing. "I don't know why she's so sensitive about that, but I back off on it. I can say anything I want to about her cooking, her appearance, her mothering—whatever. But not her skiing."

One of my favorite exercises with families is to ask them to reflect upon 38 phrases they most like to hear and those they least like to hear. Recently, I invited seventy-five fourth- and fifth-graders to submit the words they most like to hear from their mothers. Here are the five big winners:

"I love you."

"Yes."

"Time to eat."

"You can go."

"You can stay up late."

And on the children's list of what they least like to hear from one another are 39 the following:

"I'm telling."

"Mom says!"

"I know something you don't know."

"You think you're so big."

"Just see if I ever let you use my bike again."

It can be worthwhile for a family to list the phrases members like most and 40 least to hear, and post them. Often parents aren't even aware of the reaction of their children to certain routine comments. Or keep a record of the comments heard most often over a period of a week or two. It can provide good clues to the level of family sensitivity. If the list has a lot of "shut ups" and "stop its," that family needs to pay more attention to its relationships, especially the role that communication plays in them.

The Family Interrupts, but Equally

When Dr. Jerry M. Lewis began to study the healthy family, he and his staff video- 41 taped families in the process of problem solving. The family was given a question, such as, "What's the main thing wrong with your family?" Answers varied, but what was most significant was what the family actually did: who took control, how individuals responded or reacted, what were the put-downs, and whether some members were entitled to speak more than others.

The researchers found that healthy families expected everyone to speak 42 openly about feelings. Nobody was urged to hold back. In addition, these family members interrupted one another repeatedly, but no one person was interrupted more than anyone else.

Manners, particularly polite conversational techniques, are not hallmarks of 43 the communicating family. This should make many parents feel better about their family's dinner conversation. One father reported to me that at their table people had to take a number to finish a sentence. Finishing sentences, however, doesn't seem all that important in the communicating family. Members aren't sensitive to being interrupted, either. The intensity and spontaneity of the exchange are more important than propriety in conversation.

The Family Develops a Pattern of Reconciliation

"We know how to break up," one man said, "but who ever teaches us to make 44 up?" Survey respondents indicated that there is indeed a pattern of reconciliation in healthy families that is missing in others. "It usually isn't a kiss-and-make-up situation," explained one family therapist, "but there are certain rituals developed over a long period of time that indicate it's time to get well again. Between husband and wife, it might be a concessionary phrase to which the other is expected to respond in kind. Within a family, it might be that the person who stomps off to his or her room voluntarily reenters the family circle, where something is said to make him or her welcome."

When I asked several families how they knew a fight had ended, I got remark- 45 ably similar answers from individuals questioned separately. "We all come out of our rooms," responded every member of one family. Three members of another family said, "Mom says, 'Anybody want a Pepsi?'" One five-year-old scratched his head and furrowed his forehead after I asked him how he knew the family fight was over. Finally, he said, "Well, Daddy gives a great big yawn and says, 'Well . . .'" This scene is easy to visualize, as one parent decides that the unpleasantness needs to end and it's time to end the fighting and to pull together again as a family.

Why have we neglected the important art of reconciling? "Because we have 46 pretended that good families don't fight," says one therapist. "They do. It's essential to fight for good health in the family. It gets things out into the open. But we need to learn to put ourselves back together—and many families never learn this."

Close families know how to time divisive and emotional issues that may 47 cause friction. They don't bring up potentially explosive subjects right before they go out, for example, or before bedtime. They tend to schedule discussions rather than allow a matter to explode, and thus they keep a large measure of control over the atmosphere in which they will fight and reconcile. Good families know that they need enough time to discuss issues heatedly, rationally, and completely—and enough time to reconcile. "You've got to solve it right there," said one father. "Don't let it go on and on. It just causes more problems. Then when it's solved, let it be. No nagging, no remembering."

The Family Fosters Table Time and Conversation

Traditionally, the dinner table has been a symbol of socialization. It's probably the 48 one time each day that parents and children are assured of uninterrupted time with one another.

Therapists frequently call upon a patient's memory of the family table during 49 childhood in order to determine the degree of communication and interaction there was in the patient's early life. Some patients recall nothing. Mealtime was either so unpleasant or so unimpressive that they have blocked it out of their memories. Therapists say that there is a relationship between the love in a home and life around the family table. It is to the table that love or discord eventually comes.

But we are spending less table time together. Fast-food dining, even within 50 the home, is becoming a way of life for too many of us. Work schedules, individual organized activities, and television all limit the quantity and quality of mealtime interaction. In an informal study conducted by a church group, 68 percent of the families interviewed in three congregations saw nothing wrong with watching television while eating.

Families who do a good job of communicating tend to make the dinner meal 51 an important part of their day. A number of respondents indicated that adults in the healthiest families refuse dinner business meetings as a matter of principle and discourage their children from sports activities that cut into mealtime hours. "We know which of our swimmers will or won't practice at dinnertime," said a coach, with mixed admiration. "Some parents never allow their children to miss dinners. Some don't care at all." These families pay close attention to the number of times they'll be able to be together in a week, and they rearrange schedules to be sure of spending this time together.

The family that wants to improve communication should look closely at its 52 attitudes toward the family table. Are family table time and conversation important? Is table time open and friendly or warlike and sullen? Is it conducive to sharing more than food—does it encourage the sharing of ideas, feelings, and family intimacies?

We all need to talk to one another. We need to know we're loved and appreci- 53 ated and respected. We want to share our intimacies, not just physical intimacies but all the intimacies in our lives. Communication is the most important element of family life because it is basic to loving relationships. It is the energy that fuels the caring, giving, sharing, and affirming. Without genuine sharing of ourselves, we cannot know one another's needs and fears. Good communication is what makes all the rest of it work.

VOCABULARY IN CONTEXT

1. The word *aghast* in "One parent was aghast to discover that his family's most familiar comments were 'What's on?' and 'Move'" (paragraph 14) means
   a. horrified.
   b. satisfied.
   c. curious.
   d. amused.

2. The word *engrossing* in "as the discussion became more engrossing to them, they turned the sound down so that they could continue their conversation" (paragraph 17) means

    a. disgusting.

    b. intellectual.

    c. foolish.

    d. interesting.

READING COMPREHENSION QUESTIONS

1. Which of the following would be the best alternative title for this selection?

    a. Successful Communication

    b. How to Solve Family Conflicts

    c. Characteristics of Families

    d. Hallmarks of the Communicating Family

2. Which sentence best expresses the article's main point?

    a. Television can and often does destroy family life.

    b. More American families are unhappy than ever before.

    c. A number of qualities mark the healthy and communicating family.

    d. Strong families encourage independent thinking.

3. *True or false?* _____ According to the article, healthy families have no use for television.

4. Healthy families

    a. never find it hard to communicate.

    b. have no conflicts with each other.

    c. know how to reveal their feelings.

    d. permit one of the parents to make all final decisions.

5. The author has found that good families frequently make a point of being together

    a. in the mornings.

    b. after school.

    c. during dinner.

    d. before bedtime.

6. *True or false?* _____ The article implies that the most troublesome nonverbal signal is silence.

7. The article implies that

    a. verbal messages are always more accurate than nonverbal ones.

    b. in strong families, parents practice tolerance of thoughts and feelings.

    c. parents must avoid arguing with their adolescent children.

    d. parents should prevent their children from watching television.

8. From the article, we can conclude that

   a. a weak marital relationship often results in a weak family.

   b. children should not witness a disagreement between parents.

   c. children who grow up in healthy families learn not to interrupt other family members.

   d. parents always find it easier to respond to their children than to react to them.

DISCUSSION QUESTIONS

About Content

1. What are the nine hallmarks of a successfully communicating family? Which of the nine do you feel are most important?

2. How do good parents control television? How do they make television a positive force instead of a negative one?

3. In paragraph 20, the author says, "It is usually easier to react than to respond." What is the difference between the two terms *react* and *respond*?

4. Why, according to Curran, is a "pattern of reconciliation" (paragraph 44) crucial to good family life? Besides those patterns mentioned in the essay, can you describe a reconciliation pattern you have developed with friends or family?

About Structure

5. What is the thesis of the selection? Write here the number of the paragraph in which it is stated: _____

6. What purpose is achieved by Curran's introduction (paragraphs 1–2)? Why is a reader likely to feel that her article will be reliable and worthwhile?

7. Curran frequently uses dialogue or quotations from unnamed parents or children as the basis for her examples. The conversation related in paragraphs 16–17 is one instance. Find three other dialogues used to illustrate points in the essay and write the numbers below:

   Paragraph(s) _____

   Paragraph(s) _____

   Paragraph(s) _____

About Style and Tone

8. Curran enlivens the essay by using some interesting and humorous remarks from parents, children, and counselors. One is the witty comment in paragraph 5 from a marriage counselor: "And when I share this complaint with their husbands, they don't hear *me*, either." Find two other places where the author keeps your interest by using humorous or enjoyable quotations, and write the numbers of the paragraphs here:

   _____   _____

WRITING ASSIGNMENTS

Assignment 1: Writing a Paragraph

Write a definition paragraph on the hallmarks of a *bad* family. Your topic sentence might be, "A bad family is one that is _____, _____, and _____."

To get started, you should first reread the features of a good family explained in the selection. Doing so will help you think about what qualities are found in a bad family. Prepare a list of as many bad qualities as you can think of. Then go through the list and decide on the qualities that seem most characteristic of a bad family.

Assignment 2: Writing a Paragraph

Curran tells us five phrases that some children say they most like to hear from their mothers (paragraph 38). When you were younger, what statement or action of one of your parents (or another adult) would make you especially happy—or sad? Write a paragraph that begins with a topic sentence like one of the following:

A passing comment my grandfather once made really devastated me.

When I was growing up, there were several typical ways my mother treated me that always made me sad.

A critical remark by my fifth-grade teacher was the low point of my life.

My mother has always had several lines that make her children feel very pleased.

You may want to write a narrative that describes in detail the particular time and place of a statement or action. Or you may want to provide three or so examples of statements or actions and their effect on you.

To get started, make up two long lists of childhood memories involving adults—happy memories and sad memories. Then decide which memory or memories you could most vividly describe in a paragraph. Remember that your goal is to help your readers see for themselves why a particular time was sad or happy for you.

Assignment 3: Writing an Essay

In light of Curran's description of what healthy families do right, examine your own family. Which of Curran's traits of communicative families fit your family? Write an essay pointing out three things that your family is doing right in creating a communicative climate for its members. Or, if you feel your family could work harder at communicating, write the essay about three specific ways your family could improve. In either case, choose three of Curran's nine "hallmarks of the successfully communicating family" and show how they do or do not apply to your family.

In your introductory paragraph, include a thesis statement as well as a plan of development that lists the three traits you will talk about. Then present these traits in turn in three supporting paragraphs. Develop each paragraph by giving specific examples of conversations, arguments, behavior patterns, and so on, that illustrate how your family communicates. Finally, conclude your essay with a summarizing sentence or two and a final thought about your subject.

Do It Better!

Ben Carson, M.D., with Cecil Murphey

PREVIEW	WORDS TO WATCH
If you suspect that you are now as "smart" as you'll ever be, then read the following selection. Taken from the book **Think Big**, it is about Dr. Ben Carson, who was sure he was "the dumbest kid in the class" when he was in fifth grade. Carson tells how he turned his life totally around from what was a path of failure. Today he is a famous neurosurgeon at the Johns Hopkins University Children's Center in Baltimore, Maryland.	parochial (20) trauma (20) tenement (20) reluctantly (56) indifferent (58) acknowledged (67) obsidian (74)

1   "Benjamin, is this your report card?" my mother asked as she picked up the folded white card from the table.

2   "Uh, yeah," I said, trying to sound casual. Too ashamed to hand it to her, I had dropped it on the table, hoping that she wouldn't notice until after I went to bed.

3   It was the first report card I had received from Higgins Elementary School since we had moved back from Boston to Detroit, only a few months earlier.

4   I had been in the fifth grade not even two weeks before everyone considered me the dumbest kid in the class and frequently made jokes about me. Before long I too began to feel as though I really was the most stupid kid in fifth grade. Despite Mother's frequently saying, "You're smart, Bennie. You can do anything you want to do," I did not believe her.

5   No one else in school thought I was smart, either.

6   Now, as Mother examined my report card, she asked, "What's this grade in reading?" (Her tone of voice told me that I was in trouble.) Although I was embarrassed, I did not think too much about it. Mother knew that I wasn't doing well in math, but she did not know I was doing so poorly in every subject.

7   While she slowly read my report card, reading everything one word at a time, I hurried into my room and started to get ready for bed. A few minutes later, Mother came into my bedroom.

8   "Benjamin," she said, "are these your grades?" She held the card in front of me as if I hadn't seen it before.

9   "Oh, yeah, but you know, it doesn't mean much."

10   "No, that's not true, Bennie. It means a lot."

11   "Just a report card."

12   "But it's more than that."

13   Knowing I was in for it now, I prepared to listen, yet I was not all that interested. I did not like school very much and there was no reason why I should. Inasmuch as I was the dumbest kid in the class, what did I have to look forward to? The others laughed at me and made jokes about me every day.

14   "Education is the only way you're ever going to escape poverty," she said. "It's the only way you're ever going to get ahead in life and be successful. Do you understand that?"

15   "Yes, Mother," I mumbled.

"If you keep on getting these kinds of grades you're going to spend the rest of [16] your life on skid row, or at best sweeping floors in a factory. That's not the kind of life that I want for you. That's not the kind of life that God wants for you."

I hung my head, genuinely ashamed. My mother had been raising me and my [17] older brother, Curtis, by herself. Having only a third-grade education herself, she knew the value of what she did not have. Daily she drummed into Curtis and me that we had to do our best in school.

"You're just not living up to your potential," she said. "I've got two mighty [18] smart boys and I know they can do better."

I had done my best—at least I had when I first started at Higgins Elementary [19] School. How could I do much when I did not understand anything going on in our class?

In Boston we had attended a parochial• school, but I hadn't learned much [20] because of a teacher who seemed more interested in talking to another female teacher than in teaching us. Possibly, this teacher was not solely to blame— perhaps I wasn't emotionally able to learn much. My parents had separated just before we went to Boston, when I was eight years old. I loved both my mother and father and went through considerable trauma• over their separating. For months after ward, I kept thinking that my parents would get back together, that my daddy would come home again the way he used to, and that we could be the same old family again—but he never came back. Consequently, we moved to Boston and lived with Aunt Jean and Uncle William Avery in a tenement• building for two years until Mother had saved enough money to bring us back to Detroit.

Mother kept shaking the report card at me as she sat on the side of my bed. [21] "You have to work harder. You have to use that good brain that God gave you, Bennie. Do you understand that?"

"Yes, Mother." Each time she paused, I would dutifully say those words. [22]

"I work among rich people, people who are educated," she said. "I watch how [23] they act, and I know they can do anything they want to do. And so can you." She put her arm on my shoulder. "Bennie, you can do anything they can do—only you can do it better!"

Mother had said those words before. Often. At the time, they did not mean [24] much to me. Why should they? I really believed that I was the dumbest kid in fifth grade, but of course, I never told her that.

"I just don't know what to do about you boys," she said. "I'm going to talk to [25] God about you and Curtis." She paused, stared into space, then said (more to herself than to me), "I need the Lord's guidance on what to do. You just can't bring in any more report cards like this."

As far as I was concerned, the report card matter was over. [26]

The next day was like the previous ones—just another bad day in school, an- [27] other day of being laughed at because I did not get a single problem right in arithmetic and couldn't get any words right on the spelling test. As soon as I came home from school, I changed into play clothes and ran outside. Most of the boys my age played softball, or the game I liked best, "Tip the Top."

We played Tip the Top by placing a bottle cap on one of the sidewalk cracks. [28] Then taking a ball—any kind that bounced—we'd stand on a line and take turns throwing the ball at the bottle top, trying to flip it over. Whoever succeeded got two points. If anyone actually moved the cap more than a few inches, he won five points. Ten points came if he flipped it into the air and it landed on the other side.

When it grew dark or we got tired, Curtis and I would finally go inside and [29] watch TV. The set stayed on until we went to bed. Because Mother worked long hours, she was never home until just before we went to bed. Sometimes I would awaken when I heard her unlocking the door.

Two evenings after the incident with the report card, Mother came home 30 about an hour before our bedtime. Curtis and I were sprawled out, watching TV. She walked across the room, snapped off the set, and faced both of us. "Boys," she said, "you're wasting too much of your time in front of that television. You don't get an education from staring at television all the time."

Before either of us could make a protest, she told us that she had been praying 31 for wisdom. "The Lord's told me what to do," she said. "So from now on, you will not watch television, except for two preselected programs each week."

"Just *two* programs?" I could hardly believe she would say such a terrible 32 thing. "That's not—"

"And *only* after you've done your homework. Furthermore, you don't play out- 33 side after school, either, until you've done all your homework."

"Everybody else plays outside right after school," I said, unable to think of 34 anything except how bad it would be if I couldn't play with my friends. "I won't have any friends if I stay in the house all the time—"

"That may be," Mother said, "but everybody else is not going to be as success- 35 ful as you are—"

"But, Mother—" 36

"This is what we're going to do. I asked God for wisdom, and this is the an- 37 swer I got."

I tried to offer several other arguments, but Mother was firm. I glanced at 38 Curtis, expecting him to speak up, but he did not say anything. He lay on the floor, staring at his feet.

"Don't worry about everybody else. The whole world is full of 'everybody 39 else,' you know that? But only a few make a significant achievement."

The loss of TV and play time was bad enough. I got up off the floor, feeling as 40 if everything was against me. Mother wasn't going to let me play with my friends, and there would be no more television—almost none, anyway. She was stopping me from having any fun in life.

"And that isn't all," she said. "Come back, Bennie." 41

I turned around, wondering what else there could be. 42

"In addition," she said, "to doing your homework, you have to read two books 43 from the library each week. Every single week."

"Two books? Two?" Even though I was in fifth grade, I had never read a whole 44 book in my life.

"Yes, two. When you finish reading them, you must write me a book report 45 just like you do at school. You're not living up to your potential, so I'm going to see that you do."

Usually Curtis, who was two years older, was the more rebellious. But this 46 time he seemed to grasp the wisdom of what Mother said. He did not say one word.

She stared at Curtis. "You understand?" 47

He nodded. 48

"Bennie, is it clear?" 49

"Yes, Mother." I agreed to do what Mother told me—it wouldn't have occurred 50 to me not to obey—but I did not like it. Mother was being unfair and demanding more of us than other parents did.

The following day was Thursday. After school, Curtis and I walked to the lo- 51 cal branch of the library. I did not like it much, but then I had not spent that much time in any library.

We both wandered around a little in the children's section, not having 52 any idea about how to select books or which books we wanted to check out.

The librarian came over to us and asked if she could help. We explained that 53 both of us wanted to check out two books.

"What kind of books would you like to read?" the librarian asked. 54

"Animals," I said after thinking about it. "Something about animals."   55

"I'm sure we have several that you'd like." She led me over to a section of   56
books. She left me and guided Curtis to another section of the room. I flipped
through the row of books until I found two that looked easy enough for me to
read. One of them, *Chip, the Dam Builder*—about a beaver—was the first one I had
ever checked out. As soon as I got home, I started to read it. It was the first book I
ever read all the way through even though it took me two nights. Reluctantly* I
admitted afterward to Mother that I really had liked reading about Chip.

Within a month I could find my way around the children's section like some-   57
one who had gone there all his life. By then the library staff knew Curtis and me
and the kind of books we chose. They often made suggestions. "Here's a delightful
book about a squirrel," I remember one of them telling me.

As she told me part of the story, I tried to appear indifferent,* but as soon as   58
she handed it to me, I opened the book and started to read.

Best of all, we became favorites of the librarians. When new books came in   59
that they thought either of us would enjoy, they held them for us. Soon I became
fascinated as I realized that the library had so many books—and about so many
different subjects.

After the book about the beaver, I chose others about animals—all types of   60
animals. I read every animal story I could get my hands on. I read books about
wolves, wild dogs, several about squirrels, and a variety of animals that lived
in other countries. Once I had gone through the animal books, I started reading
about plants, then minerals, and finally rocks.

My reading books about rocks was the first time the information ever became   61
practical to me. We lived near the railroad tracks, and when Curtis and I took the
route to school that crossed by the tracks, I began paying attention to the crushed
rock that I noticed between the ties.

As I continued to read more about rocks, I would walk along the tracks,   62
searching for different kinds of stones, and then see if I could identify them.

Often I would take a book with me to make sure that I had labeled each stone   63
correctly.

"Agate," I said as I threw the stone. Curtis got tired of my picking up stones   64
and identifying them, but I did not care because I kept finding new stones all the
time. Soon it became my favorite game to walk along the tracks and identify the
varieties of stones. Although I did not realize it, within a very short period of time,
I was actually becoming an expert on rocks.

Two things happened in the second half of fifth grade that convinced me of   65
the importance of reading books.

First, our teacher, Mrs. Williamson, had a spelling bee every Friday afternoon.   66
We'd go through all the words we'd had so far that year. Sometimes she also called
out words that we were supposed to have learned in fourth grade. Without fail, I
always went down on the first word.

One Friday, though, Bobby Farmer, whom everyone acknowledged* as the   67
smartest kid in our class, had to spell "agriculture" as his final word. As soon as
the teacher pronounced his word, I thought, *I can spell that word.* Just the day before, I had learned it from reading one of my library books. I spelled it under my
breath, and it was just the way Bobby spelled it.

If I can spell "agriculture," I'll bet I can learn to spell any other word in the world. I'll   68
bet I can learn to spell better than Bobby Farmer.

Just that single word, "agriculture," was enough to give me hope.   69

The following week, a second thing happened that forever changed my life.   70
When Mr. Jaeck, the science teacher, was teaching us about volcanoes, he held up
an object that looked like a piece of black, glass-like rock. "Does anybody know
what this is? What does it have to do with volcanoes?"

Immediately, because of my reading, I recognized the stone. I waited, but none 71 of my classmates raised their hands. I thought, *This is strange. Not even the smart kids are raising their hands.* I raised my hand.

"Yes, Benjamin," he said. 72

I heard snickers around me. The other kids probably thought it was a joke, or 73 that I was going to say something stupid.

"Obsidian,• " I said. 74

"That's right!" He tried not to look startled, but it was obvious he hadn't ex- 75 pected me to give the correct answer.

"That's obsidian," I said, "and it's formed by the supercooling of lava when 76 it hits the water." Once I had their attention and realized I knew information no other student had learned, I began to tell them everything I knew about the subject of obsidian, lava, lava flow, supercooling, and compacting of the elements.

When I finally paused, a voice behind me whispered, "Is that Bennie 77 Carson?"

"You're absolutely correct," Mr. Jaeck said, and he smiled at me. If he had an- 78 nounced that I'd won a million-dollar lottery, I couldn't have been more pleased and excited.

"Benjamin, that's absolutely, absolutely right," he repeated with enthusiasm 79 in his voice. He turned to the others and said, "That is wonderful! Class, this is a tremendous piece of information Benjamin has just given us. I'm very proud to hear him say this."

For a few moments, I tasted the thrill of achievement. I recall thinking, *Wow,* 80 *look at them. They're all looking at me with admiration. Me, the dummy! The one everybody thinks is stupid. They're looking at me to see if this is really me speaking.*

Maybe, though, it was I who was the most astonished one in the class. Al- 81 though I had been reading two books a week because Mother told me to, I had not realized how much knowledge I was accumulating. True, I had learned to enjoy reading, but until then I hadn't realized how it connected with my schoolwork. That day—for the first time—I realized that Mother had been right. Reading is the way out of ignorance, and the road to achievement. I did not have to be the class dummy anymore.

For the next few days, I felt like a hero at school. The jokes about me stopped. 82 The kids started to listen to me. *I'm starting to have fun with this stuff.*

As my grades improved in every subject, I asked myself, "Ben, is there any 83 reason you can't be the smartest kid in the class? If you can learn about obsidian, you can learn about social studies and geography and math and science and everything."

That single moment of triumph pushed me to want to read more. From then 84 on, it was as though I could not read enough books. Whenever anyone looked for me after school, they could usually find me in my bedroom—curled up, reading a library book—for a long time, the only thing I wanted to do. I had stopped caring about the TV programs I was missing; I no longer cared about playing Tip the Top or baseball anymore. I just wanted to read.

In a year and a half—by the middle of sixth grade—I had moved to the top of 85 the class.

VOCABULARY IN CONTEXT

1. The word *trauma* in "I loved both my mother and father and went through considerable trauma over their separating. For months afterward, I kept thinking that my parents would get back together . . . but he never came back" (paragraph 20) means

a. love.

b. knowledge.

c. distance.

d. suffering.

2. The word *acknowledged* in "One Friday, though, Bobby Farmer, whom everyone acknowledged as the smartest kid in our class, had to spell 'agriculture' as his final word" (paragraph 67) means

a. denied.

b. recognized.

c. forgot.

d. interrupted.

READING COMPREHENSION QUESTIONS

1. Which of the following would be the best alternative title for this selection?

a. The Importance of Fifth Grade

b. The Role of Parents in Education

c. The Day I Surprised My Science Teacher

d. Reading Changed My Life

2. Which sentence best expresses the main idea of this selection?

a. Children who grow up in single-parent homes may spend large amounts of time home alone.

b. Because of parental guidance that led to a love of reading, the author was able to go from academic failure to success.

c. Most children do not take school very seriously, and they suffer as a result.

d. Today's young people watch too much television.

3. Bennie's mother

a. was not a religious person.

b. spoke to Bennie's teacher about Bennie's poor report card.

c. had only a third-grade education.

d. had little contact with educated people.

4. To get her sons to do better in school, Mrs. Carson insisted that they

a. stop watching TV.

b. finish their homework before playing.

c. read one library book every month.

d. all of the above.

5. *True or false?* _____ Bennie's first experience with a library book was discouraging.

6. We can conclude that Bennie Carson believed he was dumb because

a. in Boston he had not learned much.

b. other students laughed at him.

c. he had done his best when he first started at Higgins Elementary School, but still got poor grades.

d. all of the above.

7. We can conclude that the author's mother believed
   a. education leads to success.
   b. her sons needed to be forced to live up to their potential.
   c. socializing was less important for her sons than a good education.
   d. all of the above.

8. From paragraphs 70–80, we can infer that
   a. Bennie thought his classmates were stupid because they did not know about obsidian.
   b. Mr. Jaeck knew less about rocks than Bennie did.
   c. this was the first time Bennie had answered a difficult question correctly in class.
   d. Mr. Jaeck thought that Bennie had taken too much class time explaining about obsidian.

DISCUSSION QUESTIONS

About Content

1. How do you think considering himself the "dumbest kid in class" affected Bennie's schoolwork?

2. The author recalls his failure in the classroom as an eight-year-old child by writing, "Perhaps I wasn't emotionally able to learn much." Why does he make this statement? What do you think parents and schools can do to help children through difficult times?

3. How did Mrs. Carson encourage Bennie to make school—particularly reading—a priority in his life? What effect did her efforts have on Bennie's academic performance and self-esteem?

4. As a child, Carson began to feel confident about his own abilities when he followed his mother's guidelines. How might Mrs. Carson's methods help adult students build up their own self-confidence and motivation?

About Structure

5. What is the main order in which the details of this selection are organized—time order or listing order? Locate and write below three of the many transitions that are used as part of that time order or listing order.

   _____   _____   _____

6. In paragraph 65, Carson states, "Two things happened in the second half of fifth grade that convinced me of the importance of reading books." What two transitions does Carson use in later paragraphs to help readers recognize those two events? Write those two transitions here:

   _____   _____

About Style and Tone

7. Instead of describing his mother, Carson reveals her character through specific details of her actions and words. Find one paragraph in which this technique

is used, and write its number here: _____. What does this paragraph tell us about Mrs. Carson?

8. Why do you suppose Carson italicizes sentences in paragraphs 67, 68, 71, 80, and 82? What purpose do the italicized sentences serve?

WRITING ASSIGNMENTS

Assignment 1: Writing a Paragraph

The reading tells about some of Carson's most important school experiences, both positive and negative. Write a paragraph about one of your most important experiences in school. To select an event to write about, try asking yourself the following questions:

> Which teachers or events in school influenced how I felt about myself?

> What specific incidents stand out in my mind as I think back to elementary school?

To get started, you might use freewriting to help you remember and record the details. Then begin your draft with a topic sentence similar to one of the following:

> A seemingly small experience in elementary school encouraged me greatly.

> If not for my sixth-grade teacher, I would not be where I am today.

> My tenth-grade English class was a turning point in my life.

Use concrete details—actions, comments, reactions, and so on—to help your readers see what happened.

Assignment 2: Writing a Paragraph

Reading helped Bennie, and it can do a lot for adults, too. Most of us, however, don't have someone around to make us do a certain amount of personal reading every week. In addition, many of us don't have as much free time as Bennie and Curtis had. How can adults find time to read more? Write a paragraph listing several ways adults can add more reading to their lives.

To get started, simply write down as many ways as you can think of—in any order. Here is an example of a prewriting list for this paper:

> Situations in which adults can find extra time to read:
> Riding to and from work or school
> In bed at night before turning off the light
> While eating breakfast or lunch
> Instead of watching some TV
> In the library

Feel free to use items from the list above, but see if you can add at least one or two of your own ideas as well. Use descriptions and examples to emphasize and dramatize your supporting details.

Assignment 3: Writing an Essay

Mrs. Carson discovered an effective way to boost her children's achievement and self-confidence. There are other ways as well. Write an essay whose thesis statement is "There are several ways parents can help children live up to their potential." Then, in the following paragraphs, explain and illustrate two or three methods parents can use. In choosing material for your supporting paragraphs, you might consider some of these areas, or think of others on your own:

Assigning regular household "chores" and rewarding a good job

Encouraging kids to join an organization that fosters achievement: Scouts, Little League, religious group, or neighborhood service club

Going to parent-teacher conferences at school and then working more closely with children's teachers—knowing when assignments are due, and so on

Giving a child some responsibility for an enjoyable family activity, such as choosing decorations or food for a birthday party

Setting up a "Wall of Fame" in the home where children's artwork, successful schoolwork, and so on, can be displayed

Setting guidelines (as Mrs. Carson did) for use of leisure time, homework time, and the like

Draw on examples from your own experiences or from someone else's—including those of Bennie Carson, if you like.

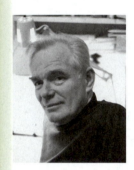

Anxiety: Challenge by Another Name

James Lincoln Collier

PREVIEW	WORDS TO WATCH
What is your basis for making personal decisions? Do you aim to rock the boat as little as possible, choosing the easy, familiar path? There is comfort in sticking with what is safe and well known, just as there is comfort in eating bland mashed potatoes. But James Lincoln Collier, author of numerous articles and books, decided soon after leaving college not to live a mashed-potato sort of life. In this essay, first published in *Reader's Digest*, he tells how he learned to recognize the marks of a potentially exciting, growth-inducing experience, to set aside his anxiety, and to dive in.	fabled (2) pampas (2) daunted (2) wavered (7) venture (10) corollary (15) insistent (15)

Between my sophomore and junior years at college, a chance came up for me 1 to spend the summer vacation working on a ranch in Argentina. My roommate's father was in the cattle business, and he wanted Ted to see something of it. Ted said he would go if he could take a friend, and he chose me.

The idea of spending two months on the fabled• Argentine pampas• was ex- 2 citing. Then I began having second thoughts. I had never been very far from New England, and I had been homesick my first weeks at college. What would it be like in a strange country? What about the language? And besides, I had promised to teach my younger brother to sail that summer. The more I thought about it, the more the prospect daunted• me. I began waking up nights in a sweat.

In the end I turned down the proposition. As soon as Ted asked somebody 3 else to go, I began kicking myself. A couple of weeks later I went home to my old summer job, unpacking cartons at the local supermarket, feeling very low. I had turned down something I wanted to do because I was scared, and I had ended up feeling depressed. I stayed that way for a long time. And it didn't help when I went back to college in the fall to discover that Ted and his friend had had a terrific time.

In the long run that unhappy summer taught me a valuable lesson out of 4 which I developed a rule for myself: *do what makes you anxious; don't do what makes you depressed.*

I am not, of course, talking about severe states of anxiety or depression, which 5 require medical attention. What I mean is that kind of anxiety we call stage fright, butterflies in the stomach, a case of nerves—the feelings we have at a job interview, when we're giving a big party, when we have to make an important presentation at the office. And the kind of depression I am referring to is that downhearted feeling of the blues, when we don't seem to be interested in anything, when we can't get going and seem to have no energy.

I was confronted by this sort of situation toward the end of my senior year. As 6 graduation approached, I began to think about taking a crack at making my living as a writer. But one of my professors was urging me to apply to graduate school and aim at a teaching career.

I wavered.• The idea of trying to live by writing was scary—a lot more scary 7 than spending a summer on the pampas, I thought. Back and forth I went, making my decision, unmaking it. Suddenly, I realized that every time I gave up the idea of writing, that sinking feeling went through me; it gave me the blues.

The thought of graduate school wasn't what depressed me. It was giving up 8 on what deep in my gut I really wanted to do. Right then I learned another lesson. To avoid that kind of depression meant, inevitably, having to endure a certain amount of worry and concern.

The great Danish philosopher Søren Kierkegaard believed that anxiety always arises when we confront the possibility of our own development. It seems 9 to be a rule of life that you can't advance without getting that old, familiar, jittery feeling.

Even as children we discover this when we try to expand ourselves by, say, 10 learning to ride a bike or going out for the school play. Later in life we get butterflies when we think about having that first child, or uprooting the family from the old hometown to find a better opportunity halfway across the country. Any time, it seems, that we set out aggressively to get something we want, we meet up with anxiety. And it's going to be our traveling companion, at least part of the way, in any new venture.•

When I first began writing magazine articles, I was frequently required to 11 interview big names—people like Richard Burton, Joan Rivers, sex authority William Masters, baseball great Dizzy Dean. Before each interview I would get butterflies and my hands would shake.

At the time, I was doing some writing about music. And one person I particu- 12 larly admired was the great composer Duke Ellington. On stage and on television, he seemed the very model of the confident, sophisticated man of the world. Then I learned that Ellington still got stage fright. If the highly honored Duke Ellington, who had appeared on the bandstand some ten thousand times over thirty years, had anxiety attacks, who was I to think I could avoid them?

I went on doing those frightening interviews, and one day, as I was getting 13 onto a plane for Washington to interview columnist Joseph Alsop, I suddenly realized to my astonishment that I was looking forward to the meeting. What had happened to those butterflies?

Well, in truth, they were still there, but there were fewer of them. I had ben- 14 efited, I discovered, from a process psychologists call "extinction." If you put an individual in an anxiety-provoking situation often enough, he will eventually learn that there isn't anything to be worried about.

Which brings us to a corollary• to my basic rule: *you'll never eliminate anxiety by* 15 *avoiding the things that caused it.* I remember how my son Jeff was when I first began to teach him to swim at the lake cottage where we spent our summer vacations. He resisted, and when I got him into the water he sank and sputtered and wanted to quit. But I was insistent.• And by summer's end he was splashing around like a puppy. He had "extinguished" his anxiety the only way he could—by confronting it.

The problem, of course, is that it is one thing to urge somebody else to take on 16 those anxiety-producing challenges; it is quite another to get ourselves to do it.

Some years ago I was offered a writing assignment that would require three 17 months of travel through Europe. I had been abroad a couple of times on the usual "If it's Tuesday this must be Belgium"* trips, but I hardly could claim to know my way around the continent. Moreover, my knowledge of foreign languages was limited to a little college French.

I hesitated. How would I, unable to speak the language, totally unfamiliar with 18 local geography or transportation systems, set up interviews and do research? It seemed impossible, and with considerable regret I sat down to write a letter begging off. Halfway through, a thought—which I subsequently made into another corollary to my basic rule—ran through my mind: *you can't learn if you don't try.* So I accepted the assignment.

There were some bad moments. But by the time I had finished the trip I was 19 an experienced traveler. And ever since, I have never hesitated to head for even the most exotic of places, without guides or even advance bookings, confident that somehow I will manage.

The point is that the new, the different, is almost by definition scary. But each 20 time you try something, you learn, and as the learning piles up, the world opens to you.

I've made parachute jumps, learned to ski at forty, flown up the Rhine in a 21 balloon. And I know I'm going to go on doing such things. It's not because I'm braver or more daring than others. I'm not. But I don't let the butterflies stop me from doing what I want. Accept anxiety as another name for challenge, and you can accomplish wonders.

VOCABULARY IN CONTEXT

1. The word *daunted* in "The more I thought about [going to Argentina], the more the prospect daunted me. I began waking up nights in a sweat" (paragraph 2) means

   a. encouraged.

   b. interested.

   c. discouraged.

   d. amused.

2. The word *corollary* in "Which brings us to a corollary to my basic rule: *you'll never eliminate anxiety by avoiding the things that caused it*" (paragraph 15) means

   a. an idea that follows from another idea.

   b. an idea based on a falsehood.

   c. an idea that creates anxiety.

   d. an idea passed on from one generation to another.

*Reference to a film comedy about a group of American tourists who visited too many European countries in too little time.

READING COMPREHENSION QUESTIONS

1. Which of the following would be the best alternative title for this selection?
   a. A Poor Decision
   b. Don't Let Anxiety Stop You
   c. Becoming a Writer
   d. The Courage to Travel

2. Which sentence best expresses the main idea of the selection?
   a. The butterflies-in-the-stomach type of anxiety differs greatly from severe states of anxiety or depression.
   b. Taking on a job assignment that required traveling helped the author get over his anxiety.
   c. People learn and grow by confronting, not backing away from, situations that make them anxious.
   d. Anxiety is a predictable part of life that can be dealt with in positive ways.

3. When a college friend invited the writer to go with him to Argentina, the writer
   a. turned down the invitation.
   b. accepted eagerly.
   c. was very anxious about the idea but went anyway.
   d. did not believe his friend was serious.

4. *True or false?* _____ As graduation approached, Collier's professor urged him to try to make his living as a writer.

5. *True or false?* _____ The philosopher Søren Kierkegaard believed that anxiety occurs when we face the possibility of our own development.

6. *Extinction* is the term psychologists use for
   a. the inborn tendency to avoid situations that make one feel very anxious.
   b. a person's gradual loss of confidence.
   c. the natural development of a child's abilities.
   d. the process of losing one's fear by continuing to face the anxiety-inspiring situation.

7. The author implies that
   a. it was lucky he didn't take the summer job in Argentina.
   b. his son never got over his fear of the water.
   c. Duke Ellington's facing stage fright inspired him.
   d. one has to be more daring than most people to overcome anxiety.

8. The author implies that
   a. anxiety may be a signal that one has an opportunity to grow.
   b. he considers his three-month trip to Europe a failure.
   c. facing what makes him anxious has eliminated all depression from his life.
   d. he no longer has anxiety about new experiences.

DISCUSSION QUESTIONS

About Content

1. Collier developed the rule "Do what makes you anxious; don't do what makes you depressed." How does he distinguish between feeling anxious and feeling depressed?

2. In what way does Collier believe that anxiety is positive? How, according to him, can we eventually overcome our fears? Have you ever gone ahead and done something that made you anxious? How did it turn out?

About Structure

3. Collier provides a rule and two corollary rules that describe his attitude toward challenge and anxiety. Below, write the location of that rule and its corollaries.

   Collier's rule: paragraph _____

   First corollary: paragraph _____

   Second corollary: paragraph _____

   How does Collier emphasize the rule and its corollaries?

4. Collier uses several personal examples in his essay. Find three instances of these examples and explain how each helps Collier develop his main point.

About Style and Tone

5. In paragraph 3, Collier describes the aftermath of his decision not to go to Argentina. He could have just written, "I worked that summer." Instead he writes, "I went home to my old summer job, unpacking cartons at the local supermarket." Why do you think he provides that bit of detail about his job? What is the effect on the reader?

6. Authors often use testimony by authorities to support their points. Where in Collier's essay does he use such support? What do you think it adds to his piece?

7. In the last sentence of paragraph 10, Collier refers to anxiety as a "traveling companion." Why do you think he uses that image? What does it convey about his view of anxiety?

8. Is Collier just telling about a lesson he has learned for himself, or is he encouraging his readers to do something? How can you tell?

RESPONDING TO IMAGES

In his famous painting *The Scream*, expressionist painter Edward Munch creates an emotionally true (rather than logically realistic) landscape. Using specific details, write a paragraph that supports the main point in the previous sentence (which you can use as your topic sentence). *Hint:* Look up **expressionist** in a dictionary or online.

WRITING ASSIGNMENTS

Assignment 1: Writing a Paragraph

Collier explains how his life experiences made him view the term *anxiety* in a new way. Write a paragraph in which you explain how a personal experience of yours has given new meaning to a particular term. Following are some terms you might consider for this assignment:

Failure

Friendship

Goals

Homesickness

Maturity

Success

Here are two sample topic sentences for this assignment:

I used to think of failure as something terrible, but thanks to a helpful boss, I now think of it as an opportunity to learn.

The word *creativity* has taken on a new meaning for me ever since I became interested in dancing.

Assignment 2: Writing a Paragraph

The second corollary to Collier's rule is "you can't learn if you don't try." Write a paragraph using this idea as your main idea. Support it with your own experience, someone else's experience, or both. One way of developing this point is to compare two approaches to a challenge: One person may have backed away from a frightening opportunity while another person decided to take on the challenge. Or you could write about a time when you learned something useful by daring to give a new experience a try. In that case, you might discuss your reluctance to take on the new experience, the difficulties you encountered, and your eventual success. In your conclusion, include a final thought about the value of what was learned.

Listing a few skills you have learned will help you decide on the experience you wish to write about. To get you started, below is a list of things adults often need to go to some trouble to learn.

Driving with a stick shift

Taking useful lecture notes

Knowing how to do well on a job interview

Asking someone out on a date

Making a speech

Standing up for your rights

Assignment 3: Writing an Essay

Collier describes three rules he follows when facing anxiety. In an essay, write about one or more rules, or guidelines, that you have developed for yourself through experience. If you decide to discuss two or three such guidelines, mention or refer to them in your introductory paragraph. Then go on to discuss each in one or more paragraphs of its own. Include at least one experience that led you to develop a given guideline, and tell how it has helped you at other times in your life. You might end with a brief summary and an explanation of how the guide-lines as a group have helped. If you decide to focus on one rule, include at least two or three experiences that help to illustrate your point.

To prepare for this assignment, spend some time freewriting about the rules or guidelines you have set up for yourself. Continue writing until you feel you have a central idea for which you have plenty of interesting support. Then organize that support into a scratch outline, such as this one:

Thesis: I have one rule that keeps me from staying in a rut—Don't let the size of a challenge deter you; instead, aim for it by making plans and taking steps.

Topic sentence 1: I began to think about my rule one summer in high school when a friend got the type of summer job that I had only been thinking about.

Topic sentence 2: After high school, I began to live up to my rule when I aimed for a business career and entered college.

Topic sentence 3: My rule is also responsible for my having the wonderful boyfriend (*or* girlfriend *or* spouse *or* job) I now have.

Let's Really Reform Our Schools
Anita Garland

PREVIEW	WORDS TO WATCH
A few years ago, a National Commission on Excellence in Education published *A Nation at Risk*, in which the commission reported on a "rising tide of mediocrity" in our schools. Other studies have pointed to students' poor achievement in science, math, communication, and critical thinking. What can our schools do to improve students' performance? Anita Garland has several radical ideas, which she explains in this selection. As you read it, think about whether or not you agree with her points.	prowl (1) remedies (2) curriculum (2) affluent (6) subliminal (9) elite (9) epitome (10) implore (10)

American high schools are in trouble. No, that's not strong enough. American 1 high schools are disasters. "Good" schools today are only a rite of passage for American kids, where the pressure to look fashionable and act cool outweighs any concern for learning. And "bad" schools—heaven help us—are havens for the vicious and corrupt. There, metal detectors and security guards wage a losing battle against the criminals that prowl• the halls.

Desperate illnesses require desperate remedies.• And our public schools are 2 desperately ill. What is needed is no meek, fainthearted attempt at "curriculum• revision" or "student-centered learning." We need to completely restructure our thinking about what schools are and what we expect of the students who attend them.

The first change needed to save our schools is the most fundamental one. Not 3 only must we stop *forcing* everyone to attend school; we must stop *allowing* the attendance of so-called students who are not interested in studying. Mandatory school attendance is based upon the idea that every American has a right to basic education. But as the old saying goes, your rights stop where the next guy's begin. A student who sincerely wants an education, regardless of his or her mental or physical ability, should be welcome in any school in this country. But "students" who deliberately interfere with other students' ability to learn, teachers' ability to teach, and administrators' ability to maintain order should be denied a place in the classroom. They do not want an education. And they should not be allowed to mark time within school walls, waiting to be handed their meaningless diplomas while they make it harder for everyone around them to either provide or receive a quality education.

By requiring troublemakers to attend school, we have made it impossible to 4 deal with them in any effective way. They have little to fear in terms of punishment. Suspension from school for a few days doesn't improve their behavior. After all, they don't want to be in school anyway. For that matter, mandatory attendance is, in many cases, nothing but a bad joke. Many chronic troublemakers are absent so often that it is virtually impossible for them to learn anything. And when they *are* in school, they are busy shaking down other students for their lunch money or jewelry. If we permanently banned such punks from school, educators could turn their attention away from the troublemakers and toward those students who realize that school is a serious place for serious learning.

You may ask, "What will become of these young people who aren't in school?" 5 But consider this: What is becoming of them now? They are not being educated. They are merely names on the school records. They are passed from grade to grade, learning nothing, making teachers and fellow students miserable. Finally they are bumped off the conveyor belt at the end of twelfth grade, oftentimes barely literate, and passed into society as "high school graduates." Yes, there would be a need for alternative solutions for these young people. Let the best thinkers of our country come up with some ideas. But in the meanwhile, don't allow our schools to serve as a holding tank for people who don't want to be there.

Once our schools have been returned to the control of teachers and genu- 6 ine students, we could concentrate on smaller but equally meaningful reforms. A good place to start would be requiring students to wear school uniforms. There would be cries of horror from the fashion slaves, but the change would benefit everyone. If students wore uniforms, think of the mental energy that could be redirected into more productive channels. No longer would young girls feel the need to spend their evenings laying out coordinated clothing, anxiously trying to create just the right look. The daily fashion show that currently absorbs so much of students' attention would come to a halt. Kids from modest backgrounds could stand out because of their personalities and intelligence, rather than being tagged as losers because they can't wear the season's hottest sneakers or jeans. Affluent● kids might learn they have something to offer the world other than a fashion statement. Parents would be relieved of the pressure to deal with their offspring's constant demands for wardrobe additions.

Next, let's move to the cafeteria. What's for lunch today? How about a Milky 7 Way bar, a bag of Fritos, a Coke, and just to round out the meal with a vegetable, maybe some french fries. And then back to the classroom for a few hours of intense mental activity, fueled on fat, salt, and sugar. What a joke! School is an institution of education, and that education should be continued as students sit down to eat. Here's a perfect opportunity to teach a whole generation of Americans about nutrition, and we are blowing it. School cafeterias, of all places, should demonstrate how a healthful, low-fat, well-balanced diet produces healthy, energetic, mentally alert people. Instead, we allow school cafeterias to dispense the same junk food that kids could buy in any mall. Overhaul the cafeterias! Out with the candy, soda, chips, and fries! In with the salads, whole grains, fruits, and vegetables!

Turning our attention away from what goes on during school hours, let's con- 8
sider what happens after the final bell rings. Some school-sponsored activities
are all to the good. Bands and choirs, foreign-language field trips, chess or skiing
or drama clubs are sensible parts of an extracurricular plan. They bring together
kids with similar interests to develop their talents and leadership ability. But other
common school activities are not the business of education. The prime example of
inappropriate school activity is in competitive sports between schools.

Intramural sports are great. Students need an outlet for their energies, and 9
friendly competition against one's classmates on the basketball court or baseball diamond is fun and physically beneficial. But the wholesome fun of sports is
quickly ruined by the competitive team system. School athletes quickly become
the campus idols, encouraged to look down on classmates with less physical ability. Schools concentrate enormous amounts of time, money, and attention upon
their teams, driving home the point that competitive sports are the *really* important part of school. Students are herded into gymnasiums for "pep rallies" that
whip up adoration of the chosen few and encourage hatred of rival schools. Boys'
teams are supplied with squads of cheerleading girls . . . let's not even get into
what the subliminal° message is *there.* If communities feel they must have competitive sports, let local businesses or even professional teams organize and fund
the programs. But school budgets and time should be spent on programs that
benefit more than an elite° few.

Another school-related activity that should get the ax is the fluff-headed, 10
money-eating, misery-inducing event known as the prom. How in the world did
the schools of America get involved in this showcase of excess? Proms have to be
the epitome° of everything that is wrong, tasteless, misdirected, inappropriate,
and just plain sad about the way we bring up our young people. Instead of simply
letting the kids put on a dance, we've turned the prom into a bloated nightmare
that ruins young people's budgets, their self-image, and even their lives. The pressure to show up at the prom with the best-looking date, in the most expensive
clothes, wearing the most exotic flowers, riding in the most extravagant form of
transportation, dominates the thinking of many students for months before the
prom itself. Students cling to doomed, even abusive romantic relationships rather
than risk being dateless for this night of nights. They lose any concept of meaningful values as they implore° their parents for more, more, more money to throw
into the jaws of the prom god. The adult trappings of the prom—the slinky dresses,
emphasis on romance, slow dancing, nightclub atmosphere—all encourage kids
to engage in behavior that can have tragic consequences. Who knows how many
unplanned pregnancies and alcohol-related accidents can be directly attributed to
the pressures of prom night? And yet, not going to the prom seems a fate worse
than death to many young people—because of all the hype about the "wonder"
and "romance" of it all. Schools are not in the business of providing wonder and
romance, and it's high time we remembered that.

We have lost track of the purpose of our schools. They are not intended to be 11
centers for fun, entertainment, and social climbing. They are supposed to be institutions for learning and hard work. Let's institute the changes suggested here—
plus dozens more—without apology, and get American schools back to business.

VOCABULARY IN CONTEXT

1. The word *affluent* in "Kids from modest backgrounds could stand out because
   of their personalities and intelligence. . . . Affluent kids might learn they have
   something to offer the world other than a fashion statement" (paragraph 6)
   means

a. intelligent.

b. troubled.

c. wealthy.

d. poor.

2. The word *implore* in "They lose any concept of meaningful values as they implore their parents for more, more, more money to throw into the jaws of the prom god" (paragraph 10) means

a. beg.

b. ignore.

c. pay.

d. obey.

READING COMPREHENSION QUESTIONS

1. Which of the following would be the best alternative title for this selection?

a. America's Youth

b. Education of the Future

c. Social Problems of Today's Students

d. Changes Needed in the American School System

2. Which sentence best expresses the main idea of the selection?

a. Excesses such as the prom and competitive sports should be eliminated from school budgets.

b. Major changes are needed to make American schools real centers of learning.

c. Attendance must be voluntary in our schools.

d. The best thinkers of our country must come up with ideas on how to improve our schools.

3. Garland believes that mandatory attendance at school

a. gives all students an equal chance at getting an education.

b. allows troublemakers to disrupt learning.

c. is cruel to those who don't really want to be there.

d. helps teachers maintain control of their classes.

4. Garland is against school-sponsored competitive sports because she believes that

a. exercise and teamwork should not have a role in school.

b. they overemphasize the importance of sports and athletes.

c. school property should not be used in any way after school hours.

d. they take away from professional sports.

5. We can infer that Garland believes

a. teens should not have dances.

b. proms promote unwholesome values.

c. teens should avoid romantic relationships.

d. proms are even worse than mandatory education.

6. The author clearly implies that troublemakers
   a. are not intelligent.
   b. really do want to be in school.
   c. should be placed in separate classes.
   d. don't mind being suspended from school.

7. *True or false?* _____ We can conclude that the author feels that teachers and genuine students have lost control of our schools.

8. The essay suggests that the author would also oppose
   a. school plays.
   b. serving milk products in school cafeterias.
   c. the selection of homecoming queens.
   d. stylish school uniforms.

DISCUSSION QUESTIONS

About Content

1. What reforms does Garland suggest in her essay? Think back to your high school days. Which of the reforms that Garland suggests do you think might have been most useful at your high school?

2. Garland's idea of voluntary school attendance directly contradicts the "stay in school" campaigns. Do you agree with her idea? What do you think might become of students who choose not to attend school?

3. At the end of her essay, Garland writes, "Let's institute the changes suggested here—plus dozens more." What other changes do you think Garland may have in mind? What are some reforms you think might improve schools?

About Structure

4. The thesis of this essay can be found in the introduction, which is made up of the first two paragraphs. Find the thesis statement and write it here:

   _____

   _____

5. The first point on Garland's list of reforms is the elimination of mandatory (that is, required) education. Then she goes on to discuss other reforms. Find the transition sentence that signals that she is leaving the discussion about mandatory education and going on to other needed changes. Write that sentence here:

   _____

   _____

6. What are two transitional words that Garland uses to introduce two of the other reforms?

   _____   _____

About Style and Tone

7. Garland uses some colorful images to communicate her ideas. For instance, in paragraph 5 she writes, "Finally [the troublemakers] are bumped off the conveyor belt at the end of twelfth grade, oftentimes barely literate, and passed into society as 'high school graduates.'" What does the image of a conveyor belt imply about schools and about the troublemakers? What do the quotation marks around *high school graduates* imply?

8. Below are three other colorful images from the essay. What do the italicized words imply about today's schools and students?

    . . . don't allow our schools to serve as a *holding tank* for people who don't want to be there. (paragraph 5)

    A good place to start would be requiring students to wear school uniforms. There would be cries of horror from the *fashion slaves* . . . (paragraph 6)

    Students are *herded* into gymnasiums for "pep rallies" that whip up adoration of the chosen few . . . (paragraph 9)

9. To convey her points, does the author use a formal, straightforward tone or an informal, impassioned tone? Give examples from the essay to support your answer.

WRITING ASSIGNMENTS

Assignment 1: Writing a Paragraph

Write a persuasive paragraph in which you agree or disagree with one of Garland's suggested reforms. Your topic sentence may be something simple and direct, like these:

    I strongly agree with Garland's point that attendance should be voluntary in our high schools.

    I disagree with Garland's point that high school students should be required to wear uniforms.

Alternatively, you may want to develop your own paragraph calling for reform in some other area of American life. Your topic sentence might be like one of the following:

    We need to make radical changes in our treatment of homeless people.

    Strong new steps must be taken to control the sale of guns in our country.

    Major changes are needed to keep television from dominating the lives of our children.

Assignment 2: Writing a Paragraph

If troublemakers were excluded from schools, what would become of them? Write a paragraph in which you suggest two or three types of programs that troublemakers could be assigned to. Explain why each program would be beneficial to the troublemakers themselves and society in general. You might want to include in your paragraph one or more of the following:

    Apprentice programs

    Special neighborhood schools for troublemakers

Reform schools

Work-placement programs

Community service programs

Assignment 3: Writing an Essay

Garland suggests ways to make schools "institutions for learning and hard work." She wants to get rid of anything that greatly distracts students from their education, such as having to deal with troublemakers, overemphasis on fashion, and interschool athletics. When you were in high school, what tended most to divert your attention from learning? Write an essay explaining in full detail the three things that interfered most with your high school education. You may include any of Garland's points, but present details that apply specifically to you. Organize your essay by using emphatic order—in other words, save whatever interfered most with your education for the last supporting paragraph.

It is helpful to write a sentence outline for this kind of essay. Here, for example, is one writer's outline for an essay titled "Obstacles to My High School Education."

Thesis: There were three main things that interfered with my high school education.

Topic sentence 1: Concern about my appearance took up too much of my time and energy.

a. Since I was concerned about my looking good, I spent too much time shopping for clothes.

b. In order to afford the clothes, I worked twenty hours a week, drastically reducing my study time.

c. Spending even more time on clothes, I fussed every evening over what I would wear to school the next day.

Topic sentence 2: Cheerleading was another major obstacle to my academic progress in high school.

a. I spent many hours practicing in order to make the cheerleading squad.

b. Once I made the squad, I had to spend even more time practicing and then attending games.

c. Once when I didn't make the squad, I was so depressed for a while that I couldn't study, and this had serious consequences.

Topic sentence 3: The main thing that interfered with my high school education was my family situation.

a. Even when I had time to study, I often found it impossible to do so at home, since my parents often had fights that were noisy and upsetting.

b. My parents showed little interest in my schoolwork, giving me little reason to work hard for my classes.

c. When I was in eleventh grade, my parents divorced; this was a major distraction for me for a long time.

To round off your essay with a conclusion, you may simply want to restate your thesis and main supporting points.

As an alternative to the above assignment, you can write about current obstacles to your college education.

How They Get You to Do That

Janny Scott

PREVIEW	WORDS TO WATCH
So you think you're sailing along in life, making decisions based on your own preferences? Not likely! Janny Scott brings together the findings of several researchers to show how advertisers, charitable organizations, politicians, employers, and even your friends get you to say "yes" when you should have said "no"—or, at least, "Let me think about that."	propaganda (2) wielding (3) compliance (4) pervasive (4) proliferates (8) teeming (11) jujitsu (15) peripheral (23) dapper (24) inveterate (24) reciprocity (28) deference (37)

1   The woman in the supermarket in a white coat tenders a free sample of "lite" cheese. A car salesman suggests that prices won't stay low for long. Even a penny will help, pleads the door-to-door solicitor. Sale ends Sunday! Will work for food.

2   The average American exists amid a perpetual torrent of propaganda.° Everyone, it sometimes seems, is trying to make up someone else's mind. If it isn't an athletic shoe company, it's a politician, a panhandler, a pitchman, a boss, a billboard company, a spouse.

3   The weapons of influence they are wielding° are more sophisticated than ever, researchers say. And they are aimed at a vulnerable target—people with less and less time to consider increasingly complex issues.

4   As a result, some experts in the field have begun warning the public, tipping people off to precisely how "the art of compliance°" works. Some critics have taken to arguing for new government controls on one pervasive° form of persuasion— political advertising.

5   The persuasion problem is "the essential dilemma of modern democracy," argue social psychologists Anthony Pratkanis and Elliot Aronson, the authors of *Age of Propaganda: The Everyday Use and Abuse of Persuasion.*

6   As the two psychologists see it, American society values free speech and public discussion, but people no longer have the time or inclination to pay attention. Mindless propaganda flourishes, they say; thoughtful persuasion fades away.

7   The problem stems from what Pratkanis and Aronson call our "message-dense environment." The average television viewer sees nearly 38,000 commercials a year, they say. "The average home receives . . . [numerous] pieces of junk mail annually and . . . [countless calls] from telemarketing firms."

8   Bumper stickers, billboards and posters litter the public consciousness. Athletic events and jazz festivals carry corporate labels. As direct selling proliferates,° workers patrol their offices during lunch breaks, peddling chocolate and Tupperware to friends.

9   Meanwhile, information of other sorts multiplies exponentially. Technology serves up ever-increasing quantities of data on every imaginable subject, from home security to health. With more and more information available, people have less and less time to digest it.

10   "It's becoming harder and harder to think in a considered way about anything," said Robert Cialdini, a persuasion researcher at Arizona State University

in Tempe. "More and more, we are going to be deciding on the basis of less and less information."

Persuasion is a democratic society's chosen method for decision making 11 and dispute resolution. But the flood of persuasive messages in recent years has changed the nature of persuasion. Lengthy arguments have been supplanted by slogans and logos. In a world teeming• with propaganda, those in the business of influencing others put a premium on effective shortcuts.

Most people, psychologists say, are easily seduced by such shortcuts. Humans 12 are "cognitive misers," always looking to conserve attention and mental energy— leaving themselves at the mercy of anyone who has figured out which short- cuts work.

The task of figuring out shortcuts has been embraced by advertising agencies, 13 market researchers, and millions of salespeople. The public, meanwhile, remains in the dark, ignorant of even the simplest principles of social influence.

As a result, laypeople underestimate their susceptibility to persuasion, psy- 14 chologists say. They imagine their actions are dictated simply by personal prefer- ences. Unaware of the techniques being used against them, they are often unwit- tingly outgunned.

As Cialdini tells it, the most powerful tactics work like jujitsu•: They draw 15 their strength from deep-seated, unconscious psychological rules. The clever "compliance professional" deliberately triggers these "hidden stores of influence" to elicit a predictable response.

One such rule, for example, is that people are more likely to comply with a 16 request if a reason—no matter how silly—is given. To prove that point, one re- searcher tested different ways of asking people in line at a copying machine to let her cut the line.

When the researcher asked simply, "Excuse me, I have five pages. May I use 17 the Xerox machine?" only 60 percent of those asked complied. But when she added nothing more than, "because I have to make some copies," nearly every one agreed.

The simple addition of "because" unleashed an automatic response, even 18 though "because" was followed by an irrelevant reason, Cialdini said. By asking the favor in that way, the researcher dramatically increased the likelihood of get- ting what she wanted.

Cialdini and others say much of human behavior is mechanical. Automatic 19 responses are efficient when time and attention are short. For that reason, many techniques of persuasion are designed and tested for their ability to trigger those automatic responses.

"These appeals persuade not through the give-and-take of argument and de- 20 bate," Pratkanis and Aronson have written. " . . . They often appeal to our deep- est fears and most irrational hopes, while they make use of our most simplistic beliefs."

Life insurance agents use fear to sell policies, Pratkanis and Aronson say. Par- 21 ents use fear to convince their children to come home on time. Political leaders use fear to build support for going to war—for example, comparing a foreign leader to Adolf Hitler.

As many researchers see it, people respond to persuasion in one of two ways: 22 If an issue they care about is involved, they may pay close attention to the argu- ments; if they don't care, they pay less attention and are more likely to be influ- enced by simple cues.

Their level of attention depends on motivation and the time available. As Da- 23 vid Boninger, a UCLA psychologist, puts it, "If you don't have the time or moti- vation, or both, you will pay attention to more peripheral• cues, like how nice somebody looks."

Cialdini, a dapper• man with a flat Midwestern accent, describes himself as 24 an inveterate• sucker. From an early age, he said recently, he had wondered what made him say yes in many cases when the answer, had he thought about it, should have been no.

So in the early 1980s, he became "a spy in the wars of influence." He took a 25 sabbatical and, over a three-year period, enrolled in dozens of sales training programs, learning firsthand the tricks of selling insurance, cars, vacuum cleaners, encyclopedias, and more.

He learned how to sell portrait photography over the telephone. He took a 26 job as a busboy in a restaurant, observing the waiters. He worked in fund-raising, advertising, and public relations. And he interviewed cult recruiters and members of bunco squads.

By the time it was over, Cialdini had witnessed hundreds of tactics. But he 27 found that the most effective ones were rooted in six principles. Most are not new, but they are being used today with greater sophistication on people whose fast-paced lifestyle has lowered their defenses.

Reciprocity•. People have been trained to believe that a favor must be repaid in 28 kind, even if the original favor was not requested. The cultural pressure to return a favor is so intense that people go along rather than suffer the feeling of being indebted.

Politicians have learned that favors are repaid with votes. Stores offer free 29 samples—not just to show off a product. Charity organizations ship personalized address labels to potential contributors. Others accost pedestrians, planting paper flowers in their lapels.

Commitment and Consistency. People tend to feel they should be consistent— 30 even when being consistent no longer makes sense. While consistency is easy, comfortable, and generally advantageous, Cialdini says, "mindless consistency" can be exploited.

Take the "foot in the door technique." One person gets another to agree to 31 a small commitment, like a down payment or signing a petition. Studies show that it then becomes much easier to get the person to comply with a much larger request.

Another example Cialdini cites is the "lowball tactic" in car sales. Offered a 32 low price for a car, the potential customer agrees. Then at the last minute, the sales manager finds a supposed error. The price is increased. But customers tend to go along nevertheless.

Social Validation. People often decide what is correct on the basis of what other 33 people think. Studies show that is true for behavior. Hence, sitcom laugh tracks, tip jars "salted" with a bartender's cash, long lines outside nightclubs, testimonials, and "man on the street" ads.

Tapping the power of social validation is especially effective under certain 34 conditions: When people are in doubt, they will look to others as a guide; and when they view those others as similar to themselves, they are more likely to follow their lead.

Liking. People prefer to comply with requests from people they know and like. 35 Charities recruit people to canvass their friends and neighbors. Colleges get alumni to raise money from classmates. Sales training programs include grooming tips.

According to Cialdini, liking can be based on any of a number of factors. 36 Good-looking people tend to be credited with traits like talent and intelligence.

People also tend to like people who are similar to themselves in personality, background, and lifestyle.

Authority. People defer to authority. Society trains them to do so, and in many 37 situations deference● is beneficial. Unfortunately, obedience is often automatic, leaving people vulnerable to exploitation by compliance professionals, Cialdini says.

As an example, he cites the famous ad campaign that capitalized on actor Rob- 38 ert Young's role as Dr. Marcus Welby, Jr., to tout the alleged health benefits of Sanka decaffeinated coffee.

An authority, according to Cialdini, need not be a true authority. The trap- 39 pings of authority may suffice. Con artists have long recognized the persuasive power of titles like doctor or judge, fancy business suits, and expensive cars.

Scarcity. Products and opportunities seem more valuable when the supply is 40 limited.

As a result, professional persuaders emphasize that "supplies are limited." 41 Sales end Sunday and movies have limited engagements—diverting attention from whether the item is desirable to the threat of losing the chance to experience it at all.

The use of influence, Cialdini says, is ubiquitous.   42

Take the classic appeal by a child of a parent's sense of consistency: "But you 43 said . . ." And the parent's resort to authority: "Because I said so." In addition, nearly everyone invokes the opinions of like-minded others—for social validation—in vying to win a point.

One area in which persuasive tactics are especially controversial is political 44 advertising—particularly negative advertising. Alarmed that attack ads might be alienating voters, some critics have begun calling for stricter limits on political ads.

In Washington, legislation pending in Congress would, among other things, 45 force candidates to identify themselves at the end of their commercials. In that way, they might be forced to take responsibility for the ads' contents and be unable to hide behind campaign committees.

"In general, people accept the notion that for the sale of products at least, there 46 are socially accepted norms of advertising," said Lloyd Morrisett, president of the Markle Foundation, which supports research in communications and information technology.

"But when those same techniques are applied to the political process—where 47 we are judging not a product but a person, and where there is ample room for distortion of the record or falsification in some cases—there begins to be more concern," he said.

On an individual level, some psychologists offer tips for self-protection.   48

- Pay attention to your emotions, says Pratkanis, an associate   49
  professor of psychology at UC Santa Cruz: "If you start to feel
  guilty or patriotic, try to figure out why." In consumer transactions,
  beware of feelings of inferiority and the sense that you don't
  measure up unless you have a certain product.

- Be on the lookout for automatic responses, Cialdini says.   50
  Beware foolish consistency. Check other people's responses
  against objective facts. Be skeptical of authority, and look out for
  unwarranted liking for any "compliance professionals."

Since the publication of his most recent book, *Influence: The New Psychology* 51 *of Modern Persuasion,* Cialdini has begun researching a new book on ethical uses of influence in business—addressing, among other things, how to instruct salespeople and other "influence agents" to use persuasion in ways that help, rather than hurt, society.

"If influence agents don't police themselves, society will have to step in to reg- 52 ulate . . . the way information is presented in commercial and political settings," Cialdini said. "And that's a can of worms that I don't think anybody wants to get into."

VOCABULARY IN CONTEXT

1. The word *wielding* in "The weapons of influence they are wielding are more sophisticated than ever" (paragraph 3) means
   a. handling effectively.
   b. giving up.
   c. looking for.
   d. demanding.

2. The word *peripheral* in "As David Boninger . . . puts it, 'If you don't have the time or motivation, or both, you will pay attention to more peripheral cues, like how nice someone looks'" (paragraph 23) means
   a. important.
   b. dependable.
   c. minor.
   d. attractive.

READING COMPREHENSION QUESTIONS

1. Which of the following would be the best alternative title for this selection?
   a. Automatic Human Responses
   b. Our Deepest Fears
   c. The Loss of Thoughtful Discussion
   d. Compliance Techniques

2. Which sentence best expresses the selection's main point?
   a. Americans are bombarded by various compliance techniques, the dangers of which can be overcome through understanding and legislation.
   b. Fearful of the effects of political attack ads, critics are calling for strict limits on such ads.
   c. With more and more messages demanding our attention, we find it harder and harder to consider any one subject really thoughtfully.
   d. The persuasion researcher Robert Cialdini spent a three-year sabbatical learning the tricks taught in dozens of sales training programs.

3. *True or false?* _____ According to the article, most laypeople think they are more susceptible to persuasion than they really are.

4. According to the article, parents persuade their children to come home on time by appealing to the children's sense of
   a. fair play.
   b. guilt.
   c. humor.
   d. fear.

5. When a visitor walks out of a hotel and a young man runs up, helps the visitor with his luggage, hails a cab, and then expects a tip, the young man is depending on which principle of persuasion?
   a. reciprocity
   b. commitment and consistency
   c. social validation
   d. liking

6. An inference that can be drawn from paragraph 49 is that
   a. Anthony Pratkanis is not a patriotic person.
   b. one compliance technique involves appealing to the consumer's patriotism.
   c. people using compliance techniques never want consumers to feel inferior.
   d. consumers pay too much attention to their own emotions.

7. One can infer from the selection that
   a. the actor Robert Young was well known for his love of coffee.
   b. Sanka is demonstrably better for one's health than other coffees.
   c. the actor Robert Young was also a physician in real life.
   d. the TV character Marcus Welby, Jr., was trustworthy and authoritative.

8. We can conclude that to resist persuasive tactics, a person must
   a. buy fewer products.
   b. take time to question and analyze.
   c. remain patriotic.
   d. avoid propaganda.

DISCUSSION QUESTIONS

About Content

1. What unusual method did Robert Cialdini apply to learn more about compliance techniques? Were you surprised by any of the ways he used his time during that three-year period? Have you ever been employed in a position in which you used one or more compliance techniques?

2. What are the six principles that Cialdini identifies as being behind many persuasion tactics? Describe an incident in which you were subjected to persuasion based on one or more of these principles.

3. In paragraph 16, we learn that "people are more likely to comply with a request if a reason—no matter how silly—is given." Do you find that to be true? Have you complied with requests that, when you thought about them later,

were backed up with silly or weak reasons? Describe such an incident. Why do you think such requests work?

4. In paragraphs 44–47, the author discusses persuasive tactics in political advertising. Why might researchers view the use of such tactics in this area as "especially controversial"?

About Structure

5. What is the effect of Janny Scott's introduction to the essay (paragraphs 1–2)? On the basis of that introduction, why is a reader likely to feel that the selection will be worth his or her time?

6. Which of the following best describes the conclusion of the selection?

   a. It just stops.

   b. It restates the main point of the selection.

   c. It focuses on possible future occurrences.

   d. It presents a point of view that is the opposite of views in the body of the selection.

   Is this conclusion effective? Why or why not?

About Style and Tone

7. Why might Robert Cialdini have identified himself to the author as an "inveterate sucker"? How does that self-description affect how you regard Cialdini and what he has to say?

8. The author writes, "People defer to authority. Society trains them to do so; and in many situations deference is beneficial." Where does the author herself use the power of authority to support her own points? In what situations would you consider authority to be beneficial?

RESPONDING TO IMAGES

How does this photograph articulate a cause-and-effect relationship?

WRITING ASSIGNMENTS

Assignment 1: Writing a Paragraph

According to the article, "laypeople underestimate their susceptibility to persuasion. . . . They imagine their actions are dictated simply by personal preferences. Unaware of the techniques being used against them, they are often unwittingly outgunned." After having read the selection, do you believe that statement is true of you? Write a paragraph in which you either agree with or argue against the statement. Provide clear, specific examples of ways in which you are or are not influenced by persuasion.

   Your topic sentence might be like either of these:

   After reading "How They Get You to Do That," I recognize that I am more influenced by forms of persuasion than I previously thought.

   Many people may "underestimate their susceptibility to persuasion," but I am not one of those people.

Assignment 2: Writing a Paragraph

Think of an advertisement—on TV, on the Internet, in print, or on a billboard—that you have found especially memorable. Write a paragraph in which you describe it. Provide specific details that make your reader understand why you remember it so vividly. Conclude your paragraph by indicating whether or not the advertisement persuaded you to buy or do what it was promoting.

Assignment 3: Writing an Essay

Robert Cialdini identifies "social validation" as a strong persuasion technique. Social validation involves people's need to do what they hope will get approval from the crowd, rather than thinking for themselves. The essay provides several examples of social validation, such as laughing along with a laugh track and getting in a long line to go to a nightclub.

Choose a person you know for whom the need for social validation is very strong. Write an essay about that person and how the need for social validation has impacted several areas of his or her life. Develop each paragraph with colorful, persuasive examples of the person's behavior. (You may wish to write about an invented person, in which case, feel free to use humorous exaggeration to make your points.)

Here is a possible outline for such an essay:

Thesis statement: My cousin Nina has a very strong need for social validation.

Topic sentence 1: Instead of choosing friends because of their inner qualities, Nina chooses them on the basis of their popularity.

Topic sentence 2: Nina's wardrobe has to be made up of the newest and most popular styles.

Topic sentence 3: Instead of having any real opinions of her own, Nina adopts her most popular friend's point of view as her own.

End your essay with a look into the future of a person whose life is ruled by the need for social validation.

Alternatively, write about the most independent thinker you know, someone who tends to do things his or her way without worrying much about what others say.

Dealing with Feelings
Rudolph F. Verderber

PREVIEW	WORDS TO WATCH
Do you hide your feelings, no matter how strong they are, letting them fester inside? Or do you lash out angrily at people who irritate you? If either of these descriptions fits you, you may be unhappy with the results of your actions. Read the following excerpt from the college textbook *Communicate!* Sixth Edition (Wadsworth) to discover what the author recommends as a better approach to dealing with your emotions.	decipher (2) seethe (2) neuroses (3) psychoses (3) detrimental (4) wedge (14)

An extremely important aspect of self-disclosure is the sharing of feelings. We **1** all experience feelings such as happiness at receiving an unexpected gift, sadness about the breakup of a relationship, or anger when we believe we have been taken advantage of. The question is whether to disclose such feelings, and if so, how. Self-disclosure of feelings usually will be most successful not when feelings are withheld or displayed but when they are described. Let's consider each of these forms of dealing with feelings.

Withholding Feelings

Withholding feelings—that is, keeping them inside and not giving any verbal or **2** nonverbal clues to their existence—is generally an inappropriate means of dealing with feelings. Withholding feelings is best exemplified by the good poker player who develops a "poker face," a neutral look that is impossible to decipher.• The look is the same whether the player's cards are good or bad. Unfortunately, many people use poker faces in their interpersonal relationships, so that no one knows whether they hurt inside, are extremely excited, and so on. For instance, Doris feels very nervous when Candy stands over her while Doris is working on her report. And when Candy says, "That first paragraph isn't very well written," Doris begins to seethe,• yet she says nothing—she withholds her feelings.

Psychologists believe that when people withhold feelings, they can develop **3** physical problems such as ulcers, high blood pressure, and heart disease, as well as psychological problems such as stress-related neuroses• and psychoses.• Moreover, people who withhold feelings are often perceived as cold, undemonstrative, and not much fun to be around.

Is withholding ever appropriate? When a situation is inconsequential, you **4** may well choose to withhold your feelings. For instance, a stranger's inconsiderate behavior at a party may bother you, but because you can move to another part of the room, withholding may not be detrimental.• In the example of Doris seething at Candy's behavior, however, withholding could be costly to Doris.

Displaying Feelings

Displaying feelings means expressing those feelings through a facial reaction, **5** body response, or spoken reaction. Cheering over a great play at a sporting event, booing the umpire at a perceived bad call, patting a person on the back when the person does something well, or saying, "What are you doing?" in a nasty tone of voice are all displays of feelings.

Displays are especially appropriate when the feelings you are experiencing **6** are positive. For instance, when Gloria does something nice for you, and you experience a feeling of joy, giving her a big hug is appropriate; when Don gives you something you've wanted, and you experience a feeling of appreciation, a big smile or an "Oh, thank you, Don" is appropriate. In fact, many people need to be even more demonstrative of good feelings. You've probably seen the bumper sticker "Have you hugged your kid today?" It reinforces the point that you need to display love and affection constantly to show another person that you really care.

Displays become detrimental to communication when the feelings you are **7** experiencing are negative—especially when the display of a negative feeling appears to be an overreaction. For instance, when Candy stands over Doris while she is working on her report and says, "That first paragraph isn't very well written," Doris may well experience resentment. If Doris lashes out at Candy by screaming, "Who the hell asked you for your opinion?" Doris's display no doubt will hurt Candy's feelings and short-circuit their communication. Although displays of negative feelings may be good for you psychologically, they are likely to be bad for you interpersonally.

Describing Feelings

Describing feelings—putting your feelings into words in a calm, nonjudgmen- 8
tal way—tends to be the best method of disclosing feelings. Describing feelings
not only increases chances for positive communication and decreases chances for
short-circuiting lines of communication; it also teaches people how to treat you.
When you describe your feelings, people are made aware of the effect of their behavior. This knowledge gives them the information needed to determine whether
they should continue or repeat that behavior. If you tell Paul that you really feel
flattered when he visits you, such a statement should encourage Paul to visit you
again; likewise, when you tell Cliff that you feel very angry when he borrows your
jacket without asking, he is more likely to ask the next time he borrows a jacket.
Describing your feelings allows you to exercise a measure of control over others'
behavior toward you.

Describing and displaying feelings are not the same. Many times people think 9
they are describing when in fact they are displaying feelings or evaluating.

If describing feelings is so important to communicating effectively, why don't 10
more people do it regularly? There seem to be at least four reasons why many
people don't describe feelings.

1. Many people have a poor vocabulary of words for describing the various 11
feelings they are experiencing. People can sense that they are angry; however,
they may not know whether what they are feeling might best be described as annoyed, betrayed, cheated, crushed, disturbed, furious, outraged, or shocked. Each
of these words describes a slightly different aspect of what many people lump
together as anger.

2. Many people believe that describing their true feelings reveals too much 12
about themselves. If you tell people when their behavior hurts you, you risk their
using the information against you when they want to hurt you on purpose. Even
so, the potential benefits of describing your feelings far outweigh the risks. For
instance, if Pete has a nickname for you that you don't like and you tell Pete that
calling you by that nickname really makes you nervous and tense, Pete may use
the nickname when he wants to hurt you, but he is more likely to stop calling you
by that name. If, on the other hand, you don't describe your feelings to Pete, he is
probably going to call you by that name all the time because he doesn't know any
better. When you say nothing, you reinforce his behavior. The level of risk varies
with each situation, but you will more often improve a relationship than be hurt
by describing feelings.

3. Many people believe that if they describe feelings, others will make them 13
feel guilty about having such feelings. At a very tender age we all learned about
"tactful" behavior. Under the premise that "the truth sometimes hurts" we learned
to avoid the truth by not saying anything or by telling "little" lies. Perhaps when
you were young your mother said, "Don't forget to give Grandma a great big kiss."
At that time you may have blurted out, "Ugh—it makes me feel yucky to kiss
Grandma. She's got a mustache." If your mother responded, "That's terrible—your
grandma loves you. Now you give her a kiss and never let me hear you talk like
that again!" then you probably felt guilty for having this "wrong" feeling. But the
point is that the thought of kissing your grandma made you feel "yucky" whether
it should have or not. In this case what was at issue was the way you talked about
the feelings—not your having the feelings.

4. Many people believe that describing feelings causes harm to others or to 14
a relationship. If it really bothers Max when his girlfriend, Dora, bites her fin-

gernails, Max may believe that describing his feelings to Dora will hurt her so much that the knowledge will drive a wedge• into their relationship. So it's better for Max to say nothing, right? Wrong! If Max says nothing, he's still going to be bothered by Dora's behavior. In fact, as time goes on, Max will probably lash out at Dora for other things because he can't bring himself to talk about the behavior that really bothers him. The net result is that not only will Dora be hurt by Max's behavior, but she won't understand the true source of his feelings. By not describing his feelings, Max may well drive a wedge into their relationship anyway.

If Max does describe his feelings to Dora, she might quit or at least try to quit **15** biting her nails; they might get into a discussion in which he finds out that she doesn't want to bite them but just can't seem to stop, and he can help her in her efforts to stop; or they might discuss the problem and Max may see that it is a small thing really and not let it bother him as much. The point is that in describing feelings the chances of a successful outcome are greater than they are in not describing them.

To describe your feelings, first put the emotion you are feeling into words. Be **16** specific. Second, state what triggered the feeling. Finally, make sure you indicate that the feeling is yours. For example, suppose your roommate borrows your jacket without asking. When he returns, you describe your feelings by saying, "Cliff, I [indication that the feeling is yours] get really angry [the feeling] when you borrow my jacket without asking [trigger]." Or suppose that Carl has just reminded you of the very first time he brought you a rose. You describe your feelings by saying, "Carl, I [indication that the feeling is yours] get really tickled [the feeling] when you remind me about that first time you brought me a rose [trigger]."

You may find it easiest to begin by describing positive feelings: "I really feel **17** elated knowing that you were the one who nominated me for the position" or "I'm delighted that you offered to help me with the housework." As you gain success with positive descriptions, you can try negative feelings attributable to environmental factors: "It's so cloudy; I feel gloomy" or "When the wind howls through the cracks, I really get jumpy." Finally, you can move to negative descriptions resulting from what people have said or done: "Your stepping in front of me like that really annoys me" or "The tone of your voice confuses me."

VOCABULARY IN CONTEXT

1. The word *detrimental* in "For instance, a stranger's inconsiderate behavior at a party may bother you, but because you can move to another part of the room, withholding may not be detrimental" (paragraph 4) means

   a. useful.

   b. private.

   c. helpless.

   d. harmful.

2. The word *wedge* in "Max may believe that describing his feelings to Dora will hurt her so much that the knowledge will drive a wedge into their relationship" (paragraph 14) means

   a. something that divides.

   b. loyalty.

   c. friendship.

   d. many years.

READING COMPREHENSION QUESTIONS

1. Which of the following would be the best alternative title for this selection?
   a. Effective Communication
   b. Negative Feelings
   c. The Consequences of Withholding Feelings
   d. Emotions: When and How to Express Them

2. Which sentence best expresses the article's main point?
   a. Everyone has feelings.
   b. There are three ways to deal with feelings; describing them is most useful for educating others about how you want to be treated.
   c. Withholding feelings means not giving verbal or nonverbal clues that might reveal those feelings to others.
   d. Psychologists have studied the manner in which people deal with their feelings.

3. You are most likely to create physical problems for yourself by
   a. withholding your feelings.
   b. displaying your positive feelings.
   c. describing your positive feelings.
   d. describing your negative feelings.

4. The author uses the term "describing your feelings" to refer to
   a. keeping your feelings inside.
   b. giving a nonverbal response to feelings.
   c. putting your feelings into words calmly.
   d. telling "little" lies.

5. Shouting angrily at a person who has stepped in front of you in line is an example of
   a. withholding feelings.
   b. displaying feelings.
   c. describing feelings.
   d. self-disclosing.

6. From the reading, we can conclude that describing feelings
   a. is usually easy for people.
   b. is often a good way to solve problems.
   c. should be done only for positive feelings.
   d. should make you feel guilty.

7. Which sentence can we infer is an example of describing a feeling?
   a. Although Mrs. Henderson hates going to the mountains, she says nothing as her husband plans to go there for their vacation.
   b. Neil calls Joanna the day after their date and says, "I want you to know how much I enjoyed our evening together. You're a lot of fun."
   c. Raoul jumps out of his seat and yells joyfully as the Packers make a touchdown.

d. Peggy's office-mate chews gum noisily, cracking and snapping it. Peggy shrieks, "How inconsiderate can you be? You're driving me crazy with that noise!"

8. *True or false?* _____ We can infer that people who describe their feelings tend to be physically healthier than those who withhold feelings.

DISCUSSION QUESTIONS

About Content

1. What is the difference between describing feelings and expressing them? How might Doris describe her feelings to Candy after Candy says, "That first paragraph isn't very well written" (paragraph 2)?

2. Why do you think Verderber emphasizes describing feelings over the other two methods of dealing with feelings?

3. What are some examples from your own experience of withholding, expressing or displaying, and describing feelings? How useful was each?

About Structure

4. What method of introduction does Verderber use in this selection?
   a. Broad to narrow
   b. Anecdote
   c. Beginning with a situation opposite to the one he will describe
   d. Question

   Is his introduction effective? Why or why not?

5. Verderber divides the body of his essay into three parts: first about withholding feelings, second about displaying feelings, and finally about describing feelings. He further divides the third part by introducing a list. What is that list about? How many items does he include in it?

6. What devices does the author use to emphasize the organization of his essay?

7. How many examples does Verderber provide for withholding feelings? Displaying feelings? Describing feelings?

About Style and Tone

8. What type of evidence does the author use to back up his points throughout the selection? What other types of support might he have used?

WRITING ASSIGNMENTS

Assignment 1: Writing a Paragraph

Write a paragraph about a time when you withheld or displayed feelings, but describing them would have been a better idea. Your topic sentence might be something like either of these:

An argument I had with my boyfriend recently made me wish that I had described my feelings rather than displaying them.

Withholding my feelings at work recently left me feeling frustrated and angry.

Then narrate the event, showing how feelings were withheld or displayed and what the result was. Conclude your paragraph by contrasting what really happened with what *might* have happened if feelings had been described.

Assignment 2: Writing a Paragraph

"Dealing with Feelings" lists and discusses several ways to cope with emotions. Write a paragraph in which you present three ways to do something else. Your tone may be serious or humorous. You might write about three ways to do one of the following:

Cut expenses

Meet people

Get along with a difficult coworker

Ruin a party

Embarrass your friends

Lose a job

Here is a possible topic sentence for this assignment:

To ruin a party, you must follow three simple steps.

Assignment 3: Writing an Essay

At one time or another, you have probably used all three methods of communicating described by Verderber: withholding, displaying, and describing. Write an essay that describes a situation in which you have used each of those methods. In each case, narrate the event that occurred. Then explain why you responded as you did and how you ended up feeling about your response. Finish your essay with some conclusion of your own about dealing with feelings.

Here's a sample outline for such an essay:

Thesis statement: At different times, I have withheld my feelings, displayed my feelings, and described my feelings.

Topic sentence 1: Dealing with a rude store clerk, I withheld my feelings.

Topic sentence 2: When another driver cut me off in traffic, I displayed my feelings.

Topic sentence 3: When my mother angered me by reading a letter I'd left lying on the dining-room table, I described my feelings.

Conclusion: When it comes to dealing with people I care about, describing my feelings works better than withholding or displaying them.

A Change of Attitude

Grant Berry

PREVIEW	WORDS TO WATCH
Every college has them: students the same age as some of their professors, students rushing into class after a full day at work, students carrying photographs—not of their boyfriends or girlfriends, but of the children they too seldom see. In many cases, these students are as surprised as anyone to find themselves in college. In this essay, one such student describes his development from a bored high schooler to a committed college student.	decades (3) striven (3) suavely (4) immaculately (4) cliques (5) tedious (6) trudging (6) nil (6) smugly (8) deprivation (16) scowl (21) battering (22)

1 For me to be in college is highly improbable. That I am doing well in school teeters on the illogical. Considering my upbringing, past educational performance, and current responsibilities, one might say, "This guy hasn't got a chance." If I were a racehorse and college were the track, there would be few who would pick me to win, place, or show.

2 When I told my dad that I was going back to school, the only encouragement he offered was this: "Send me anywhere, but don't send me back to school." For my father, school was the worst kind of prison, so I was raised believing that school at its best was a drag. My dad thought that the purpose of graduating from high school was so you never had to go back to school again, and I adopted this working stiff's philosophy.

3 I followed my dad's example the way a man who double-crosses the mob follows a cement block to the bottom of the river. My dad has been a union factory worker for more than two decades,• and he has never striven• to be anything more than average. Nonetheless, he is a good man; I love him very much, and I respect him for being a responsible husband and father. He seldom, if ever, missed a day of work; he never left his paycheck at a bar, and none of our household appliances were ever carted off by a repo-man. He took his family to church each week, didn't light up or lift a glass, and has celebrated his silver anniversary with his first, and only, wife. However, if he ever had a dream of being more than just a shop rat, I never knew about it.

4 On the other hand, my dreams were big, but my thoughts were small. I was not raised to be a go-getter. I knew I wanted to go to work each day in a suit and tie; unfortunately, I could not define what it was I wanted to do. I told a few people that I wanted to have a job where I could dress suavely• and carry a briefcase, and they laughed in my face. They said, "You'll never be anything," and I believed them. Even now I am envious of an immaculately• dressed businessman. It is not the angry type of jealousy; it is the "wish it were me" variety.

5 Since I knew I was not going to further my education, and I didn't know what I wanted to do except wear a suit, high school was a disaster. I do not know how my teachers can respect themselves after passing me. In every high school there are cliques• and classifications. I worked just hard enough to stay above the bottom, but I did not want to work hard enough to get into the clique with the honor roll students.

Also, I had always had a problem with reading. When I was a kid, reading **6** for me was slow and tedious.• My eyes walked over words like a snail trudging• through mud. I couldn't focus on what I was reading, and this allowed my young, active mind to wander far from my reading material. I would often finish a page and not remember a single word I had just read. Not only was reading a slow process, but my comprehension was nil.• I wasn't dumb; in fact, I was at a high English level. However, reading rated next to scraping dog poop from the tread of my sneakers. I didn't yet know that reading could be like playing the guitar: the more you do it, the better you get. As far as reading was concerned, I thought I was stuck in the same slow waltz forever.

In junior high and high school, I read only when it was absolutely essential. **7** For example, I had to find out who Spider-Man was going to web, or how many children Superman was going to save each month. I also had to find out which girls were popular on the bathroom walls. I'm ashamed to say that my mother even did a book report for me, first reading the book. In high school, when I would choose my own classes, I took art and electronics rather than English.

Even though I was raised in a good Christian home, the only things I cared **8** about were partying and girls. I spent all of my minimum-wage paycheck on beer, cigarettes, and young ladies. As a senior, I dated a girl who was twenty. She had no restrictions, and I tried to keep pace with her lifestyle. I would stay out drinking until 3:00 A.M. on school nights. The next morning I would sleep through class or just not show up. It became such a problem that the school sent letters to my parents telling them that I would not be joining my classmates for commencement if I didn't show up for class once in a while. This put the fear of the establishment in me because I knew the importance of graduating from high school. Nonetheless, I never once remember doing homework my senior year. Yet in June, they shook my hand and forked over a diploma as I smugly• marched across the stage in a blue gown and square hat.

Since I felt I didn't deserve the piece of paper with the principal's and super- **9** intendent's signatures on it, I passed up not only a graduation party but also a class ring and a yearbook. If it were not for my diploma and senior pictures, there would not be enough evidence to convince a jury that I am guilty of attending high school at all. I did, however, celebrate with my friends on graduation night. I got loaded, misjudged a turn, flattened a stop sign, and got my car stuck. When I pushed my car with my girlfriend behind the steering wheel, mud from the spinning tire sprayed all over my nice clothes. It was quite a night, and looking back, it was quite a fitting closure for the end of high school.

After graduation I followed my father's example and went to work, plung- **10** ing into the lukewarm waters of mediocrity. All I was doing on my job bagging groceries was trading dollars for hours. I worked just hard enough to keep from getting fired, and I was paid just enough to keep from quitting.

Considering the way my father felt about school, college was a subject that **11** seldom came up at our dinner table. I was not discouraged, nor was I encouraged, to go to college; it was my choice. My first attempt at college came when I was nineteen. I had always dreamed of being a disk jockey, so I enrolled in a broadcasting class. However, my experience in college was as forgettable as high school. My habit of not doing homework carried over, and the class was such a yawner that I often forgot to attend. Miraculously, I managed to pull a C, but my dream was weak and quickly died. I did not enroll for the next term. My girlfriend, the one who kept me out late in high school, became pregnant with my child. We were married two days after my final class, and this gave me another excuse not to continue my education.

My first job, and every job since, has involved working with my hands and **12** not my head. I enjoyed my work, but after the money ran out, the month would keep going. One evening my wife's cousin called and said he had a way that we could increase our income. I asked, "How soon can you get here?" He walked us through a six-step plan of selling and recruiting, and when he was finished, my wife and I wanted in. Fumbling around inside his large briefcase, he told us we needed the proper attitude first. Emerging with a small stack of books, he said, "Read these!" Then he flipped the books into my lap. I groaned at the thought of reading all those volumes. If this guy wanted me to develop a good attitude, giving me books was having the opposite effect. However, I wanted to make some extra cash, so I assured him I would try.

I started reading the books each night. They were self-help, positive mental-attitude manuals. Reading those books opened up my world; they put me in touch with a me I didn't know existed. The books told me I had potential, possibly even greatness. I took their message in like an old Chevrolet being pumped full of premium no-lead gasoline. It felt so good I started reading more. Not only did I read at night; I read in the morning before I went to work. I read during my breaks and lunch hour, when waiting for signal lights to turn green, in between bites of food at supper, and while sitting on the toilet. One of the books I read said that there is no limit to the amount of information our brains will hold, so I began filling mine up.   **13**

The process of reading was slow at first, just as it had been when I was a kid, but it was just like playing the guitar. If I struck an unclear chord, I would try it again, and if I read something unclear, I would simply read it again. Something happened: the more I read, the better I got at it. It wasn't long before I could focus in and understand without reading things twice. I began feeling good about my reading skills, and because of the types of books I was reading, I started feeling good about myself at the same time.   **14**

The income from my day job blossomed while the selling and recruiting business grew demanding, disappointing, and fruitless. We stopped working that soil and our business died, but I was hooked on reading. I now laid aside the self-help books and began reading whatever I wanted. I got my first library card, and I subscribed to *Sports Illustrated.* I found a book of short stories, and I dived into poetry, as well as countless newspaper articles, cereal boxes, and oatmeal packages. Reading, which had been a problem for me, became a pleasure and then a passion.   **15**

Reading moved me. As I continued to read in a crowded lunchroom, sometimes I stumbled across an especially moving short story or magazine article. For example, a young Romanian girl was saved from starvation and deprivation• by an adoptive couple from the United States. I quickly jerked the reading material to my face to conceal tears when she entered her new home filled with toys and stuffed animals.   **16**

Not only did reading tug at my emotions; it inspired me to make a move. All those positive-mental-attitude books kept jabbing me in the ribs, so last fall, at age twenty-seven, I decided to give college another try. Now I am back in school, but it's a different road I travel from when I was a teenager. Mom and Dad paid the amount in the right-hand column of my tuition bill then, but now I am determined to pay for college myself, even though I must miss the sound of the pizza delivery man's tires on my blacktop driveway. I hope to work my way out of my blue collar by paying for school with blue-collar cash.   **17**

As a meat-cutter, I usually spend between 45 and 50 hours a week with a knife in my hand. Some weeks I have spent 72 hours beneath a butcher's cap. In one two-week period I spent 141 hours with a bloody apron on, but in that time I managed to show up for all of my classes and get all of my homework done (except being short a few bibliography cards for my research paper).   **18**

Working full time and raising a family leave me little free time. If I am not in class, I'm studying linking verbs or trying to figure out the difference between compound and complex sentences.   **19**

There are other obstacles and challenges staring me in the face. The tallest 20
hurdle is a lack of time for meeting all my obligations. For instance, my wife works
two nights a week, leaving me to care for my two daughters. A twelve-hour day at
work can lead to an evening coma at home, so when Mom's punching little square
buttons on a cash register, I hardly have the energy to pour cornflakes for my kids,
let alone outline a research paper.

Going to college means making choices, some of which bring criticism. My 21
neighbors, for example, hate my sickly, brown lawn sandwiched between their
lush, green, spotless plots of earth, which would be the envy of any football field.
Just walking to my mailbox can be an awful reminder of how pitiful my lawn
looks when I receive an unforgiving scowl● from one of the groundskeepers who
live on either side of me. It is embarrassing to have such a colorless lawn, but it will
have to wait because I want more out of life than a half-acre of green turf. Right
now my time and money are tied up in college courses instead of fertilizer and
weed killer.

But the toughest obstacle is having to take away time from those I love most. 22
I am proud of the relationship I have with my wife and kids, so it tears my guts
out when I have to look into my daughter's sad face and explain that I can't go
to the Christmas program she's been practicing for weeks because I have a final
exam. It's not easy to tell my three-year-old that I can't push her on the swings because I have a cause-and-effect paper to write, or tell my seven-year-old that I can't
build a snowman because I have an argument essay to polish. As I tell my family
that I can't go sledding with them, my wife lets out a big sigh, and my kids yell,
"Puleeze, Daddy, can't you come with us?" At these times I wonder if my dream
of a college education can withstand such an emotional battering,● or if it is even
worth it. But I keep on keeping on because I must set a good example for the four
little eyes that are keeping watch over their daddy's every move. I must succeed
and pass on to them the right attitude toward school. This time when I graduate,
because of the hurdles I've overcome, there will be a celebration—a proper one.

VOCABULARY IN CONTEXT

1. The word *cliques* in "In every high school there are cliques and classifications.
   I worked just hard enough to stay above the bottom, but I did not want to work
   hard enough to get into the clique with the honor roll students" (paragraph 5)
   means

   a. grades.

   b. schools.

   c. groups.

   d. sports.

2. The word *scowl* in "Just walking to my mailbox can be an awful reminder of
   how pitiful my lawn looks when I receive an unforgiving scowl from one of
   the groundskeepers who live on either side of me" (paragraph 21) means

   a. sincere smile.

   b. favor.

   c. angry look.

   d. surprise.

READING COMPREHENSION QUESTIONS

1. Which sentence best expresses the central idea of the selection?

    a. The author was never encouraged to attend college or to challenge himself mentally on the job.

    b. After years of not caring about education, Berry was led by some self-help books to love reading, gain self-esteem, and attend college.

    c. The author's wife and children often do not understand why he is unable to take part in many family activities.

    d. The author was given a high school diploma despite the fact that he did little work and rarely attended class.

2. Which sentence best expresses the main idea of paragraph 13?

    a. Influenced by self-help books, the author developed a hunger for reading.

    b. People who really care about improving themselves will find the time to do it, such as during the early morning, at breaks, and during the lunch hour.

    c. Self-help books send the message that everyone is full of potential and even greatness.

    d. There is no limit to the amount of information the brain can hold.

3. Which sentence best expresses the main idea of paragraph 22?

    a. The author's decision to attend college is hurting his long-term relationship with his wife and daughters.

    b. The author has two children, one age three and the other age seven.

    c. The author enjoys family activities such as attending his children's plays and building snowmen.

    d. Although he misses spending time with his family, the author feels that graduating from college will make him a better role model for his children.

4. The author's reading skills

    a. were strong even when he was a child.

    b. improved as he read more.

    c. were strengthened considerably in high school.

    d. were sharpened by jobs he held after high school graduation.

5. The author's father

    a. was rarely home while the author was growing up.

    b. often missed work and stayed out late at bars.

    c. was a college graduate.

    d. disliked school.

6. In stating that his graduation night "was quite a fitting closure for the end of high school," Berry implies that

    a. he was glad high school was finally over.

    b. car troubles were a common problem for him throughout high school.

    c. his behavior had ruined that night just as it had ruined his high school education.

    d. despite the problems, the evening gave him good memories, just as high school had given him good memories.

7. We can infer from paragraph 21 that the author

  a. does not tend his lawn because he enjoys annoying his neighbors.

  b. receives a lot of mail.

  c. is willing to make sacrifices for his college education.

  d. has neighbors who care little about the appearance of their property.

8. We can infer that the author believes children

  a. should be passed to the next grade when they reach a certain age, regardless of their test scores.

  b. should not require a great deal of time from their parents.

  c. fall into two categories: "born readers" and those who can never learn to read very well.

  d. benefit from having role models who care about education.

DISCUSSION QUESTIONS

About Content

1. The author looks back at this period of reading self-help books as one in which his attitude improved, eventually leading to his enrollment in college. Has a particular occurrence ever sharply changed your outlook on life? Was it something that you read, observed, or directly experienced? How did it happen? How did it change your point of view?

2. Berry writes that his father did not encourage him to go on to college. Nevertheless, he sees many positive things about his father. In what ways was his father a positive role model for him? In other words, is Berry's positive behavior as an adult partly a result of his father's influence? What do you see in your own adult behavior that you can attribute to your parents' influence?

3. Berry discusses some of the difficulties he faces as a result of being in college—struggling to find time to meet his obligations, giving up lawn care, spending less time with his family. What difficulties do you face as a result of fitting college into your life? What obligations must you struggle to fulfill? What activities remain undone?

About Structure

4. In most of his essay, Berry uses time order, but in some places he uses listing order. For example, what does Berry list in paragraphs 20–22?

_____

5. In closing his essay, Berry writes that at his college graduation, "there will be a celebration—a proper one." With what earlier event is he contrasting this graduation?

_____

About Style and Tone

6. In explaining that he followed his father's example, the author compares himself to "a man who double-crosses the mob [and] follows a cement block to the bottom of the river." In this comparison, Berry strikingly makes the point

that his own actions led him to an undesirable situation. Find two other places where the author uses a richly revealing comparison. Write those images below, and explain what Berry means by each one.

Image: _____

_____

Meaning: _____

Image: _____

_____

Meaning: _____

7. In the first sentence of Berry's essay, he tells us that it is "highly improbable" for him to be in college. What is his tone in this sentence and in the paragraph that follows?

RESPONDING TO IMAGES

Consider how this photograph of assembly line workers is structured. Why do you think the photographer chose to take the picture from this particular angle?

WRITING ASSIGNMENTS

Assignment 1: Writing a Paragraph

Children are strongly influenced by the example of their parents (and other significant adults in their lives). For instance, the author of this essay followed his father's example of disliking school and getting a job that did not challenge him mentally.

Think about your growing-up years and about adults who influenced you, both positively and negatively. Then write a paragraph that describes one of these people and his or her influence on you. Supply plenty of vivid examples to help the reader understand how and why this person affected you.

The topic sentence of your paragraph should identify the person (either by name or by relationship to you) and briefly indicate the kind of influence he or she had on you. Here are some examples of topic sentences for this paper:

My aunt's courage in difficult situations helped me to become a stronger person.

My father's frequent trouble with the law made it necessary for me to grow up in a hurry.

The pastor of our church helped me realize that I was a worthwhile, talented person.

Assignment 2: Writing a Paragraph

Write a paragraph about one way that reading has been important in your life, either positively or negatively. To discover the approach you wish to take, think for a moment about the influence of reading throughout your life. When you were a child, was being read to at bedtime a highlight of your day? Did reading out loud in elementary school cause you embarrassment? Do you adore mysteries or true-crime books? Do you avoid reading whenever possible? Find an idea about the role of reading in your life that you can write about in the space of a paragraph. Your topic sentence will be a clear statement of that idea, such as:

I first learned to read from watching *Sesame Street*.

One key experience in second grade made me hate reading out loud in class.

My parents' attitude toward reading rubbed off on me.

Reading to my child at bedtime is an important time of day for both of us.

Books have taught me some things I never would have learned from friends and family.

There are several reasons why I am not a good reader.

A wonderful self-help book has helped me build my self-esteem.

Develop your main idea with detailed explanations and descriptions. For example, if you decide to write about reading to your child at bedtime, you might describe the positions you and your child take (Is the child in bed? On the floor? On your lap?), one or two of the stories the child and you have loved, some of the child's reactions, and so on.

Assignment 3: Writing an Essay

Berry's graduation-night celebration was a dramatic one and, he states, "a fitting closure for the end of high school." What was your senior prom or high school graduation celebration like? Did you participate in any of the planning and preparation for the events? Were finding a date and shopping for clothing for the prom fun or nerve-racking experiences? Was the event itself wonderful or disappointing? Write an essay telling the story of your graduation celebration from start to finish. Use many sharp descriptive details to help your readers envision events, decorations, clothing, cars, the weather, and so on. In addition, add meaning to your story by telling what you were thinking and feeling throughout the event.

You might try making a list as a way of collecting details for this paper. At first, don't worry about organizing your details. Just keep adding to your list, which might at one point look like this:

decorations committee

considered asking my cousin to go with me, if necessary

shopping for prom dress with Mom (and arguing)

afraid I'd be asked first by someone I didn't want to go with

talk of being up all night

pressed orchid corsage afterward

florist busy that week

working on centerpieces

feet hurt

Eventually, you will have enough information to begin thinking about the organization of your essay. Here's what the scratch outline for one such essay looks like:

Central idea: My high school prom was a mixture of fun and disappointment.

(1) Before the dance

Work on the decorations com. (theme: sky's the limit)

Anxiety over getting a date, finally relief

Worn out shopping for a dress

Last-minute preparations (getting flowers, having hair done, decorating ballroom)

(2) Night of the dance
Picture-taking at home
Squeezing gown into car, hem gets stuck in car door and grease
rubs on it
Beautiful ballroom
Rotten meal
Great band (even teachers yelling requests)
After two dances had to take off heels
Date kept dancing with others
Danced with my brother, who came with my girlfriend
Early breakfast served at hotel

(3) After the dance
Total exhaustion for two days
Extensive phone analysis of dance with girlfriends
Never went out with that date again
Several years later, prom dress, wrapped in a garbage bag, went to Salvation
Army

Perhaps you don't remember your prom or graduation night celebration very well, or don't wish to. Feel free to write about another important social event instead, such as a high school reunion, a family reunion, or your own or someone else's wedding.

Let's Get Specific

Beth Johnson

PREVIEW	WORDS TO WATCH
Some people are better writers than others. That's obvious to anyone who reads. There are writers whose material you just can't put down—and there are writers whose material you can't put down fast enough. One of the biggest differences between the skillful writer and the poor one is this: the successful writer uses specific, concrete language. Journalist and teacher Beth Johnson explains the power of specific language and demonstrates how any writer can become more skilled in its use.	instinctive (2) prospective (2) vividly (2) glaze (3) blandly (7) intuitively (8) swayed (8) parody (8) crave (9) anecdote (12) compelling (16) sustain (17)

Imagine that you've offered to fix up your sister with a blind date. "You'll like   1
him," you tell her. "He's really nice." Would that assurance be enough to satisfy her? Would she contentedly wait for Saturday night, happily anticipating meeting this "nice" young man? Not likely! She would probably bombard you with questions: "But what's he like? Is he tall or short? Funny? Serious? Smart? Kind? Shy? Does he work? How do you know him?"

Such questions reveal the instinctive• hunger we all feel for specific detail. Be-   2
ing told that her prospective• date is "nice" does very little to help your sister picture him. She needs concrete details to help her vividly• imagine this stranger.

The same principle applies to writing. Whether you are preparing a research **3** paper, a letter to a friend, or an article for the local newspaper, your writing will be strengthened by the use of detailed, concrete language. Specific language energizes and informs readers. General language, by contrast, makes their eyes glaze● over.

The following examples should prove the point.   **4**

Dear Sir or Madam:

Please consider my application for a job with your company. I am a college graduate with experience in business. Part-time jobs that I have held during the school year and my work over summer vacations make me well-qualified for employment. My former employers have always considered me a good, reliable worker. Thank you for considering my application.

Sincerely,
Bob Cole

Dear Sir or Madam:

I would like to be considered for an entry-level position in your purchasing department. I graduated in June from Bayside College with a 3.5 GPA and a bachelor's degree in business administration. While at Bayside, I held a part-time job in the college's business office, where I eventually had responsibility for coordinating food purchasing for the school cafeteria. By encouraging competitive bidding among food suppliers, I was able to save the school approximately $2,500 in the school year 1998–1999. During the last three summers (1997–1999), I worked at Bayside Textiles, where I was promoted from a job in the mailroom to the position of assistant purchasing agent, a position that taught me a good deal about controlling costs. Given my background, I'm confident I could make a real contribution to your company. I will telephone you next Tuesday morning to ask if we might arrange an interview.

Sincerely,
Julia Moore

Which of the preceding letters do you think makes a more convincing case **5** for these job seekers? If you're like most people, you would choose the second. Although both letters are polite and grammatically acceptable, the first one suffers badly in comparison with the second for one important reason. It is *general* and *abstract*, while the second is *specific* and *concrete*.

Let's look at the letters again. The differing styles of the two are evident in the **6** first sentence. Bob is looking for "a job with your company." He doesn't specify what kind of job—it's for the employer to figure out if Bob wants to work as a groundskeeper, on an assembly line, or as a salesperson. By contrast, Julia is immediately specific about the kind of job she is seeking—"an entry-level position in your purchasing department." Bob tells only that he is "a college graduate." But Julia tells where she went to college, what her grade point average was, and exactly what she studied.

The contrast continues as the two writers talk about their work experience. 7
Again, Bob talks in vague, general terms. He gives no concrete evidence to show
how the general descriptions "well-qualified" and "good, reliable worker" apply
to him. But Julia backs up her claims. She tells specifically what positions she's
held (buyer for cafeteria, assistant purchasing clerk for textile company), gives
solid evidence that she performed her jobs well (saved the school $2,500, was pro-
moted from mailroom), and explains what skills she has acquired (knows about
controlling costs). Julia continues to be clear and concrete as she closes the letter.
By saying, "I will telephone you next Tuesday morning," she leaves the reader
with a helpful, specific piece of information. Chances are, her prospective employer will be glad to take her call. The chances are equally good that Bob will
never hear from the company. His letter was so blandly• general that the employer will hardly remember receiving it.

Julia's letter demonstrates the power of specific detail—a power that we all ap- 8
preciate intuitively.• Indeed, although we may not always be aware of it, our opinions and decisions are frequently swayed• by concrete language. On a restaurant
menu, are you more tempted by a "green salad" or "a colorful salad bowl filled
with romaine and spinach leaves, red garden-fresh tomatoes, and crisp green pepper rings"? Would being told that a movie is "good" persuade you to see it as
much as hearing that it is "a hilarious parody• of a rock documentary featuring a
fictional heavy-metal band"? Does knowing that a classmate has "personal problems" help you understand her as well as hearing that "her parents are divorcing,
her brother was just arrested for selling drugs, and she is scheduled for surgery to
correct a back problem"?

When we read, all of us want—even crave•—this kind of specificity. Concrete 9
language grabs our attention and allows us to witness the writer's world almost
firsthand. Abstract language, on the other hand, forces us to try to fill in the blanks
left by the writer's lack of specific imagery. Usually we tire of the effort. Our attention wanders. We begin to wonder what's for lunch and whether it's going to rain,
as our eyes scan the page, searching for some concrete detail to focus on.

Once you understand the power of concrete details, you will gain consider- 10
able power as a writer. You will describe events so vividly that readers will feel
they experienced them directly. You will sprinkle your essays with nuggets of
detail that, like the salt on a pretzel, add interest and texture.

Consider the following examples and decide for yourself which came from a 11
writer who has mastered the art of the specific detail.

Living at Home

Unlike many college students, I have chosen to live at home with my
parents. Naturally, the arrangement has both good and bad points. The most
difficult part is that, even though I am an adult, my parents sometimes still
think of me as a child. Our worst disagreements occur when they expect me
to report to them as though I were still twelve years old. Another drawback
to living with my parents is that I don't feel free to have friends over to "my
place." It's not that my parents don't welcome my friends in their home, but
I can't tell my friends to drop in anytime as I would if I lived alone.

But in other ways, living at home works out well. The most obvious plus
is that I am saving a lot of money. I pay room and board, but that doesn't
compare to what renting an apartment would cost. There are less measurable
advantages as well. Although we do sometimes fall into our old parent-child
roles, my parents and I are getting to know each other in new ways. Generally,
we relate as adults, and I think we're all gaining a lot of respect for one another.

The Pros and Cons of Living at Home

Most college students live in a dormitory or apartment. They spend their hours surrounded by their own stereos, blaring hip-hop or rock music; their own furnishings, be they leaking beanbag chairs or Salvation Army sofas; and their own choice of foods, from tofu-bean sprout casseroles to a basic diet of Cheetos. My life is different. I occupy the same room that has been mine since babyhood. My school pictures, from gap-toothed first-grader to cocky senior, adorn the walls. The music drifting through my door from the living room ranges from Lawrence Welk to . . . Lawrence Welk. The food runs heavily to Mid-American Traditional: meatloaf, mashed potatoes, frozen peas.

Yes, I live with my parents. And the arrangement is not always ideal. Although I am twenty-four years old, my parents sometimes slip into a time warp and mentally cut my age in half. "Where are you going, Lisa? Who will you be with?" my mother will occasionally ask. I'll answer patiently, "I'm going to have pizza with some people from my psych class." "But where?" she continues. "I'm not sure," I'll say, my voice rising just a hair. If the questioning continues, it will often lead to a blowup. "You don't need to know where I'm going, OK?" I'll say shrilly. "You don't have to yell at me," she'll answer in a hurt voice.

Living at home also makes it harder to entertain. I find myself envying classmates who can tell their friends, "Drop in anytime." If a friend of mine "drops in" unexpectedly, it throws everyone into a tizzy. Mom runs for the dustcloth while Dad ducks into the bedroom, embarrassed to be seen in his comfortable, ratty bathrobe.

On the other hand, I don't regret my decision to live at home for a few years. Naturally, I am saving money. The room and board I pay my parents wouldn't rent the tiniest, most roach-infested apartment in the city. And despite our occasional lapses, my parents and I generally enjoy each other's company. They are getting to know me as an adult, and I am learning to see them as people, not just my parents. I realized how true this was when I saw them getting dressed up to go out recently. Dad was putting on a tie, and Mom one of her best dresses. I opened my mouth to ask where they were going when it occurred to me that maybe they didn't care to be checked up on any more than I did. Swallowing my curiosity, I simply waved good-bye and said, "Have a good time!"

Both passages could have been written by the same person. Both make the 12 same basic points. But the second passage is far more interesting because it backs up the writer's points with concrete details. While the first passage merely *tells* that the writer's parents sometimes treat her like a child, the second passage follows this point up with an anecdote• that *shows* exactly what she means. Likewise with the point about inviting friends over: the first passage only states that there is a problem, but the second one describes in concrete terms what happens if a friend does drop in unexpectedly. The first writer simply says that her room and board costs wouldn't pay for an apartment, but the second is specific about just how inadequate the money would be. And while the first passage uses abstract language to say that the writer and her parents are "getting to know each other in new ways," the second shows what that means by describing a specific incident.

Every kind of writing can be improved by the addition of concrete detail. Let's 13
look at one final example: the love letter.

Dear April,

I can't wait any longer to tell you how I feel. I am crazy about you. You
are the most wonderful woman I've ever met. Every time I'm near you I'm
overcome with feelings of love. I would do anything in the world for you
and am hoping you feel the same way about me.

Love,
Paul

Paul has written a sincere note, but it lacks a certain something. That some- 14
thing is specific detail. Although the letter expresses a lot of positive feelings, it
could have been written by practically any love-struck man about any woman. For
this letter to be really special to April, it should be unmistakably about her and
Paul. And that requires concrete details.

Here is what Paul might write instead.   15

Dear April,

Do you remember last Saturday, as we ate lunch in the park, when I
spilled my soda in the grass? You quickly picked up a twig and made a tiny
dam to keep the liquid from flooding a busy anthill. You probably didn't
think I noticed, but I did. It was at that moment that I realized how totally
I am in love with you and your passion for life. Before that I only thought
you were the most beautiful woman in the world, with your eyes like
sparkling pools of emerald water and your chestnut hair glinting in the sun.
But now I recognize what it means when I hear your husky laugh and I feel a
tight aching in my chest. It means I could stand on top of the Empire State
Building and shout to the world, "I love April Snyder." Should I do it? I'll be
waiting for your reply.

Paul

There's no guarantee that April is going to return Paul's feelings, but she cer- 16
tainly has a better idea now just what it is about her that Paul finds so lovable, as
well as what kind of guy Paul is. Concrete details have made this letter far more
compelling.•

Vague, general language is the written equivalent of baby food. It is adequate; 17
it can sustain• life. But it isn't very interesting. For writing to have satisfying
crunch, sizzle, and color, it must be generously supplied with specifics. Whether
the piece is a job application, a student essay, or a love letter, it is concrete details
that make it interesting, persuasive, and memorable.

VOCABULARY IN CONTEXT

1. The word *swayed* in "our opinions and decisions are frequently swayed by concrete language" (paragraph 8) means
    a. hidden.
    b. repeated.
    c. influenced.
    d. shown to be wrong.

2. The word *compelling* in "she certainly has a better idea now just what it is about her that Paul finds so lovable. . . . Concrete details have made this letter far more compelling" (paragraph 16) means
    a. forceful and interesting.
    b. long and boring.
    c. empty and vague.
    d. silly but amusing.

READING COMPREHENSION QUESTIONS

1. Which sentence best expresses the central idea of the selection?
    a. Communication skills of all types are useful throughout life.
    b. Always be specific when applying for a job.
    c. Specific language will strengthen your writing.
    d. Most people need help with their writing skills.

2. Main ideas may cover more than one paragraph. Which sentence best expresses the main idea of paragraphs 6–7?
    a. In letters of application for a job, Bob and Julia have included their background and job goals.
    b. Bob and Julia have written letters of application for a job.
    c. While Bob says only that he's a college graduate, Julia goes into detail about where and what she studied and her grades.
    d. While Bob's job-application letter is probably too vague to be successful, Julia's very specific one is likely to get a positive response.

3. Which sentence best expresses the main idea of paragraph 8?
    a. Julia's letter is a good example of the power of specific details.
    b. Our opinions and decisions are often influenced by specific language.
    c. We want to hear exactly what's in a salad or movie before spending money on it.
    d. When we know just what someone's "personal problems" are, we understand him or her better.

4. Johnson states that abstract language
    a. is rare.
    b. lets us clearly see what the writer's world is like.
    c. tends to lose our attention.
    d. makes us want to read more of the writer's piece.

5. Johnson feels that concrete language

   a. is hard to follow.

   b. makes readers' eyes glaze over.

   c. helps readers picture what the author is writing about.

   d. is not appropriate for a menu or a parody.

6. In paragraphs 6–7, the author suggests that Bob Cole

   a. is not qualified to enter the business world.

   b. is lying about his education and work experience.

   c. should have written a less wordy letter.

   d. should have written a more detailed letter.

7. Which of the following sentences can we assume Beth Johnson would most approve of?

   a. Shore City is an amusing but expensive place.

   b. Shore City is an interesting place to spend a bit of time.

   c. Shore City has an amusement park and racetrack, but all the hotel rooms cost over $100 a day.

   d. There is a city near the shore that has some interesting attractions, but its hotels are quite expensive.

8. We can infer from the reading that specific details would be very important in

   a. a novel.

   b. a history textbook.

   c. a biography.

   d. all of the above.

DISCUSSION QUESTIONS

About Content

1. At some earlier point in school, did you learn the importance of writing specifically? If so, do you remember when? If not, when do you think you should have been taught about the power of specific details in writing?

2. Johnson provides three pairs of examples: two job-application letters, two passages about living at home, and two love letters. Which pair most effectively makes her point for you about the value of writing specifically?

3. What kinds of writing will you be doing over the next few weeks, either in or out of school? Will it be papers for other classes, answers to essay questions, reports at work, letters of application for jobs, letters to friends, or other types of writing? Name one kind of writing you will be doing, and give an example of one way you could make that writing more specific.

About Structure

4. Essays often begin with an introduction that prepares readers for the author's central idea. How does Johnson begin her essay? Why do you think she chose this kind of introduction?

_____

_____

_____

5. The authors of the papers on living at home are essentially using listing order. What are they listing?

_____

6. Johnson takes her own advice and uses many concrete details in her essay. Locate two particularly strong examples of specific details in the reading that are not in the three pairs of samples, and write them below:

_____

_____

_____

About Style and Tone

7. Johnson opens her essay in the second-person point of view. As a reader, how do you respond to being addressed directly? Why might Johnson have chosen this approach?

_____

_____

_____

8. In paragraph 10, Johnson writes: "You will sprinkle your essays with nuggets of detail that, like the salt on a pretzel, add interest and texture." What kind of language is she using here?

_____

_____

_____

Allen Swerling. Used with permission.

RESPONDING TO IMAGES

The writer in this illustration plans to use three specific scenes to tell her story. How might the scenes be connected? What story do they tell? Be creative in your response, but make sure your ideas are based on specific visual details in the cartoon.

WRITING ASSIGNMENTS

Assignment 1: Writing a Paragraph

Using the same level of detail as Julia's application letter in the reading, write a one-paragraph letter of application for a part-time or a full-time job. Like Julia Moore, be sure to include the following in your paragraph:

What kind of job you are applying for

Where you have worked previously

What positions you have held

Evidence that you performed your job well

Which skills you have acquired

Assignment 2: Writing a Paragraph

In this reading, "The Pros and Cons of Living at Home" is a strong example of a "pro and con" analysis—one that details the advantages and disadvantages of something. Think of a topic about which you have conflicting views. It could be a decision you are struggling with, such as changing jobs or moving to a larger (or smaller) house or apartment. Or it could be a situation in which you already find yourself, such as attending school while holding a job or having an elderly parent living with you. Write a paragraph in which you explain in detail what the pros and cons of the issue are.

Once you've chosen a topic, do some prewriting. A good strategy is to make two lists; one of the advantages, the other of the disadvantages. Here is a sample:

Advantages of moving to a smaller apartment

Save money on rent ($325 a month instead of $400 a month)

Save money on utilities (smaller heating bill)

Less space to clean (one bedroom instead of two)

Disadvantages of moving to a smaller apartment

Less space for all my furniture (big chest of drawers, sofa bed)

No spare bedroom (can't have friends sleep over)

Will get more cluttered (little space to display all my trophies, souvenirs, and sports equipment)

If you are not sure about which issue to write about, make lists for two or three topics. Then you'll have a better idea of which one will result in a better paper.

Use the lists of advantages and disadvantages as an outline for your paragraph, adding other ideas as they occur to you. Begin with a topic sentence such as "_____ has both advantages and disadvantages" or "I'm having a hard time deciding whether or not to _____." Next, write the supporting sentences, discussing first one side of the issue and then the other.

Be sure to include plenty of specific details. For inspiration, reread "The Pros and Cons of Living at Home" before writing your essay.

Assignment 3: Writing an Essay

Johnson uses sharp, concrete details to make a point she feels strongly about—that specific language gives writing real power. Write an essay persuading readers of the importance of something you believe in strongly. Be sure to include at least one or two concrete, convincing examples for every point that you make. You might write about the value of something, such as:

Regular exercise

Volunteer work

Reading for pleasure

Gardening

Spending time with young (or grown) children

Periodic intense housecleaning

Alternatively, you can write about the negative aspects of something, such as:

Excessive television watching

Compulsive shopping

Tabloid journalism

Procrastinating

Smoking

Following is an example of an informal outline for this assignment. As the writer developed this outline into paragraphs, she added, subtracted, and re-arranged some of her examples.

Central idea: Cleaning out closets every now and then can be rewarding.

(1) I get rid of things I no longer need, or never needed:

Pair of ten-year-old hiking boots, which I kept because they were expensive but that are thoroughly worn out

Portable TV that no longer works

Yogurt maker given to me by my first husband on our anniversary

(2) I make room for things I do need:

All my shoes and pocketbooks, which can be arranged in neat rows on the shelves instead of crammed into cartons

Christmas presents I buy for my family in July and want to hide

(3) I find things that I thought were lost forever or that I forgot I ever had:

Box of photographs from our first family vacation

My bowling trophy

Presents I bought for last Christmas and forgot about

Old Before Her Time

Katherine Barrett

PREVIEW	WORDS TO WATCH
Most of us wait for our own advanced years to learn what it is like to be old. Patty Moore decided not to wait. At the age of twenty-six, she disguised herself as an eighty-five-year-old woman. What she learned suggests that to be old in our society is both better and worse than is often thought. This selection may give you a different perspective on the older people in your life—on what they are really like inside and on what life is really like for them.	donned (3) gerontology (4) throng (4) nonentity (4) lark (4) anathema (14) jauntily (21) abysmally (24)

1 This is the story of an extraordinary voyage in time, and of a young woman who devoted three years to a singular experiment. In 1979, Patty Moore—then aged twenty-six—transformed herself for the first of many times into an eighty-five-year-old woman. Her object was to discover firsthand the problems, joys, and frustrations of the elderly. She wanted to know for herself what it's like to live in a culture of youth and beauty when your hair is gray, your skin is wrinkled, and no men turn their heads as you pass.

2 Her time machine was a makeup kit. Barbara Kelly, a friend and professional makeup artist, helped Patty pick out a wardrobe and showed her how to use latex to create wrinkles and wrap Ace bandages to give the impression of stiff joints. "It was peculiar," Patty recalls, as she relaxes in her New York City apartment. "Even the first few times I went out, I realized that I wouldn't have to act that much. The more I was perceived as elderly by others, the more 'elderly' I actually became. . . . I imagine that's just what happens to people who really are old."

3 What motivated Patty to make her strange journey? It was partly her career— as an industrial designer, Patty often focuses on the needs of the elderly. But the roots of her interest are also deeply personal. Extremely close to her own grandparents—particularly her maternal grandfather, now ninety—and raised in a part of Buffalo, New York, where there was a large elderly population, Patty always drew comfort and support from the older people around her. When her own marriage ended in 1979 and her life seemed to be falling apart, she dived into her "project" with all her soul. In all, she donned° her costume more than two hundred times in fourteen states. Here is the remarkable story of what she found.

4 Columbus, Ohio, May 1979. Leaning heavily on her cane, Pat Moore stood alone in the middle of a crowd of young professionals. They were all attending a gerontology° conference, and the room was filled with animated chatter. But no one was talking to Pat. In a throng° of men and women who devoted their working lives to the elderly, she began to feel like a total nonentity.° "I'll get us all some coffee," a young man told a group of women next to her. "What about me?" thought Pat. "If I were young, they would be offering me coffee, too." It was a bitter thought at the end of a disappointing day—a day that marked Patty's first appearance as "the old woman." She had planned to attend the gerontology conference anyway, and almost as a lark° decided to see how professionals would react to an old person in their midst.

Now, she was angry. All day she had been ignored . . . counted out in a way 5
she had never experienced before. She didn't understand. Why didn't people help
her when they saw her struggling to open a heavy door? Why didn't they include
her in conversations? Why did the other participants seem almost embarrassed by
her presence at the conference—as if it were somehow inappropriate that an old
person should be professionally active?

And so, eighty-five-year-old Pat Moore learned her first lesson: The old are 6
often ignored. "I discovered that people really do judge a book by its cover," Patty
says today. "Just because I looked different, people either condescended to me or
totally dismissed me. Later, in stores, I'd get the same reaction. A clerk would turn
to someone younger and wait on her first. It was as if he assumed that I—the older
woman—could wait because I didn't have anything better to do."

New York City, October 1979. Bent over her cane, Pat walked slowly toward 7
the edge of the park. She had spent the day sitting on a bench with friends, but
now dusk was falling and her friends had all gone home. She looked around nervously at the deserted area and tried to move faster, but her joints were stiff. It was
then that she heard the barely audible sound of sneakered feet approaching and
the kids' voices. "Grab her, man." "Get her purse." Suddenly an arm was around
her throat and she was dragged back, knocked off her feet.

She saw only a blur of sneakers and blue jeans, heard the sounds of mocking 8
laughter, felt fists pummeling her—on her back, her legs, her breasts, her stomach.
"Oh, God," she thought, using her arms to protect her head and curling herself
into a ball. "They're going to kill me. I'm going to die. . . ."

Then, as suddenly as the boys attacked, they were gone. And Patty was left alone, 9
struggling to rise. The boys' punches had broken the latex makeup on her face, the
fall had disarranged her wig, and her whole body ached. (Later she would learn that
she had fractured her left wrist, an injury that took two years to heal completely.) Sobbing, she left the park and hailed a cab to return home. Again the thought struck her:
What if I really lived in the gray ghetto? . . . What if I couldn't escape to my nice safe
home . . . ?

Lesson number two: The fear of crime is paralyzing. "I really understand now 10
why the elderly become homebound," the young woman says as she recalls her
ordeal today. "When something like this happens, the fear just doesn't go away.
I guess it wasn't so bad for me. I could distance myself from what happened . . .
and I was strong enough to get up and walk away. But what about someone who is
really too weak to run or fight back or protect herself in any way? And the elderly
often can't afford to move if the area in which they live deteriorates, becomes un-
safe. I met people like this, and they were imprisoned by their fear. That's when
the bolts go on the door. That's when people starve themselves because they're
afraid to go to the grocery store."

New York City, February 1980. It was a slushy, gray day, and Pat had labori- 11
ously descended four flights of stairs from her apartment to go shopping. Once
outside, she struggled to hold her threadbare coat closed with one hand and ma-
nipulate her cane with the other. Splotches of snow made the street difficult for
anyone to navigate, but for someone hunched over, as she was, it was almost impossible. The curb was another obstacle. The slush looked ankle-deep—and what
was she to do? Jump over it? Slowly, she worked her way around to a drier spot,
but the crowds were impatient to move. A woman with packages jostled her as
she rushed past, causing Pat to nearly lose her balance. If I really were old, I would
have fallen, she thought. Maybe broken something. On another day, a woman had
practically knocked her over by letting go of a heavy door as Pat tried to enter
a coffee shop. Then there were the revolving doors. How could you push them
without strength? And how could you get up and down stairs, on and off a bus,
without risking a terrible fall?

Lesson number three: If small, thoughtless deficiencies in design were cor- **12** rected, life would be so much easier for older people. It was no surprise to Patty that the "built" environment is often inflexible. But even she didn't realize the extent of the problems, she admits. "It was a terrible feeling. I never realized how difficult it is to get off a curb if your knees don't bend easily. Or the helpless feeling you get if your upper arms aren't strong enough to open a door. You know, I just felt so vulnerable—as if I was at the mercy of every barrier or rude person I encountered."

Fort Lauderdale, Florida, May 1980. Pat met a new friend while shopping, and **13** they decided to continue their conversation over a sundae at a nearby coffee shop. The woman was in her late seventies, "younger" than Pat, but she was obviously reaching out for help. Slowly, her story unfolded. "My husband moved out of our bedroom," the woman said softly, fiddling with her coffee cup and fighting back tears. "He won't touch me anymore. And when he gets angry at me for being stupid, he'll even sometimes . . ." The woman looked down, too embarrassed to go on. Pat took her hand. "He hits me; . . . he gets so mean." "Can't you tell anyone?" Pat asked. "Can't you tell your son?" "Oh, no!" the woman almost gasped. "I would never tell the children; they absolutely adore him."

Lesson number four: Even a fifty-year-old marriage isn't necessarily a good **14** one. While Pat met many loving and devoted elderly couples, she was stunned to find others who had stayed together unhappily—because divorce was still an anathema● in their middle years. "I met women who secretly wished their husbands dead, because after so many years they just ended up full of hatred. One woman in Chicago even admitted that she deliberately angered her husband because she knew it would make his blood pressure rise. Of course, that was pretty extreme. . . ."

Patty pauses thoughtfully and continues. "I guess what really made an im- **15** pression on me, the real eye-opener, was that so many of these older women had the same problems as women twenty, thirty, or forty—problems with men . . . problems with the different roles that are expected of them. As a 'young woman' I, too, had just been through a relationship where I spent a lot of time protecting someone by covering up his problems from family and friends. Then I heard this woman in Florida saying that she wouldn't tell her children their father beat her because she didn't want to disillusion them. These issues aren't age-related. They affect everyone."

Clearwater, Florida, January 1981. She heard the children laughing, but she **16** didn't realize at first that they were laughing at her. On this day, as on several others, Pat had shed the clothes of a middle-income woman for the rags of a bag lady. She wanted to see the extremes of the human condition, what it was like to be old and poor, and outside traditional society as well. Now, tottering down the sidewalk, she was most concerned with the cold, since her layers of ragged clothing did little to ease the chill. She had spent the afternoon rummaging through garbage cans, loading her shopping bags with bits of debris, and she was stiff and tired. Suddenly, she saw that four little boys, five or six years old, were moving up on her. And then she felt the sting of the pebbles they were throwing. She quickened her pace to escape, but another handful of gravel hit her and the laughter continued. They're using me as a target, she thought, horror-stricken. They don't even think of me as a person.

Lesson number five: Social class affects every aspect of an older person's ex- **17** istence. "I found out that class is a very important factor when you're old," says Patty. "It was interesting. That same day, I went back to my hotel and got dressed as a wealthy woman, another role that I occasionally took. Outside the hotel, a little boy of about seven asked if I would go shelling with him. We walked along the beach, and he reached out to hold my hand. I knew he must have a grandmother who walked with a cane, because he was so concerned about me and my footing. 'Don't put your cane there; the sand's wet,' he'd say. He really took responsibility for my welfare. The contrast between him and those children was really incredible—the little ones who were throwing pebbles at me because they didn't see me as human, and then the seven-year-old taking care of me. I think he would have responded to me the same way even if I had been dressed as the middle-income woman. There's no question that money does make life easier for older people, not only because it gives them a more comfortable lifestyle, but because it makes others treat them with greater respect."

New York City, May 1981. Pat always enjoyed the time she spent sitting on the 18 benches in Central Park. She'd let the whole day pass by, watching young children play, feeding the pigeons and chatting. One spring day she found herself sitting with three women, all widows, and the conversation turned to the few available men around. "It's been a long time since anyone hugged me," one woman complained. Another agreed. "Isn't that the truth. I need a hug, too." It was a favorite topic, Pat found—the lack of touching left in these women's lives, the lack of hugging, the lack of men.

In the last two years, she found out herself how it felt to walk down Fifth Av- 19 enue and know that no men were turning to look after her. Or how it felt to look at models in magazines or store mannequins and know that those gorgeous clothes were just not made for her. She hadn't realized before just how much casual attention was paid to her because she was young and pretty. She hadn't realized it until it stopped.

Lesson number six: You never grow old emotionally. You always need to feel 20 loved. "It's not surprising that everyone needs love and touching and holding," says Patty. "But I think some people feel that you reach a point in your life when you accept that those intimate feelings are in the past. That's wrong. These women were still interested in sex. But more than that, they—like everyone—needed to be hugged and touched. I'd watch two women greeting each other on the street and just holding onto each other's hands, neither wanting to let go. Yet, I also saw that there are people who are afraid to touch an old person; . . . they were afraid to touch me. It's as if they think old age is a disease and it's catching. They think that something might rub off on them."

New York City, September 1981. He was a thin man, rather nattily dressed, 21 with a hat that he graciously tipped at Pat as he approached the bench where she sat. "Might I join you?" he asked jauntily.• Pat told him he would be welcome and he offered her one of the dietetic hard candies that he carried in a crumpled paper bag. As the afternoon passed, they got to talking . . . about the beautiful buds on the trees and the world around them and the past. "Life's for the living, my wife used to tell me," he said. "When she took sick, she made me promise her that I wouldn't waste a moment. But the first year after she died, I just sat in the apartment. I didn't want to see anyone, talk to anyone or go anywhere. I missed her so much." He took a handkerchief from his pocket and wiped his eyes, and they sat in silence. Then he slapped his leg to break the mood and change the subject. He asked Pat about herself, and described his life alone. He belonged to a "senior center" now, and went on trips and had lots of friends. Life did go on. They arranged to meet again the following week on the same park bench. He brought lunch—chicken salad sandwiches and decaffeinated peppermint tea in a thermos—and wore a carnation in his lapel. It was the first date Patty had had since her marriage ended.

Lesson number seven: Life does go on . . . as long as you're flexible and open to 22 change. "That man really meant a lot to me, even though I never saw him again," says Patty, her eyes wandering toward the gray wig that now sits on a wig stand on the top shelf of her bookcase. "He was a real old-fashioned gentleman, yet not afraid to show his feelings—as so many men my age are. It's funny, but at that point I had been through months of self-imposed seclusion. Even though I was in a different role, that encounter kind of broke the ice for getting my life together as a single woman."

In fact, while Patty was living her life as the old woman, some of her young **23** friends had been worried about her. After several years, it seemed as if the lines of identity had begun to blur. Even when she wasn't in makeup, she was wearing unusually conservative clothing, she spent most of her time with older people, and she seemed almost to revel in her role—sometimes finding it easier to be in costume than to be a single New Yorker.

But as Patty continued her experiment, she was also learning a great deal **24** from the older people she observed. Yes, society often did treat the elderly abysmally°; . . . they were sometimes ignored, sometimes victimized, sometimes poor and frightened, but so many of them were survivors. They had lived through two world wars, through the Depression, and into the computer age. "If there was one lesson to learn, one lesson that I'll take with me into my old age, it's that you've got to be flexible," Patty says. "I saw my friend in the park, managing after the loss of his wife, and I met countless other people who picked themselves up after something bad—or even something catastrophic—happened. I'm not worried about them. I'm worried about the others who shut themselves away. It's funny, but seeing these two extremes helped me recover from the trauma in my own life, to pull my life together."

Today, Patty is back to living the life of a single thirty-year-old, and she rarely **25** dons her costumes anymore. "I must admit, though, I do still think a lot about aging," she says. "I look in the mirror and I begin to see wrinkles, and then I realize that I won't be able to wash those wrinkles off." Is she afraid of growing older? "No. In a way, I'm kind of looking forward to it." She smiles. "I know it will be different from my experiment. I know I'll probably even look different. When they aged Orson Welles in *Citizen Kane* he didn't resemble at all the Orson Welles of today."

But Patty also knows that in one way she really did manage to capture the **26** feeling of being old. With her bandages and her stooped posture, she turned her body into a kind of prison. Yet inside she didn't change at all. "It's funny, but that's exactly how older people always say they feel," says Patty. "Their bodies age, but inside they are really no different from when they were young."

VOCABULARY IN CONTEXT

1. The word *nonentity* in "But no one was talking to Pat. In a throng of men and women who devoted their working lives to the elderly, she began to feel like a total nonentity. . . . All day she had been ignored" (paragraphs 4–5) means

   a. expert.

   b. nobody.

   c. experiment.

   d. leader.

2. The word *abysmally* in "society often did treat the elderly abysmally; . . . they were sometimes ignored, sometimes victimized, sometimes poor and frightened" (paragraph 24) means

   a. politely.

   b. absentmindedly.

   c. very badly.

   d. angrily.

READING COMPREHENSION QUESTIONS

1. Which of the following would be the best alternative title for this selection?
   a. How Poverty Affects the Elderly
   b. Similarities between Youth and Old Age
   c. One Woman's Discoveries about the Elderly
   d. Violence against the Elderly

2. Which sentence best expresses the main idea of the selection?
   a. The elderly often have the same problems as young people.
   b. Pat Moore dressed up like an elderly woman over two hundred times.
   c. By making herself appear old, Pat Moore learned what life is like for the elderly in the United States.
   d. Elderly people often feel ignored in a society that glamorizes youth.

3. *True or false?* _____ As they age, people need others less.

4. Pat Moore learned that the elderly often become homebound because of the
   a. fear of crime.
   b. high cost of living.
   c. availability of in-home nursing care.
   d. lack of interesting places for them to visit.

5. One personal lesson Pat Moore learned from her experiment was that
   a. she needs to start saving money for her retirement.
   b. by being flexible she can overcome hardships.
   c. she has few friends her own age.
   d. her marriage could have been saved.

6. From paragraph 2, we can infer that
   a. behaving like an old person was difficult for Moore.
   b. many older people wear Ace bandages.
   c. people sometimes view themselves as others see them.
   d. Barbara Kelly works full time making people look older than they really are.

7. The article suggests that fifty years ago
   a. young couples tended to communicate better than today's young couples.
   b. divorce was less acceptable than it is today.
   c. verbal and physical abuse was probably extremely rare.
   d. the elderly were treated with great respect.

8. We can conclude that Moore may have disguised herself as an elderly woman over two hundred times in fourteen states because
   a. she and her friend Barbara Kelly continuously worked at perfecting Moore's costumes.
   b. her company made her travel often.
   c. she was having trouble finding locations with large numbers of elderly people.
   d. she wanted to see how the elderly were seen and treated all over the country, rather than in just one area.

DISCUSSION QUESTIONS

About Content

1. Why did Moore decide to conduct her experiment? Which of her discoveries surprised you?

2. Using the information Moore learned from her experiment, list some of the things that could be done to help the elderly. What are some things you personally could do?

3. How do the elderly people Moore met during her experiment compare with the elderly people you know?

4. Lesson number seven in the article is "Life does go on . . . as long as you're flexible and open to change" (paragraph 22). What do you think this really means? How might this lesson apply to situations and people you're familiar with—in which people either were or were not flexible and open to change?

About Structure

5. Most of the selection is made up of a series of Pat Moore's experiences and the seven lessons they taught. Find the sentence used by the author to introduce those experiences and lessons, and write that sentence here:

   _____

6. The details of paragraph 21 are organized in time order, and the author has used a few time transition words to signal time relationships. Find two of those time words, and write them here:

   _____   _____

About Style and Tone

7. What device does the author use to signal that she is beginning a new set of experiences and the lesson they taught? How does she ensure that the reader will recognize what each of the seven lessons is?

8. Do you think Barrett is objective in her treatment of Moore? Or does the author allow whatever her feelings might be for Moore to show in her writing? Find details in the article to support your answer.

RESPONDING TO IMAGES

What is the tone of this photograph, and how is it established? What is the photographer's attitude toward her subject?

WRITING ASSIGNMENT

Assignment 1: Writing a Paragraph

In her experiment, Moore discovered various problems faced by the elderly. Choose one of these areas of difficulty and write a paragraph in which you discuss what could be done in your city to help solve the problem. Following are a few possible topic sentences for this assignment:

Fear of crime among the elderly could be eased by a program providing young people to accompany them on their errands.

The courthouse and train station in our town need to be redesigned to allow easier access for the elderly.

Schools should start adopt-a-grandparent programs, which would enrich the emotional lives of both the young and the old participants.

Assignment 2: Writing a Paragraph

What did you learn from the selection, or what do you already know, about being older in our society that might influence your own future? Write a paragraph in which you list three or four ways you plan to minimize or avoid some of the problems often faced by elderly people. For instance, you may decide to do whatever you can to remain as healthy and strong as possible throughout your life. That might involve quitting smoking and incorporating exercise into your schedule. Your topic sentence might simply be: "There are three important ways in which I hope to avoid some of the problems often faced by the elderly."

Assignment 3: Writing an Essay

Lesson number seven in Barrett's article is "Life does go on . . . as long as you're flexible and open to change" (paragraph 22). Think about one person of any age whom you know well (including yourself). Write an essay in which you show how being (or not being) flexible and open to change has been important in that person's life. Develop your essay with three main examples.

In preparation for writing, think of several key times in your subject's life. Select three times in which being flexible or inflexible had a significant impact on that person. Then narrate and explain each of those times in a paragraph of its own. Here are two possible thesis statements for this essay:

My grandmother generally made the most of her circumstances by being flexible and open to change.

When I was a teenager, I could have made life easier for myself by being more flexible and open to change.

Your conclusion for this essay might summarize the value of being flexible or the problems of being inflexible, or both, for the person you are writing about.

Assignment 4: Writing an Essay Using Internet Research

As Moore studied the elderly people around her, she recognized that some were "survivors"—people who adapted successfully to the challenges of aging—and some were not. What can people do, both mentally and physically, to make their later years active and happy? Go online to see what some experts have suggested. Then write an essay on three ways that people can cope well with old age.

Using Google (or another search engine), try one of the following phrases or some related phrase:

growing older and keeping active and happy

happy healthy aging

elderly people and healthy living

You may, of course, use a simple phrase such as "growing older," but that will bring up too many items. As you proceed, you'll develop a sense of how to "track down" and focus a topic by adding more information to your search words and phrases.

The Most Hateful Words

Amy Tan

PREVIEW	WORDS TO WATCH
For years, a painful exchange with her mother lay like a heavy stone on Amy Tan's heart. In the following essay, Tan, author of best-selling novels, including *The Joy Luck Club* and *The Kitchen God's Wife*, tells the story of how that weight was finally lifted. This essay is from her memoir, *The Opposite of Fate*.	stricken (2) tormented (3) forbade (3) impenetrable (3) bequeathed (15)

1   The most hateful words I have ever said to another human being were to my mother. I was sixteen at the time. They rose from the storm in my chest and I let them fall in a fury of hailstones: "I hate you. I wish I were dead. . . ."

2   I waited for her to collapse, stricken• by what I had just said. She was still standing upright, her chin tilted, her lips stretched in a crazy smile. "Okay, maybe I die too," she said between huffs. "Then I no longer be your mother!" We had many similar exchanges. Sometimes she actually tried to kill herself by running into the street, holding a knife to her throat. She too had storms in her chest. And what she aimed at me was as fast and deadly as a lightning bolt.

3   For days after our arguments, she would not speak to me. She tormented• me, acted as if she had no feelings for me whatsoever. I was lost to her. And because of that, I lost, battle after battle, all of them: the times she criticized me, humiliated me in front of others, forbade• me to do this or that without even listening to one good reason why it should be the other way. I swore to myself I would never forget these injustices. I would store them, harden my heart, make myself as impenetrable• as she was.

4   I remember this now, because I am also remembering another time, just a few years ago. I was forty-seven, had become a different person by then, had become a fiction writer, someone who uses memory and imagination. In fact, I was writing a story about a girl and her mother, when the phone rang.

5   It was my mother, and this surprised me. Had someone helped her make the call? For a few years now, she had been losing her mind through Alzheimer's disease. Early on, she forgot to lock her door. Then she forgot where she lived. She forgot who many people were and what they had meant to her. Lately, she could no longer remember many of her worries and sorrows.

6   "Amy-ah," she said, and she began to speak quickly in Chinese. "Something is wrong with my mind. I think I'm going crazy."

7   I caught my breath. Usually she could barely speak more than two words at a time. "Don't worry," I started to say.

8   "It's true," she went on. "I feel like I can't remember many things. I can't remember what I did yesterday. I can't remember what happened a long time ago, what I did to you. . . ." She spoke as a drowning person might if she had bobbed to the surface with the force of will to live, only to see how far she had already drifted, how impossibly far she was from the shore.

9   She spoke frantically: "I know I did something to hurt you."

10   "You didn't," I said. "Don't worry."

11   "I did terrible things. But now I can't remember what. . . . And I just want to tell you . . . I hope you can forget, just as I've forgotten."

I tried to laugh so she would not notice the cracks in my voice. "Really, don't 12
worry."

"Okay, I just wanted you to know."   13

After we hung up, I cried, both happy and sad. I was again that sixteen-year- 14
old, but the storm in my chest was gone.

My mother died six months later. By then she had bequeathed● to me her most 15
healing words, as open and eternal as a clear blue sky. Together we knew in our
hearts what we should remember, what we can forget.

VOCABULARY IN CONTEXT

1. The word *stricken* in "I waited for her to collapse, *stricken* by what I had just
   said" (paragraph 2) means

   a. wounded.

   b. amused.

   c. annoyed.

   d. bored.

2. The word *bequeathed* in "By then she had *bequeathed* me her most healing words,
   those that are as open and eternal as a clear blue sky" (paragraph 15) means

   a. denied.

   b. sold.

   c. given.

   d. cursed.

READING COMPREHENSION QUESTIONS

1. Which sentence best expresses the central idea of the selection?

   a. Because of Alzheimer's disease, the author's mother forgot harsh words
      the two of them had said to each other.

   b. Amy Tan had a difficult relationship with her mother that worsened over
      the years.

   c. Years after a painful childhood with her mother, Amy Tan was able to real-
      ize peace and forgiveness.

   d. Despite her Alzheimer's disease, Amy Tan's mother was able to apologize
      to her daughter for hurting her.

2. Which sentence best expresses the main idea of paragraphs 1–2?

   a. Amy Tan's mother was sometimes suicidal.

   b. Amy Tan wanted to use words to hurt her mother.

   c. It is not unusual for teenagers and their parents to argue.

   d. Amy Tan and her mother had a very hurtful relationship.

3. Which sentence best expresses the main idea of paragraphs 8–9?

   a. The author's mother was deeply disturbed by the thought that she had
      hurt her daughter.

   b. Alzheimer's disease causes people to become confused and unable to re-
      member things clearly.

   c. The author's mother could not even remember what she had done the day before.
   d. The author's mother had changed very little from what she was like when Tan was a child.

4. After arguing with her daughter, the author's mother
   a. would say nice things about her to others.
   b. would immediately forget they had argued.
   c. would refuse to speak to her.
   d. would apologize.

5. When she was a girl, the author swore that she
   a. would never forget her mother's harsh words.
   b. would never be like her mother.
   c. would publicly embarrass her mother by writing about her.
   d. would never have children.

6. The first sign that the author's mother had Alzheimer's disease was
   a. forgetting where she lived.
   b. being able to speak only two or three words at a time.
   c. forgetting people's identities.
   d. forgetting to lock her door.

7. We can infer from paragraph 2 that
   a. the author wished her mother were dead.
   b. the author immediately felt guilty for the way she had spoken to her mother.
   c. the author's mother was emotionally unstable.
   d. the author's mother was physically abusive.

8. The author implies, in paragraphs 9–15, that
   a. she was pleased by her mother's sense of guilt.
   b. her love and pity for her mother were stronger than her anger.
   c. she did not recall what her mother was talking about.
   d. she was annoyed by her mother's confusion.

DISCUSSION QUESTIONS

About Content

1. How would you describe Amy Tan's mother? What kind of mother does she appear to have been?

2. In the discussion at the end of the essay, Tan chooses to keep her emotions hidden from her mother. Why do you think she does this?

3. What does Tan mean by her last line, "Together we knew in our hearts what we should remember, what we can forget."

About Structure

4. Tan makes effective use of parallel structure in writing her story. What are two examples of parallelism that help make her sentences clear and easy to read?

5. Tan begins her essay from the point of view of a sixteen-year-old girl but finishes it from the perspective of a woman in her late forties. Where in the essay does Tan make the transition between those two perspectives? What words does she use to signal the change?

6. Paragraph 5 describes a sequence of events, and the writer uses several transition words to signal time relationships. Locate three of those transitions and write them here:

_____   _____   _____

About Style and Tone

7. What effect does Tan achieve by using so many direct quotations?

8. Tan uses images of the weather throughout her essay. Find three instances in which Tan mentions weather and list them below. What does she accomplish with this technique?

_____   _____   _____

WRITING ASSIGNMENTS

Assignment 1: Writing a Paragraph

Despite being an adult, Tan recalls feeling like a sixteen-year-old girl again when she speaks to her mother. Think about something in your life that has the power to reconnect you to a vivid memory. Write a paragraph in which you describe your memory and the trigger that "takes you back" to it. Begin your paragraph with a topic sentence that makes it clear what you are going to discuss. Then provide specific details so that readers can understand your memory. Here are sample topic sentences.

> Whenever I see swings, I remember the day in second grade when I got into my first fistfight.

> The smell of cotton candy takes me back to the day my grandfather took me to my first baseball game.

> I can't pass St. Joseph's Hospital without remembering the day, ten years ago, when my brother was shot.

Assignment 2: Writing a Paragraph

In this essay, we see that Tan's relationship with her mother was very complicated. Who is a person with whom you have a complex relationship—maybe a relationship you'd describe as "love-hate" or "difficult"? Write a paragraph about that relationship. Be sure to give examples or details to show readers why you have such difficulties with this person.

Your topic sentence should introduce the person you plan to discuss. For example:

To me, my mother-in-law is one of the most difficult people in the world. (*Or,* My mother-in-law and I have contrasting points of view on several issues.)

While I respect my boss, he is simply a very difficult person.

Even though I love my sister, I can't stand to be around her.

Be sure to provide specific examples or details to help your reader understand why the relationship is so difficult for you. For example, if you decide to write about your boss, you will want to describe specific behaviors that show just why you consider him or her difficult.

Assignment 3: Writing an Essay

Like Tan's mother, most of us have at some time done something we wish we could undo. If you had a chance to revisit your past and change one of your actions, what would it be? Write an essay describing something you would like to undo.

In your first paragraph, introduce exactly what you did. Here are three thesis statements that students might have written:

I wish I could undo the night I decided to drive my car while I was drunk.

If I could undo any moment in my life, it would be the day I decided to drop out of high school.

One moment from my life I would like to change is the time I picked on an unpopular kid in sixth grade.

Be sure to provide details and, if appropriate, actual words that were spoken so that your readers can "see and hear" what happened. Once you've described the moment that you wish to take back, write three reasons why you feel the way you do. Below is a scratch outline for the first topic.

I wish I could undo the night I decided to drive my car while I was drunk.

1. Caused an accident that hurt others.

2. Lost my license, my car, and my job.

3. Affected the way others treat me.

To write an effective essay, you will need to provide specific details explaining each reason you identify. For instance, to support the third reason above, you might describe new feelings of guilt and anger you have about yourself as well as provide examples of how individual people now treat you differently. To end your essay, you might describe what you would do today if you could replay what happened.

Rudeness at the Movies
Bill Wine

PREVIEW	WORDS TO WATCH
When you're at a movie theater, do loud conversations, the crinkling of candy wrappers, and the wailing of children make you wish you'd gone bowling instead? Do you cringe when your fellow viewers announce plot twists moments before they happen? If so, you'll find a comrade in suffering in the film critic and columnist Bill Wine, who thinks people have come to feel far too at home in theaters. In the following essay, which first appeared as a newspaper feature story, Wine wittily describes what the movie-going experience all too often is like these days.	ecstatic (2) epidemic (14) galling (14) malodorous (15) superfluous (16) reluctance (18) prescient (20) gregarious (25)

1   Is this actually happening or am I dreaming?

2   I am at the movies, settling into my seat, eager with anticipation at the prospect of seeing a long-awaited film of obvious quality. The theater is absolutely full for the late show on this weekend evening, as the reviews have been ecstatic• for this cinema masterpiece.

3   Directly in front of me sits a man an inch or two taller than the Jolly Green Giant. His wife, sitting on his left, sports the very latest in fashionable hairdos, a gathering of her locks into a shape that resembles a drawbridge when it's open.

4   On his right, a woman spritzes herself liberally with perfume that her popcorn-munching husband got her for Valentine's Day, a scent that should be renamed "Essence of Elk."

5   The row in which I am sitting quickly fills up with members of Cub Scout Troop 432, on an outing to the movies because rain has canceled their overnight hike. One of the boys, demonstrating the competitive spirit for which Scouts are renowned worldwide, announces to the rest of the troop the rules in the Best Sound Made from an Empty Good-n-Plenty's Box contest, about to begin.

6   Directly behind me, a man and his wife are ushering three other couples into their seats. I hear the woman say to the couple next to her: "You'll love it. You'll just love it. This is our fourth time and we enjoy it more and more each time. Don't we, Harry? Tell them about the pie-fight scene, Harry. Wait'll you see it. It comes just before you find out that the daughter killed her boyfriend. It's great."

7   The woman has more to say—much more—but she is drowned out at the moment by the wailing of a six-month-old infant in the row behind her. The baby is crying because his mother, who has brought her twins to the theater to save on babysitting costs, can change only one diaper at a time.

8   Suddenly, the lights dim. The music starts. The credits roll. And I panic.

9   I plead with everyone around me to let me enjoy the movie. All I ask, I wail, is to be able to see the images and hear the dialogue and not find out in advance what is about to happen. Is that so much to expect for six bucks, I ask, now engulfed by a cloud of self-pity. I begin weeping unashamedly.

10 Then, as if on cue, the Jolly Green Giant slumps down in his seat, his wife removes her wig, the Elk lady changes her seat, the Scouts drop their candy boxes on the floor, the play-by-play commentator takes out her teeth, and the young mother takes her two bawling babies home.

Of course I am dreaming, I realize, as I gain a certain but shaky consciousness. 11 I notice that I am in a cold sweat. Not because the dream is scary, but from the shock of people being that cooperative.

I realize that I have awakened to protect my system from having to handle 12 a jolt like that. For never—NEVER—would that happen in real life. Not on this planet.

I used to wonder whether I was the only one who feared bad audience behav- 13 ior more than bad moviemaking. But I know now that I am not. Not by a long shot. The most frequent complaint I have heard in the last few months about the movie-going experience has had nothing to do with the films themselves.

No. What folks have been complaining about is the audience. Indeed, there 14 seems to be an epidemic° of galling° inconsiderateness and outrageous rudeness.

It is not that difficult to forgive a person's excessive height, or malodorous° 15 perfume, or perhaps even an inadvisable but understandable need to bring very young children to adult movies.

But the talking: that is not easy to forgive. It is inexcusable. Talking—loud, 16 constant, and invariably superfluous°—seems to be standard operating procedure on the part of many movie patrons these days.

It is true, I admit, that after a movie critic has seen several hundred movies in 17 the ideal setting of an almost-empty screening room with no one but other politely silent movie critics around him, it does tend to spoil him for the packed-theater experience.

And something is lost viewing a movie in almost total isolation—a fact that 18 movie distributors acknowledge with their reluctance° to screen certain audience-pleasing movies for small groups of critics. Especially with comedies, the infectiousness of laughter is an important ingredient of movie-watching pleasure.

But it is a decidedly uphill battle to enjoy a movie—no matter how suspense- 19 ful or hilarious or moving—with nonstop gabbers sitting within earshot. And they come in sizes, ages, sexes, colors, and motivations of every kind.

Some chat as if there is no movie playing. Some greet friends as if at a picnic. 20 Some alert those around them to what is going to happen, either because they have seen the film before, or because they are self-proclaimed experts on the predictability of plotting and want to be seen as prescient° geniuses.

Some describe in graphic terms exactly what is happening as if they were do- 21 ing the commentary for a sporting event on radio. ("Ooh, look, he's sitting down. Now he's looking at that green car. A banana—she's eating a banana.") Some audition for film critic Gene Shalit's job by waxing witty as they critique the movie right before your very ears.

And all act as if it is their constitutional or God-given right. As if their admis- 22 sion price allows them to ruin the experience for anyone and everyone else in the building. But why?

Good question. I wish I knew. Maybe rock concerts and ball games—both 23 environments which condone or even encourage hootin' and hollerin'—have conditioned us to voice our approval and disapproval and just about anything else we can spit out of our mouths at the slightest provocation when we are part of an audience.

But my guess lies elsewhere. The villain, I'm afraid, is the tube. We have seen 24 the enemy and it is television.

We have gotten conditioned over the last few decades to spending most of our 25 screen-viewing time in front of a little box in our living rooms and bedrooms. And when we watch that piece of furniture, regardless of what is on it—be it commercial, Super Bowl, soap opera, funeral procession, prime-time sitcom, Shakespeare play—we chat. Boy, do we chat. Because TV viewing tends to be an informal, gregarious,° friendly, casually interruptible experience, we talk whenever the spirit moves us. Which is often.

All of this is fine. But we have carried behavior that is perfectly acceptable in 26 the living room right to our neighborhood movie theater. And that *isn't* fine. In fact, it is turning lots of people off to what used to be a truly pleasurable experience: sitting in a jammed movie theater and watching a crowd-pleasing movie. And that's a first-class shame.

Nobody wants Fascist-like ushers, yet that may be where we're headed of necessity. Let's hope not. But something's got to give. 27

Movies during this Age of Television may or may not be better than ever. 28 About audiences, however, there is no question.

They are worse. 29

VOCABULARY IN CONTEXT

1. The word *ecstatic* in "The theater is absolutely full . . . as the reviews have been ecstatic for this cinema masterpiece" (paragraph 2) means

   a. clever.

   b. disappointing.

   c. a little confusing.

   d. very enthusiastic.

2. The word *malodorous* in "It is really not that difficult to forgive a person's . . . malodorous perfume" (paragraph 15) means

   a. pleasant.

   b. expensive.

   c. bad-smelling.

   d. hard-to-smell.

READING COMPREHENSION QUESTIONS

1. Which of the following would be the best alternative title for this selection?

   a. Television-Watching Behavior

   b. Today's Movie Audiences

   c. Modern Films

   d. The Life of a Movie Critic

2. Which sentence best expresses the main idea of the selection?

   a. Ushers should now make movie audiences keep quiet.

   b. People talk while they watch television or sports.

   c. Rude audiences are ruining movies for many.

   d. Films have changed in recent years.

3. The author states that in his dream

   a. he had come to the movies with a friend.

   b. he wore a tall hat and sat in front of a person shorter than he is.

   c. the Cub Scouts stopped making noises with empty candy boxes.

   d. the popcorn was too salty.

4. *True or false?* _____ The experience that Wine describes in the first eight paragraphs of this article is typical of what really happens at the movies today.

5. The most frequent complaint the author has heard about movies is that
   a. they are too long.
   b. they are too expensive.
   c. the audiences are too noisy.
   d. the audiences arrive too late.

6. The author suggests that watching television
   a. has affected the behavior of movie audiences.
   b. should be done in silence.
   c. is more fun than seeing movies in a theater.
   d. is a good model for watching movies in theaters.

7. From the selection, we can conclude that the author feels
   a. films aren't as good as they used to be.
   b. teenagers are the rudest members of movie audiences.
   c. talking during a movie is much more common now than it used to be.
   d. tall people should be seated in the back of a theater.

8. In paragraph 27, the author implies that unless audiences become quieter,
   a. movie theaters will be closed.
   b. everyone will watch less television.
   c. movies will get worse.
   d. ushers will have to force talkers to be quiet or leave.

DISCUSSION QUESTIONS

About Content

1. According to Wine, what are some possible causes for people's rude behavior at movies? Of these, which does Wine consider the most likely cause?

2. Do you agree with Wine's theory about why some people are rude at the movies? Why or why not? What might theater operators and other audience members do to control the problem?

3. Have you noticed the problem of noisy audiences in a movie theater? If so, what exactly have you experienced? What, if anything, was done about the problems you encountered?

About Structure

4. Wine writes about a problem. Write here the paragraphs in which Wine presents details that explain and illustrate what that problem is: paragraphs _____ ____ to _____.

5. Wine discusses reasons for the problem he writes about. Write here the paragraphs in which he discusses those reasons: paragraphs _____ to _____.

6. Wine suggests one possible but unwelcome solution for the problem he writes about. Write here the number of the paragraph in which he mentions that solution: _____.

About Style and Tone

7. Wine provides exaggerated descriptions of audience members—for example, he refers to the tall man sitting in front of him as "an inch or two taller than the Jolly Green Giant." Find two other examples of this humorous exaggeration.

_____

_____

Besides making readers smile, why might Wine have described the audience in this way?

_____

_____

8. Wine tends to use informal wording and sentence structure. In paragraphs 22–26, for instance, find two examples of his informal wording.

_____

_____

In the same paragraphs, find an example of his informal sentence structure.

_____

RESPONDING TO IMAGES

How do you know that this photograph was staged? How, specifically, would you suggest that the actors pose more convincingly next time?

WRITING ASSIGNMENTS

Assignment 1: Writing a Paragraph

Which do you prefer—watching a movie on your DVD player or TV at home or seeing it in a movie theater? Drawing on your own experiences, write a paragraph in which you explain why you prefer one viewing location over the other. Provide a strong example or two for each of your reasons. For instance, below is one reason with a specific example to support it.

Reason: One reason I prefer going to a movie theater is that it is definitely more peaceful than watching a film at home.

Supporting example: For instance, when I tried watching _Titanic_ at home the other night, I had to check on a crying baby or a fussy toddler every ten minutes. Can you imagine what it is like just as two pairs of lips on the screen are getting close enough to meet, to hear, "Mommy, my tummy hurts." If I go out to the movies, I leave my kids and their diapers in the care of my husband or mother.

Assignment 2: Writing a Paragraph

Using exaggeration and humor, Wine gives his impressions of people's looks and behavior at a movie theater. Write a paragraph describing your impressions of people's looks and behavior at a specific event or place. For instance, you might describe how people look and act at a rock concert, in an elevator, in a singles' hangout, or in a library. Like Wine, use colorful descriptions and quotations. Your topic sentence might be similar to the following:

How people behave on an elevator reveals some key personal qualities.

Try listing ideas to develop your supporting details. For example, below is a list of possible supporting points for the topic sentence above.

Shy people tend to avoid eye contact.

Very friendly people smile and may say something.

Helpful people will keep the elevator from leaving when they see someone rushing toward it.

A romantic couple won't notice anyone else on the elevator.

Impatient people may push the number of their floor more than once.

Assignment 3: Writing an Essay

Rudeness, unfortunately, is not limited to the movie theater. We have all observed rude behavior in various places we often go to. Write an essay on this topic. You might use one of the following thesis statements:

Rude behavior is all too common in several places I often go to.

A common part of life at my neighborhood supermarket is the rude behavior of other shoppers.

In an essay with the first central point, you could write about three places where you have seen rude behavior. Develop each paragraph with one or more vivid examples.

In an essay on the second central point, you would need to come up with two or three general types of rude behavior to write about. Below is one student's outline for an essay with that topic sentence.

Central idea: A common part of life at my neighborhood supermarket is the rude behavior of other shoppers.

(1) Getting in the way of other shoppers

Blocking the aisle with a cart

Knocking things down and not picking them up

"Parking" in front of all the free samples

(2) Misplacing items

Putting unwanted frozen food on a shelf instead of back in a freezer

Putting unwanted meat on a shelf instead of in a refrigerated section

(3) Unreasonably making others wait at the checkout line

Bringing a bulging cartload to the express line

Keeping a line waiting while running to get "just one more thing" (instead of stepping out of line)

Keeping a line waiting while deciding what not to buy to keep the total price down (instead of keeping track while shopping)

My Daughter Smokes
Alice Walker

PREVIEW	WORDS TO WATCH
Alice Walker is a famous writer, probably best known for her novel *The Color Purple*. In "My Daughter Smokes," her daughter's habit is a stepping stone to a broader discussion of smoking than the title suggests. She goes on to also tell of her father's experience with tobacco and from there slips into a discussion of tobacco that moves through the centuries and across continents.	consort (2) pungent (3) dapper (4) perennially (6) ritual (12) emaciated (13) eradicating (14) futility (16) empathy (17) venerated (17) denatured (17) mono-cropping (17) suppressed (18) redeem (18) cajole (20)

1   My daughter smokes. While she is doing her homework, her feet on the bench in front of her and her calculator clicking out answers to her algebra problems, I am looking at the half-empty package of Camels tossed carelessly close at hand. Camels. I pick them up, take them into the kitchen, where the light is better, and study them—they're filtered, for which I am grateful. My heart feels terrible. I want to weep. In fact, I do weep a little, standing there by the stove holding one of the instruments, so white, so precisely rolled, that could cause my daughter's death. When she smoked Marlboros and Players I hardened myself against feeling so bad; nobody I knew ever smoked these brands.

2   She doesn't know this, but it was Camels that my father, her grandfather, smoked. But before he smoked "ready-mades"—when he was very young and very poor, with eyes like lanterns—he smoked Prince Albert tobacco in cigarettes he rolled himself. I remember the bright-red tobacco tin, with a picture of Queen Victoria's consort,• Prince Albert, dressed in a black frock coat and carrying a cane.

3   The tobacco was dark brown, pungent,• slightly bitter. I tasted it more than once as a child, and the discarded tins could be used for a number of things: to keep buttons and shoelaces in, to store seeds, and best of all, to hold worms for the rare times my father took us fishing.

4   By the late forties and early fifties no one rolled his own anymore (and few women smoked) in my hometown, Eatonton, Georgia. The tobacco industry, coupled with Hollywood movies in which both hero and heroine smoked like chimneys, won over completely people like my father, who were hopelessly addicted to cigarettes. He never looked as dapper• as Prince Albert, though; he continued to look like a poor, overweight, overworked colored man with too large a family; black, with a very white cigarette stuck in his mouth.

5   I do not remember when he started to cough. Perhaps it was unnoticeable at first. A little hacking in the morning as he lit his first cigarette upon getting out of bed. By the time I was my daughter's age, his breath was a wheeze, embarrassing to hear; he could not climb stairs without resting every third or fourth step. It was not unusual for him to cough for an hour.

It is hard to believe there was a time when people did not understand that 6 cigarette smoking is an addiction. I wondered aloud once to my sister—who is perennially* trying to quit—whether our father realized this. I wonder how she, a smoker since high school, viewed her own habit.

It was our father who gave her her first cigarette, one day when she had taken 7 water to him in the fields.

"I always wondered why he did that," she said, puzzled, and with some 8 bitterness.

"What did he say?" I asked. 9

"That he didn't want me to go to anyone else for them," she said, "which never 10 really crossed my mind."

So he was aware it was addictive, I thought, though as annoyed as she that he 11 assumed she would be interested.

I began smoking in eleventh grade, also the year I drank numerous bottles of 12 terrible sweet, very cheap wine. My friends and I, all boys for this venture, bought our supplies from a man who ran a segregated bar and liquor store on the outskirts of town. Over the entrance there was a large sign that said COLORED. We were not permitted to drink here, only to buy. I smoked Kools, because my sister did. By then I thought her toxic darkened lips and gums glamorous. However, my body simply would not tolerate smoke. After six months I had a chronic sore throat. I gave up smoking, gladly. Because it was a ritual* with my buddies—Murl, Leon, and "Dog" Farley—I continued to drink wine.

My father died from "the poor man's friend," pneumonia, one hard winter 13 when his bronchitis and emphysema had left him low. I doubt he had much lung left at all, after coughing for so many years. He had so little breath that, during his last years, he was always leaning on something. I remembered once, at a family reunion, when my daughter was two, that my father picked her up for a minute— long enough for me to photograph them—but the effort was obvious. Near the very end of his life, and largely because he had no more lungs, he quit smoking. He gained a couple of pounds, but by then he was so emaciated* no one noticed.

When I travel to Third World countries I see many people like my father 14 and daughter. There are large billboards directed at them both: the tough, "take-charge," or dapper older man, the glamorous, "worldly" young woman, both puff-ing away. In these poor countries, as in American ghettos and on reservations, money that should be spent for food goes instead to the tobacco companies; over time, people starve themselves of both food and air, effectively weakening and addicting their children, eventually eradicating* themselves. I read in the news-paper and in my gardening magazine that cigarette butts are so toxic that if a baby swallows one, it is likely to die, and that the boiled water from a bunch of them makes an effective insecticide.

My daughter would like to quit, she says. We both know the statistics are 15 against her; most people who try to quit smoking do not succeed.*

There is a deep hurt that I feel as a mother. Some days it is a feeling of futil- 16 ity.* I remember how carefully I ate when I was pregnant, how patiently I taught my daughter how to cross a street safely. For what, I sometimes wonder; so that she can wheeze through most of her life feeling half her strength, and then die of self-poisoning, as her grandfather did?

But, finally, one must feel empathy* for the tobacco plant itself. For thousands 17 of years, it has been venerated* by Native Americans as a sacred medicine. They have used it extensively—its juices, its leaves, its roots, its (holy) smoke—to heal wounds and cure diseases, and in ceremonies of prayer and peace. And though the plant as most of us know it has been poisoned by chemicals and denatured*

*Three months after reading this essay, my daughter stopped smoking.

by intensive mono-cropping• and is therefore hardly the plant it was, still, to some modern Indians it remains a plant of positive power. I learned this when my Native American friends, Bill Wahpepah and his family, visited with me for a few days and the first thing he did was sow a few tobacco seeds in my garden.

Perhaps we can liberate tobacco from those who have captured and abused 18 it, enslaving the plant on large plantations, keeping it from freedom and its kin, and forcing it to enslave the world. Its true nature suppressed,• no wonder it has become deadly. Maybe by sowing a few seeds of tobacco in our gardens and treating the plant with the reverence it deserves, we can redeem• tobacco's soul and restore its self-respect.

Besides, how grim, if one is a smoker, to realize one is smoking a slave.   19

There is a slogan from a battered women's shelter that I especially like: "Peace 20 on earth begins at home." I believe everything does. I think of a slogan for people trying to stop smoking: "Every home a smoke-free zone." Smoking is a form of self-battering that also batters those who must sit by, occasionally cajole• or complain, and helplessly watch. I realize now that as a child I sat by, through the years, and literally watched my father kill himself; surely one such victory in my family, for the rich white men who own the tobacco companies, is enough.

VOCABULARY IN CONTEXT

1. The word *eradicating* in "over time, people starve themselves of both food and air, effectively weakening and addicting their children, eventually eradicating themselves" (paragraph 14) means

   a. curing.

   b. feeding.

   c. destroying.

   d. controlling.

2. The word *venerated* in "For thousands of years, it has been venerated by Native Americans as a sacred medicine. They have used it extensively" (paragraph 17) means

   a. honored.

   b. ignored.

   c. ridiculed.

   d. forgotten.

READING COMPREHENSION QUESTIONS

1. Which of the following sentences best expresses the central idea of the essay?

   a. Most people who try to quit smoking are not successful.

   b. Pained by her daughter's cigarette addiction and the misdeeds of the tobacco companies, Walker urges people to stop smoking.

   c. Native Americans have used the tobacco plant for thousands of years as a sacred medicine and in ceremonies of prayer and peace.

   d. Tobacco advertisements that show healthy, attractive people are misleading.

2. Which sentence best expresses the main idea of paragraph 4?

   a. For Walker's father and others, the reality of smoking was very different from the images shown in ads and movies.

   b. Walker's father smoked because he wanted to be as stylish as Prince Albert.

   c. No one rolled his or her own cigarettes by the 1950s.

   d. Walker's father was poor, overweight, and overworked.

3. Which sentence best expresses the main idea of paragraph 5?

   a. Walker does not know when her father began to cough.

   b. When Walker was her daughter's age, she was embarrassed to hear her father wheezing.

   c. Walker's father's cough began quietly but grew to become a major problem.

   d. Walker's father had great difficulty climbing stairs.

4. Walker is especially upset that her daughter smokes Camel cigarettes because

   a. she believes Camels to be especially bad for people's health.

   b. Camels are the brand that Walker herself smoked as a teenager.

   c. Walker's father, who died as a result of smoking, smoked Camels.

   d. Camels' advertisements are glamorous and misleading.

5. When Walker's father picked up his granddaughter at a family reunion, he

   a. burned the child with his cigarette.

   b. put her down quickly so he could have another cigarette.

   c. warned her against smoking.

   d. was too weak to hold her for long.

6. We can infer that Walker

   a. believes people who are poor, uneducated, and nonwhite have been especially victimized by the tobacco industry.

   b. believes that tobacco should be made illegal.

   c. blames her father for her daughter's decision to smoke.

   d. believes Native Americans were wrong to honor the tobacco plant.

7. We can infer that, for Walker, smoking as a teenager

   a. was strictly forbidden by her parents.

   b. was an exciting experiment.

   c. was quickly habit-forming.

   d. was the end of her friendship with Murl, Leon, and "Dog" Farley.

8. We can infer that Walker's daughter

   a. did not care that her mother was concerned about her smoking.

   b. may have been helped to quit smoking by her mother's essay.

   c. remembered her grandfather well.

   d. did not believe that smoking was harmful to people's health.

DISCUSSION QUESTIONS

About Content

1. How would you deal with a friend who engages in self-destructive behavior, such as smoking, excessive drinking, or taking drugs? Would you ignore the behavior or try to educate the friend about its dangers? Is letting a friend know you are concerned worth risking the friendship?

2. The dangers of smoking are well documented. Study after study shows that smoking leads to a variety of illnesses, including cancer, emphysema, and heart disease. Newer studies are proving that secondhand smoke—smoke that nonsmokers breathe when they are around smokers—is dangerous as well. If you had the power to do so, would you make smoking illegal? Or do you believe that smoking should continue to be an individual's right?

3. Imagine learning that your sixteen-year-old child has begun smoking or drinking, or has become sexually active. Which discovery would worry you most? Would it make a difference if the child were a girl or a boy? What fears would each of these discoveries raise in you? How would you respond to your child?

About Structure

4. In which parts of her essay does Walker use time order? _____

_____

5. Write down what you think are two of the most vivid images in Walker's essay. Then explain how each helps to further her central idea.

_____

_____

_____

6. How does Walker enlarge the significance of her essay so that it becomes more than the story of her daughter's smoking?

_____

_____

_____

_____

_____

_____

About Style and Tone

7. How does Walker's tone contribute to the strength of her argument in this essay?

8. What are some of the richest descriptions in this essay? Why do you think Walker chose to render these particular images in such detail?

RESPONDING TO IMAGES

Describe this photograph in a sentence; then list one or two details that grabbed your attention. Next, compare your description and details with those of at least two other classmates. How did your interpretations and descriptions differ? Did you each mention the same aspects, or did you focus on different ones?

WRITING ASSIGNMENTS

Assignment 1: Writing a Paragraph

Write a paragraph in which you try to persuade a friend to quit smoking. Explain in detail three reasons you think he or she should quit. Use transitions such as *first of all*, *second*, *another*, and *finally* as you list the three reasons.

Assignment 2: Writing a Paragraph

In her essay, Walker is critical of the glamorous, healthy image presented by cigarette advertisements. Write a paragraph in which you describe what you think an honest cigarette advertisement would look like. Who would appear in the ad? What would they be doing? What would they be saying? Use the following as a topic sentence, or write one of your own.

> The elements of an honest cigarette "advertisement" would tempt people not to smoke.

In preparation for this assignment, you might study two or three cigarette ads, using them as inspiration for this assignment. Use the name of a real cigarette or make up a name.

Assignment 3: Writing an Essay

What bad habits do *you* have? Write an essay explaining how you believe you acquired one of those habits, how you think it harms you, and how you could rid yourself of it. You might begin by making a list or questioning to help you find a bad habit you wish to write about. (We all have plenty of bad habits, such as smoking, drinking too much, spending money impulsively, biting our nails, eating too much food, and so on.)

Remember to write an informal outline to guide you in your writing. Here, for example, is one possible outline for this assignment:

Central idea: A bad habit I intend to change is studying for tests at the last minute.

(1) I acquired the habit in high school, where studying at the last minute was often good enough.

For example, I studied for spelling tests in the hallway on the way to class.

Even history tests were easy to study for because our teacher demanded so little.

(2) I've learned the hard way that last-minute studying doesn't work well in college.

During my first quarter, I got the first D I've ever gotten.

I thought memorizing a few names would get me through my first business class, but was I ever wrong.

(3) I took a study skills course, and what I learned is helping me get on the right track.

I learned the benefits of taking class notes, and I'm trying to get better at getting down a written record of each lecture.

I also learned that keeping up with readings and taking notes on a regular basis are needed for some classes.

The writer of the preceding outline still has to come up with many more details to expand each of her points. For instance, why did she get the D, and how did that help motivate her to improve her study habits? Also, what techniques is she experimenting with in her effort to improve her note-taking? She could add such details to her outline, or she could begin working them into her essay when she starts writing.

Six appendixes follow. Appendix A consists of Parts of Speech, and Appendix B is a series of ESL pointers. Appendixes C and D consist of a diagnostic test and an achievement test that measure many of the sentence skills in this book. The diagnostic test can be taken at the outset of your work; the achievement test can be used to measure your progress after you have studied these topics. Appendix E supplies answers to the introductory activities and practice exercises in Part 3. The answers, which you should refer to only after you have worked carefully through each exercise, give you responsibility for testing yourself. (To ensure that the answer key is used as a learning tool only, answers are not given for the review tests. These answers appear only in the Instructor's Manual; they can be copied and handed out at the discretion of your instructor.) Finally, Appendix F provides space for you to record ideas and notes, including a vocabulary list, in A Writer's Journal.

Parts of Speech

www.mhhe.com/langan

Words—the building blocks of sentences—can be divided into eight parts of speech. *Parts of speech* are classifications of words according to their meaning and use in a sentence.

This appendix will explain the eight parts of speech:

nouns	prepositions	conjunctions
pronouns	adjectives	interjections
verbs	adverbs	

Nouns

A *noun* is a word that is used to name something: a person, a place, an object, or an idea. Here are some examples of nouns:

NOUNS			
woman	city	pancake	freedom
Alice Walker	street	diamond	possibility
Steve Martin	Chicago	Corvette	mystery

Most nouns begin with a lowercase letter and are known as *common nouns.* These nouns name general things. Some nouns, however, begin with a capital letter. They are called *proper nouns.* While a common noun refers to a person or thing in general, a proper noun names someone or something specific. For example, *woman* is a common noun—it doesn't name a particular woman. On the other hand, *Alice Walker* is a proper noun because it names a specific woman.

ACTIVITY 1	Using Nouns

Insert any appropriate noun into each of the following blanks.

1. The shoplifter stole a(n) _____ from the department store.

2. _____ threw the football to me.

3. Tiny messages were scrawled on the _____ .

4. A _____ crashed through the window.

5. Give the _____ to Keiko.

Singular and Plural Nouns

A *singular noun* names one person, place, object, or idea. A *plural noun* refers to two or more persons, places, objects, or ideas. Most singular nouns can be made plural with the addition of an *s.*

Some nouns, like *box,* have irregular plurals. You can check the plural of nouns you think may be irregular by looking up the singular form in a dictionary.

SINGULAR AND PLURAL NOUNS

Singular	Plural
goat	goats
alley	alleys
friend	friends
truth	truths
box	boxes

- For more information on nouns, see "Subjects and Verbs," pages 154–161.

Identifying Nouns   ACTIVITY 2

Underline the three nouns in each sentence. Some are singular, and some are plural.

1. Two bats swooped over the heads of the frightened children.

2. The artist has purple paint on her sleeve.

3. The lost dog has fleas and a broken leg.

4. Tiffany does her homework in green ink.

5. Some farmers plant seeds by moonlight.

Pronouns

A *pronoun* is a word that stands for a noun. Pronouns eliminate the need for constant repetition. Look at the following sentences:

www.mhhe.com/langan

The phone rang, and Malik answered the phone.

Lisa met Lisa's friends in the music store at the mall. Lisa meets Lisa's friends there every Saturday.

The waiter rushed over to the new customers. The new customers asked the waiter for menus and coffee.

Now look at how much clearer and smoother these sentences sound with pronouns.

The phone rang, and Malik answered it.

(The pronoun *it* is used to replace the word *phone.*)

Lisa met her friends in the music store at the mall. She meets them there every Saturday.

(The pronoun *her* is used to replace the word *Lisa's.* The pronoun *she* replaces *Lisa.* The pronoun *them* replaces the words *Lisa's friends.*)

The waiter rushed over to the new customers. They asked him for menus and coffee.

(The pronoun *they* is used to replace the words *the new customers.* The pronoun *him* replaces the words *the waiter.*)

Following is a list of commonly used pronouns known as *personal pronouns:*

PERSONAL PRONOUNS

I	you	he	she	it	we	they
me	your	him	her	its	us	them
my	yours	his	hers		our	their

ACTIVITY 3   **Using Personal Pronouns**

Fill in each blank with the appropriate personal pronoun.

1. André feeds his pet lizard every day before school. _____ also gives _____ flies in the afternoon.

2. The reporter interviewed the striking workers. _____ told _____ about their demand for higher wages and longer breaks.

3. Students should save all returned tests. _____ should also keep _____ review sheets.

4. The pilot announced that we would fly through some air pockets. _____ said that we should be past _____ soon.

5. Adolfo returned the calculator to Sheila last Friday. But Sheila insists that _____ never got _____ back.

There are several types of pronouns. For convenient reference, they are described briefly in the box on the following page.

TYPES OF PRONOUNS

Personal pronouns can act in a sentence as subjects, objects, or possessives.

> *Singular:* I, me, my, mine, you, your, yours, he, him, his, she, her, hers, it, its

> *Plural:*   we, us, our, ours, you, your, yours, they, them, their, theirs

Relative pronouns refer to someone or something already mentioned in the sentence.

> who, whose, whom, which, that

Interrogative pronouns are used to ask questions.

> who, whose, whom, which, what

Demonstrative pronouns are used to point out particular persons or things.

> this, that, these, those

> **Note:** Do not use *them* (as in *them* shoes), *this here, that there, these here,* or *those there* to point out.

Reflexive pronouns are those that end in *-self* or *-selves*. A reflexive pronoun is used as the object of a verb (as in *Cary cut **herself***) or the object of a preposition (as in *Jack sent a birthday card to **himself***) when the subject of the verb is the same as the object.

> *Singular:* myself, yourself, himself, herself, itself

> *Plural:*   ourselves, yourselves, themselves

Intensive pronouns have exactly the same forms as reflexive pronouns. The difference is in how they are used. Intensive pronouns are used to add emphasis. (*I **myself** will need to read the contract before I sign it.*)

Indefinite pronouns do not refer to a particular person or thing.

> each, either, everyone, nothing, both, several, all, any, most, none

Reciprocal pronouns express shared actions or feelings.
> each other, one another

- For more information on pronouns, see pages 250–272.

Verbs

Every complete sentence must contain at least one verb. There are two types of verbs: action verbs and linking verbs.

Action Verbs

An *action verb* tells what is being done in a sentence. For example, look at the following sentences:

Mr. Jensen *swatted* at the bee with his hand.

Rainwater *poured* into the storm sewer.

The children *chanted* the words to the song.

In these sentences, the verbs are *swatted*, *poured*, and *chanted*. These words are all action verbs; they tell what is happening in each sentence.

- For more about action verbs, see "Subjects and Verbs," pages 154–161.

| ACTIVITY 4 | Using Action Verbs |

Insert an appropriate word in each blank. That word will be an action verb; it will tell what is happening in the sentence.

1. The surgeon _____ through the first layer of skin.

2. The animals in the cage _____ all day.

3. An elderly woman on the street _____ me for directions.

4. The boy next door _____ our lawn every other week.

5. Our instructor _____ our papers over the weekend.

Linking Verbs

Some verbs are *linking verbs*. These verbs link (or join) a noun to something that is said about it. For example, look at the following sentence:

The clouds *are* steel gray.

In this sentence, *are* is a linking verb. It joins the noun *clouds* to words that describe it: *steel gray*.

Other common linking verbs include *am, is, was, were, look, feel, sound, appear, seem,* and *become.*

- For more about linking verbs, see "Subjects and Verbs," pages 154–161.

| ACTIVITY 5 | Using Linking Verbs |

In each blank, insert one of the following linking verbs: *am, feel, is, look, were.* Use each linking verb once.

1. The important papers _____ in a desk drawer.

2. I _____ anxious to get my test back.

3. The bananas _____ ripe.

4. The grocery store _____ open until 11:00 p.m.

5. Whenever I _____ angry, I go off by myself to calm down.

Helping Verbs

Sometimes the verb of a sentence consists of more than one word. In these cases, the main verb will be joined by one or more *helping verbs*. Look at the following sentence:

The basketball team *will be leaving* for their game at six o'clock.

In this sentence, the main verb is *leaving*. The helping verbs are *will* and *be*.

Other helping verbs include *do, has, have, may, would, can, must, could,* and *should*.

- For more information about helping verbs, see "Subjects and Verbs," pages 154–161, and "Irregular Verbs," pages 219–229.

Using Helping Verbs	ACTIVITY 6

In each blank, insert one of the following helping verbs: *does, must, should, could, has been.* Use each helping verb once.

1. You _____ start writing your paper this weekend.

2. The victim _____ describe her attacker in great detail.

3. You _____ rinse the dishes before putting them into the dishwasher.

4. My neighbor _____ arrested for drunk driving.

5. The bus driver _____ not make any extra stops.

Prepositions

A *preposition* is a word that connects a noun or a pronoun to another word in the sentence. For example, look at the following sentence:

A man *in* the bus was snoring loudly.

In is a preposition. It connects the noun *bus* to *man*. Here is a list of common prepositions:

PREPOSITIONS				
about	before	down	like	to
above	behind	during	of	toward
across	below	except	off	under
after	beneath	for	on	up
among	beside	from	over	with
around	between	in	since	without
at	by	into	through	

The noun or pronoun that a preposition connects to another word in the sentence is called the *object* of the preposition. A group of words beginning with a preposition and ending with its object is called a *prepositional phrase*. The words *in the bus*, for example, are a prepositional phrase.

Now read the following sentences and explanations.

An ant was crawling *up the teacher's leg.*

The noun *leg* is the object of the preposition *up. Up* connects *leg* with the word *crawling*. The prepositional phrase *up the teacher's leg* describes *crawling*. It tells just where the ant was crawling.

The man *with the black moustache* left the restaurant quickly.

The noun *moustache* is the object of the preposition *with*. The prepositional phrase *with the black moustache* describes the word *man*. It tells us exactly which man left the restaurant quickly.

The plant *on the windowsill* was a present *from my mother.*

The noun *windowsill* is the object of the preposition *on*. The prepositional phrase *on the windowsill* describes the word *plant*. It describes exactly which plant was a present.

There is a second prepositional phrase in this sentence. The preposition is *from*, and its object is *mother*. The prepositional phrase *from my mother* explains *present*. It tells who gave the present.

- For more about prepositions, see "Subjects and Verbs," pages 154–161, and "Sentence Variety II," pages 300–313.

ACTIVITY 7	Using Prepositions

In each blank, insert one of the following prepositions: *of, by, with, in, without*. Use each preposition once.

1. The letter from his girlfriend had been sprayed _____ perfume.

2. The weedkiller quickly killed the dandelions _____ our lawn.

3. _____ giving any notice, the tenant moved out of the expensive apartment.

4. Donald hungrily ate three scoops _____ ice cream and an order of French fries.

5. The crates _____ the back door contain glass bottles and old newspapers.

Adjectives

An *adjective* is a word that describes a noun (the name of a person, place, or thing). Look at the following sentence.

The dog lay down on a mat in front of the fireplace.

Now look at this sentence when adjectives have been inserted.

The *shaggy* dog lay down on a *worn* mat in front of the fireplace.

The adjective *shaggy* describes the noun *dog;* the adjective *worn* describes the noun *mat.* Adjectives add spice to our writing. They also help us to identify particular people, places, or things.

Adjectives can be found in two places:

1. An adjective may come before the word it describes (a *damp* night, the *moldy* bread, a *striped* umbrella).

2. An adjective that describes the subject of a sentence may come after a linking verb. The linking verb may be a form of the verb *be* (he *is* **furious**, I *am* **exhausted**, they are **hungry**). Other linking verbs include *feel, look, sound, smell, taste, appear, seem,* and *become* (the soup *tastes* **salty**, your hands *feel* **dry**, the *dog seems* **lost**).

   *   For more information on adjectives, see "Adjectives and Adverbs," pages 274–280.

Using Adjectives

ACTIVITY 8

Write any appropriate adjective in each blank.

1. The _____ pizza was eaten greedily by the _____ teenagers.

2. Melissa gave away the sofa because it was _____ and _____.

3. Although the alley is _____ and _____, Jian often takes it as a shortcut home.

4. The restaurant throws away lettuce that is _____ and tomatoes that are _____.

5. When I woke up in the morning, I had a(n) _____ fever and a(n) _____ throat.

Adverbs

An *adverb* is a word that describes a verb, an adjective, or another adverb. Many adverbs end in the letters *-ly*. Look at the following sentence:

The canary sang in the pet store window as the shoppers greeted each other.

Now look at this sentence after adverbs have been inserted.

The canary sang *softly* in the pet store window as the shoppers *loudly* greeted each other.

The adverbs add details to the sentence. They also allow the reader to contrast the singing of the canary and the noise the shoppers are making.

Look at the following sentences and the explanations of how adverbs are used in each case.

The chef yelled **angrily** at the young waiter.

(The adverb *angrily* describes the verb *yelled.*)

My mother has an **extremely** busy schedule on Tuesdays.
(The adverb *extremely* describes the adjective *busy*.)

The sick man spoke **very** faintly to his loyal nurse.
(The adverb *very* describes the adverb *faintly*.)

Some adverbs do not end in *-ly*. Examples include *very, often, never, always,* and *well.*

- For more information on adverbs, see "Adjectives and Adverbs," pages 274–280.

ACTIVITY 9	Using Adverbs

Fill in each blank with any appropriate adverb.

1. The water in the pot boiled _____ .

2. Carla _____ drove the car through _____ moving traffic.

3. The telephone operator spoke _____ to the young child.

4. The game show contestant waved _____ to his family in the audience.

5. Wes _____ studies, so it's no surprise that he did _____ poorly on his finals.

Conjunctions

A *conjunction* is a word that connects. There are two types of conjunctions: coordinating and subordinating.

Coordinating Conjunctions

Coordinating conjunctions join two equal ideas. Look at the following sentence:

Kevin *and* Steve interviewed for the job, *but* their friend Anne got it.

In this sentence, the coordinating conjunction *and* connects the proper nouns *Kevin* and *Steve.* The coordinating conjunction *but* connects the first part of the sentence, *Kevin* and *Steve interviewed for the job,* to the second part, *their friend Anne got it.*

Following is a list of all the coordinating conjunctions. In this book, they are simply called *joining words.*

COORDINATING CONJUNCTIONS (JOINING WORDS)			
and	so	nor	yet
but	or	for	

- For more on coordinating conjunctions, see information on joining words in "Run-ons," pages 179–194, and "Sentence Variety I," pages 195–208.

Using Coordinating Conjunctions

ACTIVITY 10

Write a coordinating conjunction in each blank. Choose from the following: *and, but, so, or, nor.* Use each conjunction once.

1. Either Jerome _____ Alex scored the winning touchdown.

2. I expected roses for my birthday, _____ I received a vase of plastic tulips from the discount store.

3. The cafeteria was serving liver and onions for lunch, _____ I bought a sandwich at the corner deli.

4. Marian brought a pack of playing cards _____ a pan of brownies to the company picnic.

5. Neither my sofa _____ my armchair matches the rug in my living room.

Subordinating Conjunctions

When a *subordinating conjunction* is added to a word group, the words can no longer stand alone as an independent sentence. They are no longer a complete thought. For example, look at the following sentence:

Karen fainted in class.

The word group *Karen fainted in class* is a complete thought. It can stand alone as a sentence. See what happens when a subordinating conjunction is added to a complete thought:

When Karen fainted in class

Now the words cannot stand alone as a sentence. They are dependent on other words to complete the thought:

When Karen fainted in class, we propped her feet up on some books.

In this book, a word that begins a dependent word group is called a *dependent word*. Subordinating conjunctions are common dependent words. Below are some subordinating conjunctions.

SUBORDINATING CONJUNCTIONS			
after	even if	unless	where
although	even though	until	wherever
as	if	when	whether
because	since	whenever	while
before	though		

Following are some more sentences with subordinating conjunctions:

After she finished her last exam, Irina said, "Now I can relax."

(*After she finished her last exam* is not a complete thought. It is dependent on the rest of the words to make up a complete sentence.)

Lamont listens to audiobooks **while** he drives to work.

(*While he drives to work* cannot stand by itself as a sentence. It depends on the rest of the sentence to make up a complete thought.)

Since apples were on sale, we decided to make an apple pie for dessert.

(*Since apples were on sale* is not a complete sentence. It depends on *we decided to make an apple pie for dessert* to complete the thought.)

- For more information on subordinating conjunctions, see information on dependent words in "Fragments," pages 162–178; "Run-ons," pages 179–194; "Sentence Variety I," pages 195–208; and "Sentence Variety II," pages 300–313.

ACTIVITY 11	Using Subordinating Conjunctions

Write a logical subordinating conjunction in each blank. Choose from the following: *even though, because, until, when, before.* Use each conjunction once.

1. The bank was closed down by federal regulators _____ it lost more money than it earned.

2. _____ Paula wants to look mysterious, she wears dark sunglasses and a scarf.

3. _____ the restaurant was closing in fifteen minutes, customers sipped their coffee slowly and continued to talk.

4. _____ anyone else could answer it, Leon rushed to the phone and whispered, "Is that you?"

5. The waiter was instructed not to serve any food _____ the guest of honor arrived.

Interjections

An *interjection* is a word that can stand independently and is used to express emotion. Examples are *oh, wow, ouch,* and *oops.* These words are usually not found in formal writing.

"*Hey!*" yelled Maggie. "That's my bike."

Oh, we're late for class.

A Final Note

A word may function as more than one part of speech. For example, the word *dust* can be a verb or a noun, depending on its role in the sentence.

I *dust* my bedroom once a month, whether it needs it or not. (verb)

The top of my refrigerator is covered with an inch of *dust.* (noun)

ESL Pointers

This section covers rules that most native speakers of English take for granted but that are useful for speakers of English as a second language (ESL or ESOL).

Articles

Types of Articles

An *article* is a noun marker—it signals that a noun will follow. There are two kinds of articles: indefinite and definite. The indefinite articles are *a* and *an*. Use *a* before a word that begins with a consonant sound:

a desk, **a p**hotograph, **a u**nicycle

(*A* is used before *unicycle* because the *u* in that word sounds like the consonant *y* plus *u*, not a vowel sound.)

Use *an* before a word beginning with a vowel sound:

an error, **an o**bject, **an h**onest woman

(*Honest* begins with a vowel sound because the *h* is silent.)

The definite article is *the.*

the sofa, **the** cup

An article may come right before a noun:

a magazine, **the** candle

Or an article may be separated from the noun by words that describe the noun:

a popular magazine, **the** fat red candle

> **TIP** There are various other noun markers, including quantity words (*a few, many, a lot of*), numerals (*one, thirteen, 710*), demonstrative adjectives (*this, these*), adjectives (*my, your, our*), and possessive nouns (*Raoul's, the school's*).

Articles with Count and Noncount Nouns

To know whether to use an article with a noun and which article to use, you must recognize count and noncount nouns. (A *noun* is a word used to name something—a person, place, thing, or idea.)

Count nouns name people, places, things, or ideas that can be counted and made into plurals, such as *pillow, heater,* and *mail carrier* (*one pillow, two heaters, three mail carriers*).

Noncount nouns refer to things or ideas that cannot be counted and therefore cannot be made into plurals, such as *sunshine, gold,* and *toast.* The box below lists and illustrates common types of noncount nouns.

COMMON NONCOUNT NOUNS

Abstractions and emotions: justice, tenderness, courage, knowledge, embarrassment

Activities: jogging, thinking, wondering, golf, hoping, sleep

Foods: oil, rice, pie, butter, spaghetti, broccoli

Gases and vapors: carbon dioxide, oxygen, smoke, steam, air

Languages and areas of study: Korean, Italian, geology, arithmetic, history

Liquids: coffee, kerosene, lemonade, tea, water, bleach

Materials that come in bulk or mass form: straw, firewood, sawdust, cat litter, cement

Natural occurrences: gravity, sleet, rain, lightning, rust

Other things that cannot be counted: clothing, experience, trash, luggage, room, furniture, homework, machinery, cash, news, transportation, work

---

The quantity of a noncount noun can be expressed with a word or words called a *qualifier,* such as *some, more, a unit of,* and so on. In the following two examples, the qualifiers are shown in *italic* type, and the noncount nouns are shown in **boldface** type.

How *much* **experience** have you had as a salesclerk?

Our tiny kitchen doesn't have *enough* **room** for a table and chairs.

Some words can be either count or noncount nouns depending on whether they refer to one or more individual items or to something in general:

Three **chickens** are running around our neighbor's yard.

(This sentence refers to particular chickens; *chicken* in this case is a count noun.)

Would you like some more **chicken?**

(This sentence refers to chicken in general; in this case, *chicken* is a noncount noun.)

Using *a* or *an* with Nonspecific Singular Count Nouns Use *a* or *an* with singular nouns that are nonspecific. A noun is nonspecific when the reader doesn't know its specific identity.

> **A** photograph can be almost magical. It saves a moment's image for many years.
>
> (The sentence refers to any photograph, not a specific one.)
>
> **An** article in the newspaper today made me laugh.
>
> (The reader isn't familiar with the article. This is the first time it is mentioned.)

Using *the* with Specific Nouns In general, use *the* with all specific nouns—specific singular, plural, and noncount nouns. A noun is specific—and therefore requires the article *the*—in the following cases:

- When it has already been mentioned once:

  An article in the newspaper today made me laugh. **The** article was about a talking parrot who frightened away a thief.

  (*The* is used with the second mention of *article*.)

- When it is identified by a word or phrase in the sentence:

  The song that is playing now is a favorite of mine.

  (*Song* is identified by the words *that is playing now*.)

- When its identity is suggested by the general context:

  The service at Joe's Bar and Grill is never fast.

  (*Service* is identified by the words *at Joe's Bar and Grill*.)

- When it is unique:

  Some people see a man's face in **the** moon, while others see a rabbit.

  (Earth has only one moon.)

- When it comes after a superlative adjective (for example, *best*, *biggest*, or *wisest*):

  The funniest movie I've seen is *Young Frankenstein*.

Omitting Articles Omit articles with nonspecific plurals and nonspecific noncount nouns. Plurals and noncount nouns are nonspecific when they refer to something in general.

> Stories are popular with most children.
>
> Service is almost as important as food to a restaurant's success.
>
> Movies can be rented from many supermarkets as well as video stores.

Using *the* with Proper Nouns

Proper nouns name particular people, places, things, or ideas and are always capitalized. Most proper nouns do not require articles; those that do, however, require *the*. Following are general guidelines about when not to use *the* and when to use *the*.

Do not use *the* for most singular proper nouns, including names of the following:

- *People and animals* (Tom Cruise, Fluffy)
- *Continents, states, cities, streets, and parks* (South America, Utah, Boston, Baker Street, People's Park)
- *Most countries* (Cuba, Indonesia, Ireland)
- *Individual bodies of water, islands, and mountains* (Lake Michigan, Captiva Island, Mount McKinley)

Use *the* for the following types of proper nouns:

- *Plural proper nouns* (the Harlem Globetrotters, the Marshall Islands, the Netherlands, the Atlas Mountains)
- *Names of large geographic areas, deserts, oceans, seas, and rivers* (the Midwest, the Kalahari Desert, the Pacific Ocean, the Sargasso Sea, the Nile River)
- *Names with the format "the _____ of _____ "* (the king of Morocco, the Strait of Gibraltar, the University of Illinois)

ACTIVITY 1	**Using Articles**

Underline the correct word or words in parentheses.

1. (Map, The map) on the wall is old and out of date.
2. To show (affection, the affection), a cat will rub against you and purr.
3. This morning my daughter sang (a song, the song) I had not heard before.
4. She had learned (a song, the song) in her kindergarten class.
5. When Javier takes a test, he always begins by answering (the easiest, easiest) questions.
6. (Nile River, The Nile River) has been used for irrigation in Egypt since 4,000 BC.
7. Although (Sahara Desert, the Sahara Desert) is very hot during the day, it can get terribly cold at night.
8. The reason we don't fall off the Earth is the pull of (gravity, the gravity).
9. (Patience, The patience) is not always a virtue.
10. Don't forget to put the (garbage, garbages) out to be picked up Wednesday morning.

Subjects and Verbs

Avoiding Repeated Subjects

In English, a particular subject can be used only once in a word group with a subject and a verb (that is, a clause). Don't repeat a subject in the same word group by following a noun with a pronoun.

Incorrect: My *parents they* live in Miami.

Correct: My **parents** live in Miami.

Correct: **They** live in Miami.

Even when the subject and verb are separated by several words, the subject cannot be repeated in the same word group.

Incorrect: The *windstorm* that happened last night *it* damaged our roof.

Correct: The **windstorm** that happened last night **damaged** our roof.

Including Pronoun Subjects and Linking Verbs

Some languages omit a subject that is a pronoun, but in English, every sentence other than a command must have a subject. In a command, the subject *you* is understood: (You) Hand in your papers now.

Incorrect: The soup tastes terrible. *Is* much too salty.

Correct: The soup tastes terrible. **It is** much too salty.

Every English sentence must also have a verb, even when the meaning of the sentence is clear without the verb.

Incorrect: The table covered with old newspapers.

Correct: The table **is** covered with old newspapers.

Including *There* and *Here* at the Beginning of Sentences

Some English sentences begin with *there* or *here* plus a linking verb (usually a form of *to be: is, are,* and so on). In such sentences, the verb comes before the subject.

There are ants all over the kitchen counter.
(The subject is the plural noun *ants,* so the plural verb *are* is used.)

Here is the bug spray.
(The subject is the singular noun *spray,* so the singular verb *is* is used.)

In sentences like those above, remember not to omit *there* or *here.*

Incorrect: *Are* several tests scheduled for Friday.

Correct: **There are** several tests scheduled for Friday.

Not Using the Progressive Tense of Certain Verbs

The progressive tenses are made up of forms of *be* plus the *-ing* form of the main verb. They express actions or conditions still in progress at a particular time.

The garden **will be blooming** when you visit me in June.

However, verbs for mental states, the senses, possession, and inclusion are normally not used in the progressive tense.

Incorrect: I **am knowing** a lot about auto mechanics.

Correct: I **know** a lot about auto mechanics.

Incorrect: Gerald **is having** a job as a supermarket cashier.

Correct: Gerald **has** a job as a supermarket cashier.

Common verbs not generally used in the progressive tense are listed in the following box.

COMMON VERBS NOT GENERALLY USED IN THE PROGRESSIVE

Verbs relating to thoughts, attitudes, and desires: agree, believe, imagine, know, like, love, prefer, think, understand, want, wish

Verbs showing sense perceptions: hear, see, smell, taste

Verbs relating to appearances: appear, look, seem

Verbs showing possession: belong, have, own, possess

Verbs showing inclusion: contain, include

Using Gerunds and Infinitives after Verbs

Before learning the rules about gerunds and infinitives, you must understand what they are. A *gerund* is the *-ing* form of a verb that is used as a noun:

Reading is a good way to improve one's vocabulary.

(*Reading* is the subject of the sentence.)

An *infinitive* is *to* plus the basic form of the verb (the form in which the verb is listed in the dictionary), as in **to eat.** The infinitive can function as an adverb, an adjective, or a noun.

On weekends, Betsy works at a convenience store **to make** some extra money.

(*To make some extra money* functions as an adverb that describes the verb *works*.)

My advisor showed me a good way **to study** for a test.

(*To study for a test* functions as an adjective describing the noun *way*.)

To forgive can be a relief.

(*To forgive* functions as a noun—it is the subject of the verb *can be*.)

Some verbs can be followed by only a gerund or only an infinitive; other verbs can be followed by either. Examples are given in the following lists. There are many others; watch for them in your reading.

Verb + gerund (*enjoy + skiing*)
Verb + preposition + gerund (*think + about + coming*)

Some verbs can be followed by a gerund but not by an infinitive. In many cases, there is a preposition (such as *for, in,* or *of*) between the verb and the gerund. Following are some verbs and verb-preposition combinations that can be followed by gerunds but not by infinitives:

admit	deny	look forward to
apologize for	discuss	postpone
appreciate	dislike	practice
approve of	enjoy	suspect of
avoid	feel like	talk about
be used to	finish	thank for
believe in	insist on	think about

Incorrect: The governor *avoids to make* enemies.

Correct: The governor **avoids making** enemies.

Incorrect: I *enjoy to go* to movies alone.

Correct: I **enjoy going** to movies alone.

Verb + infinitive (*agree + to leave*)

Following are common verbs that can be followed by an infinitive but not by a gerund:

agree	decide	manage
arrange	expect	refuse
claim	have	wait

Incorrect: I *arranged paying* my uncle's bills while he was ill.

Correct: I **arranged to pay** my uncle's bills while he was ill.

Verb + noun or pronoun + infinitive (*cause + them + to flee*)

Below are common verbs that are first followed by a noun or pronoun and then by an infinitive, not a gerund.

cause	force	remind
command	persuade	warn

Incorrect: The flood *forced them leaving* their home.

Correct: The flood **forced them to leave** their home.

Following are common verbs that can be followed either by an infinitive alone or by a noun or pronoun and an infinitive:

ask	need	want
expect	promise	would like

Rita **expects to go** to college.

Rita's parents **expect her to go** to college.

Verb + gerund or infinitive (*begin + packing* or *begin + to pack*)

Following are verbs that can be followed by either a gerund or an infinitive:

begin	hate	prefer
continue	love	start

The meaning of each verb in the box above remains the same or almost the same whether a gerund or an infinitive is used.

I love **to sleep** late.

I love **sleeping** late.

With the verbs below, the gerunds and the infinitives have very different meanings.

forget	remember	stop

Yuri **forgot putting money** in the parking meter.
(He put money in the parking meter, but then he forgot that he had done so.)

Yuri **forgot to put money** in the parking meter.
(He neglected to put money in the parking meter.)

ACTIVITY 2 — Using Subjects and Verbs

Underline the correct word or words in parentheses.

1. The coffee table (wobbles, it wobbles) because one leg is loose.

2. The firewood is very dry. (Is, It is) burning quickly.

3. (Are knives and forks, There are knives and forks) in that drawer.

4. Olivia (seems, is seeming) sad today.

5. Our instructor warned us (studying, to study) hard for the exam.

6. When the little boy saw his birthday presents, he (very excited, became very excited).

7. Do you (feel like walking, feel like to walk) home?

8. A vegetarian (refuses eating, refuses to eat) meat.

9. The alarm on my watch (it started beeping, started beeping) in the middle of the church service.

10. I like small parties, but my boyfriend (prefers, is preferring) large, noisy ones.

Adjectives

Following the Order of Adjectives in English

www.mhhe.com/langan

Adjectives describe nouns and pronouns. In English, an adjective usually comes directly before the word it describes or after a linking verb (a form of *be* or a "sense" verb such as *look, seem,* or *taste*), in which case it modifies the subject of the sentence. In each of the following two sentences, the adjective is **boldfaced** and the noun it describes is *italicized*.

Marta has **beautiful** *eyes.*

Marta's *eyes* are **beautiful.**

When more than one adjective modifies the same noun, the adjectives are usually stated in a certain order, though there are often exceptions. Following is the typical order of English adjectives:

TYPICAL ORDER OF ADJECTIVES IN A SERIES

1. Article or other noun marker: a, an, the, Helen's, this, seven, your

2. Opinion adjective: rude, enjoyable, surprising, easy

3. Size: tall, huge, small, compact

4. Shape: triangular, oval, round, square

5. Age: ancient, new, old, young

6. Color: gray, blue, pink, green

7. Nationality: Greek, Thai, Korean, Ethiopian

8. Religion: Hindu, Methodist, Jewish, Islamic

9. Material: fur, copper, stone, velvet

10. Noun used as an adjective: book (as in *book report*), picture (as in *picture frame*), tea (as in *tea bag*)

Here are some examples of the order of adjectives:

an exciting new movie

the petite young Irish woman

my favorite Chinese restaurant

Greta's long brown leather coat

In general, use no more than two adjectives after the article or another noun marker. Numerous adjectives in a series can be awkward: **that comfortable big old green velvet** couch.

Using the Present and Past Participles as Adjectives

The present participle ends in *-ing*. Past participles of regular verbs end in *-ed* or *-d*; a list of the past participles of many common irregular verbs appears on pages 220–222. Both types of participles may be used as adjectives. A participle used as an adjective may come before the word it describes:

> There was a **frowning** *security guard.*

A participle used as an adjective may also follow a linking verb and describe the subject of the sentence:

> The *security guard* was **frowning.**

While both present and past participles of a particular verb may be used as adjectives, their meanings differ. Use the present participle to describe whoever or whatever causes a feeling:

> a **disappointing** *date*
>
> (The date *caused* the disappointment.)

Use the past participle to describe whoever or whatever experiences the feeling:

> the **disappointed** *neighbor*
>
> (The neighbor *is* disappointed.)

Here are two more sentences that illustrate the differing meanings of present and past participles.

> The waiter was **irritating.**
>
> The diners were **irritated.**
>
> (The waiter caused the irritation; the diners experienced the irritation.)

The following box shows pairs of present and past participles with similar distinctions.

annoying / annoyed	exhausting / exhausted
boring / bored	fascinating / fascinated
confusing / confused	surprising / surprised
depressing / depressed	tiring / tired
exciting / excited	

ACTIVITY 3   Using Adjectives

Underline the correct word or wording in parentheses.

1. When my grandfather died, he left me his (big old oak, old big oak) seaman's chest.

2. The guest lecturer at today's class was a (young Vietnamese Buddhist, Vietnamese Buddhist young) nun.

3. Yolanda's family lives in a (gray huge stone, huge gray stone) farmhouse.

4. Doesn't working all day and studying at night make you very (tired, tiring)?

5. The (fascinated, fascinating) children begged the magician to tell them how he made a rabbit disappear.

Prepositions Used for Time and Place

The use of a preposition in English is often not based on its common meaning, and there are many exceptions to general rules. As a result, correct use of prepositions must be learned gradually through experience. Following is a chart showing how three of the most common prepositions are used in some customary references to time and place:

USE OF *ON*, *IN*, AND *AT* TO REFER TO TIME AND PLACE

Time

On a specific day: on Wednesday, on January 11, on Halloween

In a part of a day: in the morning, in the daytime (but *at* night)

In a month or a year: in October, in 1776

In a period of time: in a second, in a few days, in a little while

At a specific time: at 11:00 p.m., at midnight, at sunset, at lunchtime

Place

On a surface: on the shelf, on the sidewalk, on the roof

In a place that is enclosed: in the bathroom, in the closet, in the drawer

At a specific location: at the restaurant, at the zoo, at the school

---

Using Prepositions ACTIVITY 4

Underline the correct preposition in parentheses.

1. May I come see you (on, at) Saturday?

2. We will eat dinner (on, at) 7:00 p.m.

3. I found this book (on, in) the library.

4. Alex will be leaving for the army (in, at) a week.

5. David and Lisa met each other (on, at) the post office.

REVIEW TEST

Underline the correct word or words in parentheses.

1. I had to pull off the road because of the heavy (hail, hails).

2. (Are, There are) fresh cookies on the kitchen table.

3. Theresa does not like living alone—she becomes (frightening, frightened) at every little sound.

4. Have you gotten used to working (in, at) night?

5. Carla (practiced to give, practiced giving) her speech at least ten times.

6. What a (pretty red, red pretty) scarf you are wearing today!

7. That antique car (belongs to, is belonging to) my cousin.

8. Fireworks are set off (on, in) the Fourth of July to commemorate the American Revolution.

9. The newlyweds' apartment does not contain much (furnitures, furniture).

10. Paul's favorite pastime is going to (the rock concerts, rock concerts).

Sentence-Skills Diagnostic Test

Part 1

This diagnostic test will help check your knowledge of a number of sentence skills. In each item below, certain words are underlined. Write *X* in the answer space if you think a mistake appears at the underlined part. Write *C* in the answer space if you think the underlined part is correct.

The headings within the text ("Fragments," "Run-ons," and so on) will give you clues to the mistakes to look for. However, you do not have to understand the heading to find a mistake. What you are checking is your own sense of effective written English.

Fragments

_____ 1. Because I didn't want to get wet. I waited for a break in the downpour. Then I ran for the car like an Olympic sprinter.

_____ 2. The baby birds chirped loudly, especially when their mother brought food to them. Their mouths gaped open hungrily.

_____ 3. Trying to avoid running into anyone. Cal wheeled his baby son around the crowded market. He wished that strollers came equipped with flashing hazard lights.

_____ 4. The old woman combed out her long, gray hair. She twisted it into two thick braids. And wrapped them around her head like a crown.

Run-ons

_____ 5. Irene fixed fruits and healthy sandwiches for her son's lunch, he traded them for cupcakes, cookies, and chips.

_____ 6. Angie's dark eyes were the color of mink they matched her glowing complexion.

_____ 7. My mother keeps sending me bottles of vitamins, but I keep forgetting to take them.

_____ 8. The little boy watched the line of ants march across the ground, he made a wall of Popsicle sticks to halt the ants' advance.

Standard English Verbs

_____ 9. When she's upset, Mary tells her troubles to her houseplants.

_____ 10. The street musician counted the coins in his donations basket and pack his trumpet in its case.

_____ 11. I tried to pull off my rings, but they was stuck on my swollen fingers.

_____ 12. Belle's car have a horn that plays six different tunes.

Irregular Verbs

_____ 13. I've swam in this lake for years, and I've never seen it so shallow.

_____ 14. The phone rung once and then stopped.

_____ 15. Five different people had brought huge bowls of potato salad to the barbecue.

_____ 16. The metal ice cube trays froze to the bottom of the freezer.

Subject-Verb Agreement

_____ 17. The songs in my iPod is arranged in alphabetical order.

_____ 18. There was only one burner working on the old gas stove.

_____ 19. My aunt and uncle gives a party every Groundhog Day.

_____ 20. One of my sweaters have moth holes in the sleeves.

Consistent Verb Tense

_____ 21. After I turned off the ignition, the engine continued to sputter for several minutes.

_____ 22. Before cleaning the oven, I lined the kitchen floor with newspapers, open the windows, and shook the can of aerosol foam.

Pronoun Reference, Agreement, and Point of View

_____ 23. All visitors should stay in their cars while driving through the wild animal park.

_____ 24. At the library, they showed me how to use the microfilm machines.

_____ 25. As I slowed down at the scene of the accident, you could see long black skid marks on the highway.

Pronoun Types

_____ 26. My husband is more sentimental than me .

_____ 27. Andy and I made ice cream in an old-fashioned wooden machine.

Adjectives and Adverbs

_____ 28. Brian drives so reckless that no one will join his carpool.

_____ 29. Miriam pulled impatiently at the rusty zipper.

_____ 30. I am more happier with myself now that I earn my own money.

_____ 31. The last screw on the license plate was the most corroded one of all.

Misplaced Modifiers

_____ 32. I stretched out on the lounge chair wearing my bikini bathing suit.

_____ 33. I replaced the shingle on the roof that was loose.

Dangling Modifiers

_____ 34. While doing the dishes, a glass shattered in the soapy water.

_____ 35. Pedaling as fast as possible, Todd tried to outrace the snapping dog.

Faulty Parallelism

_____ 36. Before I could take a bath, I had to pick up the damp towels on the floor, gather up the loose toys in the room, and the tub had to be scrubbed out.

_____ 37. I've tried several cures for my headaches, including drugs, meditation, exercise, and massaging my head.

Capital Letters

_____ 38. This fall we plan to visit Cape Cod.

_____ 39. Vern ordered a set of tools from the sears catalog.

_____ 40. When my aunt visits us, she insists on doing all the cooking.

_____ 41. Maureen asked, "will you split a piece of cheesecake with me?"

Numbers and Abbreviations

_____ 42. Before I could stop myself, I had eaten 6 glazed doughnuts.

_____ 43. At 10:45 a.m., a partial eclipse of the sun will begin.

_____ 44. Larry, who is now over six ft. tall, can no longer sleep comfortably in a twin bed.

End Marks

_____ 45. Jane wondered if her husband was telling the truth.

_____ 46. Does that stew need some salt?

Apostrophes

_____ 47. Elizabeths thick, curly hair is her best feature.

_____ 48. I tried to see through the interesting envelope sent to my sister but couldnt.

_____ 49. Pam's heart almost stopped beating when Roger jumped out of the closet.

_____ 50. The logs' in the fireplace crumbled in a shower of sparks.

Quotation Marks

_____ 51. Someone once said, "A lie has no legs and cannot stand."

_____ 52. "This repair job could be expensive, the mechanic warned."

_____ 53. "My greatest childhood fear," said Sheila, "was being sucked down the bathtub drain."

_____ 54. "I was always afraid of everybody's father, said Suzanne, except my own."

Commas

_____ 55. The restaurant's "sundae bar" featured bowls of whipped cream chopped nuts and chocolate sprinkles.

_____ 56. My sister, who studies karate, installed large practice mirrors in our basement.

_____ 57. When I remove my thick eyeglasses the world turns into an out-of-focus movie.

_____ 58. Gloria wrapped her son's presents in pages from the comics section, and she glued a small toy car atop each gift.

Spelling

_____ 59. When Terry practices scales on the piano, her whole family wears earplugs.

_____ 60. I wondered if it was alright to wear sneakers with my three-piece suit.

_____ 61. The essay test question asked us to describe two different theorys of evolution.

_____ 62. A thief stole several large hanging plants from Marlo's porch.

Omitted Words and Letters

_____ 63. After dark, I'm afraid to look in the closets or under the bed.

_____ 64. I turned on the television, but baseball game had been rained out.

_____ 65. Polar bear cubs stay with their mother for two year.

Commonly Confused Words

_____ 66. Before your about to start the car, press the gas pedal to the floor once.

_____ 67. The frog flicked it's tongue out and caught the fly.

_____ 68. I was to lonely to enjoy the party.

_____ 69. The bats folded their wings around them like leather overcoats.

Effective Word Choice

_____ 70. If the professor gives me a break, I might pass the final exam.

_____ 71. Harry worked like a dog all summer to save money for his tuition.

_____ 72. Because Monday is a holiday, sanitation engineers will pick up your trash on Tuesday.

_____ 73. Our family's softball game ended in an argument, as usual.

_____ 74. As for my own opinion, I feel that nuclear weapons should be banned.

_____ 75. This law is, for all intents and purposes, a failure.

Part 2 (Optional)

Do the following at your instructor's request. This second part of the test will provide more detailed information about skills you need to know. On a separate piece of paper, number and correct all the items that you marked with an X in Part I. For example, suppose you had marked the word groups below with an X. (Note that these examples are not taken from the actual test.)

4. When I picked up the tire. Something in my back snapped. I could not stand up straight.

7. The phone started ringing, then the doorbell sounded as well.

15. Marks goal is to save enough money to get married next year.

29. Without checking the rearview mirror the driver pulled out into the passing lane.

Here is how you should write your corrections on a separate sheet of paper:

4. When I picked up the tire, something in my back snapped.

7. The phone started ringing, and then the doorbell sounded as well.

15. Mark's

29. mirror, the driver

There are over forty corrections to make in all.

Sentence-Skills Achievement Test

Part I

This achievement test will help you check your mastery of a number of sentence skills. In each item below, certain words are underlined. Write *X* in the answer space if you think a mistake appears at the underlined part. Write *C* in the answer space if you think the underlined part is correct.

The headings within the test ("Fragments," "Run-ons," and so on) will give you clues to the mistakes to look for.

Fragments

_____ 1. When the town's bully died. Hundreds of people came to his funeral. They wanted to make sure he was dead.

_____ 2. Suzanne adores junk foods, especially onion-flavored potato chips. She can eat an entire bag at one sitting.

_____ 3. My brother stayed up all night. Studying the rules in his driver's manual. He wanted to get his license on the first try.

_____ 4. Hector decided to take a study break. He picked up *TV Guide.* And flipped through the pages to find that night's listings.

Run-ons

_____ 5. Ronnie leaned forward in his seat, he could not hear what the instructor was saying.

_____ 6. Our television set obviously needs repairs the color keeps fading from the picture.

_____ 7. Nick and Fran enjoyed their trip to Chicago, but they couldn't wait to get home.

_____ 8. I tuned in the weather forecast on the radio, I had to decide what to wear.

Standard English Verbs

_____ 9. My sister Louise walks a mile to the bus stop every day.

_____ 10. The play was ruined when the quarterback fumble the handoff.

_____ 11. When the last guests left our party, we was exhausted but happy.

_____ 12. I don't think my mother have gone out to a movie in years.

Irregular Verbs

_____ 13. My roommate and I seen a double feature this weekend.

_____ 14. My nephew must have growed six inches since last summer.

_____ 15. I should have brought a gift to the office holiday party.

_____ 16. After playing touch football all afternoon, Al drank a quart of Gatorade.

Subject-Verb Agreement

_____ 17. The cost of those new tires are more than I can afford.

_____ 18. Nick and Fran give a New Year's Eve party every year.

_____ 19. There was only two slices of cake left on the plate.

_____ 20. Each of the fast-food restaurants have a breakfast special.

Consistent Verb Tense

_____ 21. After I folded the towels in the basket, I remembered that I hadn't washed them yet.

_____ 22. Before she decided to buy the wall calendar, Joanne turns its pages and looked at all the pictures.

Pronoun Reference, Agreement, and Point of View

_____ 23. All drivers should try their best to be courteous during rush hour.

_____ 24. When Bob went to the bank for a home improvement loan, they asked him for three credit references.

_____ 25. I like to shop at factory outlets because you can always get brand names at a discount.

Pronoun Types

_____ 26. My brother writes much more neatly than me.

_____ 27. Vonnie and I are both taking Introduction to Business this semester.

Adjectives and Adverbs

_____ 28. When the elevator doors closed sudden, three people were trapped inside.

_____ 29. The homeless woman glared angrily at me when I offered her a dollar bill.

_____ 30. Frank couldn't decide which vacation he liked best, a bicycle trip or a week at the beach.

_____ 31. I find proofreading a paper much more difficult than writing one.

Misplaced Modifiers

_____ 32. The car was parked along the side of the road with a flat tire.

_____ 33. We bought a television set at our neighborhood discount store that has stereo sound.

Dangling Modifiers

_____ 34. While looking for bargains at Target, an exercise bike caught my eye.

_____ 35. Hurrying to catch the bus, Donna fell and twisted her ankle.

Faulty Parallelism

_____ 36. Before she leaves for work, Agnes makes her lunch, does fifteen minutes of calisthenics, and her two cats have to be fed.

_____ 37. Three remedies for insomnia are warm milk, taking a hot bath, and sleeping pills.

Capital Letters

_____ 38. Every Saturday I get up early, even though I have the choice of sleeping late.

_____ 39. We stopped at the drugstore for some crest toothpaste.

_____ 40. Rows of crocuses appear in my front yard every spring.

_____ 41. The cashier said, "sorry, but children under three are not allowed in this theater."

Numbers and Abbreviations

_____ 42. Our train finally arrived—2 hours late.

_____ 43. Answers to the chapter questions start on page 293.

_____ 44. Three yrs. from now, my new car will finally be paid off.

End Marks

_____ 45. I had no idea who was inside the gorilla suit at the Halloween party.

_____ 46. Are you taking the makeup exam.

Apostrophes

_____ 47. My fathers favorite old television program is _Star Trek._

_____ 48. I couldnt understand a word of that lecture.

_____ 49. My dentist's recommendation was that I floss after brushing my teeth.

_____ 50. Three house's on our street are up for sale.

Quotation Marks

_____ 51. Garfield the cat is fond of saying, "I never met a carbohydrate I didn't like."

_____ 52. "This restaurant does not accept credit cards, the waiter said."

_____ 53. Two foods that may prevent cancer," said the scientist, "are those old standbys spinach and carrots."

_____ 54. "I can't get anything done," Dad complained, if you two insist on making all that noise."

Commas

_____ 55. The snack bar offered overdone hamburgers rubbery hot dogs and soggy pizza.

_____ 56. My sister, who regards every living creature as a holy thing, cannot even swat a housefly.

_____ 57. When I smelled something burning I realized I hadn't turned off the oven.

_____ 58. Marge plays the musical saw at parties, and her husband does Dracula imitations.

Spelling

_____ 59. No one will be admitted without a valid student identification card.

_____ 60. Pat carrys a full course load in addition to working as the night manager at a supermarket.

_____ 61. Did you feel alright after eating Ralph's special chili?

_____ 62. My parents were disappointed when I didn't enter the family busines.

Omitted Words and Letters

_____ 63. Both high schools in my hometown offer evening classes for adults.

_____ 64. I opened new bottle of ketchup and then couldn't find the cap.

_____ 65. Visiting hour for patients at this hospital are from noon to eight.

Commonly Confused Words

_____ 66. Shelley has always been to self-conscious to speak up in class.

_____   67. Its not easy to return to college after raising a family.

_____   68. "Thank you for you're generous contribution," the letter began.

_____   69. Nobody knew whose body had been found floating in the swimming pool.

Effective Word Choice

_____   70. My roommate keeps getting on my case about leaving clothing on the floor.

_____   71. Karla decided to take the bull by the horns and ask her boss for a raise.

_____   72. Although Lamont accelerated his vehicle, he was unable to pass the truck.

_____   73. When the movie ended suddenly, I felt I had been cheated.

_____   74. In light of the fact that I am on a diet, I have stopped eating between meals.

_____   75. Personally, I do not think that everyone should be allowed to vote.

Part 2 (Optional)

Do the following at your instructor's request. This second part of the test will provide more detailed information about which skills you have mastered and which skills you still need to work on. On a separate piece of paper, number and correct all the items that you marked with an X in Part I. For example, suppose you had marked the word groups below with an X. (Note that these examples were not taken from the actual test.)

4. When I picked up the tire. Something in my back snapped. I could not stand up straight.

7. The phone started ringing, then the doorbell sounded as well.

15. Marks goal is to save enough money to get married next year.

29. Without checking the rearview mirror the driver pulled out into the passing lane.

Here is how you should write your corrections on a separate sheet of paper:

4. When I picked up the tire, something in my back snapped.

7. The phone started ringing, and then the doorbell sounded as well.

15. Mark's

29. mirror, the driver

There are over forty corrections to make in all.

Answers to Activities in Part 3

This answer key can help you teach yourself. Use it to find out why you got some answers wrong—you want to uncover any weak spot in your understanding of a given skill. By using the answer key in an honest and thoughtful way, you will master each skill and prepare yourself for many tests in this book that have no answer key.

CHAPTER 6: Subjects and Verbs

Introductory Activity (page 154)

Activity 1: Finding Subjects and Verbs (page 156)

1. Carl spilled
2. ladybug landed
3. Nick eats
4. waitress brought
5. I found
6. Diane stapled
7. audience applauded
8. boss has
9. I tasted
10. paperboy threw

Activity 2: Subject and Linking Verbs (page 156)

1. parents are
2. I am
3. Tri Lee was
4. dog becomes
5. Estelle seems
6. hot dog looks.
7. people appear
8. students felt
9. cheeseburger has
10. telephone seemed

Activity 3: Subjects and Verbs (page 157)

1. rabbits ate
2. father prefers
3. restaurant donated
4. Stanley looks
5. couple relaxed
6. Lightning brightened
7. council voted
8. throat kept
9. sister decided
10. I chose

Activity 4: Subjects and Prepositional Phrases (page 158)

1. By accident, Anita dropped her folder into the mailbox.
2. Before the test, I glanced through my notes.
3. My car stalled on the bridge at rush hour.
4. I hung a photo of Whitney Houston above my bed.
5. On weekends, we visit my grandmother at a nursing home.
6. During the movie, some teenagers giggled at the love scenes.
7. A pedestrian tunnel runs beneath the street to the train station.
8. The parents hid their daughter's Christmas gifts in the garage.

9. All the teachers, except Mr. Blake, wear ties to school.
10. The strawberry jam in my brother's sandwich dripped onto his lap.

Activity 5: Verbs of More than One Word (page 159)

1. Ellen has chosen
2. You should plan
3. Felix has been waiting
4. We should have invited
5. I would have preferred
6. Classes were interrupted
7. Sam can touch
8. I have been encouraging
9. Tony has agreed
10. students have been giving

Activity 6: Compound Subjects and Verbs (page 160)

1. Boards and bricks make
2. We bought and finished
3. fly and bee hung
4. twins look, think, act, and dress
5. salmon and tuna contain
6. I waited and slipped
7. girl waved and smiled
8. bird dived and reappeared
9. Singers, dancers, and actors performed
10. magician and assistant bowed and disappeared

CHAPTER 7: Fragments

Introductory Activity (page 162)

1. verb
2. subject
3. subject . . . verb
4. express a complete thought

Activity 1: Correcting Dependent Word Fragments (*page 165*)

Activity 2: Combining Sentences to Correct Dependent Word Fragments (*page 166*)

1. When the waitress coughed in his food, Frank lost his appetite. He didn't even take home a doggy bag.
2. Our power went out during a thunderstorm.
3. Tony doesn't like going to the ballpark. If he misses an exciting play, there's no instant replay.
4. After the mail carrier comes, I run to our mailbox. I love to get mail even if it is only junk mail.
5. Even though she can't read, my little daughter likes to go to the library. She chooses books with pretty covers while I look at the latest magazines.

Activity 3: Correcting -ing Fragments (*page 168*)

1. Vince sat nervously in the dentist's chair, waiting for his X-rays to be developed.
2. Looking through the movie ads for twenty minutes, Lew and Marian tried to find a film they both wanted to see.
3. As a result, it tipped over.

Activity 4: Correcting -ing or to Fragments (*page 169*)

1. Some workers dug up the street near our house, causing frequent vibrations inside.
2. I therefore walked slowly into the darkened living room, preparing to look shocked.
   or: I was preparing to look shocked.
3. Dribbling skillfully up the court, Luis looked for a teammate who was open.
4. Wanting to finish the dream, I pushed the snooze button.
5. To get back my term paper, I went to see my English instructor from last semester.

Activity 5: Identifying and Correcting Fragments (*page 170*)

1. For example, she waits until the night before a test to begin studying.
2. My eleventh-grade English teacher picked on everybody except the athletes.
3. For example, he bought an air conditioner in December.

Activity 6: Identifying and Correcting Added-Detail Fragments (*page 171*)

1. I find all sorts of things in my little boy's pockets, including crayons, stones, and melted chocolate.
2. There are certain chores I hate to do, especially cleaning windows.
3. The meat loaf, for instance, is as tender and tasty as shoe leather.
4. By midnight, the party looked like the scene of an accident, with people stretched out on the floor.
5. For example, the smiles of game show hosts look pasted on their faces.

Activity 7: Correcting Missing Subject Fragments (*page 172*)

1. Artie tripped on his shoelace and then looked around to see if anyone had noticed.
   or: Then he looked around to see if anyone had noticed.
2. I started the car and quickly turned down the blaring radio.
   or: And I quickly turned down the blaring radio.
3. Its orange-red flames shot high in the air and made strange shadows all around the dark room.
4. She also forgot to take my name.
5. She places herself in front of a seated young man and stands on his feet until he gets up.
   or: And she stands on his feet until he gets up.

CHAPTER 8: Run-Ons

Introductory Activity (*page 179*)

1. period
2. *but*
3. semicolon
4. *Although*

Activity 1: Correcting Fused Sentences (*page 181*)

1. month. Its
2. porch. They
3. make. It
4. do. He
5. shirt. A
6. B.C. The
7. cheaply. She
8. desk. She
9. fireplace. The
10. traffic. Its

Activity 2: Correcting Run-ons: Fused Sentences and Comma Splices (*page 182*)

1. man. He
2. mailbox. Then
3. common. The
4. tiny. A
5. greyhound. It
6. Chinese. She
7. working. Its
8. lovely. It
9. drink. One
10. times. For

Activity 3: Writing the Next Sentence (*page 183*)

Activity 4: Connecting Two Thoughts (*page 185*)

1. , but
2. , and
3. , and
4. , so
5. , but
6. , so
7. , for
8. , but
9. , so
10. , for

Activity 5: Using Commas and Joining Words (*page 185*)

Activity 6: Using Semicolons (*page 186*)

1. dessert; I
2. ate; the
3. me; her
4. ground; old
5. queens; birth

Activity 7: Using Logical Transitions (*page 187*)

1. drive; however, the
2. art; otherwise, it
3. gasoline; as a result, spectators (*or* thus *or* consequently *or* therefore
4. started; however, all
5. feelers; consequently, they (*or* as a result *or* thus *or* therefore)

Activity 8: Using Semicolons and Commas (*page 188*)

1. store; nevertheless, she
2. candy; as a result, he
3. strangers; however, he
4. schedule; otherwise, he
5. children; furthermore, she

Activity 9: Using Dependent Words (*page 189*)

1. since
2. Unless
3. because
4. After
5. although

Activity 10: Using Subordination (*page 189*)

1. Although I want to stop smoking, I don't want to gain weight.
2. Because it was too hot indoors to study, I decided to go down to the shopping center for ice cream.
3. While the puppy quickly ate, the baby watched with interest.
4. When the elderly woman smiled at me, her face broke into a thousand wrinkles.
5. Although this world map was published only three years ago, the names of some countries are already out of date.

CHAPTER 9: Sentence Variety I

Activity 1: The Simple Sentence (*page 195*)

Activity 2: The Compound Sentence (*page 196*)

1. Cass tied the turkey carcass to a tree, and she watched the birds pick at bits of meat and skin.
2. I ran the hot water faucet for two minutes, but only cold water came out.
3. Nathan orders all his Christmas gifts through the Internet, for he dislikes shopping in crowded stores.
4. I need to buy a new set of tires, so I will read *Consumer Reports* to learn about various brands.
5. I asked Cecilia to go out with me on Saturday night, but she told me she'd rather stay home and watch TV.

Activity 3: Writing Compound Sentences (*page 197*)

Activity 4: Creating Complex Sentences (*page 198*)

1. When Cindy opened the cutlery drawer, a bee flew out.
2. Although I washed the windows thoroughly, they still looked dirty.

3. Because I never opened a book all semester, I guess I deserved to flunk.
4. When Manny gets up in the morning, he does stretching exercises for five minutes.
5. After my son spilled the pickle jar at dinner, I had to wash the kitchen floor.

Activity 5: Using Subordination (*page 199*)

1. As Carlo set the table, his wife finished cooking dinner.
2. Although Maggie could have gotten good grades, she did not study enough.
3. After I watered my drooping African violets, they perked right up.
4. Though the little boy kept pushing the "down" button, the elevator didn't come any more quickly.
5. I never really knew what pain was until I had four impacted wisdom teeth pulled at once.

Activity 6: Using Who, Which, or That (*page 200*)

1. Karen, who is an old friend of mine, just gave birth to twins.
2. The tea, which was hotter than I expected, burned the roof of my mouth.
3. I dropped the camera that my sister had just bought.
4. Ernie, who is visiting from California, brought us some enormous oranges.
5. Liz used a steam cleaner to shampoo her rugs, which were dirtier than she realized.

Activity 7: Writing Complex Sentences (*page 201*)

Activity 8: Using Joining Words and Dependent Words (*page 201*)

1. After . . . for
2. When . . . but
3. when . . . and
4. Because . . . so
5. but . . . because

Activity 9: Writing Compound-Complex Sentences (*page 202*)

Activity 10: Using Subordination or Coordination (*page 202*)

1. Though Sidney likes loud music, his parents can't stand it, so he wears earphones.
2. After the volcano erupted, the sky turned black with smoke. Nearby villagers were frightened, so they clogged the roads leading to safety.
3. After Glenda had a haircut today, she came home and looked in the mirror. Then she decided to wear a hat for a few days because she thought she looked like a bald eagle.
4. When I ran out of gas on the way to work, I discovered how helpful strangers can be. A passing driver saw I was stuck, so he drove me to the gas station and back to my car.

5. Our dog often rests on the floor in the sunshine while he waits for the children to get home from school. As the sunlight moves along the floor, he moves with it.

6. Because my father was going to be late from work, we planned to have a late dinner. But I was hungry before dinner, so I secretly ate a salami and cheese sandwich.

7. A baseball game was scheduled for early afternoon, but it looked like rain. So a crew rolled huge tarps to cover the field, and then the sun reappeared.

8. Cassy worries about the pesticides used on fruit, so she washes apples, pears, and plums in soap and water. Because she doesn't rinse them well, they have a soapy flavor.

9. Charlene needed to buy stamps, so she went to the post office during her lunch hour, when the line was long. After she waited there for half an hour, she had to go back to work without stamps.

10. After the weather suddenly became frigid, almost everyone at work caught a cold, so someone brought a big batch of chicken soup. She poured it into one of the office coffeepots, and the pot was empty by noon.

CHAPTER 10: Standard English Verbs

Introductory Activity (*page 210*)

played . . . plays

hoped . . . hopes

juggled . . . juggles

1. past time . . . *-ed* or *-d*
2. present time . . . *-s*

Activity 1: Using Standard Verb Forms (*page 212*)

1. drives
2. gets
3. practices
4. makes
5. brushes
6. falls
7. C
8. comes
9. watches
10. buzzes

Activity 2: Using Present Tense -s Verb Endings (*page 212*)

My little sister wants to be a singer when she grows up. She constantly hums and sings around the house. Sometimes she makes quite a racket. When she listens to music on the radio, for example, she sings very loudly in order to hear herself over the radio. And when she takes a shower, her voice rings through the whole house because she thinks nobody can hear her from there.

Activity 3: Using Standard Verb Forms: -d and -ed Endings (*page 213*)

1. spilled
2. jailed
3. burned
4. tied
5. measured
6. C
7. smashed
8. constructed
9. leveled
10. realized

Activity 4: Using Past Tense Verb Endings (*page 213*)

My cousin Joel completed a course in home repairs and offered one day to fix several things in my house. He repaired a screen door that squeaked, a dining room chair that wobbled a bit, and a faulty electrical outlet. That night when I opened the screen door, it loosened from its hinges. When I seated myself in the chair Joel had fixed, one of its legs cracked off. Remembering that Joel had also fooled around with the electrical outlet, I quickly called an electrician and asked him to stop by the next day. Then I prayed the house would not burn down before he arrived.

Activity 5: Standard Forms of Irregular Verbs (*page 216*)

1. is
2. do
3. has
4. is
5. have
6. are
7. has
8. do
9. were
10. does

Activity 6: Identifying and Correcting Nonstandard Verbs (*page 216*)

1. ~~does~~ do
2. ~~be~~ is
3. ~~be~~ are
4. ~~has~~ have
5. ~~were~~ was
6. ~~have~~ had
7. ~~was~~ were
8. ~~done~~ did
9. ~~do~~ does
10. ~~have~~ has

Activity 7: Using Standard Forms of *Be, Have,* and *Do* (*page 217*)

My cousin Rita has decided to lose thirty pounds, so she has put herself on a rigid diet that does not allow her to eat anything that she enjoys. Last weekend, while the family was at Aunt Jenny's house for dinner, all Rita had to eat was a can of Diet Delight peaches. We were convinced that Rita meant business when she joined an exercise club whose members have to work out on enormous machines and do twenty sit-ups just to get started. If Rita does reach her goal, we are all going to be very proud of her. But I would not be surprised if she does not succeed, because this is her fourth diet this year.

CHAPTER 11: Irregular Verbs

Introductory Activity (*page 219*)

1. R . . . screamed . . . screamed
2. I . . . wrote . . . written
3. I . . . stole . . . stolen
4. R . . . asked . . . asked
5. R . . . kissed . . . kissed
6. I . . . chose . . . chosen
7. I . . . rode . . . ridden
8. R . . . chewed . . . chewed
9. I . . . thought . . . thought
10. R . . . danced . . . danced elevator.

Activity 1: Identifying Incorrect Verb Forms (*page 222*)

1. came
2. stood
3. built
4. swum
5. held
6. drove
7. written
8. blew
9. bought
10. knew

Activity 2: Using Present Tense, Past Tense, and Past Participle Verbs (*page 223*)

1. (a) sleeps
   (b) slept
   (c) slept
2. (a) rings
   (b) rang
   (c) rung
3. (a) write
   (b) wrote
   (c) written
4. (a) stands
   (b) stood
   (c) stood
5. (a) swims
   (b) swam
   (c) swum
6. (a) buys
   (b) bought
   (c) bought
7. (a) choose
   (b) chose
   (c) chosen
8. (a) eats
   (b) ate
   (c) eaten
9. (a) freezes
   (b) froze
   (c) frozen
10. (a) give
    (b) gave
    (c) given

Activity 3: Using Lie and Lay (*page 225*)

1. lies
2. Lying
3. laid
4. laid
5. lay

Activity 4: Using Set and Sit (*page 226*)

1. Set
2. sitting
3. sat
4. Set
5. setting

Activity 5: Using Rise and Raise (*page 227*)

1. rises
2. raised
3. rose
4. risen
5. raise

CHAPTER 12: Subject-Verb Agreement

Introductory Activity (*page 230*)

Correct: The pictures in that magazine are very controversial.

Correct: There were many applicants for the job.

Correct: Everybody usually watches the lighted numbers in an elevator

1. pictures . . . applicants
2. singular . . . singular

Activity 1: Words between Subjects and Verbs (*page 231*)

1. trail ~~of bloodstains~~ leads
2. clothes ~~in the hall closet~~ take
3. basket ~~of fancy fruit and nuts~~ was
4. instructions ~~for assembling the bicycle~~ were
5. Smoke ~~from the distant forest fires~~ is
6. Workers ~~at that automobile plant~~ begin
7. date ~~on any of the cemetery gravestones~~ appears
8. line ~~of cars in the traffic jam~~ seems
9. boxes ~~in the corner of the attic~~ contain
10. bags ~~with the new insulation material~~ protect

Activity 2: Verbs that Precede Subjects (*page 232*)

1. is noise
2. are berries
3. were cans
4. sits cabin
5. were students
6. stands cutout
7. was shape
8. were sneakers
9. are magazines
10. was row

Activity 3: Using Verbs with Indefinite Pronouns (*page 233*)

1. keeps
2. works
3. pays
4. have
5. slips
6. leans
7. expects
8. was
9. stops
10. has

Activity 4: Using Verbs with Compound Subjects (*page 234*)

1. sadden
2. need
3. have
4. continue
5. tears

Activity 5: Using Who, Which, or That with Verbs (*page 235*)

1. has
2. goes
3. become
4. taste
5. are

CHAPTER 13: Consistent Verb Tense

Introductory Activity (*page 239*)

Mistakes in verb tense: Alex discovers . . . calls . . . present . . . past

Activity 1: Avoiding Unnecessary Tense Shifts (*page 240*)

1. rolled
2. purchased
3. stepped
4. crashed
5. snatched
6. covered
7. lifted
8. argues
9. swallowed
10. glowed

CHAPTER 14: Additional Information About Verbs

Activity 1: Using the Correct Verb Tense (*page 245*)

1. had dried
2. had planned (*or* were planning)
3. is growing
4. had thrown
5. was carving (*or* had carved)
6. had opened
7. is caring
8. has watched
9. had walked
10. were trying

Activity 2: Using Infinitives, Participles, and Gerunds (*page 246*)

1. *P*
2. *G*
3. *I*
4. *G*
5. *P*

6. *I*
7. *G*
8. *I*
9. *P*
10. *P*

Activity 3: Making Sentences Active (*page 247*)

1. A man with a live parrot on his shoulder boarded the bus.
2. A large falling branch broke the stained-glass window.
3. The entire team autographed baseballs for hospitalized children.
4. A fire that started with a cigarette destroyed the hotel.
5. Doctors must face the pressures of dealing with life and death.
6. A sophisticated laser system directed the missile to its target.
7. A thick layer of yellowish grease covered the kitchen shelves.
8. A group of volunteers removed trash in the neighborhood park.
9. The state police captured most of the escaped convicts within a mile of the jail.
10. The judges awarded prizes for hog-calling and stone-skipping.

CHAPTER 15: Pronoun Reference, Agreement, and Point of View

Introductory Activity (*page 250*)

1. b
2. b
3. b

Activity 1: Pronoun Reference (*page 252*)

1. Fran removed the blanket from the sofa bed and folded the blanket up.
2. The defendant told the judge, "I am mentally ill."
3. Before the demonstration, the leaders passed out signs for us to carry.
4. Cindy complained to Rachel, "My (*or* Your) boyfriend is being dishonest."
5. Because I didn't rinse last night's dishes, my kitchen smells like a garbage can.
6. A film on endangered species really depressed the students.
    Or: Watching a film on endangered species really depressed the students.
7. The veterinarian said that if I find a tick on my dog, I should get rid of the tick immediately.
8. My sister removed the curtains from the windows so that she could wash the curtains.
    Or: So that she could wash the curtains, my sister removed them from the windows.
    Or: My sister removed the curtains from the windows so that she could wash the windows.
    Or: So that she could wash the windows, my sister removed the curtains from them.

9. Richard said his acupuncture therapist could help my sprained shoulder, but I don't believe in acupuncture.
10. I discovered when I went to sell my old textbooks that publishers have put out new editions, and nobody wants to buy my textbooks.
    Or: I discovered when I went to sell my old textbooks that nobody wants to buy them because publishers have put out new editions.

Activity 2: Pronoun Agreement (*page 253*)

1. they
2. their
3. it

4. them
5. their

Activity 3: Using Pronouns Correctly (*page 255*)

1. his
2. his
3. its
4. her
5. them

6. his or her
7. her
8. he
9. her
10. his or her

Activity 4: Correcting Inconsistent Pronouns (*page 257*)

1. my blood
2. they know
3. they have
4. they should receive
5. I can avoid
6. their hands
7. he can worry . . . his own
8. we could
9. she can still have . . . her day
10. our rights

CHAPTER 16: Pronoun Types

Introductory Activity (*page 261*)

Correct sentences:

Andy and I enrolled in a computer course.

The police officer pointed to my sister and me.

Lola prefers men who take pride in their bodies.

The players are confident that the league championship is theirs.

Those concert tickets are too expensive.

Our parents should spend some money on themselves for a change.

Activity 1: Identifying Subject and Object Pronouns (*page 264*)

1. her (*O*)
2. She (*S*)
3. me (*O*)
4. her and me (*O*)
5. he (*S*)

6. I (*am* is understood) (*S*)
7. they (*S*)
8. me (*O*)
9. We (*S*)
10. I (*S*)

Activity 2: Using Subject or Object Pronouns (*page 264*)

1. I
2. him *or* me
3. they
4. I *or* we
5. us
6. I *or* he *or* she *or* they *or* we
7. they *or* he *or* she
8. I *or* he *or* she *or* they *or* we
9. I *or* he *or* she *or* they *or* we
10. us *or* them

Activity 3: Identifying Correct Relative Pronouns (*page 267*)

1. that
2. that
3. who
4. which
5. whom

Activity 4: Using Relative Pronouns (*page 267*)

Activity 5: Correcting Possessive Pronouns (*page 268*)

1. yours
2. his
3. theirs
4. your
5. mine

Activity 6: Correcting Demonstrative Pronouns (*page 269*)

1. This town
2. those seats
3. That dress
4. those chocolates
5. those potholes

Activity 7: Using Demonstrative Pronouns (*page 270*)

Activity 8: Using Reflexive Pronouns (*page 271*)

1. themselves
2. herself
3. himself
4. ourselves
5. themselves

CHAPTER 17: Adjectives and Adverbs

Introductory Activity (*page 274*)

adjective . . . adverb . . . *ly* . . . *er* . . . *est*

Activity 1: Using Comparatives and Superlatives (*page 276*)

tougher	toughest
more practical	most practical
quieter	quietest
more aggressive	most aggressive
clearer	clearest

Activity 2: Using the Correct Comparative and Superlative Forms (*page 276*)

1. best
2. dirtier
3. more considerate
4. worse
5. scariest
6. less
7. more stylish
8. sillier
9. slowest
10. most fattening

Activity 3: Using Adjectives or Adverbs (*page 277*)

1. badly
2. harshly
3. steep
4. frequently
5. truthfully
6. peacefully
7. bright
8. loudly
9. carefully
10. nicely

Activity 4: Using Well or Good (*page 278*)

1. well
2. good
3. well
4. good
5. well

CHAPTER 18: Misplaced Modifiers

Introductory Activity (*page 281*)

1. Intended: The farmers were wearing masks.
   Unintended: The apple trees were wearing masks.
2. Intended: The woman had a terminal disease.
   Unintended: The faith healer had a terminal disease.

Activity 1: Fixing Misplaced Modifiers (*page 282*)

1. At the back of his cage, the tiger growled at a passerby.
2. Lee hung colorful scarves made of green and blue silk over her windows.
3. Standing on our front porch, we watched the fireworks.
4. Jason has almost two hundred baseball cards.
5. With a smile, the salesclerk exchanged the blue sweater for a yellow one.
6. We all stared at the man with curly purple hair in the front row of the theater.
7. I love the cookies with the chocolate frosting from the bakery.
8. During their last meeting, the faculty decided to strike.
9. Larry looked on with disbelief as his car burned.
10. My cousin sent me instructions in a letter on how to get to her house.

Activity 2: Placing Modifiers Correctly (*page 283*)

1. My mother sat lazily with a glass of lemonade in the hot sun, watching her grandchildren play.
2. My father agreed over the phone to pay for the car repairs.
   Or: Over the phone, my father agreed to pay for the car repairs.
3. I found a note from Jeff on the kitchen bulletin board.
4. The fires destroyed almost the entire forest.
5. During class, Jon read about how the American Revolution began.
   Or: Jon read during class about how the American Revolution began.

CHAPTER 19: Dangling Modifiers

Introductory Activity (*page 286*)
1. Intended: The giraffe was munching leaves from a tall tree.
   Unintended: The children were munching leaves.
2. Intended: Michael was arriving home after ten months in the army.
   Unintended: The neighbors were arriving home after ten months in the army.

Activity 1: Correcting Dangling Modifiers (*page 288*)

1. A security guard pointed to the priceless painting that was hanging safely on a wall.
2. When I was five, my mother bought me a chemistry set.
3. C
4. Since the milk had turned sour, I would not drink it.
5. While I was talking on the phone, my hot tea turned cold.
6. Pete hated to look at the kitchen sink, which was piled high with dirty dishes.
7. Because I locked my keys in the car, the police had to open it for me.
8. Because the plants were drooping and looking all dried out, the children watered them.
9. After I sat through a long lecture, my foot was asleep.
10. Since I was late, stopping for coffee was out of the question.

Activity 2: Placing Modifiers Correctly (*page 289*)

CHAPTER 20: Faulty Parallelism

Introductory Activity (*page 292*)
Correct sentences:

I use my TV remote control to change channels, to adjust the volume, and to turn the set on and off.

One option the employees had was to take a cut in pay; the other was to work longer hours.

The refrigerator has a cracked vegetable drawer, a missing shelf, and a strange freezer smell.

Activity 1: Using Parallelism (*page 293*)
1. (example: fast service)
2. howling dogs
3. rude
4. hiking
5. poor security
6. cleaned the apartment
7. having fun
8. inexpensive desserts
9. on the closet floor
10. sings in the church choir

Activity 2: Creating Nonparallel Sentences (*page 294*)
1. waited
2. cramming
3. illness
4. late buses
5. attracting
6. to suffocate
7. interrupted
8. financial security
9. birds chirping
10. breathed fire

Activity 3: Writing Parallel Sentences (*page 295*)

CHAPTER 21: Sentence Variety II

Activity 1: Combining Sentences with -*ing* Words (*page 300*)

1. Picking up their cameras, the tourists began to leave the bus.
2. Jogging on the street, I was almost hit by a car.
3. Wincing with pain, Barbara untangled her snarled hair from the brush.
4. Waving her arms at the excited crowd, the singer ran to the front of the stage.
5. Losing by one point with thirty seconds left to play, the team braced itself for a last-ditch effort.

Activity 2: Using -*ing* Word Groups (*page 300*)

Activity 3: Combining Sentences with -*ed* Words (*page 301*)

1. Mary, startled by a thunderclap, sat up suddenly in bed.
2. Married for fifty years, my parents decided to have a second wedding.
3. Frightened by the large dog near the curb, Erica wouldn't leave her car.
4. Dotted with mold, the old orange felt like a marshmallow.
5. Ernie, determined to have plenty to eat during the movie, made a huge sandwich and popped popcorn.

Activity 4: Using -*ed* Word Groups (*page 302*)

Activity 5: Combining Sentences with -*ly* Words (*page 303*)
1. Noisily, we ate raw carrots and celery sticks.
2. Gently, Cliff spoke to his sobbing little brother.
3. Tenderly, the father picked up his baby daughter.
4. Anxiously, I paced up and down the hospital corridor.
5. Frantically, Anita repeatedly dived into the pool to find her engagement ring.

Activity 6: Using -*ly* Words (*page 304*)

Activity 7: Combining Sentences with *to* Word Groups (*page 304*)
1. To make the tub less slippery, Sally put a thick towel on the bottom.
2. To keep raccoons away, we now keep our garbage in the garage.
3. To count his pulse, Bill pressed two fingers against the large vein in his neck.
4. To steam her face, my aunt opens her dishwasher when it begins drying.
5. To help out the homeless, we looked through our closets for unused clothing.

Activity 8: Using -*to* (*page 305*)

Activity 9: Combining Sentences by Opening with Prepositional Phrases (*page 305*)

1. About once a week, we have dinner with my parents at a restaurant.
2. Before company came, I put the dirty cups away in the cupboard.
3. During my English exam, my eyes roamed around the room until they met the instructor's eye.
4. For twenty minutes, the little boy drew intently in a comic book without stopping once.
5. At the zoo, a playful young orangutan wriggled in a corner under a paper sack.

Activity 10: Using Prepositional Phrases (*page 306*)

Activity 11: Using Adjectives in a Series (*page 307*)

1. The old, peeling shingles blew off the roof during the blustery storm.
2. The lean, powerful dancer whirled across the stage with his graceful, elegant partner.
3. A large, furry rat scurried into the crowded kitchen of the restaurant.
4. The full, golden moon lit up the cloudy sky like a huge floating streetlamp.
5. The oval plastic doorbell of the large, ornate house played a loud rock tune.

Activity 12: Writing with Adjectives in a Series (*page 308*)

Activity 13: Combining Sentences with Verbs in a Series (*page 309*)

1. The flea-ridden dog rubbed itself against the fence, bit its tail, and scratched its neck with its hind leg.
2. I put my homework on the table, made a cup of coffee, and turned the radio up full blast.
3. The driver stopped the school bus, walked to the back, and separated two children.
4. I rolled up my sleeve, glanced at the nurse nervously, shut my eyes, and waited for the worst to be over.
5. The parents applauded politely at the program's end, looked at their watches, exchanged looks of relief, and reached for their coats.

Activity 14: Using Verbs in a Series (*page 310*)

CHAPTER 22: Paper Format

Introductory Activity (*page 315*)

In "A," the title is capitalized and has no quotation marks around it; there is a blank line between the title and the body of the paper; there are left and right margins around the body of the paper; no words are incorrectly hyphenated.

Activity 1: Correcting Formatting Errors (*page 317*)

1. (example: Break words at correct syllable divisions (sis-ter))
2. Do not use quotation marks around the title.
3. Capitalize the major words in the title ("Being a Younger Sister").
4. Skip a line between the title and first line of the paper.
5. Indent the first line of the paper.
6. Keep margins on both sides of the paper.

Activity 2: Writing Titles (*page 317*)

1. Benefits of Pets
2. Learning How to Budget
3. The Value of a Study Group
4. A Special Relationship *or* Grandparents and Grandchildren
5. A Wise Decision

Activity 3: Rewriting Dependent Sentences (*page 318*)

1. The best children's television shows educate while they entertain, and they are not violent.
2. Women have made many gains in the workplace in the last decade.
3. The generation gap results from differing experiences of various age groups.
4. Correct
5. One of my important accomplishments was to finish high school despite my parents' divorce.

CHAPTER 23: Capital Letters

Introductory Activity (*page 320*)

1–13: Answers will vary, but all should be capitalized.

14–16: On . . . "Let's . . . I

Activity 1: Capitalizing Names and Titles (*page 322*)

1. I . . . Boy Scouts
2. Friday . . . Thanksgiving . . . Target
3. Regal Cinema . . . If
4. New England . . . Republicans . . . Democrats
5. State Farm . . . Nationwide . . . Prudential Building
6. *Time* . . . *Newsweek* . . . California
7. Valentine's Day . . . Mother's Day
8. Pepsis . . . Fritos . . . Macintosh
9. Ford Taurus . . . Saturday
10. Broadway . . . *My Fair Lady*

Activity 2: Where Is Capitalization Needed? (*page 325*)

1. Hundred Years' War
2. Aunt Sophie . . . Polish
3. Independence Hall . . . Liberty Bell
4. World History . . . Middle Ages
5. Cuban . . . Spanish . . . Hispanic

Activity 3: Where Is Capitalization Unnecessary? (*page* 325)

1. grandmother . . . spaghetti . . . meatballs
2. high school . . . basketball coach
3. shop . . . fashion magazines
4. parents' groups . . . ads . . . maniac
5. manager . . . restaurant . . . dessert

CHAPTER 24: Numbers and Abbreviations

Introductory Activity (*page* 329)

Correct choices:

First sentence: 8:55 . . . 65 percent
Second sentence: Nine . . . forty-five
Second sentence: brothers . . . mountain
Second sentence: hours . . . English

Activity 1: Using Numbers (*page* 330)

1. 6:15
2. nine o'clock
3. July 28, 2004
4. six
5. 1600 Pennsylvania Avenue
6. Forty-three
7. $930.20
8. 60 . . . 64
9. 27 . . . 52
10. 50 percent

Activity 2: Using Abbreviations (*page* 331)

1. newspaper . . . telephone
2. bushels . . . market . . . Route
3. Monday . . . September
4. psychology . . . England
5. chicken . . . macaroni
6. ounce . . . tablespoon
7. chemistry . . . Sunday . . . hours
8. January . . . company . . . year
9. license . . . medical
10. veteran . . . business . . . college

CHAPTER 25: End Marks

Introductory Activity (*page* 334)

1. depressed.
2. paper?
3. parked.
4. control!

Activity 1: Using End Punctuation (*page* 335)

1. drown?
2. redhead.
3. me.
4. it!"
5. "vidiots."
6. accurate.
7. life?
8. truck!"
9. forward?"
10. married.

CHAPTER 26: Apostrophes

Introductory Activity (*page* 337)

1. In each case, the 's indicates possession or ownership.
2. The apostrophes indicate omitted letters and shortened spellings.
3. In the first sentence, s indicates a plural noun; in the second sentence, 's indicates possession.

Activity 1: Combining Words (*page* 338)

you've	we're	couldn't
haven't	you'll	they'll
he's	we'd	doesn't

Activity 2: Forming Contractions (*page* 338)

1. didn't . . . wasn't
2. doesn't . . . she's
3. You're . . . can't
4. isn't . . . you've
5. We'd . . . don't

Activity 3: Using the Apostrophe (*page* 339)

Activity 4: Using Apostrophes Correctly (*page* 340)

1. It's . . . your
2. whose . . . who's
3. You're . . . your
4. There . . . their
5. It's . . . their

Activity 5: Using 's to Show Possession (*page* 341)

1. singer's voice
2. Dawn's garage
3. Murphy's law
4. computer's memory
5. my wife's mother
6. yesterday's meat loaf
7. My sister's promotion
8. Alexis's bratty little brother
9. the referee's call
10. the tanker's hull

Activity 6: Identifying Possessive Nouns (*page* 342)

1. horse's
2. brother's
3. son's
4. comedian's
5. landlord's
6. Ted's
7. teller's
8. people's
9. studio's
10. girl's

Activity 7: Making Words Possessive (*page* 343)

1. (example: Cary's)
2. teacher's
3. insect's
4. husband's
5. salesperson's

Activity 8: Apostrophes vs. Simple Plurals (*page 344*)

1. parlors: parlor's, meaning "belonging to the parlor"

   aromas: simple plural meaning more than one aroma

   vents: simple plural meaning more than one vent

2. cars: car's, meaning "belonging to the car"

   streets: simple plural meaning more than one street

   buildings: simple plural meaning more than one building

3. Karens: Karen's, meaning "belonging to Karen"

   plants: simple plural meaning more than one plant

   stakes: simple plural meaning more than one stake

4. lakes: lake's, meaning "belonging to the lake"

   officials: simple plural meaning more than one official

5. positions: simple plural meaning more than one position

   exterminators: exterminator's, meaning "belonging to an exterminator"

6. candlelights: candlelight's, meaning "belonging to the candlelight"

   plates: simple plural meaning more than one plate

   goblets: simple plural meaning more than one goblet

7. Crackers: simple plural meaning more than one cracker

   slices: simple plural meaning more than one slice

   fathers: father's, meaning "belonging to my father"

8. insects: insect's, meaning "belonging to the insect"

   eggs: simple plural meaning more than one egg

   worms: simple plural meaning more than one worm

9. Seabirds: simple plural meaning more than one seabird

   oceans: ocean's, meaning "belonging to the ocean"

   surfers: simple plural meaning more than one surfer

10. daughters: daughter's, meaning "belonging to my daughter"

    prayers: simple plural meaning more than one prayer

    schools: simple plural meaning more than one school

Activity 9: Missing Apostrophes (*page 345*)

1. nurses' union
2. sisters' feet
3. lions' keeper
4. The Tylers' new television set
5. parents' wedding pictures

CHAPTER 27: Quotation Marks

Introductory Activity (*page 349*)

1. Quotation marks set off the exact words of a speaker.
2. Commas and periods following quotations go inside quotation marks.

Activity 1: Using Quotation Marks (*page 351*)

1. The chilling bumper sticker read, "You can't hug children with nuclear arms."
2. "One day we'll look back on this argument, and it will seem funny," Bruce assured Rosa.
3. "Hey, lady, this is an express line!" shouted the cashier to the woman with a full basket.
4. My grandfather was fond of saying, "Happiness is found along the way, not at the end of the road."

5. "When will I be old enough to pay the adult fare?" the child asked.
6. On his deathbed, Oscar Wilde is supposed to have said, "Either this wallpaper goes or I do."
7. The sign on my neighbor's front door reads, "Never mind the dog. Beware of owner."
8. "I'm not afraid to die," said Woody Allen. "I just don't want to be there when it happens."
9. My son once told me, "Sometimes I wish I were little again. Then I wouldn't have to make so many decisions."
10. "I don't feel like cooking tonight," Eve said to Adam. "Let's just have fruit."

Activity 2: Formatting Quotations (*page 351*)

1. Simon said, "Take three giant steps forward."
2. "Please don't hang up before leaving a message," stated the telephone recording.
3. Clark Kent asked a man on the street, "Where is the nearest phone booth?"
4. "You dirtied every pan in the kitchen just to scramble some eggs," Rico said in disgust.
5. "Nothing can be done for your broken little toe," the doctor said. "You have to wait for it to heal."

Activity 3: Writing with Quotation Marks (*page 352*)

Activity 4: Using Dialogue (*page 353*)

1. (example: Agnes said to me as we left work, "Herb got a raise.")
2. I said, "That's hard to believe, since Herb is a do-nothing."
3. Agnes replied, "Even so, he's gone up in the world."
4. I told her, "You must be kidding."
5. Agnes laughed and said, "Herb was moved from the first to the fourth floor today."

Activity 5: Converting Quotations into Indirect Statements (*page 353*)

1. My doctor said that I need to lose weight.
2. Lola asked Tony if he ever washes his car.
3. The police officer asked if I knew how fast I was going.
4. Janie whispered that Harold's so boring he lights up a room when he leaves it.
5. The instructor said that movies are actually a series of still pictures.

Activity 6: Using Quotations in Titles (*page 355*)

1. My sister just bought a TiVo so she won't have to miss any more episodes of General Hospital.
2. Rita grabbed the National Enquirer and eagerly began to read the article "I Had a Space Alien's Baby."
3. Our exam will cover two chapters, "The Study of Heredity" and "The Origin of Diversity," in our biology textbook, Life.
4. The last song on the bluegrass program was called "I Ain't Broke but I'm Badly Bent."
5. The classic 1980s movie Stand by Me was actually based on "The Body," a short story written by Stephen King.
6. At last night's performance of Annie Get Your Gun, the audience joined the cast in singing "There's No Business Like Show Business."

7. A typical article in <u>Cosmopolitan</u> will have a title like "How to Hook a Man without Letting Him Know You're Fishing."

8. One way Joanne deals with depression is to get out her <u>Man of La Mancha</u> album and play the song "The Impossible Dream."

9. I read the article "How Good Is Your Breakfast?" in <u>Consumer Reports</u> while munching a doughnut this morning.

10. According to a <u>Psychology Today</u> article titled "Home on the Street," there are 36,000 people living on New York City's sidewalks.

CHAPTER 28: Commas

Introductory Activity (*page* 360)

1. a: card, . . . check, . . . ; ants, roaches,
2. b: car, . . . ; hiking,
3. c: leeches, . . . blood, . . . ; Derek, . . . arrested,
4. d: easy, . . . ; trees,
5. e: asked, . . . ; work, . . . said,
6. f: 1,500,000; Newark, New Jersey, . . . August 26, 2004,

Activity 1: Commas between Items in a Series (*page* 362)

1. work, food, or a place to live
2. Ice cream, crushed candy, Pepsi, and popcorn
3. eight hours, four hundred miles, and three rest stops

Activity 2: Necessary and Unnecessary Commas (*page* 362)

1. pennies, and a sock hidden under the seats
2. Squirrels, . . . and clouds of mosquitoes populate
3. spun to his left, . . . arms of the Panthers' center

Activity 3: Commas after Introductory Clauses (*page* 363)

1. done,   2. tape,   3. time,

Activity 4: More Necessary and Unnecessary Commas (*page* 363)

1. presents, . . . ribbon and tied
2. aisle, I saw a bead of sweat roll from her forehead
3. For example, I wrote a note to remind me that

Activity 5: Commas that Set Off Interruptions (*page* 364)

1. dancer, aided by members of the chorus,
2. Anderson, who were married on the Fourth of July,
3. repairman, unaware of the grease on his shoes,

Activity 6: More Necessary and Unnecessary Commas (*page* 365)

1. gigantic, . . . the rest is deadwood
2. council, in a rare fit of wisdom
3. presidents of the United States,
4. aunt, a talkative woman,

Activity 7: Commas that Connect Complete Thoughts (*page* 366)

1. spacious, but
2. thunderstorm, so
3. C
4. space, for
5. C
6. supermarket, but
7. C
8. college, but
9. schoolwork, but
10. C

Activity 8: Setting Off Quotations with Commas (*page* 367)

1. said,
2. temptation," Oscar Wilde advised,
3. family,"

Activity 9: More Necessary and Unnecessary Commas (*page* 367)

1. poster in the subway station,
2. fine," . . . forgetting to kick."
3. think," the judge asked the defendant,

Activity 10: Adding Commas (*page* 368)

1. me, madam,
2. 6,000 . . . 15,000
3. 15, 1912.
4. Teresa, . . . Love,
5. Washington, D.C., . . . 50,000 . . . 6,500

Activity 11: Eliminating Unnecessary Commas (*page* 369)

1. We grew a pumpkin last year that weighed over one hundred pounds.
2. Anyone with a failing grade must report to the principal.
3. Last weekend a grizzly bear attacked a hiker who got too close to its cubs.
4. After watching my form on the high diving board, Mr. Riley, my instructor, asked me if I had insurance.
5. Rosa flew first to Los Angeles, and then she went to visit her parents in Mexico City.
6. The tall muscular man wearing the dark sunglasses is a professional wrestler.
7. Onions, radishes, and potatoes seem to grow better in cooler climates.
8. Whenever Vincent is in Las Vegas, you can find him at the blackjack table or the roulette wheel.
9. While I watched in disbelief, my car rolled down the hill and through the front window of a Chinese restaurant.
10. The question, sir, is not whether you committed the crime but when you committed the crime.

CHAPTER 29: Other Punctuation Marks

Introductory Activity (*page* 374)

1. list:
2. life-size
3. (1856–1939)
4. track;
5. breathing—but alive

Activity 1: Using Colons (*page* 375)

1. diet:
2. summer:
3. columns:

Activity 2: Using Semicolons (*page* 376)

1. night; consequently,
2. raining; all
3. vegetarian; my . . . diabetic; and

Activity 3: Using the Dash (*page* 376)

1. sea—shivering
2. —her third in three years—
3. time—eight

Activity 4: Using Hyphens (*page* 377)

1. slow-moving . . . no-passing
2. sugar-free . . . double-cheese
3. hard-hearted . . . teary-eyed

Activity 5: Using Parentheses (*page* 378)

1. Americans (80 percent) had
2. hours (3:00 to 4:00 p.m.) are
3. often (1) make a list and then (2) check off items I have done.

CHAPTER 30: Dictionary Use

Introductory Activity (*page* 381)

1. fortutious (fortuitous)
2. hi/er/o/glyph/ics
3. be
4. oc/to/ge/naŕ/i/an (primary accent is on *nar*)
5. (1) identifying mark on the ear of a domestic animal
   (2) identifying feature or characteristic

Answers to the practice activities are in your dictionary. Check with your instructor if you have any problems.

Activity 1: Using a Dictionary (*page* 382)

welcome . . . quitting . . . concentration . . . professional . . . receiving . . . arranged . . . extremely . . . necessary . . . exciting . . . persistent . . . performance . . . opportunity . . . decision . . . roommate . . . involvement . . . difference . . . category . . . privilege

Activity 2: Marking Syllable Divisions (*page* 382)

2 . . . 3 . . . 4 . . . 5 . . .

Activity 3: Understanding Vowel Sounds (*page* 383)

pet . . . pie . . . pot . . . toe . . . cut . . . boot

Activity 4: Using the Schwa (*page* 384)

Activity 5: Using a Dictionary's Abbreviations Key (*page* 385)

plural . . . singular . . . adjective . . . adverb

Activity 6: Principal Parts (*page* 386)

choose - chose - chosen - choosing
know - knew - known - knowing
speak - spoke - spoken - speaking

Activity 7: Writing Plural Forms (*page* 386)

thieves . . . cavities . . . heroes . . . theses

Activity 8: Using Sentence Context (*page* 386)

Dictionary definitions:

1. Of foremost importance
2. requiring skillful or tactful handling
3. expressed objections or criticisms in bitter, harsh, or abusive language

Activity 9: Etymology (*page* 387)

magazine: from a French word meaning "storehouse"
anatomy: from the Greek anatome, meaning "dissection"
frankfurter: after Frankfurt, Germany

Activity 10: Usage (*page* 388)

informal . . . informal . . . informal . . . nonstandard . . . slang

Activity 11: Synonyms (*page* 388)

desire: covet, crave, want, wish
ask: question, inquire, query, interrogate, examine, quiz
cry: weep, wail, whimper, sob, blubber

CHAPTER 31: Spelling Improvement

Introductory Activity (*page* 390)

Misspellings:

akward . . . exercize . . . buisness . . . worryed . . . shamful . . . begining . . . partys . . . sandwichs . . . heros

Activity 1: Using Correct Endings (*page* 392)

1. hurried
2. admiring
3. denies
4. jabbing
5. magnified
6. committed
7. diving
8. hastily
9. propelling
10. nudges

Activity 2: Using Plural Endings or Forms (*page* 393)

1. buses
2. groceries
3. potatoes
4. taxis
5. themselves
6. theories
7. passersby
8. alumni
9. sandwiches
10. mice

CHAPTER 32: Omitted Words and Letters

Introductory Activity (*page* 397)

bottles . . . in the supermarket . . . like a wind-up toy . . . his arms . . . an alert shopper . . . with the crying

Activity 1: Adding Missing Words (*page 398*)

1. I grabbed a metal bar on the roof of the subway car as the train lurched into the station.
2. For most of our country's history, gold was the basis of the monetary system.
3. Maggie made about a quart of French-toast batter—enough to soak a few dozen slices.
4. Several pairs of sneakers tumbled around in the dryer and banged against the glass door.
5. To err is human and to forgive is divine, but never to make a mistake in the first place takes a lot of luck.
6. Raccoons like to wash their food in a stream with their nimble, glove-like hands before eating.
7. When I got to the grocery store, I realized I had left my shopping list in the glove compartment of my car.
8. Game shows are an inexpensive way for networks to make a high profit.
9. Soap operas, on the other hand, are very expensive to produce because of the high salaries of many cast members.
10. One memorable Friday the thirteenth, a friend of mine bought a black cat and a broken mirror and walked under a ladder. He had a wonderful day!

Activity 2: Using -s Endings (*page 399*)

1. sightseers . . . ghouls
2. sets . . . names
3. Dozens . . . beetles
4. dentists . . . restaurants . . . lines
5. workers . . . departments
6. lights . . . games . . . cars . . . persons
7. games . . . balls
8. shoes . . . jeans . . . months
9. stamps . . . pens
10. Workers . . . logs . . . chunks . . . chips

Acitivity 3: Writing with Plural Forms (*page 400*)

CHAPTER 33: Commonly Confused Words

Introductory Activity (*page 402*)

1. Incorrect: your	Correct: you're
2. Incorrect: who's	Correct: whose
3. Incorrect: there	Correct: their
4. Incorrect: to	Correct: too
5. Incorrect: Its	Correct: It's

Activity 1: Homonyms (*page 403*)

all ready . . . already
break . . . brake
course . . . coarse
here . . . hear
whole . . . hole
its . . . it's
new . . . knew
know . . . no

pair . . . pear
passed . . . past
peace . . . piece
plain . . . plane
principal . . . principle
right . . . write
then . . . than
there . . . their . . . they're
through . . . threw
two . . . too . . . to
where . . . wear
weather . . . whether
who's . . . whose
you're . . . your

Activity 2: Commonly Confused Words (*page 410*)

an . . . a
except . . . accept
advice . . . advise
affect . . . effect
Among . . . between
beside . . . besides
can . . . may
cloths . . . clothes
desert . . . dessert
dose . . . does
fewer . . . less
former . . . latter
learn . . . teach
loose . . . lose
quite . . . quiet
though . . . thought

Activity 3: Incorrect Word Forms (*pages 414–415*)

being that
1. Since (*or* Because) our stove doesn't work
2. since (*or* because) they don't speak to each other
3. since (*or* because) it's my birthday

can't hardly / couldn't hardly
1. I can hardly
2. James could hardly
3. You could hardly

could of
1. you could have
2. you could have
3. I could have

irregardless
1. Regardless of your feelings
2. regardless of the weather
3. regardless of age

must of / should of / would of

1. I must have
2. he would have
3. You should have

CHAPTER 34: Effective Word Choice

Introductory Activity (*page 418*)

Correct sentences:

1. After a disappointing movie, we devoured a pizza.
2. Mourning the death of his best friend, Tennyson wrote the moving poem "In Memoriam."
3. Psychological tests will be given on Wednesday in the Student Center.
4. I think the referee made the right decision.

    1 . . . 2 . . . 3 . . . 4

Activity 1: Avoiding Slang (*page 419*)

1. If you keep overeating, you're going to be fat.
2. My parents always refuse when I ask them for some money to buy new clothes.
3. The entire city was excited when the basketball team beat its opponent in the playoffs.
4. If Ellen would get less serious and stop talking about her troubles, a date with her wouldn't be so depressing.
5. I'm going to have to wait anxiously for the next couple of days, hoping the boss doesn't discover the mistake I made.

Activity 2: Avoiding Clichés (*page 421*)

1. Substitute In brief for To make a long story short.
2. Substitute Very quickly for As quick as a wink.
3. Substitute is ignored for goes in one ear and out the other.
4. Substitute was delighted for felt like a million dollars.
5. Substitute rare for few and far between.

Activity 3: Avoiding Pretentious Words (*page 422*)

1. Please ask one of our salespeople.
2. The weather is terrible today.
3. My parents want me to get a college degree.
4. Do not put your arm out of the car, or an accident might happen.
5. Many fires are caused by the careless use of portable heaters.

Activity 4: Omitting Unnecessary Words (*page 424*)

1. There is no cure for the common cold.
2. My main point is that our state should legalize gambling.
3. Because Chen's car wouldn't start, he took a bus to work.
4. Even when I was a boy, my goal was to be a stockbroker.
5. Susan's daily exercises energize her.

A Writer's Journal

Photo Credits

Pages 1 and 2	© Merri Cyr/Nonstock
Page 3	© Greg Friedler/Jupiter Images
Page 12	© Ryan McVay/Photodisc Green/Getty Images
Page 14	© Steven Weinberg/Stone/Getty Images
Page 15	© Bettmann/CORBIS
Page 31	© David Young Wolff/Photo Edit
Page 41	© Jeff Greenberg
Pages 46 and 48	© Royalty-Free/Corbis
Pages 46 and 48	© Francis Miller//Time Life Pictures/Getty Images
Page 49	© Robert W. Hoopes
Page 49	Photri MicroStock(tm)/A.Kaplan
Page 49	©Photo Network Stock / Grant Heilman Photography—All rights reserved.
Page 54	Darren Hopes/Getty Images
Page 54	© Frank May/dpa/Corbis
Page 54	© Nick White/Digital Vision/Getty Images
Page 54	© Amanda Edwards/Getty Images
Page 54	© David Young Wolff/Photo Edit
Page 83	Library of Congress
Page 84	top © Mario Tama/Getty Images; bottom © Mark Wilson/Getty Images
Page 84	© Mario Tama/Getty Images
Page 84	© Michael Ainsworth/Dallas Morning News/Corbis
Page 84	© A.J. Sisco/Corbis
Page 100	© David Buffington/Getty Images
Page 100	© McGraw-Hill Companies, Inc./Gary He, photographer
Page 124	© Angela Gaul
Page 124	© Angela Gaul
Page 125	© Alinari/Art Resource, NY
Page 125	© Reunion des Musees Nationaux/Art Resource, NY
Page 146	© The Bridgeman Art Library/Getty Images
Page 146	© Jim Zuckerman/Corbis
Page 146	© Vatican Museums and Galleries, Vatican City, Italy/Getty Images
Pages 150 and 152	© Bob Daemmrich/The Image Works
Page 153	© Andrew Walsh
Page 153	© Sheryl Stephen
Page 209	© Natalie Hummel
Page 314	© Oren Levine
Page 314	© Glenn Loos-Austin
Page 314	© Ryan Caiazzo
Page 380	© Lisa Beebe
Page 380	© James Yu
Page 430	© Lee Snider/The Image Works
Page 430	© Livia Corona/Taxi/Getty Images
Page 430	© Apply Pictures / Alamy
Page 435	Courtesy of the Franciscan Sisters of Little Falls, Minnesota
Page 439	© Ryan McVay/Taxi/Getty Images
Page 453	© Jim CooperAP Photo
Page 468	© JOE GIZA/Reuters/Corbis
Page 476	Courtesy of James Lincoln Collier
Page 480	Edvard Munch (1863-1944) © ARS, NY. The Scream. 1893. Photo Erich Lessing/Art Resource, NY
Page 489	© Mark Peterson/Corbis
Page 495	© Left Lane Productions/Left Lane Productions/Corbis
Page 503	Courtesy of Marcus, Larry, of Minneapolis, Minnesota
Page 509	© Louie Psihoyos/CORBIS
Page 527	© ImageSource
Page 529	© Frank Capri/Hulton Archive/Getty Images
Page 534	© Kelly & Massa
Page 538	© Fabio Cardoso/zefa/Corbis
Page 540	© Jean Weisinger, 1991
Page 545	© Larry Mangino/The Image Works

Text Credits

p. 435   Sister Helen P. Mrosla, O. S. F., "All the Good Things." Originally published in *Proteus,* Spring 1991. Reprinted by permission as edited and published by *Reader's Digest* in October, 1991.

p. 441   Paul Logan, "Rowing the Bus." Copyright © 1997. Reprinted by permission of the author.

p. 447   Marta Salinas, "The Scholarship Jacket," from *Nosotros: Latina Literature Today,* 1986, edited by Maria del Carmen Boza, Beverly Silva, and Carmen Valle. Copyright Bilingual Press, Arizona State University, Tempe, AZ.